"RACE" IS A FOUR-LETTER WORD

The Genesis of the Concept

C. Loring Brace
University of Michigan

New York   Oxford
OXFORD UNIVERSITY PRESS
2005

Oxford University Press

Oxford   New York
Auckland   Bangkok   Buenos Aires   Cape Town   Chennai
Dar es Salaam   Delhi   Hong Kong   Istanbul   Karachi   Kolkata
Kuala Lumpur   Madrid   Melbourne   Mexico City   Mumbai   Nairobi
São Paulo   Shanghai   Taipei   Tokyo   Toronto

Published by Oxford University Press, Inc.
198 Madison Avenue, New York, New York 10016
www.oup.com

Oxford is a registered trademark of Oxford University Press

Library of Congress Cataloging-in-Publication Data

Brace, C. Loring.
  "Race" is a four-letter word : the genesis of the concept / C. Loring Brace.
    p. cm.
  Includes bibliographical references and index.
  ISBN 13: 978-0-19-517352-9 (cloth : acid-free paper) — ISBN 13: 978-0-19-517351-2
    (paper : acid-free paper)

  1. Race. 2. Physical anthropology. 3. Race awareness—United States—History. I. Title.

GN269B73 2005
305.8—dc22

                                                                    2004052081

Printed in the United States of America
on acid-free paper

Dedicated to the Memory of
Ashley Montagu, 1905–99
who understood most of this a full half-century ago

CONTENTS

PREFACE

My first encounter with Ashley Montagu was in Santa Barbara, California, in the fall of 1961, where I had begun teaching anthropology at the local branch of the University of California. Montagu was famous, or in the minds of some "infamous," for his book *Man's Most Dangerous Myth: The Fallacy of Race* (1942), which I had read in spite of the fact that my mentors did not think much of it. Over half a century later, it was to be my great privilege to be asked to write a foreword to the 6th edition of that splendid work (1997). The point of that book was to show that "race" was not only a useless concept but also positively pernicious.

Rumor had it that he was considering moving to Santa Barbara, so I got in touch with him to welcome him to our small but aspiring group of anthropologists. We felt that the addition of a person of such renown to our community would have given our anthropological ethos a real boost. He visited our department, gave a talk for our Anthropology Club, and charmed virtually everyone. It was the beginning of a lifelong friendship, and to our great pleasure he stayed with us on repeated visits.

In the end, he did not move to Santa Barbara, but I was able to get the faculty to allot Regents Professorship funds to bring him in for a term as a visiting lecturer a year later. The position of lecturer is the lowest rung in the British academic hierarchy, and, as a person who had gotten his initial university education in his native England, it continued to amuse him that he was both a regents professor and a lecturer at the same time at the University of California Santa Barbara. His congenial presence led to collaboration with me on an introductory textbook (Brace and Montagu 1965), which evolved into *Human Evolution: An Introduction to Biological Anthropology* (Brace and Montagu 1977).

Early in 1967, however, the governor of California, Ronald Reagan, fired the president of the university with the following words: "The State of California has no business subsidizing intellectual curiosity" (Smith 1968, 112). Since all university faculty members assume that intellectual curiosity is an essential component of the learning environment they have been hired to promote, it became obvious to some of us that we had no future in California, and that was why I moved to Michigan.

For over a third of a century here, I have been teaching a course somewhat awkwardly entitled "Problems of Race." Actually, I inherited the topic and title from my long-time colleague Frank Livingstone. I was initially hired at the University of Michigan to provide coverage of the fossil evidence for human evolution, which was and has continued to be a main focus of my professional activities. I had also been interested in the picture of the biological variation of living human populations. That variation, of course, has its roots in the prehistoric ancestors of the various groups in question. As a student of the human past, I had a related interest in the legacy it had bequeathed to the present. Frank, for his part, as a student of variation in living humans, had a parallel interest in the past sources of that variation. After I had been at Michigan for a few years, we agreed to try swapping courses. He would deal with fossils, and I would extend my coverage to living human biological differences.

It was Frank Livingstone who first produced the aphorism "There are no races, there are only clines" (1962, 279), and he was absolutely right. *Clines* are simply gradations in the distribution of individual biological traits, and in our treatment of a course dealing with human variation, we both use the tactic of showing how clines of human biological traits can be understood only by dispensing with the concept of "race" right at the beginning. I do this in the first chapter here simply to illustrate why such an approach is necessary. In the course I have taught for the last three decades, I spend much more time dealing with the biology of human variation. Chapter 1 is just a hint at what that covers, but I felt I had to do at least that bit so the general reader would realize that my dismissal of "race" is not merely "political correctness" but rooted in basic biological understanding. The same point has been clearly made with an extensive treatment of the biology involved by a genetically qualified biological anthropologist (Graves 2001), and the misuses to which that biologically indefensible concept have been put in the last century have been eloquently treated by another fully qualified anthropologist (Baker 1998).

The following question then immediately presents itself: If there is no biological justification for such a construct, how on earth did it come to be accepted as something that virtually everyone regards as self-evident? There are plenty of sources that can be used to deal with the biology of human variation, but there is much less available that attempts to document the circumstances leading to the growth of the belief in the concept of "race," in the first place, and its application in the promotion of social injustice, in the second (Smedley 1993 being one of the few). I devote the last half of my course to this topic, and I have generated this book so that it should have formal written coverage. The "bigot brigade" is a fact of contemporary existence, and, however much we may regret it, it deserves recognition and treatment.

ACKNOWLEDGMENTS

What enabled me to produce this book was tenure, an institution that has come under attack recently in some quarters. I had gained that nearly four decades ago, when it was nowhere near so difficult as it has since become. Even 20 years ago I was warned by my department chair that my professional activities would not qualify me for tenure if I had not previously gained it and that this would "impact" my "merit raise" possibilities. Such was indeed the case, and my "merit" raises ceased from that time on. After J. Philippe Rushton received his fellowship from the John Simon Guggenheim Foundation to produce his denunciation of the intellectual capabilities of people with pigment in their skins, I had thought that they might just supply support to someone who intended to produce a rebuttal. However, they indicated that they had no interest in such an effort and rejected my application, but with tenure, I could not be fired unless I actually refused to meet the classes I had been assigned to teach. I like teaching and continued with my classes. My research time I could devote to preparing the manuscript which appears here. It was tenure then that allowed me to get it done. As always, the reference librarians at the Graduate, Science, and the Medical School libraries at the University of Michigan provided invaluable service. I owe special thanks to my long-time friend Dr. Richard J. Kaplan of the Rand Corporation in Santa Monica, California, for vetting some of the sections on intelligence testing. An anthropologist ventures into that realm with a certain amount of angst since it has been the fiefdom of psychology for a full century now. Dick Kaplan got his graduate initiation into that domain at Columbia University, when the outspoken advocate of scientific racism, Henry Garrett, was still chair of the department there, so he has been aware of the outlook, the assumptions, and the accomplishments of that realm for far longer than I have. I have also benefited enormously from the encyclopedic knowledge of my long-term colleague and half brother-in-law Stanley M. Garn (he is indeed a whole person, but we married half-sisters who are also whole people but with different mothers). Finally, for whatever semblance of readability there may be in the ensuing manuscript, I owe an enormous debt of gratitude to the literate good sense of my wife, Mary L. Brace. Wherever it lapses back into the awkward plodding of standard academic prose, it is because I was not smart enough to follow her advice.

INTRODUCTION

Race is such an ever-present issue and generates such an emotional response that it will come as a matter of some astonishment to many to be told that there is no coherent biological entity that corresponds to what most people assume is meant by the term. Of course, the meaning evoked by that word will vary from one part of the world to another. The German dictator of World War II, Adolf Hitler, used the term to refer to people who were not obviously different in appearance from the spectrum visible in ordinary Germans. His vision of the ideal "Aryan" was satirized at the time as being as tall as Goebbels, as lean as Goering, and as blond as Hitler. The first was short by any standards, the second was positively ponderous, and Hitler, of course, was anything but blond. The English have used the term *race* to refer to the Irish, the Welsh, and the Scots, who are not visibly distinguishable from the English themselves.

Americans, however, assume that recognizable differences in physical appearance are an essential part of what is meant by "race." Although Americans are largely unaware of it, they are spreading their own assumptions of what is meant by "race" to much of the rest of the world (Lewis 1990, 17). This is quite unwitting and merely a reflection of the influence the country has as a result of its economic and military power. Since I am American, the reader would normally expect me to reflect some version of what the country means when the term is used. Indeed, I have no trouble grasping what Americans mean when they ascribe "racial" identity to themselves and others, but I repeat that it is a concept that has no coherent biological validity.

At that point, most Americans, and indeed many others, will query, "What kind of arcane academic wordplay is that?" Is it "political correctness" carried to a level that simply transcends biological reality? The answer is that the common perception of "biological reality" is itself based on a misconception of how the dimensions of human variation are distributed. It would be possible to produce a book-length treatment of how adaptively important biological traits are distributed without regard to each other or to supposed "racial" boundaries. This, however, is not my intention. I do think it is important to show how a few such traits are distributed in a completely nonracial fashion so that the reader can see why I have said that my position is grounded in biological understanding and has nothing to do with political correctness. This is the rationale behind Chapter 1. That it can be used by those who have been accused of being politically correct is another matter entirely but one I have left to other people with other purposes (see the admirable treatment by Appiah and Gutmann 1996).

There is one more thing that needs to be dealt with before going on to the substance of what I have treated in this book and that also is covered in Chapter 1: the view that all of the human populations in the world today should be expected to have the same level of intellectual capability. Individuals will show inherited differences within each group, but there should be no average differences between groups. This expectation has been derided as the "equalitarian dogma" and blamed on "communists (and their supporters)" possibly qualifying it as "the hoax of the century" (Garrett 1961, 483, 484). The blame has also been assigned to Christianity, especially the Catholic Church (Pearson 1996, 116–117), and to political correctness of a left-wing or radical nature (Pearson 1996, 102). To counter that, I should make it clear from the start that I have no political or religious ties or motivations. My expectations of the similarities of the average mental capabilities of all the various human groups in the world is based on an assessment of the nature of the selective forces that they have faced over the past 2 million years. The expectation, then, is based on an appraisal of what the archaeological record can tell us about the nature of human life-ways and subsistence activities during that long sweep of time when the species *Homo sapiens* emerged from its nonhuman predecessors (Brace 1995, 1999a). That also is dealt with in Chapter 1.

Having shown that the concept of "race" has no biological justification, the following question arises: "Then why is it so universally believed?" One of the things that will come as a surprise is the fact that no such concept existed in the world of antiquity until the end of the Middle Ages. It has even been observed that no concept of "race" existed before the 17th century (Hannaford 1996). The way human variation was perceived in the ancient world was conditioned by what can be called the "peasant perspective" (see Chapter 2). I make the case that, curiously, this was a more accurate appreciation than that of the subsequent world, right up to and including the present day.

Travelers in the ancient world could and did go great distances, but they did so on foot or on horse- or camelback. The average day's journey was on the order of 25 miles. Nowhere in the world are people 25 miles away noticeably different in biological appearance. Even in a month of steady traveling it would be hard to encounter obvious differences, and when they became perceptible, it was by such gradual degrees that they were not thought about in categorical fashion.

All that changed dramatically in the European Renaissance. With the construction of ocean-going ships and the attainment of navigational skills, people could set off across an ocean and arrive at a shore some thousands of miles away without having seen anything or anyone in between. Inevitably, the inhabitants appeared categorically distinct from those in the country from which the ship had embarked. Consequently, they were described in categorical fashion, and the seeds of the "race" concept were duly planted in the minds of readers.

Even so, the habits of thought that began to treat other people in categorical fashion were largely based on vicarious information. The resulting treatment of human differences tended to be somewhat arbitrary. The great 18th-century systematizer Carolus Linnaeus (1707–78) organized the human spectrum almost in flat-earth fashion as though there were a set four corners to the world–north, south, east, and west. His human embodiments were Europeans, Africans, Asians, and Native Americans.

The Enlightenment treatment of human diversity remained largely an arbitrary abstraction in its European home. However, it was an everyday reality in the minds of the European colonists in other parts of the globe. By far the largest part of that colonial entity was the Western Hemisphere. For reasons considered in Chapter 2, that formalization was a product of the Protestant-dominated milieu that became the United States of

America. There, the everyday reality was that populations relatively recently removed from categorically separate parts of the world—northwest Europe, West Africa, and northeast Asia—faced each other on terms of manifest social inequality. A hierarchical concept of "race" was the inevitable result.

The exporting of that concept to a receptive Europe, where it formed the rationale for establishing anthropology as a formal academic discipline, is a somewhat unexpected twist to the story. The eclipse of American anthropology as a result of the Civil War (treated in Chapters 9 and 10) and its reimportation as a manifestation of continental sophistication in World War I (see Chapter 12) are further previously unappreciated turns in the course of its development. At that time, the outlook of "eugenics," developed by the Englishman Sir Francis Galton, was adopted by Americans to determine who should be forced to undergo sterilization for what was said to be the good of society. Adolf Hitler adopted the American program with enthusiasm as soon as he gained power in 1933 and pushed it to its ghastly extremes with the gas chambers of the Holocaust, and many of his views are alive and well in the 21st century.

Before plunging into the meat of the matter, I should define a couple of key terms that crop up again and again. These are *racialism* and the pejorative term *racism* (Fredrickson 2002, 155). *Racialism* is the belief that there are inherited traits possessed by all members of a given group which they do not share with members of any other group. Groups characterized by the possession of inherited traits that are not shared with others are what are considered to be *races* (Todorov 1986, 1993; Appiah 1990, 4–5; Fredrickson 2002, 153–154). "Racialism is not, in itself, a doctrine that must be dangerous." It "is false; but by itself . . . seems to be a cognitive rather than a moral problem" (Appiah 1990, 5).

On the other hand, *racism*—"the *ism* of the Modern World" (Benedict 1945, 3)— has been called "the evil twin of ethnocentrism" (Fredrickson 2002, 155). It is the application of a racialist outlook as the basis for invidious "racial" comparisons and treatment. "Racialists do not become racists until they make such convictions the basis for claiming privileges for members of what they consider to be their own race, and for disparaging and doing harm to those deemed racially Other" (Fredrickson 2002, 154). For those who know the excellent treatment of the subject by Michael Banton, I should note that we are defining *racism* and *racialism* in an opposite fashion. He defined *racialism* as the practice, rather than the ideology, of racism, whereas our usage treats *racialism* more as the ideology and *racism* as the practice of racial prejudice (Banton 1967, 8; also Banton 1998, 1, 26–27, 170 ff.).

Because of the unconsciously implemented power and influence of America at the present time, the ethnocentrism that has been perceived in the context of racialism has actually contributed to a heightened level of racism as the new millennium has begun. When it is finally realized that there is no coherent biological entity that corresponds with what people generally assume is meant by "race," all those claims extolling or denigrating various aspects of racial worth will be deprived of any validity. Race, then, is a social construct that should be dealt with solely on the basis of the conventions that govern social behavior. At this point, science ceases to be relevant. The governing conventions are then entirely in the realms of ethics and politics, where all rights and claims are absolutely equal.

1

THE BIOLOGY OF HUMAN VARIATION

BACKGROUND OF A BELIEF

The thesis that underlies the approach taken in this book is based on the realization that there is no biological justification for the concept of "race." To the general reader, particularly the average American reader, this assertion is so counterintuitive that it is apt to be greeted with frank incredulity. Even those with a scientific or professional background are apt to react with patent disbelief. The physician, for example, can counter "Of course races exist: I see them in my practice every day!" This recalls the somewhat analogous instance, sometimes attributed to Mark Twain, of the response given when a Maine farmer was asked if he believed in baptism. The reply was "Believe in it, why, I've seen it done!" (Gilbert 1998). In neither case, however, is there any assurance of a larger meaning inherent in what was seen. The great 19th century naturalist Thomas Henry Huxley yielded to his wife's wishes to have their children christened, although neither one had much confidence in its formal significance. As Huxley said of his wife's insistence, "I am afraid she is not very orthodox but looks upon the process as a kind of spiritual vaccination without which the youngsters might catch Sin in worse forms as they grow up" (Clark 1968, 95).

My point is that one can observe the phenomena of baptism and christening without necessarily believing that they have long-term consequences for the "souls" of the people involved. As the protagonists realized, there was no potential harm in going along with those practices whether or not there was anything really to them. Here, however, our analogy breaks down because there is a simply incalculable amount of harm that has been done in the name of "race." With this in mind, some of the critics of the view that "race" has no biological basis have jumped to the conclusion that those of us who have maintained this view have done so solely in order to counter the possibility of using that concept for the differential promotion or denigration of the various human groups subsumed under that term. Our stance, then, is viewed as what has been called "political correctness."

I cannot deny that it is comforting to know that invidious comparisons are impossible if the groups at which they are aimed have no basic biological validity, but that was not the prime mover behind the viewpoint we have developed. At bottom, our intent was to come to grips with the underlying nature of the fundamental dimensions of human biology and how these intersect to produce the picture of human variation that we can actually see. It was the pursuit of this enterprise that led to the realization that the concept of "race" can only prevent us from understanding the nature and meaning of human biological variation. While most of this book is about what is believed in regard to that concept and how that concept came into existence in the first place, I shall begin with a synopsis of how one actually deals with the nature of human variation. Although it is a bit of a dose of hard biology right at the beginning, the illustrations of how it works are so striking that they should be able to get the point across right at the start and then leave the field clear for dealing with the actual subject matter that is the point of the book.

ADAPTIVE TRAITS: CLINES

In the 1940s, field zoologists began to realize that trait variation in widespread but re-productively continuous species occurred in graded fashion. The gradation in a given trait is called a *cline,* and its graded variation reflects the varying intensity of the selective force to which it represents an adaptation. Separate studies on amphibians (leopard or meadow frogs: Moore 1944, 1949), birds (red-eyed towhee: Dickinson 1952; Huntington 1952), insects (butterflies: Brown 1955; Gillham 1956), and mammals (pine marten: Hagmeier 1958) showed that what had once been regarded as valid subspecies graded into each other to such an extent that a number of zoologists formally gave up the subspecies concept (Wilson and Brown 1953). Most awkwardly, the clines in different traits went in different directions and did not coincide with each other.

The concept of "cline" was first articulated by the British biologist Julian Huxley in 1938, although it is clear from his presentation that he did not fully understand the evolutionary implications of what he had proposed: "I propose the word *cline,* meaning a gradient in a measurable character" (Huxley 1938, 219). As the title of his contribution suggested—"An Auxiliary Taxonomic Principle"—he was more interested in working out ways of labeling things than in finding out the dynamics and the meaning associated with trait distribution. Even though Huxley was one of the first to raise biological objections to the use of the concept of "race" in dealing with human variation (Huxley and Haddon 1936), ironically he missed the fact that it was the investigation of clines that really documented the fact that, zoologically, there really is no such thing as "race." The full realization of that first came more than 10 years later in the assessment of zoological field data: "one can detect gradual clines, step clines, and sudden mid-distribution cline reversals for each character, and the clines obviously do not all have the same axes lying along the same compass directions" (Wilson and Brown 1953, 101).

Yet another decade further on, this insight was picked up by biological anthropology and articulated in unequivocal fashion by Frank Livingstone at the University of Michigan: "There are no races, there are only clines" (Livingstone 1962, 279). That was before I joined the anthropology faculty at the University of Michigan myself, but it explains why I did so when the opportunity arose. In any case, I quickly seconded Livingstone's declaration: *"The most important thing for the analysis of human variation is the appreciation of the selective pressures which have operated to influence the expression of each trait separately"* (Brace 1964a, 107, italics in original). Even though we know the human spectrum better than we do those of frogs or butterflies, it still is not intuitively obvious to us that human adaptive traits have distributions that are completely unrelated to each other and cannot be studied coherently if we start with what we perceive to be "racial" distributions. At this point, it would be instructive to look at a few adaptive traits and see how they are distributed.

Skin Color

Human beings belong to the zoological Order Primates, and like the average member of that concatenation, we rely primarily on our visual sense to orient us in the world. As a result, we are highly sensitive to what our eyes tell us. As we contemplate the appearance of the people of the world, we are particularly aware of differences in the color of the skin. These are almost entirely due to different quantities of the pigment melanin (Montagna et al. 1993). The main function of pigment in the skin is to prevent the penetration of mid-range ultraviolet B (UVB) radiation, the main factor in producing basal cell skin cancer (Friedman et al. 1991; Robins 1991; Holick 2002). Since UV radiation is at its most intense at the equator between the tropic of Cancer and the tropic of Capricorn, it is no surprise to discover that human skin pigment is darkest among those people who have longest resided in the tropics (Fig. 1–1).

There are other factors besides crude latitude that influence how much UVB reaches the surface of the earth. Cloud cover and dense vegetation can intervene. As a consequence, while human pigmentation does reach its maximum in the tropics, it is not a uniform phenomenon (Jablonski and Chaplin 2000). I have left out the Western Hemisphere from Figure 1–1. Human beings did not get into the Western Hemisphere

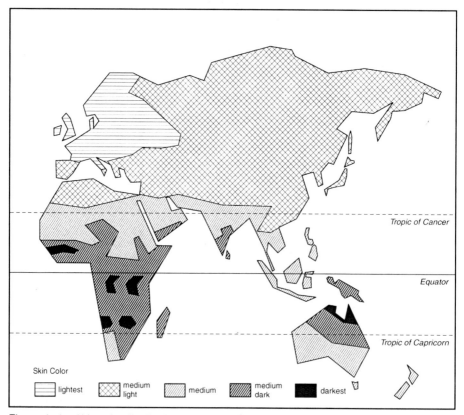

Figure 1–1   Skin color distribution in the Old World (Biasutti 1959, 8, table IV, 192–193; Brace 1964a, 109; 1996a, 116; 2002, 244; Brace and Seguchi in press).

until late in the Pleistocene, not much more than 15,000 years ago (Goebel et al. 2003), and that is not enough time for a significant skin color cline to have evolved (Brace et al. 2001). Human skin pigmentation decreases in proportion to the distance both north and south of the equator. The evolutionary mechanism that produced this reduction is in dispute (Brace 1996a; Jablonski and Chaplin 2000), but all would agree that the decrease is related to the reduced intensity of UV radiation.

Tooth Size

Differences in skin color are easy enough for us to understand, but we are less aware that there are systematic differences in the size of the teeth. The role of teeth has been primarily in the processing of food. During most of the Pleistocene, people throughout the inhabited parts of the Old World were eating essentially the same kind of thing and there was no systematic difference in human tooth size. In fact, it remained essentially the same wherever people lived from nearly 2 million years ago until just before the last glaciation about 150,000 years ago. All of the differences that characterize the teeth of different living populations have developed since that time. Those differences are the result of dental reductions that have occurred earlier in some places than in others.

The reductions in turn have been because of traditions of food processing that were necessary for survival in some areas but not in others. Although humans have descended from tropical ancestors, starting about 500,000 years ago they have extended their area of occupation up into the Temperate Zone. As facultative carnivores, there was an abundance of available game for them to exploit. The only hitch was coping with Temperate Zone temperatures with what remained essentially a tropical mammalian physiology. One of the things that allowed them to do this was the control of fire (Straus 1989).

Recently, claims have been advanced that control of fire and its use in cooking goes all the way back to the beginning of the Pleistocene, 1.9 million years ago (Wrangham et al. 1999); but in the almost complete absence of evidence, this requires a bigger speculative leap of faith than most of us are willing to make. From 150,000 years ago, however, the evidence is reasonably abundant. Not only that, but for the first time there are clear indications that fire was being used in the preparation of food.

It was unlikely that even the hungriest band of Neanderthals could eat a whole Paleolithic cow at a single sitting, and during a Pleistocene winter, it was more than likely to have frozen before the next time it could be served as dinner. Before that happened, it was butchered into individually usable hunks. By what I have referred to as "obligatory cooking" (Brace 1995, 228), those portions could be thawed subsequently for further meals. This procedure had the unintended by-product of reducing the amount of chewing that was normally necessary to process the food ingested. Selection maintaining fully mid-Pleistocene-sized teeth was reduced and, simply by random mutations that were not selected against, tooth size itself reduced in proportion to the length of time that cooking had been used in the preparation of food (Brace et al. 1991).

The mechanism for reduction with the relaxation or cessation of selection is something I have called the "probable mutation effect" (Brace 1963). The essence of that process and its consequences was appreciated by Hermann J. Muller, the geneticist who earned a Nobel Prize for his work showing that radiation could produce genetic mutations. In appraising the consequences of mutations under conditions of reduction in the forces of selection, he observed that "an actual cessation of selection for a character would in time lead to its complete disappearance" (Muller 1949, 465). Essentially the same perception was expressed by Julian Huxley (1951) and by biologists working with island or cave-dwelling creatures (Carson et al. 1982; Wilkens 1988). Although it has been recognized as being compatible with the outlook of molecular geneticists, especially those who have pioneered what has been called the "neutral theory" (Ohno 1970), biological anthropologists are often less comfortable with the outlook of evolutionary biology and have tended to reject it (Holloway 1966), even regarding it as "improbable" (Wolpoff et al. 2000, 134).

The most likely change in the basic genetic material is the alteration of a single component or nucleotide in DNA, something referred to as a "single-nucleotide polymorphism," or SNP. The most likely result of that is the alteration of a single component or amino acid in the structure of a protein. A random change of a single amino acid has the likely consequence that the protein will not work as well as it did before modification. If that protein is one of the enzymes that control the production of melanin in the skin or the growth of a tooth, then a random change is most likely to result in less pigment or less tooth unless it is selected against.

Where selection for skin pigment or tooth size is strong, such random mutations will be weeded out. Individuals who display them will not have such a good chance to survive and reproduce. However, if circumstances change and a full amount of skin pigment or larger tooth size is no longer essential for survival, then the random changes that occur by chance will not be weeded out and skin color or tooth size will reduce in proportion to the length of time that selection for the original condition has been eased. The most likely result of the most likely mutation—the probable mutation effect—is structural reduction.

Figure 1–2 shows the distribution of tooth size in the world today. Evidently, the populations whose ancestors first used the techniques that allowed them to survive in the Temperate Zone are those whose teeth have undergone the greatest reduction from the common Middle Pleistocene level that characterized all humans 150,000 years ago. In many respects, the cline for tooth size and the cline for skin color run in parallel. The maximum reduction in both is associated with the length of residence in the Temperate Zone. UV levels have nothing to do with tooth size, and cooking has nothing to do with skin color; and the reversal of that northern parallelism can be clearly seen in Australia.

People have been in Australia for only about 50,000 years (Roberts et al. 1994), and while some depigmentation has occurred south of the tropic of Capricorn, it has evidently not proceeded as far as at comparable latitudes north of the tropics at the western end of the Old World (Henneberg and Brace 2000). Evidently, it takes much longer than 50,000 years of residence in situ at temperate latitudes for the full amount of pigment reduction observed in the north to actually take place. While the first Australians were fully familiar with making and maintaining fire, they did not use it extensively for earth-oven cooking until less than 15,000 years ago (Pretty 1977). Australian tooth size, then, remained at Middle Pleistocene levels until that time. From then on, it began reducing at the same rate documented for people elsewhere in the world starting at earlier times. Cooking evidently entered Australia from the north and spread slowly southward. Tooth size in Australia, then, gets larger toward the south, where skin color is its lightest (Brace 1980a; Henneberg and Brace 2000). This is the complete opposite of the association of those two traits in the Northern Hemisphere.

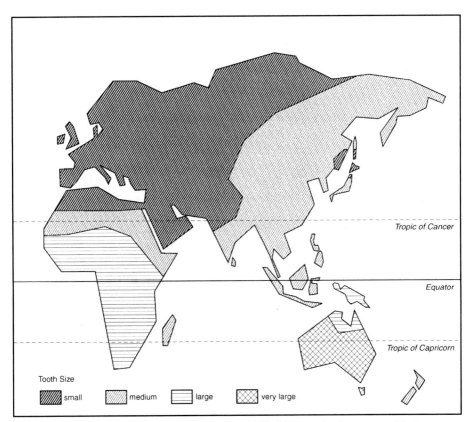

Figure 1-2   Human tooth size variation in the Old World (from the data reported in Brace et al. 1991, 38–41; Brace 1996a, 123; Brace and Seguchi in press).

Hemoglobin S

Skin color and, to a lesser extent, tooth size are assessable by eye; but now I am going to turn to a few traits that are obviously under selective force control but which we have no immediate way of perceiving short of laboratory tests. The first to be considered is hemoglobin variation. Hemoglobin is a protein molecule in red blood cells that is responsible for picking up oxygen in the lungs and carrying it to the sites where it is used in active metabolic functions. It gives up the oxygen at the site of metabolic activity, picks up carbon dioxide, and takes it back to the lungs to be exhaled. As with all single-gene traits, the locus on the chromosome (chromosome 16 in the case of hemoglobin) contains one allele (gene) from the mother and one from the father. Normal hemoglobin is called *hemoglobin A,* and most people will have an A from each parent. That is they will be AA, or homozygous for A. The hemoglobin molecule is actually a four-chain structure with two α chains and two β chains, each being over 140 amino acids long. The change of a single amino acid at position 6 of the β chain, substituting valine for glutamic acid, will produce hemoglobin S (Honig and Adams 1986).

Hemoglobin S is the source of sickle cell anemia, but in order to get the full manifestation of the disease, one needs to have an S from both parents, or to be homozygous

for S. In such cases, when the red cell gives up its oxygen at the site of metabolic functioning, the abnormal hemoglobin molecules will tie to each other in the cytoplasm of
the cell, forming long, stiff rods. These distort the soft, round shape of the red blood cell
into jagged crescents. The first physicians who identified these under the microscope
thought they looked like sickle blades, hence the term *sickle cell.* These stiffened and
jagged red cells clog the capillaries at the peripheries of circulation, creating painful
swellings and blocking circulation. The body's response is to lyse, or destroy, the of-
fending cells. The loss of red cells is *anemia,* by definition, and that is why a person who
inherits an S gene from each parent will have sickle cell anemia.

Under normal circumstances, there is nothing good to say about sickle cell anemia.
The probability of living past childhood is low, growth is stunted, and the condition is
painful. As it happens, the heterozygote, that is the person with an AS genotype, has
something of an advantage in coping with the effects of a particularly noxious kind of
malaria. This is caused by infection with a single-celled creature called *Plasmodium
falciparum,* which takes over the body's red blood cells and uses them as shelters for its
own reproduction. After growing and maturing in the red blood cell, the infecting manifestations, called *merozoites,* burst the cell's surrounding membrane. Each new mero-
zoite seeks out another red cell to infect and continue the cycle. Some of these infected
red cells are picked up when a person is bitten by a particular kind of mosquito. The
plasmodia then complete their reproductive cycle in the stomach walls of the mosquito,
and their offspring migrate to the mosquito's salivary glands and await the mosquito's
bite of another person, when they head off into the human bloodstream to start the cycle
all over again.

A person with AA hemoglobin is at risk of dying from malaria, an SS person is at
risk of dying from anemia, but an AS person has a chance of surviving. The latter has
enough A hemoglobin so as not to be seriously anemic, and the S blood cells sickle and
dump their contents into the bloodstream. If those cells have been infected with malarial parasites, the latter get dumped into the blood plasma before those parasites are
mature enough to seek the shelter of another red blood cell. In the plasma they are identified by the white blood cells, the phagocytes, which seek out and destroy infecting
microorganisms. That way, the AS person can reduce the amount of malarial infection.
Malaria is not prevented, but it is kept down to sublethal levels (Livingstone 1967).

In both the medical profession and the segment of the public that knows the story I
have just told, there is a widespread assumption that sickle cell anemia is an African
"racial" marker. Figure 1–3 shows that it certainly has its highest frequencies in Africa.
However, it may very well have gotten into Africa from outside and only reached those
high frequencies fairly recently (Livingstone 1989). The origin of agriculture in the
Middle East produced a population density that allowed continuous infection. The greatest genetic diversity associated with hemoglobin S occurs there, and it is the likely
source from which it spread along with agriculture into sub-Saharan Africa. Agricultural
spread led to the establishment of sedentary populations as a reservoir for the disease.
The farming techniques also generated ideal breeding grounds for the mosquitoes involved, and it is no surprise that falciparum malaria took hold in Africa on a large scale
(Livingstone 1958). However, both falciparum malaria and sickle cell anemia run across
the Mediterranean from Greece to southern Italy and in the other direction to the Persian
Gulf and South Asia (Cavalli-Sforza and Bodmer 1971).

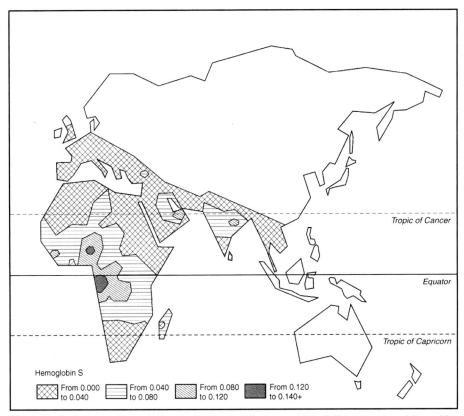

Figure 1–3   The distribution of gene frequencies for hemoglobin S (from Brace and Seguchi in press, adapted from Cavalli-Sforza and Bodmer 1971). In the white portions of the map there is no hemoglobin S.

Blood Groups

It should be obvious from comparing Figures 1–1, 1–2, and 1–3 that traits under separate selective force control have independent distributions. Just to emphasize this, I present the distributions of the main manifestations of the ABO blood group system. There are other systems with completely different distributions, but this should suffice to make the point in unambiguous fashion. More is known about the distribution of the genes for the ABO system than for practically any other human biological trait. Ironically, however, very little attention has been paid to why there are different frequencies in different regions or what the whole picture means. The reason for this is that the medical profession is principally concerned with making sure that there is compatibility between donor and recipient in the instance of a transfusion. Blood group O can be donated to a person with any other blood group, but an A or a B cannot give blood to each other or to an O. Quite properly, the issue of compatibility is uppermost in the minds of clinicians, to the extent that there has been comparatively little interest in the question of why there are any differences in the first place.

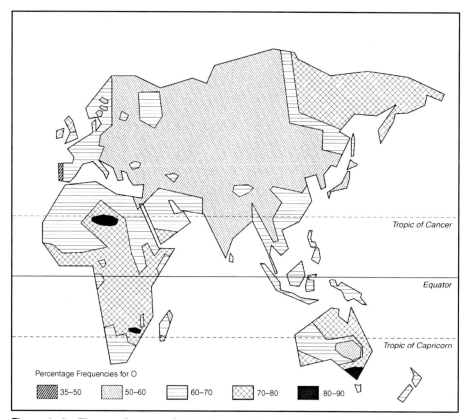

Figure 1–4   The gene frequency for blood group O in the Old World (adapted from Race and Sanger 1975).

The gene for blood group O is the most widely distributed, although because it is re-cessive to both A and B it is not perceived as easily. Figure 1–4 shows its distribution in the Old World. Some work has indicated that those with blood group A are less likely to survive smallpox than those with blood group O (Basu 1969; Vogel and Chakravarti 1971; Adelsteinsson 1985); however, that does not help us account for why A is rela-tively high in certain parts of the world, as indicated in Figure 1–5. Likewise, blood group B is high in certain parts of Asia, as can be seen in Figure 1–6, but, again, we have no idea why.

Clusters and Nonadaptive Traits

When the 20th century rediscovered Darwin back in the 1930s and linked the outlook of genetics, laboratory and field biology, and paleontology in what was sometimes called "neo-Darwinism" or "evolutionary synthesis" (Mayr 1982, 2000), some of the partici-pants went so far as to take it as a given that natural selection had been responsible for the nuances of form of all biological traits even if we could not see how. This was labeled "hyperselectionism" in a witty and erudite critique by the late Stephen Jay Gould and his

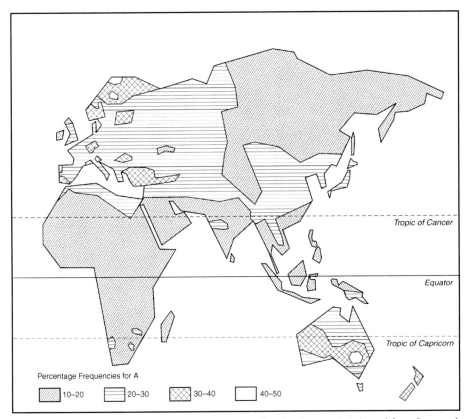

Figure 1-5   The distribution of the gene frequency for blood group A (adapted from Race and Sanger 1975).

colleague Richard Lewontin, who compared such faith in the all-pervasive power of natural selection to the faith of Voltaire's caricature Dr. Pangloss in his satire *Candide* (Gould and Lewontin 1979; Gould 1980). Dr. Pangloss defends the view that all is for the best in this best of all possible worlds (Voltaire [1759] 1957).

The critique was well done, although many felt that it went too far and denied any significant role for natural selection in shaping the course of organic evolution (Kellog 1988; Dennett 1995). Actually, as the realm of molecular genetics became more a part of the outlook of evolutionary biology, the realization grew that changes with predictable consequences could occur at the molecular level that would influence the course of evolution even without being controlled by natural selection (Brace 1963; Kimura 1968, 1969; King and Jukes 1969). It came as something of a surprise to discover that over 97% of the genome does not code for anything, leading to the suggestion that much of it was simply "junk" DNA (Ohno 1972). Geneticists could then focus on parts of the genome that were not under selective force control and study the nature and the rates of the changes that occurred. By studying the homologous parts of the genome in different organisms with an understanding of how long it took certain kinds of change to occur, they could estimate how long ago certain related groups had split apart.

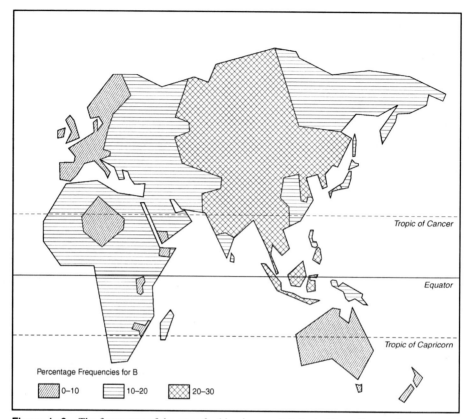

Figure 1–6   The frequency of the gene for blood group B (adapted from Race and Sanger 1975).

Ultimately, the fossil record provides the clock for establishing how long it took for the observed differences to come about. For example, the ancient continent of Gondwanaland included what is now Africa, Madagascar, India, Antarctica, Australia, and South America. It split up between 150 and 160 million years ago (Sampson et al. 1997), so the genetic separation of the Australian and South American marsupials has to date back that far. There is more than a little guesswork in suggesting the dates for the splits in related lineages, but a great deal of comparative work is being enthusiastically pursued at the present time. Not a little of this is focused on human populations in different parts of the world. Comparisons of nuclear DNA (Tishkoff et al. 2000), mitochondrial DNA (Cann et al. 1987; Wallace et al. 1997), and DNA from the non-recombining part of the Y chromosome (Hammer and Zegura 1996; Hammer et al. 2001) have been made and estimates offered for the length of time that such diverse groups as Europeans, Asians, and Australians split off from their African ancestors.

Depending on which DNA segment is being studied and how the fossil record is interpreted, estimates of how long ago given regional populations separated range from 40,000 to 600,000 to over a million years. The dates proposed depend more on the mind-set and assumptions of the scholar than they do on the actual evidence at hand. Many of the dates currently being asserted are starkly at odds with what is known of the archaeological record. This will all be worked out in time, but for the moment the general reader should be skeptical of any of the claims currently being offered no matter how confident the author seems to be.

Time estimates aside, however, the various DNA comparisons allow the construction of very plausible trees depicting the relationships of all the populations. Not surprisingly, adjacent populations in a particular part of the world are closer to each other than they are to those in distant areas. When nonadaptive traits are used for comparison, what one gets is a picture of relationship. Informally we get the same impression when we contemplate the physical appearance of the human spectrum. If that is the case, then there is reason to suggest that traits that allow us to see the relatedness of people in a given region also have no adaptive significance.

This dawned on me rather slowly a couple of decades ago. I had been collecting tooth measurements to show how teeth reduced in time after the selective forces that had maintained their size in the Pleistocene lessened. The picture was consistent in place after place where I could get my calipers on prehistoric and recent samples—Europe, the Middle East, Australia, Southeast Asia, China—until I got to Japan. There, the teeth of living Japanese are clearly larger than those of their prehistoric predecessors, the Jōmon of the Late Pleistocene to the arrival of rice farmers approximately 2,300 years ago. However, a good look at the form of those prehistoric people quickly convinced me that they were not the ancestors of the modern Japanese. When I first voiced my suspicions to a senior and very gracious Japanese anthropologist, his comment to me was "Oh, I hope you're wrong."

Hunches can be useful starting points, but they remain matters of opinion until they are tested against hard and preferably quantified data. So when I returned to Japan a subsequent year, I took a series of craniofacial measurements on prehistoric and recent Japanese cranial material. I was still operating on the neo-Darwinian assumption that those dimensions were under selective force control even if it was difficult to imagine how. Since I was pretty sure that nose length and height were indeed controlled by selection, I included nasal measurements in the battery I applied. It would be interesting, I thought, if I could get a correlation between the variation in nasal dimensions with regional differences in temperature and humidity (Negus 1958, 1965). For a variety of reasons, that hunch never worked out, but I was able to show conclusively that those prehistoric Japanese people were not the ancestors of the ones who live there now. When I stuck to the prehistoric Jōmon specimens, I was able to show that their teeth did indeed get smaller over the last 8,000 years (Brace et al. 1989).

I was disappointed in my inability to show clines of nasal measurements. When we look at the people of the world, we can clearly see that northern people and desert-dwelling people have larger noses than others. So I added more nasal measurements to my battery and remeasured a whole series of samples in Japan, China, Europe, and America. I still was unable to get the nasal clines I had hoped to find, but what I discovered was that every time I added another measurement, however unimportant it appeared to be, my ability to discriminate between the people in different areas improved. When one uses measurements to create a tree diagram, or dendrogram, samples from a given portion of the world will cluster together as twigs on a single branch. Eventually,

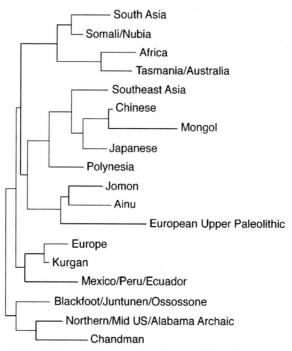

Figure 1–7　A neighbor-joining dendrogram based on craniofacial measurements depicting the relationships of a series of geographically disparate people with Late Pleistocene representatives from both the western and the eastern edges of the Old World (from Brace et al. 2001). To help the viewer with some of the unfamiliar names, *Kurgan* is the name of the Bronze Age culture in the Crimea of southern Russia, and *Chandman* is the Bronze Age of Mongolia, both about 4,000–4,500 years ago. *Blackfoot* is from the western Great Plains, *Juntunen* is a recent northern Michigan site, and *Ossossone* is also a recent site from nearby Ontario, Canada.

all branches join together at the base; but the lower down that union occurs, the more distantly related are the clusters at the end of those long branches.

The cluster diagrams we have produced from our craniofacial measurements on samples of all the regional populations of the world (see Fig. 1–7) are strikingly similar to the ones produced by those using DNA data as input. As with the DNA data, natural selection has played no role in controlling the distribution of what is being measured. In both cases, what we get is a picture that I have called "family resemblance writ large" (Brace 1996a, 136; 2000, 22, 320). When we are dealing with biological aspects that are inherited but have little or no adaptive value, their distribution is going to be controlled exclusively by relatedness. Neighbors then will be more closely associated on a dendrogram that depicts relationships than groups that are from different parts of the world.

2

THE PERCEPTION OF HUMAN DIFFERENCES IN THE PAST

WHAT SHALL WE CALL "THEM"?

At one of the sessions in a scientific meeting some years ago, I listened to a series of reports by geneticists discussing the differences between human populations in the configuration and base-pair sequence of mitochondrial DNA. They casually referred to the populations with which they were dealing as "Australoid," "Caucasoid," "Mongoloid," and so forth. At the end of each paper, there is routinely a short period for discussion, where questions and comments from the audience are in order.

After several such papers had been given, I rose to make the point that it would be preferable to use a geographical rather than a "racial" designation in describing human groups. The point is that the use of a "racial" designation runs the risk of perpetuating the hint of derogatory stereotypes that were classically part of the baggage of "racial" terminology. Names of the traditional sort assume some kind of implied descriptive aspect. Geographic terms, in contrast, tend to carry less of that implication and are just as useful in referring to human populations. In fact, they are even more useful because they can be expanded or contracted and specified with greater precision. This is one of the points that I hope this book will illustrate in convincing fashion.

Traditions die hard, however, and I was immediately opposed by a one-time protégé, who addressed the session as follows: "I apologize for my colleague Dr. Brace. It's all right to use the word 'Mongoloid.' . . . if the term has meaning, and it seems to . . . we should go on using the word 'Mongoloid.' If it's a fish, let's call it a fish." I repeat these words here because they serve as a poignant illustration of the dangers that inhere in the use of racial designations. In one utterance, the people of Asia were referred to in terms still used to characterize a kind of mental deficiency—"Mongolian" or "Mongoloid idiocy," more appropriately called Down syndrome (Nadel and Rosenthal 1991). As one of the audience remarked to me privately somewhat later, "Comments like that could set anthropology back fifty years."

As can be seen in Figure 1–7, the clusters bear a superficial resemblance at first glance to the "races" in a traditional classification. That is because I chose groups that came from the cores of the areas used to create the traditional taxonomy. If I had chosen to add groups from between these core areas, it would have produced a pattern showing how each area grades without break into the area adjacent to it. Even in Figure 1–7 itself, one can see that the Somali/Nubia sample of northeast Africa is actually closer to the South Asian sample than it is to the samples used for the Africa twig. If I were to put in our Egyptian sample, it would be even more remote from the twig labeled "Africa."

If you use every group, including those from the edges of the areas, then the cline would be apparent.

17

The more samples, the bushier the picture becomes and the harder it is to identify anything that could stand for the relationships indicated. Mongols, for example, are the least typical of the samples from East Asia. "Mongoloid" then is not a good way to characterize the cluster of Asian people. If one starts with samples from the Caucasus between southern Russia and northern Iran and Iraq, one would see that samples from England and Norway are sufficiently separated so they would have trouble qualifying as "Caucasoid." Osama Bin Laden would fit in nicely; however, Prince Philip of Britain would not. Likewise, Somalia and West Africa are not close to each other, even though the people are equally dark in skin color. "Negroid" then falls apart.

There is really a very simple solution. Instead of using the name of a people or their assumed characteristics, one can simply refer to the peoples of the world by the actual geographic name of where they are found. In the simplest possible way, we can refer to Africa, Europe, East Asia, South Asia, Australia, and North and South America. Then, if we want to be more specific, we can speak of West Africa, Northwest Europe, the Middle East, Southeast Asia, South Australia, and so forth. That way we can be as general or as narrowly specific as we like and no unwarranted assumptions are implied. In this manner, we can deal with the reality of human biological differences without any of the preconceptions introduced by the concept of "race." This book, however, was not intended as a treatment of human biological variation. I had to do just enough of that so that the reader could see why the concept of "race" prevents us from understanding the nature of human biological variation.

THE PEASANT PERSPECTIVE

Until very recently, the average human inhabitant of planet Earth lived on the family farm. Few of us even now are more than two or three generations removed from a farming way of life. Not only were they typically farmers, but most were unable to read and write. Knowledge about the world and the places and people in it was compounded from personal experience and the stories of parents and grandparents, whose own personal experiences were similarly limited.

Personal familiarity with the world was largely confined to the distance one could walk in a day or two. The average person rarely went more than 25 miles or so from the natal farm. Thus, the normal range of human experience was limited to what could be seen in that segment of the world lying within a radius of little more than 25 miles of the place of one's birth.

Roads were rudimentary, mere paths in many instances. There was no such thing as "public" transportation, horse-and-buggy travel was for the prosperous few, and books could be read and owned only by the educated well-to-do. Even the family Bible, like that rarefied urban phenomenon the newspaper, was possible only after the invention of the printing press in the middle of the 15th century.

It is still true that human appearance is essentially the same between any adjacent 25 mile circles. What differences are perceived tend to relate to customs of dress and traditions of behavior and speech. Variations in accent and even different languages can be encountered in adjacent districts in many parts of the world, but discernible differences in appearance just do not occur.

Today, if one were to start off on foot from Norway at the northwest edge of Europe and walk to Nigeria in equatorial Africa by way of Russia and the Middle East, there would be no single segment of that trip where the people in any 25 mile stretch were different enough from the people 25 miles farther on so that the traveler would take notice. Yet, obviously, there is a marked difference in the physical appearance of the people of Norway and the people of Nigeria, and Americans today accept this as "racial." The reason that Herodotus, Marco Polo, Ibn Battutah, and other such travelers of yesteryear never perceived human differences in categorical fashion is that they got from place to place largely over land—25 mile segment by 25 mile segment (Edwards 2001, 16)—and the gradation of one human group into another is so continuous that no boundaries are discernible. Even when they went by boat, it tended to be along a coastline and they would put in at port or anchor for the night rather than keep on going in the dark. The perception of human variation then was essentially the same as it was for the land traveler.

ANTIQUITY ✳

Now, if the reader has grasped the implications of what I have presented so far, the question inevitably comes up "If 'race' has no biological justification, how is it that we all grow up in the confident belief that this is just the way things are?" When I say that we all grow up confident that human "races" are valid biological categories, I am talking about the world of the present day. Most of us do not realize that what we now take for granted was not always the way that people thought about things. In fact, it is an outlook that has emerged only since the Renaissance in the 15th and 16th centuries and attained the status of accepted truth only within the last 200 years. It comes as something of a surprise to find out that this is not how people thought about the world prior to the Renaissance. As one French anthropologist put it late in the 19th century, "Neither the notion nor the word existed in Antiquity," and it was not used by Aristotle or Hippocrates (Topinard 1879, 589 [my translation]). It is not that people were unaware of human differences in the Middle Ages or the more remote worlds of classical antiquity. True, relatively fewer were able to gain their impressions of human variation firsthand since travel opportunities were much more limited. There were, however, some very assiduous and energetic travelers who produced detailed and vivid written accounts of their adventures, and these became well known.

It is interesting that, for all the accurate descriptions and records of human differences they contained, there is no mention of anything that we could call "race." In fact, there is nothing that would correspond with what we would regard as a "racial" designation in any of the writings of antiquity. Egyptian hieroglyphic accounts describe human appearance all the way from southern Russia to the equator, but there is no word or concept that corresponds to "race." Nor is there any such in the Judeo-Christian Bible, and it is completely missing from the writings of that classical Greek Herodotus (ca. 484–25 B.C.E.), the "father of history." To be sure, some of the translations of Herodotus's many-volumed *Histories* (see the 1990 edition) do use the term *race* in some places, but that is just an example of the translator reading his or her own slant into the Greek word for "people." "The ancient Arabs showed an acute awareness of ethnic, but very little consciousness of racial differences" (Lewis 1990, 43). Over 1,500 years later, the same can still be said for the writings of those phenomenal medieval travelers Marco Polo (1254–1324) of Venice and his Moroccan counterpart Ibn Battutah (1304–68) (see the 1931 and 1968 translations of Polo and the 1982 edition of Battutah).

Marco Polo went all the way across central Asia to China, then back via Southeast Asia and India before writing of his experiences (see the 1931 and 1968 translations). Somewhat later, his travels were surpassed by those of the Islamic geographer Ibn Battutah, the "Tangerine" (he was from Tangiers, Morocco [Mackintosh-Smith 2001]), who also visited the Balkans, the Black Sea and southern Russia, China, India, the Middle East, Egypt, and North Africa. He further visited the western Mediterranean as far as Gibraltar and Spain, and he made a trek across the Sahara to West Africa before settling in Fez to write his memoirs (see the 1982 edition).

The concept of "race" is significantly absent from the writings of these two great travelers, and they used no term that could be employed to represent it, although their translators regularly insert the term *race* where a word meaning "group" or "people" was used in the original. The only kinds of categorizing word that they used were more in the nature of religious designations, such as *Saracens, idolaters,* and *infidels.* Certainly, they encountered people whom Americans would regard as belonging to different "races," but it never occurred to them to think about human differences in such a fashion and for an obvious reason. Both were also fully aware of differences in human pigmentation and described them regularly. Polo (1931) referred to the people of Japan as "white, courteous and handsome" (p. 270). He also called the Mongol Tartars "most beautiful and white" (p. 114). He referred to the southwest Chinese as a "very handsome people, not quite white, but brown" (p. 205) and the people of the southeast coast of India as "black" and of the opinion that "he who is blackest is thought most of and held superior to those who are not so black" (p. 312). Scandinavians, he stated, were "very tall, and shapely, but they are also pale and colourless" (p. 388). Ibn Battutah was somewhat less charitable. He did not like the pink and blotchy complexion of the people of the coast of northwest Europe or the dark pigmentation of sub-Saharan Africa, feeling that what Allah had really intended was the medium brown of his native Tangiers in Morocco. Non-Muslims he invariably referred to as *infidels.*

To be completely accurate, the Italian version of Marco Polo's *Travels* does occasionally use the term *razze,* but while the English word *race* is a cognate, the implications of the Italian word are rather different from the accepted connotations in English. Polo mentioned the presence of "three races"—*tre razze*—in "Turcomania" (Polo 1998, 9). The three are Turks, Armenians, and Greeks; and he used the term *popoli*—"peoples"— to refer to the latter two. In other contexts, he used the word *uomini*—"humans." Some English translations use the word *classes.* The Latin translation uses the word *genera*— not in the formal sense of zoological taxonomy but to mean "kinds" or "classes." The French translations use *gens,* which simply indicates "people." In any case, the context of Polo's occasional use of the term *razze* shows that it does not have the implications that are at the core of the concept of "race" in the present world.

It is not that those ancient authors were unobservant or quaintly obtuse. In fact, quite the opposite; and one could suggest that they actually recorded a more accurate picture of the world than the one that has subsequently become accepted because they were forced to see it as it is, rather than skip steps as has since become the rule.

However, since human differences had been perceived as the result of such gradual means, they were never dealt with in categorical fashion. The world of human biological variation, then, was perceived as a graded phenomenon and not one comprised of discrete or distinct units. As we look back on things now, it is evident that their perceptions of the human world were actually more sophisticated and more faithful to reality than those of their successors.

RENAISSANCE

The advent of the Renaissance, however, was to change all that. The basic cause of that change was improvement in maritime technology and navigational capabilities. No longer was it necessary to poke along the coast in a modified fishing boat. The Renaissance mariner of the 15th century could set out from a port in western Europe and see nothing but water until raising the coast of an entirely different continent. Of course, the people encountered were immediately perceived as categorically distinct from those at the point of origin, and, for the first time, human variation began to be described in terms of categories instead of gradients. It is no accident that the peoples used to exemplify the nature of the human biological spectrum in subsequent accounts were just those encountered at the ends of the major Renaissance trade routes. These still serve as the exemplars of "the races" that most people now think constitute an adequate representation of the nature of biological variation in the species *Homo sapiens.*

For Europeans, this was largely an academic exercise, but such was not the case in the New World, the lands of the Western Hemisphere (Harris 1964). In those parts of the hemisphere under the control of the Roman Catholic Church, that is, much of what is called "Latin America," decisions about the status and treatment of the native inhabitants were theoretically made by the ecclesiastical authorities in the Old World— ultimately by the pope in Rome. In practice, the enforcement of subject status onto the indigenes by the European colonizers was driven by the Europeans' assumption of their own superiority. This was made possible by their possession of firearms and inadvertently hastened by the introduction of diseases to which the New World inhabitants had no immunity (Diamond 1997). Even within the Church itself there was a split between those who regarded all the Native Americans as the descendants of Adam and Eve and those who regarded them as belonging to Aristotle's category of people who were born to be slaves. The standoff between these two positions was epitomized by the inconclusive debate between the bishop of Chiapas, Bartolomé de Las Casas, and the Spanish jurist Juan Gines de Sepúlveda at Valladolid, Spain, in 1550 (Hanke 1974). The ambivalence which characterized the outcome of that debate remained evident in the Latin world for the next three centuries.

Finally, the short circuit in perceptions begun by the transoceanic Renaissance packet was simply reemphasized by advances in transportation and communications technology. The steamship kept on doing the same kind of thing that the sailing ship had started—that is, get people from their starting point to destinations however distant without seeing anything in between. When photography was invented, it simply recorded what people saw at those end points and presented this to the world as a frozen picture of what the whole presumably looked like. Acquisition of this disjointed picture of the world has simply been speeded up by the jumbo jet and magnified through the lens of the television camera, but the fundamental misperception of the world remains essentially the same.

Not only was human variation perceived in categorical fashion for the first time, but the Aristotelian tradition of logical division, adopted from Neoplatonism by medieval churchmen, was taken over and applied with increasing rigor to the natural world. Fundamental to this was the assumption that the world was essentially categorical in nature. Categorical perceptions lent themselves with seductive ease to categorical modes of description, and the categorical tradition of classification was the inevitable result. The classic example of this is the *Systema Naturae* (1735) of the Swedish botanist/ naturalist Carolus Linnaeus. In this, especially in its definitive tenth edition of 1758, the technique of the medieval *logica materialis* was applied to arranging the living species of the world in a named hierarchy, what has been called the "Great Chain of Being."

ENLIGHTENMENT: THE "AGE OF REASON"

The post-Renaissance world of the 18th century is known as the Enlightenment, or the "Age of Reason" to give it the name by which it was designated in the title of Thomas Paine's book in 1796. As with most other periods, it has no precise dates of demarcation. Furthermore, a good case can be made that it simply represents the working out of themes that were established in the preceding Renaissance. Still, there is utility in recognizing the Age of Reason, and it plays a very important, if somewhat curious, role in the development of the concept of "race."

The Renaissance had been responsible for a renewed interest in the thinking of the ancient Greeks, who had assumed that the world operated in terms of a rational moral set of principles. The collapse of the Greek city states and the subsequent collapse of the usurper of that legacy, the Roman Empire, had seen the eclipse of those ancient Greek views and their replacement by the rise of Christianity, in which "revelation" represented a higher truth than that which could be discerned by the use of reason alone. In the medieval Christianity of Saint Thomas Aquinas (1225–74), the reason of Aristotelian logic was much admired, but it was seen as subordinate to and supportive of revelation rather than being separate or in conflict (Aquinas 1994).

With the Protestant Reformation, the picture of the world provided by everyday human common sense was seen to be superior to at least some of the judgments offered by the hierarchy of the Church (Merton 1938, 451). Once more, as in ancient Greece, there was an increase in the faith that reason, judiciously applied, was sufficient to make sense out of the phenomena of the natural as well as the human world. The ascendancy of this faith during the 17th and 18th centuries is why this period is referred to as the "Enlightenment." Given the nature of the trends in thinking started by Martin Luther, it is not surprising to find that the flourishing of Enlightenment themes was particularly evident in the parts of Europe and America under Protestant domination. France might be seen as an exception to this generalization, but it was only partially an exception.

Early Enlightenment figures include Sir Francis Bacon (1561–1626) in England, René Descartes (1596–1650) in France, and Benedict Spinoza (1632–77) in Holland. Descartes, however much he stressed the use of logic, assumed a world of given entities very much in the fashion of his intellectual predecessor, Thomas Aquinas. Loyal to the Church of Rome, he exemplified "the metaphysics of a Catholic mathematician" (Shapiro 1991, 457). The full momentum of Enlightenment thought can be seen in the parallel careers of Sir Isaac Newton (1642–1727) in England and Gottfried Wilhelm Leibniz (1646–1716) in the German-speaking area.

SCIENCE AND THE GREATNESS OF GOD

Sir Francis Bacon, in contrast to his Catholic predecessors and contemporaries, excluded the consideration of "final causes" (really a code word for acts of God) from natural science and insisted that the "natural philosopher" (the words *science* and *scientist* had not been coined yet) become "as a little child" before "nature." In his view, to study nature was to glorify the God whose outward manifestation it is (Losee 1980). Bacon is widely regarded as the root from which modern science arose, and he exemplified the Enlightenment faith that the practice of science can only reveal the greatness of the God who created the wondrous world in which we find ourselves.

He also, as did most of the others who can be identified as Enlightenment figures, assumed that there could be no contradiction between what an individual investigator could find out by his own efforts and what was written in the accepted Christian Scriptures. If particular research efforts produced conclusions that were at odds with the biblical account, then this only indicated that the research had not been pursued far enough. Coupled with the idea that the world had been created specifically for human benefit, this assumption provided a powerful incentive for the pursuit of scientific research. It is no accident that the flourishing of science as a career and the pace of scientific discovery are disproportionately associated with countries that have a predominantly Protestant outlook (Merton 1970).

THE LIMITS OF REASON

In Catholic countries, there tended to be a much greater degree of skepticism concerning the powers of human reason. Since the human mind is finite and of far less capacity than the mind of God, it was deemed unlikely that the true nature of divine intent could be discovered as a result of human research and the application of human reason. In fact, there was a general feeling that to find out the ultimate nature of reality by the efforts of individual mortals could only lead to an incomplete and erroneous picture of what God actually intended. It would be best then to confine research to problems of limited scope that could be kept under tight control, leaving aside the large issues under the assumption that they were beyond the bounds of human ken. God made things the way they are in His infinite wisdom, and we mere mortals should accept that on faith since we can never gain more than an incomplete and flawed understanding by the use of our own imperfect capacities.

Unlike the previously mentioned conflict between Las Casas and Sepúlveda over whether Native Americans deserved to be regarded as real people or not, where it is quite clear that Las Casas was right and Sepúlveda was wrong, there is no obvious and clear-cut "right" and "wrong" to the differences between the approach toward science taken between the Catholic and Protestant societies during the Enlightenment. Although it is my own preference to push our efforts to the limit in trying to figure out what makes things tick in this world, when I look at the mess that people have made where the subject of "race" is concerned, I have more than a little sympathy with the skepticism embodied in the Catholic outlook.

Still, the point of this book is to apply an essentially Enlightenment approach to dealing with the nature of human biological differences, and I hope that the reader will agree that it is indeed within our power to find out what is significant in what ways and what is not. Although the main locus of the Enlightenment was in northern Europe, the region of the New World that was to become the United States of America was under northern European domination during that period, and the political and social history of the nation that was to emerge was heavily conditioned by the central currents of Enlightenment thought. Finally, of course, it was principally in the Western Hemisphere that populations of different continental origins confronted each other on a daily basis and provided a constant goad to the thought processes of those who were committed to making logical sense out of the world of their perception.

An essentially Enlightenment orientation can be found in the writings of one of the most unlikely people in colonial Boston, that fiery Puritan and Congregational minister Cotton Mather (1663–1728). Certainly the terms *reason* and *enlightened* hardly come to mind when we think back on the ethos of fear and hysteria to which he contributed at the time of the Salem witch trials in 1692. Still, he was much interested in science (Silverman 1984). He founded the Boston Benefit Societies that influenced the young Benjamin Franklin, a true and obvious Enlightenment figure; he was elected a Fellow of the Royal Society in 1713, and he led the Boston campaign for smallpox inoculations in 1721 (Imperato 1984). In classic Protestant Enlightenment fashion, he took the stance that science was "no *Enemy,* but a mighty and wondrous *Incentive* to Religion" (Mather 1721, 1).

LINNAEUS AND CLASSIFICATION

If America was the workshop in which the concept of "race" was to be cobbled together to resemble what is now accepted on a worldwide basis, the intellectual framework that served as a guide was entirely European. Furthermore, that framework, both in its substance and in the processes by which that substance was treated, came from the traditions of Enlightenment scholarship that gave rise to science as we know it.

Newton, giving full credit to his predecessors—the "giants" on whose shoulders he said that he stood—provided the foundation for subsequent physics and astronomy. Newton and Leibniz simultaneously but independently launched a major realm of mathematics, calculus (Kreiling 1968). Their counterpart in the natural sciences, the figure whose work underlies all subsequent accomplishments in biology, was the Swedish botanist Carl von Linné (1707–78), better known to us by the Latinized version of his name, Carolus Linnaeus (Fig. 2–1).

While Linnaeus started as a botanist, he extended his interests to encompass all living things, including human beings. It was his ambition to devise a system that could make order out of the apparent chaos of the manifestations of organic life. In the course

Figure 2-1   Carl von Linné, or Carolus Linnaeus, 1707–78, in 1775 (from the frontispiece of Blunt 2001).

of time, he succeeded in doing this in his *Systema Naturae (System of Nature)* first published in 1735. In subsequent editions, he used the techniques and categories that medieval churchmen had resuscitated from Aristotelian logic and took the final step of applying these to the arrangement of the categories of plants and animals in the living world. It was Linnaeus who established the now universal tradition of referring to a given organic entity by its generic and specific name.

In the two-name, or binomial, classification he devised, human beings are classed as genus *Homo* and species *sapiens.* The domestic dog is called *Canis familiaris,* and the wolf from which it was derived is *Canis lupus.* (Dogs and wolves interbreed without any problem, and recent work in molecular genetics has supported the view that dogs in fact are just a variety of wolf and should properly be classified as *Canis lupus familiaris* [Wayne 1993].) Linnaeus also gave each plant a generic and a specific name, such as *Acer saccharum* for the sugar maple and *Rudbeckia hirta* for the black-eyed susan. In the latter case, Linnaeus gave that name in honor of his patron, Olof Rudbeck, who was also a colleague on the faculty of the University of Uppsala in Sweden, where Linnaeus was professor of botany.

Inspired by the roster of categories in the Aristotelian logic of the Middle Ages, Linnaeus arranged the living world into named units in descending order of increasing distinctiveness. The five categories were class, order, genus, species, and variety. He realized that there was an element of the arbitrary in doing this, but he felt that a system of some sort was better than none at all (Larson 1971).

It was a truly monumental undertaking, and by 1758 when Linnaeus produced the tenth edition of his famous *Systema Naturae,* with some 12,000 plants and animals duly named and arranged, he clearly merited the fame he had acquired. Even so, more than a few of his contemporaries and subsequent biographers have commented on his vanity and self-interest, "All animals are beautiful, but money is more beautiful" being one cited example (Gilbert 1984, 106). Another example of his ego is found in his aphorism "God created, Linnaeus arranges" and his reference to himself as "God's Registrar" (Gilbert 1984, 112, 114).

Although it may be true that there were less than admirable aspects evident in Linnaeus the man, it seems quite clear from his writings that he honestly felt that his effort in naming all the plants and animals he could identify in the world was a genuine act of piety (Lindroth 1983). To him, the act of naming was equated with the practice of science itself, which in effect simply meant giving recognition to the magnitude of divine creation. This can be clearly seen in the words he used in the introduction to all the later editions of his *Systema Naturae:* "I saw the infinite, all-knowing and all-powerful God from behind as He went away and I grew dizzy. I followed His footsteps over nature's fields and saw everywhere an eternal wisdom and power, an inscrutable perfection" (quoted by Lindroth 1973, 380). This, like the words of Sir Francis Bacon and Cotton Mather, demonstrates the strength of an Enlightenment Protestant's conviction that the study of the natural world was an exercise in honoring the God who made it.

Linnaeus and the Classification of the Human Species

In the famous tenth edition of his *Systema Naturae,* Linnaeus ([1758] 1956) placed *Homo sapiens* in the order Primates, where it has remained ever since. He also included apes and monkeys in the order, as well as, for good measure, bats. He did this strictly on the grounds of shared anatomical characteristics, a procedure that has been followed by natural scientists ever since. There was no intention of indicating actual relationships in terms of common ancestry or heritage, although the use of a common term to include other forms along with humans in a single scheme of classification made some of his contemporaries distinctly uncomfortable.

For example, the noted English zoologist Thomas Pennant (1726–98) stated, with rather transparent honesty, "I REJECT his first division, which he calls *Primates,* or Chiefs of Creation, because my vanity will not suffer me to rank mankind with *Apes, Monkies, Maucaucos* and *Bats,* the companions LINNAEUS has allotted us" (Pennant 1781, iii–iv). Considering the obvious quantity of unacknowledged vanity that lurks in the classifications of so many naturalists—with recent paleoanthropologists heading the list—it is refreshing indeed to read a scholar who candidly admits that his taxonomic preferences are controlled by that emotion. From a strictly scientific point of view, of course, "vanity" is an inadmissible reason for the ranking of similarities and differences, so more recent scholars have done their best to deny that their egos have had anything to do with the often arcane systems they have erected and defended with clouds of terminological obfuscation.

In contemplating the list that Linnaeus included among the Primates, the perspicacious reader may wonder whether he slipped a cog by including bats. In fact, many zoologists from the time of Linnaeus on have noted that the Primates show many simi-larities to the Insectivora—moles, shrews, and the like—and that bats can properly be regarded as specialized flying insectivores. Not long ago, a study of the neural pathways between the eye and the brain plus some other features of fruit bats led to the suggestion that they are more closely related to the Primates than they are to insect-eating bats—in effect, flying Primates (Pettigrew 1986, 1991). Linnaeus could not have known neu-roanatomical details of this kind, but whether either assessment is correct or not, the fact that the issue of Primate–bat relationships is still being given serious consideration today only points up the insight that he had in the assessment of gross morphological details.

When Linnaeus turned his attention to human biological variation, he picked up on the ideas of a late 17th-century French physician, François Bernier (1620–88), who ad-vocated using the "four quarters" of the globe as the basis of providing labels for human differences. In a sense, it was something of a holdover of the way of thinking about the world dating from before the realization that the earth was a sphere rather than a flat plane with four edges. Linnaeus's perception of the nature of geography was a bit more encompassing than that of Bernier, and the four varieties of human beings that he rec-ognized were *Homo sapiens europaeus, H. sapiens asiaticus, H. sapiens americanus,* and *H. sapiens afer,* representing Europe, Asia, America, and Africa, respectively. Emphasizing his quadripartite division, he attributed a predominance of the four "humors" of the Greco-Roman physician Claudius Galen (ca. 130–220 C.E.), inspired in turn from the four "elements" of Aristotle (Needham 1993, 31; Nutton 2002). Galen's humors were blood, phlegm, yellow bile, and black bile, and he attributed what he as-sumed to be the characteristics of the various human groups to an excess of one or an-other of these humors. Thus, Europeans tended to be "sanguine," Asians "melancholic," Americans "choleric," and Africans "bilious" (Temkin 1973).

Linnaeus did not stop with the four supposed geographic varieties of human popu-lations; he also mentioned other human or semihuman groups of which he had heard mention but had no direct experience. Included were certain supposed "wild men," "men" with tails, and *Homo monstrosus.* As we shall see shortly, Linnaeus did not consider the order of the groups to be random. In fact, his whole scheme was part of a fundamentally hierarchical view of things.

The Great Chain of Being

Linnaeus was an Enlightenment figure to the extent that he held it as an incontrovertible item of faith that the pursuit of science was one of the most productive ways of demon-strating the glory of God. To be sure, like his modern intellectual descendants in various aspects of paleontology, he was convinced that science was confined to the giving of names (Larson 1971, 144). In this respect, Linnaeus reflected the world view of the me-dieval scholastics. He was a thoroughgoing Platonic essentialist. The reality in the world he depicted consisted in the fixed and separate species whose perfect representations were to be found only in the mind of God.

In this sense, Linnaeus was a classic creationist. His monumental effort at naming simply gave honor to the act of creation by which the living world was assumed to have been produced. Since Linnaeus had taken his scheme of classification from the structure of Aristotelian logic enshrined in medieval thought, it was inevitable that the categories he set up could be treated in terms of similarity or difference by application of that very same logic. This could be extended to generate a dendrogram.

It is easy enough now to see that dendrograms based on similarities and differences can be regarded as depicting actual lineage relationships. In the middle of the 19th century, Charles Darwin actually used them in this sense, and biologists have been doing so ever since. I also did just that in Figure 1–7. This, however, was not implied in the pre-Darwinian use of the dendrogram concept.

When early Christian scholastics took over the idea of tree construction implicit in the logic of Neoplatonism, they conceived of the hierarchy that such diagrams inevitably produce as indicating proximity to and distance from the perfection of the divine. They united such views with repeated biblical assertions that human beings are superior to all other forms of life and were given dominion over them by divine fiat. In the King James version of the Bible, one of the most famous passages asserting this position is found in Psalms 8:4–9.

> **4** What is man that thou art mindful of him?
> and the son of man, that thou visitest him?
>
> **5** For thou hast made him a little lower than the angels,
> And hast crowned him with glory and honour.
>
> **6** Thou madest him to have dominion over the works of thy hands;
> Thou hast put all *things* under his feet:
>
> **7** All sheep and oxen, yea, and the beasts of the fields;
>
> **8** The fowl of the air and the fish of the sea,
> And *whatsoever* passeth through the paths of the seas.
>
> **9** O Lord our Lord, how excellent *is* thy name in all the earth!

The assumption that the world was hierarchically arranged pervaded medieval Christian thought and continued without question in the outlook of Enlightenment thinkers as well. Linnaeus and his contemporaries simply took that general view and provided a more specific picture of all aspects of the world arranged in a series of steps running from God at the top down through the various entities of the living world to the inorganic—"base" metals—at the bottom. This arrangement was referred to as the *scala naturae* or "Great Chain of Being."

Like most of his Enlightenment colleagues, Linnaeus thought of the Great Chain as a series of discrete steps, each occupying a unique position in the hierarchy in relation to God at the top and the adjacent steps above and below and each essential as a part of the structure of the world that God had created. It was a perfectly fixed and static structure, and, in the somewhat simplistic euphoria of Enlightenment rationalizing where "All is for the best in this the best of all possible worlds," each step had an essential role to perform in maintaining the integrity of the chain as a whole (Voltaire [1759] 1957; Jerrold 1930, xiii).

The 18th-century vision of the fixed and perfect *scala naturae* was captured in verse by the English writer Alexander Pope (1688–1744) in epistle I of his *Essay on Man* ([1734] 1969, 19).

Vast chain of Being! Which from God began,
Natures Ethereal, human, Angel, Man,
Beast, bird, fish, insect; what no eye can see,
No glass can reach: from Infinite to thee,
From thee to Nothing.—On superior pow'rs
Were we to press, inferior might on ours;
Or in the full Creation leave a Void,
Where, one step broken, the great Scale's destroy'd:
From Nature's Chain whatever link you strike,
Tenth or ten thousandth, breaks the chain alike.

For those who viewed the world as God-created, fixed, and perfect, the idea that one of the entities of God's creation could cease to exist was simply impossible. The possibility of extinction, then, was denied in principle. The loss of even one of the steps in that Great Chain would mean that the perfection of the world had been diminished, and of course if an all-powerful divinity had allowed such an event to occur, then either the world had not been created perfect in the first place or God was not all-powerful. Neither possibility was compatible with orthodox Enlightenment thinking, which was why the contemplation of evidence for extinction was so profoundly disturbing to the 18th-century mind.

Enter the dodo, or rather, exit the dodo. It has often been said that the name was from the Portuguese word for "stupid," but it is more likely to derive from the Dutch for "sluggard" or "fat rear" (Gould 1996a, 27). The dodo was a large, flightless relative of the pigeons that lived on Mauritius in the middle of the Indian Ocean between South Africa and India when that island was discovered in 1505. The Dutch also called it *walckvögel*, or "nausea bird," and evidently did not care to eat them even though they were hopelessly inept at avoiding capture (Quammen 1996). In 1628, the Dutch landed some pigs on Mauritius "to maintain God-fearing shipwrecked sailors," and these multiplied so rapidly that the outcompeted dodo became extinct early in the 1680s (Guggisberg 1970).

No gastronomic or other regrets are recorded on behalf of the Dutch sailors, but the eventual realization of the demise of the dodo caused more than a little mental anguish to those Enlightenment scholars who felt that this should not have been possible in the perfect God-created world. Despite all their protestations, however, it was patently demonstrable that there were no more dodos, and the realists who insisted on pointing this out to the discomfiture of their philosophical colleagues in the Age of Reason are remembered in the phrase that has lasted as a memento of their debate: "as dead as a dodo."

The Great Chain of Being that was assumed by Linnaeus and his followers—and there were many—was a categorical phenomenon. It was made up of individual entities that were clearly distinct and nonoverlapping, hierarchically ranked from the highest of living forms represented by the Primates with human beings crowning the list and running down to the inorganic at the bottom. The distinct categories were the same as the ideal essences in the pre-Christian formulation of Plato and his school, now incorporated into the Christian ethos so that they were considered to be representations of the ideas in the mind of God.

This was why the demise of the dodo was so disturbing. If the dodo existed because God had the idea in his mind, what did it imply when the dodo ceased to exist? Human beings, after all, could still think about the now defunct dodo, and if human beings could think of something, surely the all-powerful divine mind could think of it too or else it would be less than all-powerful. If the divine mind thinks *dodo,* then dodo there is; but there was no more dodo! Did that mean a diminution in the powers of the mind of God? These were disturbing thoughts to the pious Protestants of the Age of Reason. Catholic thinkers, on the other hand, were much less bothered by them. In the Catholic view, the ways of God were beyond the powers of the human mind to understand, and it was simply a waste of effort worrying about what was inscrutable. If the dodo was extinct, *requiescat in pace.*

BUFFON AND CONTINUITY

Although Linnaeus and others thought of the world as made up of a finite series of distinct and hierarchically ranked categories, there was in fact another and very persuasive way of looking at things. This was powerfully articulated by the French naturalist Georges Louis Leclerc, Comte de Buffon (1707–88), who was an exact contemporary of Linnaeus. Buffon was born of bourgeois parents in Montbard, Burgundy. His mother had inherited a comfortable fortune, which his father used to acquire his noble title. He was educated in a Jesuit school and later trained in law at Dijon, where his father was a member of the Burgundian Parliament.

In 1732, Buffon came into his mother's fortune and moved to Paris, where, in 1739, he became keeper in the Jardin du Roi (Garden of the King), renamed the Jardin des Plantes (Garden of Plants) during the French Revolution. This was more than just a botanic garden since it later included the Paris Zoo, and a portion of it was used in 1793 as the site for the Muséum d'Histoire Naturelle, now called the Muséum National d'Histoire Naturelle, the chief focus for the study of natural history in France.

In Paris, Buffon devoted part of his efforts to the pursuit of business interests and succeeded in building a substantial fortune. What he is best remembered for, however, is his monumental efforts in the field of natural history. Starting in 1749, the first of his multivolume tour de force *Histoire Naturelle* appeared in print. By the time of his death in 1788, 36 volumes had been produced. Another eight were published posthumously (Roger 1970). The effect of this on his contemporaries was enormous, and he has been assessed as "the greatest naturalist of the eighteenth century" (Rudwick 1972, 930). In the words of one of the giants in the natural sciences of the 20th century, "It is no exaggeration to claim that initially all the well-known writers of the Enlightenment . . . were Buffonians, either directly or indirectly" (Mayr 1982, 330).

In classic Enlightenment fashion, Buffon had tried to produce a rational treatment of the whole of natural history, but his perspective was quite different from that of Linnaeus, who felt that his task would be complete when he had classified everything in creation. On his part, Buffon noted the correspondence between aspects of the environment in particular regions and the form of the plants and animals that lived there—today, we would say that he was aware of both ecology and adaptation. He accepted the evidence for a vast time scale and the fact that the similarity between the differently adapted forms in given regions suggests some kind of actual relationship. Although he rejected the idea of organic evolution in essential features, he at least brought it up as a topic for discussion. Throughout his writings, there was a continual concern for the processes by which organic form is shaped, something that was completely missing in the writings of Linnaeus.

The most fundamental difference between Buffon and Linnaeus, however, lay in their attitudes toward the identity of the basic units of the biological world. Linnaeus simply assumed the reality of the named categories he had adopted from the *logica materialis* of medieval theology. Buffon, on his part, resurrected the skepticism of the nominalist critics of Aquinas and the medieval scholastics. He considered that Linnaeus's use of those logical categories to represent the organic world had the effect of rendering "the language of science more difficult than science itself" (quoted in Larson 1971, 149). All those hierarchical names that Linnaeus had used were, in Buffon's eyes, human creations for the sake of human convenience. "In fact, in nature there are only individuals; genera, orders, and classes exist only in our imagination" (quoted in Nordenskiöld 1928, 222).

During his mid-career in the early 1760s, Buffon even went so far as to reject the reality of species. Although the phrase "individuals alone exist in nature" continued to appear in all the editions of his *Histoire Naturelle* even long after his death, he did note that "We should regard two animals as belonging to the same species if, by means of copulation, they can perpetuate themselves and preserve the likeness of the species" (1799, II:10). Although the rejection of the reality of species may seem to border on the indefensible, it is squarely in line with the conclusions of none other than Charles Darwin a century later, when he noted the amount of decision making and judgment needed to define a species. As Darwin observed, "In short we shall have to treat species in the same manner as those naturalists treat genera, who admit that genera are merely artificial combinations made for convenience" (Darwin 1859, 485). Darwin concluded "This may not be a cheering prospect; but we shall at least be freed from the vain search for the undiscovered and undiscoverable essence of the term species" (Darwin 1859, 485).

Buffon had rejected the Platonic essentialism of Linnaeus and his medieval predecessors. Because of Linneaus's preoccupation with the giving of names, Buffon regarded him as a "nomenclateur" rather than what we would now refer to as a "scientist." Much the same could be said about recent writers who deal with the fossil record of human evolution (e.g., Tattersall 2001). Buffon's own position was in line with Baconian empiricism, although he did not lapse into the atheism of some of his contemporaries. Instead, he remained within that Enlightenment tradition that maintained the compatibility between science and religion. In the classic 18th-century sense of accepting God as manifest in nature and the operation of natural laws, Buffon was a "deist." One could say very much the same thing for Darwin a century later.

If Buffon did not accept the a priori categories that Linnaeus assumed, he did accept as a fact that the world of living things was hierarchically arranged from the divine down to the inorganic. Resembling the formulation of the English philosopher and empiricist John Locke (1632–1704), his version of the Great Chain of Being, however, was that of a continuous gradation and not that of rungs on a ladder or links in a chain (Lovejoy 1936, 184). The view of the Great Chain as a continuum rather than a series of discrete steps was bolstered by the development of calculus by Leibniz and Newton, and it also received support from another aspect of the medieval Platonism that flourished during the Enlightenment. This was the idea of "plenitude." If God were indeed all-good and all-powerful, not only was this therefore the best of all possible worlds, but everything

Buffon's argument counters Linneus

that could in fact must exist. It was implicit in Platonism that no genuine potentiality for existence could remain unfulfilled. In the Christian version of this, if a human could think of a logical kind of being, surely God, with his more powerful mind, had already thought of it. If God had thought of it, it must therefore exist.

These aspects of 18th-century faith had the curious effect of leading to a search for "missing links." So thoroughly has the Great Chain of Being been incorporated into general evolutionary expectations in the post-Darwinian world of a century and more later that we tend to think of "missing links" in the sense of something in-between living and fossil forms. This, however, was far from the original meaning of the term. Instead, it was entirely promoted by the idea that somewhere there should be a form that came right between obviously "higher" and "lower" ranks on the scale of beings that ran from the inert at the bottom to God at the top. It was really from the idea that creation was filled with every possibility that the vision of the chain as an unbroken continuum was initially derived.

After the end of the 18th century, the very idea of the Great Chain of Being was called into question by secular scholars, and it has essentially been dismissed in the subsequent world of science. This was not the end of it, however, and it has lingered on as a powerful if unrecognized organizer in Western perceptions of the world. The whole subject of its roots and origins, its categorical versus its continuous manifestations, and its surviving influence has been treated in magisterial fashion in *The Great Chain of Being: A Study in the History of an Idea,* originally delivered in 1933 as the William James Lectures at Harvard University by Professor Arthur O. Lovejoy of Johns Hopkins University (Lovejoy 1936). As the definitive treatment of its subject, it has rightly been called "one of the masterpieces of twentieth century scholarship" (Nisbet 1980, x).

CAMPER AND THE FACIAL ANGLE

If I have done little more than summarize Lovejoy's treatment of the general matter of the Great Chain of Being, it should be obvious that much more can be said about the influence such an idea has had on assessments of the meaning of human biological variation. Many European naturalists during the Enlightenment had only a second-hand knowledge of human variation throughout the world. Much of Linnaeus's information, for example, had been gained from his students, who had brought him back specimens and descriptions from their field expeditions so that he could add material to his growing "system." Bringing back a representative collection of human specimens was not quite as easily accomplished, so some of his synthesis was based on descriptions by other people. Inevitably, this resulted in the incorporation of hearsay ideas and in a reduction in the accuracy of some of what was printed.

Those European countries attempting to maintain colonial empires tended to provide more direct access for their scholars to the data of natural history in other parts of the world. They also provided greater opportunity for direct observation on the original human inhabitants of their colonial domains. One such was Holland. It is no accident, for example, that Linnaeus produced the first edition of his *Systema Naturae* during a prolonged stay in Holland, where he earned his M.D. Subsequently, when asked about the categorical distinction between human and ape, Linnaeus wrote in despair: "I demand of you, and of the whole world, that you show me a generic character . . . by which to distinguish between Man and Ape. I myself most assuredly know of none. I wish somebody would indicate one to me" (quoted in Greene 1909, 25). Not too surprisingly, it was a Dutch anatomist, Pieter Camper (1722–89), who provided what he believed to be just such a categorical distinction. Because of the presence of Dutch colonial forces in what is now Indonesia, aspects of the flora and fauna of Southeast Asia were readily available, and Camper had dissected five specimens of the Southeast Asian great ape, the orangutan. Linnaeus's own information was taken from the published accounts of others, and he had actually included the orangutan in the human genus as *Homo sylvestris orang outang*. Camper, however, was able to show that the forward part of the palate in apes, the part that bears the upper incisor teeth, is separated from the rest of the tooth-bearing part of the maxilla by a suture that is not present in human beings. In most mammals, that separate bone at the front of the palate is called the *intermaxillary bone* or the *premaxilla* and the suture that separates it from the maxilla proper is the *premaxillary suture*.

Camper is much more famous, however, for his comparison of the angles of the facial profile between monkeys, apes, and humans. His famous "facial angle" is produced by drawing a tangent touching the forehead and the upper lip and measuring the angle made by that line—the *facial line*—and a line that runs through the ear opening and the juncture of the upper lip and the lower border of the nose. He had noticed that the heads carved by ancient Greek sculptors had a steeper profile than those painted by Dutch and Flemish artists, and using his computed facial angle, he extended the comparison to other human populations and to apes and monkeys (Fig. 2–2).

When he compared Europeans, Africans, and central Asians (Kalmucks) with a monkey and an orangutan, he commented upon the "marked analogy between the head of the Negro and that of the ape" (quoted in Greene 1959, 190; see Fig. 2–3). As far as the variation in the angle between the human samples he used was concerned, he claimed that it fell between 70 and 80 degrees: "Everything above eighty degrees belonged to the realm of art, everything below seventy degrees to the animal kingdom." Starting from the relatively vertical ancient Greek profile, he observed that "when I inclined that line backwards, I produced a Negro physiognomy, and definitely the profile of an ape, of a Chinese, of an idiot in proportion as I inclined this same line more or less to the rear" (quoted in Greene 1959, 190–191).

Here, then, is a clear use of a morphological attribute to place different human groups on different levels of an assumed hierarchy, and it is an example that has been repeated endlessly over the last 200 years to justify differences in worth between the various modern populations of *Homo sapiens*. At least Camper did not make categorical distinctions between his various human populations of the kind that would have allowed them to have been viewed as different species. If they could be put on a hierarchy of worth as was almost universally assumed, it was a hierarchy in which each group graded into the next without break—in fact, an interpretation of the Great Chain of Being as a continuum.

Others followed Camper's lead, and one of the most cited of these was the English "surgeon" (British for what Americans call a "doctor") Charles White (1728–1813). The title of his book of 1799 is worth quoting in full because, if one reads it without understanding the Great Chain of Being context in which it was written, the title sounds more

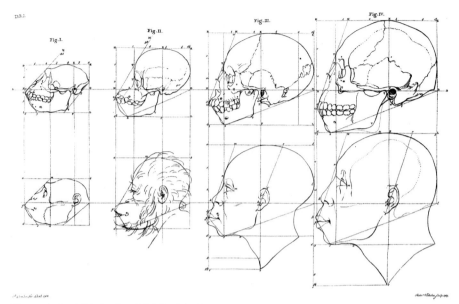

Figure 2–2   This is plate I (TAB. I) in Camper (1791, 37), showing the differences in his famous "facial angle." This was measured by drawing a line through the top of the ear opening and the bottom of the nose and another line running from the forehead to the juncture of the lips and measuring the angle between them. Camper's fig. I is of an Old World monkey of unknown species; his fig. II is of a juvenile orangutan before the eruption of any of its permanent teeth. Camper refers to his fig. III as a "young Negro," actually one bordering on adolescence. The second permanent molar is in place, but the second upper premolar, or "bicuspid," has yet to emerge. Camper labeled the specimen in fig. IV a "Kalmouk," presumably from central Asia north of the Caspian Sea, although I have to confess that it does not look anything like the some dozens of Calmuck crania that I have seen. Camper's facial angle actually simply measures the extent to which the tooth-bearing part of the cranium projects forward of the brain-enclosing part. As such, it represents a complex interplay of the relations between brain size and tooth size, each of which is under a separate and unrelated set of selective pressures.

than slightly bizarre. He called his book *An Account of the Regular Gradation in Man, and in Different Animals and Vegetables; and from the Former to the Latter.* His commitment to a noncategorical and graded view of the *scala naturae* is shown in his introductory words: "From man down to the smallest reptile, Nature exhibited to our view an immense chain of being, endued with various degrees of intelligence and active powers, suited to their stations in the general system" (White 1799, iii). Even more explicitly, he continued: "Nature would not employ gradation in only one instance, but would adopt it as a general principle" (White 1799, iii). In White's version of the chain, not only was "man" at the top but the very first link was composed of European "whites."

The reality and "logic" of the Great Chain of Being were accepted by virtually all Enlightenment thinkers. For a while, the influence of Buffon was such that the view of the Chain as a continuum held sway. It was certainly apparent in Pieter Camper and Charles White, and it was also prominent in the thinking of two even more important writers, Samuel Stanhope Smith and Johann Friedrich Blumenbach, who are treated at

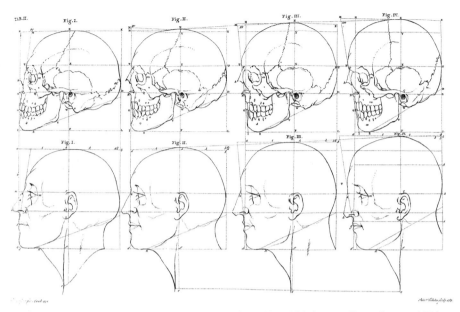

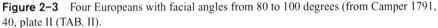

Figure 2-3   Four Europeans with facial angles from 80 to 100 degrees (from Camper 1791, 40, plate II (TAB. II).

greater length in the pages to come. These were the authors who turned their attention most specifically to the description and interpretation of human biological variation late in the 18th century. Other writers dealt with variation in the nonhuman components of the biological world, but that is not the focus of this book so they have been passed over without mention.

ASSESSING THE MEANING OF HUMAN DIFFERENCES

There remained a major commitment to reconciling the rapidly accumulating information brought back by the expanding mercantile network with what could be read in the Christian Bible (Berlin 1980). Where human beings were concerned, this meant trying to figure out how the progeny of Adam and Eve had come to look like Africans, Asians, Australians, and all the rest in the few thousand years assumed to have elapsed since creation (Smith [1787] 1965).

Resolute efforts to reconcile the findings of science with a traditional Christian framework were built into the outlook of the Protestant world, and it was not unexpected that this was particularly a matter of concern to those parts of the New World that were under Protestant domination (Hooykaas 1972; Steinberg 1989). If this was to lead to inherently unresolvable conflicts for the literalists, there was the further problem that there was nothing about the human populations of the Western Hemisphere that could possibly be used to make sense out of the variation perceived, although no one at that time— or since—really recognized that. Yet, there they were, populations derived from three narrowly restricted parts of the world, thrown together on a daily basis, with the dominant segment committed to an effort to make sense out of it. The ultimate result was the reification of a concept of "race" derived from somewhat poorly examined Protestant compulsions and a biologically nonsensical database—the artificially assembled population blocs of the New World. Adding strain to the whole picture was the blatant contradiction posed by the reality of African slavery in a country which professed to embody the principles of equalitarian democracy.

Martin Luther's challenge to the authority of the Church, initiated in 1517, had promoted the view that each individual was fully able to make the moral decisions essential for the pursuit of a proper Christian life without the aid of a priest or other churchly authority figure (Poliakov 1974). In a way, it was somewhat like opening Pandora's box. From this, it was but a step to a faith that ordinary human beings also were perfectly competent to make decisions concerning their own governance, and the seeds of political democracy grew from there (Huntington 1985). Combined with an Enlightenment assumption that the world was logical and knowable, there was a surge in deliberate scientific endeavor along with a confident expectation that the results would be not only evident and understandable by all but also compatible with Christian traditions (Berlin 1980). It was no accident that these themes flourished in those parts of Europe under Protestant domination and that they characterized the outlook of the portion of the New World that was conquered and colonized by Protestant Europeans.

By the end of the 18th century in Europe, confidence in some of these Enlightenment themes had started to crumble and give way to the emerging currents of Romanticism. It was not that the Age of Reason gave way to unreason, but an uneasy feeling began to grow that there were aspects of the world that were simply beyond the power of reason to dissect and yet within the grasp of human intuition (Lovejoy 1936; Hook 1975, 126; Horsman 1981, 159). These trends had a parallel course in the young United States of America, and nothing illustrates this better than the development of the concept of "race."

3

ONE ORIGIN OR MANY?

THE ROOTS OF "POLYGENISM"

The Enlightenment is sometimes said to end with the French Revolution of 1789–92. Like the other historical periods already treated, it is not so easy to put exact dates on beginnings and endings. The storming of the Bastille on July 14, 1789, did put in motion events that were to change the way people thought about the world. However, the French Revolution had been inspired in part by the previous American Revolution of 1776, so neither July 14, 1789, nor January 21, 1793, when Louis XVI lost his head to the guillotine, actually signaled by itself the beginning or the end of an era (Higonnet 1988). The final years of the 18th century and the beginning of the next did see a major alteration in outlook. This will be examined in greater detail in the next section, but one of the things that can serve to symbolize that major change was the increasing willingness of people to abandon a commitment to traditional views just because they were traditional.

One of these fragments of traditional "wisdom" was the acceptance of the "unity of mankind" that had been a key element in the thinking of Samuel Stanhope Smith, the American Enlightenment figure who is treated at some length in Chapter 4. Like most of his predecessors and contemporaries, he accepted that position primarily because the words of the Bible allowed no alternative. Of course, the obvious fecundity that followed from sexual coupling between males and females of the most visibly divergent human populations provided a basic biological confirmation for that scripturally sanctified stance. Recall for a moment that the biblical account was based on the traditional wisdom of the "peasant perspective." This was rooted in the outlook of nonliterate farmers and herdsmen whose experience of other people and places was limited to the distance they could walk in a day or two.

Starting with the Renaissance "age of discovery," however, travelers who were to write their impressions of the world away from home increasingly came to do so on the basis of voyages made by boat. Even commentators on the world who had not traveled themselves based their analyses on the reports of those who had gained their experiences from seafaring expeditions. To an increasing extent, the readers of their accounts were presented with descriptions of all kinds of things that were never mentioned in the Bible. Furthermore, their words spoke of the discrete differences between the people at home—Renaissance Europe—and the people at the various ports of call visited by the marine voyager.

Not surprisingly, questions began to arise as to whether the biblical account was the whole story or not. The possibility suggested itself that the various human populations of the world may have descended from different "original pairs" created in different places. Within the realm of Christendom, occasional and somewhat offhand suggestions of this sort began to be made as the Renaissance gathered momentum. Predictably enough, the proposers were charged with blasphemy, if not outright heresy.

Paracelsus

The most noted Renaissance polygenist or proponent of multiple human origins—although the adjective *notorious* is probably more appropriate—is remembered by the name of Paracelsus (ca. 1493–1541). Born in Switzerland as Theophrastus Bombastus von Hohenheim, he opted for the name Philippus Aureolus Paracelsus, presumably to indicate his equivalence to the first-century Roman medical writer Celsus, author of the famous work *De Medicina*. Paracelsus had studied medicine at various universities, including Ferrara in Italy, but may never have earned a degree (Temkin 1952; Pagel 1974). Today, we react with alarm at the thought of people practicing medicine without a degree, but traditionally the great majority of physicians gained their training as apprentices to those already in practice. Of the 3,500 "doctors" in the American army during the Revolution, 90% lacked medical doctorates and had been apprentice-trained (Norwood 1966, 20).

Controversy surrounded Paracelsus from beginning to end. He lectured on medicine at the University of Basel between 1526 and 1528 and created something of a sensation by beginning his performance with a solemn burning of the classical medical texts of the Greco-Roman physician Galen (ca. 130–220 C.E. [Sarton 1966]) and the Persian Neoplatonist physician Avicenna (980–1037 C.E.), after which he proceeded to push his own system. His lectures were in the German vernacular rather than the formal Latin of tradition, and he advocated a curious mystical combination of Neoplatonism, astrology, and alchemy. On the positive side, he established the importance of chemistry in medicine, earning himself recognition as one of the principal founders of pharmacology. It was he who pioneered the use of powders, tinctures, and alcoholic extracts, which went on to take their place in the standard pharmacopoeia (Saunders and O'Malley 1950, 21).

The Basel printer Johannes Oporinus, who produced the brilliant and beautifully illustrated books of the Renaissance anatomist Andreas Vesalius (1514–64), studied medicine for a while with Paracelsus but abandoned his efforts because of the erratic behavior of his teacher, whom he came to regard as "an impious sot" (Saunders and O'Malley 1950, 21). Paracelsus was referred to by his contemporaries as "the Luther of medicine" (Webster 1982, 4). A rather vivid appraisal described him as "Personally . . . unbearable. Like Luther, whom he despised, he was a crude peasant—obscene, insulting, exasperating—and, most annoyingly, like Luther, he was right—about some things. Maybe" (White 1983, 50).

It is hardly surprising that so iconoclastic a figure was not reluctant to challenge the traditional view of a single creation or "monogenism." In 1520, he wrote "I cannot abstain in this place from making mention of those who have been found in out-of-the-way islands, and still remain, and are to be met with there. No one will easily believe that they are the posterity of Adam and Eve, for the sons of Adam by no means departed into out-of-the-way islands. It is probable that they are descended from another Adam" (quoted by Bendyshe 1865, 353). Those "out-of-the-way islands," by the way, refer to what Columbus had encountered in the Caribbean. At the time Paracelsus was writing, it was still not understood that Columbus had discovered a whole new continent. Paracelsus's claims for "non-Adamical Men" remained a topic for commentary—largely condemnatory—over the next several centuries.

Given his evidently combative nature, it was hardly unexpected that he should have come into conflict with the authorities at Basel. He lost his position and his property and was forced to leave in 1528. After a difficult and peripatetic period, he received an invitation from the bishop of Salzburg, Ernst of Wittelsbach, to come to that city in Germany, and there he spent the rest of his life. Even the manner of his death has been a matter of controversy. His critics claimed that it was the consequence of a "drunken debauch," but others maintained that jealous physicians and apothecaries arranged to have him hurled down "a steep incline" (Adair 1970). The polygenism that he espoused was just one among many issues that made him a controversial figure, but because he had advocated polygenism, it meant that the taint of the other controversies in which he had been involved tended to adhere to and emphasize the controversial nature of polygenism as well.

Peyrère

The polygenism of Paracelsus was really only an incidental aspect of his troubled career. A full-scale advocacy of polygenism by itself, however, could create all kinds of problems for its author, as is shown by the case of Isaac de la Peyrère (1594–1676) a century later. Peyrère had been born in Bordeaux in a noble family of "Marrano" Calvinists. Marranos were Spanish Jews who had been expelled at the same time that the Moors had been thrown out toward the end of the 15th century. He spent much of his life in the service of the Prince de Condé, the leading Huguenot family of the royal house of Bourbon (Niceron 1732). This was during the time following the Edict of Nantes (1598), which had granted formal toleration of Protestantism in France; but it was also the period when Cardinal Richelieu was successfully whittling away at Protestant rights, anticipating their complete suspension by Louis XIV barely a decade after Peyrère's death. When de Condé removed from France to Flanders—a region that includes much of what is Belgium today—Peyrère followed and remained for several years. During that interval, he wrote a book entitled *Systema Theologica ex Praeadamitarum Hypothesi*, which was published in Amsterdam in 1655 and immediately translated into English as *A THEOLOGICAL SYSTEME Upon That PRESUPPOSITION That MEN Were Before ADAM*. In this, he maintained that Adam and Eve were indeed the ancestors of the Jews but not of the gentiles, who he suggested had descended from people who had lived before Adam. This, he claimed, was sustained by his reading of Saint Paul's Epistle to the Romans.

His book was denounced by the bishop of Namurs in December 1655 without any mention of the author since Peyrère had published anonymously, but Peyrère's arrest in Brussels followed anyway, in February 1656. He remained in prison for 6 months and was released upon his promise to abjure his errors and publish a formal retraction. Meanwhile, when his book appeared in Paris, it was ordered to be burned by the "public executioner" (Niceron 1732, 66–68, 78; Casson 1939, 114; McKee 1944, 458).

Supported by the credit of his master, the Prince de Condé, Peyrère traveled to Rome, where he gained an audience with Pope Alexander VII. There, on March 11, 1657, at "the feet of the Pope," he abjured not only all his "heresies" but also his Calvinism. His formal retraction was written in Latin, although after he subsequently returned to the service of de Condé, he continued to maintain privately that the Scriptures did not show that his views had been false. For some years, he served as librarian for his prince, and finally retired toward the end of his long life to a monastery near Paris (Niceron 1732, 68–69, 82).

It was Peyrère more than anyone else who started people thinking seriously about the possibility of multiple origins for the human populations of the world (Allen 1949, 133). Even though he is not mentioned by Voltaire in the next century, he has been credited with having made a real contribution to the deism that flourished in France and later in the English-speaking world in the latter part of the 18th century (McKee 1944, 459).

After these somewhat unpropitious beginnings, polygenism gained a great many somewhat tentative adherents as the Enlightenment came to an end. Even as early as 1735, the British naval surgeon John Atkins wrote "tho' it be a little Heterodox, I am persuaded that the black and white Race have, *ab origine,* sprung from different-coloured first Parents" (quoted in Jordan 1968, 17). Note that, as a Navy man, Atkins would have gained his experience of human variation as a result of encounters separated by long periods at sea. The result was that distinctions were perceived in discrete and categorical fashion quite different from the gradations between one population and another that had characterized the experiences of the land travelers from the time of Herodotus through the Middle Ages. During the last quarter of the 18th century, Lord Kames and Charles White wrote at considerable length promoting the idea of separate origins, and Voltaire (1694–1778), that extraordinary French deist and man of letters, opined that "only the blind could doubt" the original distinction of human "races" (1773, I:6).

There were a number of other writers in the latter part of the 18th century who reflected a polygenist outlook. Most are relatively unimportant, but one of them, Edward Long (1734–1813), an English plantation owner in Jamaica, expressed a series of views that were to exert a considerable influence in the subsequent era. In *The History of Jamaica* (1774), Long concluded that whites and blacks belonged to different species and that their "hybrids" were therefore of reduced fertility and would eventually die out. Blacks, he declared, were closer to apes, mentally inferior to whites, and characterized by all kinds of unpleasant attributes. He described Africans as inherently bloody, brutish, crafty, idle, intellectually inferior, and superstitious and added many more derogatory adjectives (Long 1774, II:351–354). The focus on the categorical distinction between Europeans and Africans was characteristic of reflections on the nature of human differences by an observer whose experience came solely from the confrontation of representatives of those two population blocs—uprooted as they were, facing each other out of context in the Western Hemisphere, and under conditions of brutally enforced inequality.

As the 19th century got under way, polygenist formulations proliferated without the ringing denunciations that had accompanied them in earlier centuries but also without attracting as much attention and critical interest as had previously been the case. Most of these were published in France, which, following the revolution late in the 18th century, had seen a cessation of the previous ties between the conduct of public affairs and the judgments of the Catholic Church (Higonnet 1994). In the newly secular state, publications that would have been judged contrary to established religion in a former time were no longer necessarily illegal.

The first of these was entitled *Histoire Naturelle du Genre Humain* (2 volumes, 1801; 2nd revised edition in three large volumes, 1824) by the French military pharmacist/ physician Julien-Joseph Virey (1775–1846) (Erickson 1986, 109; Léonard 1988). Virey was a follower of Buffon and has been described as "a minimally polygenist author" (Blanckaert 1988a, 100; 1988b, 31), who recognized the gradations of one human population into another without break but divided the human spectrum into two distinct categories in spite of this. As will be developed further in the next section, this is fully consistent with the growing outlook of Romanticism that was on the upswing at this time.

Virey divided the human genus into two "species." The first includes four "races:" white, yellow, copper, and dark brown (in which he included Malays and Polynesians). The second includes black and "blackish" races, where the latter refers to Hottentots and Papuans. Virey's publications have been called "characteristic" of French anthropology by Egon Freiherr von Eickstedt (1892–1965), one of the most prolific of the "racial an-thropologists" in Nazi Germany (von Eickstedt 1937–40, 331). One should remember, however, that the French word for "species," *espèce,* does not have the same formal tax-onomic significance as its English counterpart and is widely used to indicate "sort" or "kind" of whatever is being named.

Next, Colonel Jean Baptiste Bory de Saint-Vincent (1778–1846) produced his *L'Homme (Homo: Essai Zoologique sur le Genre Humain)* in two volumes initially in 1825. Bory, chief of the scientific commission in Algeria (Blanckaert 1988b, 42), has been described as an "eccentric naturalist-voyager, army officer, and early evolutionist" (Appel 1987, 171). Citing Virey's scheme, Bory labeled Virey's two species "lank-haired" (*Léiotriques*) and "crispy-haired" (*Ulotriques*), a division later to be used by the English naturalist Thomas Henry Huxley and his German contemporary Ernst Haeckel. Going one step further than Virey, however, Bory recognized 15 groups within those two divisions, each one of which he regarded as a proper "species." Like Virey also, he was somewhat offhand about ultimate origins, although he did mention the "certainty" that "each Adam had to have had his own particular locale (literally, 'cradle')" (Bory 1827, II:151).

His "evolution," such as it was, followed along the lines of Lamarck and the French Romantic era biologist Etienne Geoffroy Saint-Hilaire (1772–1844). Geoffroy was one of the most interesting figures in 19th-century science but his story does not really bear on the subject of this book, so I shall not add further details of his fascinating career to this account. The famous confrontation he had with his contemporary, Georges Cuvier (1769–1832), before the French Academy of Sciences in 1830 has been well told by Toby A. Appel in *The Cuvier–Geoffroy Debate: French Biology in the Decades Before Darwin* (1987). Some of her generalizations can be questioned, but I urge any who are interested to consult this well-written book.

Following the schemes presented by Virey and Bory, but not citing either, is the *Histoire Naturelle des Races Humaines* of Louis-Antoine Desmoulins (1796–1828). Antoine Desmoulins divided humans into 16 "species" and 25 "races," and he rejected the possibility that environmental circumstances or climate could produce any changes in the observed spectrum of human biological differences. Human "species" and "races," he declared, invariably preserve all the traits which they "indubitably had since the beginning" wherever they have remained "pure and without mixture" (1826, 158).

A decade later, the French physician Pierre-Paul Broc (1782–1848)—not to be confused with Pierre Paul Broca (1824–80), treated at length in Chapter 11—published his *Essai sur les Races Humaines* (1837), which was actually more of a pamphlet than a book. In substance, it was very much like the writings of the other early 19th-century French polygenists, although the usual derogatory comments about the intellectual abilities of people with dark skin are completely missing.

The picture presented by the French polygenists is divorced from the need to coordinate the findings of science with a reading of the Bible, but at the same time, in spite of the presumably secular context within which they published, the view of the world presented is one in which reality is made up of Platonic essences that can be analyzed by the use of Aristotelian logic. The result can then be considered in a hierarchical fashion, from the worthy to the less worthy. In effect, the outlook is precisely the same as that of medieval Christian thought. The only difference is in the removal of all of the traditional verbalizations of formal Christianity, where "worthiness" is expressed in terms of approximation to an idea in the mind of God and origins are tied to original pairs located in the Garden of Eden.

The ultimate irony is that with the publication of Charles Darwin's *Origin of Species* in 1859 it should have been obvious that a modified version of the monogenism of Johann Friedrich Blumenbach and Samuel Stanhope Smith, treated at some length in Chapter 4, was the only framework within which human biological variation could be understood. Monogenism, however, was summarily rejected because of its theological associations. What survived and went on to underlie the approach toward "race" taken by the emergent anthropological profession was in fact a much more direct product of medieval Christian theology than was the monogenism that it replaced. The eventual triumph of polygenism is treated subsequently in Chapters 7 and 12.

MONOGENISM

Up until the end of the Enlightenment, few writers saw any incompatibility between the accounts in the Christian Scriptures and the findings of science. With a few exceptions, all who contemplated the question of human origins started with the assumption that all living human beings were the lineal descendants of the biblical first pair, Adam and Eve in the Garden of Eden. The term *monogenism* simply means "the doctrine of single origins," and the vast majority of the Christian inhabitants of Europe and its colonies were unquestioning monogenists. To be sure, there were an occasional few who questioned the prevailing orthodoxy, but they were the exception and tended to encounter the fate that generally befell heretics. Those who rejected monogenism felt that the differences between modern human populations were so great that they could not all have descended from that hypothetical original pair. The periodically resurrected suggestion that the different "races" came from different original pairs is the doctrine called *polygenism*.

Historians of science have generally treated the dispute between the monogenists and the polygenists as a kind of "tempest-in-a-teapot," a trivial sort of argument between opponents who were equally ill-informed. As we shall see later, this seriously underestimates the significance of the dispute. Although no historian has previously recognized this, the polygenists actually triumphed in spite of the fact that their viewpoint is scientifically indefensible. The concept of "race" that is now generally accepted throughout the world is the direct legacy of the polygenist winners of the debate that ran throughout the first half of the 19th century. Polygenism is a fascinating topic in itself, and it is treated later in its own section. The full-scale development of monogenist thinking was independently produced in Europe and America by Johann Friedrich Blumenbach and Samuel Stanhope Smith, respectively, each writing initially without knowledge of the other.

Blumenbach's doctoral dissertation was originally published in 1775, but his major impact came with the publication of his third (revised and greatly expanded) edition in 1795. Smith's *Essay* of 1787 was revised in 1810 with recognition of the contribution not only of Blumenbach but also of Buffon, Leibniz, and Kant. Blumenbach and Smith represent not only the first full-scale development of monogenist thinking but also its high point and its end. Blumenbach was clearly the more scientific of the two and had a major, if overrated, influence on the subsequent development of the field of biological anthropology. Smith, for his part, represents the first major contribution of America to scholarship on questions regarding the matter of human biological variation. Although it was a contribution that had no lasting impact, it did mark the fact that scientific attention to the meaning of "race" was soon to become dominated by the situation in America, and American scholarship was to play a major role in establishing the interpretations subsequently accepted by so much of the world.

4

ANTHROPOLOGY IN THE ENLIGHTENMENT

BLUMENBACH AND "DEGENERATION"

The German physician and anatomist Johann Friedrich Blumenbach (1752–1840) pursued his happy and influential career in the university city of Göttingen. There, he published his doctoral dissertation in 1775, *De Generis Humani Varietate Nativa* (*On the Natural Varieties of Mankind*), printed for the public in 1776, and served as professor of medicine for the rest of his long and productive life (Blumenbach [1865] 1969; Fig. 4–1). Among his many students, perhaps the most notable was Alexander von Humboldt (1769–1859), whose research and travel reports were later to be of such importance in stimulating the young Charles Darwin to pursue his own travels and research. Although he was critical of what he called the "artificial method" of Linnaeus, preferring his own "natural method" of classification, he nonetheless accepted Linnaeus's division of the human species into four "varieties": European, Asian, American, and African (for which he generally preferred the term *Ethiopian*). His subsequent modifications of his thesis were also influenced by the writings of the German philosopher and advocate of the mind as a transcendental phenomenon beyond the realm of "pure reason" Immanuel Kant (1724–1804).

Kant also accepted Linnaeus's four-part division of the human species, but he attempted to add something in the nature of an explanation for differentiation somewhat along the lines of Buffon. Blumenbach actually went even further in this direction than Kant, although neither recognized human biological differentiation as the equivalent of specific distinction. By the time he published the second edition of his work, Blumenbach had divided Linnaeus's Asian variety into Mongolian and Malay groups.

Of all Blumenbach's contributions, the most enduring was his use of the term *Caucasian* to refer to people of European origin. In this, he was influenced in part by the writings of the well-to-do French Protestant/English traveler of the previous century Sir John Chardin (1643–1713), who had proclaimed the inhabitants of the Republic of Georgia, situated in the Caucasus, the most beautiful people in the world (Jordan 1965, 261). In Blumenbach's own words:

> I have taken the name of this variety from Mount Caucasus, both because its neighborhood, and especially its southern slope, produces the most beautiful race of men, I mean the Georgian; and because all physiological reasons converge to this, that in that region,

44

Figure 4-1 Johann Friedrich Blumenbach of Göttingen, 1752–1840 (Brace and Montagu 1977, 22).

if anywhere, it seems we ought with the greatest probability to place the autochthones of mankind. For in the first place, that stock displays . . . the most beautiful form of the skull, from which, as from a mean and primeval type, the others diverge by most easy gradations on both sides. . . . white . . . we may fairly assume to have been the primitive colour of mankind. (translated by Bendyshe 1865, 269)

While it was not spelled out in his statement, the significance of his reference to the "neighborhood" of Mount Caucasus was not lost on his readers. The Caucasus Mountains share their name with the peninsula between the Black and Caspian seas, where Russia extends down toward Iraq in the southeast and Turkey in the southwest; and it was somewhere in the southwestern part of that region that, according to the account in the Bible, Noah's Ark landed on Mount Ararat. In the minds of his pious Christian readership, it was from just such a location that the ancestors of all living people would be expected to have derived. *Early Thoughts on Man's origins*

Blumenbach recorded his pointed opposition to Great Chain of Being formulations in his celebrated letter to Sir Joseph Banks (1743–1820), the naturalist on the first voyage (1768–71) of the English explorer Captain James Cook and wealthy patron of scientific enterprises in England at the end of the Enlightenment. Blumenbach had spent time in England and was a Fellow of the Royal Society as well as "Court Physician to the King of Great Britain." Actually, his opposition to the Great Chain of Being was based on the recognition, shared by many others, that the arbitrary and artificial framework of medieval logic did not necessarily coincide with the vagaries and realities of the natural world (his letter to Banks is quoted in Bendyshe 1865, 150–151). As far as practicality was concerned, he felt that "the ideas of chain, scale, progression etc. in Nature" are "useful in the methodical part of the study of Natural History, as they form the basis of a (so-called) Natural System" (Blumenbach 1825, 5).

In Blumenbach's treatment of the human species, he adopted a limited version of the Great Chain as continuum. While he recognized five "varieties" of *Homo sapiens,* he noted that since each grades into the others "by such an insensible transition," it is arbitrary where one chooses to draw the lines. In his words, "It is very clear they are all related, or only differ from each other in degree" (Bendyshe 1865, 264). He went on to declare that "even among these arbitrary kinds of divisions, one is said to be better and preferable to another" (Bendyshe 1865, 264). Having said that, he declared that his five-part scheme seemed best to him. For the next two centuries, those who have attempted to "classify" human biological variation have inevitably built on the scheme proposed by Blumenbach.

It is obvious from his writings that Blumenbach's primary motivation was that of a good Enlightenment scientist. His work included the most detailed and accurate descriptions of human biological variation that had been published up to that time, and he carefully produced drawings of the skulls of the major human "varieties." Still, it is also clear that he accepted the biblical account of ultimate origins. He repeatedly commented on the distances by which the various living human populations were separated from the region of the Caucasus and the differences in the conditions for life affecting them now as opposed to before their dispersal. Although all humans originally had the same "germs" of potential, the *nisus formativus,* or vital force, caused by differences in climate, nutrition, and mode of life over many generations had led to changes in form from that present in the beginning—assumed to be represented by his "Caucasians"—to what was presently visible in areas remote from the Caucasus. These changes from the assumed original form he labeled "degenerations" (in Bendyshe 1865, 188), even though they were not enough to remove their representatives from full membership in *Homo sapiens.* Despite his celebrated opposition to the Great Chain of Being, his view of human biological variation was completely shaped by the continuum version of that picture of the world. "Caucasians" represented the closest approximation of God's intent for human form, and other human populations were "degenerate" to the extent that they departed from that manifestation of the ideal.

Here, I should say a word in defense of Blumenbach's use of the term *degeneration.* That term has taken on a pejorative meaning, which he certainly did not intend. Just as *monogenesis* and *polygenesis* mean "single creation" and "multiple creation," respectively, we should realize that *degeneris* in Latin signifies "removed from one's origin." When Blumenbach stated that the differences visible between the various geographic populations of modern humans had occurred by "degeneration," all he meant was that distance and circumstances had combined to change their appearance from what it had been "in the beginning." One could easily translate what is rendered as "degeneration" by the term *evolution.* Blumenbach's *De Generis Humani . . .* (literally "of the Human Kind . . .") was originally written in Latin, and when it was translated, the word *degenerent* was rendered in English as "they degenerated" under the assumption that readers would understand the literal Latin implications. Unfortunately, fewer people today have the background that allows them that automatic insight into the intent of the original Latin, and more tend to understand Blumenbach's use of "degeneration" as indicating a lessening in worth of some sort, with possible implications of moral decay and/or physical deterioration. That people would automatically think this way is in itself an indicator of just how strong the notion of the world-as-hierarchy—the Great Chain of Being—remains today. Few indeed realize that the images generally brought to mind by the use of terms such as *degeneration* are direct, if unrecognized, survivors from medieval theology.

THE SCOTTISH ENLIGHTENMENT COMES TO AMERICA

If Blumenbach's outlook was primarily that of a scientist who also assumed the validity of Christian scripture, the outlook of his American contemporary Samuel Stanhope Smith (1751–1819) was primarily that of a Protestant divine who also assumed that the findings of science would serve to bolster his Christian belief. In the eyes of most Europeans, America was still a land of wilderness, "savages," and poorly educated colonists who were little better than unsophisticated bumpkins. No one expected that anything thought and communicated on the basis of American experience could alter the way the world would come to think about itself. While the work of Samuel Stanhope Smith was ultimately rejected by both Americans and Europeans alike and, as such, does not really represent the contribution which American experience would make to the world outlook, it did create enough stir to stimulate a European rebuttal. In this sense, it was a harbinger of the fact that, in the succeeding generation, the American intellectual tail was going to end up wagging the European dog.

In the middle of the 18th century, the grim Calvinism of Cotton Mather's era, with its focus on "innate depravity" and "predestination," gave way to the effects of the Scottish Enlightenment, with its "Philosophy of Common Sense" that reflected the teachings of Francis Hutcheson (1694–1746) and of Thomas Reid and his followers, James Beattie and Dugald Stewart of Aberdeen. According to this school, which has also been called "Scottish realism," the extremes of skepticism, on the one hand, and "idealism," on the other, could be countered by the common sense with which everyone is endowed (Wood 2000).

In good Protestant Enlightenment fashion, every human being was considered to have the common sense to determine the difference between the good and the bad, the beautiful and the ugly, and the true and the false. It simply required sufficient education and application. There was also the assumption that decisions reached collectively (i.e., held in common) were more reliable than those reached individually. This, of course, is the basis of relying on the decisions of a jury in legal cases. Martin Luther initiated the Protestant Reformation with the claim that a person did not need a priest to discern the difference between right and wrong. This not only became the impetus for the growth of professional science but also underlay the establishment of democratic systems of government.

Curiously, this Scottish outlook incorporated an acceptance of a certain amount of intuition in that belief in common sense that was similar to the intuition in the philosophy of Descartes against which it was objecting (Buchler 1940, ix). This made Scottish philosophy popular in France in the early part of the succeeding (19th) century and was the basis for the approach used by the German philosopher Immanuel Kant, himself of Scottish ancestry, in his *Kritik der reinen Vernunft (Critique of Pure Reason)* (1781), where he rejected the extremes of skepticism of David Hume (1711–76). Hume actually was a member of that group of thinkers who constitute the Scottish Enlightenment, even though his denial of induction and the logical extent to which he carried his skeptical arguments were rejected by the majority of his contemporaries.

Following the "union" of Scotland with England in 1707, the Scots dealt with their sense of backwardness and cultural inferiority by stressing self-improvement through the kind of liberal education that enabled individuals to improve their intellectual powers. Among the forces promoting this was the struggle of large portions of the country to learn the English language.

The collapse of the revolt called the "Forty-Five," led by the Stuart Prince Charles Edward, the "Young Pretender" or "Bonnie Prince Charlie," at Culloden in April 1746 and the dispossession of so many rural Scots caused by the "Highland Clearances" and the "enclosures" produced a substantial exodus from Scotland (Sloan 1971). The consequences are still clearly apparent in the modern populations of Australia and New Zealand, to an extent in the English-speaking segment of the South African population, and of course, as the name indicates, in Nova Scotia. This also had a major effect on the colonial predecessor to the United States of America to the extent that approximately one-quarter of the English-speaking American colonials were of Scottish ancestry at the time of the American Revolution. These were among the reasons why the thinking of the Scottish Enlightenment took root and flourished on American soil with such vigor (Howe 1970, 31; Hook 1975). The case has been ably made that the ideas and phrases that Thomas Jefferson (1743–1826) used in the Declaration of Independence in 1776 were not taken from John Locke (1632–1704), as is often presumed (Wills 1978, 173–174). They were inspired rather by Thomas Reid (1710–96) in his *An Inquiry into the Human Mind on the Principles of Common Sense* (1764). If Reid and his fellow countryman Francis Hutcheson served as the inspiration for Thomas Jefferson, it was also Reid and his cohort who stimulated the intellectual currents that led to the domination of the Harvard Divinity School by Unitarians in the second decade of the 19th century (Howe 1970; Sloan 1971).

The thinking of the Scottish Philosophy of Common Sense clearly pervaded the political and intellectual life of the emerging nation (Hook 1975, 36). In the 18th century certainly and well into the 19th, "intellectual life" and religion were generally tied together. With one exception—the University of Pennsylvania, which was directly modeled on the nondenominational University of Edinburgh in Scotland (Norwood 1966, 22)—colleges and universities were denominational and had been founded for the express purpose of producing clergymen of the denomination that had paid to establish them. Harvard College, as America's oldest institution of higher learning, began in 1636 as a training school for Congregational ministers (Howe 1970, 175).

As the initial attitude of grim Calvinism gave way to a more intellectual atmosphere, there was some dissatisfaction among the more devout, who felt that "true faith" was being diluted. Amongst these was Cotton Mather, whose father had been president of Harvard; and it was at his urging that Elihu Yale provided the money for the establishment of Yale College (1701) (Silverman 1984). The growth of evangelical Protestant religious fervor in the subsequent decades of the 18th century has been called the "Great Awakening," and it was particularly identified with the "hell-fire and brimstone" sermons of the New England Congregationalist preacher Jonathan Edwards (1703–58) (Noll 1994).

During that time of religious "revival," the Presbyterian synod of Philadelphia started a movement to found a college to rival the New England establishments of Harvard and Yale in America's northeast. By 1746, the Middle Atlantic state of New Jersey had granted a charter, and in 1752 an "academy" was begun at Princeton (Hook 1975, 32). Its formal title was The College of New Jersey, although it became increasingly known as Princeton College. Eventually, a century and a half later (1896), it formally took on the name of Princeton University (Wertenbaker 1946). Reflecting the evangelical fervor that accompanied its founding, it had attracted none other than Jonathan Edwards himself, who was president at Princeton at the time of his death. It may seem a little curious that Edwards, a Congregationalist, was chosen to be president of a Presbyterian school; however, both Congregationalists and Presbyterians accepted the doctrinal standards of the "Westminster Confession" of 1648, and the good Presbyterian trustees of Princeton clearly recognized a kindred soul in Jonathan Edwards.

One of the more eminent 18th-century graduates of Princeton (1760) was the famed Philadelphia physician Benjamin Rush (1745–1813). Rush had gone to Scotland, where he studied under William Cullen in Edinburgh's famous medical school (Shryock 1960, 1966; Hook 1975). While Rush was in Scotland, he helped with the arrangements that brought the Reverend John Witherspoon (1723–94) to Princeton in 1768 to be the president of the College of New Jersey (Noll 1989, 113). Witherspoon was selected by the Presbyterian-dominated board of trustees at least partially because he was identified as an "Evangelical Presbyterian" clergyman, and this would presumably make him compatible with the approach championed by the late Jonathan Edwards. However, the splits in Presbyterianism in Scotland were not quite the same as those in American Presbyterianism, and Witherspoon was "conservative" principally in that he represented the part of the Scottish Enlightenment that opposed the radical skepticism of David Hume (Noll 1989, 31).

Far from the fervent hymn singing and the rabble-rousing emotionalism of "revivalist" preaching, Witherspoon brought the full-scale faith in the compatibility of reason with revelation that characterized the Scottish Philosophy of Common Sense. He had graduated from Edinburgh University in 1739 and absorbed the views advocated by Thomas Reid in *An Inquiry into the Human Mind on the Principles of Common Sense* (1764). It was this that he managed to make the successful heart of the educational program at Princeton, where he enjoyed the title of president until the end of his life (Noll 1989, 23 ff.). Witherspoon was very much the right man in the right place at the right time. He evidently was a warm and earthy person who established rapport with his students, even though they sometimes had trouble understanding his sermons because of his strong Scottish burr; and he fit right into events as they were unfolding on the American scene in the latter third of the 18th century.

Parenthetically, Princeton, like other American institutions called "colleges," was really more the equivalent of what now would be ranked as a secondary school. Students tended to arrive in their early or middle teens and to graduate before they were 20. Cotton Mather, for example, was only 11 and a half years old when he matriculated at Harvard in 1674, and, although it is also true that he was the youngest ever admitted, his father, Increase Mather, had been admitted at the age of 12 (Silverman 1984, 15). Rapport with the head of the institution, then, was of more immediate importance than is the case with the larger and more impersonal organizations that we now think of as "colleges."

During Witherspoon's tenure, the embryonic nation moved from colonial status, through war, and on into independence. Witherspoon became an immediate and ardent patriot. He was selected as a New Jersey delegate to the Continental Congress in June 1776 and became a signer of the Declaration of Independence on the fourth of July. Subsequently, he served as a member of Congress until 1783. Given his Scottish background, it is more than possible that the long history of clashes between his countrymen and the rule of England imposed by military force may have played a role in determining where his loyalties lay. In any case, Princeton was regarded as a "seminary of sedition" as America approached its revolution, and the college and its buildings suffered the ravages of war (Noll 1989, 50, 73 ff.).

SAMUEL STANHOPE SMITH: "RACE" FROM THE PERSPECTIVE OF THE AMERICAN ENLIGHTENMENT

Whereas Harvard and Yale drew their students mainly from narrowly regional New England constituencies, Princeton served students from New York and Pennsylvania down through the Middle Atlantic states and the states of the American South. The latter, especially, have sometimes been referred to as the "slave states," and the moral issues raised by the presence of the institution of slavery inevitably loomed larger than was generally true at educational establishments in the American North. This was even more the case at an institution which was devoted to the position that—in addition to matters of science—ethical, moral, and religious issues could be decided by the application of common sense. The question did not arise in any formal way during the period John Witherspoon was engaged in active teaching, but it was addressed by his successor, Samuel Stanhope Smith (Fig. 4–2).

Smith was born in Lancaster County, some 40 miles west of Philadelphia, Pennsylvania. His father had been born in Ireland of Scottish parents and had migrated to America in 1730, eventually to become pastor of the Presbyterian church in Pequea, Pennsylvania, where Samuel and his brother, John Blair Smith—later to join him at Princeton—were born. The family connection with Princeton goes right back to the beginning since his uncle, Samuel Blair, was one of the founding trustees of the College of New Jersey. His father, Robert Smith, exactly the same age as John Witherspoon, became a Princeton trustee in 1772. Samuel Stanhope Smith came to Princeton as a junior in 1767, 1 year before Witherspoon was installed. Immediately after the new president arrived, young Smith—aged 17 and beginning his senior year—adopted the Scottish Philosophy of Common Sense and went on to be valedictorian of his class in 1769. During the subsequent year, he assisted his father at the Pequea Grammar School and then returned to Princeton as a tutor in 1770.

In 1773, he contracted the tuberculosis that was to affect his health for the rest of his life. This was one of the reasons that led him to move south to Virginia for a while. One of the other reasons was the number of Scottish Presbyterian immigrants spreading down east of the crest of the Blue Ridge Mountains in western Virginia. Smith served as an itinerant clergyman to minister to their religious needs and earned an increasing reputation as an effective preacher. In 1774, the Presbytery in Prince Edward County, Virginia, had raised enough money to found an "academy"—later to become Hampden-Sydney College—and they chose Samuel Stanhope Smith to be its first rector. The next

Figure 4-2   Samuel Stanhope
Smith, 1751–1819 (from a painting
by Charles B. Lawrence in
Monk 1946).

year, he returned briefly to Princeton to marry Ann Witherspoon, John Witherspoon's
oldest surviving child, who he brought back to Virginia with him when he returned to resume his duties. Subsequently as instruction was initiated in 1776, he recruited as teachers three recent Princeton graduates, including his brother and his brother-in-law, David
Witherspoon. Enrollment had burgeoned and things were going well, although the onset
of the Revolutionary War was to slow down subsequent development at his school.

   Then, in the fall of 1779, he was called back to Princeton to teach moral philosophy,
and there he stayed for the remainder of his active career. His father-in-law retained his
title as president even when he was away on his congressional duties and when his eye-
sight failed in his last years. Smith served as acting president during that time and, after
Witherspoon's death in 1794, was elected president by unanimous vote of the trustees in
May 1795, a post he held until a new age was ushered in and he was forced to resign
in 1812.

   Samuel Stanhope Smith was a polished and able promoter of the Scottish philosophy he had learned from his father-in-law, and he wrote up and published the lectures he
gave at Princeton perpetuating that position (Jordan 1965, xvii; Noll 1989, 118, 123).
Evidently, he was better organized and a more systematic scholar than Witherspoon,
whose position is best known through the ambitious and extensive writings of his son-
in-law (Noll 1989, 191). The lasting claim to fame of Samuel Stanhope Smith was his
application of the Christian Common Sense position to the vexing question of the significance of human biological differences. He had become known informally for his position on the meaning and origin of "racial" differences, and in 1785 he was elected to

membership in the American Philosophical Society in Philadelphia, an organization established in 1769 by the merger of two earlier "mutual improvement" societies founded by Benjamin Franklin (1706–90) on the model of the benefit societies created by Cotton Mather in the Boston of Franklin's youth.

Not long after his election, Smith was invited to present his findings in the form of an "oration" at the meetings of the Philosophical Society in Philadelphia in 1787 (Noll 1989, 118). The manuscript from which he delivered his oration was duly published as *An Essay on the Causes of the Variety of Complexion and Figure in the Human Species,* to which are added *Strictures on Lord Kaims's Discourse, on the Original Diversity of Mankind* (Jordan 1965, xiii). In this, Smith assumed the biblical assertion that all the peoples of the world had a common origin and are therefore of one species. He marshaled the available factual information to show that all kinds of humans are capable of effective sexual reproduction with each other, thus demonstrating that science and Scripture were in agreement. The visible differences in appearance arose, Smith argued, after human populations had become dispersed into different parts of the world under the influence of the differences in climate and the different social conditions in which they found themselves.

In many respects, the picture painted by Smith was quite compatible with the one developed independently and, in effect, simultaneously by Blumenbach in Germany. When Smith eventually gained access to the third edition of Blumenbach's *De Generis Humani Varietate Nativa,* he mined it for data and references to bolster the revised edition of his own *Essay,* which he published in 1810. The difference in emphasis between the parallel schemes of Blumenbach and Smith foretells the impact that the American experience was going to have upon the world at large later in the 19th century. Blumenbach's formulation was an abstract undertaking based largely on vicarious gleanings, whereas Smith's was stimulated by questions raised from the ongoing confrontation of three very different populations. In the words of the most perceptive of his biographers, "Smith's book reveal[s] how very much more immediate the problem of human physical and cultural diversity had become for transplanted Europeans who lived with it than for those who sat reading about it in the comfortable home of civilization" (Jordan 1965, xli). Blumenbach, of course, was a representative of the latter.

Smith, for his part, had produced "an American book shaped by an American dilemma which still remains unresolved" (Jordan 1965, xxvii). In the subsequent 200 years, that dilemma has increasingly become a problem for the whole world. Whereas Blumenbach had invoked a kind of vitalism in the production of visible differences, Smith contended for a more active role played by surrounding circumstances. In his discussion, he ranged between advocating a kind of inheritance of acquired characteristics in the fashion that has been dubbed "Lamarckian" in a somewhat facile way and arguments that assumed the operation of an almost Darwinian kind of selection. He spoke of the effects of the tropical sun in increasing skin pigmentation near the equator, and he noted the advantages in the possession of shortened extremities as a guard against frostbite in arctic regions. He also spoke of the intellectual and behavioral refinements discernible in all people who were raised to live in "civilized" circumstances.

In effect, Samuel Stanhope Smith presented a picture in which "race" as an essence did not exist at all. What we see is just the product of circumstances, and if these are changed, then human form will change as well. As examples, he offered the case of

Smith here argues there is no such thing as race

the differences in appearance between the African Americans serving as "house" slaves and those used as "field" slaves. His scheme had the further implication that, with the installation of African American and European American people side by side in the New World, they would come to resemble each other in the course of the next several generations or at least in a century or two. It was a wondrously utopian vision, and, for a brief time, it captured some of the spirit of the new country, now fully independent and committed to the ideals enshrined in the Constitution and its Bill of Rights. Supported by the twin pillars of reason and faith adopted from the Scottish Enlightenment, all Americans could look forward to a future in which biological and social distinctions would fade away and, as in the concluding words of the archetypical European fairy story, all would "live happily ever after."

Unfortunately, this was not to be. From what we know today, Blumenbach and Smith were both quite correct in noting that human populations grade into each other in such an imperceptible manner that the drawing of lines and assigning of labels is an arbitrary matter of "convenience" only—if indeed it is that. However, they were both badly off target in their assessment of how long it takes to transform the configuration visible in one given population into that recognizable in another. They essentially assumed a time scale for human existence reckoned from the "begats" in the Bible, and although they avoided attempts at calculating the time in actual years, no one ever dreamed that it was much more than a few thousand. Now, we know that regional configurations persist between 50,000 and 100,000 years and that the time taken for major changes to occur can be far longer than that.

The other major flaw in the similar schemes of Blumenbach and Smith was in the hierarchical assumptions still present in what they assumed to be the recently generated and perhaps reversible differences visible in the human world. Both took it as a given that "white" Europeans were as close as it was possible to come to what God had intended people to be. Others could be brought "up" to that level to the extent that they could be altered to look and act like Europeans. Now, 200 years later, the self-satisfied and ethnocentric flaws in those views are all too evident.

Curiously, however, it was not the real weaknesses in their parallel schemes that led to their demise. Instead, their downfall was the product of a major change of outlook between the Enlightenment that had produced them and the era of Romanticism that was to follow. The Age of Reason was coming to an end, and, although the succeeding period did not actually espouse irrationalism, it became increasingly suspicious of schemes that sought to encompass the whole of creation or even any substantial segment thereof. It was actually the hint of coming problems that led Smith to write his *Essay* in the first place.

Smith appended a section to his work entitled "Strictures on Lord Kaims's Discourse, on the Original Diversity of Mankind." The reference is to a publication called *Sketches of the History of Man,* first presented in 1774 by the Scottish judge Lord Kames (1696–1782). Born Henry Home and a relative of David Hume, Lord Kames was another of the somewhat fractious representatives of the Scottish Enlightenment. Kames belonged to the same end of the Common Sense spectrum that included his skeptical kinsman David Hume, and John Witherspoon had tangled with him in print long before leaving Scotland for Princeton. In part, it may have been as a champion of Witherspoon that Smith entered the fray. Lord Kames came close to representing the view that there really had been a plurality of creations. Certainly, it was his position that "there are different species of men," a phenomenon that came about by the action of God at the time of the legendary attempt to construct the Tower of Babel (Kames 1774, I:119). To Smith, of course, this was manifestly poor science as it was a misrepresentation of the words of Scripture. His *Essay,* then, was his response to the manifestation of "infidelity" that he perceived in Kames's *Sketches.*

The time had not yet come for intellectual developments in America to produce a major impact on the parent cultures of Europe, but this time, at least, the latter did begin to take notice. Charles White's *Account of the Regular Gradation in Man* in 1799 was a specific rebuttal of Samuel Stanhope Smith. While I have mentioned White's *Account* earlier as a lovely illustration of the Great Chain of Being as a gradual continuum, White in fact treated human populations as different species. Kames and then White gave preliminary hints of what was to become the full-scale development of polygenism in America in the 19th century, a movement that was then exported to establish the categorical reality of "race" in the minds of the world. Samuel Stanhope Smith then used the ammunition furnished him in Blumenbach's book to prepare the final edition of his own, in 1810, where he once again took aim at Lord Kames and replied at some length to matters that had been raised by White. It was an ably prepared effort with an admirable command of what had been published concerning the evidence relating to human biological variation at that time, and, as before, it was motivated by an ethical sense that was equal in its excellence to the caliber of the science represented. Unfortunately, instead of providing a platform to be revised and improved for the support of future research into the nature of human biological variation, it served as the swan song of the Philosophy of Common Sense.

Early in his career as president of Princeton, Smith had attempted to introduce Princeton students to the nature and uses of reason as an approach to dealing with the world at large. Toward this end, he hired the Scottish chemist John Maclean (1771–1814) in 1796 as the first professor of chemistry and "natural philosophy" (as "science" was called in that era) in an American college (Hudnutt 1956, 541). Maclean had been part of the reform movement in Glasgow and had fled the Tory persecutions for Philadelphia in 1795, where Benjamin Rush was instrumental in arranging for his position at Princeton (Hook 1975, 241; Brown 1989, 101). Although science was to encounter a setback at Princeton, Maclean's protégé Benjamin Silliman (1779–1864) was successful in making it an integral part of the curriculum at Yale (Brown 1989).

In the 1810 edition of his *Essay,* Smith wrote "Genuine philosophy has ever been found the friend of true religion" (1965, 3). He continued to the last to put equal stress on science and religion, but he had outlived his era. The students of 20 years earlier had welcomed and understood his message; however, the Age of Reason was now in the past, and the freedoms that it had engendered had led to a focus on the individual, with individual rights and privileges given higher value than the rights of society as a whole. The nature of what happened was analyzed apropos of quite a different situation by the distinguished historian of ideas Arthur O. Lovejoy: "It is one of the instructive ironies of the history of ideas that a principle introduced by one generation in the service of a tendency or philosophic mood congenial to it often proves to contain, unsuspected, the germ of a contrary tendency—to be by virtue of its hidden implications, the destroyer of that Zeitgeist to which it was meant to minister" (Lovejoy 1936, 288). Lovejoy was referring to how the structures of thought of the 18th-century creationists were adopted by the 19th-century Darwinian evolutionists, but the same kind of thing can be said for the stress on individual accomplishments emphasized by the Romantics as an outgrowth of the Enlightenment insistence that each individual human being had the requisite common sense to understand the ways of God and the world.

Samuel Stanhope Smith had become increasingly out of touch with the currents of his times. Ideologically, he was an intellectual liberal; at the same time, he was a social conservative. He felt that the right to vote should be tied to the possession of property and that "magistrates" and others who could be called "patricians" deserved some sort of special consideration (Jordan 1965, xxii–xxiii; Noll 1989, 148–149). With others like him, he felt that the excesses of the "terror" in the French Revolution had been the inevitable result of popular democracy. As a consequence, his sympathies were for the Federalists during the early days of the Republic, and he was convinced that Jeffersonian democracy would spell doom for the nation. One cannot help but wonder also about what his ideas on "race" did for his credibility in the eyes of his students, an increasing number of whom were from well-to-do southern families whose very wealth and position were the products of a system that was based on assumptions of "racial" inequality and exploitation of the labor of African people.

There is no evidence to suggest that this contributed to the problems that Smith experienced as the new century got under way, although it appears that he no longer commanded the respect of the students as he had right after the Revolutionary War. Adding to his troubles was the fact that the number of Princeton students becoming Presbyterian ministers had plummeted from the nearly 50% in the early reign of John Witherspoon to less than 10% in the first decade of the 19th century, and the board of trustees was becoming increasingly unhappy (Noll 1989, 172). The "freedom" enjoyed by some of the students was increasingly aided by the use of alcohol, and instances of disruptive and destructive behavior increased. Nassau Hall was burned in 1802, and a full-scale riot in the spring of 1807—the "Great Rebellion"—led the trustees to step in and suspend nearly three-quarters of the student body and send letters to other colleges to prevent those students from being able to enroll anywhere else (Hudnutt 1956, 542; Jordan 1965, xxii–xxiii; Noll 1989, 232–235). As the trustees stepped in and took control, they blamed Smith for being lax as a disciplinarian, and indeed his tubercular condition put limits on his strength and what he could accomplish.

They also were less than enthusiastic about his stress on science and felt that a return to religious fundamentals was in order. In line with the changing intellectual currents of the age, they were increasingly suspicious of the good that could come from the pursuit of reason. Ultimately, they felt—with a certain amount of justification—it could lead to the questioning of things they felt should not be questioned. Better a return to the Bible and the Confession of Faith. In 1812, the board of trustees forced the resignation first of Professor Maclean and then of President Smith. The era of Common Sense was over at Princeton, although some vestiges of the tradition did maintain their continuity. Professor Maclean's son, also John Maclean (1800–86), served as president of Princeton later in the century (1854–68) and wrote the first full history of the college (1877).

Then, a full century after the arrival of John Witherspoon, Scotland was once again tapped for leadership, and James McCosh (1811–94) became Princeton's president in 1868 (Noll 1989, 290). By this time, however, the era of Common Sense had ended in Scotland (Hook 1975, 198). When he arrived in Princeton, McCosh brought in a version of philosophical idealism that represented a return to what the Common Sense philosophy of Witherspoon and Smith had explicitly opposed. It is interesting to reflect on the fact that the repression exerted in 1812 was so successful that biological anthropology was absent from the Princeton curriculum throughout the remainder of the 19th and all of the 20th centuries. Samuel Stanhope Smith may count as America's first biological anthropologist (Hudnutt 1956, 544), but he was also the last one to have been a member of the Princeton faculty until the new millennium.

5

THE TRIUMPH OF FEELING
OVER REASON

ROMANTICISM

The Enlightenment belief in a rational, knowable, and good world crumbled toward the end of the 18th century. The Age of Reason gave way to the outlook called Romanticism, and this was to gain momentum and strength as the 19th century got under way. That change pervaded all aspects of the culture of the Western world to a greater or lesser extent, although it was most apparent in literature and the arts.

German poetry and drama showed the way under the impetus of Johann Gottfried von Herder (1744–1803), his friend Johann Wolfgang von Goethe (1749–1832), and his friend in turn Friedrich Schiller (1759–1805). They advocated an "abandonment of reason for feeling and personal experience" (Stein 1950, 7–8). They and their contemporaries produced works that were characterized by *Sturm und Drang*—"storm and stress"—as a device for indicating the intensity of personal involvement in the events portrayed. In the matter of style alone, this was a sharp departure from the serenity and order of Enlightenment modes of expression. Goethe's first novel, *The Sorrows of Young Werther* (1774), was described by the English Germanophile Thomas Carlyle as giving voice to "nameless unrest and longing discontent" (Wilkinson 1970, 524). If this brings to mind the mid-20th-century James Dean and *Rebel Without a Cause,* that is just one of the many things that indicates a closer affinity between the outlook of the Romantics and that of the modern world than between either and the Enlightenment.

Parallel changes occurred in painting and music as well. The supremely structured celebration of a divinely rational world in Johann Sebastian Bach (1685–1750) gave way to the thunderous dramatics of Ludwig van Beethoven (1770–1827) and later to the cumulative harmonic transformations of Richard Wagner (1813–83). The studied classicism of 18th-century painting epitomized in the tableaux of Jacques Louis David (1748–1825) yielded to the dramatic turbulence of storm and shipwreck and of Parliament in flames in the canvases of J. M. W. Turner (1775–1851) (Hamilton 2003).

Spilling over from the arts into attitudes expressed in daily life were a sense of disillusion and dissatisfaction with present conditions and an impulse toward protest and revolt. Coupled with these was a heightened focus on the individual and the originality of individual accomplishments and an objection to restraints on individual freedoms. It was the actions of students in the grip of just such an ethos that brought about the demise of that Enlightenment figure Samuel Stanhope Smith at Princeton. The inevitable stress on egoism generated by these trends was further complicated by the drive toward absolutes in the realms of thought, art, society, and love impelled by a yearning for the infinite, which of course is unattainable by definition.

This is why the Romantic drama always ends in tragedy: the soprano dies of consumption, flings herself from a parapet, or stabs herself; and Valhalla goes up in flames at the end of Wagner's *Ring* cycle, extinguishing the whole panoply of gods, goddesses, Valkyries, heroes, and heroines who had been declaiming their unrequitable yearnings in stentorian competition with echoing peals of evolving orchestral sound over a span of four very long and very loud operas. Perhaps the fact that fully developed Romanticism never took root in America to quite the extent that it had in Europe is what is really being indicated in Mark Twain's appraisal: "Wagner's music is better than it sounds" (http://www.brainyquote.com/quotes/quotes/m/q101909.html).

The term *Romanticism* sometimes evokes an image of simplistic and mindless sentimentality, but, while that was indeed an occasional by-product, it is hardly a fair characterization of the movement as a whole. Perhaps the most succinct assessment of the changes in outlook that occurred at the end of the Enlightenment was made by the late historians Will and Ariel Durant:

> But what shall we mean by the Romantic movement? The rebellion of feeling against reason, of instinct against intellect, of sentiment against judgment, of the subject against the object, of subjectivism against objectivity, of solitude against society, of imagination against reality, of myth and legend against history, of religion against science, of mysticism against ritual, of poetry and poetic prose against prose and prosaic poetry, of neo-Gothic against neoclassical art, of the feminine against the masculine, of romantic love against the marriage of convenience, of "Nature" and the "natural" against civilization and artifice, of emotional expression against conventional restraints, of individual freedom against social order, of youth against authority, of democracy against aristocracy, of man versus the state—in short, the revolt of the nineteenth century against the eighteenth . . . all these are waves of the great Romantic tide that swept Europe between Rousseau and Darwin. (Durant and Durant 1967, 887)

To that list of contrasts, but very much in the same spirit, Lovejoy had previously noted that one could add: "the revulsion against simplicity; the distrust of . . . universal formulas in politics; the aesthetic antipathy to standardization; . . . the cultivation of individual, national, and *racial* peculiarities; the depreciation of the obvious and the general high valuation (wholly foreign to most earlier periods) of originality, and the usually futile and absurd self-conscious pursuit of that attribute" (Lovejoy 1936, 293–294; italics added). Lovejoy concluded that these changes "consisted in the substitution of what may be called diversitarianism for uniformitarianism as the ruling preconception in most of the normative provinces of thought." This transformation "perhaps, more than any other *one* thing has distinguished, both for better and worse, the prevailing assumptions of the mind of the nineteenth and of our own [meaning the 20th] century from those of the preceding period in the intellectual history of the West" (Lovejoy 1936, 294). Although he wrote this at a time that was closer to the 19th century than it is to today, nothing has happened to change the nature of his conclusion.

I added the italics to the phrase quoted from Lovejoy to highlight the tendency in the Romantic movement to elevate the racialism it encouraged to a frank out-and-out racism. The author of that recent controversially flawed tour de force *Black Athena*,

Martin Bernal, has spoken in a similar vein of "the tidal wave of ethnicity and racialism . . . that engulfed Northern Europe with the Romantic movement at the end of the
18th century" (Bernal 1987, 29). Lovejoy himself was quite explicit in his statement:

> [Romanticism] lent itself all too easily to the service of man's egotism, and especially—
> in the political and social sphere—of the kind of collective vanity which is nationalism
> or *racialism*. The belief in the sanctity of one's idiosyncrasy—especially if it be a group
> idiosyncrasy, and therefore sustained and intensified by mutual flattery—is rapidly con-
> verted into belief in its superiority. More than one great people in the course of the past
> century and a half, having first made a god of its own peculiarities, good or bad or both,
> presently began to suspect that there was no other god. . . . The tragic outcome has been
> seen, and experienced, by all of us in our own time. (Lovejoy 1936, 313; italics added)

When that passage was written, World War II had not yet broken out, *Kristallnacht*
was yet to occur (November 9, 1938), and the Holocaust was still in the future. The
handwriting was clearly on the wall, however: In Nazi Germany, Jews were being put
under arrest, their property was being confiscated, and it was quite clear that much worse
things were in store—all in the name of "race." What actually was meant by "race" had
not been settled in either the scholarly or the public mind at the beginning of the
Romantic era, although the term was increasingly being pressed into use, as can be seen
in the works of the French polygenists already mentioned.

The uniquely Romantic framing of the definition of "race" came later in the 19th
century and is attributed to the school of anthropology that flourished in Paris. I am not
going to discuss that definition in detail at present any more than to say that it fits perfectly into that characteristic Romantic emotional state which Lovejoy has identified as
"the pathos of the esoteric." "How exciting and how welcome is the sense of initiation
into hidden mysteries:" the philosophers who offered this pleasure to their admiring
public promoted what Lovejoy called the "metaphysical pathos"—"the pathos of sheer
obscurity, the loveliness of the incomprehensible" (Lovejoy 1936, 11). When we actually consider the definition of "race" used by the anthropologists concerned with the nature of human biological differences up to well after the end of World War II, we shall
see that it is a splendid manifestation of both the "esoteric" and the "metaphysical
pathos."

It would be quite wrong, however, to characterize the mistrust of reason in
Romanticism as tantamount to enshrining the irrational. The source of that mistrust was
the feeling of having been misled by Enlightenment claims that all the problems of the
world could be solved by the strict and dispassionate application of logic. As one analyst
has noted, "Romantics felt that there was an intellectual arrogance in the Enlightenment,
and that the champions of the application of disciplined reason had failed to produce
that utopian world of happiness, prosperity and peace that had been the object of their
efforts" (Pulzer 1964, 42). In a sense, it was an earlier manifestation of a crisis in rising
expectations.

The disappointment that came as a result of the feeling that the Age of Reason had
not delivered on its promises led to the thought that there must be something more to be
gained that was beyond the realm encompassed by reason alone. Immanuel Kant, for example, felt that the human mind was beyond the realm of reason itself, and this was the
implication behind the words in the title of his famous *Critique of Pure Reason* (1781).

The idea that humans could achieve insights that transcended the bounds of mere reason gave rise to what has been called "transcendentalism."

Perhaps the most famous exponent of this was the German philosopher Friedrich Schelling (1775–1854), whose *System des Transcendentalen Idealismus* (*System of Transcendental Idealism*) (1800) started the new century off with a splendidly prolix manifestation of German Romanticism. The appeal of the transcendental aspect of Romanticism had different effects in different places. In England, it was manifest in the increasing emphasis on symbolic ritual in High Church Anglicanism, as seen in the Oxford Movement of 1833 through the middle 1840s. This culminated with the defection of John Henry Newman to the Roman Catholic Church in 1845; ultimately, he was made a cardinal in 1879 by Pope Leo XIII (Weatherby 1973). The return of Roman Catholicism to a position of acceptance and growing respectability in England was clearly aided by the tides of Romanticism.

In America, we noted the growing effects of Romanticism among the undergraduates at Princeton during the last years of the presidency of Samuel Stanhope Smith, but in general, "America preferred . . . its romanticism to be of a reasonably safe and undisturbing nature" (Hook 1975, 126). The leading adherent of transcendentalism, as the main manifestation of Romanticism in America, was the "lapsed Unitarian clergyman" Ralph Waldo Emerson (1803–82), who expressed a typically Romantic enthusiasm for "spontaneity, poetic imagination, and intuitive insight" (Livingstone 1987a, 16–18). Emerson, a characteristically tame American Romantic, even preferred the gentler Romanticism in the painting of the Hudson River School, as in Frederick E. Church (1826–1900), to the more turbulent works of Turner in England (Nicholson 2002).

The Enlightenment lasted somewhat longer in Scotland than it did elsewhere, and the consequences were to be of extraordinary importance in the sciences—physics (Olson 1975), chemistry (Cardwell 1968), and biology (Mayr 1982, 396). It was no accident that the scientific style of Charles Darwin had more of the Enlightenment in it than of Romanticism since the crucial years of Darwin's scientific training came while he attended medical school in Edinburgh (1825–27) just before the end of the Scottish Enlightenment (Brace 1997b). By 1830, however, the Scotland of Sir Walter Scott had supplanted the previously dominant ethos of Common Sense. The epic, Ossianic poems and Scott's historical novels embodied a "Scottish literary romanticism" characterized by "the romantic emotions of regret and nostalgia" that "are in the end quite harmless" and safely appealing to a "broadly conservative society" (Hook 1975, 126).

In Germany, where Romanticism began and achieved its greatest power, the movement penetrated the sciences as well. Interestingly enough, the figure who helped to inject it into a scientific context was none other than Goethe himself, one of the fountainheads of the movement as a whole. As a child of the Enlightenment, Goethe supported scientific enterprise, but he did so for very romantic reasons. One of the slogans of Romanticism was "unity in diversity," and Goethe was a supporter of the idea of broad aspects of unity in nature. In his mind, "nature used a single archetype in constructing" living forms (Wells 1967, 357). In 1790, he published a monograph demonstrating the extent to which many aspects of plant form can be traced to modifications of the basic leaf. It actually was quite an insightful effort, although it did not work when the question of roots was brought into consideration.

Looking at animals and noting the various forms that the elements of the backbone could take, he suggested that the skull at the top of the spinal column is just a modified vertebra, a view that was later to become part of the teachings of the German *Naturphilosophe* Lorenz Oken (1779–1851). This led Goethe to the splendid Romantic declaration "Der Mensch ist ein Wirbel," "man is a vertebra" (O'Hanlon 1982, 654). His assumptions concerning the unity of plan led him to question Camper's assertion that the absence of the intermaxillary bone constitutes the definitive distinction between human and nonhuman form. As a result of his own research efforts—and these involved procuring specimens and dissecting them, not an easy task in that era—he found that there were clear traces of the maxilla–premaxillary suture in the prenatal human fetus. Although these are obliterated before birth, he felt that he had demonstrated the unity of human and animal form according to his expectations.

Actually, this was hardly new information. During the Renaissance, Vesalius had correctly demonstrated that the anatomical work of the Greco-Roman physician Galen had been based on his dissections of nonhuman primates rather than human beings because Galen had depicted an intermaxillary bone in his drawings of the human skull. Vesalius noted that humans generally lack a separate intermaxillary bone, although traces do occur for varying periods of time during the prenatal period. Some of Vesalius's contemporaries denounced him for criticizing Galen's work, which had nearly taken on the status of sacred writ in anatomy. Goethe's work also was the source of conflicting interpretations. In fact, the whole history of the debate concerning the status and meaning of the intermaxillary bone has given us a phrase that has passed into the language largely separated from the situation that generated it in the first place: the intermaxillary bone is the original "bone of contention."

As a result of Goethe's ideals and efforts—some successful and others less so—the biological sciences in Germany entered the 19th century with a strong Romantic aura. The movement labeled *Naturphilosopie* had a powerful impact on the course of German biology and biological thinking elsewhere in Europe. This book is not really the place to go into the topic, however fascinating it may be, but the legacy of Naturphilosophie was one of the reasons Darwin was so readily accepted in Germany as opposed to his rejection in France. At the same time, it is also one of the reasons the German version of evolution, with its "strivings," "urges," "directional forces," and other aspects of romantic mysticism, was so completely at variance with the impersonal mechanism envisioned by Darwin himself.

As a scientist, Goethe had his limitations. He was passionately opposed to the kind of science represented by Newton and anyone else who used mathematics. "Physics must be divorced from mathematics. It must be completely independent, and try to penetrate with all its living, reverent, pious force into nature and its holy life; quite regardless of what mathematics accomplishes and does" (quoted by Cassirer 1945, 62).

In assessing his approach to science, Goethe said of himself "Trennen und zählen lag nicht in meiner Natur" (distinguishing and counting is not in my nature). In the views of a modern scientist, this is more than a slight hindrance since the most spectacular subsequent scientific achievements, ranging from the splitting of the atom to the cracking of the genetic code, have all been based on insights gained from the use of precisely quantified information. The weaknesses of Goethe as a scientist were thoughtfully and sensitively assessed by the great 19th-century English supporter of Darwin Thomas Henry Huxley (1825–95), writing at the end of his own life: "the worst faults of later speculative morphologists are no less visible in his writings than their great merits. In the artist–philosopher there was, at best, a good deal more artist than philosopher; and when Goethe ventured into the regions which belong to pure science, this excess of a virtue had all the consequences of a vice" (Huxley 1894, 292).

I cannot leave the topic of Romanticism without saying something about its role in leading to a separation between the intellectual worlds of the arts and the sciences. A couple of generations ago, that dichotomy had proceeded to such an extent that the distinguished English scientist and novelist C. P. Snow made it the subject of his Rede Lecture at Cambridge University in 1959. In this, he noted that literary people as far apart as London and New York used essentially the same kind of language to speak about the same things with the same level of expectation and understanding of the world as though there were no ocean separating them, whereas the intellectual gulf between them and scientists at institutions such as M.I.T. (Massachusetts Institute of Technology) was every bit as large as one would expect if there were indeed an intervening ocean.

Lord Snow's lecture was published under the title *The Two Cultures and the Scientific Revolution* (1959). In this, he warned that problems would surely arise in the future as a result of the evident level of scientific illiteracy in so many of the highly educated people of the world. Snow, as a participating member of both the scientific and the literary worlds, could command a hearing from each. In his judgment, however, it was science that would generate the wave of the future, while the ills of the recent past, including Auschwitz and other such manifestations of unpleasantness, could be traced to the less structured and less logical reasoning of a world dominated by people trained principally in literature and the humanities. The apparent implications of his position were that the world would be better off run by people trained in the sciences than by people lacking in a scientific background. Not surprisingly, his lecture called down the wrath of the literary establishment upon his head.

The voice of outrage was most evident in the Richmond Lecture given by the acclaimed English literary critic F. R. Leavis at Downing College of Cambridge University 3 years later. Leavis called it "The Two Cultures?—The Significance of C. P. Snow," and it was subsequently published in *The Spectator* (March 9, 1962). His denunciation took the form of denigrating the competence of Snow himself, charging that "He knows nothing of history" and that "he is utterly without a glimmer of what creative literature is, or why it matters" (Leavis 1962, 299–300). Leavis further cast aspersions on the conceptual level of Snow's efforts at argument and concluded that "*The Two Cultures* exhibits an utter lack of intellectual distinction and an embarrassing vulgarity of style" (Leavis 1962, 297).

When Leavis stated that "criticism of the style, here, becomes, as it follows down into analysis, criticism of the thought," he put his finger on the major source of the dispute, although, having said it, he was himself completely unaware of the significance of his statement. At bottom, the argument between Snow and Leavis comes down to a matter of style. Although Snow was a practicing novelist despite Leavis's expostulation that "as a novelist he doesn't exist," he was in fact trained as a physicist. Leavis's background was in history and English, and he was on the English faculty at Cambridge until he retired not long after giving his Richmond Lecture in 1962. Each man was loyal to the intellectual style in which he had been trained and intolerant of any other. By an ironic twist, however, Snow wrote with a skill characteristic of the literary world and Leavis framed his critique with all the vulgarity he had professed to see in Snow.

Each, however, belonged to an intellectual tradition which had pursued such a separate course that their representatives no longer talked to each other with much effort in the way of tolerance and mutual understanding. Snow, representing continuity from the Enlightenment, exemplified the somewhat complacent and self-satisfied faith that all our problems can be handled by the systematic application of the scientific method to their solution. Representing the continuity of the Romantic movement, on the other hand, Leavis belonged to the tradition which felt that the essence of what is human disappears when the quantified and impersonal techniques of the scientist are applied.

A kind of mediator appeared in the form of the novelist Aldous Huxley (1894–1963) of *Brave New World* fame, brother of the equally famous scientist Sir Julian Huxley (1887–1975). Aldous Huxley's attempt at mediation was entitled *Literature and Science* (1963), a title that was as appropriate as was he as its author since the same title had been used by his great uncle, Matthew Arnold (1822–88), for his Rede Lecture of 1882. The very next year, his grandfather, Thomas Henry Huxley, presented something of a different emphasis when he in turn gave the Rede Lecture at Cambridge on the very day that the university bestowed an honorary doctorate on Matthew Arnold.

Whereas Leavis and Snow, respectively, maintained the continuing threads of Romanticism and the Enlightenment in a posture of hardened hostility, this was not the case for Arnold and T. H. Huxley. Arnold, a professor of poetry at Oxford, was famous for his defense of the importance of "culture" in the conduct of human affairs. By culture, he meant "the best which has been thought and said in the world" (1869, xi); but the thoughts and utterances included those coming from the realms of "art, science, poetry, philosophy, history [and] religion," and he made a point of writing to Huxley and stressing the fact that he included science in that roster of recorded human experience which he considered essential (Armytage 1953, 352).

Huxley indeed felt that science deserved a more important role in the curriculum than that given to it by Arnold, but he continued to stress the importance of reading the Bible as literature, of reading Shakespeare, and of training in modern languages. Huxley and Arnold may have disagreed on emphasis, but each fully respected the position of the other. They were members of the same distinguished London club, they corresponded with each other when they were away from town, and they remained lifelong friends (Armytage 1953). Symbolizing that friendship of these two very different people, Huxley's son married Arnold's niece, and they in turn became the parents of the famous Huxley brothers (Aldous and Julian) who attempted to mediate the increasingly bitter conflict between "the two cultures" in the middle of the 20th century. Science + Religion

The split between the "two cultures" actually began in the 18th century and the distinguished British philosopher, the late Sir Isaiah Berlin (1980, 80–110) has held up the figures of the relatively unknown Italian thinker, Giambattista Vico (1668–1744) and the universally acclaimed French writer Voltaire (1694–1778) as exemplifying the Romantic and Enlightenment styles of thought, respectively. At the end of the 18th century, a person could still be simultaneously a pillar of both the scientific and the literary establishments. Goethe, in fact, was one such prominent example. Fueled by the currents of Romanticism, however, the two domains began to part company. The rise of professional science represented a continuation of Enlightenment ideals from which the separate course of the literary Romantics progressively diverged. Since most of the historians responsible for evaluating the outlook of the 19th century are products of the literary establishment, the fact that the sciences represent an unbroken and continuing manifestation of the Enlightenment has often been overlooked.

Occasionally, when a scientist such as Darwin commanded a wider span of attention than was the usual case, this is regarded by surprised literary historians as a kind of aberration. As one commentator wrote, "the impact of Charles Darwin's discoveries caused a gaping rent in the intellectual fabric spun by the romantics" (Wilshire 1968, 214). Darwin, of course, did nothing of the sort. The "gaping rent" which he represented is only portrayed as such because the divergence between the literary and scientific worlds had proceeded to such an extent by the middle of the 19th century that it took a scientist of Darwin's magnitude to bring home to the educated reader the fact that the inductive–deductive, research-and-testing intellectual style that guides scientific behavior had simply continued from the previous era while the style in the world of literature had come to lay increased stress on emotions, personal feelings, and intuitive leaps.

In the middle of the 19th century, occasional realizations of this sort were possible because the two cultural traditions were still talking to each other. Darwin was read and understood by his Romantic literary contemporaries. The *Origin of Species,* for example, was reviewed for *Blackwood's* magazine by George Henry Lewes, an editor, critic, and novelist and the first major biographer of Goethe (Barzun 1958, 34). Lewes in turn loaned his advance copy to his "common-law wife" Mary Ann Evans, better known as the novelist George Eliot (1819–80); and she recorded the pleasure it gave her in her diary entry for November 24, 1859. Although literary people like Eliot and Lewes read Darwin, they were distinctly uncomfortable with what they perceived as the "materialism" in the evolutionary mechanics of his overall picture. Darwin for his part read Eliot's *Adam Bede* when it first appeared and "gave it the rarest of the comments in the booklists: 'Excellent' (Notebook 128)" (Beer 1983, 266). Then, as now, first-rate scientists are often fully aware of what is going on in the literary world. The reverse, however, is less often the case. That continues to be so, as is shown in the "Sokal hoax," a particularly amusing incident that I recount in Chapter 19.

By the middle of the 20th century, however, the separation had gone to the extent that people of the stature of a Leavis and a Snow could no longer communicate in terms other than those of misunderstanding, mistrust, and dislike. The dominant literary culture, carrying on the traditions of Matthew Arnold, still tends to feel that a person thoroughly grounded in the humanities is sufficiently qualified to report on the products of any intellectual endeavor including science. Although specialties within the humanistic camp are recognized and treatment is ceded to those with suitable backgrounds, this kind of recognition is not so readily given to the various divisions of the scientific realm.

For example, in such widely read periodicals as the *New York Times Book Review,* poetry is always reviewed by poets, fiction by novelists, history by historians, economics by economists, and so on. For books in the various divisions of the sciences, however, the reviewer all too often is identified as "a writer" who deals with whatever the subject might be—anthropology to zoology. Sometimes a particular scientist may make a name writing for the public and be asked to review works in other parts of the scientific spectrum, with the evident feeling that, after all, so-and-so is a scientist and writes reasonably well and, therefore, can handle virtually anything of a scientific nature. These are the reasons reviews of serious works in science written for the general reading public are usually of a distinctly lower quality than reviews of works that emanate from the humanities in the first place.

The divergent legacies of Romanticism, on the one hand, and the Enlightenment, on the other hand, have had an interesting effect on the development of the concept of "race." The rise of Romanticism captured the imagination of the public at large, and historians have generally accepted the idea that the Enlightenment faded away and disappeared late in the 18th century and early in the 19th century. That the general public came to accept the idea that categorical "racial" distinctions were intuitively obvious is hardly surprising, particularly in those parts of the world where that "general public" was made up of people who had been uprooted from the regions of their origins and then faced each other on a daily basis. This, of course, was the case for the inhabitants of the Western Hemisphere.

It is perhaps less to be expected that the nascent anthropological profession should also have come to the same intuitive conclusion. Anthropology, however, had its origins in just those countries that had a major involvement in the colonial enterprises that followed after the Renaissance Age of Discovery. The efforts by English-speaking observers to deal with the meaning of the human biological differences in the colonial situations with which they were involved were phrased with the Enlightenment commitment to the compatibility of reason with the Bible as we have already seen in the monogenism of Samuel Stanhope Smith.

The field of anthropology in Great Britain was launched by James Cowles Prichard (1786–1848), who earned his M.D. in 1808 in an Edinburgh still in the full grip of the Scottish Enlightenment. In 1813, he expanded his dissertation and published it as *Researches into the Physical History of Mankind.* Dedicated to Blumenbach and acknowledging the earlier work of Smith in America, it was written in defense of monogenism and in opposition to the tide of polygenism that was rising in France. Prichard's driving motivation was very similar to that of Smith, although as a physician rather than a clergyman, he followed Blumenbach's emphasis and devoted somewhat less space to specifically religious considerations.

Prichard revised and expanded his *Researches* several times, and by the time of his death, the fourth edition ran to five volumes (Prichard 1851). Prichard's contemporary, Sir William Lawrence (1783–1867), also a physician, followed in the same vein with his *Lectures on Physiology, Zoology, and the Natural History of Man* (1819), delivered at the Royal College of Surgeons in London. This also went through multiple editions by the mid-19th century. Between Prichard and Lawrence, English anthropology was stamped in the mold of monogenism following the lead of Blumenbach and Smith, and it remained in this form until approximately the time of the American Civil War.

Mention of that pivotal event can serve to remind us that the crucial areas where the concept of "race" was established as a categorical reality in the minds of the subsequent world were just those where populations of different origins faced each other on a daily basis and where the dominant Protestant outlook demanded a logical explanation for the origin and significance of the human biological differences observed. This locale was specifically the United States of America. From Blumenbach and the subsequent English monogenists to Bory and the subsequent French polygenists, the discussions had been more a matter of academic interest than a reflection of immediate and daily involvement. As the Enlightenment gave way to Romanticism in America, however, contemplations about "race" were constant and unavoidable, and the whole matter was brought to a level of even more intense concern because of the institution of slavery.

- Full development of Race & Racism begins in the US. (Slavery perpetuates this)

6

PHRENOLOGY — *Character based on features*

The currents of Romanticism emanating from Europe starting late in the 18th century brought with them some odd manifestations of nonscience. One of these was called "physiognomik," from the *Physiognomica* of Aristotle, and involved the claim that a person's character could be judged from an assessment of the shape of his or her features. While this movement had a previous history in the 16th century linked with astrology, it was promoted in all seriousness by a clergyman in Zurich, Switzerland, Johann Caspar Lavater (1741–1801). His *Physiognomische Fragmente* of 1775 enjoyed something of a following on the Continent and was translated into English before the end of the century (see Lavater [1775] 1968–9). Herder and Goethe took it up briefly; however, it exuded too much in the way of mysticism for even such a prototypical Romantic as Goethe, and he turned away from it (von Eickstedt 1937–40, 290–292).

A lingering influence of Lavater's claims almost prevented Charles Darwin from being accepted as a shipmate on the round-the-world voyage of the *Beagle*. Before that ultimately famous trip (1831–36), Darwin was interviewed by the ship's captain, Robert FitzRoy, who was a believer in physiognomik. As Darwin later wrote, "he doubted whether any one with my nose could possess sufficient energy and determination for the voyage. But I think he was afterwards well satisfied that my nose had spoken falsely" (printed in F. Darwin 1961, 43).

Building upon some of the elements of physiognomik, the Viennese physician Franz Joseph Gall (1758–1828) launched a "science" that came to be called "phrenology" (Davies 1971, 7). Gall reasoned that since the brain was the organ of thought and since certain areas are associated with specific capacities, one should be able to discover a good deal about the abilities of a given person by the relative development of the various areas of the brain as shown by nuances in the shape of the overlying skull.

Localization of brain function has been abundantly borne out by subsequent neuroanatomical research but in a fashion quite other than that claimed by phrenology. If anything, the claims of phrenology, by their very extravagance and silliness, may have served to impede the development of scientific neurology. With a few exceptions, such as J. Philippe Rushton and his claim of determining "intelligence" by applying a tape measure to the circumference of the head (and see Chapter 18), there are no reputable scientists today who would defend the idea that any aspect of the external form of the cranium can tell us anything whatsoever about the capabilities of the brain enclosed. It has been more than a century since the claims of phrenology were shown to be completely without merit, and now "it is classified with alchemy and astrology" (Davies 1971, x) as a pseudoscience (Wrobel 1987).

At the beginning of the 19th century, however, phrenology rode the rising tide of Romanticism to a position of surprising respectability and popular favor. It was first advocated in the lectures of the German "mystic" Gall in Vienna (Gross 1887, II:298). The twin arbiters of acceptability in Vienna at that time were Emperor Franz I and the Roman Catholic Church. Both made their disapproval of Gall a matter of public record. His transgression was the crime of "materialism." In the view of the Austrian emperor, anyone who claimed that he could determine a person's morals, ethics, and capabilities by an examination of physical characteristics might just use such an approach to determine who had the right to be emperor. Franz I wrote to the state chancellor in December 1801, "Perhaps those who have spoken of this head-teaching ('*Kopflehre*') with enthusiasm should lose their own heads. This doctrine leads to materialism and seems to contradict the first principles of morality and religion, so you will prohibit these private readings" (quoted in Neuburger 1916, 56–57).

Evidently Austria was no longer safe for Gall, so, along with his disciple the one-time theology student Johann Gaspar Spurzheim (1776–1832), he left Vienna for an extended and highly successful lecture tour through Europe before settling down in Paris in 1807, where he established a lucrative medical practice catering to the socially prominent. There, he began a regular course of lectures at the Atheneum, which he continued to give until his death and which were attended by many visitors to Paris over the years (Ackerknecht and Vallois 1955, 6). In addition, he put his position before the reading public in a volume translated from the German and entitled *Craniologie,* to be followed by a four-volume series starting in 1810, *Anatomie et Physiologie du Système Nerveux en Général, et du Cerveau en Particulier, avec des Observations sur la Possibilité de Reconnoître Plusieurs Dispositions Intellectuels et Morales de l'Homme et des Animaux par la Configuration de Leurs Têtes,* the first two volumes written jointly with his flamboyant follower Spurzheim.

It was Spurzheim who actually christened the approach "phrenology," which he defined as the "science of mind," a step Gall was unwilling to take (Davies 1971, 8). Gall's pre-Freudian vision of "anatomy as destiny" was just as unappealing to continental Romantics as it had been to the emperor and the Church in Vienna since it seemed to contradict the Romantic ideal of unfettered freedom (Temkin 1947, 278). It would be wrong to leave the reader with the impression that Gall's scheme was restricted to the simplistic effort to assay the meaning of the various "bumps" on the skull to which it has been reduced so often in historical accounts. Gall in fact advocated the systematic testing of his claims that specific capacities were associated with specific areas of the brain in order to see whether they could be verified or not. This still counts as classic scientific procedure, and it is thanks to the efforts of his successors to follow up on his suggestion that we have been able to learn as much about the localization of cerebral functioning as we know today.✓

Gall rejected the Enlightenment ideas that all humans are created with equal potential and that the mind of each human being at birth is a blank slate—a *tabula rasa*—on which experience writes to shape the endless human differences that we can observe in the world. It was with the appearance of Gall's work that the ongoing nature-vs.-nurture arguments began, which continue unabated today. He also rejected the "speculative philosophy" of Romanticism and the belief that ego is all that is necessary to "create" the world (Temkin 1947, 281). In his view, cultural and educational influences could neither create nor abolish behavioral characteristics, but they could be used to develop or suppress them according to what was deemed desirable after "scientific study" of how an individual was constructed (Temkin 1947, 288).

Gall was neither an egalitarian nor a democrat, and he held, with Aristotle, that some are born to dominate and others are born to obey (Temkin 1947, 307). Furthermore, he felt that all humans possessed the faculty of "evil" to a greater or lesser extent—in essence, a version of "original sin" (Temkin 1947, 305)—and he was dubious about world views that stressed "ever progressing perfection." It was a "peculiar combination of science and theology" (Temkin 1947, 305), and it fit right in between many of the contrasting positions of the Enlightenment and Romanticism in concept as well as date.

Spurzheim, however, was able to reshape phrenology in such a way that it had great appeal to the relatively pragmatic Romanticism of the British Isles and North America. He added poetic, religious, and metaphysical "faculties," among others, to Gall's list, producing a total of 35 that could be associated with specific areas of the brain. Most important of all, however, was his removal of any "evil faculty" from the roster. The presence of evil, when it could be detected, came, he suggested, from the abuse of other faculties. With the removal of any vestige of Calvinistic predestination and the hope-filled prospect of using phrenological self-knowledge for self-improvement, Spurzheim was well equipped to cater to the remnants of the faith element of the Philosophy of Common Sense that Scotland and America retained from the Enlightenment.

Gall complained that Spurzheim "too frequently deviated from the pure path of observation and had thrown himself into ideal-metaphysical and even theological reveries" (quoted in Temkin 1947, 309). This, however, was just the kind of Romanticism that Anglo-American audiences wanted to hear, and Spurzheim was too good a showman not to take advantage of the opportunity. He mastered English in short order, although not without retaining a strong German accent, and embarked on a lecture tour of Great Britain in 1814. After phrenology had been denounced by the reviewer of Gall and Spurzheim's volumes of 1810 and 1812 in *The Edinburgh Review* in 1815 as "a piece of *thorough quackery* from beginning to end" ([Gibbon?] 1815), he went to Scotland to confront his adversaries. Although the review was unsigned, as was the accepted tradition for reviews at that time, it was known to have been written by Dr. John Gibbon. Before he returned to Paris, Spurzheim delivered presentations which made a lasting impression on the Scottish barrister George Combe (1788–1858) (Gibbon 1878, I:94–95; Davies 1971, 9–10). Combe and his physician brother Andrew (1797–1847) helped found the Phrenological Society in Edinburgh in 1820 and *The Phrenological Journal* in 1823; and G. Combe's phrenological volume of 1834, *The Constitution of Man,* became extremely popular as the Scottish Enlightenment faded to a close.

Later, both Spurzheim and, subsequently, Combe were to have a direct impact on America; but the first attempt to present phrenology to the reading public on the western shores of the Atlantic was made by an American who had attended Gall's lectures and made the acquaintance of Spurzheim when visiting Paris in 1821. This was Charles Caldwell, M.D. (1772–1853), a professor of medicine at Transylvania University. No, this Transylvania was not the Romanian Province of Bram Stoker, it was Transylvania University in Lexington, Kentucky. And although Charles Caldwell bore no resemblance to the sinister Count Dracula—"Vlad the Impaler"—of Stoker's novel, he certainly has to rank as one of the most peculiar and enigmatic characters in the entire sweep of the history that I am attempting to cover.

Charles Caldwell was born to Presbyterian emigrants from northern Ireland in western North Carolina and received his medical training under the famous Dr. Benjamin Rush at the University of Pennsylvania in Philadelphia during the 1790s. He followed the clinical tradition of bleeding, blistering, and purging that Rush had himself learned from his own teacher, William Cullen, in Edinburgh; but he was at odds with Rush about the latter's doctrine of the "unity of disease." During the defense of his doctoral thesis in 1796, Caldwell publicly disagreed with Rush and later, in his posthumously published autobiography, declared that it was this dispute that prevented him from succeeding to the chair of medicine that Rush held at the University of Pennsylvania Medical School (Caldwell 1855, 238, 248).

It seems more likely, however, that it was not just the substance of his disagreement with Rush that kept him from being considered as a successor but the style he used. In a series of subsequent critiques that Caldwell published involving many other figures, he evidently relished the pose of high dudgeon and the language of scathing denunciation: "happy in controversy, he apparently tried to wound as well as defeat his opponents" (Horine 1960, 16). If, in his doctoral defense, he had used anything like the phrases he employed in his later disputations, then there is no wonder that he lost Rush's support.

Regarding his autobiographical account of his attack on Rush during his doctoral defense, one early biographer noted that "the impudence" displayed by his words "is as reprehensible as it must have been distasteful" (Gross 1887, II:285). As that same one-time colleague went on, "An overweening vanity was the specific characteristic of this extraordinary man," and further "If conceit could have made him greater, he would assuredly have occupied the loftiest of pedestals" (Gross 1887, II:287). A more recent biographer has observed that "His *Autobiography,* so replete with self-adulation, obscures to a marked degree his unusual abilities and accomplishments" (Horine 1960, 4). The same writer added that "Aside from unlimited egotism, Caldwell's greatest fault . . . was his undue readiness to take offense and to precipitate arguments" (Horine 1960, 16).

Caldwell started his long record of published disputations with an unsigned review of the last edition (1810) of Samuel Stanhope Smith's *Essay,* which he published in the *American Review* in July 1811. In his appraisal of the agencies that Smith had offered to account for change in human biological form, he opined that "it is our deliberate belief that those principles are unsound and the conclusions fallacious" ([Caldwell] 1811, 133). In his critique of Smith, he exemplified the Romantic-era complaint that Enlightenment figures had sought to offer all-inclusive accounts of what was beyond our power to explain; and in a subsequent expansion of his original denunciation, he charged Smith with "not discriminating between the laws of living and of dead matter—the laws of mechanics and those of physiology" (Caldwell 1814, 18). Caldwell, in fact, was a vitalist and a defender of spontaneous generation (Erickson 1981, 253), and his attack on Smith's mechanistic explanation was a precursor of the skepticism voiced by the Romantic elements in French biology in response to Darwin during the following generation.

He made disparaging remarks about the tone and style used in Smith's *Essay,* declaring that "In its air and manner it is unbecomingly authoritative and dogmatical. It lacks much of that liberal sentiment and tolerant spirit" and that "It is marked in many of its pages with a harshness of language" ([Caldwell] 1811, 133). Those words, however, are a far more accurate description of the writings of Caldwell himself than they are of Smith. Certainly, they hardly reflect the stance of the "simple unassuming Christian" that Caldwell claimed to be in his subsequent expansion of that review (Caldwell 1814, 149). At that, Caldwell had not risen to the heights of invective that were to characterize some of his later controversies, where he charged his opponents with such faults as "plagiarism," "deception," "falsehood," "bloated pretension," "perverted quotation," "moral delinquencies," and "depravity" (Caldwell 1838, 1, 6, 7, 18).

Although Caldwell was not the only writer to pen an unfavorable review of Smith's *Essay*, he certainly was the most energetic. His attack was expanded in a prolonged series of installments in 1814 on the pages of *The Port Folio*, a leading American literary journal which he edited in Philadelphia at that time. The denunciations of Smith extended over a period of 5 months, and although they were unsigned as was the custom, there was little public doubt as to the identity of the author. At least one historian has accepted Caldwell's own claim that his denunciation led to Smith's attacks of paralysis, which culminated in his death in 1819 (Caldwell 1855, 272; Stanton 1960, 23). I have already reported, however, that Smith's health had been precarious for quite different reasons. The most recent treatment of Smith in the context of his times noted that, after his forced retirement in 1812, he faded slowly but enjoyed "a beautiful old age" (Noll 1989, 288). No mention is made there of "attacks of paralysis," and the orotund denunciations of Caldwell would seem to have been the least of Smith's concerns. Since Caldwell was notoriously inaccurate in assessing his own impact on and importance in the world (Horine 1960, v), there may be some reason to question his smugly indignant assertion that "I was charged with being essentially instrumental in his death" (Caldwell 1855, 272).

While Caldwell denounced Smith's monogenism as having been based essentially on religion and not science, he did not offer a solution at that time. However, in his 1830 book *Thoughts on the Original Unity of the Human Race*, aimed principally at the more recently articulated monogenism of James Cowles Prichard (whom he consistently misspells as "Pritchard"), Caldwell produced the first explicitly polygenist work written in English. He was contemptuous of those who clung to the faith that all humans were descended from Adam and Eve since that would have required the sons to cohabit with their sisters and "that was incest; against which the punishment of death was afterward proclaimed by Moses himself, at the express command of the Deity." He was equally incredulous concerning the story of Noah's Ark as the refuge for all the kinds of animal in the world: "crammed with living beings of every description, with all of their discharges, solid, liquid, and aeriform, in full play, and ventilated by one door, and one *small* window. . . . As a human residence, the 'BLACK HOLE OF CALCUTTA' was a paradise to it.]Yet Noah and his family, and the hosts of animals enshrined with them in the horrid dormitory, without air, without light, and filthier far than the Augean stables, emerged from it in health, after soaking in it of a hundred and fifty days" (Caldwell 1852, 163). Accepting the categorical distinction of the "races" mentioned by Linnaeus, he declared in rhetorical fashion: "Is it not probable, then, that each of these four races of mankind is descended from an original pair, as each of the numerous species of baboons, apes, monkies, and animals of the equine race?" (Caldwell 1852, 41).

[While this little book had an importance for the subsequent development of polygenism in America that has been largely overlooked, it was Caldwell's previous conversion to and promotion of phrenology that took center stage and came to define the way he was perceived by his contemporaries and by history. In 1821, Transylvania University sent him to Europe with $17,000, a very large sum of money for that time, and the mission to buy books, charts, anatomical models, and chemical apparatus to equip the medical school he had been hired to establish in Lexington (Horine 1960, 11). He made his way to Paris via Liverpool and London, and he purchased over 1,100 volumes as well as the requisite laboratory equipment; however, he also attended the lectures being given by Gall and further made the acquaintance of Spurzheim. As a result, he became a convert to phrenology, and he remained unshakably loyal to it for the rest of his long and contentious life.

After his return to Kentucky, Caldwell set to work and produced the first book on phrenology written by an American (Horine 1960, 11). His volume, *Elements of Phrenology* (1824), was printed at his own expense in Lexington. Phrenology then became the core of Caldwell's medical teaching (Gross 1887, II:283), and he embarked on a series of lecture tours to promote it that took him from Massachusetts to Louisiana. Despite some saying that "His language was scholarly and ponderous," his contemporaries regarded him as "unmistakably a great lecturer" (Gross 1887, II:283). He has been described as "Dignified, pompous and vain" (Stanton 1960, 20), and he was an imposing figure on the lecture platform. With his aura of dignity and self-confidence, apparently he was able to hold the interest of his audiences.

Still, one wonders how he was able to get away with some of his more extravagant manifestations of conceit. In a phrenological presentation before a "large and select audience" in Lexington, Kentucky, he is quoted as having declared "There are only three great heads in the United States: one is that of Daniel Webster; another that of Henry Clay; and the last," pointing to his own, "modesty prevents me from mentioning" (quoted by Gross 1887, II:287). Modesty, it scarcely needs to be said, was singularly lacking in the make-up of Charles Caldwell.

Caldwell's less-than-admirable qualities are perfectly obvious. Further, the fact that he was so visibly associated with what eventually became discredited as a pseudoscientific fad has contributed to the assessment of Caldwell as one of those minor curiosities who made no lasting mark. All of this has served to divert our attention from the fact that it was he who started the twin currents of phrenology and polygenism in America. Those two dimensions became an integral part of the incipient field of biological anthropology, which grew in strength and importance as the 19th century progressed. Although biological anthropologists in the last half of the 20th century would unanimously and vehemently deny any validity to either polygenism or phrenology, the most fundamental tenets of both continued to play a major but unrecognized role in shaping how the profession in particular and the public in general thought about "race."

Meanwhile, Spurzheim had already become another in a series of self-promoters who had discovered a lucrative new market to exploit. The infant Industrial Revolution was in the course of generating a class of nouveaux riches, a burgeoning middle class, and a working class with a spendable income. One must remember also that this was a time before moving pictures, radio, and television and that the most exciting event of an average week was the oratorical show put on by the minister in church on Sunday. The hell-fire-and-brimstone sermon given by a Great Awakening preacher was both therapy and entertainment for the parishoners, but a good public speaker with a new and different message could rent a hall for Saturday night, charge admission, and make quite a handsome income for himself. His counterpart today is the rock musician, although the latter rarely makes any pretense at appealing to the "higher sensibilities" that was de rigueur a century and a half ago.

The Industrial Revolution was generating wealth and social stratification in the American northeast at that time as well, and Spurzheim tried to cash in on the opportunity. Toward that end, he scheduled an American lecture tour beginning in August 1832. After arriving in New York, he went to Yale for the commencement exercises, staying with the renowned Benjamin Silliman while he was in New Haven. Spurzheim's lectures at Yale were a great success, and Silliman became an enthusiastic convert to phrenology (Stanton 1960, 37; Davies 1971, 16).

He arrived in Boston on August 20, where the prominent clergyman William Ellery Channing declared that the excitement aroused by his performances was "unequaled . . . by any since the days of the Declaration of Independence" (Walsh 1972, 187). Boston, which had considered itself "the Hub of the universe" since Cotton Mather had asserted its centrality in God's struggle with Satan, provided an endless opportunity for Spurzheim's public lecturing. In addition to his public presentations in Boston and his appearances before the Boston Medical Society, he crossed the river to Cambridge, where he gave addresses at the Harvard commencement, to Harvard College, to the Phi Beta Kappa Society, as well as to the general public.

Spurzheim's own book, *Phrenology, or the Doctrine of the Mental Phenomena* (1832), had just been published in Boston; and he was obviously riding the crest of a wave of popularity. The phrenology he advocated, however, had been transformed almost beyond recognition from the field that had been initiated by Gall at the beginning of the century. As one recent author has remarked, "it had all but ceased being primarily a medical science. Rather, it came to resemble a social science, its bright and cheerful patchwork of scientific, religious, and moralistic doctrine promising a rationalistic means for describing man's place in society and his relation to nature's laws" (Wrobel 1987, 124). As his book clearly shows, "To Spurzheim, science, religion and morality became one. Phrenology was the science which revealed the laws of man as an intelligent and moral being. To obey these laws was to serve the will of the Creator as well as to improve humanity" (Temkin 1947, 308).

Obviously, to a secular but still pious America where common sense and self-improvement were being leavened with intuitive aspirations, the message being marketed by Spurzheim had immense appeal. American demands for the Spurzheim product, however, proved to be more than he was capable of providing, although he literally died in the effort to satisfy them. After 6 weeks of keeping to an exhausting schedule of lectures and social engagements, his health began to give way. At first, he refused to curtail his program, and, what with the unaccustomed dank chill of the Boston climate in late autumn and the drain caused by his engagements, he contracted a fever, which proved to be fatal on November 10, 1832. One report called it "typhus fever" (Walsh 1972, 194), another called it "typhoid fever" (Warren 1921, 3, 8), and yet another did not specify (Gibbon 1878, 276).

As we look back from the perspective of more than a century and a half, what happened after his death was just as extraordinary as the events which led up to it. Harvard's president, Josiah Quincy, led a discussion among Spurzheim's friends and mourners to determine the procedures for settling his estate and handling his remains. In accordance with their arrangements, a public autopsy was performed on Spurzheim's cadaver in "a crowded theatre" by Dr. John Collins Warren, professor of anatomy and surgery at Harvard, temporarily a convert to phrenology and later to become famous for performing the first operation using ether as an anesthetic (Horine 1960, 12).

Spurzheim's funeral took place on November 17 in the Old South Meeting House in Boston, and his funeral procession was made up of some 3,000 mourners, with the Boston Medical Society marching as a body in their midst (Davies 1971, 17). After interment at Mount Auburn Cemetery in Cambridge, his loyal followers met that very evening to found the Boston Phrenological Society. The collection of that august body was initiated with the skull and the embalmed brain of Johann Gaspar Spurzheim. When the society disbanded 15 years later, Professor Warren purchased its collection for the Department of Anatomy, and Spurzheim's cranium is still in the possession of the Harvard Medical School.

Gall had died 4 years earlier, and, according to his instructions, his skull had been added to the specimens in his own collection, which is still preserved in the Musée de l'Homme in Paris (Ackerknecht and Vallois 1955, 2, 65). With the passing of Spurzheim, the principal avatar of phrenology became George Combe of Edinburgh. Now, it was his turn to undertake an American tour; and following Spurzheim's footsteps, he made his way to Boston in 1838, where "Warned of Spurzheim's unhappy demise," he was careful not to undertake more than his constitution could sustain (Davies 1971, 20).

Combe was "feted by the Bostonian and Philadelphian elite" (Erickson 1977, 93) and was one of the first of a burgeoning number of itinerant lecturers to extend his travels beyond the Allegheny Mountains to what was then "The West"—Ohio and Kentucky. Combe's reason, however, was not to pursue an expanding market but to visit "America's leading phrenologist," Charles Caldwell (Gibbon 1878, II:96; Davies 1971, 46). Combe's 18-month-long visit to America denoted what has been called "the high-water mark in phrenology, at least among the upper classes of the United States" (Davies 1971, 20), and certainly he was treated with the greatest of admiration and respect. He was introduced to the president of the United States, Martin Van Buren (Gibbon 1878, II:51), and he had his portrait painted by Rembrandt Peale (1778–1860), the son of Charles Willson Peale (1741–1827), whose unflattering portrait of George Washington is one of the best-known representations of America's first president (Gibbon 1878, II:56).

His lectures were given to audiences of between 300 and 500, and he was guaranteed a fee of $750 for each, a sum that was well over the average annual income of all but the well-to-do. In the end, he broke even since he had invested a portion of his wife's inheritance and all of his spare capital in the United States Bank, which failed, and he was just able to cover the losses with his earnings on books and lectures. In any case, it is clear that Combe was not just another opportunist on the make. He has been described as "a sincere and conscientious adherent of phrenology," and his "infusion of Scottish philosophy into the phrenological movement" was part of what made it so well received in America (Wrobel 1975, 41). Among the many friends he made in America was the "father of American public education," Horace Mann (1796–1859), secretary of the Massachusetts Board of Education and later the first president of Antioch College, who was so taken with phrenology and George Combe that he named his only son George Combe Mann (Wilson 1956, 223).

Of all the contacts that he made in America, however, perhaps the most consequential was the meeting with his long-term correspondent Samuel George Morton in Philadelphia in 1839. As I shall discuss in the next chapter, Morton was to become the heart of what was informally called The American School of Anthropology. In 1839, he was working on his most important contribution, *Crania Americana,* and, as a result of Combe's visit, he aspired to include something of the outlook of phrenology. Since he did not feel qualified to write on the subject himself, he managed to get Combe to examine the Native American crania on which his monograph was based and write an appendix that was included when the work was published later that year. This will be treated at greater length in the section that follows.

Combe finished his American tour with a visit to Benjamin Silliman at Yale and returned to Scotland in June 1840. His reputation was such that he was asked to do phrenological analyses of the children of Queen Victoria and Prince Albert (Gibbon 1878, II:299), but the strength of phrenology as a fad had begun to wane. Phrenology as a respectable enterprise could be said to have "died with Combe in 1858," although "it left. . . a legacy to anthropology" (Erickson 1977, 92). Combe himself had lacked the credentials of either scientific or medical training, although that was partially made up for by the support of his physician brother, Andrew. George Combe, however, was not really a scientist at all, and he could have served as a case in point for Huxley's opposition to Matthew Arnold's claim that it was enough to be able to talk about what science presumably had shown without needing to understand what it was actually about.

Even before his trip to America, Combe had been offered the chair of mental and moral philosophy at the fledgling University of Michigan in 1837. Fortunately for the future of that distinguished institution, he declined the offer (Gibbon 1878, II:9). The number of eminent Americans who became enthusiastic supporters serves as a measure of the lack of intellectual sophistication of the young country: President James A. Garfield, distinguished college presidents Horace Mann and Josiah Quincy, prominent clergymen Henry Ward Beecher and William Ellery Channing, noted physicians Philip Syng Physick and John Collins Warren, and admired poets Edgar Allen Poe and Walt Whitman as well as many others became enthusiastic converts. Not all eminent Americans, however, were taken in. One former American president, John Quincy Adams, and John Collins Warren's younger but even more eminent Harvard medical colleague Oliver Wendell Holmes, Sr. spotted phrenology for the fraud that it was. Even though, for a while, it was "at the core of Transcendental inquiry rather than at the periphery," the preeminent American transcendentalist Ralph Waldo Emerson eventually consigned it to "the lunatic fringe along with nudism, wearing beards and eating 'aspiring' vegetables" (Wilson 1956, 221).

Encouraged by the endorsements of such prominent and respected people, phrenology was being taken up and peddled for public consumption by people with no obvious qualifications at all. This was becoming evident even to people who were inclined to believe in phrenology itself. One of the more amusing anecdotes demonstrating this was provided by the American humorist Mark Twain. When he went incognito to a well-known phrenological operator, he was told that the presence of a depression instead of a bulge over his "organ of mirthfulness" indicated "the total absence of a sense of humor." However, when he went back again later under his own famous name, he was declared to possess a veritable "Mount Everest" for his "bump of humor" (Gribben 1972, 64).

On the more serious side, not long before Combe's American tour, the distinguished German scholar Friedrich Tiedemann (1781–1861), professor of anatomy and physiology at Heidelberg, had published a massive compilation of information on the size of the brain of the five "races" recognized by Blumenbach. He had personally collected all of the data himself, using a most ingenious technique, and his sources included, among many others, the crania assembled in the phrenological collection in Edinburgh.

Despite the repeated phrenological disparagement of the brains of "negroes" and other non-European human groups, Tiedemann found that "The common doctrine, that the African brain, and particularly that of the Negro, is greatly smaller than the European, is false" (Tiedemann 1836, 511). When he separately measured the different major components of the brain, he was able to sustain the same conclusion. Finally, he dissected the tissues of the various divisions of the brain and spinal cord and, again, found no noticeable difference between any of the human groups in his sample.

Efforts to claim inferiority for African brains have continued from that day to this, but none is based on original comparative research. Whether those attempts to denigrate the brains of different non-European groups are based on supposed "phrenological" grounds or on what running a tape measure around the skull would presumably show, the invariable underlying assumption is that skin color somehow can tell us something about the structure and function of the brain. In this regard, it is instructive to quote the conclusion Tiedemann reached as a result of his own original research: "As . . . there are no well-marked and essential differences between the brain of the Negro and the European, we must conclude that no innate difference in the intellectual faculties can be admitted to exist between them" (1836, 520).

Unfortunately, ideas and attitudes concerning "race" were increasingly being determined by those who were confronted with the issue on a daily basis in the context of a tradition that demanded some kind of acceptable account of what was observed. Nowhere was this more clear than in the United States of America, and nowhere was a less coherent account likely to arise. The artificial juxtaposition of peoples uprooted from different parts of the globe created categorical distinctions out of what had originally been continuous and graded variations. Furthermore, after initially using force to ensure their privileged position, the dominant Europe-derived part of the resulting mix accepted the consequent social hierarchy as a reflection of the innate worth of the constituent components. Although it is unfair to blame the framers of the emerging "race" concept for having created the conditions that produced the artificial picture they described, it would be equally shortsighted not to examine that picture in some detail, for, as we shall see, it is just that picture which underlies the accepted if unexamined concept of "race" that is held by the greater part of the literate world at the present time.

7

THE FOUNDING OF THE AMERICAN SCHOOL OF ANTHROPOLOGY

THE POSTCOLONIAL UNITED STATES OF AMERICA

Following the termination of the American Revolutionary War, which began in 1776, the hard feelings between Britain and America continued for several generations. These were not eased when British armed forces made an incursion up the Potomac and burned the White House during the War of 1812 (August 24, 1814). That war sticks in American minds more vividly than in European ones since it was really only a minor diversion during the period when Napoleon was rampaging across the Continent and threatening to invade England. For a 50- or 60-year stretch in the late 18th and early 19th centuries, there was something of a rupture in the ties between the former colonies and the country from which they derived their language and culture.

Through the efforts of the Marquis de Lafayette (Marie Joseph Paul Yves Roch Gilbert du Motier, 1757–1834), France had aided the American cause during the Revolutionary War and thereby assured a feeling of friendliness that has lasted in one form or another ever since. From the point of view of cold reality, however, French assistance had been given not out of any particular liking for Americans or sympathy with American ideals but, rather, as a means of contributing to the embarrassment of the British, with whom the French had been feuding off and on for 700 years. In fairness, it should be said that Lafayette's mixture of liberal democratic ideals and sheer military competence compelled the personal admiration of both French as well as American citizens.

The positive feelings that Americans had for France in the abstract meant that Paris was a more likely destination than London for those who had the money and the leisure to travel overseas. However, American education, then as now, provided little competence in dealing with the French language; and the culture of France was sufficiently different from that of postcolonial America so that more than a little suspicion was directed at those Americans who fancied some aspects of the French way of life: Thomas Jefferson, for example, was regarded as being affected when he adopted elements of French dining habits. "Frenchified" was the epithet of opprobrium sometimes applied.

If Americans going overseas tended to find the style of life in France a bit alien and to feel uncomfortable with the English as their recent enemies, they had no such reservations about Scotland. Despite the differences in pronunciation, the language was still the English that they could understand, and the ideals of the Scottish Enlightenment had played a dominant role in shaping the way that Americans thought about politics and life. The Medical School at the University of Edinburgh had earned recognition as being the best in the world during the 18th century, and it continued to attract aspiring students from such overseas places as America during the remaining life of the Scottish Enlightenment over the first three decades of the 19th century.

As the century proceeded, however, Scotland increasingly came to be perceived as falling behind the times. In a world where up-to-dateness and "progress" had become positive values for the first time, Americans, feeling somewhat backward themselves, were anxious to catch up with those parts of the world that set the trend. That trend was propelled by the winds of Romanticism, and for Americans, its most beguiling source was the European continent. As one reviewer phrased it, "Civilization, like commerce, has its trade routes, and the United States has traditionally regarded France as its favorite station, whether for luxury (the fork comes to us from Bordeaux), recipes, fashion or ideas (equality, existentialism, structuralism)" (Davenport 1979, 9). For the first decades of the 19th century, however, Scotland continued to be a major influence on how Americans looked at the world.

SAMUEL GEORGE MORTON AND THE AMERICAN ORIGIN OF BIOLOGICAL ANTHROPOLOGY

Throughout this book, I have repeatedly noted the importance of the role played by America in generating the concept of "race" as it is now generally accepted. America not only provided the stage on which the issues were raised that led to the fixation of that concept, but it essentially generated the profession that took "race" as its topic of study. One of the most thorough chroniclers of phrenology, J. D. Davies, declared that "Physical anthropology is peculiarly an American science, and largely because of the continuous attack upon a single problem—the eternal presence and challenge of the American Indian" (Davies 1971, 145–146). However, he did not go quite far enough. There was another "eternal presence and challenge" that was just as omnipresent and just as much of a stimulus to the genesis of the field of biological anthropology. Beyond the American "Indian" issue was the burden of conscience imposed by the unavoidable presence of large numbers of people of African origin in a position of enforced servitude—that is, slavery. As one of the biographers of America's first physical anthropologist observed "Here, three of the five races, into which Blumenbach divided mankind, are brought together to determine the problem of their destiny as best they may" (Patterson 1855, xxxii). Not only did America constitute the crucible in which the "race" concept was forged, it also generated the anthropologists who established the traditions of its study. The first to summarize the history of the field in America observed that "the actual birth of the science took place in Philadelphia" (Hrdlička 1943, 61; supported by Hallowell 1967, 47).

At the beginning of the 19th century, Philadelphia was America's largest city, and its only rival as a center for cultural and intellectual distinction was Boston (Baltzell 1979). Philadelphia had been the seat of the revolutionary government before the building of Washington, D.C., and, with the most available access to the American interior, it benefited financially from its position as the largest American port serving the import and export trade. This latter advantage was ceded to New York when the Erie Canal, completed in 1825, forged a direct water linkage from the sea via the Hudson River to the Great Lakes and the resources of the heartland in the American Midwest. Until this happened, however, Philadelphia maintained its place as the richest and most populous American city.

There was another, less touted aspect of Philadelphia, however: it was one of the unhealthiest American cities. Part of the reason was the relative density of the population, and part was the fact that, on the border between the American north and south, the winters were not cold enough to serve as a fully effective barrier to diseases normally associated with somewhat warmer climates. The repeated epidemics of yellow fever at the end of the 18th century were responsible for the deaths of many thousands of people at each onset and the flight of many more. One of the other consequences of the health problems repeatedly associated with life in Philadelphia was the genesis of an unusually flourishing medical establishment. The Medical School of the University of Pennsylvania, the oldest in America, was founded in 1765, and it, like the university as a whole, was also modeled on its counterpart at the University of Edinburgh in Scotland (Norwood 1966, 20; Hook 1975, 23). Others soon arose; even today, there are more well-known medical schools in Philadelphia than in any other American city of comparable size, and in the past, the number was still greater (Abrahams 1966).

It was into this context that Samuel George Morton (1799–1851) was born and raised to be a physician (Fig. 7–1). His father, George Morton, was the youngest son of an Anglican family in Clonmel, County Tipperary, in the southern part of Ireland.

Figure 7–1   Samuel George Morton, 1799–1851 (from the frontispiece of Meigs 1851).

He emigrated to America, set up a business in Philadelphia, married a Quaker "lady" and started a family. Of the nine children born to this union, only two lived to adult-hood—a grim picture but not atypical for colonial and immediately postcolonial America. George Morton died when his youngest child, Samuel George Morton, was just 6 months old. Jane Cummings Morton later remarried back into the faith, and young Samuel George was duly educated in Quaker schools. Subsequently, he spent a period as an apprentice in a mercantile house in Philadelphia, during which time his mother contracted a lingering ailment that led to her death in 1816 (Wood 1859, 437–439).

During her illness, she was attended by some of the most highly regarded physicians in Philadelphia, including Caspar Wistar, professor of anatomy at the University of Pennsylvania, and the exemplary Quaker physician, Dr. Joseph Parrish (1779–1840). This contact had a permanent effect in shaping the career of her youngest child. After her death, he became apprenticed to Parrish and began his training in medicine. At that time, the usual route to entering medical practice was apprenticeship to a practicing physician, with medical school generally coming afterward, if at all. During the American Revolution, for example, about 90% of the 3,500 doctors in the Continental Army were apprentice-trained. Of the approximately 10% who were institutionally trained, most came from London, Leyden, Paris, and, especially, Edinburgh (Norwood 1966, 20). During his apprenticeship, Morton simultaneously gained his actual medical degree under the tutelage of Philip Syng Physick (1768–1837), professor of surgery and anatomy at the University of Pennsylvania Medical School.

With the long history of ties between the Philadelphia medical world and the University of Edinburgh, it was almost to be expected that young Morton should aspire to go there to earn his doctorate. In America up to the end of the 18th century, as in England today, the degree earned by attending medical school and qualifying for practice was not a doctorate but a baccalaureate in medicine. An M.D. was a research degree conferred after the defense and publication of a doctoral dissertation (Wood 1859, 344). Pennsylvania had abandoned that requirement by the end of the previous century, however; and the degree that Morton acquired in Philadelphia in 1820 was an American M.D. American medical practitioners ever since have been granted a doctorate in the absence of the production and defense of a research dissertation.

Morton's Irish uncle had urged him to come for a visit after his graduation, and during the summer of 1820, he made his way to Ireland, where he was warmly welcomed by a host of congenial kin. They were dubious about the significance of his American diploma and urged him to go to Edinburgh and get a "real" degree, which he was able to do because of financial support from his wealthy uncle, James Morton of Clonmel, whose fortune he ultimately inherited (Stanton 1960, 25–44). In Scotland in the fall of 1820, however, he found that they also were dubious about the equivalence of American training to their own, and he was required to repeat another year of undergraduate studies. Even though Edinburgh still retained some of the prestige of its earlier medical standing, Paris by this time had moved to the forefront in medical matters; during the winter of 1821–22, Morton went there for a season of clinical training (Meigs 1851, 15). During the spring and summer, he traveled throughout France and made a ceremonial pilgrimage to Italy, where Vesalius had been teaching when he wrote the *Fabrica*. He returned to Edinburgh in the autumn of 1822 to work on his doctorate. In the summer of

1823, he finished his M.D. thesis, *De Corporis Dolore* (On Pain of the Body), which he dedicated to his former preceptor at the University of Pennsylvania, Philip Syng Physick (Spencer 1983, 324). Thus prepared, he returned to Philadelphia in 1824 to establish what eventually was described as a "lucrative" medical practice (Wood 1859, 452).

Prestigious qualifications and financial security allowed Morton to move in the best of social and academic circles, and his situation gave him the leisure to devote some of his attention to matters beyond the basic need of earning a living. His interests turned to matters of science. Right after earning his M.D. in 1820, he had been elected to the prestigious Academy of Natural Sciences in Philadelphia, with which he was to remain associated for the rest of his life. He became recording secretary in 1825, moving on to corresponding secretary in 1831, then vice president in 1840; and he was president at the time of his death in 1851 (Meigs 1851, 14; Hrdlička 1943, 62). Morton became one of the most outstanding representatives of the first American generation of professional scientists and achieved full recognition as such among his scientific contemporaries in Europe as well as America.

To be sure, his primary professional orientation was toward medicine. By 1830, he had become a teacher of anatomy at the school established by his former preceptor, Joseph Parrish. That school evolved into the Medical Department of Pennsylvania College, where he served as professor of anatomy from 1839 to 1843. This was not the University of Pennsylvania, with which it is sometimes confused, but another of those many medical schools that flourished in Philadelphia but did not survive the impact of the American Civil War of the 1860s.

His scientific contributions, however, began in the mid-1820s and continued to the time of his premature death in 1851. My primary concern here of course is with his anthropological publications, but he made his presence felt with research contributions ranging from medicine through geology, paleontology, and zoology. Nor were these simply the productions of an unprofessional dabbler. In each of the fields to which he contributed, his work counted as state-of-the-art scholarship. In medicine, he dealt with nutrition, pharmacology, and the treatment of tuberculosis in addition to the teaching texts in gross and microscopic anatomy and in pathology with which he was associated.

Over a 20-year span, Morton produced a stream of works in both vertebrate and invertebrate paleontology. These were triggered by the material that was unearthed during the construction of the Chesapeake and Delaware Canal. This had been duly sent to Philadelphia for study since, at that time, the city was the recognized center for scientific research. In his efforts to name and identify the specimens on which he was working, he engaged in correspondence with leading European authorities in the field. Among these was the English physician and paleontologist Gideon Mantell (1790–1852), famous for having given the name *Iguanodon* to a Mesozoic reptile tooth found by his wife near Brighton. Morton was so appreciative of Mantell's help that he dedicated his most ambitious paleontological work to him, *Synopsis of the Organic Remains of the Cretaceous Group of the United States* (1834). Morton, in fact, launched the science of paleontology in the United States and projected Philadelphia into a position of prominence in that field, which it was to retain for the remainder of the 19th century (Abrahams 1966, 49).

He had been sent two hippopotamus skulls from Liberia when he was compiling his collection of human and animal crania, and he immediately recognized that they clearly belonged to a different species from the standard hippopotamus. Morton was the first to publish a description of the skull of the West African pygmy hippopotamus, which is indeed a separate species from *Hippopotamus amphibius*. Initially, Morton proposed calling it *Hippopotamus minor* (Morton 1844b, 407), but, as a good cautious scholar, he checked with the leading authorities in the field. Using his friend, Sir Charles Lyell, as a courier, he sent his two specimens to London to be examined by Sir Richard Owen and Dr. Hugh Falconer at the British Museum. Falconer wrote him back that Cuvier had already used the name *H. minor* to describe a fossil specimen, but recognizing that Morton had indeed identified a new living species of hippopotamus, he accepted *H. liberiensis* (Morton) as the proper designation. Morton then published Falconer's letter along with his own technical description (Morton 1849, 4, 7, 10). His species name is still used for the pygmy hippopotamus, although it is now regarded as belonging in a separate genus.

In spite of these and other contributions, however, the enduring fame of Samuel George Morton rests on his role as a pioneer in anthropology. In the summer of 1830, he started his anatomy course with the lecture "The Five Races of Men," using Blumenbach's scheme; but he remarked in retrospect "Strange to say, I could neither buy nor borrow a cranium of each of these races." Looking back on that occasion, he reported that as a consequence "I at once resolved to make a collection for myself; and now, after a lapse of sixteen years, I have deposited in the Academy of Natural Sciences, a series embracing upwards of seven hundred human crania, and an equal number of inferior animals" (Morton 1848, 218). If all that focus on skulls leads the reader to suspect an underlying commitment to phrenology, it must be realized that the 1830s represented the peak of enthusiasm for that enterprise. Morton did flirt with phrenology, as we shall see; and although he never accepted the list of localized "faculties" claimed by Gall and his followers, he did not definitively separate himself from the field and its practitioners. In the long run, this was one of the factors that helped obscure the nature of his accomplishments.

The cranial collection that he assembled in Philadelphia was occasionally referred to by his contemporaries as "The American Golgotha" (Stanton 1960, 28), *Golgotha* being the Aramaic word for Calvary, or "the place of a skull," (Matthew 37:33; Mark 15:22) where Christ was crucified; and it continued to grow until Morton's death, at which time it contained representative samples of all five of Blumenbach's "races." It still exists today at the University Museum in Philadelphia, where it is maintained by the Department of Anthropology at the University of Pennsylvania as part of one of the most important and certainly longest-enduring anthropological research resources in the world.

Morton announced his intention to expand on the craniological approach started by Blumenbach in his *Decades . . . Craniorum* (1790–1828) and devote a major volume to the treatment of cranial form in the native populations of the Western Hemisphere. This was completed in 1839 and entitled *Crania Americana; or, a Comparative View of the Skulls of Various Aboriginal Nations of North and South America; to which Is Prefixed an Essay on the Varieties of the Human Species*. With nearly 300 pages plus over 70 elegantly produced plates, the book made a most impressive appearance. As was true of most books published at that time, the author was responsible for the costs of publication. In order to meet these expenses, Morton was backed by "subscribers" at the

Academy of Natural Sciences in Philadelphia and by the money of his father's brother in Ireland. The purchase price was $20, more than a month's wages for the average person, and 500 copies were divided between its simultaneous publication in London and Philadelphia. The English edition was identical to the American one with the exception of the dedication. The former was jointly inscribed to Dr. James Cowles Prichard and the author's uncle, James Morton, Esq.

Despite what we would now regard as two serious intellectual flaws, it remains a monumental piece of scholarship, and it immediately projected Samuel George Morton into a position of international eminence. The universally admired German naturalist Alexander von Humboldt (1769–1859) wrote him an effusive letter in French, which was translated in his obituary: "Your work is equally remarkable for the profundity of its anatomical views, the numerical detail of the relations of organic conformation, and the absence of those poetical reveries which are the myths of modern physiology" (quoted in Meigs 1851, 48).

The Swedish anatomist Anders Retzius (1796–1860) wrote him in a similar vein (in Patterson 1855, xxxiii) and later stated that Morton's book was more valuable than anything of its kind written in Europe since Blumenbach's work at the end of the previous century. The book was reviewed in all the leading scholarly journals on both sides of the Atlantic, and it was generally regarded with respect and admiration, although phrenological reviewers were evidently disappointed that it did not reflect the use of their perspective except in the appendix, which had been written by George Combe himself. Sales were successful, and the investment of Morton's backers was amply rewarded.

Morton had consulted the descriptions and accounts of travelers and historians from the time of Herodotus right up to his own to gain information on the life-ways of all the major populations of the world. That aspect of his work alone was a major piece of scholarship, although it followed right in the tradition of Buffon, Blumenbach, Bory, Lawrence, and Prichard, all of whom he cited. Unlike Caldwell, he noted his disagreement with the positions of scholars such as Blumenbach and Prichard without impugning their motives or competence. Not only was he a first-rate scholar but he was a thoroughly decent person, a kindly gentleman in the best sense of that word, and renowned for the hospitality that his relative wealth allowed him to provide (Wood 1859, 452).

The original and enduring contribution that Morton made was in the invention and application of a battery of measurements that he used to compare large numbers of specimens from many parts of the world. Morton devised more than a dozen cranial measurements and basically initiated the use of metrics in comparing human biological forms. Many of the measurements Morton devised continue to be used for comparative purposes in biological anthropology today (e.g., Brace et al. 1993, 2001). Morton, then, deserves recognition as one of the founders of the field of biological anthropology as a whole and not just its American manifestation.

He assembled and used samples from more than 40 localities in North and South America. These included a series of North American populations as well as samples from Mexico, Peru, and Tierra del Fuego at the southern tip of South America. As a result of his comparisons, Morton demonstrated that the Native Americans deserved recognition as a separate group equivalent in their distinction to the other major geographical populations of the world. Furthermore, Morton had acquired skulls from burials associated with the fortified but abandoned settlements that seemed to be such an enigma to the European immigrants then moving into the American Midwest. Through his metric analysis, Morton demonstrated that these prehistoric people were indistinguishable from the living Native American groups from which he had obtained samples. The mysterious "Mound Builders" were in fact simply American "Indians" after all, dispelling those myths of the "lost tribes of Israel" and other such fantasies.

In the essay on classification with which he opens his *Crania Americana,* Morton discussed the major schemes that had been offered by previous scholars. He made reference to the French workers Virey, Bory, and Broc as well as to Cuvier (Morton 1839, 4), whose tripartite classification—Caucasian, Mongolian, and Ethiopian—has been so pervasive in the folklore of Western civilization. However, the system that he adopted and modified was that of Blumenbach. Morton accepted Blumenbach's five "varieties" of human form, renamed them "races" (Morton 1839, 5), and "races" they have been ever since.

Constituting these five "races," Morton recognized 22 "families." His American race, for example, consisted of the American and the Toltecan families; his Malay race was made up of the Malay and Polynesian families; the Caucasian race had seven families; the Ethiopian race, six families; and the Mongolian race, five families. All subsequent classifications of human "races" have basically been derivatives of the system presented by Morton in his *Crania Americana* (e.g., Coon et al. 1950; Coon 1963; Coon and Hunt 1965; Baker 1974).

Although Morton took his five "races" from Blumenbach's "varieties," giving the Göttingen professor full credit for his original formulation, there was one fundamental respect in which Morton's scheme was radically different from the one on which it was modeled. Whereas Blumenbach had said that "no variety exists . . . so singular as not to be connected with others of the same kind by such an imperceptible transition, that it is very clear they are all related, or only differ from each other in degree" (in Bendyshe 1865, 264), to Morton the "races" were categorically distinct and unrelated to each other. In part, this was the result of the Neoplatonic legacy of essentialism in Western thought, and in part it was the fact that Morton, as an American, was reacting to the artificial situation that had come about because of the way in which human populations from three separate parts of the world had been uprooted and brought into daily confrontation on the western shores of the Atlantic Ocean.

Further, whereas Blumenbach felt that human varieties had come to differ in their characteristic way through a process of "degeneration" under the influence of differences in climate, nutrition, and mode of life, Morton assumed "that the physical characteristics which distinguish the different Races . . . are independent of external causes" (Morton 1839, 3). It was Morton's view that "each Race was adapted from the beginning to its peculiar local destination" (Morton 1839, 3) by the agency of an "all-wise Providence." Morton was brought to that conclusion by contemplating the assertion of Charles Caldwell that, since it was accepted to be some 4,179 years "since Noah and his family," assumed to be "Caucasian," "came out of the ark" and since Ethiopians, assumed to have been dark of skin, "were known to have existed" 3,445 years ago, if that latter were: "of the stock of Noah, the change must have been completed and a new race formed in seven hundred and thirty-three years, and probably in a much shorter period" (Caldwell 1852, 72).

This "knowledge" about the antiquity of Ethiopians of which both Caldwell and Morton spoke with such assurance was based on the information available in ancient

Egyptian written records. The famous Rosetta Stone, found by Napoleon's forces in the Nile Delta in 1799, had finally been deciphered by Jean François Champollion in 1822, and this allowed interested scholars to read and understand ancient Egyptian hieroglyphics (James 1988, 16). That was what allowed Morton to say the following:

> The recent discoveries in Egypt give additional force to [Caldwell's] preceding statement, inasmuch as they show beyond all question that the Caucasian and Negro races were as perfectly distinct in that country upwards of three thousand years ago as they are now: whence it is evident that if the Caucasian was derived from the Negro, or the Negro from the Caucasian, by the action of external causes, the change must have been effected in at most a thousand years: a theory which the subsequent evidence of thirty centuries proves to be a physical impossibility; and we have already ventured to insist that such a commutation could be effected by nothing short of a miracle. (Morton 1839, 88)

Even while Morton was in the midst of writing his *Crania Americana,* he was beginning to assemble the material for his next major anthropological contribution, his *Crania Ægyptiaca* (Morton 1844a). In 1837, he initiated correspondence with George Robins Gliddon (1809–57), who had been sent to New York by the Ottoman viceroy of Egypt, Mohammed Ali—no relation to the American pugilist—on a mission to gather information and machinery to assist in the development of the Egyptian cotton industry (Patterson 1855, xxxv). Gliddon was a glib and charming self-promoter, born to an English mercantile family, who spent his short and frenetic life involved in one marginal scheme after another, ever on the lookout for the big success that always seemed to elude him.

From the middle of the second decade of the 19th century on, the expanding community of western Europeans in Alexandria led every European country of consequence plus the United States to station consuls in Egypt to see to their interests. The United States had fewer experienced Mediterranean hands to oversee their affairs, so they contracted out the consulship to interested Englishmen. George Gliddon's father, John Gliddon, served without pay as the honorary U.S. consul, first at Alexandria and then at Cairo, between 1832 and 1844. George Gliddon himself served as U.S. vice-consul in Cairo from 1832 until he came to the United States more or less permanently in 1840. It was in Cairo in the early 1830s that he met and became friends with John Lowell, Jr., the scion of "New England's first cotton-mill millionaire" (Stanton 1960, 46–48; Howard 1975, 123). It was the cotton connection that prompted Mohammed Ali to send George R. Gliddon on his mission to America.

Morton was unable to go to New York in 1837 to meet Gliddon, but he knew of his visit and wrote to ask him if he would procure a sampling of the skulls of ancient Egyptians for his growing collection. Morton promised to pay for the collection and shipping, and Gliddon was glad to oblige when he returned to Egypt in 1838 (Patterson 1855, xxxv). In time, Gliddon was able to provide Morton with 137 Egyptian crania, which proved to be ample for his monograph of 1844 (Morton 1846, 93).

The fascination that Egypt held for such figures as Caldwell, Gliddon, and Morton was related to the newly realized antiquity of the fabled civilization of the Valley of the Nile. The justly celebrated Rosetta Stone had allowed scholars to read the recorded history of that ancient culture and to reckon its actual dates with considerable precision.

By that time, it was correctly realized that Egyptian written accounts went back to 3000 B.C.E. (Gregersen 1977, 176). This, of course, was barely 1,000 years less than the date of creation calculated from the "begats" in the Bible—4004 B.C.E.—commonly, if erroneously, attributed to the Anglican Archbishop of Armagh, James Ussher in 1650 (Rudwick 1972, 70). It is a curious irony that both Caldwell and Gliddon, who were so scornful of the biblical roots of monogenism, accepted a biblically based time scale for the antiquity of the earth without second thoughts.

It is curious also that Morton accepted this as well since he had attended the Edinburgh lectures by the Scottish geologist Robert Jameson (1774–1854). This is particularly puzzling because Morton professed to have admired Jameson's lectures, yet he seems to have completely missed the perspective of infinite time that had entered the outlook of geology in Scotland following the famous observation of James Hutton in 1795 that, as a result of his investigations into the structure and shaping of the earth, he could see "no vestige of a beginning,—no prospect of an end" (Hutton 1795, I:200) and that "time, which . . . is often deficient in our schemes, is to nature endless" (Hutton 1795, I:15). Oddly enough, Charles Darwin also attended Jameson's lectures a few years later, although he soon stopped because he found them intolerably "dull." That short and unappreciated exposure, however, was enough to give him the perspective of an effective infinity of geological time that pervaded everything else he was to do for the rest of his life.

That total failure to grasp the implications of the breathtaking enormity involved in the extent of geological time was one of the principal flaws in the anthropology of Samuel George Morton. He correctly concluded that the prehistoric skeletons buried at the bottom of the Midwestern mounds were essentially the same as living American "Indians" and that ancient Egyptians were essentially the same as living Egyptians. Ancient Egyptians could be dated to as far back as 3000 B.C.E., and he took this to mean that Egyptians had remained unchanged since barely more than 1,000 years from the instant of creation. Furthermore, he was aware that the paintings on the walls of ancient Egyptian tombs portrayed facial features characteristic of sub-Saharan Africans as far back as the written records extended.

From all of this, he felt modestly certain that the only conclusion that science would allow was that human "racial" distinctions had been established "in the beginning" and that no natural agency could possibly have transformed the characteristic appearance of one known human population into that of another within the span of time he assumed to have elapsed since the creation of the world. It was simply beyond his grasp that the actual age of the earth is not just ten or a hundred but fully a million times greater than what was commonly accepted, although this was clearly the import of Hutton's famous dictum of the previous century; and it was this realization that Morton's friend, Sir Charles Lyell, was largely instrumental in bringing to the attention of the reading public.

Where Morton actually controlled his data, his work was exemplary and he was fully in control of his anatomical assessments. His *Crania Ægyptiaca* of 1844 was just as solid an appraisal of Egyptians and their relations to their neighbors as was his *Crania Americana* of 1839. He reported on the observations of travelers and writers as far back as Herodotus, and he appraised the comparative anatomical treatments of Blumenbach, Cuvier, Lawrence, Prichard, and von Soemmering before he produced an assessment based on his own quantitative analysis. He concluded that Egyptians are closely akin to modern Libyans (Morton 1844a, 42) and show similarities to the people of the Indian subcontinent (Morton 1844a, 53). After further thought and comparison, he concluded that "the Egyptians had no national affiliation with the Negro race" (Morton 1848, 220). It is a measure of the solid nature of Morton's comparative anatomical work that, if one substitutes "sub-Saharan African" for his term "Negro race," the gist of that conclusion is essentially identical to those recently reached by the use of much more extensive lists of measurements on massive worldwide samples aided by the latest computerized statistical treatment (Keita 1990; Brace et al. 1993, 2001).

Because he was so far afield in his understanding of geological time and its implications, Morton accepted it as self-evident that the "races" simply derived from the *"primeval diversities* among men" (Morton 1847, 40), but he continued to worry about his definition. As he said later in words very similar to those previously used by Caldwell, "But it is necessary here to explain what is meant by the word *race*. I do not use it to imply that all its divisions are derived from a single pair; on the contrary, I believe that they have originated from several, perhaps even from many pairs, which were adapted from the beginning, to the varied localities they were designed to occupy" (Morton 1848, 219). Then, still later, he revised things further: "The *five races of men*, would more appropriately be called *groups* . . . each of these is again divisible into a greater or smaller number of primary races, each of which expanded from an original nucleus or centre" (Morton 1850c, 246, 248). Finally, when he defined a biological species as "a primordial organic form" that "may be regarded by some naturalists as a *primitive variety*" (Morton 1851, 275–276), the confusion was complete. Since he had repeatedly referred to "races" as "primeval diversities" (Morton 1839, 3; 1844a, 37; 1847, 40), any possible distinction between "race" and species had vanished.

Morton was grappling with some of the problems that were receiving attention from the best natural scientists of his time, and although he badly muddied the distinctions between genus, species, and variety or "race," he really did no worse than most of his eminent peers. Only Charles Darwin was able to transcend the morass of "the species problem" that had entrapped so many of the best minds of the age, but, then, Darwin was a genius whose stature is still being contemplated with wonderment and awe (Browne 1995, 2002). We can only look back with regret that Morton's untimely death deprived him of the opportunity to absorb the import of the revolution in outlook that Darwin was to produce 8 years later.

Meanwhile, Morton was wrestling with his unsatisfactory definition of "race." In the course of this, he turned his attention to the question of hybrid sterility, which had been used by John Ray in the 17th century and Buffon in the 18th century to define specific distinction. After culling the available published sources, he produced a major paper entitled "Hybridity in Animals, Considered in Reference to the Question of the Unity of the Human Species" (Morton 1847), which was published in the *American Journal of Science and Arts,* founded and edited by the Yale chemist Benjamin Silliman, one-time student of John Maclean at the College of New Jersey (later to become Princeton; Morton 1847). At the time, this was the most prestigious scientific journal in America, and it was colloquially referred to as "Silliman's Journal." Silliman, in his role as editor, recognized that Morton's treatment of the subject of hybridity and his attempt to apply his conclusions to an assessment of the human condition was likely to be controversial, noting all of this in a footnote while disclaiming any responsibility for Morton's argument on the part of the editor or the journal itself.

The classic example of hybrid sterility illustrating species difference between the contributing parents, of course, is the cross between a horse and a donkey. The resulting mule is perfectly viable, but it is unable to reproduce. Other species of mammals and birds also illustrate the same point, although normally the experiment is carried out only under the artificial conditions encountered in captivity. Morton tried to set up a typology of species ranging from those that never produce hybrids—"*Remote species*"—through those that produce sterile offspring—"*Allied species*"—to "*Proximate species*" that produce fertile offspring (re-emphasized in Morton 1850a, 82; 1851, 276). The typological essentialism and arbitrariness involved in any fixed definition of a biological species was fully realized by Darwin just over a decade later (1859, 52), and this problem has drawn the attention of biologists ever since; however, Morton's treatment of the issue did not constitute a positive contribution to the question in general, and it had less than laudable consequences for considerations regarding the human species in particular.

Morton concluded his paper with a series of generalizations based on the more or less anecdotal evidence for prolific hybrids between various species and even genera. He asserted that domestication "evolves" this "faculty" and that the capacity for hybridity indicates an aptitude for domestication. His final two points declared that "hybridity ceases to be a test of specific affiliation" and that "Consequently, the mere fact that the several races of mankind produce with each other, a more or less fertile progeny, constitutes in itself, no proof of the unity of the human species" (Morton 1847, 212). In the end, Morton never produced a definition of species based on criteria that could be used to test whether or not a given group would warrant specific recognition, and he offered no guidelines to distinguish between a species and a "race." At most, he evidently assumed that if recognizable morphological distinctions could be identified 5,000 years ago, this was so close to the presumed date of creation that it could be regarded as "primordial" and therefore would warrant named recognition of some sort. The idea of an average species "half-life" of just less than 10 million years (Raup 1986, 1532) would have seemed simply inconceivable to him.

In his treatment of the species question in general and its possible application to the human condition in particular, Morton went beyond the solid, observational science that had characterized his comparative anatomical treatment. The "data" on which he based his conclusions concerning species, "races," and hybridity had not been acquired as a result of his own controlled efforts; and some of what he used to support his views was clearly unreliable hearsay. For example, he concluded that domestic dogs do not descend from one "primitive form, but from many" (1850a, 82) and that there were "many species of primordial dogs" (1850b, 89). Again, his perception that very divergent dog breeds were present in ancient Egypt led him to conclude that these differences had to have been present from the beginning. Today, as a result of a wealth of solid information, we know that all domestic dogs have descended from a single species, the wolf, and that all the different forms have been produced by selective breeding (Olsen 1985); these differences, however, do not warrant separate specific labels (Vilà et al. 1997).

Morton then extended the "logic" of his hybridity assumptions to instances of interbreeding between different human populations. He had made some effort to get information on "hybrids" between Australian aboriginals and the European settlers in Australia, and he assembled this in tabular form showing how ostensibly rare such offspring are. As he stated, "Perhaps no two human races are more remote from each other than the European and the Australian; and where two such extremes are blended, reason and analogy lead us to expect only a limited fertility" (Morton 1851, 175). While Europe and Australia are indeed just about as remote from each other as it is possible to be in the sense of geographic distance, there is no evidence whatever of a lowering of fertility associated with sexual union between native Australians and Europeans.

Having assumed that fertility between Europeans and Australians was limited, Morton continued "we may therefore ask, is not the real cause the *difference in race,* the disparity of primordial organization" (Morton 1851, 175). By his own definition, then, he was advancing the claim that Australians and Europeans belong to different species. His information came from his correspondence with various figures in Australia, and it was second hand at best, with no way to check its accuracy and no consideration given for the effects of the diseases of contact which had had just as devastating an impact on the survival and fertility of Native Australians as on Native Americans (Rowley 1970). Indicative of the shaky nature of what Morton was willing to accept as fact was his relation of the claim made by a "Polish traveler" in Australia that after an aboriginal woman had given birth to a child fathered by a European, she could not subsequently become pregnant by an Australian but only by a European male (1851, 175). Although Morton was not the source of both the racism and sexism that pervaded accounts such as this, it is clear that it was not the scientist in him that was operating when he included such information in his published reports.

Some pages back, I mentioned that Morton's failure to understand the magnitude of geological time was one of the principal flaws in his anthropology. The other main flaw was the latent racism that pervaded his thinking. Actually, neither one had any impact on the comparative work on which he reported in his *Crania Americana* and *Crania Ægyptiaca,* although both—particularly the racism—helped to negate the attempts at theoretical synthesis in his essays on species and hybridity. In fact, the racism in his thinking was simply a reflection of the general outlook of the society of which he was a part; and although our recent attempts to repudiate the commonly held racist assumptions of a century and a half ago are indirectly related to the eclipse that his reputation suffered after his death, his own somewhat genteel manifestation of that racism had nothing directly to do with the fact that he has almost become the forgotten man in the history of biological anthropology. Today, when he is remembered at all, it is usually for the wrong reasons.

A quarter of a century ago, in his otherwise admirable book *The Mismeasure of Man,* the late Stephen Jay Gould, a Harvard paleontologist and recent president of the American Association for the Advancement of Science, accused Morton of engaging in "a patchwork of fudging and finagling in the clear interest of controlling a priori convictions" (Gould 1978, 504; 1981, 54; 1996b, 86). Gould was obviously aware of the racism in Morton's general make-up and assumed that it influenced his reporting on the measurements of cranial volume in the various groups. After thus having assured damnation, Gould then tendered his faint praise: "Yet—and this is the most intriguing aspect of the case—I find no evidence of conscious fraud; indeed, had Morton been a conscious fudger, he would not have published his data so openly" (Gould 1978, 504; 1981, 54; 1996b, 86).

Most curious of all, however, is that the phrases I have quoted make a splendid description of the treatment of Samuel George Morton by Stephen Jay Gould, but they simply do not apply to the work of Morton himself. Morton's collection still exists at the

University of Pennsylvania, and John S. Michael, an enterprising honors student in geology at Macalester College, St. Paul, Minnesota, went through it and used a substantial sampling to duplicate the measurements that Morton had taken. He also recalculated the summaries Morton himself had made and published from his own measurements. Michael then compared the results of both his and Morton's efforts with what Gould had reported from his own recalculations. Although Michael's measurements showed a slight but constant difference from those made by Morton, this was almost certainly due to the nature of the homemade measuring equipment that Morton had used and was quite unrelated to any possible bias toward the different samples measured.

As Michael discovered, there were minor "miscalculations and omissions" in the *Catalogue of Skulls of Man and the Inferior Animals* published by Morton in 1849, but Morton's summaries "are reasonably accurate and there is no clear evidence that he doctored those tables for any reason" (Michael 1988, 354). Whatever "fudging and finagling" had been done was produced by Gould in an effort to show the presence of the bias that he assumed must have conditioned Morton's reporting. Yet, Gould himself appears to have been just as innocent of conscious fraud as he concludes Morton to have been. Somewhat belatedly and relegated to a footnote, he admitted that he had generalized from a Xerox copy of Morton's data and accepted a mean value for African American brain size that was actually below the bottom of the reported range of variation (footnote to Gould 1993, 109).

It appears that his denigration of Morton was even more obviously a product of his own bias about his subject than the distortions that he erroneously attributed to Morton were a product of the latter's racism. It is a bit ironic to realize that the term *Mismeasure* in the title of Gould's book is a better description of Gould's failure to "take the measure" of Samuel George Morton than it is of the efforts of the latter to present a metric description of the various human populations of the world.

Gould's incautious and unreflective treatment is an absolutely classic textbook illustration of one of the banes that afflict writers who deal with the past: it exemplifies what the historian Sir Herbert Butterfield has called *The Whig Interpretation of History* in his delightful little book of that name written in 1931. The Whig view of history, sometimes called "presentism," looks at the past from the perspective of a "direct and perpetual reference to the present" (Butterfield 1931, 11) and assesses the figures of yesteryear as either "the friends or the enemies of progress" (Butterfield 1931, 5). The Whig historian, having examined things out of context, then makes value judgments and counts them "as the verdict of history" (Butterfield 1931, 105).

This is precisely what Stephen Jay Gould did in his treatment of Samuel George Morton. Since Gould has written extensively on the history of science and has even warned repeatedly about the dangers inherent in presentism (Gould 1989, 16), it is all the more ironic that he himself has produced such a clear-cut example of the misperception that can arise from an incautious lapse into a whiggish interpretation of history, although others have previously detected this tendency in various samples of his writing (Hull 1984, 923; Trefil 1989, 36). Gould never acknowledged the flaw in his treatment that Michael had pointed out, but he did react when another, more senior scholar pointed out the actual error he had made in reporting Morton's data. He had claimed a mean value of cranial capacity of 80 cubic inches for people of African origin when the lowest value in the range was actually 84. As he said in a footnote, "The reason for this is embarrassing. I never saw the inconsistency—presumably because a low value of 80 fit my hopes" (1993, 109). None of this was mentioned, however, when he later produced a revised edition of *The Mismeasure of Man* (1996b), which continued to blame Morton for "fudging and finagling."

Morton, of course, did live in a society that was racially biased, and some of his private correspondence makes his own acceptance of that bias quite clear. At the same time, Morton was an exemplary scientist, and a careful analysis of his work shows that his "racial" bias had no effect at all on the major pieces of anthropological investigation that he published.

Morton produced the first full-scale quantified biological descriptions of geographically circumscribed human populations. This actually should have counted as the professional beginnings of biological anthropology; however, his name is hardly recalled today, and when it is, it is usually remembered for the tinge of phrenology or racism that history has attributed to his work. It has even been suggested that "his anthropology was, to a large extent, an extension of the doctrine of physiological vitalism that formed an intrinsic component of medical theory at the beginning of the 19th century" (Spencer 1983, 338). A quick rundown of these suggestions will show that none of them can suffice to account for the obscurity into which his memory lapsed.

It was true that physiological vitalism had been at the core of medical teaching during the era of Benjamin Rush at the University of Pennsylvania and that it continued to be a factor during the time immediately after his death when Morton was beginning his training. For all the personal animosity that had affected the relations between Rush and Charles Caldwell, vitalism continued to dominate Caldwell's medical outlook and clearly played a role in his enthusiasm for phrenology. Although Morton does cite with approval Caldwell's argument in favor of polygenism, this in itself had little, if anything, to do with vitalism. One could argue that the idea that there is a behavioral or spiritual "essence" associated with each "race" is compatible with the Romantic vitalism of the early 19th-century outlook; but then that aspect of Romanticism is an integral part of the "race" concept that survives to the present day, so it could hardly account for the eclipse of the reputation of Samuel George Morton.

Morton's flirtation with phrenology also has been repeatedly cited as a reason his work is not remembered (Hrdlička 1919, 10; Erickson 1977). Certainly, the advocates of phrenology in Edinburgh "must have been in the very fervor of their first love during Morton's residence there" (Patterson 1855, xxxii), and Morton has been reported as having attended the meetings of the "fledgling Phrenological Society" at that time (Spencer 1983, 324, citing a manuscript by Paul Erickson, who notes that this has not yet been substantiated). Although two of the most recent considerations of Morton's involvement with phrenology have suggested that he was more serious about it than Stanton's balanced account had concluded (Erickson 1977, 93; Spencer 1983, 337), no solid evidence has been produced to overturn Stanton's judgment that he was not as interested in the phrenological study of crania as has been alleged (Stanton 1960, 29).

It is true that he solicited a phrenological essay to append to his *Crania Americana* and asked his long-time correspondent George Combe to write it when the original author declined because of illness (Morton 1839, iii). As for his own views concerning phrenology, he wrote that "In this study I am yet a learner . . . the brain is the organ of the mind, and that its different parts perform different functions . . . [he had been] slow to acknowledge the details of Cranioscopy as taught by Dr. Gall" (Morton 1839, i). Like Stanton, I am inclined to agree with the biographer who wrote that "Morton's collection was ethnographic in its aim from the outset; nor can I find that he ever committed himself fully to Phrenology" (Patterson 1855, xxxii). It seems, then, that his involvement with phrenology was no more likely than his alleged physiological vitalism to have been the source of the taint to his reputation.

That leaves the matter of his racism. When he referred to the Caucasian as "the noblest race" (Morton 1839, 4), there was no doubt that he accepted the same "racial" hierarchy that animated the schemes of Blumenbach, Smith, Prichard, Lawrence, and virtually everyone else who wrote about the nature and meaning of human biological differences in the 18th and 19th centuries. In his private correspondence, he was even more explicit. On May 30, 1846, he wrote to George R. Gliddon: "it makes little difference whether the mental inferiority of the Negro, the Samoiyede, or the Indian, is natural or acquired; for, if they ever possessed equal intelligence with the Caucasian, they have lost it; and if they never had it, they had nothing to lose. One party would arraign Providence for creating them originally different, another for placing them in circumstances by which they inevitably became so. Let us search out the truth, and reconcile it afterwards" (quoted in Patterson 1855, lii).

While we can hardly applaud the egregious and ethnocentric racism in that statement, it was no different from the feelings and expressions of his predecessors and contemporaries; and it continued to characterize the writings of such figures as Paul Broca in France and Thomas Henry Huxley in England, whose reputations, while slightly tarnished by it, hardly suffered the kind of eclipse that was to be Morton's fate. Even the one 20th-century figure who reappraised Morton's contributions without seeing them as being diminished by the racism in his assumptions, despite his admiration, failed to give Morton his full due. This was Aleš Hrdlička (1869–1943), the person whose efforts led to the founding of the American Association of Physical Anthropologists in 1930 and who was the founding editor of the *American Journal of Physical Anthropology* a dozen years earlier.

In the very first appearance of the journal that he founded and edited in 1918, Hrdlička surveyed the history and status of biological anthropology. This was slightly revised and published as a separate book in 1919, *Physical Anthropology, Its Scope and Aims; Its History and Present Status in the United States.* In this, Hrdlička accorded more recognition to Samuel George Morton than he has received at the hands of any other writer: "it is plain that Morton may justly and with pride be termed the father of American anthropology; yet it must be noted with regret that, like others later on, he was a father who left many friends to the science and even followers, but no real progeny, no disciples who would continue his work as their special or life vocation" (Hrdlička 1919, 41).

It was a handsome and merited tribute, but it completely missed the mark. As will become evident in Chapter 11, the anthropology that Morton introduced was eagerly picked up as the life vocation of the dominant figures who established the field as a legitimate profession during the latter half of the 19th century—that is, Paul Broca and his associates—although, as we shall also see, none of them was American. Hrdlička himself, despite the American segment of his background, was a product of this European tradition, although ironically he completely missed the role played by Morton in its establishment. If Morton was one of the principal pioneers in founding biological anthropology, it is also clear that his name has been removed from the roster of the honored ancestors of the field.

The reason for this should become clear in the next section. It is my contention that this was not due to the strains of whatever vitalism or phrenology may have been infused in his work or even to the more evident nature of his own racism. On the other hand, it seems quite clear that racism was at the bottom of it. Samuel George Morton had never enjoyed robust good health, but his death in 1851 after a short illness was not expected. At that point, his work was adopted by self-appointed disciples and vigorously promoted as "scientific" justification for the perpetuation of the slavery of people of African ancestry in the American South.

A decade later, the festering issue of slavery became the principal impetus for the American Civil War. The defenders of slavery in the American South eventually lost the war, slavery was abolished, and the efforts that had been marshaled as intellectual justification for that "peculiar" institution were discredited because of their association with the lost cause. Among these were the anthropology that Morton had begun and which was posthumously retailored and offered to the South with his name attached.

Actually, Morton had been put in touch with an outspoken slavery proponent, the South Carolina politician John C. Calhoun, through the efforts of the peripatetic Englishman George R. Gliddon in 1844 (Nott and Gliddon 1854, 50). Gliddon had visited the State Department in Washington on business matters for his father, who was acting as U.S. Consul in Egypt, and the Secretary of State in the Tyler administration was John C. Calhoun (1782–1850). Calhoun had been secretary of war for James Monroe at the time of the War of 1812, and he served as vice president under both John Quincy Adams and Andrew Jackson. His presidential ambitions were curbed because of his strong identification with regional issues (Freehling 1965, 226), but he served as senator for South Carolina from 1833 until his death in 1850. As a result of his correspondence with Morton, the latter sent him both his *Crania Americana* and *Crania Ægyptiaca* (Nott and Gliddon 1854, 51). These confirmed Calhoun's racial bigotry and gave the grounding for his stance when he declared in a speech before the U.S. Senate "Ours, sir, is the government of a white race" (Calhoun 1848, 98). As a champion of states' rights, "he did more than any other individual to bring the South to the fever pitch of civil war," even though he died more than a decade before that event actually took place (Nevin 1992, 97).

The resulting stigma was such that the memory of Morton's career and his actual work have been buried along with the institutionalized racism that is such an embarrassing specter in the baggage of American history. Morton surely did not deserve such an unhallowed interment; however, he has never been the subject of a full-scale biographical study, and, as Hrdlička noted at the end of his own life, of the several biographical sketches available, "all are more or less wanting" (Hrdlička 1943, 61). Perhaps what I have written here will provide stimulus enough so that someone will undertake the work that will finally give to Samuel George Morton the recognition that is clearly his due.

8

PASSING THE TORCH

LOUIS AGASSIZ, ARCHETYPICAL AMERICAN

After Morton's death in 1851, his memory was kept alive by three figures who were considered to embody the "American School of Anthropology" in the eyes of European scientists and scholars. These were Louis Agassiz, George Robins Gliddon, and Josiah Clark Nott. Of these, Nott, both by himself and in collaboration with Gliddon, had the greatest impact in America and abroad, but the presence of Agassiz added a prestige to the group that could not be commanded by the others. Finally, his European connections made the productions of the American School more readily acceptable to the intellectual establishment in the Old World.

Louis Agassiz (1807–73) was the son of a Protestant minister in French Switzerland (Fig. 8–1). After schooling in Lausanne, he received his university training at Zürich, Heidelberg, Erlangen, and Munich just as the influences of Romanticism and *Naturphilosophie* were at their height (Lurie 1960). That kind of multiple-university exposure possible in the 19th-century German academic sphere was a sort of intellectual Camelot that has evoked a note of nostalgia on the part of those who were privileged to take part in it, but it was not to last. The rise of the sense of regional identity culminating in the kind of nationalism not previously present was accompanied by an increase in the formalities associated with local academic requirements, and the once relatively open system ceased to be.

Writing in later years of his teacher, Lorenz Oken (1779–1851) of Munich, where he earned his M.D., Agassiz recalled that "he exercised an almost irresistible influence . . . constructing the universe out of his own brain . . . deducing from *a priori* conceptions *all* the relations . . . of living beings. . . . It seemed to us . . . that the slow, laborious process of accumulating pieces of detailed knowledge could only be the work of drones, while a . . . commanding spirit might build the world of its own powerful imagination" (quoted in Lurie 1960, 50). Ironically, Agassiz's main contributions to the world of science were in just that realm of accumulating data. With one major exception, Agassiz neither added to nor understood the major theoretical contributions that were the products of the scientific imagination of the 19th century. On the other hand, he achieved overwhelming international acclaim as the very embodiment of natural science.

Agassiz focused his research on zoology, geology, and paleontology and became particularly well known among scientists for his work on fossil fish. In 1831, he was welcomed by the elderly Georges Cuvier (1769–1832) at the Muséum d'Histoire Naturelle in Paris, where he was given access to the extensive fossil collections that Cuvier would never have time to work up and put into print (Lurie 1960, 54). In effect, he became Cuvier's last student, and he continued to reflect the rigid Platonic essentialism and the

Figure 8–1   Louis Agassiz, 1807–73, in 1855 (from Lurie 1960).

outlook of "natural theology" that had been at the core of the thinking of the great French naturalist (Lurie 1960, 283; Rudwick 1972, 153).

He picked up another aspect of Cuvier's outlook, and this was the assumption that geological changes had taken place in sudden and catastrophic fashion. One of Cuvier's most influential publications was his "Discours sur les Révolutions de la Surface du Globe" (Cuvier 1821). Earlier, the term *revolution* had had more of a Newtonian implication, represented by planets revolving around the sun; "In a revolutionary era, however, the word took on new overtones of sudden violence, and it was in this sense that Cuvier came to view the history of the Earth as punctuated by 'revolutions'" (Rudwick 1972, 109). Cuvier had lived through the French Revolution, and he clearly did not mean gradual transformation when he applied the term to characterize the episodes of topographical change that had taken place in the geological past. It was a view that the professor of moral philosophy and master of Trinity College, Cambridge, William Whewell (1794–1866, pronounced "Hule") was later to call "catastrophism" (Whewell 1832). The catastrophist mind-set was not congenial to expectations that geological and indeed biological change was produced gradually by the forces currently at work in the world. It is no surprise, then, that the continuity of the thought patterns characteristic of Cuvier and Agassiz is represented by so many individuals and institutions that have rejected a Darwinian outlook.

With Cuvier's approval, Agassiz set to work with a will and produced a stream of publications, printed largely at his own expense; and although this was the foundation of a scientific credibility that was to last for the rest of his life, it put him in something of a financial bind. Volumes devoted to the technical descriptions of fossil fish simply do not produce the monetary returns generated by best-selling novels, and since the income from his modest professorship in Neuchâtel, Switzerland, was not sufficient to support the "scientific factory" he was running, Agassiz was soon in financial difficulties (Lurie 1960, 109–113).

The one major theoretical contribution with which Agassiz was associated also provided the basis for a way out of his financial troubles. During his summer vacation in 1836, Jean de Charpentier (1786–1855), a Swiss geologist "of considerable reputation" (Lurie 1960, 102), showed Agassiz how mountain glaciers had shaped the floors and sides of Alpine valleys and how they could transport rocks a distance of many miles. Agassiz had originally been skeptical, but he was converted by Charpentier's demonstrations and logic. A year later, Agassiz expanded upon this in a presentation to the Swiss Society of Natural History (Lurie 1960, 94). Although he knew that Charpentier was in the course of publishing his theory, Agassiz beat him into print, gaining credit for priority but losing a friend in the process.

When he went to Scotland in 1840 to attend the meetings of the British Association for the Advancement of Science in Glasgow, Agassiz accompanied William Buckland (1784–1856), the Oxford geologist, on a visit to Glen Roy in Argyll on the northern flanks of the Grampian Hills in the western highlands. Just a year earlier, Charles Darwin had published an account suggesting that the configuration of that valley must have been shaped by marine action (Darwin 1839), but Agassiz correctly recognized that the parallel beach-like structures, or "roads," that Darwin had observed were just what one would expect to find at the edges of a glacial lake. Of course, there is no glacier there now; but at the Glasgow meetings, Agassiz proposed that the landscape of Scotland, England, and much of the adjacent continent from the arctic to the Mediterranean had been shaped by glacial action in prehistoric times (Agassiz 1840).

In this instance, Agassiz was right and Darwin was wrong. Darwin, who had met him at the Glasgow meetings, subsequently wrote him that "I have enjoyed reading your work on glaciers, which has filled me with admiration" (quoted in Lurie 1960, 100). The roles were to be reversed 19 years later when Darwin published his *Origin*. That book fundamentally reshaped the way in which the biological world was subsequently conceptualized, but it was a view that Agassiz was unable to share. He did not reciprocate with an admiring letter to Darwin after reading his epoch-making work.

The public was intrigued by the idea of an "Ice Age" preceding the emergence of the modern world. Actually, we now know that there was not just one Ice Age but a whole series of episodes of glaciation recurring at intervals of approximately 100,000 years over the last million years and more, but it took several more generations of geological field work before this became apparent. Previously, some of the phenomena that Agassiz explained by the action of an immense prehistoric glaciation had been attributed to the biblical flood, but Agassiz was sufficiently in command of the facts to defend his glaciation hypothesis with great skill. At the same time, because of his status as a minister's son and an avowed Christian, he was not perceived as offering views that were contrary to accepted, common religious beliefs. His feelings in fact were quite compatible with those of his friend William Buckland, reader in geology at Oxford and later dean of Westminster Cathedral (Rudwick 1972, 135).

Buckland was confident that God had placed iron, coal, and limestone in the British Isles specifically to ensure Britain's place as the supreme manufacturing country in the world, which at that time it was (Hitchcock 1852). In the same vein, Agassiz interpreted prehistoric glacial action as the means by which God had distributed fertile soil for the particular benefit of those chosen human populations that lived in the temperate regions of the globe. As he put it, "The glacier was God's great plough" (quoted by Lurie 1960, 98). Both Agassiz and Buckland accepted the teleologically egocentric stance of traditional Christianity, which regarded human beings as the object and end of divine creation and assumed that the world and its contents had been put there specifically to be exploited for human use. In good Protestant fashion, they felt that active efforts to discover what was in the world and how it worked were necessary steps prior to harnessing the resources of nature for human benefit.

Both also subscribed to the movement that has been called "natural theology," which found evidence for the existence of God in the wonders of the world that He had created. That in itself was sufficient to justify the pursuit of science as an activity which could not be incompatible with religion. As Agassiz was later to say, "Our task is . . . complete as soon as we have proven His existence" (1857, 132). Although Agassiz came from a background that was culturally French—or at least French Swiss—his basic Protestant orientation made him fully acceptable in the English-speaking world.

This suggested a way out of the financial bind in which he found himself. As a magnetic and appealing personality, he was capable of holding the attention of an audience with ease, and a good public lecturer could command a not insignificant income. Following the pattern previously established by Spurzheim, Agassiz honed his skills in English during his visits to Britain; and with recommendations from such prominent figures as Sir Charles Lyell, he proposed to undertake a trip to America in an effort to rid himself of his burden of debt. Lyell had given the Lowell Institute Lectures in Boston, 1840–41, and his influence was helpful in getting Agassiz invited to deliver them in 1846 (Lurie 1960, 116).

The Lowell Institute had been endowed by the "proper" Bostonian John Lowell, Jr., with a bequest of $250,000. This was a very large sum of money for that time, as can be seen from the fact that, despite significant expenditures, it had grown by the residual interest alone to the level of eight million dollars by 1966 (Weeks 1966, 13). The lecture series was initiated on January 3, 1840, by Benjamin Silliman of Yale (Weeks 1966, 40–41). By tradition, the lectures were given by socially acceptable speakers on topics that were of general interest but not likely to be upsetting or controversial. William Lloyd Garrison, the passionate abolitionist, for example, was too much a figure of controversy to be considered acceptable; so, too, was Ralph Waldo Emerson, who had become controversial because he left the pulpit of the Second Church in Boston when his conscience would not allow him to pretend that he believed in the supernatural efficacy of the communion ceremony (Weeks 1966, 40; Goodman 1990, 34). Given these circumstances, the Romantic "feel-good" approach of Agassiz, with its confident "God's-in-His-Heaven-and-all's-right-with-the-world" ambience, seemed to be just the kind of thing that would appeal to the pious Bostonians.

George R. Gliddon, who had earlier befriended the late John Lowell, Jr., in Egypt, had given the Lowell Lectures in 1843 and had used this to generate a career of lecturing to American audiences. With similar thoughts in mind, Agassiz headed off to America at the end of the summer in 1846 and, although this had hardly been his intent, began an entirely new career for himself. His initial hopes for his American tour were amply realized, and he earned nearly $6,000 in less than 6 months just from his lectures in New England (Lurie 1960, 129). To put this in perspective, when Agassiz later became a top-ranked Harvard professor, his salary was $1,500 per year, which was very handsome for the time (Lurie 1960, 138).

The new life that Agassiz constructed made him into an American. He repeatedly returned to Europe, but America was to remain his home for the rest of his life. Although he was internationally famous and far better educated than the average immigrant who became an American, there are many ways in which Louis Agassiz was perfectly typical of the immigrant American who created the national identity that still characterizes the United States to this day. The intellectual tradition in which he had been raised was that of northwest Europe, with all the baggage of Neoplatonic essentialism that this entailed. Further, as a Protestant, he had inherited the post-Reformation Enlightenment faith that the exercise of reason could only demonstrate the glories of God and the world that He had created. Perhaps the best expression of that outlook was penned by Archdeacon William Paley from the English Midlands in his *Natural Theology* (Paley 1802). This had been an important source for the orientation of the young Charles Darwin, although he outgrew it later on since it really belonged to the scientific outlook of the 18th century (Rudwick 1972, 154). Like Buckland and the other authors of the *Bridgewater Treatises* of the 1830s, Agassiz remained faithful to this style of thinking for the rest of his life (Mayr 1959, 165).

Finally, as a properly indoctrinated Christian, he took it as a matter of course that all humans were descended from Adam and Eve in the Garden of Eden—he was, in fact, an orthodox monogenist. In Neuchâtel, a year before he came to America, he had published a small volume entitled *Notice sur la Géographie des Animaux*. A decade later, this was translated into English by the Rev. John Bachman, the embattled monogenist in Charleston, South Carolina, along with a reprint of the original French. In a key passage, Agassiz declared that "Whilst the lower animals are of distinct species in different zoological provinces to which they belong; man, notwithstanding the diversity of his races, constitutes only one, and the same over all the surface of the globe. In this respect as well as in so many others, man seems to us to form an exception to the general rule in this creation, of which he is at the same time the object and the end" (translated by Bachman 1855c, 491).

Agassiz, however, had never met face to face with representatives of the various non-European inhabitants of the earth. The shock he was to feel on coming to America led to a conversion experience, and this too was typical for the average immigrant who had been uprooted and plunked down out of context in the Western Hemisphere. Today, it is transparent to us that the conclusions which he drew were based not on a scientific assessment of systematically collected facts viewed in context but on his own emotional reactions.

When Agassiz first arrived in America and before he delivered his Lowell Lecture, he hastened to Philadelphia to meet America's most eminent scientist, Samuel George Morton. The Harvard botanist Asa Gray (1810–88) accompanied him and performed the introduction to Morton, whose influence on him "was second only to Cuvier" (Abrahams 1966, 49). In the dining room at his hotel in Philadelphia, he was served by the first people of African ancestry that he had ever personally encountered. As he wrote in a letter to his mother back in Switzerland, the shock was such that he could scarcely refrain from bolting out of the room: "I hardly dare to tell you the painful impression I received, so much are the feelings they gave me contrary to all our ideas of the brother-hood of man and the unique origin of our species. But truth before all. The more pity I felt at the sight of this degraded and degenerate race, the more . . . impossible it becomes for me to repress the feeling that they are not of the same blood as we are" (letter of December 2, 1846, quoted in Lurie 1960, 257). Oddly enough, Stephen Jay Gould later looked up the same letter in the Houghton Library at Harvard and claimed credit as the first to have translated it into English (1993, 95; 1996b, 76–77). Evidently, he never bothered to read Lurie's excellent biography of Agassiz.

Agassiz then went to Boston, where he began the first of his course of lectures with "The Plan of Creation in the Animal Kingdom"—properly in the spirit of the series whose full title was the Lowell Lectures on the Application of Metaphysical and Ethical Science to the Evidences of Religion, Delivered Before the Lowell Institute in Boston. The Lowell Institute, curiously enough, was an institute without a building. The endow-ment provided a stipend for the lecturer, and the usual practice was to rent a suitable hall for his presentation (Weeks 1966, 11–12). The actual invitation had been tendered by John Amory Lowell, the trustee of the Lowell Institute and both the cousin and the brother-in-law of the late John Lowell, Jr.—proper Bostonians in that bygone era had a tendency to intermarry to an extent that now would be regarded as of dubious legality, which may have had something to do with the drop in the Lowell fertility level evident at the end of the 19th century.

Agassiz's performance evidently captivated his New England audience. As an indi-cation of the attention he commanded, Benjamin Silliman traveled all the way from New Haven, Connecticut, just to be on hand (Lurie 1960, 126). It was recorded that "Upward of three thousand people turned out night after night, even in the most difficult weather and sat spellbound" (McCullough 1977, 6). He literally talked his way into the hearts of Boston society. Within a year, Abbott Lawrence (1792–1855), a kinsman of the Lowells and a fellow textile tycoon, had donated $50,000 to establish the Lawrence Scientific School at Harvard. Both the Lowell and the Lawrence families had a long history of in-volvement with the financing and administration of Harvard—Abbot Lawrence Lowell, who was president of the University for 20 years starting in 1909, was a grandson of John Amory Lowell—and had mill towns named after them in the Merrimack Valley of northeastern Massachusetts.

The Boston and Harvard communities very much wanted to keep Louis Agassiz as a permanent ornament, and Abbot Lawrence had this specifically in mind when he do-nated the money to Harvard for the Lawrence Scientific School. Harvard's president, Edward Everett, and corporation member John Amory Lowell convinced the Harvard Corporation to create a professorship to be offered to Agassiz. On October 3, 1847, Agassiz accepted the position of professor of zoology and geology and the directorship of the Lawrence Scientific School and thereby committed himself to a future as an American (Lurie 1960, 138; Livingstone 1987b, 26).

It had not been part of Agassiz's intentions to stay in America when he planned his lectures starting in 1846, and he had come without his family. He had been partially es-tranged from his invalid wife even before he undertook his "visit" to America, and in

1850, a couple of years after her death from tuberculosis, he married Elizabeth Cabot Cary, the daughter of a proper Bostonian, and stayed on at Harvard, where he enjoyed the height of esteem and support from the community (Lurie 1960, 141, 175). Eventually, again with the help of the Lowells and other supportive Bostonians, enough money was collected to finance the construction of a building to serve as the locus for his research efforts and to house the specimens brought back from the field work he pursued with his students.

The Museum of Comparative Zoology was founded in 1859, the same year that Darwin's *Origin* was published, and part of the support was given in the hope that Agassiz would prove to be an effective antidote to the perceived threat of Darwinian "materialism." When the museum was formally opened in November 1860, Harvard's president, Cornelius Conway Felton—who was Agassiz's brother-in-law, being married to Lizzie Agassiz's sister Mary—declared that it was altogether fitting that the new museum should face the Harvard Divinity School on the opposite side of Divinity Avenue, "God's word and God's works mutually illustrating each other" (McCullough 1977, 14). This was a paraphrase of the sentiment expressed by the early Enlightenment writer Francis Bacon in his *Advancement of Learning* (1605). All of this served as an effective anchor to keep Agassiz at Harvard in spite of an extraordinarily prestigious and lucrative offer from Paris in 1857, repeated in 1858 (Lurie 1960, 224).

Agassiz never reconciled himself to a Darwinian perspective, and it led to a contentious break between himself and his colleague Asa Gray (Dupree 1959, 323; Livingstone 1987b, 56). Organic evolution in general and human evolution in particular were regarded by him as anathema: "The resources of the Deity cannot be so meager that in order to create a human being endowed with reason, He must change a monkey into a man" (quoted by McCullough 1977, 14). As in many other instances, Agassiz presumed not only that he had positive knowledge of what God intended for the world but also that he had the right to pronounce upon the means by which God proposed to realize that intent. It is one of the delicious ironies in the history of science that the Museum of Comparative Zoology—professionally referred to as "the MCZ" but still known locally as the "Agassiz Museum"—went on to become a world-famous center for the study of biological evolution.

Agassiz himself, however, represented a mixture of the surviving strain of Neoplatonic essentialism of the 18th century and the Romanticism of the early 19th century. Like Linnaeus, he was a conservative creationist, who felt that in discovering and naming the fossil fish and other creatures that absorbed so much of his energy he was demonstrating the ideas in the mind of God and, therefore, the plan of creation (Lurie 1960, 270, 283). At the same time, he was "a leading exponent of the transcendentalist school of thought" (Bowler 1986, 152) and a supporter of the phrenology advocated by Spurzheim (Wilson 1956, 223). His presence and charm captivated the mass of his listeners; but the verdict of history has been that, for all his romantic energy, he actually ranked among the "drones," while it was the role of Darwin to "build the world of his own powerful imagination," even if that imagination was powered by just the kind of drudgery that Agassiz promoted.

Even some nonprofessionals who came in prolonged contact with him realized the clay in his feet. The future philosopher and founder of the field of psychology William James (1842–1910), as a Harvard undergraduate, had accompanied Agassiz on the

Thayer expedition to Brazil in 1866. James wrote back to his father: "I have profited a great deal by hearing Agassiz talk, not so much by what he says, for never did a man utter a greater amount of humbug, but by learning the way of feeling of such a vast practical engine as he is" (quoted by Gould 1988, 18).

The conversion experience Agassiz had undergone in 1846 when he visited Morton in Philadelphia took a while to reach fruition. Initially, this was not evident in his lectures in New England. A year later, in the fall of 1847, he was a visitor to the plantation of the South Carolina zoologist John Edward Holbrook (1794–1871). At that time, he delivered lectures before the Charleston Literary Club, where he presented much the same material that he had given to his Boston audiences; but he began to articulate the "separate and unequal" views with which he later became identified (Lurie 1960, 143).

Just over 3 years later, however, he publicly renounced the monogenism that had governed his thinking before he came to America. The occasion for this was the third annual meeting of the newly established American Association for the Advancement of Science (AAAS) which was held in Charleston, South Carolina, in March 1850. Using the model of its European counterparts, Agassiz had been influential in helping to create the association. This was accomplished by the transformation of an offshoot of the Academy of Natural Sciences of Philadelphia, and Agassiz had just been elected to serve as its president for 1851–53 (Lurie 1960, 132, 179). From its inception to the present day, this organization has maintained its position at the center of the American scientific community. Agassiz's election, then, symbolizes the fact that he had reached the pinnacle of scientific prestige in America.

The outbreak of the American Civil War was still a decade away, but the issues that led to it were generating intense interest. One of the most important of these was the biological status of people of African ancestry in relation to the other geographically identifiable people of the world. Agassiz's traditional monogenism, jolted by his experience on his first visit to Philadelphia, was completely overturned by his repeated visits to Charleston and other parts of the South. Agassiz reveled in the admiration accorded to him by wealthy and socially prominent southerners and quickly adopted their general attitudes toward the world. A key part of that stance was the unquestioned assumption that people of African ancestry were innately inferior to Europeans. Agassiz was a willing convert to such views and brought the luster of his scientific reputation to their support.

At the AAAS meetings in Charleston, a session was devoted to the issue of unity versus diversity in assessing the question of human origins. The session featured a paper written by Josiah Clark Nott, a physician from Mobile, Alabama, whom I treat at length in Chapters 9 and 10. Nott's medical practice had kept him tied up in Mobile, so he had his contribution read for him: "An Examination of the Physical History of the Jews, in Its Bearings on the Question of the Unity of the Races" (Nott 1850; Horsman 1987, 114).

Nott was an outspoken polygenist and, in the words of his biographer, "a bigoted, narrow-minded racist" (Horsman 1987, 42): "At bottom, Nott was a prototypical Southern racist" (Brace 1974a, 516). He had taken his first cues from Charles Caldwell, who had bolstered his stance with ideas and material derived from the publications of Samuel George Morton. Nott was actually recycling material he had largely published previously in 1844 and 1849, but the AAAS forum at Charleston enabled him to reach a much wider audience than his earlier sectional readership. After the reading was finished, Agassiz rose to declare his support for Nott's position (Horsman 1987, 114).

When Nott heard about this later, he wrote in triumph to Morton: "with Agassiz in the war, the battle is ours. This was an immense accession for we shall not only have his name, but the timid will come out of their hiding places" (quoted in Lurie 1960, 261).

With Morton's death only a year later, Josiah Clark Nott was to become the principal voice of the American School of Anthropology, but that articulation was assisted by the frenetic, if somewhat diffuse, energy of George R. Gliddon and validated by the imprimatur of Louis Agassiz. Nott's most influential contribution was entitled *Types of Mankind* (1854), which was written, patched together, edited, and produced in conjunction with Gliddon and included a contribution from Agassiz that has to rank as the most embarrassing memorial to the career of that otherwise distinguished Swiss American naturalist. The intent was to show that the institution of slavery as it existed in the United States was "justified" by the findings of science. The unabashedly racist core of Nott's thesis had been presented first in two lectures given in Mobile, Alabama, in 1844 (Nott 1844). These were subsequently expanded for a New Orleans audience in December of 1848 (Nott 1849). This material appeared in various other guises later on, and I treat this in the section on Josiah Clark Nott.

The AAAS meetings of 1850 in Charleston saw the injection of these views into mainstream American scientific thought as a result of the approval and support given by Louis Agassiz. At the same time that American scientists were meeting in Charleston, Agassiz published the first of a two-part discussion concerning human biological differences in the *Christian Examiner*, the voice of the Boston–Harvard Unitarian establishment (Lurie 1960, 259). In the March issue, to the discomfiture of his pious New England readership, he bluntly declared: "That Adam and Eve were neither the only nor the first human beings created is intimated in the statement of Moses himself where Cain is represented to us as wandering among foreign nations after he was cursed, and taking a wife from the people of Nod" (Agassiz 1850a, 184–185). Indulging in his preference for the use of the pontifical "we" he concluded with the disclaimer "it is not for us to inquire further into the full meaning of the statements of Moses. But we are satisfied that he never meant to say that all men originated from a single pair, Adam and Eve, nor that the animals had a similar origin from one common centre or from a single pair" (Agassiz 1850a, 185).

In the July issue of the *Christian Examiner*, he picked up on the same theme. Accepting the reality of "racial" behavioral and biological differences emphasized by daily experience in America, he noted the following, in reference to the biblical accounts: "But there is nowhere any mention of these physical differences characteristic of the colored races of men, such as the Mongolians and negroes. . . . Have we not, on the contrary, the distinct assertion that the Ethiopian cannot change his skin nor the leopard his spots" (Agassiz 1850b, 135). Just as physical attributes are variously distributed, so he assumed are "all the developments in the intellectual and moral world. . . . So can we conceive, and so it seems to us to be indeed the fact, that those higher attributes which characterize man in his highest development are exhibited in the several races in very different proportions, giving, in the case of the inferior races, prominence to features which are more harmoniously combined in the white race" (Agassiz 1850b, 144).

His mentor, Georges Cuvier, may have rejected the Great Chain of Being, but it is alive and well in stereotypic form in his own writings: "The indomitable, courageous, proud Indian—in how very different a light he stands by the side of the submissive, obsequious, imitative negro, or by the side of the tricky, cunning, and cowardly Mongolian!! Are not these facts indications that the different races do not rank upon one level in nature?" (Agassiz 1850b, 144). These judgments were not reached by anything remotely like scientific procedure. They were simply the assertions of opinion, and that opinion was largely a reflection of the attitudes held by Agassiz's prominent slave-owning friends in the American South.

He then continued, in most unbiblical fashion: "for our own part, we entertain not the slightest doubt that human affairs with reference to the colored races would be far more judiciously conducted, if, in our intercourse with them, we were guided by a full consciousness of the real difference existing between us and them, and a desire to foster those dispositions that are eminently marked in them, rather than by treating them on terms of equality" (Agassiz 1850b, 144). Having thus pronounced his condemnation, he declared with benevolent condescension "We conceive it to be our duty to study these peculiarities and to do all that is in our power to develop them to the greatest advantage of all parties." In his words, anything less would have been "mock-philanthropy and mock-philosophy" (Agassiz 1850b, 144).

It is somewhat depressing to read almost the same words with the same intent being pronounced more than a century later by the University of California–Berkeley educational psychologist Arthur R. Jensen: "I simply say the idea of a genetic difference is not an unreasonable one . . . because everything else that's ever been examined has shown differences and why should the brain be an exception? . . . it has not been proved in any scientifically acceptable way. I think it *could* be" (quoted by Neary 1970, 62). Somehow his "everything else" does not seem to have included such things as the structure and function of the pancreas, spleen, and lungs or the composition of the blood or many more things that are essential for human survival. Jensen went on to note that our current social and welfare policies could have unfortunate consequences unless they are aided by "eugenic foresight," and he concluded that "The possible consequences of our failure seriously to study these questions may well be viewed by future generations as our society's greatest injustice to Negro Americans" (quoted by Neary 1970, 65). Like Agassiz, Jensen adopted the position that if a genetic basis for inferiority can be demonstrated, then there could be no grounds for complaints about social and economic discrimination (Neary 1970, 64). In the views of both, human populations as groups are assumed to occupy different positions on a hierarchy of superiority to inferiority, and there is some sort of imperative that impels us to study human biological differences so that we can determine the relative ranks of the various populations of the world on that scale.

While Jensen makes a perfunctory bow toward evolutionary biology in contrast to Agassiz's assumption that everything was fixed by fiat in the beginning, there is in fact very little difference between them; and Jensen's offhand use of the concept of "adaptation" is just a way to avoid an actual consideration of the circumstances that might or might not lead to differences in intellectual capabilities between human populations. For example, Jensen approves of the idea that "intelligence is the ability to adapt to civilization and that races differ in this ability according to the civilizations in which they live" (Jensen 1969a, 14). Intelligence quotient (IQ) tests presumably measure the ability to adapt to "Western civilization" (Jensen 1969a, 14), so it should follow that such tests would be appropriate to measure the intelligence of the people whose ancestors created that civilization and not for those people who were uprooted from their own ancestral ways of life and introduced into that alien milieu.

The flaw in this reasoning, however, is that "Western civilization" has existed for only a few centuries in anything like its present form, and it takes tens of thousands of years for changes in the circumstances of living to have any detectable biological consequences. In fact, not only is no human population biologically adapted to Western civilization but no living human population is adapted to the civilization with which it is associated because virtually none is pursuing a survival strategy that bears any remote resemblance to the circumstances that actually shaped the biology that is its heritage. Jensen's assumption, then, is just as thoughtlessly creationist as was that of Louis Agassiz. For the Jensens in the middle of the 20th century, as for the Agassizs in the middle of the 19th, the basic operating assumption is that people with pigment in their skins are less intelligent than people without, and how they got that way is of no real concern. Of equally little concern is the question of just why the inherited mechanism for pigment production should have the slightest connection with the growth and maintenance of the brain. Then and now, the assumption that it does is an essentially racist stance. This is treated at some length in Chapter 18.

In contrast to Nott and Gliddon, Agassiz really had no intent to denigrate the beliefs of the religiously orthodox, and he was concerned about the malaise he produced in his New England constituency. In his July contribution to the *Christian Examiner,* he tried to soften the blow of his polygenist stance by referring to "all human races" as "equal before God." He reemphasized this by saying that "They are brethren in God, brethren in humanity, though their origin . . . is lost in the beginning of the world" (Agassiz 1850b, 120). At this point, Agassiz employed a classic gambit in the phraseology of transcendental Romanticism, the "unity in diversity" and "diversity in unity" tack. It is an argument that defies paraphrasing, so I quote it here in its entirety: "We have seen what important, what prominent reasons there are for us to acknowledge the unity of mankind. But this unity does not exclude diversity. Diversity is the complement of all unity; for unity does not mean oneness, or singleness, but a plurality in which there are many points of resemblance, of agreement, of identity. This diversity in unity is the fundamental law of nature" (Agassiz 1850b, 132). He then finished off this splendidly Romantic declaration by putting it in the context of an assumed *scala naturae:* "And this diversity in unity gradually becomes more and more prominent throughout organized beings, as we rise from their lowest to their highest forms" (Agassiz 1850b, 132).

The influence of Louis Agassiz was to last long after his death in 1873. To the American public, his pronouncements were regarded as synonymous with the findings of "science," even though the scientist at the bench increasingly came to feel that he was losing touch with the significant currents of the times. His colleague at Harvard, the distinguished botanist Asa Gray, privately complained that Agassiz was acting more like a theologian than a scientist (Lurie 1960, 278). After Darwin's *Origin* was published in 1859, Gray wrote the principal review for Silliman's *American Journal of Science and Arts* in February 1860. He had been corresponding with Darwin for years and was sympathetic with his position (Dupree 1959, 239–246). This had led to a split with Agassiz, who made it clear to his students that any communication with Gray and his camp would be regarded as "parley with the enemy" (Livingstone 1987a, 28).

The reaction of Agassiz to Darwin was couched not in the form of professional scholarship but as denunciation in the popular press. Horace Greeley had him write a series of articles for his *New York Tribune,* which reached a wide public but was regarded as essentially an evasion of a serious treatment in the eyes of the scientific community (Howard 1975, 166). Even those who were sympathetic to Agassiz's special creationism were disappointed that he did not respond to what they regarded as the threat of Darwin with a more objective marshalling of relevant data in proper scientific fashion.

Although Agassiz's prestige remained undimmed in the eye of popular esteem, his high-handed and autocratic style tended to produce strain in his relations with colleagues and underlings, and many of his former students broke with him for one reason or another. Virtually all of his one-time students eventually recognized the reality of organic evolution, although not one of them accepted Darwin's theory that natural selection had been the primary driving mechanism. In the latter half of the 19th century, most American biologists who stemmed from Agassiz's milieu at Harvard, whether directly or indirectly, adopted some form of Lamarckian explanation—attributing the source of evolutionary change to the inheritance of acquired characteristics.

It is tempting to see in this a legacy of the admiration for French scholarship that Agassiz had instilled into his students. In any case, it was another two generations before a thoroughly Darwinian perspective was accepted in American biology. In Agassiz's own primary field of paleontology, a Darwinian view of evolution is still rejected by a large number of professionals today. In *paleoanthropology* (the study of the human fossil record), Darwinian mechanism is rejected by the majority of professional practitioners in favor of a version of what I have called "hominid catastrophism" (Brace 1964b)—sudden, unexplainable change and replacement (e.g., Stringer and McKie 1997; Stringer 2000; Tattersall 2001, 2002). To be sure, this cannot be charged to the lingering influence of Louis Agassiz since it was imported via another route from the same sources that had been influential in shaping his similar views (Brace 1988; see Chapters 12 and 17).

Agassiz was even more important in his influence on American thinking about "race." Even though his views were largely a reflection of the thinking that he found in America when he arrived, his status gave it added credibility. As at the Charleston meetings of 1850, the public regarded this as "science." When the *Atlantic Monthly* added a science department in the late 1860s, it was organized by one of Agassiz's students, John Fiske (1842–1901). The treatments of "race" that it promoted in the latter part of the 19th century used the same phrases and concepts that Josiah Clark Nott and Louis Agassiz had offered before the Civil War; and when the Immigration Restriction League was founded by three wealthy graduates of the Harvard class of 1889, they persuaded Fiske to take up its presidency (Livingstone 1987b, 154).

Finally, Agassiz's protégé, Nathaniel Southgate Shaler (1841–1906), became his successor as professor of paleontology at Harvard and director of the Lawrence Scientific School. Today, his contributions to real science are almost completely forgotten. Yet, Shaler was very famous in his day. He taught over 6,000 Harvard students and greatly increased the enrollment and funding of the Lawrence Scientific School.

Shaler enjoyed "overwhelming success as a university teacher," and this is what can be regarded as "his real educational legacy" (Livingstone 1987b, 274). His Lowell Lectures of 1888–89 were collected in book form as *Nature and Man in America*

in 1891. In this, as in his contributions to the *Atlantic Monthly* and other popular maga-
zines, he produced arguments about the nature of "race" that are almost direct quotes
from the earlier writings of Louis Agassiz's friend Josiah Clark Nott, although the original source is never mentioned. His legacy, then, was to perpetuate the pre–Civil War
stance of the American School of Anthropology and ensure that this was an integral part
of the knowledge of a generation of Harvard graduates, who were to play major roles in
how America was run and what it was to contribute to the world in terms of attitudes
and ideas.

The "white man's burden" attitude of American President Theodore Roosevelt, explicitly applied to colonial ventures in Panama and the Philippines, was an example of
the application of principles he had learned at the feet of his teacher, Nathaniel
Southgate Shaler (Dyer 1980, 6–7). The same thing is true of the Chinese Exclusion Act
of 1882 and a growing list of immigration restriction laws sponsored by another of
Shaler's former students, U.S. Senator Henry Cabot Lodge (1858–1924). Shaler may
have been forgotten in the world of science, but his impact on the social fabric of the
United States has left an enduring mark. Perhaps the most significant single contribution
was the perpetuation of the concept of "race" forged in the American School of
Anthropology before the U.S. Civil War. To show how this happened, Shaler deserves a
section all to himself—lest we forget.

9

THE DEMISE OF MONOGENISM
AND THE RISE OF POLYGENISM

JOHN BACHMAN: THE LAST MONOGENIST

The defense of polygenism and "racial" inequality presented by Josiah Clark Nott and Louis Agassiz in the name of science at the American Association for the Advancement of Science (AAAS) meetings of 1850 was greeted with enthusiasm by many in the South. Curiously, there were some who were just as convinced of the rectitude of slavery as was Nott but who were angrily offended by his stance. The most outspoken of these was the Reverend John Bachman (1790–1874), pastor of St. John's Lutheran Church in Charleston, South Carolina. Bachman, and the others for whom he spoke, felt that the claims of polygenism were contrary to the account in the Bible and, therefore, must count both as untruth and as blasphemy.

One might expect such a stance from the conservative and orthodox Christian clergy, and certainly Nott had done little to help make his views acceptable to the various manifestations of the Church. As we shall see, he took a positive delight in pointing out inconsistencies in the Scriptures and the ignorance of natural history on the part of their defenders. Bachman, however, unlike many of his clerical brethren, was far from being an ignoramus in matters of science. He had made the acquaintance of the distinguished and influential German naturalist and protégé of Blumenbach Baron Alexander von Humboldt in Philadelphia in 1804 and again on visits to Berlin and Paris in 1838 (Bachman 1888, 390–393), and he was professor of natural history at the College of Charleston (Bachman 1888, 262; Neuffer 1960, 81). Although this signifies that his qualifications were legitimate, his real scientific distinction was earned by his long-term collaboration with the famous artist–naturalist John James Audubon (1785–1851).

John Bachman was born in 1790 to German Swiss/south German parents in Rhinebeck by the Hudson River halfway between New York City and Albany. He enrolled at Williams College in nearby western Massachusetts but left before graduation because of an apparent bout with tuberculosis, the scourge of so many in that era and one that was to afflict others in his family later on. Subsequently, Williams was to award him a master's degree (Bachman 1888, 19; Neuffer 1960, 31). He earned his license to preach in the Lutheran church at the same time that he was supporting himself by teaching school near Philadelphia.

It was there that he met the renowned Scottish ornithologist Alexander Wilson (1766–1813), whose name is well known today to those of us who count as bird watchers. This evidently stimulated Bachman's interest in natural history, and in the course of time, he was credited by Audubon with identifying a previously unrecognized songbird.

Bachman's warbler is now an endangered species, whose last confirmed sighting was in 1981 (Diamond 1991, 32). As an acute observer of natural history, Bachman later was the first person to report that the brown and white coat phases of the weasel were the results of two molts, one in the spring and one in the fall (Hall 1974, 47).

After a short stint as a minister in Rensselaer County, New York, near his original home, he went south for his health in 1815, becoming pastor of St. John's Lutheran Church in Charleston, South Carolina, where he was to remain for the rest of his life (Neuffer 1960, 29, 32). There, he married, raised a family, and settled into the life of a "southern gentleman," enjoying the benefits of a gracious way of living that was made possible only with the aid of slave labor. His father had owned slaves on his farm in Rhinebeck while he was growing up, and one of them chose to go with him when he moved south to Charleston (Bachman 1888, 356). Bachman, although born a northerner, came to exemplify all of the American "racial" attitudes that we now identify with the Old South. Among his various activities as a promoter of Protestant Christianity, he founded and became first president of the Lutheran Synod of South Carolina and founded the South Carolina Lutheran Seminary.

In 1831, John James Audubon and his retinue of family members and assistants came to Charleston to begin work on the southern birds to be included in his magnificent *Birds of America* (Audubon 1827–38). In the tradition of "southern hospitality," Bachman insisted that they all stay at his capacious home, and this was the beginning of a friendship between the Audubon and Bachman families that was to last for the rest of their lives. By the late 1830s, Audubon's sons John and Victor had married two of the Bachman daughters, although tragically both young women died of tuberculosis within a year of each other in 1840–1 (Neuffer 1960, 67, 69). Bachman remained in close touch with the younger Audubons as their father's energy and health began to fail during the middle 1840s and it fell to his sons to see his monumental publishing projects to completion.

After the four glorious volumes of illustrations and five of text of *The Birds of America* had been published between 1827 and 1838, Audubon embarked on another project that eventually appeared in three more volumes of illustrations and three of text between 1845 and 1853, *The Viviparous Quadrupeds of North America,* for which John Bachman did most of the writing and which Audubon did not live to see completed. Bachman had declined the offer of the presidency of South Carolina College, in part because of the time he was devoting to the research for and writing of the *Quadrupeds,* and he really deserved to be credited as a coauthor with Audubon (Elman 1976, 17).

The first volume in that series appeared in 1846, the same year that Audubon's energy failed (Mengel 1967, 156) and Bachman's wife succumbed to tuberculosis (Bachman 1888, 219). This volume earned the praise of Louis Agassiz, who met Bachman on his first visit to Charleston in the fall of 1847 (Lurie 1960, 143). At that time, Agassiz told him that European scholarship had as yet produced nothing which could count as its equal (Neuffer 1960, 77).

Although the minuses began to add up in subsequent years, among the positive events in his life was his marriage in 1848 to his late wife's talented sister Maria, who had long been a member of the extensive Bachman household along with her own as well as Bachman's widowed mother (Neuffer 1960, 85). Maria Martin had been responsible for painting the background scenes for many of Audubon's portraits of southern birds and was regarded with great affection by members of both the Audubon and Bachman families. Also on the positive side, in addition to his honorary doctorate in divinity from Pennsylvania College at Gettysburg, were his LL.D. from the University of South Carolina and an honorary Ph.D. from the University of Berlin (Neuffer 1960, 91).

By mid-century, John Bachman had all the requisite social, scientific, and religious qualifications to make him the logical candidate to stand up for those who regarded the strident claims of Josiah Clark Nott as a blasphemous threat. In 1849, he had been invited to present his analysis of the polygenism promoted by the nascent American School of Anthropology to the meetings of the same prestigious Charleston Literary Club, before which Agassiz had spoken 2 years earlier. Obviously, he was prepared to face the challenge of the presentation read on behalf of Nott at the Charleston meetings of the AAAS in 1850. However, he had not expected to be confronted with the support which Nott was to receive from the president-elect of the association, Louis Agassiz, capitalizing on the aura of his European background enhanced by the prestige of his Harvard professorial status and the favor that he had already earned in the dominant social circles in the American South.

Bachman had engaged in a published exchange of letters with Morton late in 1849 and throughout 1850 in which he respectfully pointed out what he noted were errors in the latter's hybridity argument and conveyed the gist of what he had presented to the Charleston Literary Club (Patterson 1855, liii–liv). Subsequently, he worked up the notes that he had used for his 1849 presentation to the Literary Club dealing with what he perceived to be the threat represented by the stance of Morton and his supporters. This he published as a book, *The Doctrine of the Unity of the Human Race, Examined on the Principles of Science* (1850). This was a very thoughtful and well-documented piece of scholarship, very much in the tradition of Samuel Stanhope Smith, Blumenbach, Lawrence, and James Cowles Prichard, all of whom he cited. With his extensive knowledge of natural history, he was able to point to a series of mistakes in the sources Morton had used to support his hybridity arguments. This was the last fully developed attempt to integrate a literal acceptance of the biblical account of creation with the data concerning human biological variation.

During his public exchange of letters with Morton in 1850, he continued to maintain a tone of cordial respect even as he pointed to what really were flaws in the information compiled by Morton from various sources. After Morton's unexpected death in 1851, however, the tenor of the dispute changed. In his subsequent clashes with Nott and Gliddon, his tone became increasingly harsh. The full extent of his outrage did not emerge until 1854–5, when he responded to the publication of *Types of Mankind* by Nott and Gliddon. That great, sprawling volume contained, among other things, a chapter written by Louis Agassiz entitled "Sketch of the natural provinces of the animal world and their relation to the different types of man" (Nott and Gliddon 1854, lviii–lxxvi). In scope, it was quite similar to his pamphlet published in Neuchâtel in 1845, but the monogenism of the original had been abandoned.

In his 1854 essay, Agassiz presented his by now fully developed polygenist position in a more extreme fashion than he had ever done before:

> I am prepared to show that the differences existing between the races of men are of the same kind as the differences observed between the different families, genera, and species of monkeys or other animals; and that these different species of animals differ

in the same degree one from the other as the races of men—nay, the differences between distinct races are often greater than those distinguishing species of animals one from the other. The chimpanzee and gorilla do not differ more one from another than the Mandingo and the Guinea Negro: they together do not differ more from the orang than the Malay or white man differs from the Negro. (Agassiz 1854, lxxiv–lxxv)

Bachman was called upon to write the review of the Nott and Gliddon volume for the *Charleston Medical Journal,* which he did in prolonged and thunderous fashion in a series of installments stretching over the next 2 years (Bachman 1854a, 1855a,b). Two installments were devoted specifically to Agassiz's contribution (Bachman 1854b, 1855c). From the perspective of nearly a century and a half later, with the sole exception of the issue of single versus multiple origins, the attitudes of Bachman and Nott are almost identical. Bachman's full position is best shown by an extended quote from his first full treatment (which was published later in the same year as a separate booklet [Bachman 1855c]). In keeping with the pomposity characteristic of the high-flown rhetoric of the time, he used the editorial *we* to phrase his denunciation and present his conclusions:

> The following are our views. That all the races of men, including the negro, are of one species and one origin. That the negro is a striking and now permanent variety, like the numerous varieties in domesticated animals. That varieties having become permanent, possess an organization that prevents them from returning to the original species, although other varieties may spring up among them. Thus the many breeds of domesticated animals that have arisen, some only within a few years, would never return to the form of the wild species without an intermixture. That the negro will remain as he is, unless his form is changed by amalgamation—which latter is revolting to us. That his intellect, although underrated, is greatly inferior to that of the Caucasian, and that he is therefore, as far as our experience goes, incapable of self-government. That he is thrown on our protection. That our defense of slavery is contained in the holy scriptures. That the scriptures teach the rights and duties of masters, to . . . rule their servants with justice and kindness, and enjoin the obedience of servants. (Bachman 1854a, 657)

It was one of the basic hypocrisies of the antebellum South that slaves could be referred to as "servants."

Neither in this passage nor in any of the extensive prelude and follow-up was there any attempt to deal with the nature of human biological difference in a manner that had the faintest resemblance to science. Although he had correctly assessed of Nott that "His writings, however, savour too much of the wrangler . . . and too little of the close research of the naturalist . . . and calm and dignified temper of the philosopher. He . . . delights to live in the atmosphere of controversy" (Bachman 1854a, 657). It is apparent that much the same thing could have been said of the Rev. John Bachman, at least on these matters.

The clearly unscientific objections he felt toward Nott and his colleagues were shown in his claim that their work might better have been entitled *Types of Infidelity* (Bachman 1854a, 651), a phrase that was also used by several other clerical reviewers to describe their objections to Nott and Gliddon's *Types of Mankind.* In the end, Bachman abandoned the old Enlightenment faith that there simply could be no conflict between scientific findings and religious faith. He declared, in effect, that if science (i.e., the discoverable facts) should demonstrate something that was contrary to his own religious beliefs, then so much the worse for science. As for Josiah Clark Nott, although it is perfectly clear that his claims were based on pure "racial" prejudice and nothing more, he endlessly proclaimed that "science" was his sole motivation. Bachman tacitly accepted Nott's claim that he was basing his views on science but concluded that "if they could even succeed in proving the negro of a different species, the South would gain nothing, whilst we would have abandoned all the strong arguments that are derived from the scriptures in the right of holding this species of property" (Bachman 1854a, 657).

The last part of that statement pinpoints the issue that precipitated the Civil War. Many historians of the era have offered one lame excuse after another—the supposed jealousy felt by the North over the economic benefits gained by the use of "free" slave labor in the South, for example—but the actual sticking point was the treatment of human beings as property. Despite all the attempts to see the importance of this or that unrelated issue, "Slavery, far more than any other single factor, was the cause of the Civil War" (Chesebrough 1991, 17). After the war began and numbers of slaves fled to freedom in the North, Bachman and others repeatedly claimed that the North was acting illegally in depriving southerners of their "property."

To the North, however, there was a higher law superseding the "property" rights encoded in the civil law and, at bottom, what was involved was a moral matter. It was this that was behind the stance articulated by William Lloyd Garrison in the first issue of the *Liberator,* January 1, 1831: "On this subject I do not wish to think, or speak, or write, with moderation. . . . I am in earnest—I will not equivocate—I will not excuse—I will not retreat a single inch—AND I WILL BE HEARD" (Thomas 1963, 3). Although the northern clergy had been somewhat reluctant to take sides at the beginning, to an increasing extent they came to agree that what was involved was an issue of morality and that it was fundamentally immoral for any human being to claim ownership of another as a "species of property." There is much to be said for the charge that, as one of the most uncompromising driving forces in the growing abolition movement, William Lloyd Garrison "was responsible for the atmosphere of moral absolutism which caused the Civil War and freed the slave" (Thomas 1963, 4).

JOSIAH CLARK NOTT: THE VOICE OF AMERICAN RACIALISM

If Samuel George Morton provided the "scholarship" of the American School of Anthropology and if Louis Agassiz gave it the endorsement of the scientific establishment, the verbal form in which it was presented to the world at large was articulated by Josiah Clark Nott. "At bottom, Nott was a prototypical Southern racist," and the outlook of the American School which he exemplified was driven by basic bigotry (Brace 1974a:516).

Josiah Clark Nott (1804–73) was born in Columbia, South Carolina, into a family that had its roots in New England back before the mid-point of the 17th century (Fig. 9–1). His father, Abraham Nott, graduated from Yale in 1787 and moved to the South, where he qualified in law by serving as an apprentice in the law offices of another Yale graduate in Camden, South Carolina. Abraham Nott's law practice was a success, and his career flourished along with it. He served a term in Congress, maintained an "up-country" plantation, and was appointed as a judge, becoming president of the South Carolina Court of Appeals by 1824 (Horsman 1987, 6–12).

Figure 9-1 Josiah Clark Nott, 1804–73 (from the frontispiece in Horsman, 1987).

Another branch of the Nott family went on to distinction in the North in the person of Eliphalet Nott (1773–1866) who had a long and somewhat controversial career as the president of Union College in Schenectady, New York. In that era, Union College was an institution which rivaled Harvard, Yale, and Princeton; and among Eliphalet Nott's pupils were the future presidents of Brown University and the University of Michigan. He also held the pulpit of the most prestigious church in nearby Albany and numbered Aaron Burr and Alexander Hamilton among his parishioners (Wise 1990, 27–28). When the election of Thomas Jefferson to the U.S. presidency in 1800 was thrown into Congress to break the deadlock in the Electoral College, the support given to Aaron Burr by Eliphalet's uncle, Abraham Nott, effectively spelled an end to the political career of Josiah's father (Horsman 1987, 10).

Among the children of Judge Abraham Nott, five sons became physicians, one daughter married a physician, and another son, Henry Junius, became a novelist and was professor of criticism, logic, and the philosophy of languages at South Carolina College, Columbia (Horsman 1987, 19). South Carolina College was where the sons of the South Carolina gentry were expected to go, and with his father serving on the Board of Trustees, Josiah duly enrolled as a matter of course. There, he fell under the influence of its president, the outspoken iconoclast Thomas Cooper. Later in his own life, Josiah Nott was to reflect much of the same anticlerical tenor as his former mentor, and it was one of the reasons his anthropological message was regarded with so much ambivalence in a South that was otherwise predisposed to sympathize with his stance.

After graduation in 1824, Josiah served under the preceptorship of Dr. James Davis in Columbia, then, a year later, went north to get a formal medical education. In 1825, he enrolled in the College of Physicians and Surgeons in New York, later to become part of the Columbia University Medical Center. The school was embroiled in an internal struggle for control at that time, and Nott decided that his medical education would best be served by going elsewhere. As so many others in search of first-rate medical training at that time were to do, he went to the University of Pennsylvania Medical School in Philadelphia, where he earned his M.D. in 1827. He spent two more years in Philadelphia as an intern and as a demonstrator in anatomy for Dr. William Edmonds Horner and Professor Philip Syng Physick.

In spite of the assertions of many different commentators (Jenkins 1935, 256; Lurie 1960, 258; Schiller 1979, 138; Livingstone 1987b, 123), Nott never was a student of Samuel George Morton while in Philadelphia. His actual mentors were Philip Syng Physick and the successor to Benjamin Rush, Samuel Jackson (1787–1872), both of whom had also been on the faculty of the University of Pennsylvania Medical School when Morton had been a student there (Spencer 1981, 427; Erickson 1986, 101–105). During the time that Nott was a demonstrator in anatomy, Morton was beginning to publish the works that would make his scientific reputation; thus, it is possible that Nott encountered him, but their real contact was not to take place until the middle of the 1840s.

After gaining his credentials in Philadelphia, Nott returned to set up practice in Columbia, South Carolina, in 1829. Things went well for him, and he married the daughter of a prominent plantation owner and politician, cementing his ties with the representatives of the dominant social ethos in the South in the years before the Civil War. After 6 years of practice, he took a year off in 1835 to further his education in Paris, which was then at the forefront in the movement to establish a grounding in science for medical training, which still had such a residue of superstition in its traditions.

Two of his brothers were already studying medicine in Paris, and he brought two more of his brothers plus his wife, two children, and a couple of his own medical students with him when he came in May 1835 (Horsman 1987, 43). He used the occasion to visit the British Isles also and returned briefly to Columbia in 1836. In the meantime, his father-in-law, James S. Deas, had moved to Mobile, Alabama, for reasons that I discuss later (Horsman 1987, 54). Nott followed suit and shortly set up practice in Mobile, where he was to remain until after the Civil War and to which he was to return in the last year of his life.

Although Josiah Clark Nott is now remembered almost exclusively for his role in promoting the institutionalized racism that was the root cause of the American Civil War, he also deserves recognition as one of the most distinguished physician–surgeons of the time in the South in particular and America in general (Polk 1913, 958; Carmichael 1948, 254; Horsman 1987, 134). Among his many accomplishments, he founded the institution that went on to become the University of Alabama College of Medicine and he was cited by Walter Reed as suggesting that yellow fever could be spread by an intermediary host, possibly a mosquito (Stanton 1960, 65).

Testifying to his skill, his principal biographer reported that "Nott had few equals as a surgeon in the South" (Horsman 1987, 134): "Nott had learned his surgery in the age before anesthetics, when strong nerves, decisiveness, and speed were all-important. . . . His great strength as a surgeon was the calmness and confidence he brought to the scene of the operation. Whatever went wrong, and much did in these years, Nott was usually equal to the occasion" (Horsman 1987, 135). He finished his career as a gynecological surgeon in New York City, where he served first as vice-president and then as president of the New York Obstetrical Society. All his chroniclers are unanimous in their praise for his medical competence and commitment, and the most extended biography describes him as being "extremely hardworking and conscientious" (Horsman 1987, 251): "Nott was always at his best when dealing with his own specialty—medicine," in sum, he was "a first-class physician" (Horsman 1987, 247).

I have included a testimonial to his strengths as a physician in order to show that even the most convinced and obdurate of racists could simultaneously be someone of the highest integrity and competence. Evidently, Nott could also display great charm when he chose. It has been said that "he made friends with ease" and that "In person, Nott could be a scintillating man" (Horsman 1987, 102). He was "praised on all sides as a southern gentleman of the best type" (Horsman 1987, 200), and he clearly represented a specimen of that storied phenomenon. Louis Agassiz, himself a practiced master of discriminating social appraisal, wrote to his friend the Yale geologist James Dwight Dana, "Nott is a man after my heart, for whose private character I have the highest regard" (Horsman 1987, 177).

Although Nott was as far from being an "average" Southerner as Louis Agassiz was from being an "average" immigrant, in many ways he can be used to stand for the attitudes of the South in the era before the Civil War in much the same way that I used Agassiz to stand for the American immigrant in general. Agassiz was a white, Protestant male, and although he was not Anglo-Saxon, he was of western European origin, with all of the cultural baggage that this implies. Nott also was a white, Protestant male, and although he was born in the American South, his family roots were from the American Northeast and ultimately from the Anglo-Saxon edge of northwestern Europe.

The specific aspects of Nott's outlook that initially distinguished the way he looked at the world from the way Agassiz regarded it were derived from the experience of growing up in the American South, where three groups of people of distinct and different continental origin faced each other on a daily basis, out of context and under conditions of imposed social inequality. As it happened, the South Carolina coastal region where Nott was born and brought up had the largest proportion of slaves in America, and their numbers had increased dramatically early in the 19th century as South Carolina reopened the African slave trade (Horsman 1987, 6).

The idea that both categorical distinctions and the linked differences in social level were inherent to the human condition was accepted by Nott and the society of which he was a part as so self-evident that, as Nott put it in the last tirade he was to write about "race" after the Civil War, "I feel as if a labored argument on the subject would be an insult to the understanding of the reader" (Nott 1866b, 10). In this, he was consistent with the approach he had taken in his first contribution on "race," where he noted that the evidence for his claims concerning the supposed reduction in fertility of "hybrids" between blacks and whites would have to depend "upon my veracity alone." His biographer perceptively remarked, "As a southern gentleman, Nott expected to be believed" (Horsman 1987, 87), even though it is apparent that "he had raised his innate prejudices to the level of (what he assumed to be) scientific truth" (Horsman 1987, 296).

In the same vein, although "Nott liked to think of himself as a scientific realist . . . he was a romantic in everything but his medicine" (Horsman 1987, 255). "In writing on medical matters Nott never demonstrated the arrogant certainty that he showed in writing on race" (Horsman 1987, 137). However, it was in his writings on "race" that Nott was to have his greatest impact. That "arrogant certainty" was a major contributing factor to the war that was to break out in May 1861 and leave wounds that survive to this day, and it was to put into words a paradigm of racist thinking that also has lasted right up to the present day. Not only have those assumptions and phrases survived unaltered in the popular mind, but they were to be adopted whole by European anthropology and used essentially unchanged, even though unattributed, by well-educated writers for the influential popular press during the remainder of the 19th and well into the 20th centuries.

Nott's writings on race began in a formal sense in 1843 and continued to the outbreak of the Civil War in 1861, with another intense flurry in 1866 just after the war had ended. At the same time, he engaged in an extensive correspondence with a series of eminent figures, and key parts of this have been preserved. His public contributions were phrased in a direct and vigorous style, but the full nature of his inherent bigotry is even more clearly apparent in the irreverently zestful expressions displayed in his private letters.

In 1843, he published his claims concerning the supposed reduction in fertility and life span in the offspring from African and European American matings in the *American Journal of Medical Sciences*. This was entitled "The mulatto a hybrid; probable extermination of the two races if the whites and blacks were allowed to inter-marry." He based his case on material he reprinted from the *Boston Medical and Surgical Journal,* which itself had relied on the error-filled census of 1840. That census had included reports purporting to represent both African and European American life spans and death rates in communities that were later shown to lack any African Americans. "Mulattoes" were claimed to be the shortest-lived of any class of humans, and "free negroes" were reported to have a death rate that was fully double that of slaves.

Then, the Franklin Society of Mobile, which regularly sponsored presentations by prominent citizens on subjects of their own choosing, approached Nott and asked him to give a couple of public lectures during the winter of 1843–4. Nott gladly obliged them and began his presentations with a critique of the Bible as a chronicle of natural history. He followed this up with a discussion of the evidence for the physical history of human form, relying heavily on the portrayals from ancient Egyptian monuments and tombs.

He justified the focus of his interests with the words "I am convinced, that nothing *wise can be done* without giving due weight to the *marked differences* which exist between the races" and continued "If there be several *species* of the human race—if these species differ in the perfection of their moral and intellectual endowments . . . Is it not the *Christian's duty* to inquire into this subject?" (Nott 1844, 41). Even though he was filled with scorn concerning the historical accuracy of the biblical account, he continued as a matter of course to conceive of a world that had an antiquity of something on the nature of 6,000 years all told.

Nott added an introduction and an appendix to his lectures and published them as a small book in February 1844 entitled *Two Lectures on the Natural History of the Caucasian and Negro Races*. This was printed in Mobile and served as the model for much of what he was later to publish on the matter of "race." The volumes written with Gliddon and published in 1854 and 1857 simply represented expansions on the outline presented in his *Two Lectures* of 1844 to the extent that those two increasingly unwieldy tomes could be regarded as suffering from severe cases of bloat: the message was the same, but it was accompanied by an enormous quantity of verbal padding.

With the publication of his *Two Lectures,* Nott increasingly came to be regarded as the main articulator of Southern views regarding "race," and the public was inclined to accept his claim that his defense was based on objective "scientific" data. Right after the publication of his lectures in book form in 1844, Samuel George Morton wrote to him "I have read your remarks on the mulatto race with much pleasure and instruction" (quoted in Horsman 1987, 94). By this time, Morton had become one of the most eminent figures in American science, and Nott felt greatly encouraged by his praise. On September 4, 1845, he wrote to his old college friend James Henry Hammond, then the governor of South Carolina, that "the nigger business has brought me into a large and heterogeneous correspondence" and that he intended "to follow out the Negro, moral and physical in all his ramifications" (quoted in Jenkins 1935, 257). On June 27, 1847, he wrote to Morton "My niggerology, so far from harming me at home, has made me a greater man than I ever expected to be—I am the big gun of the profession here" (quoted in Erickson 1986, 110). He corresponded with Morton regularly for the remainder of the latter's short life, and he visited him in Philadelphia every time he went north.

Not long after that, Nott got the chance to deliver a reworked version of his two lectures in New Orleans when the Louisiana legislature met there in December 1848. Nott's brother Adolphus was on the faculty of the Medical School at the University of Louisiana—later to become Tulane University—and his friend James D. B. De Bow held the chair of political economy, commerce, and statistics there. As Nott wrote Ephriam George Squier early in September 1848, De Bow had invited Nott to take his chair during the next session of the legislature in order to "deliver a lecture for him on Niggerology" (quoted in Stanton 1960, 118–119).

Nott took him up on his offer and used the opportunity to expand his two lectures of 1844. Their order was reversed, but the points remained the same. Again, he tried to get the written version published, this time aspiring to enlist the interest of a more prestigious northern publishing firm. Lea & Blanchard in Philadelphia refused because they were concerned about the vigor of Nott's attack on the biblical Book of Genesis.

He then wrote to Squier for help, and the latter, with the aid of the secretary of the American Ethnological Society in New York, made arrangements with Bartlett & Welford in New York City. The last obstacle was surmounted when Nott agreed to subsidize the publication costs, and the expanded volume finally appeared in August 1849 (Horsman 1987, 111–112). It was this that stimulated John Bachman to generate his rebuttal before the Charleston Literary Club late in the summer of 1849 and to produce his volume based on that review, *The Doctrine of the Unity of the Human Race,* in 1850 (Horsman 1987, 113).

Nott clearly enjoyed twitting the pious pomposities of the theologically orthodox, and he could not resist citing instances in which the insistence on a literal interpretation of Scripture had proved to be a continuing embarrassment to religious authorities. He repeatedly cited the case of Galileo's problems two centuries earlier with a Church that insisted on a geocentric view of the universe: "Several other branches of science, such as astronomy, geology, & c., have had to struggle long and hard with religious prejudices, but, as all truth must, they have finally triumphed. Now we claim for the natural history of man, nothing more than the same liberal construction of the Bible which has been conceded to other scientific subjects . . . our object now is, not to war against genuine revelation, but against false texts and false interpretation" (Nott 1849, 14).

At the same time, he could not resist pointing out that if Christ were the son of God and not of Joseph, then he could not have been of the lineage of David because it was only Joseph who could lay claim to that distinction. He made the point that nowhere in the New Testament does it indicate that Mary was of the lineage of David (1849, 66–67). This of course had no direct bearing on his arguments concerning human origins, but it was certain to ruffle the feathers of his clerical readers. In further efforts to cast doubt on Christian and Jewish sacred writings, he noted that Moses could not have written the Pentateuch at the beginning of the Bible because the Jews had not yet acquired phonetic writing at the alleged time of its composition. If anything, he suggested, Moses knew Egyptian hieroglyphics by virtue of having been born and raised in Egypt, but the Jews did not acquire a phonetic script until their captivity in Babylon nearly 1,000 years later (1849, 69, 75, 106).

When he wrote to Squier in September 1848 before giving his lectures in New Orleans, he reported that he had been reading Baron von Bunsen's *Egypt's Place in Universal History,* whose first volume had just been translated into English: "He is a good authority and does give Moses some awful digs under the short ribs . . . The game is nearly played out and the parsons must look out for a new humbug" (quoted in Jenkins 1935, 259). In February 1849, however, when he was trying to get Squier to help him negotiate with the publishers, he somewhat piously declaimed that "I have no intention which would induce me to war against the Christian religion, though I was against all dogmas which conflict with the demonstrated facts of science" (Jenkins 1935, 259). As his biographer summed it up, he may have "wanted to free science from any necessity to restrict its arguments for fear of religious objections but he also delighted in irritating the clergy and shocking the orthodox" (Horsman 1987, 107). Despite his repeated protestations to the contrary, clearly "Nott thrived emotionally on the controversy he stirred up in the 1840s" (Horsman 1987, 118).

A year later, after the AAAS meetings at Charleston in March 1850, where his defense of polygenism had been read for him, Nott wrote in glee to Squier that "Morton is coming out dead against Moses and the prophets, and I think we have the game started now and will give them hell before we stop" (letter of May 4, 1850, quoted in Jenkins 1935, 260). In the same letter, he referred to Bachman as "a man of Science, but a biggoted [sic] Old Lutheran" (Horsman 1987, 118), and elsewhere he regularly referred to Bachman as "the Old Hyena" (Horsman 1987, 172, 200, 203). He triumphantly concluded his May 4, 1850, letter to Squier: "My great aim has been to get the world quarrelling about niggerology and I have at last succeeded, and I think I shall sit on the fence and enjoy the fight" (Jenkins 1935, 260).

It seems most unlikely that Nott really intended to leave the battle to others. As his biographer observed, "Although he often protested that he wanted no public controversy, in reality he delighted in raising clerical hackles" (Horsman 1987, 82). Morton, in contrast, was troubled by the thought of upsetting the clergy, and in any case, he was dead only a year later. George R. Gliddon used Morton's death as leverage, if any such were

really needed, to push Nott into the thick of the fray; and *Types of Mankind* was produced early in 1854 as a consequence.

As mentioned earlier, this triggered a prolonged and thunderous response from the
Rev. John Bachman. Not only did he complain that the book was couched in "irreverent
and offensive language" but, in his ponderous first-person plural, he declared in conclusion that "we regard the effort made by Nott and Gliddon to establish their theory by a
denial of the veracity of the historical Scripture as more dangerous to our institutions
than all the ravings of the abolitionists" (Bachman 1854a, 644, 659).

The irony is that both Nott and Bachman accepted it as a given that "races" exist as
permanently distinct categorical phenomena and that their attributes and abilities are
ranked on a hierarchical scale of differential worth on which their placement can easily
be determined by the color of the skin. Both believed that people of dark skin color are
incapable of governing their own lives and that they attain their greatest productivity and
fulfillment in a state of subservience to people of lighter skin color. Some three decades
ago, I observed that "The spectacle of two died-in-the-wool bigots engaged in a furious
altercation, each accusing the other of ignorance and intolerance and both wrong on fundamental points might afford some retrospective amusement if it were not for the fact
that the essence of their bigotry has been the cause of death and misery for literally millions of people" (Brace 1974a, 519).

SCOTLAND: DR. ROBERT KNOX

During the 1850s, there were two other contributors to ideas concerning "race" who
warrant mention. One of these was the Scottish anatomist Robert Knox (1791–1862),
whose book *The Races of Men: A Philosophical Enquiry into the Influence of Race over
the Destinies of Nations* (1st edition 1850; see Knox 1862) had less impact than it might
otherwise have gained due largely to the scandal with which its author was associated.
In fact, Josiah Clark Nott in America apparently was completely unaware of it. Knox has
been described as a "brilliant extra-mural lecturer on anatomy" and rival of Alexander
Monro III, professor of anatomy at Edinburgh University Medical School. Knox had
earned his M.D. at Edinburgh in 1814, served as a military surgeon at the battle of
Waterloo the next year, and spent the next 5 years with the British armed forces in South
Africa.

Knox spent the year of 1821–2 in Paris completing his medical studies and absorb-
ing the outlook of Cuvier and his Romantic-era rival, Geoffroy Saint-Hilaire. Part of
the appeal that Paris held for medical students was the access to dissecting room
materials—human cadavers—that were in scarce supply in the British Isles and
America. In France, people who died in hospitals and remained unclaimed by their kin
after a set period of time were turned over to medical schools for dissection and study
before being claimed by the Church for final burial. In England, however, the only legal
dissecting room "subjects" were condemned and executed criminals.

Toward the end of 1822, Knox returned to Edinburgh, apparently fired with the ambition of making it rival Paris in medical distinction. Evidently, it was also part of his
ambition to attain for himself the kind of recognition and prestige accorded to Cuvier in
Paris, but things did not work out that way. He got off to a fine start, however, and for

several years enjoyed an increasing reputation as an anatomy teacher in the private school established by his own former teacher, John Barclay (Rae 1964, 22–29). Some cadavers were imported from Ireland and the Continent, but these were supplemented by surreptitious acquisitions from nearby cemeteries provided for a fee by certain dubious characters referred to as "sack-'em-up men" or "resurrectionists" (Bridie 1931, 26).

Things got a little sticky in the spring of 1828 when one of Knox's students, William Fergusson—later Sir William, Bart., F.R.S., president of the Royal College of Surgeons in London and "serjeant–surgeon" to Queen Victoria—recognized one of the cadavers as a person he had seen only a few nights earlier, an "exceptionally beautiful" 18-year-old "woman of the town" (Rae 1964, 58). The scandal broke on Halloween that year when an elderly woman who had been alive and well at a local party during the evening was found naked, bloodied, and dead under a pile of straw by some boarders in a local rooming house. The boarders went to the authorities to report her death and the suspicious circumstances that surrounded it, but she had vanished by the time they got back with the police, only to turn up in Knox's dissecting room the next day.

It seems that the boarding house proprietors had been involved in the business of supplying Knox with subjects and that they had grown impatient with the pace at which the living became transformed into cadavers by natural means. With the aid of copious offerings of alcohol and, finally, a firmly applied pillow, they had been producing fine, fresh dissecting room specimens for the better part of a year at up to £10 per body. The two who were most directly involved in the sordid business were William Burke and William Hare, immigrants from Ireland who had originally come to Scotland to work as laborers on the construction of the Union Canal between Glasgow and Edinburgh (Rae 1964, 58–59).

The case caused an absolute sensation in Scotland, and its notoriety spread elsewhere as well and lasted long beyond the life spans of any of the people involved. Robert Louis Stevenson used it as the basis for one of his dramatic stories, "The Body Snatcher," in 1888; it served as the subject of James Bridie's play *The Anatomist* (1931) a century later; and Dylan Thomas mined it for his screen script *The Doctor and the Devils* (1966). The case went to trial the day before Christmas 1824, with Hare turning "King's evidence" and avoiding prosecution. Proceedings lasted all day and all night, and just after 9:00 Christmas morning, the jury pronounced Burke guilty; he was sentenced to be publicly hanged and dissected (Rae 1964, 84). Burke was duly hanged on January 28, 1829, at Lawnmarket in Edinburgh before an enormous crowd of onlookers and then dissected by Professor Alexander Monro.

This marked the last occurrence of the longstanding tradition of public hangings and dissections, but it hardly marked the end of interest in the case. Burke and Hare had evidently been responsible for 16 murders in 1828, and the public imagination was captured by the horror and fascination of the story. Renditions in prose, poetry, and song achieved great popularity in that pretelevision age:

> Up the close and doon the stair
> Ben the hoose wi' Burke and Hare,
> Burke's the butcher, Hare's the thief,
> Knox the boy who buys the beef.

(quoted in Bridie 1931, 52)

As that last ditty shows, Knox was not spared in the public mind. There is no indication that he had any knowledge of the fact that his suppliers were actually engaging in murder to keep him provided with cadavers. Like most anatomy teachers at that time, he had as little to do with the "resurrectionists" as he could and simply accepted their offerings for cash with no questions asked. The public, however, did not forget and did not forgive. Robert Knox's reputation was effectively ruined, although he continued teaching for several more years. Eventually he was forced to give it up, and he ended his career as a pathological anatomist at the Cancer Hospital in London. Although Knox's career went into a major eclipse as a result of the scandal, there was one positive outcome to the whole sorry affair: it highlighted the problem of getting cadavers suitable for use in the teaching of fledgling physicians. After another Burke and Hare type of incident in London, the Anatomy Act of 1832 legalized a system that was similar to what had previously been in use on the Continent, and the "resurrectionist" profession ceased to exist in the Old World (Rae 1964, 111). Half a century later, "body-snatching" scandals in Ohio and Michigan led to the adoption of similar legislation in the United States (Huelke 1961).

By all accounts, Knox was a flamboyant and effective teacher and did not deserve the public condemnation that he received. On the other hand, this meant that his book, *The Races of Men,* was not taken seriously by the reading public, and this is something for which we can only be thankful. The guiding theme of that book was articulated at the beginning: "Race is everything: literature, science, art—in a word, civilization, depends on it" (Knox 1862, v). Subsequently, he declared "Since the earliest times . . . the dark races have been the slaves of their fairer brethren. . . . there must be a physical and, consequently, a psychological inferiority in the dark races generally" (Knox 1862, 224). In fact, it was an expression of blatant, ingrained bigotry, very much in the tradition of that other work of the 1850s, the *Essay on the Inequality of Human Races* by Count Arthur de Gobineau. Knox has actually been referred to as "the Gobineau of England" in the admiring words of the Nazi anthropologist Egon Freiherr von Eickstedt (1937–40, 166), but the blight on his reputation provided by his association with Burke and Hare was such that relatively little attention was paid to his subsequent pronouncements on "race."

FRANCE: COMTE DE GOBINEAU

Unfortunately, such was not the case for Gobineau. Joseph-Arthur, Comte de Gobineau (1816–82), is chiefly remembered for his *Essai sur l'Inégalité des Races Humaines,* which was published in four volumes between 1853 and 1855. Gobineau has been referred to as "the father of racism" (Biddiss 1970, 3), and his doctrine was to have immense appeal both in America and in Europe during the latter half of the 19th and well on into the 20th centuries. Ultimately, it played an important part in the disastrous "racial" ideology of Adolf Hitler, whose "final solution" was an attempt to exterminate all of the Jews in Europe.

Gobineau was born on Bastille Day in 1816, a coincidence that was to be an annoyance to him for the rest of his life since, to the French, it commemorates the date—July 14, 1789—that is celebrated as the symbol of the French Revolution and the establishment of democracy in France. Gobineau, on his part, despised the Enlightenment ethos that spawned the French Revolution as well as democracy and rejected the concept of equality on which it was predicated (Biddiss 1970, 93). High on his list of values were "liberty" and "order," but his liberty was a privileged state enjoyed by the aristocratic elite in a hierarchical social order (Biddiss 1970, 95). In his Romantic vision of the world, that social order was a version of the Great Chain of Being, where "the liberty and interests of the superior race were served by the natural submission of the inferior" (Biddiss, 1970, 270). His own claim to aristocratic status was traced through his mother's father, who was alleged to have been an illegitimate son of the Bourbon King Louis XV (Biddiss 1970, 11). Although he had no proper right to it, he adopted the title of "count" that had been held by his uncle when the latter died in 1855.

Gobineau had a long career as an official in the French diplomatic service in Switzerland, Germany, Persia, Greece, Brazil, and Scandinavia. He had been the official secretary of Alexis de Tocqueville (1805–59) when the latter served briefly as minister of foreign affairs. Tocqueville is famous for his study *Democracy in America* (1835–40), an original and extraordinarily insightful assessment of the social and political situation in the young republic. It is a surprise that two such apparently different men should have had anything to do with each other, let alone that they should maintain a lifelong friendship. Tocqueville is generally regarded as a liberal thinker, and liberalism was anathema to the misanthropically conservative Gobineau (Biddiss 1970, 95, 147).

In fact, however, both men were aristocrats and viewed liberty and democracy as polar opposites (Biddiss 1970, 62; Moynihan 1991, 11). Those common grounds allowed them to treat each other with cordial respect while they differed on fundamental matters relating to the main theme in Gobineau's *Essai*. In Tocqueville's view, the racial determinism that was the main guiding thread in that *Essai* would abolish the possibility of free will and human liberty, and this was something that he simply could not accept (Biddiss 1970, 149). In Gobineau's mind, however, "race" was all-important. Like Robert Knox, he simply asserted it as a fact that "race" determined the destinies of nations.

Not only was "race" the primary factor, but he declared that "all civilizations derive from the white race, and that none can exist without its help" (Biddiss 1970, 117). Furthermore, he declared that the "Aryans" were the most "noble," "intelligent," and "vital" branch of the "white race" (Biddiss 1970, 123). The word *Aryan* had originally been used by Sir William Jones, a British colonial administrator in India in the previous century, to designate the language that was the common ancestor of the languages spoken today in northern India, Greece, Italy, Germany, and the better part of western Europe. Jones was the first to recognize the linguistic relationships between the members of what we now refer to as the "Indo-European" language family. Gobineau assigned innate biological and behavioral attributes to the Aryan speakers and, in doing so, effectively created the "Aryan race."

It may seem curious that a Frenchman would have identified his putative "Aryans" with an idealized Germanic, or "Teutonic," people. Gobineau, however, identified himself as a member of the French nobility; and in the way he viewed history, these were the descendants of the Germanic Franks, who conquered the Roman rulers of an already conquered Gaul. In his mind, the French nobility had come into their "superior position" by right of a "conquest that was itself the outcome of racial virtue" (Biddiss 1970, 105).

Gobineau developed his scheme to ever more improbable lengths with no effort at documentation. While he rejected polygenism because of his perception of its conflict with Catholicism, he felt that once divergence had taken place the different "racial types" were permanent (Biddiss 1970, 118). In this respect, his argument was very similar to that of John Bachman. From here on, however, things get murkier and murkier. The future of the civilized world, he suggested, depends on the "pure white race," but "racial purity" results in stagnation. The flowering of civilization can only occur as a result of the contact and communication between "superior" and "inferior stocks," but that in turn leads to "miscegenation" and ultimately, by consequence, to "degeneration" (Biddiss 1970, 116). In the end, Gobineau's message was one of paralyzing pessimism involving a picture of inevitable decline and fall. More than one observer has remarked upon the parallels between the predictions of impending doom presented in his *Essai* and the death of the gods in the fiery destruction of Valhalla at the end of *Götterdämmerung,* the final opera in the *Ring* cycle written by Gobineau's friend Richard Wagner.

Although Gobineau maintained that his views were the products of "scientific" investigation based on "well demonstrated mathematical truth" to the extent that they could count as "moral geology," the whole turgid outpouring had all the characteristics of literary Romanticism (Biddiss 1970, 111). In classic Romantic fashion, Gobineau, like Nott and Knox and other similar writers, simply asserted his conclusions out of his own inner consciousness without the benefit of anything that could remotely be called actual evidence. While Gobineau's message had obvious appeal for Romantic elitists in Europe, one has to remember that he "wrote in an age when the relations between the races were seldom a primary concern for that vast majority of Europeans who remained within their own continent" (Biddiss 1970, 267).

Tocqueville, in his extraordinarily prescient appraisal of America, had noted, however, that the most formidable threat to the future of the Union arose from the presence of large numbers of people of African origin. As things stood, they and the European Americans in the South were in the awkward position of being unable either to separate from each other or to combine in any mutually satisfactory fashion. Clearly, the issue of "race" was of immediate and enduring importance for Americans to a degree that had no parallel in Europe. It is hardly a surprise, then, that Gobineau's "racial" philosophy should have attracted a great deal of interest, especially on the part of an elite who enjoyed a privileged way of life supported by the labor of those who were perceived to be "racially" inferior. Many Americans, then, enthusiastically accepted Gobineau's message, and one of the first to declare his approval was none other than Josiah Clark Nott: "I have seldom perused a work which has afforded me such pleasure and instruction as the one of Count Gobineau . . . and regard most of his conclusions as incontrovertible" (Nott 1856, 463). Morton's biographer, the Philadelphia anatomist Charles D. Meigs, "boasted of having read the book ten times, and . . . regarded it as a kind of gospel to be preached" (Barzun 1937, 62).

Nott engaged the services of an immigrant Swiss printer, Henry Hotz, to produce an abridged translation for publication in America. This appeared in 1856 as *The Moral and Intellectual Diversity of Races with Particular Reference to their Respective Influences in the Civil and Political History of Mankind,* and it included a substantial appendix by Nott himself on the debate between monogenism and polygenism (Nott 1856). Gobineau did not altogether approve since he did not accept Nott's polygenist arguments and the translation left out reference to Gobineau's substantial comments about the American scene. Although Gobineau felt that people with dark skin color were certainly inferior, he did not support slavery; and he commented on the hypocrisy of Americans such as Washington and Jefferson, among others, for advocating freedom, on the one hand, and yet continuing to maintain slaves, on the other (Biddiss 1970, 146).

Furthermore, Gobineau had declared that "Human society can be rejuvenated . . . only through the agency of a relatively pure and young race. Such a race does not exist in America" (Biddiss 1970, 145). Under such circumstances, he concluded that "it is unimaginable that anything could result from such horrible confusion but an incoherent juxtaposition of the most decadent kinds of people" (Biddiss 1970, 144). These, however, were from the sections of his work that, as Gobineau complained to a friend, had not been included in the selective translation (Biddiss 1970, 147). This was just the first of what was to become a long history of the selective use of Gobineau's ideas to sustain the previously held convictions of people whose minds were already made up with regard to the reality and meaning of human "races." American immigration restriction legislation framed during the last quarter of the 19th and the first quarter of the 20th centuries was directly influenced by Gobineau's "reasoning," and, similarly, there was a direct lineal connection between this and the verbiage in Adolf Hitler's *Mein Kampf* of 1925 (Biddiss 1970, 258).

While Gobineau's concerns were particularly focused on the supposedly differential worth of "races," such as Aryans, Slavs, Celts, and Semites among others, the situation in America was characteristically simplified to a picture in "black and white." Nott and others in the South refused to admit that the issue of slavery was behind the conflict that crystallized as the American Civil War. While Gobineau had never advocated any course of action based on his "racial" philosophy, the Americans who used a tailored part of his dogma to sustain their own previously drawn conclusions actually went so far as to accept it as justification for going to war, at the same time denying that this was what they were doing.

"States' rights" was the watchword, with Southerners declaring that the rest of the nation had no right to meddle in their affairs and tell them how to run their society. Nott typically refused to admit that the South brought on the war in order to preserve slavery. Instead, he joined the chorus of those who claimed that it went to war only to preserve the internal institutions that it desired (Horsman 1987, 253). Of course, of paramount importance among those unspecified "institutions" was slavery. The euphemism "states' rights" was to continue in usage as a justification for what in reality was enforced unequal treatment based on "race" for more than a century after it was raised as a rallying cry for the South.

Among the aspects of Gobineau's Romantic vision was his hostility to the extension of centralized bureaucratic control at the expense of the provincial aristocracy. In his view, cities, as the centers of industry and materialism, were the seats of disorder that eroded the rights of the provincial nobility which embodied the most valuable form of social control (Biddiss 1970, 97). This, of course, was a view that was entirely congenial to the outlook of the southern "gentlemen," who objected to the efforts of the abolitionists to deprive them of their "property" (i.e., the human beings they "owned" as slaves).

On the other hand, Nott had assembled and articulated all of the ideas and "facts" that the South was to use to justify its "peculiar institution" (Stampp 1956) and published them long before he discovered the support offered, as he saw it, by the racist doctrine of Gobineau. In the words of one of the best appraisers of his role at the time, "his object was to give the people a weapon with which to oppose abolition" (Stanton 1960, 77). Even before he delivered the second version of his two lectures in New Orleans in 1848, he declared "I think we may safely conclude, that the negro attains his greatest perfection, physical and moral, and also his greatest longevity, in a state of slavery" (Nott 1847, 280). Then, commenting on the standing of the enslaved African Americans in the South, he concluded: "The negro will reach, I may say *has* reached, his highest degree of civilization, and emancipation has so far only proved what I think is inevitable, that when removed from compulsion he relapses into barbarism" (Nott 1847, 280).

He repeated and elaborated these arguments in his *Two Lectures* delivered in 1848, in which he declared that emancipation would result in "extermination" and that "Negro slavery is (as we believe) consistent with the laws of God, and with humanity" (Nott 1849, 18). This being the case, abolition would constitute an "illegal decision of our self-constituted judges . . . [should this] alternative [be] forced upon the South, she must carve her way out at any and every hazard, with the sword" (Nott 1849, 18). Throughout the 1850s he argued for the formation of a Southern Confederacy and severance from the Union. As his biographer has noted, "Ultimately his dream of a southern nation was to bring disaster to his section, his family, and himself" (Horsman 1987, 126).

Throughout the decade before the Civil War, Nott continued to promote his views with full confidence in their scientific and moral rectitude. It all seemed so clear to him that he treated his opponents as though their reluctance to accept his arguments must have been due to a deficiency in their powers of understanding, and he regularly availed himself of an active and irreverent sense of humor to twit his critics. Bachman was not the only one to splutter that *Types of Mankind* ought to have been issued as a separate work entitled *Types of Infidelity* (Bachman 1854a, 629). The work was also reviewed in the *Presbyterian Magazine,* edited in Philadelphia by the "staunchly orthodox" Cortland Van Rensselaer (Stanton 1960, 165). It was said to appear "under a sad misnomer": "It should have been not 'Types of Mankind,' but 'Types of Infidelity,' [symbolizing] the approach of the millennium of infidel ethnography" (Van Rensselaer 1854, 289). The reviewer did not stop there, however, but went on with a rhetorical flourish: "Why do not Messrs. Gliddon & Nott give us another quarto on the 'Types of Dogkind?' For all scientific purposes it would be just as pertinent, and just as logical; but it would fail to accomplish the occult and yet evident design of the book—that of discrediting revealed religion and casting contempt on the word of God" (Van Rensselaer 1854, 286). Nott happily obliged and published his "A natural history of dogs" in the *New Orleans Medical and Surgical Journal* in 1858. Actually, there was nothing new in this work, and he was simply adapting a portion of what Morton had presented in his paper "Hybridity in Animals" in 1847.

There were two main reasons for the demise of the American School of Anthropology. One, of course, was the American Civil War. Nott had offered the School's "findings" to the South specifically to justify the perpetuation of slavery, and the South ultimately lost the war. Ideas and attitudes that are associated with the defeated side in a war tend to be discredited because they are associated with the losers rather than because there is anything inherently wrong with them. That is just a matter of political reality. The "American School" basically ceased to exist because of the war, and the ideas associated with it ceased to have formal representation in the writings of recognized anthropologists in the English-speaking world for the duration of the 19th century. This does not mean that the ideas ceased to have their advocates, as we shall see later; but it does mean that they ceased to be a part of American and English anthropology for the next several generations.

The second major reason for the demise of the views of the American School of Anthropology was the publication of *On the Origin of Species by Means of Natural Selection* by Charles Darwin in 1859. In one blow, the basis for the scientifically shallow debate between the monogenists and the polygenists had been demolished. No longer was there any need to argue whether or not it was possible to derive Africans, Asians, Australians, Europeans, and the rest of the peoples of the world from a single pair within a span of only 6,000 years. The vision of slow, gradual biological change occurring by natural means over millions of years completely altered the way that people looked at the world and the different living beings which it contained.

10

TOWARD A WAR OVER SLAVERY AND AFTERWARD

GEORGE R. GLIDDON

George Robins Gliddon (1809–57) was born in Devonshire, England. His father was a businessman engaged in importing goods from the "Orient," a term used in a somewhat provincial way by the English to mean everything beyond the eastern shores of the Mediterranean, including Turkey, Syria, India, China, and Japan—in effect, over 80% of the area encompassed by the Old World. In the case of his father, John Gliddon, the focus was on Egypt and other countries bordering the eastern edge of the Mediterranean Sea. I called him a "business man" because that is what he would be called in 21st-century America; but at the time, he was referred to in England as a "merchant," and more generally, it would have been said that he was "in trade."

In the England of the 19th century, there was a stigma attached to those who earned their living "in trade," as opposed to those who had come into titles or property through no productive efforts of their own but simply by virtue of having been born into the "right" family. In the eyes of the English at that time, there was always a slight aura of the disreputable which clung to the Gliddons of the world. Americans, then as now, were much more tolerant; and George R. Gliddon eventually moved his operations to the United States when his father began to suffer business reverses as the 1830s came to an end.

Gliddon spent his childhood on Malta until the family moved to Cairo in 1818 (Gliddon 1857, 531; Stanton 1960, 46). He was sent back to England for school and for training in business. Subsequently, he spent time in Paris and made annual trips to the British Museum in London to familiarize himself with the translation of Egyptian hieroglyphics (Stanton 1960, 47). His father served without pay as the honorary U.S. consul, first at Alexandria and then at Cairo, from 1832 until his death in 1844; and George assisted him as his agent in Greece, Syria, and Cairo, also serving as U.S. vice-consul before coming to the United States more or less permanently in 1840.

Part of the question that arose concerning the reputation of the Gliddon family in England stemmed from the "experiment" in communal living, as it has sometimes been called, engaged in by the younger Gliddons at the "notorious" house on Queen's Road in Bayswater—now a section of western London north of Kensington—where Gliddon stayed during his visits to England (Stanton 1960, 47–48). The inhabitants included his brother John and sister Catherine (Kate), married, respectively, to the daughter and son of Leigh Hunt, a writer and poet of some recognition who had been sponging off Percy Bysshe Shelley in Italy the summer Shelley drowned in 1822. Another Gliddon sister,

Anastasia, and her husband, the portrait painter Samuel Lawrence, were also part of the menage.

Among the others who shared that residence were the writer, critic, and editor George Henry Lewes and his wife Agnes. At the time, Lewes edited *The Leader,* an influential socialist weekly magazine, for which the younger Hunt wrote the political section while Lewes covered theater, music, and books. A number of the Gliddons' female cousins also made up part of the household, and among these was their artistically talented cousin Anne, whom Gliddon later married. Problems arose when Kate's husband, Thornton Hunt—"that outrageous young rip" (Stanton 1960, 48)—fathered three successive children with Agnes Lewes, two of whom were born within weeks of the birth of two of the children that he fathered with Kate. Lewes continued to support Agnes and the children, but he himself left to become in effect the common-law husband of Mary Ann Evans—George Eliot—with whom he lived for the last 25 years of his life (Rose 1984, 205).

Long before the break-up of that experiment in "open" marriage, Gliddon left to try to make his fortune in America. During his first visit in 1837, he had sensed the opportunity afforded by the lecture circuit; and even before he was invited to give the prestigious Lowell Lectures in 1843, he had tried his luck on the public platform. He was an enthusiastic and flamboyant character, whose ability to generate words in profusion would surely have qualified as logorrhea. With his firsthand experiences in Egypt and his inculcation into hieroglyphic translation, he felt that he had a topic which would be sure to appeal to the lecture-going public.

He then undertook a lecture tour of the populous eastern United States in 1840, a circuit he would repeat as often as the market would bear over the next dozen years. To promote interest, he prepared an advertisement whose wording rather typifies his extraordinary verbal style:

> ILLUSTRATIONS, BRILLIANTLY COLORED,
> AND COVERING MANY THOUSAND SQUARE FEET OF SURFACE,
> COMPRISING—
>
> Hieroglyphical, Hieratic, Enchorial, Greek and Roman Texts, *Steles,* Inscriptions &c., from Scriptures, Paintings and Papyri, including the *Rosetta Stone,* the *Funereal Ritual,* the *Turin Genealogical Papyrus,* the *Tablet of Abydos, Ancestral Chamber of Carnac,* the *Zodiac of Dendera,* and all important historical documents of the Egyptians from the earliest times to the Christian era. A complete series of all the *Pyramids* . . . Panoramic views of the *Temples, Palaces,* and remarkable *Tombs* . . . Plates, illustrative of the art of embalmment, human and animal . . . Portraits of the Pharaohs in their chariots, and royal robes—Queens of Egypt in their varied and elegant costumes—*Likenesses* of forty-eight sovereigns of Egypt . . . Priests and Priestesses offering to all the Deities of Egyptian Mythology—Battle Scenes on the monuments . . . In short, Diagrams of every kind, illustrating every variety of Egyptian subjects, during a period of human history far exceeding 3,000 years, and terminating with the Romans in the 3rd century A.D. (Stanton 1960, 46–47)

Because he was repeatedly able to schedule lecture tours, it would appear that he was successful to an extent, but he was perpetually strapped for cash and forever trying one gambit or another to bail himself out. At one point, for example, he persuaded Mississippi Senator Jefferson Davis to introduce a bill proposing the use of camels in the American Southwest in the hope that he could get himself sent to Egypt to arrange for the transport of the animals (Stanton 1960, 161). Nothing worked all that well, however, and he was forever on the lookout for the next chance. As Nott's biographer said of him, "Gliddon had a bit of Mr. Micawber in him" (Horsman 1987, 221).

Because he had established contact with Samuel George Morton dating from his first trip to America in 1837 and because Morton had dedicated *Crania Ægyptiaca* to him for the acquisition of his collection of Egyptian skulls, Gliddon started off with an entrée into the highest circles of the American scientific establishment. He had no qualms about using such leverage to broaden his access to influential figures on the American scene. From his initial association with Morton, he quickly became friendly with people like the excavator of the mounds in the Midwest, Ephriam George Squier (Squier and Davis 1848), and the Mobile physician Josiah Clark Nott.

Along with Morton, these were key figures in the American School of Anthropology, and Gliddon was to join them as a kind of junior associate. The most insightful account of that American School is the one written by William Stanton in *The Leopard's Spots: Scientific Attitudes Towards Race in America, 1815–59*. In Stanton's words, Gliddon was "a name-dropper, a sponger, a swinger on the shirttails of the great, a braggart, pretender, and scatologist . . . [but also] courageous, generous, warm-hearted and loyal, and a friend worth having" (1960, 46).

When Gliddon visited Nott in Mobile early in 1848, the two became instant friends and remained so for the balance of Gliddon's brief life. Nott arranged for him to give a set of nine lectures under the sponsorship of the Franklin Society. Their sense of common interest was reinforced when Agassiz came out in support of Nott at the Charleston meetings of the American Association for the Advancement of Science (AAAS). Nott, on his part, had spoken of the hope to get Morton actively involved. Morton's death just over a year later changed the situation. From that point on, George R. Gliddon, ever the opportunist, sensed that the time was ripe to get Nott and others involved in generating a book that expressed the position of the emergent American School of Anthropology.

In this, he was successful, and from the summer of 1852 through the winter, spring, and summer of 1853, with lapses only for lecture trips, Gliddon plus his wife and child were supported by Nott in a cabin on the eastern shore of Mobile Bay, where Gliddon ground out his part of what was to become their joint work *Types of Mankind* (Horsman 1987, 174). Agassiz, who had spent a winter vacation in Charleston in 1852–3 (Lurie 1960, 185), visited Mobile from late March to mid-April and was inveigled by Nott and Gliddon into promising a chapter for their forthcoming book (Horsman 1987, 176). The full manuscript, illustrated by more than 300 drawings done by Gliddon's wife Anne, was finished in August, and Gliddon took it to Philadelphia to supervise its publication (Horsman 1987, 178).

Just after they finished work on the book in August 1853, disaster in the form of a yellow fever epidemic struck Mobile. Within a week in the middle of September, Josiah Clark Nott lost four of his own children plus a brother-in-law (Horsman 1987, 164). Nott was a completely dedicated medical practitioner and had expended a prodigious amount of effort on behalf of the population of Mobile. The frustration he must have felt at the futility of his efforts is only underscored by the magnitude of the personal loss he suffered. To say the least, it took some of the sense of accomplishment away from his feelings for the work he had just finished, and he left all further management of that recently completed volume to his collaborator.

Their work, dedicated to the memory of Morton, was published in March 1854; and although at 738 pages it was a veritable elephant of a book, it sold out immediately. It then went into a second printing and had sold 3,500 copies by the middle of July, a phenomenal record for that era and in spite of the $5.00 per copy price, which was "extremely high" for the 1850s (Horsman 1987, 178, 179). The *New York Herald* asked Ephriam George Squier to write a review, and he in turn asked Gliddon to supply him with a draft. Squier was a longtime friend of Nott, and their correspondence, which is preserved, provides a wonderful insight into the events and people of that time; however, even Nott was surprised at the lavish praise contained in the *Herald* review. He had not known that the words were those of his co-author, Gliddon himself, reviewing their own work (Horsman 1987, 180). Gliddon had in fact gone to considerable lengths to disguise his writing style, which under most conditions was unmistakable and often bordered on the unreadable.

That verbal style, apparent in the advertisement for his lectures, was also evident in the title of the book itself:

TYPES OF MANKIND: OR, *Ethnological Researches,* BASED UPON THE AN-CIENT MONUMENTS, PAINTINGS, SCULPTURES, AND CRANIA OF RACES, AND UPON THEIR NATURAL, GEOGRAPHICAL, PHILOLOGICAL, AND BIB-LICAL HISTORY: ILLUSTRATED BY SELECTIONS FROM THE INEDITED PA-PERS OF SAMUEL GEORGE MORTON, M.D., (LATE PRESIDENT OF THE ACADEMY OF NATURAL SCIENCES AT PHILADELPHIA) AND BY ADDI-TIONAL CONTRIBUTIONS FROM PROF. L. AGASSIZ, LL.D.; W. USHER, M.D.; AND PROF. H.S. PATTERSON, M.D.: BY J.C. NOTT, M.D., MOBILE, ALABAMA, AND GEO. R. GLIDDON, FORMERLY U.S. CONSUL AT CAIRO

Basically, the book was a hastily assembled and poorly edited pastiche of contributions by different authors with widely diverse styles of writing. I have already mentioned Agassiz's impressionistic and unscientific conclusions, so we do not need to deal with them again here. Nott based his consideration of human biological differences on the previously published work of Morton, and he included a digest of Morton's treatment of hybridity. I shall deal with that matter at greater length in a subsequent section. Patterson's portion was a longish biographical treatment of Morton. Among the sections written by Gliddon was a long and diffuse attempt to use the outline of Egyptian history, as it was becoming known from translations of hieroglyphic inscriptions, to cast ridicule on the supposed history of the earth as recorded in the Bible.

Gliddon was delighted with the successful sales of the book: it was to go through ten printings by 1871. He was so pleased, in fact, that he immediately began planning an expanded version, even though his collaborators were considerably less enthusiastic about the idea. Nott agreed to collaborate somewhat reluctantly, but when Gliddon asked for chapters from Agassiz, Ephriam George Squier, and the University of Pennsylvania anatomist and paleontologist Joseph Leidy, they politely declined. Agassiz, who had the "highest regard" for Nott, felt that Gliddon was "coarse" (Horsman 1987, 177). In the words of Nott's biographer, "As a traveling lecturer, he (Gliddon) did not have to be respected as a gentleman" (Horsman 1987, 200); but

Agassiz, with his European sensitivity to social distinctions, evidently held that against him. They may have become wary not only of Gliddon the "traveling showman" (Horsman 1987, 172) but also of the outspoken proslavery stance of Nott (Horsman 1987, 212). Agassiz and Leidy did send letters of perfunctory support, which Gliddon promptly reprinted with the finished tome and used to justify adding their names to the title page.

He did succeed in getting contributions from two obscure Europeans and from the Philadelphia anatomist J. Aitken Meigs. The vast bulk of the new volume, however, was Gliddon's own. He proposed calling the new volume *Indigenous Races of the Earth,* and when he delivered his part of the manuscript to his coauthor in the spring of 1857, Nott wrote to Squier referring to the book as "Indignant Races" and saying that they had "the right to be indignant, for Gliddon has surpassed himself in folly & confusion," adding that it was so hopelessly jumbled and confused that he had not been able to read it through (Horsman 1987, 219).

The title of Nott and Gliddon's new book alone illustrates the substance of Nott's complaint:

INDIGENOUS RACES OF THE EARTH; OR, *New Chapters of Ethnological Inquiry;* INCLUDING MONOGRAPHS ON SPECIAL DEPARTMENTS OF PHILOLOGY, ICONOGRAPHY, CRANIOSCOPY, PALEONTOLOGY, PATHOLOGY, ARCHAE-OLOGY, COMPARATIVE GEOGRAPHY, AND NATURAL HISTORY: CON-TRIBUTED BY ALFRED MAURY, BIBLIOTHÉCAIRE DE L'INSTITUT DE FRANCE; SECRÉTAIRE GÉNÉRAL DE LA SOCIÉTÉ DE GÉOGRAPHIE DE PARIS; MEMBRE DE LA SOCIÉTÉ IMPÉRIALE DES ANTIQUITAIRES DE FRANCE, DES ACADÉMIES DE BORDEAUX ET DE CAEN, DES ACADÉMIES ET SOCIÉTÉS D'ARCHÉOLOGIE DE BELGIQUE, DE PICARDIE, DE MADRID, DES SOCIÉTÉS ASIATIQUE ET MÉDICO-PSYCHOLOGIQUE DE PARIS, DE LA SOCIÉTÉ D'HISTOIRE DE LA SUISSE-ROMANDE ET DE LA SOCIÉTÉ DE LITTÉRATURE NÉERLANDAISE DE LEYDE; CHEVALIER DE L'ORDRE DE LA LÉGION D'HONNEUR, ETC. ETC. ETC., FRANCIS PULSZKY, OF LUBOCZ AND CSEFALVA, FELLOW OF THE HUNGARIAN ACADEMY; CORRESPONDENT OF THE INSTITUTO DI CORRISPONDENZA ARCHEOLOGICA DI ROMA; LATE UNDER SECRETARY OF STATE IN HUNGARY, ETC. ETC. ETC., AND J. AITKEN MEIGS, M.D., PROFESSOR OF THE INSTITUTES OF MEDICINE IN THE PHILADELPHIA COLLEGE OF MEDICINE; LIBRARIAN OF THE ACADEMY OF NATURAL SCIENCES OF PHILADELPHIA; RECORDING SECRETARY OF THE PHILADELPHIA COUNTY MEDICAL SOCIETY; FELLOW OF THE COL-LEGE OF PHYSICIANS, ETC. (With Communications from Prof. Jos. Leidy, M.D., and Prof. L. Agassiz, LL.D.) PRESENTING FRESH INVESTIGATIONS, DOCU-MENTS, AND MATERIALS; BY J. C. NOTT, M.D., MOBILE ALABAMA, AND GEO. R. GLIDDON, FORMERLY U.S. CONSUL AT CAIRO, AUTHORS OF "TYPES OF MANKIND"

Not surprisingly, it did not have the popularity or sales of its predecessor. As Nott's biographer observed, "For the most part it was an extremely tedious and ill-written work" and, especially in regard to Gliddon's 250-page stretch on Egypt, "If anything, this long section was even more unreadable than his contributions to *Types of Mankind*" (Horsman 1987, 213, 219). Nott, who had a genuine fondness for his somewhat bumptious collaborator in spite of his occasional exasperation with him, wrote to his friend Ephriam George Squier hoping that the latter could find some kind of suitable employment for the energetic Gliddon, "some *physical* employment for him, for he is not fit for book making" (Horsman 1987, 230).

Squier succeeded, and soon Gliddon had a paying post with the Honduras Interoceanic Railway Company. This, of course, was the era before the Panama Canal, and any way of saving the time and danger of running ships all the way around the tip of South America just to get goods from the Atlantic to the Pacific coasts of the United States promised to be a good investment. Even the awkwardness of unloading on one coast of the isthmus of Panama, shipping by rail to the other, and then reloading might have been an improvement over the risks of the voyage around Cape Horn. Nott wrote to Squier that he was delighted to see that Gliddon had been "transported to a country where there are no printer types." He added "for God's sake make it a part of your bargain that he is never again to afflict suffering humanity with any more books, or even title pages" (quoted in Stanton 1960, 180, 236).

Unfortunately for poor Gliddon, this new chance was to be his last one. He contracted some sort of tropical fever, possibly malaria, in Honduras. In the throes of his disease, he essayed a treatment and, in characteristic fashion, overdid things. On November 16, 1857, he died in Honduras of an overdose of opium. Nott regretted the passing of his friend and, magnanimous as always, contributed generously to the support of his widow and child.

The success of their first book had been due largely to the crisply phrased racism in Nott's section and the aura of scientific respectability given to it by Agassiz. Gliddon's own sections have been described as "opaque" at best (Horsman 1987, 219). In Stanton's more telling assessment, Gliddon was described as "hopelessly addicted to the polysyllable" and enamored of "the ponderosities of Victorian prose": "Proclaiming himself the eternal and implacable foe of humbug, he was himself a master of the art of puffing. . . . With delusions of profundity, his mind was as shallow as a mountain stream" (Stanton 1960, 46).

"RACE" AND POLITICS

When we look at the two major American political parties today, the Democrats and the Republicans, and compare their stances now to what they were 150 years ago, we cannot help being struck by the fact that they have both completely reversed their positions. Each now comes close to representing the ideological position that the other held before the American Civil War. This is never mentioned in standard works on American history, and the few on whom this realization has gradually dawned are generally at a loss to explain how it could have come about. Since I am not a professional historian and this subject is very far from my own academic specialty, I can give only the most cursory and incomplete account; but since it does bear on how the issue of "race" has been dealt with by the U.S. government, some sort of recognition of this curious state of affairs has to be accorded in a book on the subject.

Before the Civil War, the Democratic Party had its power base in the southern states, where it reflected the socially conservative stance of the elite. This, of course, was characterized by an ingrained racism, where "racial" inequality was assumed as a given and slavery was defended as part of the natural order of things. The Democratic Party used its influence to defeat efforts to appropriate tax revenues for the purpose of fostering economic growth; it successfully opposed efforts to regulate the banking system; it defeated the movement to encourage land grants; and it defeated government support for education. In the year after the Republicans succeeded in getting Abraham Lincoln elected in 1860, taxes were raised to underwrite federally supported projects, the transcontinental railroad act was passed, the Homestead Act was passed, the land-grant college act was passed, the national banking act was passed, and a progressive income tax was instituted. There were more changes where government relations with the economy were concerned than in any comparable period in American history except for the first 100 days of President Franklin D. Roosevelt's New Deal in the 1930s (McPherson 1991). Ultimately, the Emancipation Proclamation signed by Lincoln on January 1, 1863, marked the formal end of slavery for Americans of African ancestry.

Today, by contrast, the Republican Party has succeeded in removing controls from the banking system to such an extent that there has been one monstrous scandal after another, it has rolled back the progressive income tax so that the gap between the rich and the poor is greater than ever, it has attempted to return the financing of schools to the local level in spite of the vast differences in regional resources, and it has rigorously opposed raising taxes to support federal obligations. Finally, policies that attempted to redress the imbalance of African Americans in their access to educational opportunities and the bastions of money and power have been reversed, and the party has devoted its efforts to building a national power base in the southern states by playing on the fears that the "white" majority retains for the African American minority in their midst. As one analyst noted, this is an attempt "to build a political majority based on racism" (Boyd 1970, 110). More recently, the conclusion has been voiced that "the Republican Party is now . . . a natural and evidently comfortable home for white Racism in the United States" (Carter 1991).

Although Republicans have long referred to themselves as belonging to "the Party of Lincoln," the one thing that is strikingly obvious today is that the ideals exemplified by Abraham Lincoln are noted solely by their absence in the modern Republican outlook. When the party was founded in Jackson, Michigan, in 1854, it was a specifically antislavery organization (Dumond 1959, 87). It turned less liberal shortly thereafter in the hope of attracting a large enough constituency to capture the presidency (Fuller 1939, 1:311–312), and this tactic was eventually successful. The most outspoken abolitionists, such as William Lloyd Garrison, were critical of its compromises right from the beginning and refused any formal alliances (Mayer 1967, 29).

Some of the founders, however, were uncompromising antislavery ideologists. There were even some who called themselves "Radical Republicans," although this would strike us as a veritable oxymoron today. One of these was Charles Sumner (1811–74), a Bostonian descendant of the early Puritan colonists, who had argued (and lost) a court case in 1849 challenging segregation in the school system in Boston before the Civil War (Sutherland 1954, 33; Donald 1960, 180). Sumner had been elected to the U.S. Senate as a Free Soil candidate even before he had played a role in founding the Republican Party. Sumner was "inflexibly committed to a set of basic ideas as moral principles" (Donald 1960, vii–viii), and he propounded these on the floor of the Senate in oratory that was studded with Latin quotations and classical allusions. His style has been described as "highly formal," "old fashioned," and resembling the "reincarnation of some Old Testament prophet" (Donald 1960, 215–218). Evidently, however, his effectiveness was lessened by a stance of inflexible and egotistical self-righteousness.

He attacked the Kansas–Nebraska Act in a series of speeches in the Senate in 1854, calling it "a present victory of Slavery" (quoted in Donald 1960, 260), and denounced its authors, Senators Andrew Pickens Butler of South Carolina and Stephen A. Douglas of Illinois, remembered in history books as the "little giant" who subsequently engaged Abraham Lincoln in a series of famous debates. Just 2 years later, Sumner again scored Butler and the supporters of the extension of slavery into Kansas in a 2-day "oration" on the Senate floor that he published as *The Crime Against Kansas:* "The Senator from South Carolina has read many books of chivalry, and believes himself a chivalrous knight, with sentiments of honor and courage. Of course he has chosen a mistress to whom he has made his vows, and who, though ugly to others, is always lovely to him; though polluted in the sight of the world, is chaste in his sight—I mean the harlot, Slavery" (Sumner 1856, 5). Sumner was comparing Butler to Don Quixote the title figure in Cervantes's famous early 17th-century farce: "The Senator from South Carolina [Mr. BUTLER] and the Senator from Illinois [Mr. DOUGLAS] who, though unlike as Don Quixote and Sancho Panza, yet, like this couple, sally forth together on the same adventure. As the Senator from South Carolina is the Don Quixote, the Senator from Illinois is the squire of Slavery, its very Sancho Panza, ready to do all its humiliating offices" (Sumner 1856, 5, 6).

One of those who had heard at least the opening part of Senator Sumner's speech was the second-term congressman Preston S. Brooks, from South Carolina. Brooks, although a much younger man, was a cousin of Andrew P. Butler and took offense at what he perceived as an affront to both his region and his family. He declared that Sumner had "insulted South Carolina and Judge Butler grossly" (quoted in Donald 1960, 290). According to the code of behavior that was accepted in the South by those who fancied that they were "gentlemen," such an insult demanded redress, but rebuttal in kind was not considered the appropriate response. Brooks, taking his status as a "Southern gentleman" seriously, declared that he "would be obliged to flog Sumner" (Donald 1960, 290).

Two days later, after the Senate session had adjourned, Sumner lingered at his desk in the Senate chamber, signing printed copies of his speech. Brooks then entered, waited until all "ladies" had departed, approached the seated senator, and proceeded to beat him on the head with his walking stick. Sumner tried to rise after the initial onslaught, but his legs were compressed under a desk bolted to the floor. He was a tall and robust man, and eventually the fastenings broke and the desk toppled over, releasing him; however, he was dazed and bleeding, and Brooks kept up the beating until the senator was unconscious (Donald 1960, 295). There were some Southern legislators present, but they conspicuously made no attempt to restrain Brooks's attack on the unsuspecting and vulnerable Sumner.

The reactions in the North and the South were predictable. Braxton Bragg, Josiah Clark Nott's friend in Louisiana, wrote that "Were I in the House I should certainly propose a vote of thanks to Mr. Brooks" (Donald 1960, 305). In the North, however, the feeling was one of shock. A violent physical attack perpetrated without warning on an unarmed government figure in the halls of state, where by universally accepted tradition matters are decided solely on the basis of verbal credibility, was regarded as demonstrable proof of the inhumanity many had already attributed to the South. It took Sumner more than 3 years to recover (Donald 1960, 312). Meanwhile, he was reelected to his Senate seat by a landslide (Donald 1960, 322). Previous to his beating, he had been perceived with ambivalence in his own constituency, and there was more than a chance that he could not have survived a popular election. During his absence from the Senate floor, his empty seat remained a symbol of reproach. In essence, "his vacant chair was a perpetual speech" (Donald 1960, 312).

Both the aging Senator Butler and his youthful cousin—"Bully" Brooks, as he was labeled in the Northern press—died during the next year, but events had been set on their course. The claim has been fairly made that "Preston Brooks's assault upon Sumner in the Senate chamber in 1856 may be regarded as the first blow of the Civil War" (Donald 1960, vii). Bolstered by Nott and Gliddon's recently published *Types of Mankind,* southerners continued to argue not only that high civilizations could coexist with slavery but that such a situation provided the most advantages for both the "higher" and the "lower" "races" involved. The recovered Sumner replied with a 4-hour speech in June 1860, in which he declared that no such thing was possible since "Slavery must breed Barbarians," such as those who regarded human beings as "property" (Donald 1960, 354).

In arguing that slavery was being extended into Kansas simply as a result of the unwarranted use of force, Sumner mentioned the fact that slave owners maintained their system by practicing the skills needed for its application. He made the case that the solution of social problems by the use of force was barbaric, and although he did not specifically mention his own encounter with that force at the hands of Brooks, it was not hard to draw the conclusion that the code under which he had personally suffered was the code of barbarians and not of "gentlemen."

Early in Lincoln's first term, Senator Charles Sumner was made chair of the Senate Committee on Foreign Relations (Donald 1960, 384). He was thoroughly at home with European politicians and literary figures, and he had hosted such eminents as Sir Charles Lyell, Charles Dickens, and Anthony Trollope at various times. He had made wide acquaintances in England, France, Germany, and Italy, and was well-known and well-liked abroad. To all appearances, then, he should have been one of the most powerful forces in the American government. He had been "the outstanding antislavery spokesman in the Senate during the 1850's," and he was a principal architect of Reconstruction after the Civil War (Donald 1960, vii). Most of his major proposals were never passed, however; and those that survived were much altered and promoted under other leadership (McPherson 1991).

The North may have won the war, but it effectively lost the ensuing peace. A determined and unrepentant South successfully resisted everything but the actual abolition of slavery; and a backsliding North, following the path of least resistance, simply tut-tutted as the South succeeded in reinstituting slavery in everything but name by the century's end (Woodward 1966, 1969). Even before the war began, there had been clear signs of wavering in the North. As early as 1848, Sumner had suggested the existence of "a conspiracy between the Lords of the Loom and the Lords of the Lash" (Donald 1960, 269).

The Civil War letters of Major Henry Livermore Abbott—one of the Abbott, Cabot, Lawrence, Lowell relations—expressed the conviction that the North had no business meddling in the slavery of the South (Ward 1991, 37). Abbott, who died in battle in 1864, had an elitist's contempt for the common soldiers of the South and little sympathy with the lot of the slaves. His loyalty was to maintaining the integrity of the Union.

Part of the change of attitudes in the North was clearly related to the change in the structure of its society. The almost puritanical principles of a Charles Sumner had their roots in the egalitarian farming communities that had characterized New England from its first settlement up until the 19th century. By the middle of that century, however, many of those old New Englanders had become increasingly wealthy as a result of the profits made from manufacturing enterprises that were staffed by immigrant laborers. The increase in wealth led not only to a change in outlook but also to the development of a clear common interest between the textile industrialists and the managers of the plantations that produced the cotton which went into the textiles. The Republican governor of Massachusetts, John Andrews, backed the textile manufacturers' suggestion in 1865 that improved opportunities for trade and investment in the South were best promoted through alliance with the "planter class" (Bentley 1955, 31–32).

One of the most perceptive treatments of this shift in outlook was written by John S. Haller, Jr., in his *Outcasts from Evolution: Scientific Attitudes of Racial Inferiority, 1859–1900:*

> The decades after the Civil War marked the hiatus of the old New England conscience. New Englanders looked upon the wartime *cause célèbre* as having been ill conceived and blamed abolitionists for expecting too much too quickly. Unlike Le Conte, Shaler accepted no justification for slavery, but he felt too much importance had been made of the southerner's sin and not enough of the Negro's place in nature. Curiously, New Englanders, who had previously fought for the Negro and condemned southern racial ideology, approached the South during the 1880's and 1890's as a prodigal son. Both sections of the country, they felt, had a knotty race problem. Nowhere except in New England and in the south did social lines so nearly run with racial lines. It was a curious marriage of New England parochialism with the racial ideology of the sensitive southern mind. New England casuistry sought in the southerner not only an ally to stop the flow of immigrants but an understanding brother with whom it could meditate upon common problems. (Haller 1971, 173)

The co-occurrence of social and "racial" lines in the North assumes that the immigrant laborers who toiled in the mills were "racially" distinct. Initially, these were Irish, but as the century progressed, Italians joined them in increasing numbers. However, as the impact of the thinking of Gobineau and of Broca's school grew in importance, the Irish and Italians *were* thought of as being "racially" distinct and inferior.

This passage from Haller introduces the name of Joseph Le Conte (1823–1901). Both he and Nathaniel Southgate Shaler entered the Lawrence Scientific School under Agassiz at Harvard in the 1850s and had similar outlooks during the remainder of their careers. Le Conte, born in Georgia of French Huguenot parents, eventually joined the faculty of the new University of California at Berkeley (Haller 1971, 154–166). His influence, while similar to that of Shaler, was nowhere near so important. Shaler is treated at greater length subsequently.

WAR AND ITS AFTERMATH

During the winter of 1858–9 and into the succeeding summer, Josiah Clark Nott had been scouring Europe for books and equipment to start up a medical school in Mobile (Horsman 1987, 239–245). The Medical College of Alabama opened on November 14, 1859, with Nott as professor of surgery (Carmichael 1948, 253). Ten days later, Darwin's *Origin* was published, but Nott was much too busy to pay any attention until the following year. After he gave the commencement address in March 1860 (Horsman 1987, 245), Nott spent the next several months recuperating from an illness that had kept him from reading. By the end of August, however, he was able to write to Squier: "I have been well enough to skim Darwin's book—the man is clearly crazy, but it is a capital dig into the parsons—it stirs up creation and much good comes out of such thorough discussions" (quoted in Jenkins 1935, 274).

It is clear that the main point of Darwin's work had not yet been absorbed. As his principal biographer has observed, "In many ways Darwin's *Origin of Species* was too careful and too scientific for Nott . . . Nott was more a cultural anthropologist when he wrote about race. He liked books such as Gobineau's that ranged generally over the rise and fall of nations and empires" (Horsman 1987, 320). Eventually, Nott was to gain a limited understanding of the implications of Darwin's tour-de-force, and when he returned to writing about "race" for one brief blast after the end of the Civil War, he no longer used the basically pseudoscientific trappings of polygenism to justify his prejudices. He never did fully come to grips with Darwinian biology. His sense of humor eventually returned to him, and in a note to Squier near the end of his life, he remarked: "You may be kin to frogs, but I ain't" (quoted in Erickson 1986, 114).

According to conventional wisdom, the American Civil War began on April 12, 1861, when General P. G. T. Beauregard ordered the artillery barrage on Fort Sumter, a U.S. military garrison on an island at the entrance to the harbor in Charleston, South Carolina (McPherson 1982, 145). This was just the final step in the onset of America's bloodiest war since South Carolina had seceded from the Union at the end of 1860. The Ordinance of Secession had been signed and ratified at Institute Hall in Charleston on December 20 in a ceremony that had been opened by a prayer delivered by the Reverend John Bachman (Neuffer 1960, 102). South Carolina, the "hotbed" of "rebellion," was followed by Alabama, Mississippi, and Florida at the beginning of 1861; in the subsequent weeks, Georgia, Louisiana, and Texas followed suit (Horsman 1987, 253).

In spite of much belligerent verbiage on both sides, it seems that few really expected actual fighting. For example, one Civil War historian has written: "Even as late as the first part of April [1861], most abolitionists did not anticipate war. Frederick Douglass [the articulate and outspoken former slave] believed the North too cowardly and proslavery to fight" (McPherson 1964, 46). On the other side of the fence, Nott wrote Squier at the end of November 1860 and referred to himself as a "rank secessionist" and saying that he personally would volunteer to do battle for the cause (Horsman 1987, 252).

Three weeks after the firing on Fort Sumter, Nott wrote to Squier on May 3, 1861, defending the right of secession: "the Southern people will see all the whites & blacks on the globe slaughtered before they will yield this point" (Stanton 1960, 183). Even though the war had actually begun by this time, the reality had not yet come home to him, for he went on to say that he did not believe the North would risk the blood and money to go to war "without the remotest prospect of any good result" (quoted in Horsman 1987, 253). He elaborated on that thought in the same letter: "Certainly you do not expect to conquer us & make us vassals!!—This idea is too absurd to be entertained by any sane mind" (Stanton 1960, 236).

Things had gone past the point of no return by this time, however, and the war was well and truly begun. The real horror of war took some time to sink in, and both the North and the South treated it as somewhat of a lark at the beginning. Nott went to visit the southern troops in Virginia as a tourist in July 1861 and was able to set up a field station to operate on the Confederate wounded at the first battle of Bull Run (Horsman 1987, 262). In October, he joined as a surgeon in the 2nd Corps of the Confederate Army of Mississippi under the command of his friend Major General Braxton Bragg, and he served as medical director of the Confederate General Army Hospital in Mobile (Horsman 1987, 267).

My own great-grandfather, Charles L. Brace (1826–89), watched at Bull Run as a tourist from the North (E. Brace 1894, 242). He was an outspoken opponent of slavery and had written his own assessment of "race" in *The Races of the Old World* (1863) as a deliberate effort to contradict the flagrant racism displayed by Nott and Gliddon in their *Types of Mankind* (Nott and Gliddon 1854; Brace 1861, 1863). The carnage at Bull Run (or "Manassas," as it was called by the Confederates) had a sobering effect on both sides. Subsequent battles were no longer considered a spectator sport as that early engagement had been somewhat light-heartedly treated.

By the time the American flag was once again raised at Fort Sumter, South Carolina, in April 1865, effectively symbolizing the end of the Civil War, some 620,000 soldiers on both sides had lost their lives (McPherson 1982, vii). Among them were two of Nott's sons, who had fought for the South, and one of Morton's, who had fought for the North (Horsman 1987, 276, 285; Stanton 1960, 185). The Rev. John Bachman had moved his library and natural history collection to Columbia, South Carolina, for safe-keeping under the assumption that Charleston, as the original sparkplug of rebellion, would be the principal Union target. By a sad twist of fate, Charleston was spared but Columbia burned to the ground. The products of a lifetime of collecting and research were destroyed, and the venerable clergyman, aged 76, "was severely beaten by one of General Sherman's hangers-on" (Stanton 1960, 184), who was convinced that Bachman knew the location of hidden valuables (Bachman 1888, 381).

Josiah Clark Nott's medical college in Mobile stood vacant and unused because no one in the South at that moment had enough money to embark upon the education needed to become a physician. The economy of the South lay in ruins, and the long and bitter task of reconstruction was yet to begin. The jaunty banter that had provided the spice of humor to the correspondence of Nott disappeared, leaving the hard edges of his racist convictions unrepentantly exposed. Just as Nott could be taken as a kind of one-man vignette of Southern attitudes before the Civil War, so can he be taken to represent them after the war was over.

In the course of picking up the pieces of the Union, one of the principal concerns was the fate of the four million ex-slaves. The vast majority had been denied access to any form of education, with the consequence that great numbers were unable to read or write. Landless, penniless, and deprived of any experience in creating and pursuing productive lives, they represented a major potential threat to the future stability of the region. In order to face this problem, Congress passed and President Lincoln signed a bill on March 3, 1865, establishing the Bureau of Refugees, Freedmen and Abandoned Lands (Bentley 1955, 49), universally referred to as the "Freedmen's Bureau." The bill also gave "every male citizen, whether refugee or freedman" the right to rent "not more than forty acres of (abandoned or confiscated) land" with the later right of purchase (Bentley 1955, 89).

By the middle of April, however, Lincoln had been assassinated, and his successor, Andrew Johnson, embarked upon a course that had the effect of giving the South by peaceful and "legal" means everything that it had lost during the war. On May 29, 1865, Johnson issued a blanket amnesty to the former rebels, restoring "all rights of property except as to slaves" (Bentley 1955, 89). By the end of the century, the "Black Codes" enacted in state after state had whittled away the rights available to African Americans to the extent that they had been returned to a condition that amounted to slavery in everything but name (Woodward 1966; Stampp 1967, 80).

The Freedmen's Bureau undertook the task of providing clothing, medicine, food, transportation, and some manner of shelter for the recently freed slaves; but it did so under extremely difficult circumstances. The abolitionists in the Republican Party pushed in one direction, the defeated rebels in the South resisted in all ways possible, and President Johnson sided with the poor white Southerners against both the former slaves and the former plantation owners.

The role of guiding the Freedmen's Bureau fell to Major General Oliver Otis Howard, who was still in command of the Army of Tennessee at the time of Lincoln's death. Johnson honored Lincoln's choice, however, and Howard became commissioner of the Freedmen's Bureau on April 26, 1865 (Bentley 1955, 52). Howard, a pious Protestant from rural Maine, was a West Point graduate. When the Civil War began, he was a colonel in command of the 3rd Maine Volunteer Regiment, rising to become a brigadier general by the fall of 1861 (McFeely 1968, 39). He had lost his right arm in battle at the end of May 1862 (Howard 1908, I:246).

Among his other efforts on behalf of the former slaves, Howard was instrumental in helping them get the schooling that he felt underlay "every hope of success for the freedman" (quoted in Bentley 1955, 169). His name is best known today for having been memorialized in Howard University in Washington, D.C., the premier institution of its kind devoted to providing higher education for African Americans. When some influential congregational clergymen proposed founding a theological school for African Americans, Howard made Freedmen's Bureau funds available for the construction of a building that was to be called the Howard Theological Seminary. The planners had bigger ideas, however; in spite of Howard's genuinely modest objections, they developed a plan for the construction of Howard University, and it was duly chartered by Congress early in 1867 (Bentley 1955, 203).

The Freedmen's Bureau did not even have a federal budget during its first year of operations, but Howard did succeed in getting authorization to employ unused military buildings for the purpose of setting up what were referred to as "black," or freedmen's, schools (Bentley 1955, 171). In an attempt to get this program under way, Howard and his assistants canvassed the South in a search for unused structures for such purposes.

Late in 1865, they visited Mobile, Alabama, where they asked Nott about using his vacant medical building for a freedmen's school. Nott irately replied that he "would rather see the building burned to the ground than used for any such purpose" (testimony of Lt. Col. Hunter Brooks in *Report of the Joint Committee on Reconstruction* 1866, 115). In fact, the building was used in just that way until the spring of 1868, when it was returned to serve its original role as a medical school. Nott, by that time, had left Mobile and the South (Horsman 1987, 297).

Howard's visit to Mobile, however, goaded Nott into one final effort in "anthropology." This took the form of an open letter to Howard, superintendent of the Freedmen's Bureau, which he published in 1866 under a series of different titles in the *New Orleans Medical and Surgical Journal, De Bow's Review,* and *Anthropological Review* (London) and as *Instincts of Races* in a separate pamphlet in New Orleans (Nott 1866a–d). A footnote to his contribution "The Negro Race" in *Anthropological Review* identifies him as "the greatest living anthropologist of America." This was probably written by James Hunt, president of the Anthropological Society of London, editor of *Anthropological Review,* and himself a particularly poisonous racist. In his letter, Nott took it upon himself to instruct Howard on what he regarded as the basic anthropological "facts" concerning "racial" differences, and it was in this diatribe that he declared that he felt that his "conclusions" were so "self-evident" that a prolonged "argument on the subject would be an insult to the understanding of the reader" (Nott 1866c, 10).

He used slightly different wording in the various versions of his letter; but the points were essentially the same, and all had been made in his prewar writings. They had never been presented quite so bluntly, however; and this gives us a good chance to go through some of them to get at the unvarnished essence of his beliefs concerning "race." As will be seen later, these did not cease when Nott stopped writing about them, and some of them survive right up to the present day in various guises.

Treating all African Americans in classic typological fashion as if they were one and the same and offering nothing in the way of proof beyond his own assertion, he declared in patronizing fashion: "The Negro . . . is imitative, social, easily domesticated, and, as long as kept in subordination to a higher race, will ape to a certain extent its manners and customs. But the Negro rises only to a certain point of imitation—his intellect permits no approach to civilization but that of imitation, and, as soon as the race is thrown back upon itself and separated from whites . . . it becomes savage" (Nott 1866b, 8). With no more justification, he extolled what he declared to be the contrasting virtues of Europeans: "The Caucasian races have been the only truly progressive races of history. They have the largest heads, the highest instincts, the most comprehensive intellects have, in all ages, stood ahead of all others in civilization and have had no competitors in literature, art and science" (Nott 1866b, 9). The rest of the world was dismissed in offhand fashion, again without even the most rudimentary attempt at documentation: "The semi-civilization of China and India and the savagism of the red men of America, have remained stereotyped for ages" (Nott 1866b, 8). Even though the Western world has learned a great deal more about the extraordinary intellectual, literary, and artistic accomplishments of the civilizations in India and China in the century and a half since Nott wrote those words, enough was already known at that time to have raised real doubts about the credibility of anyone who would make such off-the-cuff judgments in the complete absence of any justification.

Native Americans, in addition to being relegated to "savagism," were written off as being incorrigible. As in his treatment of African Americans, Native Americans were also dismissed as though all could be encompassed in a single derogatory condemnation: "He is essentially a wild animal by nature, untamable, unimitative, uncivilizable" (Nott 1866b, 8). One of the stereotypes that Nott had about both Native and African Americans was that they failed the test of "civilization" because they lacked agriculture. In another one of his sweeping generalizations, he claimed that "The blacks, like the American Indians, Tartars and other nomadic races, are instinctively opposed to agricultural labor, and no necessity can drive them to it" (Nott 1866d, 282). That claim is patently false and, although vestiges of it are still widely held, really serves as a prime measure of the ignorance of its holders.

In the first place, the very reason that West Africans were brought over as slaves was that the African societies from which they were removed by force sustained themselves by intensive agricultural labor. Not only were they intensive farmers in their native Africa, but they were better able to cope with the diseases brought along by their captors than the Native American farmers they replaced. The okra, black-eyed peas, "Carolina" rice, yams (and these are *not* the sweet potatoes mislabeled "yams" in American stores), and watermelons so familiar to Nott and other residents of the American South had been domesticated in Africa and had served as an essential part of the subsistence base that supported the populations from which the slaves were taken (Harlan et al. 1976, 5, 14). The rice dishes identified with Southern cuisine used what has long been marketed as "Carolina rice," but that came from West Africa and not Asia. Unlike the *Oryza sativa* of China and its neighbors, the separate species *Oryza glaberrima* was independently domesticated well over 3,000 years ago in central Nigeria (Portères 1976, 445; Carney 2001). Far from being "instinctively opposed to agricultural labor," West Africans were actively sought precisely because they were raised in societies that were sustained by an agricultural system which required the expenditure of "incredible human effort" (Harlan et al. 1976, 16).

Nott's unsupported charge was equally untrue for the native inhabitants of the Western Hemisphere. The Nott household was famous for keeping a good table, and, as was true for the kitchen of every prominent Southern family, the cooking was done solely by people of African origin. It is almost certain that grits, corn bread, crawfish pie, spiced crabs from Mobile Bay, and possibly even "barbecue" were offered on a regular basis. None of them would have been possible without the Indian corn, tomatoes, capsicums—both bell peppers and chili peppers—and allspice domesticated by the ancestors of the very people Nott referred to as "uncivilizable." The very section of the United States in which Nott was born and raised had been the home of a thriving agricultural civilization. Without its contributions and the adopted elements of West African agriculture, the creole cuisine that today is the glory of New Orleans and the adjacent Gulf Coast, including Mobile, simply could not exist (Cooper 1946; Prudhomme 1984).

To be sure, Nott was only echoing a widespread prejudice on the part of European Americans. It was precisely that unwarranted and basically irrational conviction that Native Americans were "nomadic" by nature and "instinctively opposed to agricultural labor" that had led to the forcible removal of the Cherokees from their farms in Georgia 30 years earlier. Although the Native Americans of the Southeast had been tilling the soil and hence were presumably "civilized," the Georgia General Assembly had simply proclaimed that their removal would "give these sons of nature a wilderness congenial to their feelings and appropriate to their wants," although he had made no effort to find out what their feelings and wants actually were (quoted in Weinberg 1958, 88).

The election of Southerner Andrew Jackson as U.S. president and the passage of the Indian Removal Act of 1830 solved the "problem" as far as European Americans in Georgia were concerned. However, for the descendants of the people who had been growing their corn there for the previous thousand years, this represented more than just a "problem." It constituted a major disaster. During the ensuing "Trail of Tears" enforced by General Winfield Scott in 1838, more than 4,000 Native Americans lost their lives (Jahoda 1975; Rogin 1975).

As far as Nott was concerned, the "Indian problem" had been solved, but the question of the status and treatment of the large numbers of African Americans in the South after the Civil War was still unresolved; it was toward this matter that he addressed his didactic words to General O. O. Howard. He felt that, as a Northerner, Howard simply was unaware of what "every well-informed Southern man knows" (Nott 1866a, 167), so he took it upon himself to instruct the general. The "facts" he presumed to state, however, were simply a catalogue of his own prejudices, which in turn were those held in common by most European Americans in the South.

At bottom, he assumed that Africans lacked the intellectual abilities that were necessary to develop and sustain "civilization": "The negro and other inferior races have never, under the most favored circumstances, shown any capacity for self-government or civilization" (Nott 1866d, 281). Consequently, "the history of the negro race is simply a page of natural history—it has no intellectual history, because God has not endowed it with the faculties necessary to preserve written records. . . . His intellect for four thousand years has been as dark as his skin, and all attempts in and out of Africa have failed to enlighten or develop it beyond the grade for which the Creator intended it" (Nott 1866d, 270, 272).

As that passage shows, Nott was operating under the assumption that the biblical chronology which he had spent so much time attacking still served as something of a guide to the antiquity of human existence. Not only had Darwin's *Origin* of 1859 yet to affect his outlook, but it was evident that he was still unaware of the enormous extension of human antiquity demonstrated by the archaeological evidence published 3 years previously by his one-time guest Sir Charles Lyell in *The Antiquity of Man* (1863).

The intellectual deficiencies he assumed characterized people of African ancestry were due, he declared, to their supposedly smaller brains. Nott had relied on Morton for this information, but there had been no attempt to see whether the data on brain size had been corrected for possible population differences in body size or even for differences due to male/female sexual dimorphism. Instead, he simply asserted that African brain size is "less than that of the white man, and the large-headed races have always ruled the earth, and been the only repositories of true civilization" (Nott 1866d, 282). The simplistic assumption that crude brain size is an accurate measure of intelligence was used by Nott to deny that intellectual capabilities can be altered by training: "The idea that the brain of the negro or any other race can be enlarged and the intellect developed by education, continued through successive generations, has no foundation in truth or any semblance of support from history" (Nott 1866d, 282). The same raw data and the same

As As could not be educated brc as ther small brains.

simplistic assumptions are still being used today to denigrate the intellectual capacities of people of African ancestry (Rushton 1985, 1989, 1995; Lynn and Vanhanen 2002).

Nott's skepticism about the efficacy of education was applied in blanket fashion to African Americans: "The Duke of Wellington remarked that it was a great mistake to 'educate a man beyond his capacity,' as it only makes him less contented and more mischievous to society" (Nott 1866d, 270). While Wellington had meant his remarks only in the context of the European social classes, Nott applied it to his assumed hierarchy of "racial" status: "As a class, the negroes who cannot read and write are more moral, more pious, more honest, and more useful members of society than those who have received education. Like the Indians, they learn all the vices of the whites without their virtues. A little knowledge is a dangerous thing; 'drink deep or taste not,' is an old maxim, and the negro has neither the thirst nor the capacity for much of this kind of drink" (Nott 1866d, 271).

Even though Nott was just as much of an elitist as Wellington or Gobineau and had deep suspicions about the intellectual abilities of lower-class European Americans, his overriding concern with race made him theoretically generous toward extending educational benefits to all people of European ancestry: "Yet with all its risks, education must be disseminated as widely as possible in our race, because we have no means, *a priori,* of determining the *grade* of intellect of individuals. Every man who reads history will agree, that a very large proportion of the white population of this and other countries are wholly unfit to vote understandingly on the affairs of the nation, to say nothing of bribery and corruption in the lower classes" (Nott 1866d, 270–271). In spite of his Gobinesque suspicion of the worth of the average citizen, his view was that Europeans should at least be given the opportunity to see whether they could gain something from being exposed to education. It was an opportunity that he would not grant to people of African ancestry, and the legacy of his stance has denied African Americans an equal chance at self-development from that day right up to the present time.

Nott was aware that crude brain size was not a very diagnostic figure in itself, so he lapsed back into a bit of phrenology to support his conclusions: "The negro, it is true, *in the aggregate,* has a brain as capacious as that of the Chinese and Malay, and larger than that of the Hindoo; but in the negro the *posterior or animal part* of the brain greatly predominates over the *anterior or intellectual lobes.* In the other races named the anterior or intellectual lobes of the brain greatly preponderate over the posterior or animal portion. The same facts apply to the semi-civilized and barbarous tribes of Indians" (Nott 1866d, 278).

Over a generation later, one of Nott's intellectual descendants, the University of Virginia anatomist Robert Bennett Bean, tried to demonstrate the same points in a study of actual brains rather than just the nuances of their containers, the skulls (Bean 1906). A restudy of the same material, where knowledge of the "race" to which each brain belonged was not provided until after the measurements were made, provided definitive proof that Bean's conclusions were not based on the available data (Mall 1909). To Nott and his intellectual heirs, however, the inferiority of people with dark skin is taken as a given; and if the data do not support their conclusions, so much the worse for the data. In good Romantic fashion, their "knowledge" comes from a realm that transcends "mere understanding" and the mundane world of demonstrable fact.

As As were physiologically dissfent

Nott assumed a hierarchy of "racial worth" in classic Great Chain of Being fashion and applied it to his vision of predetermined relative social position: "History proves, indisputably, that a superior and inferior race cannot live together practically on any other terms than that of master and slave, and that the inferior race, like the Indians, must be expelled or exterminated. In every climate where the white man can live and prosper, he drives all others before him" (Nott 1866b, 269–270). He then applied this specifically to Africans: "History proves that the negro makes his nearest approach to civilization in slavery, or some subordinate position among the whites" (Nott 1866b, 279). Generalizing from the African American example, he claimed that "He has reached his nearest approximation to civilization in our country" (Nott 1866a, 167). His penultimate words to General Howard were that "Slavery is the normal condition of the negro, the most advantageous to him, and the most ruinous, in the end, to the white race" (Nott 1866d, 282). That pessimistic declaration sounded almost like the gloom in Gobineau's writing, and it highlighted the despair that Nott felt about the future of the South. In a bit of hypocritical double-talk, he claimed: "I have always been an emancipationist at heart—have been utterly opposed to the slave trade—have maintained that every people capable of self-government had a right to liberty. . . . Nevertheless I have not been an abolitionist; for the reason that I looked upon the emancipation of our Southern slaves as a measure leading only to misery, and the ultimate destruction of the race in this country" (Nott 1866a, 166–167). In his view, "freed blacks cannot be relied upon as an agricultural population, and that emancipation must ultimately result in their extermination" (Nott 1866a, 166).

In a classic version of the "some of my best friends are . . ." kind of bigotry, Nott declared: "No one has more kindly feeling for the blacks than I have, or is more disposed to use every effort to better their condition; but. . . . Four millions of colored population are suddenly turned loose upon us—a population ignorant, improvident and vicious" (Nott 1866d, 269). With that as a background, he thundered his concluding demand to Howard: *"Remove your bureau and the United States troops (particularly blacks) as speedily as possible from our soil, and leave the relations between the races to regulate themselves"* (Nott 1866d, 282, italics Nott's).

While he was drafting these words, he wrote to Squier that he believed that the Declaration of Independence had given Southerners "a constitutional right to niggers" (quoted in Horsman 1987, 309). Before the war, he had made much of the support that "science" presumably had given to his belief in "racial" inequality. In his admonition to Howard, however, he abandoned his references to science in favor of a more transcendental credo: "No human power can change the fiat of the Almighty. He brought the races of men and animals into existence. He gave them moral and physical laws, and all the powers of the Freedmen's Bureau, or 'gates of hell cannot prevail against them'" (Nott 1866b, 9). As always, when he expressed what were essentially the same views in private, he did so in more pungent fashion. When the Freedmen's Bureau had taken over his college building for use as a Freedmen's School, he wrote to Squier on December 5, 1865: "God Almighty made the Nigger and no dam'd Yankee on top of the earth can bleach him . . . to force the Negro to an 'equality' with the white man . . . is equally a violation of the fact of 'equality'" (quoted in Jenkins 1935, 276).

All the banter and humor had gone from his letters, leaving the raw racism starkly outlined. With this bitter blast and his dogmatic admonitions to Major-General O. O.

Howard, Josiah Clark Nott abandoned the field of "anthropology" and left the South. In that same year, 1866, he produced a book entitled *Contributions to Bone and Nerve Surgery* based on his experiences with gunshot wounds and other injuries that he had treated as a military surgeon (Nott 1866e).

Early in 1867, he wrote to Ephriam George Squier in New York: "I hope to leave Negroland to You damd Yankees—It is not now fit for a gentleman to live in" (quoted in Horsman 1987, 310). That spring, he started a medical practice in Baltimore; but feeling what he perceived as its isolation, he moved to New York in 1868, where he embarked on a very successful career as a gynecological surgeon. He continued to exchange pleasantries with his friend Squier, but he did not have the heart to continue his "anthropological" enquiries and did not participate in the activities of the Ethnological Society.

When the obvious signs of tuberculosis came on in the winter of 1871–2, he recognized the implications immediately. He set his affairs in order, asked Squier to dispose of his anthropological books, presided over the meetings of the New York Obstetrical Society for the last time in October 1872, and headed south for the winter. Death came in Mobile on his 69th birthday, March 31, 1873. It was his wife's choice that he be given an Episcopal service, in which his old friend General Braxton Bragg served as one of the pallbearers, and he was interred in the cemetery that held the graves of six of his children. Only one of the children survived his parents, but the ideas to which he gave voice have retained their vigor for over a century and haunt us still. We could but wish that some appropriate ceremony were available to exorcise that unquiet spirit. Perhaps my present efforts will mark the beginnings of a movement toward that end.

11

THE FRENCH CONNECTION

PAUL BROCA AND THE PROFESSIONALIZATION OF BIOLOGICAL ANTHROPOLOGY

Those two very different but almost simultaneous, epoch-making phenomena—the appearance of Darwin's *Origin of Species* and the outbreak of the American Civil War—combined to demolish the American School of Anthropology as a recognizable entity. Morton and Gliddon had already died; Nott ceased publishing on anthropological matters after his indignant remonstration to Major General O. O. Howard; and although Ephriam George Squier had risen to be president of the New York Anthropological Institute at the time of Nott's departure from New York, his own reputation took a beating as a result of the scandal surrounding his subsequent divorce. His wife retained two artists who "performed the function now taken over by the camera" (Stanton 1960, 184), and Squier became better known for his marital infidelity than for the merits of his anthropology.

For the remainder of the 19th century, there were no acknowledged representatives of the American School on the western side of the Atlantic. Even in their absence, however, their attitudes and words continued to be echoed in the public press as well as in the academy. I shall take a look at some of these when I return to a consideration of American attitudes toward "race" in the aftermath of the Civil War. First, however, we need to take a closer look at what really represented the continued incarnation of the American School overseas, namely, the career of Paul Broca and the Société d'Anthropologie de Paris.

The family into which Pierre Paul Broca (1824–80) was born had been associated with the traditions of Calvinistic Protestantism in southwestern France, just east of Bordeaux, ever since the Reformation (Schiller 1979, 10) (Fig. 11–1). His father was a local physician, and Paul was sent to Paris in 1841 to acquire his formal education in medicine. This determined the course of his life, and he went on to enjoy a truly distinguished medical career in Paris. By 1843, he had passed his exams for *externat* at the Hôtel Dieu—in effect, the Faculté de Médecine. He became an *interne* in 1844, and although he was briefly suspended in 1846 for "radical" political writings—really only the mildly liberal kind of iconoclasm characteristic of the student generation of his time—he went on to one success after another in the medical world. He became an *aide* in anatomy at the École Pratique in 1846, joined its Société Anatomique in 1847, was made prosector in 1848, and had his doctoral thesis accepted by the Faculté de Médecine in 1849 (Schiller 1979, 78).

In 1850, he received the Prix Portal of the Académie de Médecine for a monograph on the microscopic pathology of cancer and was elected vice-president of the Société

multiple awards

144

Figure 11-1   Paul Broca, 1824–80
(from Schiller 1979, 214).

Anatomique by unanimous vote. In 1852, he received a prize from the Académie des Sciences for an essay on rickets, and joined the Société de Chirurgie (Surgery). The next year, he passed his exams for *chirurgien des hôpitaux (du Bureau Central)* and *chirurgien agrégé* at the Hôtel Dieu (Schiller 1979, 86). Since passage of the *agrégé* exams constituted qualification to teach at the university level, this made Broca the equivalent of an assistant professor on the Faculté de Médecine, and he went on to occupy one professorial position or another for the rest of his life.

Broca was a consummate joiner and organizer. He collaborated with the celebrated French physiologist Claude Bernard to found the French Association for the Advancement of Science (*Association Française pour l'Avancement des Sciences*) in 1872, modeled on the British original; and he served as its vice-president under President Bernard (Fletcher 1882, 135; Schiller 1979, 278). At the time of his death, he had served as president of the Société de Chirurgie and vice-president and president-elect of the Académie de Médecine and he had been elected to a lifetime seat on the French *senat,* one of the highest political positions to which a French citizen could aspire (Fletcher 1882, 125; Schiller 1979, 273, 282). Evidently, Paul Broca was a figure to be reckoned with in the circles of power in Paris during the third quarter of the 19th century.

Broca used these demonstrated abilities as organizer and administrator to put anthropology on the map in a formal sense. His biographer perceptively observed that if he had not "launched anthropology on its permanent course," modern universities might never have had departments devoted to the subject (Schiller 1979, 136). Ironically, however, his vision of the scope of the subject as a whole faded out in France, where "anthropology" today means only biological anthropology. Broca's broader conception of the discipline survives mainly in the English-speaking world, most specifically in its American segment. The reasons for this Franco-American connection have been hinted at before but not fully harnessed to the task of elucidating the circumstances that shaped the field as it appears today.

From the perspective of history, however, perhaps his greatest fame stems from his neuroanatomical work and his demonstration that the posterior portion of the inferior, left, third, frontal convolution of the brain plays a crucial role in controlling the powers of articulate speech (Broca 1861a). This region is called "Broca's area" to this day, and it is clear that Broca deserves all the credit he has been given for his pioneering contribution. He knew and admired the work of Gall and recognized how it had been distorted by the phrenologists who had built upon it (Broca 1861b, 191). In his own efforts, he was able to focus on what could be dealt with scientifically in the matter of localization of brain function and to distinguish that from the transcendental quackery which characterized the wilder phrenological claims. As he put it, "if there were to be a phrenological science, it would be the phrenology of convolutions, not bumps" (quoted in Schiller 1979, 187). As in many other instances, however, he then accepted many of the conclusions that came from the work whose methods he had properly criticized (Broca 1861b, 198–199). This can be traced to the clear thread of racism that ran through his investigations of the brain and that will emerge in clearer focus when we turn to his career in anthropology.

For my purposes here, it is the source of that anthropological perspective, even more than his well-known organizational efforts on its behalf, that merits a closer look. Broca succeeded in founding the Société d'Anthropologie de Paris in the spring of 1859, although not without considerable foot-dragging on the part of the government. Even though many of the most famous French intellectuals were overtly anticlerical, to such an extent that the claim has even been made that it was hard to get elected to the Académie des Sciences without being an atheist (Pasteur 1971, 751), there was still a great deal of residual uneasiness when something so traditionally sensitive as the question of human origins was proposed as a topic for formal discussion and investigation.

Despite the claim that "France has unquestionably been less religious than any other Western country since the French revolution" (Pasteur 1971, 751), a Jesuit pamphlet published in 1843 denounced the professors at the Sorbonne and the Collège de France and supported a movement to restructure the university and insert priests as teachers. As Broca recorded in his correspondence from that time, Jesuits did invade the classes of history professors and drowned out the voices of the lecturers by whistling. Evidently, the students rallied to the support of their professors and prevented similar attempts at disruption in subsequent lectures (Schiller 1979, 25, 296).

Pressure from the Church continued, however; and in 1852, passage of the *loi Falloux* granted teaching privileges to any clergyman whether or not he had passed the qualifying exam (Schiller 1979, 285). Frédéric-Alfred-Pierre Falloux was President Louis-Napoléon Bonaparte's first minister of education. In the "freedom of higher education" debate in the *senat* in 1868, Cardinal Bonnechose, to general applause, denounced the "materialism" of Bernard, Broca, and others and concluded that "True science is religious" (Schiller 1979, 273). The "freedom" in that debate actually meant quite the opposite: "the return of the university to Catholic domination" (Schiller 1979, 273). The *loi Falloux* remained in effect until after the beginning of the 20th century, and the 1880 attempt to overturn it in the *senat* failed by a vast majority. At that time, even Broca, who was then a member, did not vote for the repeal (Schiller 1979, 273).

One must recall that this was the era when the Church was dominated by that extraordinary pope, Pius IX. *Pio Nono* in Italian, and a "No-no" he certainly was. As one eminent historian has remarked, his claims for himself were expressed in such a fashion that they would be regarded as "megalomania" in anyone but a pope (Bury 1964, 53). In 1866, he declared "I am the way, the truth and the life" (Bury 1964, 53–4), and on another occasion he boasted "Tradition is myself" (Bury 1964, 124).

When he issued the bull proclaiming the Immaculate Conception on December 8, 1854, he had virtually claimed papal infallibility (Bury 1964, 50). Fifteen years later, in commemoration of that occasion, he convened the first Vatican Council on the day of Immaculate Conception in 1869 and browbeat those good clerics into proclaiming the dogma of infallibility, which they finally did on July 18, 1870, aided by the fact that the French troops in Rome had prevented an Italian takeover until after the deed was accomplished (Bury 1964, 144).

During the period of Vatican I, he declared that "liberal Catholics are only half-Catholic" (Bury 1964, 111). This was in keeping with the denunciation in the last paragraph of his *Syllabus of Errors* published in 1864, in which he thundered "If anyone thinks that the Roman Pontiff can and should reconcile himself with progress, with liberalism and with modern civilization, let him be anathema" (quoted in Daniel-Rops 1965, 284).

Given the tenor of the times, then, the very subject matter of "anthropology" hinted at the spirit of subversion officially identified with the aborted revolutions of 1848, and the feeling persisted that there was something degrading to the immortal human soul inherent in a course of investigation that proposed to take human nature as its subject. Broca took the plans for his Société to the minister of public education under the government of Louis Napoléon, none other than Falloux himself; and he in turn passed them on to the prefect of police. That official duly dodged and sent them back to Broca. Next, Broca took his proposal to the chief of his *Préfecture*, who also happened to be a professor of legal medicine and a colleague at the Hôtel Dieu. This figure, Auguste Tardieu, has been described as a "brilliant casuist," and he used his skills to argue that gatherings of less than 20 people were not forbidden by law and that a meeting of 19 savants was inherently harmless in any case. He further suggested that they agree never to discuss politics, religion, society, church, or government and that they allow a plainclothes policeman to monitor their meetings (Schiller 1979, 134–135).

Broca readily agreed to these stipulations, and despite the nervousness of the government, the society was duly formed, with Broca acting as its secretary. Now, scientific society meetings can be fascinating occasions for the participants, but to untrained outsiders who happen to blunder in, they can easily be perceived as incomprehensible exercises in boring futility. The poor plainclothes policeman who had to attend and report on those discussions to his superiors after each session must have been less than thrilled with his duty. During one such recitation of largely anatomical trivia, he is reported to have turned to Broca and said "There will be nothing interesting today, I suppose?" and asked if he could go out and get a breath of fresh air without anything threatening to the state being said in his absence. Broca, however, with just a hint of malice in his sense of humor, replied: "No, no, my friend, you must not go for a walk: sit down and earn your pay" (Brabrook 1881, 245). Two years later, police surveillance was withdrawn and the society was officially approved by the minister of education. After 5 years, it was given full status as "a public utility" (Schiller 1979, 135).

The research papers presented at the meetings and the reports of the discussions they engendered were duly published in the *Bulletins de la Société d'Anthropologie de Paris,* which Broca had initiated to record such matters. After its first successful year of operation, the *Bulletins* summed up the status of the society and the purpose behind its existence: "The aim of the *Société d'Anthropologie de Paris* is the scientific study of human races" (Broca 1861b). The words, in essence, were the expression of Broca himself. He had created the society, and he was "the very soul of it for one and twenty years" (Fletcher 1882, 125). He remained general secretary by choice since "Not being in the President's chair made it easier for him to moderate the discussion without seeming to dominate it" and he retained control of its agenda and its publications until his death (Schiller 1979, 135).

Broca's first published treatment of what constituted "race," appeared in a series of installments of the *Journal de la Physiologie* starting in 1858. This was entitled "Mémoire sur l'hybridité en général, sur la distinction des espèces animals et sur le métis obtenu par le croisement du lièvre et du lapin" (Memoir on hybridity in general, on the distinction of animal species and on the mix obtained by crossing hares and rabbits). If this sounds remarkably like the topic explored by Morton a decade earlier and the expanded version written by Nott as Chapter XII of *Types of Mankind* in 1855, it is not surprising to find Broca paying generous tribute to those American authors (Broca 1858, 1859a, 1860a).

Originally, Broca had presented his discussion on hybridity to the Société de Biologie in 1858, but the membership was "shocked and embarrassed" by what they perceived to be a challenge to the biblical account of creation; he was asked to desist by its president. He dutifully complied, which is why his Mémoire was not published in the *Comptes Rendus* of that Société as would normally have been expected, but in the *Journal de la Physiologie* instead (Schiller 1979, 129–131). At issue was the sensitivity of the Church to controversial claims concerning human origins, and with this as a beginning, Broca was to be suspected of anticlerical leanings for the rest of his life. The troubles he encountered in presenting his views and getting them published constituted the impetus that led him to found the Société d'Anthropologie de Paris in 1859 (Vallois 1940, 1).

His extended treatment of the question of "hybridity" was published as a separate volume in Paris in 1860 (Broca 1860b). If we were to render its title directly in English, it would be *Researches on animal hybridity in general and on human hybridity in particular, considered in reference to the question of the plurality of human species.* That title alone is startlingly similar to the title of Morton's essay of 1847. An abridged English translation was produced and published under the auspices of the Anthropological Society of London as a small book in 1864 called *On the Phenomena of Hybridity in the Genus* Homo (Broca 1864). This provided the intellectual model for the outlook of that organization, which, in direct imitation of Broca's Société, had been founded in 1863 by James Hunt (1833–69) (Burrow 1963; Rainger 1978, 59), an "energetic disciple" of Robert Knox (Banton and Harwood 1975, 29; Rainger 1978, 55) and, as we have seen before, an enthusiastic champion of Josiah Clark Nott.

Broca's treatise on hybridity was the foundation on which the edifice of French anthropology was constructed, and it was also of fundamental importance for the field of biological anthropology as it grew later in Germany, England, and finally the United States of America. That contribution, however, was simply a recapitulation and extension of what Morton had written over a decade earlier. Some of the embellishing was really just a rendering in French of Nott's rhetoric, and this seems to be the source of the wording that was perceived as being anticlerical.

As his biographer observed, "Broca never attacked religion *per se* any more than he would have attacked chemistry" (Schiller 1979, 284). Clearly, he did not share Nott's delight in "parson baiting," but the idea that his approach represented "science" whereas that of his opponents represented religious sophistry was articulated by his supporters (Pouchet 1864, 3) and must have emanated in some sense from Broca himself. He was perceived to display an "antireligious orientation," and subsequently there was an organized Catholic effort to "fight against atheistic anthropology" (Paul 1974, 427), specifically against the anthropology of the school that Broca had founded at the end of 1876 (Vallois 1940, 4; Sagan 1979, 7).

It would be overly simplistic to claim that Morton was the only source of Broca's orientation. In the most judicious assessment of his intellectual debt, he has been described as "heir to both the French and American traditions of polygenism" (Stocking 1968, 40). Morton and his self-declared disciple, Nott, had both bolstered their presentations with generous citations of the earlier French polygenists, and Broca in turn paid tribute to the writings of the Americans as well as to his French predecessors. Morton and Nott, however, developed their polygenism as a consequence of the peculiarly American situation of which they were a part, and the references to the French literature were more in the nature of after-the-fact attempts to enhance their credibility with a gloss of prestige from compatible views from the older European scientific traditions. In spite of claims to the contrary, however, the direct impact of the American School in shaping Broca's approach was apparent.

The importance of Morton and the American school was repeatedly discussed by those who participated in the meetings of Broca's Société during its early years. On July 3, 1862, the physiologist Eugène Dally delivered a report on the "indigenous races" and the archaeology of the New World in which he extolled the works of Morton. He was immediately challenged by an expatriate German, Franz Ignaz Brunner, who had extensive experience in North Africa and had once been the personal physician of the Egyptian viceroy. This curious and contentious figure had become even more of a chauvinistic Frenchman than the French themselves. He still preserved the German urge for self-ennoblement, but instead of preceding his name with a "von," he hyphenated the aristocratic suffix "Bey" used in the Arab world, where he had spent so much time. Slightly modifying the spelling of his original German name and appending the Arabic designation for nobility, he presented himself in Paris as Dr. F. Pruner-Bey (Schiller 1979, 140).

At the next recorded session, July 17, 1862, Pruner-Bey declared that the Americans had only "traced a pallid copy" of a "doctrine" which is "completely and eminently French." Pruner-Bey enjoyed using French at its most flowery, and he went on to say of the representatives of the American school: "do they have the same stamp of ingenious initiative, of reflective analysis and finally of exquisite precision that have always been the inalienable endowment of the French spirit, and of which our honorable confrère [he was referring to Broca] has given us such evident proofs on many occasions?" (Pruner-Bey 1862, 421). He concluded that the "lucubrations of the American authors" cited by Dally "were only a scaffolding constructed of poorly co-ordinated borrowings" (Pruner-Bey 1862, 421). Broca then calmed things: "I shall leave it to M. Dally to undertake the defense of the American scientists . . . so severely and summarily judged. I shall restrict myself to a single comment, which is that if Germany has had a Blumenbach, and if England has had a Prichard, America has had Morton, and up to now French anthropology has had no name which can be put on a level with them" (Broca 1862a, 423). Here, I can use the privilege of nearly a century and a half of hindsight to say that the figure who was to attain that rank in France was none other than Broca himself. This was clearly his intent, and he obviously suc-ceeded; but he could hardly have foretold that the American School had already col-lapsed, the English one was mortally wounded, and the German representation was doomed by political events to become an albatross around the neck of the field as a whole in the next century. Pruner-Bey was Broca's elder by some years, however, and he stuck to his guns: "I am sorry that I cannot share M. Dally's opinion on the value of Morton's work. Without doubt, Morton was an eminent man; he devoted his life and his fortune to the study of our science; he established an important cranial col-lection at great expense. Thus he has a right to our respect. But M. Dally speaks of him as though he had founded a science. He founded absolutely nothing" (Pruner-Bey 1862, 431). (Actually, the expression that he used carries an import of contempt in French that cannot be achieved by a direct translation into English. If he had said that he considered Dally's opinion to be so much "b . . . s . . . ," then this would come somewhat closer to conveying the impact that his words would have had on a French audience.)

He concluded with the observation that craniology had previously been established by Blumenbach and that Tiedemann had preceded Morton in the measurement of cranial capacity. The only credit Pruner-Bey would allow Morton was the invention of a mea-suring gadget, a goniometer, which he declared was defective in comparison with its French counterpart (Pruner-Bey 1862, 431). As for Gliddon, he declared that he had known him in Cairo years earlier and that, although he had been an honorable merchant, he could not count as a scientific authority (Pruner-Bey 1862, 431).

Pruner-Bey was to get his comeuppance when the Société met again on August 7. At that session, Dally undertook a spirited defense of Morton and the American School. He recounted Morton's accomplishments and quoted the tributes paid to him by European scholars, including one Pruner-Bey claimed had demonstrated Morton's errors (Dally 1862, 450–455). Pruner-Bey essayed an unrepentant but somewhat feeble rebuttal, continuing to insist on the errors in Morton's work.

At that point, Broca stepped in and had the last word: "I regret that M. Pruner-Bey has given this twist to the discussion. With that kind of procedure, there is no man, how-ever eminent he may be, whom one could not demolish as he has tried to demolish Morton" (Broca 1862b, 456). He noted that, by these means, one could find errors in Blumenbach and Prichard since their works were done even earlier than Morton's. Then he queried "What does that prove?" and, answering his own rhetorical question, said it merely showed "that anthropology has progressed rapidly." Perhaps in the future, he suggested, some of the opinions of Pruner-Bey himself would be shown to have been mistaken. The accuracy of Broca's prediction was very shortly borne out since, only a year later, Pruner-Bey published the extraordinary claim that the famous Neanderthal skull was "indubitably the skull of a Celt" (Pruner-Bey 1863, 319) in which a key aspect of form "corresponds nearest . . . to that of a modern Irishman" (Pruner-Bey 1864, 223). This gaffe now counts as one of the more famous of all-time anthropological laughers.

Broca then brought a degree of perspective to bear on the issue that merits the heartfelt applause of all who deal with the history of ideas: "To appreciate the value of a man, it is necessary to put him back into his epoch and into the milieu in which he lived. When Morton began his work, there were only a few scattered ethnologists in Europe. There was not one on the other side of the Atlantic. In America today, there is a whole school of anthropology" (Broca 1862b, 456). He continued by recalling that, 25 years earlier, William Edwards, a naturalized citizen, had tried to establish an ethnological society in Paris to accomplish the same task to which the Société d'Anthropologie de Paris was dedicated but that he had been unable to overcome public indifference: "Well, what Will. Edwards was unable to do in France, what the Société d'Anthropologie has not yet fully attained, Morton, by himself, attempted to do in America, and he succeeded. Let us beware of disdaining a man who has done so much for our science. Refute him if he is mistaken, criticize him freely, but always know enough to recognize his worth" (Broca 1862b, 457).

Oddly enough, although Broca effectively founded professional anthropology in France, which in turn served as the model for much of the profession as it grew in other countries, he was not successful in making his beneficiaries aware of the debt owed by the field to the American part of its heritage. On the other hand, equally little has been said about the shaping effects of the tradition of typological essentialism inherited from medieval Neoplatonism that were such an important part of the French contribution to the field as a whole. Even though Broca was raised a Protestant, his outlook was permeated with the style of thinking of what was in essence a Catholic society. The intellectual traditions of the medieval Church played a major role in the way in which Broca's School thought about "race," although I am going to defer treatment of this until the section on his student and successor, Paul Topinard.

Unlike his colleagues, students, and successors, Broca continued to give credit to the pioneering role of Samuel George Morton. Stephen Jay Gould (1981, 84) has perceptively stated that "Morton was his hero and model." One of the things for which Broca has been remembered in anthropology is his standardization of measurements and the development of instruments by which those standard measurements can be taken on living human beings and on human skeletons. However, in this matter, he started with the measurements initiated by Morton in 1839 and simply added and elaborated. He clearly represents the continuity of what Morton began in Philadelphia, and Broca was the first to acknowledge this (Broca 1873; Gould 1981, 84).

It is also clear that his interest in "hybridity" was sparked by the attempt made by the American school to demonstrate that the ability to produce offspring was not a conclusive test of specific unity. Where Morton had categorized species as "remote," "allied," and "proximate" depending on whether they produced no offspring or produced, sterile or fertile issue, respectively, Broca expanded the typology to "agenesic," "dysgenesic," "paragenesic," and "eugenesic." In the first case, offspring produced by the crossing of such species are entirely sterile. In the second and third cases, offspring range from near sterility to partial fecundity. In the last instance, offspring are entirely fertile (Broca 1864, x). In effect, Broca simply divided Morton's "allied" species category into two parts.

This just represents embellishment, however, and does not alter the fact that Paul Broca's basic approach was taken straight from that of Samuel George Morton, and he never sought to deny it. In the midst of a long treatment of the problems inherent in using linguistics to measure the biological relationships between human populations, as advocated by James Cowles Prichard and a number of others, Broca declared as an item of faith: "I am among those who think that the great typical differences which separate human groups are primordial" (Broca 1862c, 283). This, of course, was simply Broca's rendition of Morton's declaration that "I have . . . been in favor of the doctrine of *primeval diversities* among men" (Morton 1847, 40) and his use of the term "primordial organic form" to indicate specific distinction (Morton 1851, 275).

Broca, in fact, like the members of the American School he so admired, was a thoroughgoing polygenist, although he always remained just a little cagey about saying that in so many words. The whole thrust of his "mémoire" was to demonstrate that monogenism was indefensible and that polygenic arguments were the only ones that remained consistent with the principles of science. His disciples were somewhat more direct about it than he, and one of them noted that the foundation of his Société and its *Bulletin* were "due above all to the indefatigable zeal of a partisan of the doctrines which we defend: M. P. Broca" (Pouchet 1864, 3). Those "doctrines," of course, were related to the assumption that human "races" were created separate and unequal.

Part of Broca's caginess was what he regarded as the lack of definitive information demonstrating just which human groups were specifically distinct from what other ones. He tentatively accepted the same questionable data, cited by Morton and Nott, from the Polish Count Paul Edmund de Strzelecki (1796–1873) supporting the assertion that Europeans and Native Australians produced few, if any, offspring with each other (Broca 1864, 47). Broca hedged his bets by noting that polygenists think that human groups are species and hence permanent, while monogenists think they can be modified and are only varieties: therefore, he advocated the use of the term "*races,* which prejudges nothing, and leaves the question open" (quoted in Salmon 1896, 366). Again, this was directly in the tradition of Morton, who had stated nearly 30 years earlier: "The term race has been indefinitely and conveniently used in those instances in which it is difficult to decide whether an individual of any tribe of plants or animals, is a distinct species, or only a variety of some other species" (Morton 1847, 40).

Even though Broca, like Nott in America, accepted an antiquity for human existence that was not hinted at in the biblical accounts, he—again like the Americans—was still thinking more in biblical than geological terms, and the idea that the different manifestations of human appearance could have come about by natural means over the length of time actually available just never penetrated his consciousness. Following the lead of Nott—and Morton and Caldwell before that—Broca noted that nowhere in the Bible does it say that all human beings descended from the incestuous union of the sons and daughters of Adam. Nott, in his chapter on hybridity, quoted from a letter sent to him by Morton in 1850:

> Q. Whence came that curse we call primeval sin?
> A. From Adam's children breeding in and in.
>
> (Nott 1854, 409)

Morton, unlike Nott, would express what might have been perceived as irreverence only in his private communications. It was typical of Nott, however, to quote it in a published work after Morton's death.

Broca, following the American model, suggested that the Mosaic narration applied only to the Adamites—God's people. Besides the "sons of God," he suggested, there were also the "sons of man," whose origin was not specified. In any case, as time went on, he followed the general trend in French science and regarded such questions as not provable by investigation and therefore not within the purview of science at all (editorial comment, Mr. Darwin and the French Institute, in *Nature* [London] August 18, 1870, 309).

With a vestige of the biblical time scale still lurking in his mind, Broca observed that it would make no difference whether human diversity were the result of divine fiat when people were dispersed from the Tower of Babel or whether they had been created different in the first place: "If the differences of human races and their geographic distribution had been the consequences of distinct creations or of miraculous transformations that were the equivalent of new creations, it is all the same from the point of view of the doctrine of the polygenists" (Broca 1860b, 662, my translation). He then argued that polygenism was in fact more ethical than monogenism since the latter could be used to justify slavery, to which he was opposed. If that sounds more than a little like tortured logic, his attempt to explain that stance does not help a great deal. He did observe that this in essence was the position of the Rev. John Bachman, and like his models in the American school, he took the opportunity to denounce the Charleston minister: "one could say that the polygenist doctrine assigns the inferior races of humanity to a more honorable position than does the opposing doctrine. To be inferior to another man be it in intelligence, or vigor, or beauty, is not a humiliating condition. One would blush on the contrary to have undergone a physical or moral degradation, to have descended the scale of beings, and to have lost one's rank in creation" (Broca 1860b, 663–664).

Somehow he felt that being created inferior in the first place was not sufficient justification for slavery, but if all people had originally been created the same, the presumably manifest "inferiority" of those whose ancestors had allowed themselves to degenerate was therefore somehow their own fault; consequently, they deserved to be placed "under the protection of higher races." That, as we have seen, was the position of Bachman. Putting aside the question of why modern humans should continue to be denigrated for something done by their remote ancestors, I have to confess that I cannot see why "inferiority" acquired through some presumed ancestral fall from grace would warrant slavery while an equal degree of "inferiority" present ab origine would not.

In any case, what is behind both "doctrines," as Broca called them, was the unexamined and unshaken conviction that human populations are ranked on a scale of worth and that all can be judged inferior or superior in comparison with each other. Despite Cuvier's denunciation of the *scala naturae* at the beginning of the century, it was alive and well in the anthropology of Paul Broca, as it continues to be in the 21st-century out-look of Arthur R. Jensen, J. Philippe Rushton, and others. Since Broca's anthropology became the model for all subsequent traditions that have taken the study of human biological endowments as their subject, it is hardly surprising that the idea of relative ranking survived undimmed in academic anthropology well up to the middle of the 20th century and is assumed as a matter of course in the minds of the public at large.

In the previous chapter and again at the beginning of this one, I stated that the almost simultaneous impact of Charles Darwin and the American Civil War had accomplished the destruction of the American School of Anthropology as a coherent entity. Those two portentous phenomena also had their impact in England, where Darwin was the more immediate and the American conflict over slavery the somewhat secondary impetus. Although Darwin's theories were not necessarily accepted by the English, they were not ignored; and the implications of modest selective forces operating over vast periods of time were certainly understood. The use of what was still an essentially biblical understanding of geological time by even the most anticlerical polygenists, then, was quickly perceived to be out of touch with reality (Fig. 11–2).

The fact also that polygenism in England, as in America, was offered as a justification for slavery meant that it suffered from an ethical taint that was reinforced when the proslavery forces lost the American conflict. Finally, in England, the fortuitous demise in 1869 of the flamboyant racist and misogynist James Hunt left the Anthropological Society of London leaderless at the very time that its main intellectual justifications had been pulled out from under it. The racism that had been so blatant in that Society

Figure 11–2 Charles Darwin, 1809–82, in 1863. His health worsened and he gave up shaving later that year. The result was the genesis of his famous beard (Browne 2002).

certainly did not disappear overnight, but the organization that had been set up for its promotion essentially collapsed; the vestiges joined with the Ethnological Society in 1871 in a somewhat more benign hybrid that has continued to the present day as the Royal Anthropological Institute (Burrow 1963, 139).

In France, however, it was quite a different story. In the first place, the French were far less aware of what was going on in America than were the English. Slavery had finally come to a formal end in France in 1848 (Blanckaert 1988a, 118), and the Société Ethnologique ended with it (Schiller 1979, 132). In any case, events in America were much less likely to come to the attention of the average French person than was the case in England despite the tensions between Americans and the English that had their roots in the political differences that dated from a full century earlier. The American Civil War, then, created far less notice among the French than among the English.

The other matter was Darwin and his theory of evolution by natural selection. That too had almost no impact on French intellectual life. This subject has been treated with great skill by many able writers (e.g., Stebbins 1974; Boesiger 1980; Limoges 1980; Appel 1987), and it is not my place here to discuss their fascinating syntheses. To illustrate the French reaction, I shall simply quote from one of the most comprehensive reviews: "Whatever sources may be utilized to illustrate the French reception to Darwin in a positive way, none can be as impressive as the countless books and articles where silence alone stands testimony to the French intellectual developments. . . . Silence may be harder to document than the trumpet fanfare, but in its own way it is equally impressive" (Stebbins 1974, 167).

Actually, since my whole section here is devoted to Broca and he could be taken as representative of the active, creative, and "liberal" segment of French biological and medical science, his reactions can serve as a pretty good index of the response to Charles Darwin by progressive French intellectuals. Stebbins certainly was correct that there was a prolonged silence in the French scientific literature, and that silence is as dramatically apparent in French anthropological writings as it is in the literature of any other field; this not only is true for the 19th century but has continued to be so right up to the present.

Broca was one of the very few who reacted, however; and his reaction is most interesting. He realized right away that Darwin's perspective would resuscitate the "antique dogma of the unity of the human Genus"—that monogenist specter that he thought he had put to rest. It is one of those delicious ironies of history that Broca founded his Société on the premise that monogenism was indefensible in the very same year that Darwin produced the work that demonstrated conclusively that polygenism was irrelevant.

Broca's first reaction, then, was clearly one of shock and alarm. As he put it in one of the very few published responses by a French scholar right after the appearance of Darwin's epoch-making work: "To put the permanence of species in doubt would amount to attacking respected traditions at the same time as undermining natural history at its foundations, that is to say, in its classifications; that, consequently, would upset everybody" (Broca 1860b, 435, my translation). There was no doubt that Broca himself was upset.

Two years later, when he returned to the matter, he was still evidently upset to the extent that some of the characteristic prejudices of French biological science were transparently obvious. He also showed that he was not really familiar with what Darwin had actually written. In somewhat haughty fashion, he wrote "Now, is Darwin right or wrong? I know nothing about that, I do not even wish to know. In the things that are accessible to science, I find sufficient nourishment to satisfy my curiosity without getting myself lost in the night of origins. When Darwin speaks to me about my trilobite ancestors, I am not humiliated, but I say to him: What do you know about that? You were not there. And those who refute him know more than he does" (Broca 1862c, 314, my translation). I need hardly add that Darwin never said that human beings had trilobites for ancestors. That was sheer grumpy hyperbole on Broca's part.

Eventually, Broca calmed down, considered the evidence in greater detail, and was forced to conclude that organic evolution had to have taken place. A decade later, at the end of a long discourse, he said: "I shall conclude in saying: The permanence of species would appear to be nearly impossible, it is in opposition to the mode of succession and distribution in the species of past and living beings. It is very probable then that species are variable and subject to evolution" (Broca 1870, 238, my translation).

While Broca, like most of the other French scientists, eventually came to accept the reality of evolution, he refused to accept Darwin's suggested mechanism, natural selection. That, he declared, was "no more than a brilliant mirage" (Broca 1870, 238). Evolution he was willing to accept, "But the causes, the agents of that evolution are still unknown" (Broca 1870, 238). In this regard as well, Broca was a completely characteristic representative of French science. The vitalism that had been a part of the outlook of Benjamin Rush, Charles Caldwell, and the medical world at the beginning of the century continued undiminished in French biology.

Albert Gaudry, widely credited with having been the figure who represented evolutionary thought in France late in the 19th century, rejected the idea that natural forces could have had anything to do with shaping the biological world: "Organic beings are superior to inorganic bodies, and it is not natural to suppose that the latter alone have ruled their destiny" (Gaudry 1878, 250). In a review of one of Gaudry's major works, Broca's disciple Paul Topinard wrote approvingly that while Gaudry felt it was the role of the paleontologist "to collect proofs of the doctrine of evolution, it does not belong to them . . . to explain the processes whereby the Author of the world has produced the modifications" (Topinard 1888, 473). As Gaudry (1878, 257) had previously said: "Assuredly the subject which examines the causes of modifications of beings is well worthy of the attention of naturalists. But on this subject I avow my ignorance" (my translations). The orotund pride in an avowal of "ignorance" was common among late 19th-century European scientists, who had been tinged with Romanticism. That stance has continued to characterize the majority of subsequent attempts to deal with the dynamics that have shaped the course of human evolution in particular (e.g., Groves 1989; Kimbel and Martin 1993; Tattersall 1998, 2001, 2002), and a case can be made that this was also true for a good deal of general paleontology as well. This is exemplified in the extraordinary claim put forth on behalf of one paleontological school of thought: "We believe that Darwinism . . . is . . . a theory that has been put to the test and found false" (Nelson and Platnick 1984, 143).

Since Broca had launched his Société on the basis of his commitment to polygenism, one would expect him to have been reluctant to abandon everything he had stood for, and this was indeed the case. His fully considered reaction to Darwin in the light of his own background and experience was phrased in this way: "For my part, leaving aside the darwinian explanation of natural selection and declaring that the means of the appearance of beings and the processes of the transformation of species are not yet known, I would incline towards polygenic transformism rather than towards monogenism or oligogenism, for the objections that are raised in my mind to the darwinian doctrine would no longer be valid if one attributed a considerable but as yet indeterminate number of origins to organic beings, and if one ceased considering analogy of structure as a sufficient proof of common affiliation" (Broca 1870, 192–193, my translation). Virtually all of the points Broca raised in his objection to Darwin have failed to stand the test of time.

As far as the course by which those transformations proceeded, Broca "rejected gradual continuous evolution in favor of small abrupt transformations" (Schiller 1979, 232). Again, as in the case of his having refused to give any real thought to the nature of Darwin's mechanism, the strength of the tradition that he helped to found has been such that it continues to dominate the way that the majority of students of human evolution phrase their interpretations of the human fossil record, although few of them realize that their anti-Darwinian stance simply represents a continuation of the tradition that was established by Paul Broca well over a century ago (Eldredge and Tattersall 1982; Mellars and Stringer 1989; Rightmire 1990; Tattersall 1999, 2001; Stringer 2000; Tattersall and Schwartz 2000).

In searching for an appropriate intellectual source for his proffered term, *transformisme polygénique,* he claimed that the concept might be traced back to Buffon. On a more general note, however, he rooted in the past to find a suitable French figure to serve as the source for evolutionary thinking now that its acceptability was inevitable. Even though he reluctantly granted Darwin's work the status of "greatness" (Broca 1870, 184), he was unwilling to grant authorship of so important a concept to a mere Englishman. Broca was one of the first to resurrect Lamarck as the originator of the idea of organic evolution: "It was Lamarck, I think, in his *Philosophie zoologique,* who was the first to have clearly formulated this idea (in 1809)" (Broca 1870, 171). To this day, the overwhelming majority of French biologists remain reluctant to credit natural selection with the power to shape organic evolution, and they prefer to recognize Lamarck as meriting priority in setting forth the proposition that evolution has actually taken place.

Lamarck, of course, had been ridiculed and rejected in his own day, and his ideas played no part in developing the conceptual framework of French biology. Even though Broca attempted to give him priority in establishing evolutionary thinking, neither Broca nor any of his contemporaries actually built upon any aspect of his work. Still, Lamarck's statue stands today at the south entrance of the Jardin des Plantes in Paris with the words "Au Fondateur de la Doctrine de l'Évolution" engraved beneath his name.

It was in the area of his organizational and managerial skills that Broca was to make his real contribution. He had founded his Société in 1859, and he established the Laboratoire d'Anthropologie in November 1867. When the minister of public instruction established the École Pratique des Hautes Études in 1868, this gave official recognition to Broca's Laboratory and awarded it an annual budget (Fletcher 1882, 131; Vallois 1940, 2). The Laboratory was put at the disposal of the members of the Société. Dr. Théodore-Ernest-Jules Hamy, who had already been working for Broca for several years, was installed as the official preparateur. Broca, needless to say, remained its director until his death in 1880.

In 1876, Broca had formally founded his École d'Anthropologie—his "School"—as a recognized department in the Collège de France. This was physically located in his laboratory and the real source of the influence that Broca continues to exert over the field of anthropology now more than a century after his death. From one point of view, Paul Broca, more than any other single figure, succeeded in retarding our understanding of the nature and dynamics of human evolution. However, from another point of view, no one was more successful in foreseeing the various dimensions that needed to be investigated in order to have a complete understanding of the human phenomenon and in establishing the circumstances under which these activities could be pursued.

The School that Broca founded was a testimony to a degree of insight and grasp that was completely the opposite of the closed-mindedness he displayed where evolutionary biology was concerned. He provided for all of the dimensions that we would now include in a large, well-rounded, modern university—"four-field"—department of anthropology. In Broca's School, there were chairs for zoological anthropology, general anthropology, physiological (or psychological) anthropology, prehistoric anthropology (archaeology), the history of civilization, medical geography, ethnography–philology–mythology, and demography. Several of these divisions were staffed by a number of scholars, and most of them achieved real distinction during the course of solid productive careers (Williams 1923, Chapter 1).

Nowadays, perhaps, we would divide things in slightly different ways, but no one would deny that his plan covered all the major dimensions necessary to represent anthropology in its largest and most inclusive sense, the study of humankind. Most extraordinary of all, he managed to get it permanently funded by the government and staffed with people of sufficient ability so that it became an instant and ongoing success. Even the best-laid plans cannot account for the vicissitudes of fate, and it was inevitable that the character of Broca's school would change following his death only a scant four years after he had succeeded in putting it all together.

Reflecting Broca's own training in the biomedical realm, the divisions of his School were top-heavy in the realm we would now regard as biological anthropology. As time went on, this came to represent the totality of the institution, and the study of such things as ethnography, ethnology, folklore, linguistics, and archaeology ceased to be an integral part of its program. Instead, these subjects found their niches elsewhere in the growing world of university studies in Paris, and what continued as the focus of Broca's School was the biological portion alone. In time, this altered the very meaning of the word, and the term *l'anthropologie* in France today means strictly biological anthropology. The other dimensions that Broca had originally included now have their separate labels: *l'archéologie, l'ethnologie,* and *la linguistique.* Broca's original vision of the field as a whole is now principally manifest in the structure of the major successful departments of anthropology at the university level in the United States. Unfortunately, his basic failure to understand the nature of human biological variation and the dynamics of how this has been shaped has survived along with it.

The time has come, then, to take a closer look at the person who was so important in the perpetuation of the thinking of Josiah Clark Nott in America, even though Nott's name was never mentioned as the source for the ideas that he articulated.

12

THE LEGACY OF THE AMERICAN SCHOOL IN AMERICA

NATHANIEL SOUTHGATE SHALER (1841–1906)

Earlier, I quoted Haller to the effect that the post–Civil War outlook in America was shaped by a "curious marriage of New England parochialism with the racial ideology of the sensitive southern mind" (Haller 1971, 173). It is not clear who Haller was talking about when he wrote of "the racial ideology of the sensitive southern mind." It is quite apparent, however, that the "racial ideology" which grew in strength in the North after the Civil War was along the lines of the Southern model supported by Nott, and, whatever his other virtues may have been, "sensitivity" in matters concerning "race" was not one of them. One of the principal conduits for his views in the North was Nathaniel Southgate Shaler, who can be regarded as a veritable Trojan horse. As a result of his teachings, a whole generation of those who were destined to take the reins of power as Republican leaders were trained to accept the very ideas that the party had been created to oppose in the first place.

The Shaler family left England for Jamaica in the 18th century and then came to America, where Nathaniel's father got his training at Harvard Medical School. He then settled in Kentucky, where he married Anne Hind Southgate from a prominent Virginia family that was ideologically and economically tied to the slave system. Young Nathaniel was privately instructed in Latin, Greek, and German romantic literature by a German Swiss tutor engaged by his father. He entered the Lawrence Scientific School as a sophomore at Harvard in 1859, the same year that Broca founded his Société in Paris, Humboldt died, and Darwin published his *Origin* (Livingstone 1987b, 14).

When Shaler earned his B.S. *summa cum laude* in June 1862, the Civil War was already a year old. He hurried back to Kentucky as a captain of the Fifth Kentucky Battery, "Shaler's battery" (Livingstone 1987b, 30). Curiously enough, he was on the Union side, at the urging of his slave-owning grandfather Richard Southgate (Shaler 1909, 82). Evidently, he did not find the military to his liking, and he resigned in the autumn to get married. He returned to Cambridge, Massachusetts, with his bride, and in the summer of 1864, Agassiz made him assistant in paleontology at the Museum of Comparative Zoology (Livingstone 1987b, 30). His career was tied to Harvard for the rest of his life. He became lecturer in 1869, professor in 1870, and dean of the Lawrence Scientific School in 1891 (Shaler 1909, 386) (Fig. 12–1).

Nathaniel Southgate Shaler was a popular and flamboyant classroom performer, who became "a figure of legendary stature at Harvard during America's Gilded Age"

Figure 12-1 Nathaniel Southgate Shaler, 1841–1906, in 1894 (from Livingstone 1987b, 116).

(Livingstone 1987b, 276). Despite the fact that he had been on the Northern side in the Civil War, his students—some 7,000 of them over the years—referred to him as the "Confederate General" because of his Robert E. Lee beard, his broad-brimmed hat, and the way he strolled through Harvard Yard as though it were his own plantation grounds. In fact, he did live in the Yard, on Quincy Street, in what had once been one of a series of fine faculty homes near the Harvard president's house. In another sense also, his students were quite correct. His outlook on "race" clearly had been formed in the South.

He was the only one of Agassiz's students to become a geologist as such, although he gravitated toward geography and became one of the founders of American academic geography (Livingstone 1987b, 6). With the obvious racism and crude environmental determinism in his version of geography, one gets some idea of why the field of academic geography was to be the target of so much suspicion in the century to come. Some of his enthusiasm for "anthropogeography" came from reading the works of the German anthropologist/geographer Friedrich Ratzel, such as *Anthropo-geographie* in 1882. Ratzel's subsequent *Politische Geographie* (1897) contained the concept of "Lebensraum," which the rulers of the German state used to justify their brutal attempts at military expansion that had the effect of generating both World War I and World War II (Livingstone 1987b, 135).

In 1888–89, Shaler presented "Geographical Conditions and Life" as the Lowell Lectures, and these were published as *Nature and Man in America* in 1891. This was fully in the spirit of Ratzel's anthropogeography, although he never quotes Ratzel

(Livingstone 1987b, 309). Shaler, in fact, rarely used citations to indicate where his ideas and data had come from (Livingstone 1987b, 162); and the clear debt he owed to both Gobineau, "the father of racism," and to Nott is never mentioned, either by himself or by his commentators. He did, however, record his admiration for Darwin's half-cousin Sir Francis Galton and for his new "science" of eugenics (Shaler 1893, 651; 1909, 257; Livingstone 1987b, 73). The bigotry associated with eugenic claims was to be taken to truly sordid extremes in Nazi Germany during the 1930s. I give this separate consideration later.

In his Lowell Lectures, Shaler posited a "Teutonic" origin for American democratic institutions that he traced to the English shire and ultimately back to the "primitive folk meetings deep in the heart of the old Germanic forest" (Livingstone 1987b, 191). This, of course, was a direct paraphrase of Gobineau's Aryan hypothesis, and Shaler, like Gobineau, did not feel that those "democratic institutions" were appropriate for any other people but his "Teutons." America, he argued, was suitable only for "Teutons" (Shaler 1891, 164, 283). This view was picked up with enthusiasm by William Z. Ripley, and others picked it up from him, as we shall see. In time, this became incorporated into official American immigration policy.

Shaler mixed racial and religious bigotry in the same treatment. Again without citation, he adopted Gobineau's derogatory stereotype of the Celtic "race," but he added a bit of his own Protestant prejudice that clearly was at variance with Gobineau's Catholicism. In his undocumented opinion, pure unmixed Celts, like the Irish or the Scottish Highlanders, innately maintain a backward, obdurate, conservative adherence to "the old faith of Rome." Lowland Scots, in contrast, invigorated by mixture with "strong but related peoples," achieve literary, political, and scientific excellence (Shaler 1896, 515–516). If the element of Protestant anti-Catholicism added a peculiarly American twist to Gobineau's misanthropic vision, the general outlines of his "racial" judgments were adopted almost whole from Gobineau's *Essai* (1853–55).

It was in his treatment of African Americans, however, that the full, if unacknowledged, debt to Nott can be seen. He may well have picked up some of this from his mentor, Louis Agassiz; but the latter had clearly adopted the mode of expression of Nott, who had been using those phrases himself before Agassiz even crossed the Atlantic, and kept on using them after Agassiz had ceased writing on matters relating to human "races." In their African existence, he claimed that the ancestors of the African Americans had "come to a state of arrest in their development; they had attained to a point in that process beyond which they were not fitted to go" (Shaler 1900, 44). The conditions of slavery in America, however, had "lifted a savage race nearer and more rapidly towards civilization than had ever before been accomplished" (Shaler 1904, 187). At that point, he struck the same ambivalent note that had characterized Nott's assessment in 1866 and recognized that the abuses of the system outweighed the benefits (Shaler 1904, 226).

The progress of people of African origin, he declared, depends on the imitation of "a mastering race" since biosocially they are innately deficient. Just as Nott did, he cited Haiti as an illustration of the presumed "fact" that when "such communities have remained apart from the influence of whites for a generation, they commonly show signs of a relapse towards their ancestral estate" (Shaler 1904, 138). In what is almost a direct quote from Nott's advice to Major General Howard, he concluded: "These facts (no literature, religion, social politics, nor historic ability), appear to indicate the unhappy conclusion, that the negro considered as a species is, by nature, incapable of creating or maintaining societies of an order above barbarism, and that, so far as we can discern, this feature of his nature, depending as it does on the lack of certain qualities of mind, is irremediable. Whatever we may inculcate to them in the way of commonwealth motive will remain essentially foreign and will fall away as soon as the schoolmaster is forgotten" (Shaler 1904, 138–139). This outlook continues to be expressed by racialists late in the 20th and into the 21st centuries (Lynn 1991, 284; Rushton 1995, 142; Lynn and Vanhanen 2002).

In his phrase "the negro considered as a species," it is clear that Shaler still accepted the polygenism of Josiah Clark Nott. He declared that there was hope in the fact that, with the decrease in miscegenation since the Civil War, the "short-lived" and "unfruitful half-breeds" might soon die out and leave the South with two "pure-blooded races" (Shaler 1870, 57). African European hybrids, he stated, were inferior to both parent strains (Shaler 1870, 37); and in words that were almost exactly the same as those of Nott in 1866—just 4 years earlier—he said that the "mulatto, like the man of most mixed races, is peculiarly inflammable material. From the white he inherits a refinement unfitting him for all work that has not a certain delicacy about it . . . from the black, a laxity of morals which, whether it be the result of innate incapacity for certain forms of moral culture or the result of an utter want of training in this direction, is still unquestionably a negro characteristic" (Shaler 1870, 37). While he repeatedly declared his disapproval of slavery and his support for citizenship for African Americans, he never changed from his assumption of the "natural" inferiority of people of African origin and the superiority of "whites" (Shaler 1886, 1893). Democracy could survive, he claimed, only where European superiority was recognized and maintained. He also noted the "inferiority" of European peasant immigrants to the "superior" Anglo-Saxon "race" and advocated controls on immigration. Again, he came close to quoting Nott when he opined "History makes it plain that a race oligarchy almost invariably arises wherever a superior and inferior variety of people are brought together" (Shaler 1893, 647).

The blatant color-conscious racism of Nott and the Romantic Aryanism of Gobineau were welded together in the thinking of Shaler and presented as the conclusions of "science" to a large percentage of the Harvard undergraduate student body for over a third of a century. This privileged elite went on to assume positions of power in government and industry. It was they who made up a disproportionate segment of the leadership that guided America as it emerged as a world power during the first third of the 20th century.

Nott had portrayed European expansion at the expense of the original inhabitants of the various parts of the world as an inevitable result of "racial" superiority. Senator Stephen Douglas "rejoiced" to see the Native Americans, whom he regarded as "barriers of barbarism," "fading away before the advance of civilization like snow before the vernal sun" (Current 1973, 6). This was accepted as a matter of *Manifest Destiny*—the assumption that things were fated to be that way because of the self-evident, or manifest, superiority of the European "race."

One of the wealthy young men who imbibed this world view in Shaler's classroom was Theodore Roosevelt (1858–1919). "Teddy" Roosevelt went on to become governor of New York, assistant secretary of the Navy, vice-president of the United States, and, following the assassination of President McKinley in the fall of 1901, the Republican president of the United States, to which position he was reelected in 1904. His role in Cuba during the Spanish–American War even before he gained power in Washington, D.C., and his intervention in the Panama Canal Zone as U.S. president in 1903 were actions pursued because of his implicit faith in Manifest Destiny.

Exemplifying the rapprochement of the North–South elites after the Civil War, Roosevelt's mother, Martha Bulloch, was "southern-born with a heritage that stressed membership in a superior race" (Dyer 1980, 5). Not surprisingly, Roosevelt listened with favor to the articulate bigotry of Nathanial Southgate Shaler and accepted without question the racist sentiments expressed by England's poet of empire Rudyard Kipling, who sent him an advance copy of one of his most famous verses:

The White Man's Burden

Take up the White Man's Burden,
Send forth the best ye breed;
Go, bind your sons to exile
To serve the captives' need:
To wait in heavy harness,
On fluttered folk and wild—
Your new-caught, sullen peoples,
Half-devil and half-child.

(Kipling 1899 [in Kipling 1907])

Roosevelt wrote to his friend, fellow Harvard graduate and Shaler protégé Henry Cabot Lodge, that it was "very poor poetry but made good sense from the expansion point of view" (quoted in Weston 1972, 35). Actually, Roosevelt was wrong on both accounts. There is nothing wrong with the poetry, but the sentiments are disastrously flawed.

Those sentiments, however, were right in line with the thinking of those who had inherited the outlook of what had once been the American school of anthropology. Roosevelt applied them to the milieu of expanding European American settlement with the words: "the settler and pioneer have at bottom had justice on their side; this great continent could not have been kept as nothing but a game preserve for squalid savages" (quoted in Washburn 1959, 23). Some three generations later, his "intellectual" descendant, the prominent Republican fundraiser, campaigner, and movie star John Wayne, echoed the same sentiments: "I don't feel we did wrong in taking this great country away from them. . . . There were great numbers of people who needed new land, and the Indians were selfishly trying to keep it for themselves" (Wayne 1971, 82).

One suspects, however, that John Wayne would not have been sympathetic if the barrio dwellers of Los Angeles had simply moved in and set up housekeeping on his own spacious land holdings or helped themselves to his bank account supported by the claims that they had demonstrable need, and that he was just selfishly keeping it for himself.

Shaler used his position to promote the racist views of both Nott and Gobineau. He helped frame the outlook of the Immigration Restriction League, which was founded by three wealthy Bostonian members of the Harvard class of 1889 (Chase 1977, 113); and he became one of its vice-presidents when his own contemporary, John Fiske (Harvard class of 1863), was made president (Haller 1971, 133). His defense of a "lynch law" that had emerged in the South "showed the extreme to which New England casuistry went in attempting to renounce the politics of Reconstruction and to leave the race problem in the hands of southerners" (Haller 1971, 184).

One could quibble that Shaler was not a New Englander by birth or outlook, but that does not change the fact that he played a major role in converting New England to the unsavory views that he defended. The principled conscience of an earlier generation had collapsed completely, and the palpable presence of a genuine "New England casuistry" is amply demonstrated by the fact that Harvard, to honor Shaler's "broad humanitarian instincts," awarded him an honorary LL.D. in 1903 (Livingstone 1987b, 250). Nathaniel Southgate Shaler may have represented the continuity of American thinking concerning "race" that the unrepentant South contributed to American consciousness as the new century got under way, but his legacy as the voice of "science" was to vanish almost completely.

Just before the end of his long and productive life, the eminent vertebrate paleontologist Alfred Sherwood Romer (1894–1973) visited the University of Michigan to give a series of lectures. At the time, Romer was Agassiz Professor Emeritus at the Museum of Comparative Zoology at Harvard, where he had been teaching since 1934, and he regarded himself as a kind of updated representative of the field that Louis Agassiz had created in that venerable institution. Romer, in fact, can share some of the credit with the late George Gaylord Simpson (1902–84) for introducing a thoroughly Darwinian perspective into the field of paleontology. During Romer's visit to my institution in Ann Arbor late in 1972 and as he reflected on Agassiz's pioneering role in initiating their field in America, I asked him about his views concerning Agassiz's immediate successor at Harvard and his own predecessor, Nathaniel Southgate Shaler. Romer looked at me in astonishment when I asked him that question and replied that he had never heard of him! As I sketched a brief verbal portrait of the man, I could not help but reflect "how fleeting is fame" that a figure like Shaler, with such a towering reputation in his lifetime, should have lapsed into obscurity to the extent that even his name was unknown to his own lineal successor at the same institution just a generation later.

THE FIRST WORLD WAR

Americans' perceptions of the world and their own place within it, however, were to undergo a profound shake-up only a decade after Shaler's death. As we shall see, despite all the superficial appearances of change, the basic American attitudes that had crystallized in the 19th century were simply reinforced by the intensified impressions of an outside world that impinged upon the consciousness of the nation as a consequence of its involvement in World War I. It is a classic illustration of the ironic truth in the paradoxical French phrase *plus ça change, plus c'est la même chose:* "the more things change, the more it's the same thing."

The 17th- and 18th-century settlers who populated what was later to become the United States of America were largely English speakers from the British Isles, although they did not principally think of themselves as English or even British. They were, in fact, fleeing from England's control, with the aim of generating their subsistence by their own efforts and pursuing lives governed by their own concept of Christian beliefs rather than by those of the mother country.

A strong sense of national identity had yet to develop anywhere in the world (Bell 2001). Denizens of the British Isles tended to think of themselves as Yorkshiremen or Scots or Welsh and such; those of France spoke of being Provençal or Burgundian or Breton; Italy included Sicily, Naples, Venice, and the Piedmont all under separate ruling regimes; and Germany was a set of independent principalities until well into the 19th century (Garton Ash 1993). China was a group of provinces with different languages all under the control of rulers who were not even Chinese (i.e., Manchus; Fairbank 1992). Whatever sense of "nation" there was in India owed itself to the military control exerted by the English. To this day, much of the sense of national identity in South Asia is due to the perception of difference from the British "other" (Channa *in press*). Much the same could be said for the emergence of a sense of national consciousness among the Chinese as a consequence of the opium wars of the mid-19th century and the Boxer Rebellion and the collapse of the Qing (Manchu) Dynasty early in the 20th century (Warner 1972; Fairbank 1986).

World War I (1914–18) was really a Franco–German war largely fought on French soil (Keegan 1999). Although its participants referred to it afterward as "the great war" and the "war to end all wars" (Coffman 1968), it was really a resumption of the Franco–Prussian War of 1870–71 and a prelude to World War II (1939–45). The English, somewhat to their surprise, were allies of the French from the beginning. I say "somewhat to their surprise" because ever since the Norman invasion of Britain in 1066 the French had been the "hereditary enemy" just as the English in the hearts of the French were the "*ennemi héréditaire*" (Pasteur 1971, 751). Since the defeat of Napoleon at Waterloo by combined English and Prussian forces in 1813 and going back centuries, the English had looked on the French as the main source of a possible threat to their well-being. The Germans, on the other hand, were viewed in a different light. Not only is English a Germanic language (in spite of a huge influx of French words courtesy of the Norman Conquest), but English royalty in the form of the House of Hanover, with its sequence of Georges, was of German origin. Furthermore, there was a romantic impetus to trace the roots of the traditions of government surviving in the "English shire" back to "primitive folk meetings deep in the heart of the old Germanic forest," as Nathaniel Southgate Shaler phrased it for his American audience.

So the English found themselves for the first time in over 800 years allied with the French against the emerging German threat to European peace and national integrity. Because of those centuries of hostility toward the French and amity toward the Germans, the derogatory words that the English had built up to cast slurs against the national "other" were largely aimed at the French. Wartime alliances can change things rapidly, however; and the English-speaking peoples quickly adopted French stereotypes, if not their actual vocabulary (Barzun 1965, 171–172). There is another little twist to the picture. The French may have been the traditional "enemies" of the English, but they have always occupied a curiously honored realm in English perceptions. Since the time of Norman rule, a smattering of French has always been a sign of sophistication among the socially prominent in the British Isles, although it has been completely alien to the person in the street. As World War I approached, the Francophile enthusiasms of

King Edward VII and the English upper crust created what was referred to as the "entente cordiale" (St. Aubyn 1979; Weintraub 2001). This Francophile ambience in the first decade of the 20th century facilitated the subsequent military alliance with France.

America stayed on its own side of the Atlantic until very late in the game. In spite of misgivings articulated by more than a few, Americans joined the war with enthusiasm barely a year before it was over. More than a million Americans went "over there" in the summer of 1918, and the fresh troops and armaments were sufficient to tip the balance in what had been a long drawn-out stalemate, which the Allies could not have won without their participation (Coffman 1968, 364). An armistice was signed on November 11 and the fighting stopped; but nothing was actually solved in the long run since World War II, two decades later, just picked up where World War I had ended (Kessler 1971, 117; Weinreich 1946, 239; Eisenhower and Eisenhower 2001).

Although a strain of American isolationism reasserted itself in the aftermath of World War I and delayed American entry into World War II until the bombs fell on Pearl Harbor on December 7, 1941, the impact of that earlier war on Americans' perceptions of their place in the world had produced a major change (Coffman 1968, 364). Some who went to Europe stayed on in Paris as the "lost generation" and participated in avant garde artistic and literary circles (Mellow 1974). Some returned with their perceptions permanently altered. Even those who had remained in America were influenced by the wartime contacts between the Old and New Worlds. There were many ways in which those influences manifested themselves, but two particular currents of thought contributed to the perpetuation of the concept of "race." These were the treatment of the concept of "race" that had been developing in French anthropology, on the one hand, and the eugenics movement that had been growing in England under the sponsorship of Darwin's half-cousin, Sir Francis Galton, on the other. Both of these go well back into the 19th century and were not unknown in America, but it was the events of World War I that gave them the unfortunate impetus that was to afflict so much of the world as the 20th century went on.

THE FRENCH CONNECTION AND THE CONCEPT OF "RACE"

The field of anthropology, more so than any other, has been responsible for the formal consideration of "race" in the university world, and that in turn has vetted the concept for the public at large. This is not to say that there would be no acceptance of the concept if it were not for its treatment in academia, but it was the academic milieu—and particularly anthropology—which established its supposed legitimacy.

Anthropology, however, has multiple origins, as befits a field that has so many facets. The sexist wags of yesteryear facetiously defined anthropology as 'the study of man embracing woman.' At its most comprehensive, the field does try to deal with the human phenomenon in all its dimensions: biological, cultural–ethnographic, linguistic, and prehistoric. That is a tall order, and it is no surprise to discover that the coordinated effort to present all those aspects of the human condition has often collapsed in practice. Recently, anthropology departments at places such as Stanford University, the University of California at Berkeley, and Columbia University have exhibited various manifestations of such a collapse. Other American universities, such as Johns Hopkins and Princeton, never made the attempt in the first place. The first effort to create an enterprise that involved the joint efforts of archaeologists, biologists, ethnologists, and linguists—what is commonly referred to as the "four-field approach"—was undertaken, as I have already mentioned, by Paul Broca in Paris when he established his École d'Anthropologie as a department of the Collège de France in 1876 (Williams 1923). Broca's "School" was based on the outlook of the Société d'Anthropologie de Paris, which he had founded in 1859. It did not long survive his death in 1880, and no such unified entity exists in France today. In fact, to the French, the very word *anthropologie* now means only the biological part of the field.

In the 19th century, the terms *anthropology* and *ethnology* were used more or less synonymously. The outlook of Samuel George Morton and his cohorts was alternatively called the "American school of ethnology" and the "American school of anthropology." At one point, ethnology came to be associated with the study of "race." Today, however, ethnology is regarded as the study of human cultures only and has no implications for the biological aspects of human existence. Broca himself defined ethnology as the "science of human races" and contrasted this with "la science de l'Homme ou l'*anthropologie*" (1865, IX). Literally translated, that would be "the science of man." It is one of those linguistic ironies that speakers of languages where all nouns have gender perceive no sexism in using, as the French do, the designation *l'Homme* to mean humankind as a whole while English, with no gender associated with its nouns, now finds it unacceptably sexist to use the word *man* for the species as a whole. In spite of the Mrs. Grundy–like vigilance of the gender police, even the supposedly neutral word *humankind* has a *man* imbedded in it. For that matter, so does *woman,* but so far no one has made a fuss about it.

There were ethnological societies in both France and England dating from 1839 and 1843, respectively; but they tended to be more concerned with issues relating to the question of slavery and the treatment of the inhabitants of colonized portions of the world than with more general anthropological questions. After Broca's *Société* was founded in 1859, however, it served as the model for the Anthropological Society of London, established in 1863, and for similar societies established in Germany in 1869 and 1870. No full-scale enterprises along the lines of Broca's school emerged until the 20th century, but when they finally did, they were American and recognizably derived, even if at one or two removes, from the original French model.

It is generally accepted that the most important influence in establishing the discipline of anthropology in America was that of Franz Boas (1858–1942) and his 40-year career in the Department of Anthropology at Columbia University in New York (Spier 1959, 146; Mead 1976, 903; Lewis 2001). Boas was born in Germany, earned his doctorate in physics, and became a protégé of the physician and anthropologist Rudolf Virchow (1821–1902), who was founder and head of the Berliner Gesellschaft für Anthropologie, Ethnologie und Urgeschichte and one of the founders and long time head of the Deutsche Gesellschaft für Anthropologie (von Eickstedt 1937–40, 127; Ackerknecht 1953, 232 ff.). Boas assisted Virchow in the Ethnological Museum in Berlin before coming to America in the mid-1880s in search of professional employment.

In 1896, he was appointed lecturer in physical anthropology at Columbia University through the efforts of that extraordinary organizer Frederick Ward Putnam (1839–1915), himself an Agassiz protégé, who was curator of the Peabody Museum of

American Archaeology and Ethnology at Harvard (part of the same building complex that houses the Museum of Comparative Zoology and the botany and geology museums). In 1899, Boas became professor of anthropology at Columbia. Putnam, although he was on the anthropology faculty at Harvard, played a key role in organizing the anthropological portion of the 400th celebration of Christopher Columbus's arrival in America for the World's Columbian Exposition in Chicago in 1892, and Boas assisted him. He helped create the anthropology section of the Field Museum in Chicago; he then became curator of anthropology at the American Museum of Natural History in New York (1894–1903), where he put Boas on the staff; and he went on to found the Department of Anthropology and the Anthropological Museum at the University of California, Berkeley, between 1903 and 1909—all the while retaining his Harvard professorship (Kroeber 1915; Tozzer 1936; Stocking 1968; Mark 1980; Browman 2002).

If Putnam played a key role in establishing the anthropological programs at Harvard, Columbia, Chicago, and Berkeley, it was a structural and not an intellectual contribution. The mind-set behind these programs was strongly conditioned by the outlook of Franz Boas. Ironically, from the point of view of this book, Boas's importance in the development of the modern concept of "race" did not really have its main impact until well after his death. Boas in turn had been heavily influenced by his own anthropological mentor in Berlin, Rudolf Virchow, who was practically single-handedly the creator of German anthropology.

Virchow's model of the field was the one pioneered in Paris by Paul Broca (Ackerknecht 1953; Schiller 1979). Like Broca, Virchow favored polygenism as an explanation for human "racial" differences. Boas also never used an evolutionary perspective in dealing with anthropological matters. Unlike Broca, however, Virchow did not assume that "races" were fixed and innately different in their capabilities. His protégé, Franz Boas, in fact was famous for showing the change in metric proportions between ancestors and descendants in certain groups (Boas 1899, 1912), although for those of us who have spent years testing this sort of thing, it would appear that what he really showed was that one cannot generalize reliably about the metric characteristics of groups of people from a database that considers only two dimensions (Brace and Tracer 1992; Brace et al. 1993).

Boas's outlook had an enormous impact on American anthropological thinking, and, while his perception of the scope of the field can be seen to be a modified derivative of Broca's, the part that dealt with the matter of "race" had less of an effect on either the field of anthropology or the public at large. There were a number of reasons for this. First, Boas not only was German but he took a pacifist stance during World War I. This gave him something of the aura of a subversive foreigner to a public that was grappling with the issue of evaluating immigrants of various ethnic—and "racial"—identities. In addition, Boas's family background was Jewish, and there was a pervasive anti-Semitism in America, which had increased in strength after the American Civil War and lasted through much of the 20th century (Higham 1969). Finally, Boas wrote a letter to *The Nation* in October 1919 entitled "Scientists as Spies," containing innuendos concerning the actions of certain anthropologists during the war (Boas 1919).

While Boas, as one of its founders, had been president of the young American Anthropological Association from 1902 to 1908, the governing council of the association was so upset by his spy letter that they stripped him of his membership and voted to censure him at their meeting on December 30, 1919 (Stocking 1968, 273). He weathered the storm, however, and regained his standing with his colleagues to the extent that in 1932 he was elected president of the American Association for the Advancement of Science, the principal national organization representing professional scientific activities.

WILLIAM Z. RIPLEY AND THE MAGIC THREE

If Boas's views on "race" did not influence the way it was regarded outside the realm of academia, the milieu of World War I reinforced the strong, if poorly expressed, opinions on the subject held by the American public. In 1896, William Z. Ripley (1867–1941) delivered the Lowell Institute Lectures in Boston. Ripley was simultaneously assistant professor of sociology at the Massachusetts Institute of Technology in Cambridge and, like Boas, lecturer in anthropology at Columbia University in New York.

His presentations were initially given as a course of lectures on "physical geography and anthropology" at the School of Political Science at Columbia. These appeared as "The Racial Geography of Europe" in successive issues of the *Scientific Monthly* in 1897 and 1898 and were assembled in book form as *The Races of Europe: A Sociological Study* in 1899. This was based on no original research but simply represented a typological simplification of the European section of the "racial" classification of 1889 by Joseph Deniker (1852–1918), one of Paul Broca's disciples in Paris. Deniker is best known for his massive *Les races et les peoples de la terre: éléments d'anthropologie et d'ethnographie,* published in 1900, the year after Ripley's book appeared. Ripley's presentation then introduced Americans to what was generally perceived to be the latest and most sophisticated European thinking on the concept of "race."

The principal thing for which Ripley is remembered is his division of Europeans into three "racial" entities: "Nordic," "Alpine," and "Mediterranean"—Nordic simply, being Deniker's name for the *Teutonic* category favored by Nathaniel Southgate Shaler and his Gobinesque predecessors. Although Ripley did not stress this to the extent of those who followed his lead, implicit in his scheme was the idea that there were behavioral differences and capabilities characteristic of each of the three European "races." Ripley did not elaborate on these, but, as we shall see, his followers did so with a vengeance.

The rhetorical devices Ripley used had a powerful effect on his readers even if they seem an almost risible caricature in retrospect. When one looks at what he actually did, it is apparent that his approach was more that of mystical numerology than science. His trinity of "races" and the justification for their existence depended on the repeated use of one of the most powerful magicoreligious symbols in European cultural tradition, the sacred implications in the number 3. Thus, there were three European "races," neither more nor less, although no reason was given as to why this should be. Then, assessment of the identity of each "race" was said to depend on the combination of three traits: head shape, pigmentation, and stature. For the most part, these traits in turn were treated in tripartite fashion.

To start with the first of his dimensions, he declared: "The shape of the human head—by which we mean the general proportions of length, breadth and height, irrespective of the 'bumps' of the phrenologist—is one of the best available tests of race known" (Ripley 1899, 37). This is simply a declaration of faith in the absence of any tangible support. Then, he proceeded to dispense with one of his three cranial dimensions without saying why: "The form of the head is for all racial purposes best measured by what is technically known as the cephalic index. This is simply the breadth of the head above the ears expressed as a percentage of its length from forehead to back" (Ripley 1899, 37). This and the 19th-century tradition from which it sprang led to the portrayal in caricature of the physical anthropologist, calipers in hand, chasing after people to measure their heads, as the embodiment of "scientific" inanity. At least Ripley realized that neither the proportions nor the absolute size of the human head had any direct relation to "intellectual power or intelligence" (Ripley 1899, 40–43). Unfortunately, there are still some today who are fixated on comparing head size in different human groups in an attempt to defend assumptions concerning a presumed hierarchy of relative intellectual capability (e.g., Rushton 1995; Jensen 1998; Lynn and Vanhanen 2002).

The second of Ripley's key "racial" indicators was pigmentation, and he divided that into three aspects: skin, hair, and eyes. He started with the declaration that "The colour of the skin has been from the earliest times regarded as a primary means of racial identification" (Ripley 1899, 58), and he dealt briefly with the adaptive significance of pigment variation. He went on to note that "however marked the contrasts in colour between the several varieties of the human species may be, there is no corresponding difference in anatomical structure discoverable" (Ripley 1899, 58). That is tantamount to recognizing that separate adaptive traits are distributed as independent clines. This, as we now realize, is the main reason that the concept of "race" has no coherent biological validity. However, his a priori conviction in the reality of "racial" entities remained unshaken even if he was baffled by the fact that trait distributions do not correlate with each other. He concluded that the significance of skin color is unknown. At that point he declared: "We are compelled to turn to an allied characteristic—namely the pigmentation of the hair and eyes—for more specific results" (Ripley 1899, 63). True to his guiding tactics, he observed: "There are three reasons which compel us to this action" (Ripley 1899, 63). These he listed in order, starting with the recognition that eye color, unlike skin, is not affected by the environment. The second and third aspects—lightness of hair and eye being peculiarly European and the existence of differences between Europeans in their manifestation—are sufficiently at odds with each other so that the semblance of logic in his arguments begins to come apart at the seams.

When he dealt with stature, he did not impose his three-part treatment and simply declared the innate superiority of tall populations over others. This naturally led to the conclusion that relatively affluent nations and the better-off social classes within them are inherently superior. That argument is still widely popular among those who take it as a given that there is a hierarchy of intellectual capability among the various peoples and social classes in the world (Herrnstein and Murray 1994; Lynn and Vanhanen 2002).

Having made the arbitrary declaration that three European "races" can be documented by the use of three traits, he noted: "Three stages in the development of our proof must be noted: first the distribution of separate *traits;* second their association into *types;* and, lastly, the hereditary character of these types which alone justifies the term *races*" (Ripley 1899, 105). In this particular instance, the one–two–three form of his presentation is perfectly justified. Having set up the conditions deemed necessary for his proof, however, he felt no compunction whatever at immediately abandoning them: "Let it be boldly confessed at the outset that in the greater number of cases no invariable association of traits in this way occurs" (Ripley 1899, 105). Further, he noted that if a fourth or fifth trait were added, "our proportion of pure types becomes almost infinitesimal" (Ripley 1899, 107).

In spite of the fact that reality does not conform to the conditions he declared must be met before his three-"race" model can be confirmed, his conviction in its existence remained unshaken:

> Confronted by this situation, the tyro is here tempted to turn back in despair. There is no justification for it. It is not essential to our position that we should actually be able to isolate any considerable number, nor even a single one, of our *perfect* racial types in the life. It matters not that never more than a small majority of any given population possesses even two physical characteristics in their proper association; that relatively few of these are able to add a third to the combination; and that almost no individuals show a perfect union of all traits under one head, so to speak, while contradictions and mixed types are everywhere present. Such a condition of affairs need not disturb us if we understand ourselves aright. (Ripley 1899, 108–109)

At this point, the reader has every right to wonder why on earth we should believe anything Ripley said when he had convincingly demonstrated that the conditions for the proof of his argument simply do not exist. The answer, obviously, is that we should not. Questions remain concerning the nature of his stance. Where was he coming from? What was the basis for his defense of a position that is so patently irrational? What was the "logic" behind his stance? Ripley provides a clue in his formal definition of *race*. In what he claimed to be a quote from Broca's student Paul Topinard (1879), he declared: "Race in the present state of things is an abstract conception, a notion of continuity in discontinuity, of unity in diversity. It is the rehabilitation of a real but directly unattainable thing" (Ripley 1899, 111–112). Incidentally, although Ripley attributed that statement to Paul Topinard, I have never been able to find it in anything Topinard wrote. Even the post-World War II continuity of the Broca–Topinard tradition represented by the late Henri-Victor Vallois, who quotes that statement verbatim, used Ripley's version and not the purported Topinard original (Vallois 1953, 151).

Now if Ripley's definition of "race" sounds like gobbledygook, that's because it is. That however, is a classic illustration of the antiscience stance of Romanticism, which was treated in such magisterial fashion by the historian of ideas Arthur O. Lovejoy in his William James Lectures at Harvard in 1936. Lovejoy's assessment was discussed earlier in my consideration of Romanticism. As was mentioned there, the late 19th-century definition of "race" emanating from Parisian anthropology is the very embodiment of the "pathos of the esoteric," the "insight . . . reached, not through a consecutive progress of thought guided by the ordinary logic available to every man, but through a sudden leap whereby one rises to a plane of insight wholly different in its principles from the level of mere understanding" (Lovejoy 1936). That definition also is a fine manifestation of the "metaphysical pathos . . . the pathos of sheer obscurity, the loveliness of the incomprehensible" (Lovejoy 1936, 11–12).

Ripley's synthesis did not achieve its impact through becoming a best-seller, although it was successful enough so that its publisher commissioned the Harvard anthropologist Carleton Coon to write a revised version. This was published 40 years later minus the original subtitle—*A Sociological Study*—and dedicated to William Z. Ripley (Coon 1939). Coon, to his credit, removed the dimension of behavioral elements that Ripley's followers had attributed to his three European "races," and he eliminated the anti-Semitism of Ripley's text. It was, in fact, a completely different book.

As Coon noted, it was easy for Ripley's acolytes to tack psychological characteristics onto his threefold framework and speak of the "Nordic with his genius for leadership and government," the "stolid, unimaginative, plodding but virtuous Alpine," and the "gay, artistic, and sexy Mediterranean" (Coon 1939, 284). Coon illustrated the stereotypic behavioral characteristics some had attached to Ripley's "races" by quoting the light verse satire of his scheme penned by that extraordinary Oxford critic and essayist Hilaire Belloc for the *New Statesman:*

> Behold, my child, the Nordic man,
> And be as like him as you can:
> His legs are long—his mind is slow
> His hair is lank and made of tow.
>
> And here we have the Alpine race.
> Oh! What a broad and brutal face.
> His skin is of a dirty yellow
> He is a most unpleasant fellow.
>
> The most degraded of them all
> Mediterranean we call.
> His hair is crisp and even curls
> And he is saucy with the girls.

If Ripley's book was perceived more as a technical tome than as popular reading, it stimulated a second generation of works that had a much more inflammatory effect on the public at large. It is appropriate now to turn our attention to a couple of these.

MADISON GRANT

The first of these to be considered is *The Passing of the Great Race, or the Racial Basis of European History* by Madison Grant (1916 and three more editions by 1921). Grant (1865–1937) was a Yale graduate with a Columbia law degree, although he was not a practicing lawyer. He was a socially prominent Park Avenue bachelor, who styled himself as a "sportsman" and "hunter," and he had inherited enough money to live in posh comfort without having to do anything to earn an income. As founder and chair of the New York Zoological Society, he played a key role in creating the Bronx Zoo. He was proud of his descent from colonial ancestors and suspicious of the worth of many more recent immigrants. In particular, he was outspoken in his anti-Semitism and for years tried to get Columbia University to fire Franz Boas from his position as chair of the Department of Anthropology (Chase 1977, 164). As he wrote to U.S. Senator F. M. Simmons in 1912 after Boas had published his widely cited paper showing the changes in the cranial proportions of immigrants (Boas 1911): "Dr Boas, himself a Jew, in this matter represents a large body of Jewish immigrants, who resent the suggestion that they do not belong to the white race, and his whole effort has been to show that certain physical structures, which we scientists know are profoundly indicative of race, are purely superficial" (quoted in Chase 1977, 163). That last comment was a reference to the cephalic index—the length–width proportions of the head—which Boas's 1911 paper had shown to vary between generations of the same group. With the words "we scientists," Grant made a claim that was as much pure fabrication as were his assertions concerning the behavioral characteristics genetically linked to the three European "races." Clearly, he had taken his stance on the recognition of European "racial" divisions from Ripley.

His claims concerning the genetically determined behavioral proclivities had also been taken from previous authors, but, as more than one commentator realized, these were not identified (Lindsay 1917; Boas 1918; Snyder 1939, 231; Montagu 1942, 23; Gossett 1963, 357; Stocking 1968, 68). Those sources included *The Races of Men: A Philosophical Enquiry into the Influence of Race over the Destinies of Nations* by that controversial Edinburgh figure Robert Knox (1791–1862), who had opined that "Race is everything: literature, science, art—in a word, civilization, depends on it" (Knox 1862, v). His other principal 19th-century source was the unregenerate racist, Count Joseph-Arthur de Gobineau, author of the *Essai sur l'inegalité des races humaines* (1853–5). Another uncited source was the renegade Englishman Houston Stewart Chamberlain, whose *Die Grundlagen der neunzehnten Jahrhunderts* (1909 and translated into English in 1910 as *The Foundations of the Nineteenth Century*) provided fuel for the "racial" policies of Adolf Hitler's Third Reich (Field 1981).

The final main source of Grant's outlook, to which he gave brief mention, was the eugenics movement, which had been founded in England by Francis Galton (1822–1911), who was knighted for his activities in 1909. Galton's gambit was adopted and promoted in America by Charles Benedict Davenport, director of the Carnegie Institute–supported Station for Experimental Evolution at Cold Spring Harbor on Long Island, with consequences that were to affect U.S. immigration policy for half of the 20th century. This is treated at greater length in a subsequent section.

Here, it is appropriate to take a look at Grant's appraisal of what he declared "race" to indicate. His book opened with a preface written by Henry Fairfield Osborn (1857–1935), president of the American Museum of Natural History in New York and holder of a research professorship in zoology at Columbia University. Osborn had been trained in paleontology at Princeton and was well known for his writing on that and other topics and for his leadership role at the museum. He was also known to be colossally arrogant, pompous, and vain (Rainger 1991; Colbert 1994). Like Grant, he was a member of that self-conscious social elite which prided itself in its descent from the early English colonists of America. Both Grant and Osborn considered themselves members of what they called a "native American aristocracy" of superior "Nordic" ancestry, inherently better suited to govern than "lower types." (The designation "Native American" had yet to be applied to "American Indians.") This led them and others like them to denigrate popular democratic rule in a fashion we would now regard as profoundly un-American. As Osborn said at the end of his preface for Grant's new edition of 1918: "In the new world that we are working and fighting for, the world of liberty, of justice and of humanity, we shall save democracy only when democracy discovers its own aristocracy as in the days when our Republic was founded" (Osborn 1918, xiii).

There is an odd bit of irony to this. Although there may have been a sense of the "aristocratic" among colonial Virginians, this was clearly less the case with the New Englanders, to whom Osborn traced his own ancestry. This basic difference in regional traditions prior to the Civil War was clearly recognized by one who knew both, Nathaniel Southgate Shaler (1909, 33). John Adams, the second president of the nascent United States, exemplified the tradition of subsistence farming, where one cut one's own hay and split one's own fire wood as a matter of course (McCullough 2001). A century later, the fuel for the hearth and the food for the table of the self-designated scions of what they labeled America's "own aristocracy" (Osborn 1918, xiii) were no longer provided by the householder. Instead, the work was delegated to the "hewers of wood and drawers of water," who were characterized as "lower types" or "inferior races."

Neither Madison Grant nor Henry Fairfield Osborn ever, by their own work, generated the monetary means that allowed them to indulge in the life of privilege which they enjoyed. Both, however, were fervent advocates of the view that their right to the opulence which sustained their privileged existence was justified by the superior nature of their genetic heritage. In this picture of one-hundred years of change from the self-sufficiency of a John Adams to the luxuries purchased by the inherited wealth of a Grant or an Osborn, one can see individual manifestations of how the Republican Party of Abraham Lincoln, the "rail-splitter," with its recognition of the worth of an individual human no matter what the origin, wealth or color, became transformed into an organization characterized by a promotion of the maximum benefits to those who have been the recipients of inherited money or who have profited from the labors of others. The antecedents of Enron are painfully apparent.

Americans' self-image and perception of group identity had obviously undergone an enormous change between the initial Calvinistic settlers and their descendants two centuries later. The level of self-righteousness may not have changed, but the earlier vision that the path to ultimate salvation was to be found by obeying the will of God had radically altered. Salvation was not just an individual matter. The fatalistic acceptance of predestination of the earlier Calvinists had metamorphosed into a kind of faith in group salvation determined by "racial" identity.

Grant started with Ripley's three European "races" and claimed particular behavioral attributes for each: "The great lesson of the science of race is the immutability of somatological or bodily characters, with which is closely associated the immutability of psychical predispositions and impulses" (Grant 1918, xix). "Nordics," for example, were said to be "natural rulers and administrators," which accounted for England's "extraordinary ability to govern justly and firmly the lower races" (Grant 1918, 207).

For their part, "The Alpine race is always and everywhere a race of peasants" with a tendency toward "democracy" although "submissive to authority" (Grant 1918, 227). The "Mediterranean race" was held to be inferior to both Nordics and Alpines in "bodily stamina" but superior to them in "the field of art." Mediterraneans were said to be superior to Alpines in "intellectual attainments" but far behind Nordics "in literature and in scientific research and discovery" (Grant 1918, 229). For good measure, Grant recorded his particular scorn for "the Polish Jew, whose dwarf stature, peculiar mentality and ruthless concentration on self-interest" and whose presence in "swarms" in New York City was crowding out Grant's favored "native American of Colonial descent" and "Nordic type" (Grant 1918, 16, 63, 212).

Grant was an unapologetic white supremacist. While Grant regarded his Nordic as "the white man par excellence" (Grant 1918, 27, 167), with all others repeatedly referred to as "lower types" or "inferior races," he accepted Alpines and Mediterraneans as belonging to the "Caucasian race" for convenience of contrast with "Negroes," "Indians," or "Mongols" (Grant 1918, 65–66). This was applied to his discussion of "race" crossing: "The result of the mixture of two races, in the long run, gives us a race reverting to the more ancient generalized and lower type. The cross between a white man and an Indian is an Indian; the cross between a white man and a Negro is a Negro; the cross between a white man and a Hindu is a Hindu; and the cross between any of the three European races and a Jew is a Jew" (Grant 1918, 18). Given this, it is no surprise to find him applauding the "purpose and justification" of laws supporting segregation and "social discrimination" in the southern states in America: "as long as the dominant imposes its will on the servient race and as long as they remain in the same relation to the whites as in the past, the Negroes will be a valuable element in the community but once raised to social equality their influence will be destructive to themselves and to the whites. If the purity of the two races is to be maintained they cannot continue to live side by side and this is a problem from which there can be no escape" (Grant 1918, 87–88). This stance was exactly the same as that taken by Josiah Clark Nott in his advice to General O. O. Howard right after the American Civil War just a half-century earlier and subsequently reiterated without attribution by Nathaniel Southgate Shaler, although no mention is made of Nott's or Shaler's earlier expression of these self-same opinions. Not surprisingly, Grant approved of slavery as a means of compelling a "servient race to work and to introduce it forcibly to a higher form of civilization" (Grant 1918, 8). Again, the sentiments coincided precisely with those of Nathaniel Southgate Shaler (Shaler 1904, 187), although Shaler is unmentioned in Grant's text.

Grant's book was almost entirely devoid of anything that could count as factual support. There were no references backing up any of the myriad statements and assertions. The only anthropological "authority" cited was a mention in the introduction of William Z. Ripley and his *Races of Europe,* but for all his hints at a hierarchy of "racial worth," Ripley did not assert the association of behavioral characteristics in his assumed European "races." Ripley's formulation had been based on the outlook of Broca's school in Paris, and it carried the weight of what Americans regarded as the matured traditions of European scholarship. To this day, the intellectual stances of first "structuralism" and subsequently "postmodernism" have enjoyed enthusiastic admiration in America not because of intrinsic merit but from the prestige of having emanated from the French intellectual milieu.

Americans, comrades in arms with the French during World War I, accepted the French-verified conclusions regarding "racial" identification of the populations of the world. They were preconditioned to assume the validity of those assumptions because they coincided perfectly with what had been transmitted by informal American cultural traditions. What no one realized then or now was that the outlook of Broca's School owed a major debt to America in the first place. It has been observed that the Civil War swept away both the "slave civilization of the South" and the "entire intellectual culture of the North as well," and it took a half-century for a replacement to be installed (Strouse 2001, 10). The credibility of that portion of the replacement which dealt with "race" was enhanced by its assumed European lineage, but its real strength derived from the fact that it was essentially an American turkey come home to roost.

LOTHROP STODDARD

Following on the heels of the books by Ripley and Grant, an even more inflammatory work was produced by Lothrop Stoddard (1883–1950), *The Rising Tide of Color Against White World Supremacy* (1920). Stoddard was another of that coterie of old establishment figures, such as Grant and Osborn, who had inherited money as well as social status. He had received his law degree and a Ph.D. in history from Harvard and was a friend and protégé of Madison Grant. Since Grant wrote the introduction, it is not difficult to guess the tone of the volume: "The backbone of western civilization is racially Nordic, the Alpines and Mediterraneans being effective precisely to the extent in which they have been Nordicized and vitalized" (Grant 1920, xxix). Grant then declared that Stoddard had shown how the Nordics were in danger of being swamped by the rest of the world. However, "such a catastrophe cannot threaten if the Nordic race will gather itself together in time, shake off the shackles of an inveterate altruism, discard the vain phantom of internationalism, and reassert the pride of race and the right of merit to rule" (Grant 1920, xxx). Then in an extension of the theme in his own book, he added: "Democratic ideals among an homogeneous population of Nordic blood, as in England or America, is one thing, but it is quite another for the white man to share his blood with, or intrust his ideals to, brown, yellow, black or red men. . . . This is suicide pure and simple, and the first victim of this amazing folly will be the white man himself" (Grant 1920, xxxii). The whole text of Stoddard's book, as with that of Grant's, is without the benefit of a single supporting reference. The claim that the "specialized capacities" that "mark the superior races" are "relatively recent developments" which "are highly unstable" and genetically "recessive" (Grant 1920, 300–301) is completely undocumented. The same is the case for the assertion that "the more primitive a type is, the more prepotent it is. That is why crossings with the negro are uniformly fatal. Whites, Amerindians, or Asiatics—all are alike vanquished by the invincible prepotency of the more primitive, generalized and lower negro blood" (Grant 1920, 301). It was Franz Boas, reviewing Stoddard's book in *The Nation,* who pointed out that there was virtually no evidence offered in support of any of those value-laden claims and that they were completely at variance with the known principles of genetics (Boas 1920).

Stoddard's own blatant racism concluded the volume with sentiments that are very much in line with the earlier generation of British and American writers but phrased with a florid bombast that almost becomes a caricature of itself:

> Civilization of itself means nothing. It is merely an effect, whose cause is the creative urge of superior germ-plasm. Civilization is the body; the race is the soul. (Stoddard 1920, 300)

> Unless man erects and maintains artificial barriers the various races will increasingly mingle, and the inevitable result will be the supplanting or absorption of the higher by the lower types. (Stoddard 1920, 302)

> But one element should be fundamental to all the compoundings of the social pharmacopœia. That element is *blood*. . . . It is clean, virile, genius-bearing blood, streaming down the ages through the unerring action of heredity, which, in anything like a favorable environment, will multiply itself, solve our problems, and sweep us on to higher and nobler destinies. (Stoddard 1920, 305)

Not only was the extreme of genetic determinism unsupported by anything that could be called a factual basis, but the metaphor of blood "streaming down" from generation to generation was positively dripping in serological sogginess. As one critic observed, "Stoddard was proof of the ancient axiom that while it often helps, one does not need to be an illiterate in order to be an opinionated ignoramus in science. One merely has to be arrogant" (Chase 1977, 259).

There is one matter that should puzzle the reader with regard to the central theme articulated by both Grant and Stoddard. If their noble "Nordics" were so inherently superior, why should they be so threatened by their "primitive," "generalized," and "dark" competitors? Why would the inherently less able be expected to prevail? Why would a mixture between two groups, even if there actually were average differences in capability between them, automatically produce offspring who possessed only the capabilities of the lesser endowed of the parents? Even the most rudimentary grasp of genetic principles should lead to the expectation that inherited traits, whether dominant, recessive, or neither, are randomly distributed in the offspring of parents from two different populations. There just is no way that sexual reproduction can produce a new generation that has the characteristics of only one parent.

In 1918, the United States had just become involved in World War I as one of the combatants. At the same time, an increased number of dislocated Europeans were attempting to escape the displacement that the war had produced and were seeking asylum in an America that prized itself as being the "land of opportunity," where the key to a successful future was in the will to give things a try. Not only was America faced with the need to formulate its assumptions for governing the treatment of various components of the Old World on the field of battle, it also had to agree on some way to handle the burgeoning stream of Old World immigrants. With homegrown American prejudice now reaffirmed by "science" as presented to the public by Madison Grant and Lothrop Stoddard, it was possible to use this to shape public policy.

Those two supremely self-satisfied writers achieved a large following. Former President Teddy Roosevelt wrote to Grant that his book was "the work of an American scholar and gentleman; and all Americans should be sincerely grateful to you for writing it" (1933). It was translated into German and provided ammunition for Adolf Hitler in the writing of *Mein Kampf.* Hitler subsequently wrote Grant and referred to the latter's book as his "Bible" (Kühl 1994, 85). Warren G. Harding, while running for president of the United States, praised Stoddard's book in campaign speeches; and it was subsequently praised by another American president-to-be, Herbert Hoover (Chase 1977, 642; Kühl 1994, 61). Later, Stoddard even went to Germany, where his works were quoted in Nazi school textbooks, and he arranged a meeting with the German chancellor, Adolf Hitler (Kühl 1994, 61). By 1940 he wrote approvingly that the "Jews problem" is "already settled in principle and soon to be settled in fact by the physical elimination of the Jews themselves from the Third Reich" (Stoddard 1940, 189). America had not only provided Paul Broca and the Old World intellectual milieu with the basis for reifying the concept of "race" in the realm of "science" but it had helped justify the "scientific" basis for the Holocaust in the middle of the 20th century.

13

THE ETHOS OF EUGENICS

EUGENICS

The field known as "eugenics" did not contribute to the establishment of the concept of "race," but its proponents did assume the categorical reality of "races" as a part of its very reason for existence. The attempt to put eugenics into operation resulted in some of the most appallingly inhuman horrors perpetrated in the name of "science" of the 20th century. The word *eugenics* was coined by the British dilettante Sir Francis Galton (1822–1911) in his book *Inquiries into Human Faculty and Its Development* (1883), a work whose "intention is to touch on various topics more or less connected to that of the cultivation of race, or, as we might call it, 'eugenic' questions" (Galton 1883, 24–25) (Fig. 13–1).

The term itself is derived from the Greek roots for "good" and "origins" or "breeding." As Galton phrased it, the idea of eugenics was to promote "judicious mating" in order "to give the more suitable races or strains of blood a better chance of prevailing speedily over the less suitable" (Galton 1883, 25). Not only did this take for granted the existence of coherent biological entities called "races," but it assumed that some were "more suitable" than others. Furthermore, the contrast between the "more suitable races" and the "less suitable" is presumably self-evident because no criteria other than social prominence and net financial worth were ever offered to support such a judgment. Galton subsequently declared of eugenics that "Its first object is to check the birth-rate of the Unfit" (Galton 1908b, 323). The means of identifying the "unfit" and who should make such a decision were not spelled out until the American Model Sterilization Law was formulated some years after Galton's death and subsequently adopted and made compulsory by Adolf Hitler in Nazi Germany (Gillham 2001).

In order that the "more suitable" should prevail more "speedily," the promotion of the breeding of those superior "types" was offered as part of the eugenics agenda. In addition to such a positive recommendation, it advocated that "by means of isolation, or some other less drastic yet adequate measure, a stop should be put to production of families of children likely to include degenerates" (Galton 1908a, 2; Forrest 1974, 276). In this case, the word *degenerate* did not have the descriptively neutral connotation that Blumenbach had meant in his use of the Latin term meaning "departure from original form." Instead, it had the pejorative implication that the people being designated by that term had deteriorated to a level below the acceptable standards that were implicit in the Great Chain of Being hierarchy of worth assumed in Galton's view of the human spectrum in the world. Galton's 20th-century followers put the negative part of his program into effect first by regulating immigration and subsequently with programs of involuntary sterilization. Eugenic ideals lay behind the immigration-restriction procedures put

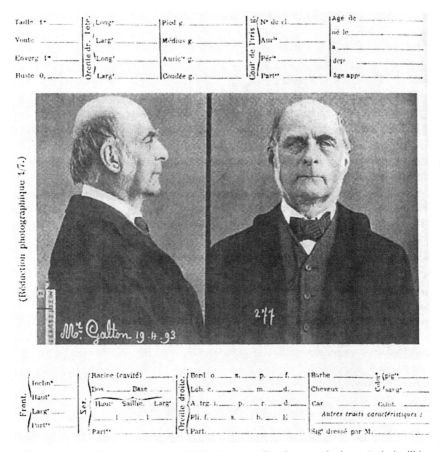

Figure 13–1   Sir Francis Galton, 1822–1911, age 71, photographed as a "criminal" in the Criminal Identification Laboratory of Alphonse Bertillon in Paris, 1893 (Gillham 2001, 234).

into place in the United States. More ominously, they were responsible for the deportation procedures in Nazi Germany and, ultimately, the extermination camps. Galton, however, was honored by the conferral of a knighthood and became Sir Francis in 1909 not long before his death (Forrest 1974, 281).

In his 1869 book *Hereditary Genius: An Inquiry into Its Laws and Consequences,* Galton had proposed a hierarchy of the peoples of the world based entirely upon his own untestable subjective assumptions. In his scheme, "the average intellectual standard of the negro race is some two grades below our own" (i.e., the Anglo-Saxon) (Galton 1869, 327). A second edition was published in 1892, which was essentially a reprint of the 1869 edition with a few errors corrected (editions of 1914 and 1962 also were reprints of the original text). Galton offered the purely subjective assertion that "The Australian type is at least one grade below the African negro" (Galton 1914, 328). In contrast, the Athenians of the fifth century B.C.E. were ranked as "very nearly two grades higher than our own," justified by the fact that they read and discussed "master-pieces" of intellectual activity that "are unsurpassed, and in many respects unequalled" (Galton 1962, 396–397). More than one commentator has noted that Galton obviously did not count the slaves, laborers, soldiers, and farmers who made up such a substantial proportion of the ancient Greek population when he was opining about the average intellectual capabilities of the people of classical Greece. When generalizing about the capabilities of his own countrymen and contemporaries, Galton declared that "the calibre of [the English] intellect is easily gauged by a glance at the contents of a railway book-stall" (Galton 1962, 398). His evaluation of the top of the spectrum of intellectual ability in the British Isles was based on his appraisal of the reputations of people of eminence: "The brains of the nation lie in the higher of our classes" (Galton 1901, 222). It is clear that in this and his other pronouncements, his conclusions were purely subjective. His assessment of the relative intellectual capabilities of Africans, Australians, Chinese, and others in his chapter "The Comparative Worth of Different Races" in his *Hereditary Genius* was simply a manifestation of ignorance and racial prejudice. He claimed to have discovered that "the Jews are specialized for a *parasitical* existence upon other nations" (quoted in Pearson 1924, 209). In a letter to the *Times* of London on June 6, 1873, he declared that Europeans were really not meant to live in Africa, but he offered a plan for improving the human situation there: "On that continent, as elsewhere, one population continually drives out another. We note how Arab, Tuarick, Fellatah, Negroes of uncounted varieties, Caffre and Hottentot surge and reel to and fro in the struggle for existence. It is into this free fight among all present that I wish to see a new competitor introduced—namely the Chinaman. The gain would be immense to the whole civilized world if he were to outbreed and finally displace the negro, as completely as the latter has displaced the aborigines of the West Indies" (quoted in Pearson 1924, 33).

Francis Galton was one of those supremely self-confident Victorian Englishmen who took his social and intellectual eminence as only fitting and proper. His father had intended him for a medical career, and he had pursued appropriate courses at Kings College in London and Trinity College in Cambridge before his father's death left him with sufficient wealth so that he never had to concern himself with the matter of earning a living. At that point, he immediately abandoned all efforts at finishing his medical training. This left him free to travel as he wished and dabble at various aspects of science for the rest of his life. He pursued weather mapping and discovered anticyclonic systems, he promoted the use of fingerprinting for personal identification (although he never gave credit to the medical missionary in Japan, Dr. Henry Faulds, who first realized the utility and devised and published the method of classifying fingerprints [Faulds 1880; Wilton 1938]), and of course he founded the eugenics movement.

In his autobiography, he declared that eugenic principles "ought to become one of the dominant motives of a civilised nation much as if they were one of its religious tenets" (Galton 1908b, 323). In fact, he looked on "eugenics not only as a science, not only as an art, but also as a national creed amounting, indeed, to a religious faith" (Pearson 1930, 3A:220). After Galton's death, one of his American disciples, Charles Benedict Davenport, actually used the title "Eugenics as a Religion" for one of his speeches in 1916 (Chase 1977, 161). As we shall see, eugenics came to play a major role in American life, and it joined with the German tradition of *Rassenhygiene* ("racial hygiene") after World War I to serve as the justification for what became the murderous policies of the Nazi government (Kühl 1994, 15). While Galton did not promote "compulsory marriage" of the genetically superior, he did promote a eugenic policy in which the "first object is to check the birth-rate of the Unfit" (Galton 1908b, 323): "I think that stern compulsion ought to be exerted to prevent the free propagation of the stock of those who are seriously afflicted by lunacy, feeble-mindedness, habitual criminality, and pauperism" (Galton 1908b, 311). The curious conceit that there are genetic backgrounds for poverty and "law-abidingness" still has its advocates (Herrnstein and Murray 1994; Rushton 1995; Lynn and Vanhanen 2002).

Galton provided financial support for the establishment of the Eugenics Record Office at the University of London in 1904 and for the Galton Laboratory of National Eugenics at University College in 1906, he founded the Eugenics Education Society in 1908, and his will endowed a chair of eugenics at University College in London. The director of the Galton Laboratory, Karl Pearson (1857–1936), subsequently became the first holder of the Galton Chair at University College (Fig. 13–2). With his conviction that intellectual ability owed far more to heredity than environment, Francis Galton has been regarded as "the progenitor of the nature–nurture controversy" (Galton 1875; Pastore 1949, 20). In his own words: "the residue with which alone I am about to deal, may be concisely and sufficiently expressed by the words 'race' and 'nurture'. . . . I look upon race as far more important than nurture" (Galton 1873, 116). This was simply stated as a given, and he never made any attempt to test for the relative contributions of

Figure 13–2 Karl Pearson, 1857–1936, pencil drawing made in 1924, reprinted in Gillham (2001, 271).

those two realms, let alone the consequences of an interaction between them. At the same time, he assumed the existence of differences in the behavioral characteristics associated with "different races," and, again, there was not even the faintest concern for setting up a test to determine whether that assumption was true or not.

Karl Pearson, Galton's self-described "disciple," was also his first biographer (Pearson 1914, 1924, 1930) and portrayed him as "one of the greatest, perhaps the greatest scientist of the nineteenth century" (1930, 3A:vi). The American psychologist who popularized use of the intelligence quotient (IQ), Lewis M. Terman, calculated that Galton had an IQ "not far from 200" and that his half-cousin Charles Darwin rated about 135 (Terman 1917, 209; 1926, 44; 1940, 294; Chase 1977, 237). This agreed with Pearson's feeling that Galton was a more important intellectual figure than Darwin, a conclusion profoundly at odds with the judgment of most historians and philosophers of science (Ghiselin 1969; Mayr 1982, 1991; Browne 1995, 2002; Dennett 1995; Brace 1997b).

A recalculation correcting for Galton's age as a child when the supposed criteria were assessed rated his IQ at 160 (Forrest 1974, 7). There are still those who refer to him as a "genius" (Forrest 1974, 288; Jensen 1998, 7). As a young man, Galton had his head assessed by a phrenologist, and he reported that "he gave me I think a very true character (self-esteem was remarkably full)" (quoted in Pearson 1914, 157). From the accounts of his life, it is clear that Francis Galton was an egocentric snob, and one would not have needed to go to the dubious expedient of examining the shape of his head to determine how pleased he was with himself. What is surprising is the number of people, both during his life and long after, who have taken his judgment of himself at face value.

On the other hand, there are real reasons to query the magnitude of his scientific reputation. His attempt to deal with heredity led him to formulate what he called the "law of ancestral heredity" (Moore 1986, 650), but it in effect was based on pre-Mendelian assumptions of blending inheritance (Gillham 2001). Galton never did attempt to incorporate the insights of the field of genetics as it grew after the rediscovery of the work of Gregor Mendel in 1900. As we have already seen, the assumptions he made concerning the levels of intelligence of different individuals and groups were sloppy in the extreme. One recent reappraisal has gone so far as to call him "an intellectual mediocrity, a sham, and a villain" (Graves 2001, 100).

If that last may seem a little strong, the late Nobel Prize biologist Sir Peter Medawar commented, in his review of a more recent biography of Galton, that "In fact, the idea that some of Galton's thinking reveals him as a spiritual fascist cannot be dismissed as an unfounded calumny" (Medawar 1975, 83). At the same time, another thoughtful critic put it like this: "Like the Bourbons, Galton forgot nothing and learned nothing during the three decades of great advances in the scientific knowledge of human heredity and development since the original publication of these pseudo-data in 1869. Thus in 1901, in his Huxley lecture . . . Galton was still measuring individuals by the size of their incomes" (Chase 1977, 103). The reference to the Bourbons was to the famous assessment made by the 18th-century French diplomat Talleyrand of the French royalty of the *ancien régime,* and a version of that same quote was used to characterize the career of one of Galton's intellectual heirs, the living American racialist Arthur R. Jensen (Brace 1999c). As far as equating "intelligence" with income or social status is concerned, "one glance at Burke's Peerage and Baronetage is enough to prove otherwise: murder, madness, incest and idiocy lurk on every page" (Bilger 2002, 18).

EUGENICS EXPORTED TO AMERICA

Galton's eugenic vision found enthusiastic converts in America. Shaler felt privileged to meet in him London and to visit various scientific and social functions "illuminated by his presence" (Shaler 1909, 257). There were two avenues by which Galtonian hubris came to the United States of America. Both were to have a long-term impact on human life in the 20th century. One was subsequently exported with lethal consequences for 6 million Jews in Nazi Europe. The other continues to affect the lives of virtually everyone in America as well as Britain and, to a lesser extent, elsewhere.

One of the most direct avenues for the transmission of Galton's views was Charles Benedict Davenport (1866–1944). Davenport met Galton in London in 1902 and, in emulation of Galton's creation of 1904, set up the Eugenics Record Office for America at Cold Spring Harbor, Long Island, New York, in 1910. Davenport was director of the Cold Spring Harbor Station for Experimental Evolution, which had been funded by the Carnegie Institution since 1904; and he continued as the head of both organizations until he retired in 1934 (Allen 1986, 227–228; Kühl 1994, 68). Further, when Madison Grant and Henry Fairfield Osborn organized the Galton Society for the Study of the Origin and Evolution of Man in the spring of 1918, Davenport was elected chair (Chase 1977, 165–166).

Davenport came from the same kind of family background as did Osborn and Grant, although without the money inherited from a previous generation's involvement with banking and industry. He was born on the family farm in Stamford, Connecticut, and farming in New England had never been a means of generating much in the way of surplus wealth. However, his father's real estate and related activities in Brooklyn Heights, New York, made it possible for him to go to Harvard, where he earned a B.A. and a Ph.D.; and after stints of teaching experimental morphology at Harvard and the University of Chicago, he moved to the Carnegie Institution–supported laboratory at Cold Spring Harbor on Long Island, where he spent the rest of his career (MacDowell 1946). He was at home in the same social milieu as Osborn and Grant and shared their outlook. When he set up the Eugenics Record Office in 1910, he hired Harry Hamilton Laughlin (1880–1943) as its superintendent. Laughlin, with what amounted to a "courtesy" doctorate in science from Princeton (Pauly 2001, 224), had been teaching agriculture at North Missouri State Normal School. Like Davenport, he was energetic, serious, "utterly humorless and rigid," and "totally dedicated to the cause of reform through eugenics" (Allen 1986, 236). The two of them in conjunction with a few other kindred souls helped ensure that Sir Francis Galton's elitist ideology continues to influence how the beneficiaries are chosen to receive what the American socioeconomic system has to offer as the twenty-first century gains momentum.

Davenport and Laughlin had no doubts that those they looked on as representatives of Galton's "unfit" were so for genetic reasons. They regarded it as sound eugenic policy and in the national interest to prevent the propagation of such innate undesirables.

Laughlin, then, formulated his "model sterilization law" to serve as a means of the "uprooting of inborn defectiveness" (Laughlin 1914, 13, 117–120; 1922, 446–451). This provided a legally phrased rationale for sterilizing people incarcerated in penal institutions for a variety of crimes assumed to be the consequences of their genetic heritage. State after state adopted variously amended versions of that "law," and involuntary sterilization became a growing practice in America. For the next six decades, approximately 1,000 people per year were involuntarily sterilized. As of 1992, there were still 22 states with sterilization laws on the books (Finkelstein 1992).

The legality of involuntary sterilization was challenged in court in Virginia in the late 1920s in the definitive case called *Buck v. Bell*. This was given to the U.S. Supreme Court to decide in 1927. Carrie Buck was an 18-years-old inmate of the State Colony for Epileptics and Feeble-Minded, whose illegitimate infant daughter had been placed in a foster home (Kevles 1985, 110). Harry H. Laughlin had testified at the earlier circuit court hearing that her sterilization was warranted because her immorality and feeblemindedness were congenital and that she was "a potential parent of socially inadequate offspring" (Laughlin 1930, 19). Her mother's marriage had been terminated because of "infidelity," and the Red Cross nurse who participated in the proceedings that committed Buck to the State Colony declared that her infant "gave evidence of mental defectiveness at an early age" (Laughlin 1930, 17). How that decision could have been made is more than slightly problematical since Buck's baby could not have been more than a couple of weeks old at the time, and judging the mental prospects of a neonate is virtually impossible. Laughlin testified that both Buck and her mother scored poorly on the Stanford-Binet intelligence test and were in the "low-grade moron" category (Laughlin 1930, 19): "These people belong to the shiftless, ignorant and worthless class of antisocial whites of the South" (Laughlin 1930, 17). The illegitimate child was said to demonstrate Buck's "immorality, prostitution and untruthfulness," which manifested themselves despite the "good environment" of her foster home (Laughlin 1930, 19; Tucker 1994b, 101).

When the case came before the U.S. Supreme Court, the chief justice, former U.S. President William Howard Taft, assigned the task of writing the majority decision to Justice Oliver Wendell Holmes. Holmes, at the end of a long and distinguished career, would be more happily remembered if he had chosen to retire somewhat earlier. The Court had accepted the argument that Buck's out-of-wedlock pregnancy had been due to her lack of competence, and Holmes phrased the justification for her sterilization in these words: "It is better for all the world, if instead of waiting to execute degenerate offspring for crime, or to let them starve for their imbecility, society can prevent those who are manifestly unfit from continuing their kind. The principle that sustains vaccination is broad enough to cover cutting the Fallopian tubes. . . . Three generations of imbeciles are enough" (quoted in Laughlin 1930, 52). The state of Virginia had suppressed the evidence that the reason for her pregnancy was that she had been raped by a relative of the foster family with whom she had been living (Gould 1984, 17). Although she had been demeaned as not having taken advantage of the "good environment" offered to her, it should have been obvious that one member of that family had evidently taken advantage of *her*. She was then placed in the State Colony for Epileptics and Feebleminded to protect the identity of her rapist. For this, she was blamed as a congenital incompetent and her sterilization was declared to be legally justified. The still-vigorous tradition of

Galtonian bigotry continues to regard her treatment as right and proper (Lynn 2001, 23–24).

GERMANY

That same year, 1927, Germany passed its first sterilization law. Then, when Hitler became chancellor in 1933, one of the first things he did was to push for making it compulsory. This was formally accomplished on what for the French was Bastille Day, July 14, 1933. It was an almost word-for-word rendition of Laughlin's "model sterilization law." In Germany, however, sterilization was carried to an extent never dreamed of in America. If 60,000 or so sounds like an appalling number of Americans to have been forcibly sterilized in the course of the 20th century, Germany had forced sterilization on some 375,000 people in the half-dozen years between the passage of its "hereditary health" law and the outbreak of World War II (Chase 1977, 350). By the time the war was over in 1945, Germany had accomplished the involuntary sterilization of some 2 million people (Chase 1977, 135). This, however, was just the tip of the iceberg. Although, as we shall see, America had been applying a eugenic perspective at the "racial" level to shape its immigration policy, Hitler and his Nazi Party were to use it first for deportation and finally for extermination.

Financial support for Nazi "racial" policy was established by the Rockefeller Foundation, which provided funds for the Kaiser Wilhelm Institute for Anthropology, Human Genetics and Eugenics in Berlin–Dahlem (Kühl 1994, 20; Watson 1998, 196). Described as "one of the Nazi regime's most notorious betrayers of scientific ethics" (Koenig 2001, 1981), that institute was later headed by Otmar von Verschuer, whose former student and protégé, Josef Mengele, became the infamous "camp doctor" at Auschwitz (Nyiszli 1960, 61; Müller-Hill 1998, 226). Mengele's equipment for his notorious "experiments" was provided by the Berlin Institute. He in return shipped body parts, organs, and blood samples back to that anthropological institute marked "War Material—Urgent" after the subjects of his "research" died from his attentions (Nyiszli 1960, 63).

After the war, the Kaiser Wilhelm Institute metamorphosed into the Max Planck Institute, and many of the participants in the sordid wartime activities of that society quietly shed their connections with its reprehensible past and were rewarded with institutional and academic positions of probity and prestige in genetics, psychiatry, and anthropology (Watson 1998, 188). None of the multitude of people interviewed for their memories of the roles of their colleagues or relatives during the Nazi era could remember any manifestation of anti-Semitism or callous racism on the part of the directors of the Institute for Anthropology, even when confronted with the blatantly racist words of its former heads, Eugen Fischer and Otmar von Verschuer. As one of von Verschuer's former protégés put it, "there was a universal amnesia" (quoted in Müller-Hill 1998, 168). Over half a century later, the Max Planck Institute has finally made a full, if belated, apology for the acts of its intellectual ancestor (Koenig 2001).

Meanwhile, in his justification for genocide, *Mein Kampf* (originally written in 1925 and 1927), Adolf Hitler declared that the nation he envisaged "*must set race in the center of all life. It must take care to keep it pure*" (1943, 403; italics Hitler's). In a 1934 conversation with Herman Rauschning, he revealed an aspect of his thinking which was years beyond that of his contemporaries at the same time that he was articulating a position of cynical barbarism that was unique:

> I know perfectly well, just as well as those tremendously clever intellectuals, that in the scientific sense there is no such thing as race. But you, as a farmer and cattle-breeder, cannot get your breeding successfully achieved without the conception of race. And I as a politician need a conception which enables the order which has hitherto existed on historic bases to be abolished and an entirely new and anti-historic order enforced and given an intellectual basis. . . . I have to liberate the world from dependence on its historic past. . . . And for this purpose the conception of race serves me well. It disposes of the old order and makes possible new associations. France carried her great Revolution beyond her borders with the conception of nation. With the conception of race, National Socialism will carry its revolution abroad and recast the world. (quoted in Rauschning 1940, 232)

Given his cynical use of words that belie the discoverable reality of the human world, it is no surprise to find that he did the same thing in regard to what he portrayed as the most important and "evil" threat to German existence, the Jews. Anticipating the comment that Judaism is simply a religion, he denounced "this first and greatest lie, that the Jews are not a race but a religion." His rebuttal was simply the unsupported assertion that "The Jew has always been a people with definite racial characteristics and never a religion" (Hitler 1943, 306–307).

In Germany, the concern for the hereditary worth of individual members of the population led to the identification of those considered "unfit" and provided the "justification" for their compulsory sterilization. Then, as World War II approached—and of course the Germans knew when it would occur because they instigated it—Hitler declared that the ultimate eugenic practice of "euthanasia" would begin as soon as the war started. While that term implies "good death" or "mercy killing," it was really a euphemism for murder. It started with children but soon was applied to adults who were considered feebleminded, epileptic, mentally disturbed, or not normal in a variety of ways. By 1941, some 70,000 people had been killed.

The sheer quantity of people who had vanished in hospitals and mental institutions led to uneasy questions about what had happened (Friedlander 1996, 39, 48, 85). To avoid that awkwardness, the killing centers were then moved eastward, mostly out of German territory and into the areas that Germany had overrun early in the war. Killing of the handicapped continued until the end of the war, but, more ominously, that earlier eugenic exercise served as a trial run for the much more drastic applications that ensued. As one observer has noted, "The euthanasia killings proved to be the opening act of Nazi genocide" (Friedlander 1996, 22). The whole procedure of disguising the gas chambers as showers, of luring the unsuspecting in with the trappings of medical examination, and then, after gassing them, of cremating the corpses in giant ovens was perfected first in the treatment of increasing quantities of the handicapped and institutionalized (Pressac 1989; Fleming 1993; Proctor 1995, 3).

From this lethal beginning, it was but a small intellectual step from dealing with large numbers of those individually deemed "unfit" to considering groups collectively to be manifestations of life unfit for living—*lebensunwerten Lebens* (Friedlander 1996, 14). Germany accepted the "racial" typology of William Z. Ripley and the characteristics attributed to those "races" by Madison Grant and Lothrop Stoddard. Under the direction of Reichsführer Schutz-Staffel (SS) Heinrich Himmler, who was also chief of the German police, and with the aid of his deputy Reinhard Heydrich, extermination camps—*Vernichtungslager*—were set up in occupied Poland and people of lesser "racial" worth than the "Nordic" Germans were brought in by the trainload for systematic annihilation. The principal victims were Jews, but Gypsies were also considered "aliens" and killed by the thousands. Slavs were also regarded by the Germans as being inferior, and quantities of them were also exterminated, as were Hungarians in some number (Levi 1959; Lengyel 1972; Wiesel 1972, 1995). As many have realized in retrospect, this was the embodiment of eugenics gone berserk (Kevles 2003).

Among the most vivid of the first-person reports on what went on in those forced labor and extermination camps is the account of the Auschwitz and Buchenwald survivor Elie Wiesel. Wiesel had been born in the town of Sighet in Transylvania, which was part of Romania and became part of Hungary by the time he left. As he described it, Sighet was a typical Hasidic Jewish *shtetl* (Wiesel 1995, 4). Yiddish was the language of the home, but he also spoke German, Romanian, and Hungarian. Later, he was to become fluent in French and, subsequently, in English. In May 1944, the whole Jewish ghetto of Sighet was rounded up by the Gestapo, put on a train, and transported to Birkenau, the reception center for Auschwitz in southern Poland (Wiesel 1972, 37). None of them had heard of Auschwitz, the German name for Oswiecim, or its reputation before they arrived. Wiesel was not quite 15 at the time and found out about the horrors of the place as soon as he got there, when he witnessed a truck full of children and babies dump its load right into a ditch that had a blazing bonfire in it (Wiesel 1972, 41). The glare from the chimneys of the crematory ovens, kept going night and day, lit up the night sky (Nyiszli 1960, 38). One Hungarian woman, who subsequently lost her husband, her two children, and their grandmother, asked about one of the ovens on her arrival and was told that it was a "camp bakery" (Lengyel 1972, 34). Later, she discovered that the Birkenau ovens, dealing with over 700 corpses per hour, were disposing of over 17,000 every 24 hours (Lengyel 1972, 81). She survived because of her skills as a physician and her resolve to write everything down after the war was over since "the world must know about this. It must know the truth" (Lengyel 1972, 79). She did indeed do this, recording that the Germans had "liquidated" over 1.3 million people at Auschwitz in the 3 months starting with Elie Wiesel's arrival in May 1944 (Lengyel 1972, 82). Subsequently, Wiesel himself wrote so effectively about the atrocities that he was awarded the Nobel Peace Prize for his efforts in 1986.

Oddly enough, however, in Germany there is a lack of written documentation of what was an agreed-upon national policy. This was in spite of the well-known German compulsion for keeping written records of all official activities. Actually, that compulsion did preserve detailed records of the design and construction of the gas chambers and industrial-sized crematory ovens. Documentation of their architecture and work slips for the construction crews plus correspondence were all preserved (Pressac 1989). What is missing is the articulation of the rationale behind their construction and intended use. Clearly, it was a policy that came from the top—that is, from Adolf Hitler himself. Hitler perceived of the Jews as the source of Germany's defeat in World War I, although he was hardly alone in such a view (Breitman 1991, 49). Anti-Semitism runs through German writings starting way before Hitler's *Mein Kampf* and going all the way back to Martin Luther's *Von den Juden und jren Lugen* (*On the Jews and Their Lies*, 1543), but it took on increasingly strident tones after Hitler's accession to power in 1933.

There were repeated references in the press to the Jewish "problem" or the Jewish "question" and endless unspecific comments about a "solution" to it.

From Hitler on down, however, that "solution" was almost always used in the form of euphemism or indirection. When Himmler sent Hitler a memorandum on March 23, 1941, declaring "I hope to see the very concept of Jewry completely obliterated," Hitler agreed but declared that the idea should remain a "top secret" (Müller-Hill 1998, 48). Shortly thereafter, Alfred Rosenberg, Reichsminister of the Occupied Eastern Territories, held a conference to mark the opening of the Frankfurt Institute for the Investigation of the Jewish Question (March 26–28, 1941). At that time, he declared that the aim of the "total solution" was "genocide (*Volkstod*) of the Jews" (Müller-Hill 1998, 49). Late in the fall of the same year, Rosenberg addressed the German press at a briefing saying that the "final solution"—*die Endlösung*—to the "Jewish Question" had begun: "the problem can only be resolved by a biological elimination of the entire Jewish population of Europe. The Jewish question will only be resolved for Germany when the last Jew has left German soil, and for Europe when no Jew remains on the European continent this side of the Urals . . . . we cannot permit ourselves to say these things in public today. It is self-evident that we should neither speak nor write about the setting of political goals" (November 18, 1941, quoted in Müller-Hill 1998, 51).

It is almost as though the organizers of the horror were showing signs of guilt in their refusal to speak of what they were actually promoting. Closer attention to their careers belies this, however, since it is apparent that they were completely without shame. They occasionally expressed complete confidence that their actions were fully justified. On the other hand, they evidently were aware of what people who do have an active conscience would think if they knew.

Most of the time Hitler and his officials used euphemisms in public. Even the notes recording the major decision to carry out mass exterminations made at the Wannsee Conference, chaired at that Berlin suburb by Heydrich on January 20, 1942, were couched in veiled language (Noakes and Pridham 1988, 1127–1135; Breitman 1991, 219, 229–231; Goldhagen 1996, 157). "Special treatment," "definite solution," and "final solution" were the favored designations. Privately, they were often more explicit. On February 2, 1942, Hitler conveyed his eugenic vision to Himmler and a number of evening guests: "Today we must conduct the same struggle that Pasteur and Koch had to fight. The cause of countless ills is a bacillus: The Jew. . . . We will become healthy if we eliminate the Jew" (quoted in Breitman 1991, 234). When the organizer of extermination for the area that included Auschwitz, the chief of police and of the SS in Lublin, was ordered to report on the progress of the operations to Hitler on October 7, 1942, he reported that Hitler's reaction was "Faster, get the whole thing over with faster!" (quoted in Müller-Hill 1998, 60).

Obviously, Hitler could hardly have been so successful without massive cooperation (Goldhagen 1996, 15). Despite the "universal amnesia" and lack of specific written records, there was both widespread knowledge of what was going on and at the same time equally widespread denial of that knowledge. As the Auschwitz survivor and chronicler Primo Levi put it, "most Germans didn't know because they didn't want to know. Because indeed, they wanted *not* to know. . . . the typical German citizen won and defended his ignorance . . . he built for himself the illusion of not knowing, hence not being an accomplice to the things taking place in front of his very door" (Levi 1986,

381). Clearly, a large portion of the German public shared Hitler's belief that Jews were inherently and unalterably different from Germans, a malevolent force of evil, and a continuing menace. As a recent German commentator put it, "Everyone knew that the Jews and the mental patients were being killed, but no one was allowed to say so. The highest, most sacred principle of German fascism, extermination, was an open secret and had to remain so. . . . Hitler allowed the German people to satisfy their desire for extermination while still being able to say they were forced into it all, and that they had known nothing" (Müller-Hill 1998, 104). The still-controversial conclusion of a major survey of the evidence is that "The inescapable, fundamental truth is that for the Holocaust to have occurred, an enormous number of ordinary Germans had to become Hitler's willing executioners" (Goldhagen 1996, 15). The German version of Galton's "religious faith" in eugenics had truly diabolical consequences.

"RACE" AND EUGENICS APPLIED TO THE SHAPING OF AMERICA

In the Western Hemisphere, social and political control is largely in the hands of people who have immigrated within the last 400 years. A concern for the nature and qualifications of the participants in the processes of government became formalized with the framing of the U.S. Constitution at the end of the 18th century. Much attention was focused on assigning the reins of governing to "native born Americans," the people identified by Madison Grant and his ilk as the American "aristocracy." The language of the Constitution referred to voters and officeholders as "men," and women were not accepted as part of the voting process until passage of the 19th Amendment in 1920 (Hole and Levine 1971, 30). Furthermore, it was taken for granted that those men in control were "white." This was such a foregone conclusion that it was not explicitly stated. Threats of "foreign" influences, presumably of a political and/or military nature, were the main worries concerning the viability of a United States of America governed by "native born Americans" expressed by the "founding fathers"—or "founding brothers" as they have recently been called (Ellis 2000)—such as George Washington, John Adams, and Thomas Jefferson. That continued to be the way things were perceived until the time of the American Civil War. At that time, it was actually stated that "only the white native and the immigrant or European population are entitled to or ever exercise the rights of citizenship" (Busey 1856, 129). This really marks the beginning of evident concern for a consideration of "race" in matters of government.

In the *Dred Scott* decision by the U.S. Supreme Court in 1857, Chief Justice Roger B. Taney, writing for the majority, declared that people of African origin "had no rights the white man was bound to respect." He added that "no one of that race has ever migrated to the United States voluntarily; all of them had been brought here as articles of merchandise" (quoted in Birnbaum and Taylor 2000, 79–80). Scott was the black slave of a person who moved from Illinois to Wisconsin and then sent him to Missouri. Wisconsin did not allow slavery, but the chief justice ruled that Congress did not have the power to deny the status of property in Missouri without due process of law as stated in the Fifth Amendment to the Constitution. Since Taney regarded all the descendants of Africans brought unwillingly to America as "property" and not as people, Scott therefore had no rights as a person.

Four years later, the Civil War was to initiate changes, although things did not quite go the way that one might have thought. President Abraham Lincoln signed the Emancipation Proclamation on January 1, 1863. The 13th Amendment, passed in 1865, abolished slavery, and the Civil Rights Act of 1866 overturned the *Dred Scott* decision (Gressman 1952, 1328). Doubts about the constitutionality of that act were removed by the 14th Amendment of 1868, which asserted that all born or naturalized citizens had equal protection under the law. Then, the 15th Amendment, enacted in 1870, declared that the right to vote could not be denied due to "race, color or previous condition of servitude" (Gressman 1952, 1333). The impetus for the passage of those amendments owed much to the efforts of that longtime antislavery figure Massachusetts senator Charles Sumner (Higginbotham 1978, 387).

Things went downhill from there, however. Federal troops were removed from the South in 1877, and Reconstruction came to an end (Horsman 1981). The Civil Rights Act of 1875 was invalidated by the Supreme Court in 1883 (Paul 1972, 2); and in the *Plessy v. Ferguson* case of 1896, the Court, citing the established existence of segregated schools among other things, promoted the principle of "separate but equal" (Birnbaum and Taylor 2000, 166). This was accepted for over half a century, until it was overturned in the decision by Chief Justice Earl Warren in the *Brown v. Board of Education* case, 1954, when he declared that "in the field of public education the doctrine of 'separate but equal' has no place. Separate educational facilities are inherently unequal" (quoted in Kluger 1977b, 573). The Confederacy may have lost the war on the battlefield, but by the end of the 19th century, it had triumphed in the political arena by instituting the sharecropping system, lynching, legalized segregation, and Black Codes. It took more than another half-century for things to get back to where they should have been in 1870. Even now, Chief Justice William Rehnquist of the U.S. Supreme Court has expressed the view that *Plessy v. Ferguson* was correct and should not have been overturned (Herbert 1999, WK21). In order to attain a position to impose his repressive convictions, it is clear that he deliberately lied to the Senate at the time of his confirmation (Dean 2001, 284). As represented by the record of that powerful legal figure who had once challenged black and Hispanic voters in Arizona and predicted that the *Brown* decision would be overturned, evidently there is still a strong undercurrent of feeling that equality of opportunity should not be protected by law (Dean 2001; Rosen 2001, 15).

Up until the time of the Civil War, perceptions of "racial" difference in effect had no bearing on issues such as citizenship and voting rights in the United States. The real indigenous Americans were simply not part of the system, and those imported from Africa were accorded the status of domestic animals—property—and not people. The legal system in Latin America derived from Roman law, which had provisions for the treatment of slaves where human rights were emphasized over the property rights of masters (Elkins 1968, 250–251). In English-speaking America, however, the formal rules governing human behavior were based on Anglo-Saxon legal traditions, and the social systems that had generated them lacked a slave category. Hence, there were no laws dealing with the treatment of slaves. Slaves in the United States then had no legal rights whatsoever.

In the northern reaches of American settlement, where African slaves were either not present or so few in number as to count as curiosities, the matter of any role that they might play in the social structure just never arose. The 17th-century Boston Puritan Cotton Mather, while not rejecting the idea of slavery, nevertheless argued for the humane treatment and Christianization of slaves. In a 1706 sermon, he admonished Boston slave-holders: "It has been cavilled by some that it is questionable whether the Negroes have Rational Souls, or no. But let that Bruitish insinuation be never Whispered any more. Certainly, their Discourse, will abundantly prove, that they have Reason. Reason showes itself in the Design which they daily act upon. The vast improvement that Education has made upon some of them, argues that they are Men, and not Beasts that you have bought, and they must be used accordingly" (quoted in Osofsky 1967, 37). From Rhode Island to New York and on southward, the increasing number of people of African origin made questions concerning their status and capabilities more likely to arise. Thomas Jefferson, for example, presented a stereotypic picture of African mental capacities in his *Notes on the State of Virginia* (1787): "it appears to me that in memory they are equal to whites; in reason much inferior, as I think one could scarcely be found capable of gracing and comprehending the investigation of Euclid; and that in imagination they are dull, tasteless and anomalous" (Jefferson [1787] 1800, 143).

Those conclusions were contradicted by the example of the freeborn black farmer Benjamin Banneker, author of a respected almanac. Banneker had taught himself astronomy and mathematics, and he sent Jefferson a copy of his almanac as proof. His skills were so highly regarded that he was employed by the architect Pierre L'Enfant to help carry out the surveys he was hired to make for the construction of the city that was to become the American capital, Washington, D.C. Banneker's competence in surveying and in astronomical calculation clearly showed a grasp of Euclid at the very least. In his letter to the then secretary of state, he chided Jefferson for failing to live up to the principles articulated in the Declaration of Independence, which Jefferson had written (Bedini 1972). Jefferson conceded Banneker's knowledge of trigonometry but regarded his letter as "very childish and trivial" (quoted in J. C. Miller 1977, 76–77). In his *Notes on Virginia,* Jefferson had also written of what he perceived as an innate lack of poetic capability in people of African ancestry and of their lack of inventiveness in narrative presentation. Even before America declared its independence, the black poet Phyllis Wheatley had been acclaimed by John Hancock and others in Boston; and the list of poets, narrators, storytellers, and novelists of African origin since that time has been a continuous contradiction to Jefferson's prejudice (Gates 1985, 7–8).

Jefferson's conclusions were based on observations of people whose lives, opportunities, and education were entirely controlled by the conditions of slavery. At the outset, he had eliminated any consideration of the evidence for intellectual accomplishments and verbal skills afforded by the residents of the areas from which American slaves had originally been derived—that is, Africa itself. Some of that evidence was not unknown to the providers of slaves for the American South.

The generalizations about black intellectual capabilities offered by the living racialist Arthur R. Jensen, professor emeritus of educational psychology at the University of California, Berkeley, are almost exactly the same as Jefferson's conclusions, although aided by a formidable statistical armamentarium. In Jensen's scheme, level I mental ability is identified as "rote memory," and African Americans are as good as anyone else. Level II refers to "reasoning," and here they do not rate so high (Jensen and Inouye

1980). Even more than was the case for Jefferson, there is no faint concern for whether the conditions from which those conclusions arose were comparable for the "black" and "white" groups.

It was the Civil War, however, that really raised the issue of "racial" intellectual capability above the level of inconsequential speculation. Constitutional amendments 13, 14, and 15 abolished slavery and generated a whole new cohort of American citizens and voters. In many instances, their lineage as "native born Americans" went back every bit as far as that of the so-called aristocracy celebrated by Madison Grant and Henry Fairfield Osborn. Amendments 14 and 15 dealing with citizenship and voting were vigorously opposed by the advocates of "states' rights," who felt that the imposition of a single federal standard on each of the individual states was a manifestation of tyranny. The rallying cry of "states' rights" goes back to the outlook of Thomas Jefferson, although it is particularly associated with the proslavery stance of John C. Calhoun (1782–1850), longtime senator from South Carolina (Gressman 1952, 1327; J. C. Miller 1977, 88, 217; Higginbotham 1978, 388; Marszalek 1998). Subsequently, the "strict construction" focus of the states' rights advocates, emphasizing the letter and not the spirit of the law, allowed the enactment of the Black Codes or "Jim Crow" laws, which by the end of the 19th century had returned the African American population to a condition that came close to slavery in everything but name (Gressman 1952, 1327; Woodward 1966). In the last decade of the 20th century and now as the 21st has begun, the United States Supreme Court under the leadership of Chief Justice William Rehnquist is ignoring the intent of the Constitution and the Congress to allow the states to act unjustly behind the shield of 'sovereign immunity' (Noonan 2002). It would appear that a majority of the Court advocates a return to the ethos of the Jim Crow era at the end of the 19th century.

The U.S. Constitution had not specified conditions for citizenship, but in 1790, the year after the Constitution was formally adopted, Congress passed a law permitting application for citizenship on the part of "free white persons." It was tacitly assumed that such would be the only people interested in citizenship, but even then there was no stipulation that applications were *restricted only* to "free white persons." The Civil War was to raise questions concerning the qualifications for citizenship and for voting rights in a manner that had never been considered by an earlier generation, and prominent among those questions was a much more emotionally charged focus on "race." Anticipating that, the aging John C. Calhoun, in a speech before the Senate on January 4, 1848, declared that "we have never dreamt of incorporating into our Union any but the Caucasian race—the free white race. . . . Ours, sir, is the Government of a white race" (Calhoun 1848, 98). In the same speech, he added "in the whole history of man, as far as my knowledge extends, there is no instance whatever of any civilized colored races being found equal to the establishment of free popular government, although by far the largest portion of the human family is composed of these races" (Calhoun 1848, 98). At that, he was talking about Mexicans and "Indians." He had yet to even imagine the implications of the 14th and 15th Amendments, and he died before the matters arose.

Another element was soon to be added to Americans' perceptions of "race" and citizenship. The earlier picture of a nation of farmers was being altered by the rise of manufacturing industries, which, to an increasing extent, were thriving with the assistance of immigrant laborers, who in due course became a new generation of Americans. Many of these were European, and initially there were no barriers to their immigration.

Along with industrial expansion came a vast proliferation of railroads. The transcontinental connection was completed in 1869. The continentwide expansion of rail lines also made extensive use of immigrant labor, and a substantial amount of this was from China. The heightened awareness of the criteria relating to citizenship that grew out of matters arising as a result of the Civil War raised concerns relating to the qualifications of immigrants that had not been pondered before. One such criterion was "race" and the idea that different abilities, strengths, and weaknesses were inherent in different "races." With post–Civil War America identifying itself to an increasing extent in "racial" terms, it followed that legislation leading to the control of immigration by "race" was only to be expected (Higham 1969, 379).

The legal importation of Africans as slaves had ceased in America in 1807 (Smedley 1993, 215), and slavery had been ended by the Civil War; but "racial" sensitivity had been raised to a level of national concern. The quantity of Chinese railroad workers generated sufficient alarm so that passage of the Chinese Exclusion Act of 1882 was only to be expected. This was the first piece of national legislation that used "race" as one of the criteria relating to immigration and potential citizenship in the United States of America (Gyory 1998, 254). In the discussion preceding its passage, the growing concern for the "racial" nature of immigrants was expressed by Maine Senator James G. Blaine: "The question lies in my mind thus: either the Anglo-Saxon race will possess the Pacific slope or the Mongolians will possess it" (speech of February 14, 1879, quoted in Gyory 1998, 3). The Chinese Exclusion Act then became the precedent for future restrictive legislation where the matter of "racial" identity became increasingly important. It was renewed in 1892, 1902, strengthened in 1904 and 1917, and then made iron-clad in 1921 and 1924, being revoked as a matter of political expediency only in the midst of World War II in 1943 (Gyory 1998, 254). Senator Blaine's verbiage was echoed much more passionately by the Sons and Daughters of the Golden West just after World War I, when they declared their dedication to the preservation of California as "it has always been and as God Himself intended it shall be—the White Man's Paradise" (quoted in Ten Broek et al. 1968, 46).

With a tide of refugees fleeing war-torn Europe late in the 19th and early in the 20th centuries and in light of the assumptions of differential "racial" worth expounded by the Nathaniel Southgate Shalers and later by the Madison Grants and Lothrop Stoddards of the country, America became increasingly involved in formulating regulations concerning who should be allowed to immigrate. In Boston in 1894, three wealthy Harvard graduates from the class of 1889 formed the Immigration Restriction League. In honor of his role in shaping their outlook, they made Shaler one of the ten vice-presidents of the league (Livingstone 1987b, 154). Grant was to be given the same honor after World War I (Günther 1927, 260). Assisting their agenda, Massachusetts Senator Henry Cabot Lodge, Harvard class of 1871 and another of Shaler's protégés, urged Congress to institute a literacy test as part of the process of qualifying for immigration. In his words, "It is found that the literacy test will bear most heavily upon the Italians, Russians, Poles, Hungarians and Greeks and very lightly, or not at all, upon English-speaking emigrants or Germans, Scandinavians, and French" (quoted in Appel 1971, 127). This was right at the time that William Z. Ripley was publishing on *The Races of Europe,* and all the countries mentioned in Lodge's speech were considered to be "racial" entities. The bias in favor of what Ripley called "Nordics" and against his other European "racial" categories is patently evident.

Congress did pass a literacy test requirement in 1896, but it was vetoed by President Grover Cleveland in 1897. Subsequent literacy test bills were passed in 1913 and 1915 and vetoed by President William Howard Taft. In 1917, anti-immigration sentiment had risen to the extent that Congress was able pass an immigration act designed to stem the tide of free immigration. It included a literacy provision and banned all Asian immigration. Support was sufficiently strong so that Congress was able to override the veto of President Woodrow Wilson.

Henry Cabot Lodge had been one of the first half-dozen to earn a Ph.D. from Harvard and had been professor of history at that university before being elected to the U.S. Senate. As head of the Senate Foreign Relations Committee and riding the tide of anti-immigrant and isolationist sentiment after the First World War, he led the Senate in rejecting President Wilson's attempt to bring the United States into the League of Nations. Whether or not that actually sped up the events that led to World War II is still considered debatable, but it certainly constituted a fatal blow to any prospects for effectiveness on the part of that ultimately powerless league.

Meanwhile, the perception of "race" in relation to immigration qualifications was becoming ever more a focus of concern. As one of the founders of the Immigration Restriction League wrote in an article entitled "The Restriction of Immigration" early in the 20th century, "The question is a race question, pure and simple . . . . it is a question as to what races shall dominate in this country" (Ward 1904, 236).

The 15th Amendment to the Constitution had removed the barrier of "race" or "color" to the qualifications for voting, but the strict constructionists could insist that, since those words were not included in the phrasing of the 14th Amendment, the provisions for naturalization of the 1790 congressional statute still applied. While former slaves were citizens by right of birth in the United States, immigrants—aliens— who were not "white" could not qualify to be naturalized citizens. In 1914, a man who had been born in Japan but graduated from high school in Berkeley, California, and attended the university there for 3 years applied for citizenship in Hawaii, where he was raising his family in an English-speaking home. His application was rejected because he was not "white" (*Takao Ozawa v. United States* in Hing 1993, 227).

Then, in 1920, a Hindu immigrant from India was granted citizenship in Oregon since he claimed identity as a "Caucasian." As was true for the case regarding the Japanese applicant, the subsequent decision for a unanimous Supreme Court was written by Justice George Sutherland, the court's "expert on racial hygiene" (Novick 1989, 357). The "racial" classifications offered by the anthropology of the time were considered, and the Court noted that since Ripley's Mediterranean category could be extended to include the people of India, the applicant's claim to "Caucasian" status could be recognized. Then, with a bit of verbal juggling that was the exact opposite of strict constructionism, the opinion concluded that, although the applicant was "Caucasian," he was not "white." His application for citizenship was rejected and his right to own property terminated. Furthermore, the immigrants from India who had become naturalized citizens over the past 15 years or so were retroactively stripped of their citizenship (*US v. Bhagat Singh Thind* in Hing 1993, 227–231; Zia 2000, 32–33).

The hair-splitting distinction between "Caucasoid" and "white" was not motivated by a regard for the literal meaning of the words themselves but by a primary concern for invidious distinctions of "race." As in the case of *Plessy v. Ferguson* a generation earlier, the issue was social perception and not biological reality. In that previous case, the plaintiff, Homer Plessy, was only one-eighth African in ancestry. In both cases, the blatant manipulation of the language to circumvent both logic and justice was a patent manifestation of racism.

Under the leadership of Republican Congressman Albert Johnson, a "rabidly anti-immigrant, anti-radical and anti-Communist from the State of Washington" (Allen 1986, 247), and with the help of Henry Cabot Lodge, a provisional Immigration Restriction Act was proposed at hearings of a committee of the U.S. House of Representatives. The provisional act of 1921 for the first time set up quotas for European immigrants. These amounted to 3% of those of the nationality in question who were present in the United States as recorded in the census of 1910 (Handlin 1959, 94).

As chair of the House Committee on Immigration and Naturalization, Representative Johnson was also chair of the Eugenics Research Association, whose secretary was Harry H. Laughlin, superintendent of Davenport's Eugenics Record Office (Kamin 1974, 19). Johnson appointed Laughlin official congressional "eugenics expert," and he testified on the "biological relationship" between certain kinds of immigrant and "social degeneracy" (Pickens 1968, 66). Grant made a deposition, and Stoddard also testified before the committee; they were regarded with admiration by Nazi Germany as the "spiritual fathers" of the immigration restriction law taken as a model by the Germans (Kühl 1994, 38). The National Origins Act of 1924—the Johnson Act of 1924, sometimes called the Johnson-Lodge Act—allotted a figure of 2% of the number of foreign-born residing in America as of the year 1890 as the number who would be permitted to immigrate from that particular country (Kamin 1974, 27). East Asians, however, were excluded from U.S. citizenship or naturalization (Hing 1993, 52). Although the Chinese were given a reprieve in 1943, the basic provisions of the National Origin Act of 1924 remained the law of the land for the next 40 years.

President Calvin Coolidge signed the act with the approving comment, echoing Madison Grant and Lothrop Stoddard, that "America must be kept American" (quoted in Chase 1977, 274). In retrospect, America would have remained just as American whether that regulation had been enacted or not. It is the nation that shapes the people rather than the other way around. Words and phrases may be added to the lexicon from a wide variety of sources, but the language remains a clearly identifiable version of English. Despite the misguided enthusiasm of the eugenicists, immigrants inevitably raise children who are completely American after a generation, no matter what the parents' origin.

After the attack on Pearl Harbor near the end of 1941, the Japanese were immediately perceived as the stereotypical "enemy." Inevitably, this made things hard for the quantities of Americans of Japanese ancestry. After the Chinese Exclusion Act of 1882 shut off the flow of immigrants from the Asian mainland, it was compensated in part by an influx of laborers from Japan seeking work in Hawaii and the western coast of the United States (Hosokawa 2002). When war with Japan was formally declared by President Roosevelt on December 8, 1941, the majority of the population—Americans of European ancestry—immediately perceived Japanese Americans as potential saboteurs or spies for Japan.

Alarm was expressed about the numbers of Japanese concentrated near military bases and airfields in California. Only later was it realized that those installations happened to be situated adjacent to prime agricultural land. It was the farming opportunities that had attracted Japanese immigration and not any nefarious intent to sabotage the American military. The alarm raised was so great, however, that it led to the perpetration of what has to count as the least admirable act of the promoter of the "New Deal," President Franklin D. Roosevelt. This was Executive Order 9066, issued February 19, 1942 (Conrat and Conrat 1972). Nearly 3 years later, the Supreme Court declared the "relocation centers" unconstitutional (Spicer et al. 1969, 253); but meanwhile well over 100,000 Japanese Americans were removed from the houses and farms they thought they owned and sent inland away from the coast to "internment" centers in Arizona, Arkansas, Colorado, Idaho, Iowa, Utah, and Wyoming (Genesway and Roseman 1987). These were de facto concentration camps, and their new inmates brought along only those possessions that could be packed into a duffle bag and two suitcases (Genesway and Roseman 1987; Irons 1989). After their eventual release, the difficulties involved in reclaiming what had once been their property proved to be largely insuperable.

When he was attorney general of California, Earl Warren testified in support of the removal of the Japanese over a decade before he was appointed to the Supreme Court. Later, he articulated his regrets (Warren 1977, 149), and it has been suggested that this may have been what lay behind his record of sympathizing with the plight of minorities in his role as chief justice (Kluger 1977a, 44). The Japanese removal was clearly a manifestation of racism, and it ultimately led to an apology from President Reagan in 1988 along with a tax-free reimbursement of $20,000 to each of those who had survived the ordeal (Bishop 1988).

14

HENRY FORD AND THE ETHOS OF THE HOLOCAUST

THE ANTI-SEMITISM OF HENRY FORD

Late in 1918, the American multimillionaire and the first to use the assembly line in the manufacture of automobiles Henry Ford (1863–1947) bought the *Dearborn Independent,* a small-town weekly newspaper. In early January 1919, it gained the subtitle *The Ford International Weekly* (Nevins and Hill 1957, 321). In order to identify his own views, he added a feature called "Mr. Ford's Own Page," although it was principally written by a Canadian-born journalist, William J. Cameron. Since Ford did not sign what was written, even on his "Own Page," he could deny that he knew about or was responsible for what was printed whenever it got him into trouble. His chief witness in a libel trial in 1927 argued that Ford had neither read nor seen the articles that had led to the charge against him (Richards 1948, 97). In fact, however, the editor and the writers were in regular communication with the owner and, although he would periodically deny that he really knew what had been proposed in its pages, the views expressed in print were his and not those of the writers (Richards 1948, 91).

As early as 1915, Ford declared that World War I had been started by "German-Jewish bankers" in order to enrich themselves (Pool and Pool 1979, 85; Baldwin 2001, 59). He also claimed that "one of the great factors that brought on the Civil War and made full settlement of the issues impossible was the Jew" (quoted in Richards 1948, 96). Then, starting in the May 22, 1920, issue of the *Dearborn Independent,* the first of more than 90 installments of virulently anti-Semitic essays appeared. The title of the first of these was "International Jew: The World's Foremost Problem" (Nevins and Hill 1957, 311). The articles were unsigned, but they may have been written by Dr. August Müller, a staff member of the *Dearborn Independent* placed there by Dr. Edward A. Rumely, a close friend of Henry Ford and an active member of a German propaganda ring in America during World War I (Cohn 1967,160). It is more likely, however, that the writer was W. J. Cameron, who shaped "Mr. Ford's Own Page" and was so visibly distraught when Ford ostensibly apologized for his anti-Semitism and halted publication of the *Dearborn Independent* in 1927 (Singerman 1981; Baldwin 2001, 242). Starting on June 26, 1920, selections from the *Protocols of the Meetings of the Learned Elders of Zion* were excerpted along with unsigned editorial commentaries (*International Jew* 1920, 1921a,b, 1922). There were 24 "protocols" in all, and they purportedly laid out the strategy of a "secret" Jewish plot to gain political and economic control of the entire world through deceit and subterfuge.

THE PROTOCOLS OF THE ELDERS OF ZION

The story of the writing and publishing of the *Protocols* is filled with contradictions and uncertainties, but one thing has been clearly established: those activities were both plagiarisms and forgeries (Bernstein 1921, 17; 1935, 18; Cohn 1967, 77–78; Segel and Levy 1995, 11). The "world-conquering plans" of the "Elders of Zion" came right out of a "trashy novel," *To Sedan*—one of a series called *Biarritz–Rome*—written by Hermann Goedsche in 1868 (Bernstein 1935, xi; Segel and Levy 1995, 61). Goedsche had been fired from a minor position in the German Post Office for being involved in a forgery aimed at smearing a liberal public figure, Benedic Waldeck, and turned to writing for a right-wing newspaper, *Die Preussiche Kreuzzeitung,* and cranking out fictional potboilers under the pseudonym "Sir John Retcliffe" to make a living (Cohn 1967, 33, 84). The rhetoric in the *Protocols* is essentially that found in Goedsche's chapter "In the Jewish Cemetery in Czech Prague" (Bernstein 1935, xi, 16–17; Segel and Levy 1995, 66). Goedsche, who had demonstrated that he had no qualms about forgery, also used the same words elsewhere and attributed them to an unnamed rabbi at an imagined Jewish congress at Lemberg, the supposed "Rabbi's Speech," which he avowed was an actual occurrence and not simply another manifestation of the fiction he had been producing (Bernstein 1935, 285–292; Cohn 1967, 269–274).

At that, Goedsche, the known forger, had engaged in plagiarism and simply copied the words from the ideas presented in a fictionalized dialogue in Hell between Machiavelli and Montesquieu that had been published 4 years earlier by the Parisian lawyer Maurice Joly, *Dialogue aux enfers entre Machiavel et Montesquieu* (1864). When both texts are printed on facing pages, the extent of the plagiarism is immediately obvious (Bernstein 1935, 371–397). All Goedsche did was to use the cynical and authoritarian stance of Machiavelli and attribute it to Jews as a plot to achieve world domination.

Joly's book was a satire on the callous and arbitrary practices of the dictatorship of Napoleon III in France, and since criticism of the government was illegal during the Second Empire (*Deuxième Empire*), he spent 15 months in prison for his efforts (Cohn 1967, 73). As it was, Joly himself has been accused of having "shamelessly copied" from an earlier novel by Eugène Sue, *Le juif errant* (*The Wandering Jew*), of 1844–45 (Eco 1989, 489). While Sue does speak of callous and mind-destroying authoritarianism, he does so only briefly and attributes it to the efforts at world domination by the Jesuits (Sue 1844, 109). Joly had almost certainly read Sue, whose novels were very popular at the time; but the words in Joly's prolonged *Dialogue* are clearly his own. That obviously was not the case for Goedsche and the generators of the *Protocols*. Joly may have built upon a longstanding anti–status quo tradition which included a Machiavellian program said to have been a source of the French Revolution late in the 18th century and subsequently carried on deliberately by Napoleon I (Webster [1924] 1967, 238, 409–414).

The *Protocols* were concocted in France during the last decade of the 19th century under the direction of Pyotr Ivanovich Rachkovsky, the head of *Okhrana* in Paris. *Okhrana* was the Russian secret police (Cohn 1967, 77). Evidently, the initial version was written in flawed French and only later translated into Russian by its fabricators. Early in the 20th century, the *Protocols* were sometimes said to have originated among the Freemasons rather than the Jews (noted in Bernstein 1935, 60). There was also the wildly unlikely view that they were a Jewish–Masonic product (Bernstein 1935, 45). That would have been only slightly less improbable than attributing them to a conjoint Judeo–Islamic undertaking.

Although more than one version of the *Protocols* was distributed as the 20th century got under way, the one that was to have the most influence was that printed by a Russian Orthodox "mystic" employee of *Okhrana,* Sergei Nilus (Bernstein 1921, 9; 1935, 30; Cohn 1967, 69). The protocols were included in the revised (second) edition, 1905, of Nilus's book *The Great in the Small and Antichrist Considered as a Near Political Possibility* (Nilus 1905; Cohn 1967, 87; Singerman 1981, 48). The revised edition of that book in 1917 was to have a far greater impact, one that has echoes which continue to the present. Both 1905 and 1917 saw revolutions in Russian political life, with the 1917 event destined to make a permanent change in the way Russia was ruled (Figes 1997). Nilus's book was supposed to bolster support for the Romanov regime of Tsar Nicholas II by creating a caricature of the alternative set up as a Jewish scapegoat. This fabrication was so successful that it influenced social and political opinions for the remainder of the 20th century and on into the 21st.

In the 1917 version, Nilus made the claim that the *Protocols* had been created and read by Theodor Herzl at the First Zionist Congress in Basel, Switzerland, late in the summer of 1897 (Bernstein 1921, 10, 60). At that time, however, the *Protocols* existed only in French, and while Herzl could speak and read French, the Congress was run entirely in German. Furthermore, it was completely open to the public, with no secret sessions (Cohn 1967, 69). Herzl, a German Jew from Hungary, had published his call for a Jewish state the previous year (Herzl 1896) and was principally responsible for organizing that congress, of which he had been elected president. Since it and his book articulated the ideals which led to the founding of the state of Israel, Herzl has been recognized as the founder of Zionism and father of the Israeli nation (Cohn 1967, 69, 229).

With the murder of Tsar Nicholas II and his family and the end of the First World War in 1918, one era closed and a new one began (Steinberg and Khrustalëv 1995; Figes 1997). However, there was no change in the issues that had led to World War I in the first place. The "Great War"—"the war to end all wars"—was really just the first act in a drama that was to resume with heightened ferocity two decades later as World War II (Coffman 1968). Germany had never accepted the reality of defeat in World War I. At the end of the conflict, Kaiser Wilhelm—and later Adolf Hitler—blamed the Jews for Germany's defeat (Field 1981, 259). "In Germany, there had been no sense that their role in generating World War I had been unjustified and there was a comparable failure to face the fact that the war had been fairly lost. Instead, the scenario was constructed that their inability to continue generating the weaponry and personnel for victory had been caused by a 'stab-in-the-back' by the 'international financial community,' a code name for 'the Jews,' themselves stigmatized as an 'inferior race'" (Brace 1997a, 13). As one perceptive analyst noted, "as soon as it became apparent that Germany was going to lose the war, those who had led the country to disaster hastened to throw the blame upon the Jews, who were held responsible both for the war itself and for Germany's failure to win it" (Cohn 1967, 130).

At the same time, the Romanov dynasty ended in Russia and Communism was imposed by a Bolshevik dictatorship. The founder of Communism, of course, was Karl Marx, who was Jewish. In the minds of many, then, Russian Communism was a manifestation of Jewish domination: "No informed person any longer doubts that Bolshevism is controlled and directed by a mysterious hierarchy of Jewish financial wizards" (Winrod n.d. [but clearly just before World War II], 22). This, of course, was precisely the view of Hitler's loyal propaganda minister Josef Goebbels (Cohn 1967, 203). It should be obvious that the paranoia in these views provided highly fertile ground for the dissemination of the inflammatory fabrication represented by the *Protocols* in Nilus's book.

After World War I was over, Nilus's rendition of the *Protocols* was translated from Russian into English, French, German, and other European languages (see the list in Cohn 1967, 292–296). One English version got into Henry Ford's hands and provided the fuel for that anti-Semitic diatribe *International Jew,* published between 1920 and 1922 in the pages of the *Dearborn Independent* and reprinted in four volumes issued by the Dearborn Publishing Company, of which Henry Ford was the president (*International Jew* 1920, 1921a,b, 1922): "All in all *The International Jew* probably did more than any other work to make the *Protocols* world famous" (Cohn 1967, 159).

Even after that outpouring was complete, the *Independent* ran a second series of anti-Semitic pieces from 1922 to 1925 (Baldwin 2001, 200 ff.). One of their targets was Aaron Sapiro, who had created the National Council of Farmer's Cooperative Marketing Associations in 1922. Ford, who cherished the memory of his own beginnings on a rural family farm, was annoyed that a Jew should be working with farmers since he accepted the common stereotype expounded in the *Protocols* that Jews were not primary producers but parasites profiting from the labors of others. In 1920, the *Independent* had flatly asserted that "The Jew is not an agriculturalist" (Baldwin 2001, 207). In 1924, a series of articles insinuated that attempts to organize farmers' marketing efforts were meant to exploit them and not to help them. Sapiro wrote Ford in January 1925 requesting a retraction. He received no answer, and the smears and unsupported denunciations in the *Independent* continued. Shortly after an article denouncing "New York Jewish bankers" and asserting "World Cotton Control by Sapiro Plan" appeared in April 1925, Aaron Sapiro sued for libel in the amount of a million dollars "to vindicate myself and my race" (Baldwin 2001, 211). The case against Henry Ford and the Dearborn Publishing Company opened in the spring of 1927, and its progress was closely followed and discussed in newspapers throughout the country.

A mistrial was declared when a Ford minion leaked to the press allegations of irregularities and a Jewish attempt to bribe one of the jurors before the case was decided. A new trial was scheduled for September; however, the negative publicity was hurting car sales, and Ford lost the will to continue airing his dirty linen (Baldwin 2001, 224). With the retirement of the Model T and the imminent appearance of the Model A, Ford wanted to counter the bad impression that the libel case had been making on the public. He then had a full apology to the Jews individually and collectively printed over his signature, promising to withdraw the *International Jew* from print and refrain from publishing any further anti-Semitic articles. He declared himself "shocked" and "mortified" by what had appeared in the *Dearborn Independent* (Bennett and Marcus 1951, 56). Actually, he had gotten Louis Marshall, the chair of the American Jewish Committee, to draft his letter of apology, which Marshall did with the help of his law partner, Samuel Untermeyer, and the Hearst journalist Arthur Brisbane. Marshall had wired Ford demanding an accounting after the very first installment of *International Jew* in May 1920 and had continued as an outspoken critic of Ford's position. As could be expected, the "apology" written for Ford was quite complete. In it, they had Ford speak of "the so-called *Protocols of the Wise Men of Zion*, which have been demonstrated, as I learn, to be gross forgeries" (quoted in Baldwin 2001, 238–239). Ford then ordered his strong-arm lieutenant Harry Bennett to forge his signature (Baldwin 2001, 237). As Bennett later boasted: "I signed Mr. Ford's signature to the document. I had always been able to sign his name as realistically as he could himself. The signature was verified, and the case was closed" (Bennett and Marcus 1951, 56). The full apology was then published in the Hearst chain of newspapers (Baldwin 2001, 238–240). Ford himself later bragged to one of his vocal supporters, the Fundamentalist preacher Gerald L. K. Smith, that he had never signed the document. After Ford's death, when Smith printed an edited and abbreviated version of *International Jew* in a single volume with no date of publication, he quoted a communication from Ford in his introduction: "Mr. Smith, my apology for publishing 'The International Jew' was given great publicity, but I did not sign the apology. It was signed by Harry Bennett" (Smith n.d., 6). In the autobiography that Ford published at the same time *International Jew* was first being printed, there is a section "Studies in the Jewish Question . . . a question which is racial at its source": "There has been observed in this country certain strains of influence which were causing a marked deterioration . . . a general letting down of standards . . . a nasty Orientalism which has insidiously affected every channel of expression . . . these influences are all traceable to one racial source" (Ford and Crowther 1922, 250–251). In spite of his published apology, it is clear that Ford retained his anti-Semitism undimmed. Years later, he intimated to Harry Bennett that he would like to publish another edition of *International Jew*, and, while he did not live to do so, Gerald L. K. Smith did it for him after his death, including the message that had been in the original Dearborn version, even if differing by a comma and an article (*International Jew* 1921, 22): "'Race or Religion?'. . . . The Jews are something more than mere 'followers of a religion,' namely they are a race, a brotherhood, a nation" (quoted in translation from a Yiddish original in both the *Dearborn Independent* version and Smith n.d., 49, 50).

International Jew had been translated into German shortly after it appeared in the early 1920s, and it was widely popular. That and Ford's autobiography were explicitly praised by the aspiring Adolf Hitler, who openly boasted of Ford's support and who had a photograph of Henry Ford hung on his Munich office wall (Leonard 1932, 208). The Dearborn outpouring, especially Ford's insistence that Jewishness was a reflection of "race" and not religion, played an important role in shaping the perspective expressed in Hitler's own manifesto, *Mein Kampf* (originally published in 1925) (Lee 1980, 64): "There is a great similarity between *The International Jew* and Hitler's *Mein Kampf*, and some passages are so identical that it has been said that Hitler copied directly from Ford's publication" (Pool and Pool 1979, 91). Hitler also read Ford's autobiography and his *Today and Tomorrow* (Ford and Crowther 1926). Germany had enough homegrown anti-Semitism to fuel the horror that was to come, but the infusion from America almost certainly speeded it up (Kevles 2003).

Ford disliked the British and admired Hitler and the Germans (Bennett and Marcus 1951, 121). As World War II approached, he refused to make aircraft engines for Britain while providing Germany with five-ton trucks (Nevins and Hill 1963, 176–178). He opposed American entry into the war and continued to sell engines and vehicles to the

Nazis until 1941. Evidently, he was glad to support any organization that would carry on the fight against the Jews (Pool and Pool 1979, 3). To express his gratitude, Adolf Hitler awarded Henry Ford the Grand Service Cross of the Supreme Order of the German Eagle (*Verdienstkreuz Deutscher Adler*), presented to Ford in his Dearborn office on his 75th birthday, July 30, 1938, by the German Consul of Cleveland, Karl Kapp, and Consul Fritz Hailer of Detroit (Pool and Pool 1979, 129; Baldwin 2001, 284). The only other non-German to have received the award was the fascist dictator of Italy, Benito Mussolini. Ford accepted it for "business reasons" and because he felt that it would annoy the American president, Franklin D. Roosevelt, whom he hated (Bennett and Marcus 1951, 120).

Ford's anti-Semitism did not cease with his 1927 "apology." Two of his admirers, the "radio priest" Father Charles E. Coughlin and the Protestant Fundamentalist preacher and radio personality Gerald L. K. Smith, promoted that version of racial prejudice on the Detroit radio station WJR in the 1930s. Starting in the early 1940s, Smith continued in this vein in his monthly *The Cross and the Flag,* the official organ of his Christian Nationalist Crusade. Smith, as I have noted, printed a shortened, single-volume version of *International Jew* after World War II was over and Ford was dead. This featured segments of the protocols heading each chapter, followed by the discussion that had been in the first Dearborn version (Smith n.d.). Father Coughlin, an isolationist Nazi and Mussolini supporter, printed an abbreviated roster of the *Protocols* in his weekly newspaper *Social Justice* from July to November 1938 (Coughlin 1938a,b).

By this time, it had been abundantly and irrefutably demonstrated that the *Protocols* were plagiarisms and forgeries. Despite this, they have continued to exhibit a hold over a segment of the popular mind that shows no sign of disappearing as the 21st century gets under way. The "logic" of this outlook was expressed by Henry Ford in an interview with Joseph H. O'Neill printed in the *New York World* of February 16, 1921, and repeated by Father Coughlin in his column "The Protocols of Zion" in *Social Justice* of July 18, 1938: "The only statement I care to make about the Protocols is that they fit in with what is going on. They are sixteen years old (at this time, 1921) and they have fitted the world situation up to this time. They fit it now" (Ford quoted by Coughlin 1938a, 5). Coughlin seconded this stance just over a month later when he said "I emphasize once more that I am not interested in the authenticity of the Protocols. I am interested in their factuality" (Coughlin 1938b, 5).

It is sobering to realize how close these views were to those articulated by Adolf Hitler, who had read the *Protocols* with great interest. When queried whether he had derived inspiration for his anti-Semitic campaign from the *Protocols,* Hitler replied "Yes, certainly, down to the veriest detail." (Rauschning 1940, 235). When his interlocutor observed that they are "a manifest forgery" and "can't possibly be genuine," Hitler replied "Why not?" He then said he "did not care two straws" whether the account "was historically true." If it was not, "its intrinsic truth was all the more convincing to him" (Rauschning 1940, 235). In the 11th edition of *Mein Kampf* (Hitler 1943, 337), he observed that news sources were "for ever moaning to the public that they [the *Protocols*] are supposed to be based on a forgery; which is the surest proof that they are genuine" (quoted in Cohn 1967, 182).

The prior commitment—prejudice—in each of those renditions is patently obvious. It is a classic case of "don't confuse me with the facts, my mind is already made up."

Supporters of anti-Semitism and racial prejudice have continued to cite the *Protocols* as evidence that the stereotypic essence designated as "the Jew" embodies a threat to the rest of the world. In the 1960s, the anti-Israeli president of Egypt Gamal Abdel Nasser asserted his acceptance of the *Protocols* (Cohn 1967, 19), and both Gerald L. K. Smith and the John Birch Society reprinted parts of Ford's version (Lee 1980, 137). The Ku Klux Klan also published the *Protocols* (Higham 1969). In the 1970s, the *Thunderbolt*, the newspaper of the National States Rights Party, issued three separate editions of the *Protocols*, including one with the annotation originally printed in *International Jew* (Segel and Levy 1995, xiv). Now, as the new millennium has gotten under way, the conservative Catholic biweekly in the Detroit area *Credo*, funded by the retired Domino's Pizza magnate Tom Monahan, has published a letter to the editor by Joseph Wira quoting from "One of the protocols authored . . . by Learned Elders of Zion," and alleging the factual nature of that forgery (Inside Ann Arbor, 2002, 11).

Although Henry Ford could hardly have known that his own parochial bigotry would contribute to the events that led to the murder of over 6 million Europeans, one of the most thorough treatments of that fraudulent document concluded that "the *Protocols* were a warrant for genocide" (Cohn 1967, 250). While the *Dearborn Independent* raised the matter of "the Jewish question" in its June 12, 1920, issue and it was clear that Ford was "anti-Semitic to the pith of his soul" (Lee 1980, 142), there is no hint that he would have accepted the "solution" that the Hitler whom he admired proposed— namely, annihilation. His solution to "the Negro problem" (Baldwin 2001, 201) was segregation. He devoted far more of his time and resources to the Jewish "problem," but there is absolutely no reason to believe that he ever entertained the idea of extermination as a possible solution.

15

THE OUTLOOK OF THE "BIGOT BRIGADE"

"RACE" AND "INTELLIGENCE"

We and They

Father, Mother, and Me,
  Sister and Auntie say,
All the people like Us are We,
  And everyone else is They:

And They live over the sea,
  While We live over the way,
But—would you believe it?—They look upon We
  As only a sort of They.

(Kipling 1926, 277)

Ethnocentrism is a human universal, and people everywhere consider that their own ways and capabilities are basically better than those of anybody else. The whole history of immigration control is simply an illustration of that generalization. For the first European settlers on America's northeast coast, the most important thing was adherence to a particular form of Christian belief. Achievement of a basic level of literacy was encouraged so that the Scriptures could be read, but no value was placed on demonstrating higher levels of intellectual accomplishment. With the national frenzy for assessing test results that is ubiquitous today, just consider what a radical change there has been.

When the initial focus on specific religious denominations faded, this was replaced by considerations of national and "racial" matters. With the establishment of a secular government after the American Revolution, literacy was seen less as a key for entrance to the Kingdom of God than as a demonstration of one's right to participate in the government of the country. That itself, however, became what one could call a secularly "sacred" belief. This was why the literacy of immigrants became a matter of increasing concern as the quantity of aspiring entrants grew late in the 19th and early in the 20th centuries. Given the ethnocentric assumption that "they" are less intellectually competent than "we" and the fear that "they" might dilute the mental caliber of the nation as a whole, it was inevitable that an attempt would be made to test the intellects of aspiring immigrants with an eye toward refusing entry to those who were considered to be mentally incompetent. The extreme lengths to which this was carried by the Nazi policies "justified" by this view were still a generation in the future.

The eugenic concern for "racial" betterment led to an interest in choosing the intellectually more fit and excluding the "dross." One of the main problems, however, is that "intelligence" is just as indefensible a biological category as "race." Does the ability to spell out and evaluate the factors that led to the outbreak of World War II have anything in common with the ability to solve differential equations in one's head? Does either have anything to do with the propensity to get lost in a shopping mall or be unable to do long division? There is an enormous spectrum of mental capacities, and many of those separate elements appear to have nothing to do with each other (Gardner 1983); yet, those separate and unrelated capabilities are always included in considerations of human intellectual capacity (Jensen 1998). Is there anything to be gained by lumping them all into a single construct called "intelligence?" Many would argue that there is not, but some have proposed that there is value in assessing the amount of variance which they share.

STATISTICAL THEOLOGY AND THE WORSHIP OF *g*

The 19th-century English dilettante Francis Galton assessed both individuals and "races" according to a single subjective ranking called "intelligence." His approach was picked up and quantified by Charles E. Spearman (1863–1945), who later succeeded Karl Pearson as one of a series of Galton-oriented professors of psychology at University College in London. Spearman identified the variance shared by different mental capabilities as "general intelligence," which he denoted as g (Spearman 1904). It was he who harnessed the matrix algebra necessary to generate that inferred entity, g. As one lifelong devotee, the Berkeley California racialist Arthur R. Jensen, has suggested: "A working definition of intelligence, then, is that it is the g factor of an indefinitely large and varied battery of mental tests" (Jensen 1980, 249).

Later, when he considered the nature of "intelligence" in another ponderous tome, entitled *The g Factor* (1998), that same Galtonian, nearly a century after the concept was proposed, opined that "psychologists are incapable of reaching a consensus on the definition. It has proved to be a hopeless quest. Therefore, the term 'intelligence' should be discarded altogether in scientific psychology, just it discarded 'animal magnetism' as the science of chemistry discarded 'phlogiston'" (Jensen 1998, 48). A generation ago, the late anthropologist Ashley Montagu referred to "race" as "the phlogiston of our time" (Montagu 1964, xii), and now it would seem that "intelligence" is slated to join it as another hypothetical entity that exists only in our imagination. One of the least helpful definitions ever proposed by a "scientist" was the "famous tautology" (Tucker 1994b, 218) offered by the Harvard psychologist and member of Yerkes's army team (discussed in Chapter 16), Edwin G. Boring: "intelligence as a measurable capacity must . . . be defined as the capacity to do well in an intelligence test. Intelligence is what the tests test" (Boring 1923, 35).

The reality of g is every bit as problematic as the reality of a single entity denoted "intelligence." It exists only in the form of loadings on the first factor of a statistical procedure called "factor analysis." The extent to which a battery of test scores covary can be rendered numerically. The roster of those numbers represents the factor which, in a classic bit of verbal mumbo-jumbo, has been called "a hypothetical variable that 'underlies' an observed or measured variable. Thus a factor is also referred to as a *latent variable*" (Jensen 1998, 55). Even the principal promoter of *g* concedes that "it is not directly observable" and "is not a tangible thing" (Jensen 1998, 55). Furthermore, there is no way to measure *g*. Others have warned that the existence of such a factor is actually a product of the statistical technique used and not a dimension of what had been measured. One of the most respected practitioners of factor analysis in the 20th century, L. L. Thurstone, gave the following warning:

> As psychologists we cannot be interested in a general factor which is only the average of any random collection of tests . . . . We must guard against the simple but common, error of merely taking a first centroid factor, a first principal component, or other mean factor, in a test battery and then calling it a general factor. Such a factor can always be found routinely for any set of positively correlated tests, and it means nothing more or less than the average of all the abilities called for by the battery as a whole. Consequently it varies from one battery to another and has no fundamental psychological significance beyond the arbitrary collection of tests that anyone happens to put together for a factor analysis. (Thurstone 1940, 208)

More recently, that warning has been reaffirmed: "When principal components analysis is used, a single major factor will be extracted from whatever measures are being analyzed. The appearance of a principal factor is a function of the factor analytic method and is not unique to tests which purport to measure intelligence" (Mercer 1988, 202).

Yet *g* has been enshrined in a place of honor and made the focus of what could almost be called a cult. Galton himself declared that eugenic principles could well be placed on a par with religious beliefs, and this clearly has been done by the worshipers of *g*. With countless papers, books, and technical journals devoted to the exegesis of *g*, the efforts have been likened to "statistical theology" where "divinity is depicted with a lower case *g*" (Brace 1980b, 334; 1996c, S157).

At almost the same time that Spearman declared his faith in *g*, the construction of a battery of test items designed to assess mental development was proposed by a French psychologist at the Sorbonne, Alfred Binet (1857–1911), in collaboration with a physician colleague, Théodore Simon (Binet and Simon 1905). The French minister of public instruction assigned Binet the task of devising a means of discovering whether particular children in the Parisian school system were mentally deficient and could profit from special treatment (Wolf 1973). He was commendably wary about assigning a definition to "intelligence," and he also rejected Spearman's Galtonian assumption that it was a simple inherited entity (Binet 1905, 623–624; Binet and Simon 1908, 74–75). As Binet realized, one had to know what was normal before one could determine what was deficient. While Binet and Simon developed a way of rating "*mental level*," they were careful to avoid the term *mental age,* and they specifically warned that the intellectual dimension being documented was not comparable to a biological datum such as stature or weight.

Performance on mental assessment tests, they noted, depended on learning as much as innate ability. The circumstances relating to that learning could have major consequences not related to inherited capacities. For example: "a normal peasant in his milieu of the fields, would be at a disadvantage in the city. In a word, retardation is a concept dependant on a multitude of circumstances which have to be taken into account to judge each particular case" (Binet and Simon 1908, 88). The usual translation quoted is the one commissioned by the American psychologist Henry H. Goddard, discussed at some length in a later section (Goddard 1980, 266–267). The French term *débile,* which I would translate as "at a disadvantage," was what Goddard chose to render as "a moron." One should note here that the term *moron* was coined by Goddard from the Greek *moros,* meaning "foolish" (Goddard 1980, 10). It has come to have such a pejorative connotation that it has tainted the entire sense of what Binet and Simon had tried to get across.

The Americans who quoted Binet and Simon's example made the simplistic and unsupported assumption that life in the fields required far less mental capacity than that needed for survival by the average urbanite. Nothing could be further from the truth. One should consider the equally valid converse: an urbanite would be considered equally "at a disadvantage"—a moron—when put in the position of trying to run a farm without the experience of having been brought up knowing the endless number of things necessary in order to make it function. The city is indeed more complicated than the farm because there are many more ways of making a living, but no single one of these requires more "intelligence" or the mastery of more information than the way of life of a successful farmer.

In addition, Binet noted that children from the working-class but not poverty-stricken wards of Paris scored below the mental level of children of well-to-do parents in Brussels, where the tests were also applied. Binet asked rhetorically, "Is this a matter of heredity? Is it a matter of education?" (Goddard 1980, 318). The difference was particularly noticeable in matters reflecting the use of language. Binet answered his own question: "This verbal superiority must certainly come from family life; the children of the rich are in a superior environment from the point of view of language; they hear a more correct language and one that is more expressive" (Goddard 1980, 320). That, of course, then as well as now, has a huge impact on the scores of those tested. In Binet's view, performance on the tests he had developed reflected a large component of learning.

Alfred Binet's approach to measuring mental capabilities was adopted with enthusiasm in both Britain and America with far-reaching consequences. Unfortunately, after his death in 1911, his cautious and nuanced style of interpretation did not survive. In England, the long-term involvement with a colonial empire had conditioned people to think automatically in terms of categorical differences in populations. Galton himself had visited the Middle East, Egypt, and sub-Saharan Africa after his university education; and his post-Renaissance means of getting there ensured that he perceived his "racial others" in categorical fashion. In America, of course, the artificial juxtaposition of people uprooted from very separate parts of the globe made the perception of the "categorical other" a matter of daily experience. Consequently, an emerging generation of British and American psychologists loyal to Galtonian eugenics applied Binet's methods of assessment to document class and "racial" distinctions which they claimed were genetically determined. What has been referred to as the "Galton School" or the "London School" of Psychology has continued at University College in London and has exerted its influence on scholarly traditions on both sides of the Atlantic (Rushton 1995, 9).

In Great Britain, it was instrumental in promoting the idea that a child's intellectual potential was fixed and could be determined by the age of 12. This was used as justification for the infamous "11-plus" examination, which determined whether a child would be admitted to a grammar school (the step toward a university), a vocational school, or a nontechnical "modern" school (Hearnshaw 1979, 112). Lifetime decisions imposed on 11-year-old children were made in the absence of any effort to assess whether their opportunities for learning prior to the imposition of judgment had been properly comparable. Binet, on the other hand, argued that "the intelligence of anyone can be improved; through exercise and training, and above all with method, one can improve attention, memory, and judgment, and become literally more intelligent than one had been before, and this continues right up to the point where one reaches one's limit" (Binet 1910, 143). To assume that a single test given at the age of 11 will show what that limit is amounts to callous indifference to very real differences in background and opportunities. The system was nominally terminated in 1965, although it had determined the fate of an entire generation and in effect continued for some time after that (Kitcher 1985).

SIR CYRIL BURT: "SCIENTIFIC" FRAUD

After the end of that program, the rationale that had sustained it suffered something of a major black eye. It was shown that the tests invoked to justify the genetic predetermination of the intelligence quotient (IQ) were in fact a fraud (Kamin 1974, 35–47; Tucker 1994a,b, 1997). The successor to Charles Spearman as professor of psychology at University College in London was Cyril Burt (1883–1971). Those efforts included his "documentation" of the idea that lower socioeconomic classes earned less because they were congenitally less bright than their social betters and that their children did not deserve equal educational opportunities because they can be assumed to have inherited the intellectual dimness of their parents. These assumptions continue to underlie opposition to "affirmative action" programs in the United States of the 21st century.

At his death in 1971, Burt had been the recipient of just about all the honors that a psychologist could have been awarded. In 1946, he had been the first psychologist to receive a knighthood for his "accomplishments" (Jensen 1972a, 116). One of his own particular disciples, the American racialist Arthur R. Jensen, had been a postgraduate student of Burt's own student and successor in London, Hans J. Eysenck; and it fell to him to write one of Burt's obituaries for a prominent psychology journal. Jensen (1972a, 117) extolled Burt with these words: "Everything about the man . . . his aura of vitality, his urbane manner . . . and, of course, especially his notably sharp intellect and vast erudition—all together leave a total impression of immense quality, a born nobleman." The "born nobleman," however was in fact a racist and a fraud. He did everything he could to prevent his own former student and protégé, Eysenck, from succeeding him in the chair of psychology at University College, denigrating him as that "German Jew at the Maudsley" (the Maudsley Hospital of the Institute of Psychiatry in London) (Hearnshaw 1979, 270; Rose 1992, 14). In Burt's mind, Jewish and Scottish people were innately acquisitive, while "some primitive races" did not have and were unable to acquire the capabilities necessary for "commercial civilization" and "industrial success" (Burt 1925, 426–427). Slum dwellers and the Irish were also considered innately intellectually inferior.

Burt's antipathy toward his successor evidently was the result of more than just anti-Semitism. As his biographer noted, "He was deeply suspicious of rivals particularly his own most able students like Cattell and Eysenck" (Cattell being the British-born American psychologist Raymond B. Cattell) (Hearnshaw 1979, 290). In the academic world, however, even in England where personal pull has traditionally been so influential, a professor has no role in choosing his successor. Eysenck's career survived, and he went on to enjoy a tenure comparable to that of his mentor, Sir Cyril Burt. As a Burt apologist, he will be remembered as an advocate of the Galtonian view that the major differences in the benefits meted out to the people of this world are mainly the consequences of differences in the genetic worth of the people in question. That they might have been born in circumstances that could be construed as representing three strikes against them, he—and the rest of the Galtonian "racial" determinists—considered irrelevant. A true product of his mentor, Eysenck was contentious, cantankerous, and given to underhanded tactics (Tucker 1994b, 234). He was also a shill for the tobacco industry and, with money from R. J. Reynolds and the Tobacco Research Council, pursued efforts aimed at demonstrating that the ailments suffered by smokers were due to their genetic predisposition and not primarily to the effects of tobacco (Eysenck 1980, 1985, 1991; Baker and Fiore 1992; Tucker 1994b, 233–234).

Burt, for his part, was almost predestined to be a Galtonian. His father had been family physician to the Galtons, and he grew up with a firsthand familiarity with the Galtonian outlook (Hearnshaw 1979, 23). With his "exaggerated egotism," "cantankerousness," and "unscrupulousness" (Hearnshaw 1979, 289), Burt "was not an easy man to like" (Scarr 1991, 200). In science, however, the value of the work has nothing to do with the likability of the scientist. In Burt's case, however, not only was he unpleasantly egocentric, but "In the end he chose to cheat rather than see his opponents triumph" (Hearnshaw 1979, 291). In his commitment to the rigid genetic determination of intelligence, he did not go through the process of collecting field data on the inheritance of IQ. Instead, he simply made them up. As one of his apologists put it, "It is almost as if Burt regarded the actual data as merely an incidental backdrop for the illustration of the theoretical issues in quantitative genetics, which, to him, seemed always to hold the center of the stage" (Jensen 1974, 25).

Burt's "data" on the correlation between the scores of identical twins raised apart and those raised together were published over a 10-year span after his retirement from University College. Some of this was presumably based on work that went back to the 1920s. Burt added to the sample sizes over the years, eventually building up the largest set of twin "data" in the literature. After Burt's death, the Princeton psychologist Leon J. Kamin pointed out that Burt had reported his correlation coefficients to three decimal places but, even though sample sizes increased, those coefficients remained absolutely the same (Kamin 1974, 38). That should have been an enormous red flag that there was something seriously wrong with what was being reported. All who have ever dealt with correlations in behavioral data know from long experience that the coefficients almost always change when more cases are added. The possibility of a coefficient remaining the same after a change in sample size cannot always be dismissed, but in Burt's case this had happened 20 times (Jensen 1974, 24). Furthermore there was no discussion of what tests were used or of the age and sex breakdown of the sample. There were other ambiguities and inconsistencies as well. After reviewing the evidence, Kamin declared: "The conclusion cannot be avoided: The numbers left behind by Professor Burt are simply not worthy of our current scientific attention" (Kamin 1974, 47).

That observation led to the demonstration that Burt's work was patently fraudulent. Kamin had claimed that the hereditarian stance of Burt and others was not supported by the available evidence but was really motivated by reactionary "political" views. One of the consequences of this claim was the emergence of "a backlash of support for Burt" from those who felt that such an argument could as easily be directed against Kamin himself (Mackintosh 1995, 132). Kamin had in fact been a victim of the witch-hunting tactics of Senator Joseph R. McCarthy in 1954, and after earning his Ph.D. at Harvard, he spent 14 years in Canada before landing at Princeton in 1969 (Tucker 1994a, 337). At that, Kamin did not print the charge against Burt that he really suspected until 2 years later, when it was obvious that Burt had simply fabricated his data. Interviewed by one of the news reporters for *Science* magazine, the flagship publication of the American Association for the Advancement of Science, the core organization of American scientists, Kamin was quoted as saying after he first read Burt's work in 1972, "The immediate conclusion I came to after ten minutes reading was that Burt was a fraud" (Wade 1976, 916).

Burt had published his "findings," occasionally with putative coauthors Margaret Howard and Jane Conway, in the *British Journal of Statistical Psychology*. For those who have gone through the inevitable struggles with editors and rewrites in response to reviewers' comments before getting a research article into print, the question arises of how Burt was able to do it over the years with fabricated data and, as it turns out, fabricated coauthors. The answer is that Cyril Burt was the founder and editor of that journal and ran it with "virtually dictatorial control" (Hearnshaw 1979, 275–276). A considerable amount of what was published in its pages was actually written by Burt himself, and he skewed the findings of the authors whose reports he chose to print (Fancher 1991, 1565–1566).

Why anyone would have believed that Burt did the field work on which his IQ correlations were said to have been based is another matter. He had contracted Ménière's disease in 1941, which left him deaf in one ear and with a poor sense of balance. From that point on, he lived a somewhat restricted life, never going abroad and cutting down on his public appearances (Hearnshaw 1979, 275 ff.). The idea of a deaf and tottery old man getting any usable information from interviewing twins, their parents, and their teachers, year after year, in the county council schools of London's the working-class sections is ludicrous. One can only conclude that people believed him because they wanted to. The claim that the actual field work was done by his coauthors comes up against the problem that there is no evidence that they even existed, at least during the period of time that the work was presumably being done (Wade 1976, 916; Gillie 1979, 1035). As for the reviews and articles published under their names, Burt's private secretary confirmed that Burt wrote them all himself (Jensen 1995a, 5).

16

THE GALTONIAN LEGACY IN AMERICA

WORLD WAR I

As the application of Galton's eugenic ideas in the realm of educational opportunities had a stifling effect on a very large proportion of the youth in the British Isles throughout the middle years of the 20th century, so it also had direct effects on who was and who was not allowed to become an American. There is a veritable rogues' gallery of figures who qualify as members of what I call the "bigot brigade" and who could collectively count as the villains of the piece (Brace 1999b,c). Three American Galtonians were largely instrumental in the development and the irresponsible application of intelligence testing in the United States. These were Henry H. Goddard (1866–1957), Lewis M. Terman (1877–1956), and Robert M. Yerkes (1876–1956). Both Goddard and Terman earned their doctorates at Clark University in Worcester, Massachusetts, under the direction of G. Stanley Hall (1844–1924), himself the first to have been awarded a Ph.D. in psychology in America (under William James at Harvard in 1879). Yerkes was Harvard-trained, in fact a protégé of Charles Benedict Davenport before the latter left for Chicago and then Cold Spring Harbor. After holding a military commission in World War I, Yerkes spent a good part of the rest of his career at Yale.

Goddard visited Binet and Simon in Paris and was responsible for importing their system of "intelligence" testing to America. He had Binet's key papers translated into English and published by the Training School for Feeble-Minded Girls and Boys at Vineland, New Jersey, where he was director of the research laboratory (see Goddard 1980). He sent a copy to his friend, Lewis M. Terman, who was professor of psychology at Stanford University in Palo Alto, California. Terman then modified the Binet-Simon scale to produce the Stanford-Binet IQ test, which is the ancestor of all the "intelligence" tests still in use today. As early as 1912, the United States Public Health Service had invited Goddard to the immigrant receiving station on Ellis Island in New York harbor to administer "intelligence" tests. Subsequently, he used the Binet and supplementary performance tests and reported that 83% of the Jews he examined were "feeble-minded" (Goddard 1913, 105; 1917, 247).

After the United States entered World War I in 1917, Yerkes, as the president of the American Psychological Association, suggested that the military test the "intelligence" of its draftees. Despite much skepticism, the charge was accepted, and psychologists were commissioned in the U.S. Army's Sanitary Corps under the leadership of Major (soon to be Colonel) Robert M. Yerkes (Kamin 1974, 17). Inspired by Binet's examples, Yerkes, Goddard, and Terman then collaborated to create the "intelligence" testing program that was applied to nearly 1.75 million American soldiers in World War I (Yoakum and Yerkes 1920, 12). This included the alpha test for those who could read and write, and the beta test for those who could not. As good Galtonians, the test creators assumed not only that "intelligence" was genetically fixed but, ignoring the cautions articulated by Binet, also that it could be calibrated for age. The intelligence quotient (IQ) is actually a ratio produced by dividing mental age by chronological age and multiplying by 100 to get rid of the decimal places. A person with a mental and chronological age of 18 would have an IQ of 100 (i.e., $18/18 = 1 \times 100$), which is "normal" by definition.

Goddard, for one, and completely contra Binet, considered "intelligence" to be a "unit character," that is, a single-gene trait inherited in simple Mendelian fashion (Goddard 1914, ix). Even the relatively straightforward melanin polymer responsible for human skin color is produced by such a complex process that the number of genes responsible is still unknown but obviously considerable (Fitzpatrick et al. 1986). The idea that the vastly more complex realm of mental functioning could be controlled by a single gene is itself so simple-minded that it could only count as a bad joke. The genetics of "intelligence" remains unknown despite nine more decades of unflagging interest and research.

Applied to the World War I draftees, the tests revealed that the average mental age of recruits of European ancestry was 13. If one considers the average chronological age of the recruits to be 18, then the average IQ would be 72. Since Goddard put the mental age of 12 at the high end of what he termed the "moron" range, this meant that a large proportion of the soldiers in the U.S. Army had to have qualified as "morons" (Goddard 1928, 220). Actually, Terman assumed that intellectual capacity became fixed at age 16, which would have given the draftees an IQ of 81, still in the dim range (Goddard 1928). However, Goddard, in his elitist view of the world, clearly felt that the average person was mentally marginal in any case (Goddard 1919, 250). He opined that the average "intelligence" of the adult American was equal to that of a 12-year-old child (Goddard 1919, 250) and that 45% of Americans belonged in the feeble-minded or "moron" class (Goddard 1920b, 427).

This led to some curious but not fully worked-out comments on the American form of government: "While we all believe in democracy . . . it would seem self-evident that the feeble-minded should not be allowed to take part in civic affairs; should not be allowed to vote" (Goddard 1920a, 99). Presumably, if nearly half the American public were morons, they should be prohibited from voting, although Goddard does not quite say that in so many words. He clearly had deep reservations about the nature of a democracy. For example: "To maintain that mediocre or average intelligence should decide what is best for a group of people in their struggle for existence is manifestly absurd. We need the advice of the highest intelligence of the group not the average any more than the lowest" (Goddard 1919, 236). His concept of "perfect government" was an aristocracy, and his model was none other than the Vineland training school for the feeble-minded, where he had been one of the appointed managers. In his words the "imbeciles and morons" did not elect their "Superintendent . . . and his associates to rule over them; *but they would do so if given the chance*" because they knew that those officials had their best interests at heart (Goddard 1920a, 98–99, italics Goddard's). In Goddard's analogy, the nation could be regarded as one vast mental asylum where the elected "devote their superior intelligence to understanding the lower mental levels." His "perfect government" then could be described as "aristocracy *in* Democracy" (Goddard 1920a, italics Goddard's).

"INTELLIGENCE" AND IMMIGRATION

If Americans were located down in the moron range in such numbers, the rankings of the foreign-born were much worse. The percentages of eastern and southern Europeans who were feeble-minded were also high: 87% of Russians, 80% of Hungarians, and 79% of Italians (Goddard 1913, 105–107; 1917, 252). Russians, Poles, and Italians scored lowest. Among other things, the designations "Russians" and "Poles" were at least in part used as euphemisms for "Jews" (Chase 1977, 267; and see the treatment by Brigham 1923, 189–190). Even though Yerkes occasionally mentioned the differences in familiarity with the American milieu (including skills with the English language), there was no hint that this could have affected the test scores (Yerkes 1921, 697, 704). Instead, the results of his survey were taken to indicate a spectrum of inherent intellectual worth in the "races" of Europe. All of this provided "proof" for the racist generalizations of Madison Grant, Lothrop Stoddard, and their followers. Not surprisingly, America applied the findings of its army survey to the matter of assessing immigrants.

Although Goddard had been using Binet's testing procedure to assess the intellectual status of immigrants at Ellis Island since 1912, it was really the tests on draftees into the U.S. Army in 1917–18 that gave America its "scientific" basis for ranking the relative worth of the various European "races." In addition to testing quantities of "native-born" Americans, both of African and of European ancestry, the program administered by Lieutenant Colonel Yerkes tested over 11,000 foreign-born Europeans (Yerkes 1921, 701). The massive collection of data was published under Yerkes's editorship as a memoir of the National Academy of Sciences in 1921. Subsequently, this was harnessed for use in "justifying" the immigration-restricting Johnson-Lodge Act of 1924. One has to feel less than confident that genetic differences in intelligence are documented by tests with questions such as "The pitcher has an important place in—tennis, football, baseball, handball;" "The Plymouth Rock is a kind of—horse, cattle, granite, fowl;" or "The Packard car is made in—Detroit, Buffalo, Toledo, Flint" (Yoakum and Yerkes 1920, 274–275). The recent arrival from Poland or Sicily is not likely to know such information, and to conclude that such a person is therefore mentally deficient is scarcely fair.

Since the Yerkes tome was an almost mindless compilation of numbers, it needed to be digested and presented in coherent fashion. One of those who did this was the Princeton psychologist Carl C. Brigham (1890–1943), who had been one of the officers assisting Yerkes on his project during World War I. His book was called *A Study of American Intelligence* (1923), and the foreword was written by none other than Yerkes himself. In the acknowledgments, Brigham declared that in his treatment of "the race hypothesis," he had relied on the "judgment" of a number of prominent figures, among them William Z. Ripley and his *Races of Europe* and Madison Grant and his *Passing of the Great Race* (Brigham 1923, xvii–xviii).

Extrapolating from the figures compiled by Yerkes and his associates, Brigham declared: "In a very definite way, the results which we obtain by interpreting the army data by means of the race hypothesis support Mr. Madison Grant's thesis of the superiority of the Nordic type" (Brigham 1923, 182). Not only did Brigham cite the test figures showing lower scores for foreign-born immigrants from southern and eastern Europe as proof of their innate intellectual inferiority, he showed that the more recent immigrants were progressively less capable than the earlier ones. The army records had allowed separate assessments of blocs of immigrants over 5-year time periods starting in 1902, and it was possible to see that the scores of the more recent entrants were lower than those of the earlier ones. Those who had been in the United States for 20 years or more at the time of testing made scores that were indistinguishable from those of native-born draftees.

Since all the draftees were between the ages of 18 and 31, those who had been in the United States for 20 years before they had been tested had become thoroughly familiar with the language and culture of the country. Since they were preteens at the time of immigration, they would have become completely fluent in colloquial American English. The more recent the immigrant arrival, the more flawed the grasp of the language, which explains the lower test scores for the more recent immigrants. This, however, was not the interpretation favored by Brigham or Yerkes and the rest. They maintained that the tests actually showed the genetically controlled capabilities of the testees and that the reduced scores of the more recent entrants indicated that, over time, those who aspired to come to America were increasingly drawn from the less competent and "degenerate" segments of those various European groups (Brigham 1923, 111, 177).

Brigham's book was extolled to the Senate Committee on Immigration, February 20, 1923, by a representative of the Immigration Restriction Society of New York, Francis H. Kinnicutt. As he told the committee chair, Republican Senator LeBaron B. Colt, "This is the most important book that has ever been written on this subject" (Kinnicutt 1923, 80). In that book, Brigham declared: "Our data from the army tests indicate clearly the intellectual superiority of the Nordic race group. . . . The Alpine race, according to our figures . . . seems to be considerably below the Nordic type intellectually" (Brigham 1923, 197). "Mediterraneans" he put another step lower (Brigham 1923, 208). Then, noting the quantity of Russians and Poles in the sample who were actually Jewish, he opined as follows: "There is no serious objection, from an anthropological standpoint, to classifying the northern Jew as an Alpine, for he has the head form, stature, and color of his Slavic neighbors. He is an Alpine Slav" (Brigham 1923, 190). As we are aware today, the attempt to represent a whole population by invoking a single male icon is completely indefensible. Given the results of the tests administered by Goddard and Yerkes, Brigham felt justified in venturing the following opinion: "Our figures, then, would rather disprove the popular belief that the Jew is highly intelligent" (Brigham 1923, 190). History has rendered a very different verdict based on the record of the rest of the 20th century, and it only goes to show how radically wrong the "bigot brigade" proponents of the "race factor" actually were.

Although the offering of Brigham's book to the Senate committee played its role, the main locus for the framing of immigration-restriction legislation was the Committee on Immigration and Naturalization in the U.S. House of Representatives, chaired by Congressman Albert Johnson, a conservative Republican from the state of Washington. "The most influential single witness" to the blatantly "racist" stance of that legislative body was the Cold Spring Harbor eugenicist and sterilization advocate Harry Hamilton Laughlin (Tucker 1994b, 94) (Fig. 16–1). Starting in 1920, Laughlin was repeatedly invited to testify before Johnson's committee, and each time he came equipped with tables, charts, graphs, and manuscripts that were printed as part of the transcripts of the sessions. On April 16–17, 1920, he entitled his contribution "Biological Aspects of Immigration" (Laughlin 1920).

Figure 16–1   Harry H. Laughlin, 1880–1943 (from Lynn 2001, 20).

Johnson was so impressed that he invited Laughlin back for the hearings on November 21, 1922 (Johnson comment in Laughlin 1922a, 731). Before his presentation, Johnson announced that Laughlin had been appointed "expert eugenics agent" for the committee. Laughlin's contribution on that occasion was "Analysis of the Metal and the Dross in America's Modern Melting Pot." Added to that description was "The Determination of the Rate of Occurrence of the Several Definite Types of Social Inadequacy in Each of the Several Present Immigrant Native Population Groups in the United States" (Laughlin 1922a). His final testimony before the committee was on March 8, 1924, and was entitled "Europe as an Emigrant-Exporting Continent and the United States as an Immigrant-Receiving Nation" (Laughlin 1924).

The first Calvinist settlers on the northeast edge of America brought with them a belief in predestination (the idea that ultimate salvation (or damnation) was determined by the will of God). They also accepted it as a given that they were God's "chosen people" and that America was their "promised land." With the adoption of the Constitution (1789) and subsequently the Bill of Rights (1791), which specified the separation of religion and politics, the earlier faith in a preordained future in the kingdom of God became subsumed in a faith in the benefits to be found in the secular state of the here-and-now. Because of the ever-present perception of "race," created and reinforced by the way in which America had been put together, the earlier views of predestination had become removed from the tests of words and works and transferred to a sense of "racial" worth. Americans still thought of themselves as the "chosen people," but the choice was no longer regarded as the act of a Calvinistic God in recognition of individual merit but, rather, as something biologically inherent in a collective "racial" identity. In Harry H. Laughlin's appearances before the House of Representatives Committee on Immigration and Naturalization, he repeated his admonition that "immigration into the United States, in the interests of national welfare, is primarily a biological problem" and added approvingly "an examination of the present American immigration situation shows the United States adopting the biological basis for its policy" (Laughlin 1924, 1339). In good Galtonian fashion, he declared "The character of a nation is based primarily upon the inborn racial traits of the inhabitants" (Laughlin 1924, 1297).

When he framed his model sterilization law in 1914, one of his chapters was called "Classification of the Socially Unfit." This started with a listing of the five Ds: Dependent, Deficient, Defective, Delinquent, and Degenerate (Laughlin 1914, 17). He then listed ten "classes" of the "socially inadequate." These included "feeble-minded," "criminalistic," "epileptic," "inebriate," and "dependent"—all said to be inherited in simple biological fashion. His initial recommendation was sterilization, but he used the same typology of supposedly inherited defects to justify barring immigration (Laughlin 1922, 730).

The bill was approved by Congress and signed into law by President Calvin Coolidge on June 30, 1924. Except for the agreement with China signed for political purposes in 1943 during World War II, the Johnson-Lodge Act governed American immigration policy until 1965. With its predecessors in 1917 and 1921, the blatant racism in that policy controlled the nature of immigration into America for a good half of the 20th century.

There are some curious bits of irony to be considered. Two of the supporters of the classification of genetically determined "social inadequacy" that underlay the thinking on immigration restriction had a complete change of heart well after it was too late to undo what their earlier testimony had helped put into place. Henry H. Goddard, having left Vineland for Ohio State University, abandoned his earlier belief in the inherent hopelessness of the teeming multitude of American "morons," who "are *not* hopeless and incurable mental defectives, but merely the lowest group of the body politic, requiring special attention and special methods in their education and training, but capable of becoming . . . regular members of the social group. . . . when I see what has been made out of the moron by a system of education, which as a rule is only *half right,* I have no difficulty in concluding that when we get an education that is entirely right there will be no morons who cannot manage themselves and their affairs and compete in the struggle for existence" (Goddard 1928, 224, 226). In effect, he wound up defending a view that was essentially identical to what Binet had proposed in the first place.

The other figure who did a complete about-face was Carl C. Brigham, who had become secretary of the College Entrance Examination Board and helped design and develop the Scholastic Aptitude Test (Kamin 1974, 22). Some of his earlier prejudice survived in that latter phenomenon and remains a problem to the present day, but his renunciation of the army tests and their application to racial classification is worth repeating:

> the army alpha test has been shown to be internally inconsistent to such a degree [that] it is absurd to go beyond this point and combine alpha, beta, the Stanford-Binet and the individual performance tests in the so-called "combined scale" or to regard a combined

scale score from one test or complex of tests as equivalent to that derived from another test or complex of tests. As this method was used by the writer in his earlier analysis of the army tests as applied to samples of foreign born in the draft, that study with its entire hypothetical superstructure of racial differences collapses completely. . . . comparative studies of various national and racial groups may not be made with existing tests, and . . . in particular that one of the most pretentious of these comparative racial studies—the writer's own—was without foundation. (Brigham 1930, 164, 165)

As was the case with Goddard's recantation, the damage caused by his earlier claims concerning genetically determined differences in individual and group worth could not be undone. Sterilization and immigration restriction proceeded in accordance with legislation based on the nature of their earlier testimony. The fact that both figures realized that their claims had been prejudicial and unwarranted had no impact on a public that had taken those views as the findings of "science."

Laughlin, however, remained unrepentantly fixed in his racist outlook to the end of his life. He applauded the "Nordic" enthusiasm of Adolf Hitler and the German compulsory sterilization law of 1933, and he used his position as editor of *Eugenical News* to aid in the dissemination of Nazi "race" propaganda (Kühl 1994, 48). He reaffirmed his 1934 views of the recognition of "race" as a qualification for immigration, recommending that "no immigrant be admitted . . . who is not a member of the white race" and adding that "for the purpose of American immigration laws, a white person be defined as one whose ancestors were members of the white or Caucasian race" (Laughlin 1939, 91). He was awarded an honorary degree of doctor of medicine from Heidelberg University on its 550th anniversary in 1936, although he did not go to Germany to receive it (Kühl 1994, 86–87). Instead, it was conferred by the German consul in New York (Watson 1998, 192).

What with his years of denouncing the various manifestations of "inborn social inadequacy," it comes as something of a surprise to realize that Laughlin was himself an epileptic. Although he regarded epilepsy as a congenital defect, he did note that some epileptics could display sterling qualities, no doubt referring to himself. After Davenport had retired as head of the laboratory in 1934, Laughlin crashed his car in Cold Spring Harbor in an epileptic seizure. Eventually, he was forced to retire when Vannevar Bush, the new director of the Carnegie Institution—the source of the financial support for the Cold Spring Harbor laboratory—was installed (Allen 1986).

LEWIS TERMAN AND GENETIC PREDESTINATION

Lewis M. Terman, the creator of the Stanford-Binet IQ test, can be considered the main figure responsible for "making IQ a household word" (Minton 1988, 262). While he did not testify before the congressional committees that specified "racial" quotas for immigrants, he was part of Yerkes's army testing group, which provided the justification for those quotas. In 1916, Terman published *The Measurement of Intelligence: An Explanation of and a Complete Guide for the Use of the Stanford Revision and Extension of the Binet-Simon Intelligence Scale,* and he dedicated it to the memory of Alfred Binet. As with Goddard's outlook, until it was way too late to fix the damage that it wrought, nothing could have been further from Binet's understanding and intent.

Terman, like Laughlin, never abandoned his commitment to the idea that performance on the tests he devised was genetically determined and that there were profound inherited differences in intelligence between the social classes and "races" in America. As a result of his single-minded devotion to the installation of testing programs in the nation's schools, the education system became fixated on ranking students as an end in itself rather than in conveying information and promoting mental skills. That fetish for comparative evaluation is as vigorous as ever now at the start of a new millennium.

One of the main consequences of Terman's outlook was the establishment of "tracking" systems, which separated students into slow-, medium-, and fast-learning groups. Having been regarded as a "gifted" child himself, Terman was particularly interested in catering to those in the gifted or genius category (Minton 1988, 266). His denigration of those at the lower part of the IQ spectrum amounted to blatant racism. In his words, this low level of intelligence "is very, very common among Spanish–Indian and Mexican families in the Southwest and also among negroes. Their dullness seems to be racial or at least inherent in the family stocks from which they come. The fact that one meets this type with such extraordinary frequency among Indians, Mexicans, and negroes suggests quite forcibly that the whole question of racial differences in mental traits will have to be taken up anew by experimental methods. The writer predicts that when this is done there will be discovered enormously significant racial differences" (Terman 1919, 91–92). His remedy was segregation from the rest of the population, and he hinted at the desirability of sterilization: "Children of this group should be segregated in special classes and be given instruction which is concrete and practical. They cannot master abstractions, but they can often be made efficient workers, able to look out for themselves. There is no possibility at present of convincing society that they should not be allowed to reproduce, although from a eugenic point of view they constitute a grave problem because of their unusually prolific breeding" (Terman 1919, 92). In almost totalitarian fashion, he looked at such people as possibly useful but not to be trusted with a role in determining the course of public affairs: "Among laboring men and servant girls there are thousands like them. They are the world's 'hewers of wood and drawers of water.' . . . uneducable beyond the merest rudiments of training. No amount of school instruction will ever make them intelligent voters or capable citizens" (Terman 1919, 91).

Terman promoted the idea of a testing program that would lead to governmental control of the lives and futures of a very large percentage of the population: "in the near future intelligence tests will bring tens of thousands of these high-grade defectives under the surveillance and protection of society. This will ultimately result in curtailing the reproduction of feeble-mindedness and the elimination of an enormous amount of crime, pauperism, and industrial inefficiency. It is hardly necessary to emphasize that the high-grade cases of the type now so frequently overlooked are precisely the ones whose guardianship it is most important for the State to assume" (Terman 1916, 6–7). Like Goddard earlier, Terman took it as a given that the average American was a marginal mental defective (although he did not use Goddard's term *moron*): "It is fairly well-established that the strictly median individual of our population meets with little success in dealing with abstractions more difficult than those represented in a typical course of study for eighth grade pupils" (Terman 1922, 35). With his promotion of intelligence testing and the tracking system and his recurrent reference to "Nordic superiority and ethnic inferiority," he helped promote racial and social class segregation in

American public schools (Chapman 1988, 175). The result was the erection of barriers to opportunity for certain segments of the population, "notably blacks and immigrants from southern and eastern Europe" (Chapman 1988, 175). What this did was to reinforce and solidify status differences in American society as a whole for three-quarters of the 20th and on into the 21st centuries.

By all accounts, Terman was a modest man and, even in his own view, "not an especially original thinker" (Minton 1988, 262): "Terman seems truly to have been a rather gray individual, whose major contributions derived from the work of others" (Fancher 1991, 1566). Another appraisal referred to him as one of "education's hucksters" and a deserving member of the "hall of shame" (Swanson 1993, 797). However, there is another point to be considered: Terman never could have succeeded in segregating the entire educational system of the United States unless society as a whole was fully convinced of the rectitude of his views. In that sense, Terman, as an exemplary organization man, played the same kind of role as did *Hitler's professors* in abetting the Holocaust in Nazi Germany (Weinreich 1946; Müller-Hill 1998).

Oddly enough, Terman considered himself a liberal (Minton 1988, 235 ff.). Backing that view of himself was his support for the presidential candidacy of Adlai E. Stevenson and his dislike of Richard M. Nixon (Minton 1988, 241). Still, his active role in eugenics organizations and his conviction, as had been the case with the Marx-admiring Karl Pearson, that the social and racial hierarchy in America and Britain was genetically determined constituted a profoundly reactionary position. At least the "Termanites" in America did not have the lethal consequences of Germany's "Hitlerites," but they did ensure that opportunities for educational and professional advancement would be constrained for large segments of the population. The legacy of segregation enforced by a rigid use of scores on the Scholastic Aptitude Test (renamed the Scholastic Assessment Test in 1993, SAT) to determine admission into undergraduate and postgraduate professional training programs continues to the present day. The SAT is a better indicator of family income and social class than it is of what subsequent school performance and earning power will be (Nairn et al. 1980, 79). To be sure, SAT scores of a certain level do predict who will and who will not be able to succeed in the programs involved. Above the level of that critical cut-off point, however, progressively higher scores are unrelated to the subsequent achievements of the testees (Bowen and Bok 1998, 65, 76, 133; T. Schwartz 1999, 51). This is an issue that still has not penetrated the consciousness of the nation as a whole.

WALTER LIPPMANN VERSUS THE TERMANITES

In spite of the invocation of "science" as a justification for the stance of the genetic determinists in their appearances before congressional committees or their writings and recommendations to the public at large, their assumptions were based on social preconceptions and not on the findings of any kind of research: "The hereditarian interpretation shared by Terman, Goddard and Yerkes did not arise as a consequence of the collection of I.Q. data. Their involvement in the eugenics movement predated the collection of such data" (Kamin 1974, 10). The unscientific nature of the prejudice in their outlook was brought to the attention of the reading public by a columnist for the *New Republic*,

Walter Lippmann (1889–1974), who went on to earn recognition as "without doubt the nation's greatest journalist" (Steel 1980, xvi). Lippmann had studied philosophy under William James and George Santayana at Harvard, where he was a classmate of some extraordinary figures including T. S. Eliot. He was a formidable intellectual figure, and he effectively skewered the claims of Brigham, Goddard, Stoddard, and Terman in a series of articles late in 1922. He denounced Brigham's book as "offering yellow science to the public" (Pastore 1978, 322). To Stoddard's statement that "The *average* mental age of Americans is only about fourteen," he retorted: "The average adult intelligence cannot be less than the adult intelligence, and to anyone who knows what the words 'mental age' mean, Mr. Stoddard's remark is precisely as silly as if he had written that the average mile was three quarters of a mile long" (Lippmann 1922a, 213). Showing an admirable grasp of the issues involved and the nature of the assumptions of the Termanites, Lippmann warned as follows: "It leads one to suspect . . . that the real promise of the investigation which Binet started is in danger of gross perversion by muddleheaded and prejudiced men" (Lippmann 1922a, 215). Time has shown that Lippmann's fears were fully justified.

Although the intelligence testers advanced their claims as the findings of "science," Lippmann pointed out that there was nothing scientific about what they were doing: "The claim that we have learned how to *measure hereditary intelligence* has no scientific foundation. We cannot measure intelligence when we have never defined it, and we cannot speak of its hereditary basis after it has been indistinguishably fused with a thousand educational and environmental influences from the time of conception to school age" (Lippmann 1922f, 10, italics Lippmann's). In one of the most insightful critiques of the intelligence testing business ever written, Lippmann observed that an intelligence test "does not weight or measure intelligence by any objective standard. It simply arranges a group of people in a series from best to worst by balancing their capacity to do certain selected puzzles, against the capacity of all others. . . . The intelligence test, then, is an instrument for classifying a group of people rather than a 'measure of intelligence'" (Lippmann 1922b, 247). Then, he warned "how easily the intelligence test can be turned into an engine of cruelty, how easily in the hands of blundering or prejudiced men it could turn into a method of stamping a permanent sense of inferiority upon the soul of a child" (1922d, 297).

The reaction of the intelligence-testing community was to denigrate Lippmann's views as those of a journalist and not a scientist, implying that he was not qualified to deal with the issues in question. Terman had written a rejoinder for the *New Republic* for the December 27 issue, but it started out with a prolonged exercise in sarcasm and avoided the actual points raised by Lippmann (Terman 1922). Lippmann in turn wrote a rebuttal for the issue of January 3, 1923, which had a grasp and flair that Terman could not match; and one commentator concluded that "Lippmann had the upper hand" (Pastore 1978, 323). Even though he made no claims to be a scientist, it is evident that he understood what was and what was not scientific better than the "scientists" about whom he was writing. He expressed his summary judgment in that rebuttal: "I hate the impudence of a claim that in fifty minutes you can judge and classify a human being's predestined fitness in life. I hate the pretentiousness of the claim. I hate the abuse of scientific method which it involves. I hate the sense of superiority which it creates, and the sense of inferiority which it imposes" (Lippmann 1923, 146).

Even though Walter Lippmann looks like a hero in retrospect, he was not perceived that way at the time. His objections had virtually no impact on the public at large, and the determinist and racist outlook of the educational testing community became accepted as the ruling orthodoxy from that point. One of the letters to the *New Republic* in response to Lippmann's critique referred to his stance as "both shallow and extremely partisan" and declared that it should really earn the magazine the title of the "*Jew*" *Republic* (Pastore 1978, 327). As much as anything else, this reference to Lippmann's ethnic roots demonstrated the inherent prejudice characteristic of the American public. Lewis Terman was elected president of the American Psychological Association just a year later, immigration-restriction legislation was enacted in 1924, involuntary sterilization was vetted by the Supreme Court in 1927, and segregation in the school system became the accepted norm. Lippmann had accurately, articulately, and very publicly pointed out the completely unscientific basis for these practices. His treatment, however, was either ignored or regarded as a manifestation of special pleading because of his residually Jewish identity.

17

"RACE" IN BIOLOGICAL ANTHROPOLOGY

ALEŠ HRDLIČKA AND THE SMITHSONIAN: ORGANIZING THE PROFESSION

The American situation of the juxtaposition of population blocs from three very different parts of the world inevitably led to their categorization in stereotypic fashion and the reification of the concept of "race." The Protestants who made up the dominant segment of the population felt that studying the nature of God's created world was an act of piety itself. It is no surprise, then, that after the United States survived its Civil War, there was a major expansion of institutions for research and teaching (Pauly 2001). Institutions such as the Academy of Natural Sciences in Philadelphia and the American Museum of Natural History in New York had nominal programs in anthropology, although for a variety of reasons these were not very active. However, the Smithsonian Institution, founded in 1846 with a major bequest from James Smithson, an English scientist who never visited America, promoted vigorous programs in a whole spectrum of sciences including anthropology. Brief reference to the establishment and growth of anthropology in America was made in Chapter 12. Now, it is time to look at the establishment of that part of anthropology which deals with the biology of human variation. Today, we generally call this "biological anthropology," but in the past it was widely known as "physical anthropology."

In January 1903, an announcement was made that there was to be a civil service exam to fill the position of assistant curator in the Division of Physical Anthropology at the Smithsonian. There were three applicants for the position: one from Harvard, one from Yale, and one who had spent the previous 4 years on field expeditions to Mexico and the American Southwest funded by financial backers of the American Museum of Natural History in New York, Aleš Hrdlička (1869–1943), who was to become one of the pillars of American biological anthropology (Fig. 17–1). The civil service exam had both a written and an oral component, and Hrdlička excelled in all aspects. In addition, he already had some 40 scientific publications (Spencer 1979, 249–250).

Aleš Hrdlička was born in Humpolec in what was then called Bohemia but now would be identified as the Czech Republic. It is a part of Europe with a very complicated social and political history, and Hrdlička's own family illustrates just that. His mother came from a family that had moved there from the southeastern German region of Bavaria in the 18th century, and her family language had been German (Spencer 1979, 17). His father was Czech, and both languages were used in the home. Beyond the elementary level, the language used in the schools was German. That portion of Bohemia

Figure 17-1   Aleš Hrdlička,
1869–1943 (from Montagu 1944).

Aleš Hrdlička

adjacent to Bavaria and Saxony to the west and north was known as the Sudetenland.
Like Hungary, Croatia, Serbia, and other southern Slav states, the Sudetenland had been
part of the Hapsburg Empire run from Vienna, Austria, for the previous century and a
half. That empire collapsed at the onset of World War I in 1914, and in the 1930s, Adolf
Hitler made it known that it was only right that the Sudetenland should be incorporated
into Germany. British Prime Minister Neville Chamberlain and other European heads of
state acceded to Hilter's wishes at a conference in Munich in the fall of 1938 in the for-
lorn hope that this would satisfy his lust for territorial expansion and thereby reduce the
risk of future armed conflict. Although historians usually cite Hitler's invasion of Poland
in 1939 as the formal onset of World War II, it had really begun with his invasion of the
Sudetenland in 1938 (Gilbert 1989).

As in so much of eastern Europe, however, there was a kind of romantic idealiza-
tion of things French. The French Revolution of 1789, with its abolition of the monar-
chy and the installation of citizen rule, reverberated strongly for those who had been
subject to the Hapsburg autocracy for a century and a half. Things French, then, had a
particular prestige; and the French language, while not widely known locally, was considered a sign of sophistication. Hrdlička learned it well enough so that later he was able
to court his first wife in French. In the early 1880s, the family moved to New York.

Hrdlička and his father did a stint in a Lower East Side factory, rolling cigars; and he referred to that episode for the rest of his life to support an image of the poor middle European immigrant who had arrived penniless in the New World but by industry and enterprise had made it up the social pyramid (Spencer 1979, 35). The family background was, in fact, far more bourgeois than that picture would lead one to believe, but he did maintain an interest in immigrants, working-class people, and liberal political causes for the rest of his life (Spencer 1979, 48). Even before he had completed his medical education, he helped found a Czech workers' educational union and showed his support for the philosophy of the Social Democratic Party (Spencer 1979, 47). Later, during World War I, he helped found the Bohemian–Czech Circle to promote Czech independence. This met at his home on the first Sunday of every month and included such luminaries as Tomas G. Masaryk, who was soon to become the first president of a free Czech Republic, and Edward Beneš, who was to be its second president (Spencer 1979, 752).

Initially, however, as a young immigrant, the first thing he had to do was learn English; and he was still young enough so that he learned to speak it fluently. Each Sunday he would go to a different church to hear the best orators and the best English available in New York, and it evidently had a powerful effect. The main biographical treatment of Hrdlička was written by my former student, the late Frank Spencer (1941–99), as his doctoral dissertation at the University of Michigan (1979, 1997b); and in the course of his research, he came upon a wax cylinder of Hrdlička speaking in public. He made a tape recording of that speech and played it for me. Spencer was English and not familiar with the various accents of American English of the late 19th and early 20th centuries, but one pair of my grandparents and some other relatives whom I remember well had been born and raised in New York City overlapping the time that Hrdlička was learning the language. As a result, I am completely familiar with the accent. It was perfectly obvious to me that his speech represented that of an educated and privileged New Yorker of the late 19th century. There was just a trace of something else, which I could not place. I asked Ashley Montagu, who had known Hrdlička well (Montagu 1944), about what that might be, and he replied that "what he did have was a slight Slavic accent" (personal communication, April 29, 1996). One has to realize, however, that Montagu himself was English and, while he spent much time in New York, did not grow up amid the sounds of an older generation of educated New Yorkers.

At a time when American medical education was still in need of reform, the family doctor, Meyer Rosenbluth, who was treating Hrdlička for a bad case of typhoid fever, encouraged him to enter the medical field. Rosenbluth was a trustee of the Eclectic Medical College of New York and arranged to have Hrdlička admitted there, where he could serve as the young man's preceptor. Hrdlička graduated at the head of his class in 1892 (Schultz 1945, 305; Spencer 1979, 38 ff.). Subsequently, he graduated at the top of his class from the New York Homeopathic Medical College in 1894 and passed his state board exams (Schultz 305). In 1895, he was an intern at the State Homeopathic Hospital for the Insane at Middleton, New York, and then became associate in anthropology at the Pathological Institute of the New York State Hospitals.

The next year he was granted leave to visit Europe, and the first thing he did there was to spend 4 months in Paris at the École and Laboratoire d'Anthropologie initially established by Paul Broca and then run by Broca's protégé and successor Léonce Pierre Manouvrier (Hrdlička 1927a; Spencer 1979, 111, 1997b). This was the only specifically anthropological training Hrdlička ever acquired, and he spent the rest of his life trying to shape American biological anthropology along the lines that Broca had accomplished in France (Spencer 1979, ix). He visited a series of European countries, including his own birthplace in Bohemia, before returning to New York. In 1898, he resigned from the Pathological Institute, which was collapsing financially. Then, he was signed on as a "field anthropologist" for the American Museum of Natural History by that extraordinary organizer of anthropological enterprises Frederic Ward Putnam, and his career in anthropology was formally launched (Spencer 1979, 172). The next stop was the Smithsonian, where he was to continue for nearly 40 years.

Over that span of time, Hrdlička carried out an extensive program of field work in many different parts of the world and produced a truly monumental corpus of published reports on what he found. Little of this is cited at the present time, and some of his most insightful and productive work is either misrepresented in caricature or never mentioned at all. This book is not the place to straighten that out since it involves aspects of evolutionary theory and of population movements and relationships that deserve full treatment at another time. If the reader wishes to get something of the flavor of Hrdlička's work, some of this is indicated in a sampling of three decades of his publications (Hrdlička 1907, 1914, 1918, 1927b, 1930, 1935). Before treating his accomplishments, it should be recorded that his views on "race" were conventionally in accord with most of what was accepted in anthropology at that time (Hrdlička 1928a,b). What was accepted in anthropology, however, especially as it was represented in the continuing ethos of Broca's school in Paris, had a strong American component, of which Hrdlička was largely unaware. He took it for granted that Africans were "lower" on an assumed gradient of intellectual capability. On the other hand, he did not accept the claims of the immigration-restriction advocates that different European populations had different levels of capability. As a person of eastern European origin himself, he recognized it as "prejudice" that Madison Grant, Congressman Albert Johnson, Harry Laughlin, Lothrop Stoddard, and their supporters believed that average American capacities were being diminished by the immigration of eastern and southern Europeans. Since he felt that all Europeans had equal capabilities on the average, he could see no disadvantage in any of the possible mixtures that might occur between the various manifestations. He did not feel the same way about mixtures with Africans, and in that regard he was a typical representative of the racist assumptions in the America of his day.

In this as in other manifestations of his thought, Hrdlička had surprisingly little influence on his contemporaries except in eastern Europe. He set up the Aleš and Marie Hrdlička Foundation in Prague to subsidize a chair in anthropology at Charles University (Montagu 1944). Biological anthropologists today would agree that his main contribution was in creating the journal that has served as the voice of the field ever since and founding the professional association to which the vast majority of its practitioners continue to belong. In 1918, he founded the *American Journal of Physical Anthropology* (AJPA), which he edited from that time through the year before his death. Initially, he subsidized publication with money from his own pocket to the tune of $1,000 per year until it achieved the status of a going concern (Spencer 1979, 700–702). Although it is not widely known, a generous yearly subsidy to support the publication of the AJPA was contributed by Mary Hooton, wife of the Harvard biological anthropologist Earnest Albert Hooton (Stanley M. Garn, personal communication). Hooton's importance and career are treated in a subsequent section. Starting in Hrdlička's last year,

1943, he passed the reins of editorship to T. Dale Stewart, who was his own protégé and successor as curator in the Division of Physical Anthropology at the Smithsonian. In recognition of the end of an era, the journal began with volume 1 of its "new series" at that time.

At the very end of 1928, at the meetings of the American Association for the Advancement of Science, Hrdlička was the spark plug in founding the American Association of Physical Anthropologists (AAPA, Hrdlička 1929). As had been the case for Broca when he founded the Société d'Anthropologie de Paris in 1859, many of the participants were trained as medical doctors, Hrdlička himself being an example. Because of those ties with the medical world, the first meetings of the AAPA were held in conjunction with the meetings of the American Association of Anatomists in May 1930. The two associations tended to meet at the same time and place for some years thereafter. Hrdlička was president through 1932 (Schultz 1945, 316), but his legacy, other than being the founder of the journal and the association, had less and less influence from that point on.

For the remainder of his life, Hrdlička faithfully attended the meetings of the association and felt compelled to comment on the papers delivered, whether he really knew anything about the subject or not. The generation that included my teachers went to the meetings, and many are the wryly humorous tales they have told. My own particular and gracious mentor, William W. Howells, has made his mark by, among other things, applying sophisticated matrix analysis and probability statistics. For any given measurement, such as stature, a population average from a small number of individuals is always going to be somewhat off what it would be if a very large number (or all) of the individuals of that population were used. There are ways of calculating how reliable the population average, or *mean,* is going to be, given the number of individuals used and their variation in dimensions. When Howells was giving a student paper at an AAPA meetings in the mid-1930s, he reported what was then a standard statistic called the "probable error" of the mean. After he had finished, Hrdlička, in his customary postpresentation commentary, announced: "When I measure a specimen, there is no probable error!" (Howells, personal communication).

Hrdlička was all in favor of measurement but famous for his antipathy to statistics. At the Philadelphia AAPA meeting in 1940, one of the presentations made extensive use of statistics. Hrdlička stood up, walked to the rear of the room, and, before leaving, whispered something to Morris Steggerda (1900–50), one of Davenport's collaborators in an ill-conceived work on "race" crossing (Davenport and Steggerda 1929). After the end of the paper, Steggerda arose and said "Dr. Hrdlička has asked me to announce that statistics will be the ruination of the science" (Lasker 1989, 615).

ACADEMIA AND THE PATTERNS OF THOUGHT IN BIOLOGICAL ANTHROPOLOGY: SIR ARTHUR KEITH

That minor example and a series of other ones of a similar nature have done more to perpetuate the picture of a Hrdlička who was out of touch with the field toward the end of his life than any consideration of what he actually accomplished. While I heard many similar anecdotes, I did not come to grips with the real nature of his contributions until well after my formal training had been completed. The substance of his contribution is not the topic of this book, but the fact that it is largely unknown is relevant to how an outlook is transmitted from one generation to the next. If Hrdlička built the framework which the practitioners of biological anthropology have used to exchange their views, he had no influence on what those views actually were. These latter actually came from a single powerful source, the Department of Anthropology at Harvard University over a 40-year time span in the 20th century. The Harvard outlook, however, was imported from a single European source, the British anatomist Sir Arthur Keith (1866–1955) (Fig. 17–2).

Keith was born near Aberdeen, Scotland, where the local accent is harder for outsiders to understand than is true for the other major Scottish cities, such as Edinburgh and Glasgow. In later life, Keith was never able to learn to get along in foreign languages (Keith 1950, 187), although evidently the extremes of Scottish dialect were toned down to such an extent that he had no trouble making himself understood in Great Britain and America. He gained his medical qualifications at the University of Aberdeen in 1888, at a time when medicine was more a healing art than anything based on science (Keith 1950, 70 ff.). He spent the next 4 years as a physician for a gold-prospecting concern in Thailand (Keith 1950,105 ff.), where he saved enough money so that he could survive in London for 3 years while angling for a paying position. During that period, he wrote a doctoral dissertation based on primate anatomical information he had collected while in Thailand. He submitted this to Aberdeen and was duly awarded his M.D. in 1894. (Remember, a British M.D. is a research degree and not comparable to the American license to practice medicine.)

Figure 17–2 Sir Arthur Keith, 1866–1955. Portrait by W. W. Ouless in 1928, when Keith was 62 (from Keith 1950).

A year later he became senior demonstrator in anatomy at the school attached to the London Hospital, and his professional career was off and running (Keith 1950, 179 ff.). In 1908, he became curator of the museum at the Royal College of Surgeons in Lincoln's Inn Fields, London, a position he held until he retired early in the 1930s. A veritable torrent of publications emerged from his pen, which, along with his genial charm and in spite of the absence of substance, brought him widespread recognition as a scientific eminent, earning him election as a fellow of the Royal Society in 1913. His first book, *Ancient Types of Man,* was published in 1911 just before he had the conversion experience that completely changed his interpretation of the course of human evolution (Keith 1911). That little book was essentially a paraphrase of a book by the Strassburg anatomist Gustav Schwalbe (1844–1916), *Studien zur Vorgeschichte des Menschen,* which presented a straightforward view of human evolution proceeding from *Homo erectus* of over a million years ago via a Neanderthal phase into modern humans (Schwalbe 1906). Characteristically, Keith made no mention of the fact that the source of the view he was presenting was Schwalbe's book. Oddly enough, the same view was represented in Hrdlička's Huxley Memorial Lecture of 1927 entitled "The Neanderthal Phase of Man" (Hrdlička 1927b). While Hrdlička cited Schwalbe's contribution, he flipped it over completely and attributed to Schwalbe the patently anti-evolutionary stance of French paleoanthropology (Hrdlička 1927b, 250; 1930, 327; Brace 1964b, 14; 1974b, 205–206; 1981, 418). In the words of his biographer: "While it is not possible to document the development of this idea in Hrdlička's writings it appears in this instance that Hrdlička's objectivity was distorted by his long-standing aversion to German culture (which had been heightened by the First World War) and his inability to transcend his deep-seated Francophilia which prevented him from evaluating dispassionately the obviously anti-evolutionary posture of Gallic paleoanthropology" (Spencer 1979, 582).

Late in the summer of 1911, Keith had what could only be called a "conversion experience." In September, he and his wife made a trip to France, being hosted by a friend in Paris for a few days first, and then exploring the lovely Dordogne region, of southwestern France, the locale where a sequence of prehistoric artifacts and human fossils had been found over the previous 40 years. They visited the Cro-Magnon site in Les Eyzies where that famous ancient "modern" had been found, the nearby La Madeleine site that had yielded Upper Paleolithic artifacts in profusion, and Le Moustier that had produced a Neanderthal skeleton plus artifacts in 1908. In 1911 also, a description of the Neanderthal skeleton found in 1908 at La Chapelle-aux-Saints in the neighboring Département of Corrèze had begun to be published by the eminent French paleontologist Marcellin Boule (1861–1936) (complete description published 1911–13). Even though Keith did not read French easily, this and the sights in the Dordogne had an overwhelming effect on his outlook. As he said in his autobiography, with a somewhat fuzzy perception of the timing:

> At the time I took office at the College of Surgeons our knowledge of the ancient inhabitants of Europe was undergoing a revolutionary change. Until then most of us had believed that in remote times Europe had been inhabited by men of the Neanderthal type, and that in the course of centuries the ape-browed Neanderthalians had evolved into men of the modern type. Discoveries had been made in the Dordogne region of France which proved that men of the modern type appeared quite abruptly in Europe, as if they had evolved elsewhere and entered as invaders. The Neanderthalians seem to have disappeared in an equally sudden manner. (Keith 1950, 318–319)

The full manifestation of Keith's change in outlook was evident in his most influential book, with a title borrowed from the 1863 work of Sir Charles Lyell, *The Antiquity of Man* (Keith 1915a, revised in 1925). Although the actual fossil and archaeological evidence provide no support for such a view, it is now held by the vast majority of those working in the field of human "evolution" today, and it is accepted as essentially self-evident by the press. When that book appeared, World War I had already broken out: "France, the traditional British enemy, suddenly became an ally; and the admiration for German scholarship . . . became unfashionable overnight" (Brace 1974b, 206). In Chapter 12, I discussed how World War I reinforced the "racial" stance of French anthropology in the English-speaking world, noting that Morton's American School played a major role in shaping that French outlook. French biology, paleontology, and anthropology, had never accepted a Darwinian perspective on evolution, and that is clearly obvious in the thinking of Sir Arthur Keith. His conversion experience of 1911, when he adopted the French antievolutionary outlook, set the stage for the treatment of human "evolution" that has dominated the English-speaking world ever since. This is more than slightly ironic since Keith lived for the last quarter of a century of his long life in a house on the Darwin estate, Down, and was regarded by the public as, and prided himself on being, the embodiment of the Darwinian perspective. As will be evident when his view on "race" is examined, nothing could be further from the truth.

As World War I came to an end, Keith's reputation soared. He had been president of the Royal Anthropological Institute, he became president of section H (anthropology) of the British Association in 1919, he was knighted in 1921 (Keith 1950, 438), and he was elected president of the British Association for the Advancement of Science (usually called just the British Association) in 1927 (Keith 1950, 494). The latter is the most important grouping of scientists in Great Britain, and election to its presidency has to be the highest accolade that can be given to a British scientist. It is true that not all of its members felt that Keith deserved the position. The Oxford geologist William J. Sollas (1849–1936), writing in July 1925 to the Scottish–South African physician and paleontologist Robert Broom (1866–1951), declared: "Sir Arthur Keith who is indeed the most arrant humbug and artful climber in the anthropological world. . . . I am truly astonished. He makes the rashest statements in the face of evidence. Never quotes an author but to misrepresent him, generalizes on single observations, and indeed there is scarcely a single crime in which he is not adept . . . journalism, pure and simple" (quoted in Findlay 1972, 53). Another, younger contemporary, Sir Solly Zuckerman (1904–93), said the following:

> And there was Arthur Keith himself, [whose] scientific qualities I usually felt were almost in inverse proportion to his widespread influence and charm. He was a distinguished looking figure who laboured assiduously in physical anthropology, and who had an outstanding ability to charm non-specialist audiences. He was immensely friendly, and the door of his conservator's room on the ground floor of the Royal College of Surgeons was always open. But I must confess that I found that the diagnostic procedures he employed in matters osteological savoured more of divine inspiration than of normally accepted scientific method. . . . I never was able to regard him as more than a superficial scientist. (Zuckerman 1973, 5, 11)

There is evidence that Zuckerman was right on the mark with his appraisal. Writing at the end of his long life, Keith declared his Darwinian loyalty: "For I believe in Darwin and Darwinism. I have lived now almost a quarter of a century in the place he made world-famous as a centre of biological research, and I have a hope that his spirit will continue to influence the work done" (Keith 1955, 289). Yet, earlier in the same volume, he stated: "the vast majority of naturalists held (rightly, in my opinion) that natural selection did not account, as Darwin believed it did, for the wonderful contrivances which Archdeacon Paley had so extolled in his *Natural Theology*" (Keith 1955, 103). This, of course, is not what the "vast majority of naturalists" accepted at all. The evolutionary synthesis of the late 1930s and 1940s effectively reaffirmed and documented everything Darwin had proposed. Even as that movement was reaching the heights of its strength, Keith was opining as follows: "To ask me to believe that the evolution of man has been determined by a series of chance events is to invite me to give credit to what is biologically unbelievable. . . . I could as easily believe the theory of the Trinity as one which maintains that living, developing protoplasm, by mere throws of chance, brought the human eye into existence. The essence of living protoplasm is its purposiveness" (Keith 1946, 217). That, of course, is about as anti-Darwinian as one can get. When his views on "race" are examined, further un-Darwinian aspects will become obvious.

I have already noted that Keith was educated in the healing arts and not in science, and he unwittingly affirmed that in speaking of his loyalties. He spoke approvingly of "the personality of Thomas Carlyle, who made so strong an appeal in my youthful years, against the personality of Charles Darwin, who engaged the wholehearted admiration of my later years" (Keith 1950, 562; also 1943, 21). As his complete mangling of Darwinian thinking suggests, it is obvious that, while he may have appreciated Darwin's gentle and nondogmatic personality, he never understood the nature of what Darwin had proposed. He continued to quote from Carlyle's *Sartor Resartus* (1838) right up to the end of his working career (Keith 1931, 27), and it is clear that his mind continued to act more like that of Thomas Carlyle (1795–1881) than that of Charles Darwin even if he did not radiate the dyspeptic gloom and anti-egalitarian elitist dogmatism for which Carlyle was famous (Heffer 1995; Wilson 1999). With this in mind, it should be of interest to check on what Darwin thought about Carlyle. In January 1839, he wrote to his cousin and wife-to-be, Emma Wedgwood: "To my mind Carlyle is the best worth listening to of any man I know" (Litchfield 1915, II:21). However, in his autobiography, published posthumously by his son Francis, he added the following: "As far as I could judge, I never met a man with a mind so ill adapted for scientific research" (F. Darwin 1887, I:64). Zuckerman might have agreed that something of that assessment could apply in the case of Sir Arthur Keith.

I do not want to leave the impression that everything that Keith did lacked merit. He made a major contribution to dental anthropology when he realized that the overbite which almost all living people possess is only a very recent phenomenon and is not the aboriginal normal way in which our jaws and teeth occlude. From his examination of human skeletons buried in certain English churches, he was able to show that the majority of the people interred up to the end of the 18th century had what is known as an "edge-to-edge bite." High-status individuals, however—those in special crypts—had the overbite that we now assume is the normal human condition (Keith 1924). He guessed correctly that the change was associated with a change in eating habits and not a genetic or evolutionary event. Until the introduction of the dinner fork in the 18th century— initially only among the relatively wealthy—food items were conveyed to the mouth with the left hand, clamped with the teeth, and sawed off at lip level by a knife held in the right hand, something I have referred to as the "stuff-and-cut school of etiquette" (Brace 1977, 199).

When Keith turned to "race," however, he was clearly at his opinionated and unscientific worst; and he did this repeatedly starting in the year he became a fellow of the Royal Society (Keith 1913, 1915b, 1916, 1919a,b, 1928b, 1931). In almost comically simple-minded fashion, he advanced his "hormonal" explanation for human differentiation: "the thyroid—or a reduction or alteration in the activity of the thyroid—has been a factor in determining some of the racial characteristics of the Mongol and the Negro races" (Keith 1919a, 304). However, he was at his most inexcusable when he expounded on "race" relations and evolution. This he did most blatantly in his Robert Boyle Lecture at Balliol College, Oxford, in 1919 (Keith 1919b); his Huxley Memorial Lecture before the Royal Anthropological Institute in 1928 (1928b); and his rectorial address at the University of Aberdeen in 1931. In the published version of his 1927 presidential address to the British Association, he reiterated a theme that pervaded much of his writing: "We cannot conceive of living matter as devoid of purpose" (Keith 1928a, 63). He emphasized this subsequently: "I have just affirmed that there are evolutionary processes inherent in living things and therefore in Nature—trends of change which are akin to human purpose and human policy" (Keith 1946, 218). Again, this is completely at variance with what Darwin had presented, and it shows that Keith's mind had not quite caught up with the middle of the 19th century. For a splendidly realized 21st-century treatment of the lack of "purpose" in Darwin's evolution, there is no better source than the recently published book *Darwin and Design: Does Evolution Have a Purpose?* (Ruse 2003).

Toward the end of his life and recalling his earlier assumptions, Keith reminisced that "races were assorted in my mind into superior and inferior; I of course was of the superior race" (Keith 1950, 119). To that he added that "like most of my fellows, I was a sober imperialist . . . Rudyard Kipling sang our creed" (Keith 1950, 228). The most complete rendering of his "racial" views is in his rectorial address at Aberdeen in 1931, and it is worth looking at some of what that contained. I have already noted that he had rejected Darwin's view that evolution proceeds by the operation of natural selection on individuals. Keith, in fact, was more a proponent of "group selection," although the main arguments promoting such a view were developed well after his death (Wynne-Edwards 1962, 1986; Gould 2002, Chapter 8). At the other extreme, the argument has been advanced that evolution takes place at the level of the gene (Dawkins 1976). Most evolutionary biologists, however, follow Darwin's original insight and recognize selection as having its effects primarily on the individual. Darwin did not completely rule out group selection, and many biologists recognize that selection can have its effects on several different levels—*hierarchical selection*—noting that selection acting on the individual can have consequences for the elimination or perpetuation of the gene as well as the population (Wimsatt 1980; Mayr 1996; Brandon 1999). Keith, however, viewed the tribe as "nature's evolutionary unit" (Keith 1916, 32): "Without a tribal organization there could have been no evolutionary progress—no ascent of man" (Keith 1931, 41). He never did say what produced that "progress," merely insisting that it could occur only if tribes were isolated from each other. If a modern breeder "were called on to evolve a new human breed he would do just what nature has done, separate Mankind into herds and tribes and keep them isolated and pure for an endless period. Each tribe in our pre-historic world would represent an evolutionary experiment. Without isolation Nature could have done nothing" (Keith 1931, 33). He then invoked the imagery of team sports, which he said had developed in imitation of the circumstances that had promoted human evolution in the past:

> Our modern masters of football have but copied the scheme of competition which Nature had set up in her ancient world. Her League of Humanity had its divisions—racial divisions—white, yellow, brown, and black. Tribes constituted her competing teams. No transfers for her; each member of the team had to be home-born and home-bred. She did not trust her players or their managers farther than she could see them! To make certain they would play the great game of life as she intended it should be played she put them into colours—not transferable jerseys, but liveries of living flesh, such liveries as the races of the modern world now wear. (Keith 1931, 34–35)

Extending the analogy still further, his "great game of life" required that hostility be-tween the players was necessary for evolution to occur: "What modern football team could face the goal-posts unless it developed as it took the field a spirit of antagonism towards the players wearing opposite colours? Nature endowed her tribal teams with the spirit of antagonism for her own purposes. It has come down to us and creeps out from our modern life in many shapes, as national rivalries and jealousies and as racial hatreds. The modern name for this spirit of antagonism is race-prejudice" (Keith 1931, 35). Not surprisingly, he extolled "race" prejudice: "Prejudices, I believe, have their purpose. Man has become what he is, not by virtue of his head, but because of his heart" (Keith 1931, 26). That contrast between the roles of the head and the heart was a common theme of the Scottish philosophy of Common Sense. That had been an Enlightenment phenomenon, but Keith was using it more in the transcendental spirit of Romanticism.

He approved not only of prejudice but also of war as a positive factor in human evo-lution (Keith 1915b): "Nature keeps her human orchard healthy by pruning; war is her pruning hook. We cannot dispense with her services" (Keith 1931, 49). This, one real-izes, was written only 2 years before Hitler took power in Germany and put into action policies that one could argue were fully compatible with Keith's outlook.

With his view that "racial" differentiation was the positive consequence of the process of evolution, it is no surprise to find that he was opposed to the idea of "racial" mixing or amalgamation. This would deprive people of their "racial birthright" (Keith 1931, 47): "If this scheme of universal deracialization ever comes before you as a mat-ter of practical politics—as the sole way of establishing peace and good will in all parts of the world, I feel certain both head and heart will rise against it. There will well up within you an overmastering antipathy of securing peace at such a price. This antipathy or race prejudice Nature has implanted within you for her own ends—the improvement of Mankind through race differentiation" (Keith 1931, 48).

Interestingly enough, Keith's ideas on "race" bore a striking similarity to those ar-ticulated by the German naturalist Ernst Haeckel (1834–1919). Haeckel has sometimes been regarded as rendering Darwin in German, but in fact his ideas on evolution were at least as unlike Darwin's as were Keith's (Gasman 1971). Not surprisingly, Keith showed an active appreciation for Haeckel (Keith 1935). Another measure of just how far off the mark Keith could be was his enthusiasm for the anthropology of Sir Francis Galton: "he will be deemed in the judgment of posterity—the greatest anthropologist produced in Europe during the 19th century" (Keith 1920, 14) and "I owe more ideas to him than to any other of my predecessors" (Keith 1950, 399).

KEITH'S INFLUENCE ON AMERICA: EARNEST ALBERT HOOTON

Sir Arthur Keith visited the United States in 1915 to lecture at Western Reserve University in Cleveland and in 1921 to lecture at Johns Hopkins University in Baltimore (Keith 1950, 375, 444). His main impact on the country, however, was via an American who had become his disciple. Earnest Albert Hooton (1887–1954), the son of a Methodist clergyman, was born and raised in Wisconsin (Laughlin 1954) (Fig. 17–3). On his graduation from Lawrence College in 1907, he qualified for a Rhodes Scholarship at Oxford University in England. He delayed acceptance for 3 years while he worked on his doctorate in classics at the University of Wisconsin. Then, in 1910, he took up his Rhodes Scholarship and held it through 1913, earning a diploma in anthropology in 1912 and a B.Litt. before he left (Howells 1954; Garn and Giles 1995; Giles 1997b). His contact with anthropology at Oxford was via Robert Ranulph Marett, rector of Exeter College, a classical scholar and one of the founders of social anthropology there (Collini 1996, 5).

To gain experience in the skeletal remains of the prehistoric inhabitants of Europe, he studied the material in the collections of the Museum of the Royal College of

Figure 17–3 Earnest Albert Hooton, 1887–1954 (from [Howells] 1954).

Surgeons in London, where Keith was the curator. In Hooton's own words: "I became, in some sense, a disciple of Arthur Keith. . . . Among the several great teachers I have had, none was his superior" (Hooton 1947, v–vi). In 1913, Hooton was hired by Harvard as an instructor in physical anthropology, which he taught there for the remainder of his life. When he joined it, the anthropology department at Harvard became the only one in the United States with a full-time biological anthropologist. As has been said, Hooton spent the next four decades "attempting to build American physical anthropology in the image of Sir Arthur Keith" (Brace 1964b, 16). That may have been just a bit of an over-statement, but there is no doubt that he retained an enormous amount of affection and respect for Sir Arthur. "The name of Sir Arthur Keith deserves to be associated with those of Charles Darwin and Thomas Huxley in the study of the evolution of man. During the last half century, Keith has been the foremost British student of human phylogeny and of fossil man, and, in the opinion of many, has exhibited the greatest mastery of the subject shown by any anthropologist" (Hooton 1947, v). No one would agree with that today, and Keith has been largely forgotten by the field, although his views on the processes and the course of evolution continue unmodified. The same kind of admiration that Hooton had for Keith was also felt by the person to whom my book is dedicated, Ashley Montagu, who learned his anatomy from Keith but whose views on "race" were radically different. Hooton, although retaining more of Keith's racial stance than Montagu, never extolled prejudice or war as playing important roles in the shaping of racial differences.

Both Hooton and Montagu exemplified the anti-Darwinian treatment of the human fossil record that Keith had adopted in the fall of 1911, and this has continued to characterize American biological anthropology right up to the present day. Starting in the early 1920s and continuing for the next two decades, Hooton supervised well over two dozen Ph.D. dissertations in biological anthropology. Just as Keith had an unparalleled influence over biological anthropology in the British Isles, so did Hooton in America. He was a marvelously fluent lecturer with a mellow baritone that brought to mind the fictional lecturer of a couple of generations prior: "The voice and accent had been carefully affected and trained in the Americanized Oxford familiar in eastern graduate schools" (G. W. Brace 1952, 34). It was not an exaggerated version, as was the case for some of its exemplars, but the Anglican aspect was clearly audible. He was undeniably an impressive figure in the classroom as I can testify since I was a teaching assistant in the course that he was giving when he died, making me in effect his last students. I would give him the same accolade that he gave Keith: among the several great teachers I have had, none was his superior.

As one of his early protégés and later eulogist put it, "we can, in an almost literal way, identify Hooton as the father of physical anthropology in this country" (Shapiro 1981, 423). Virtually every department of anthropology in America that has a subdivision which focuses on biological anthropology owes the initiation of that section either directly to a Hooton student or to the student of a Hooton student. A dilute vestige of Keith survives in the field as a whole, which is almost certainly why those biological anthropologists who study the human fossil record appear so badly out of step with the outlook of evolutionary biology. Hooton's most influential work, *Up from the Ape* (1931, 1946), reflects many of the same views defended in Keith's *The Antiquity of Man* (1915a, 1925).

Hooton's views on "race," however, are more complex. Even in the last edition of his major text, he included the statement "we are fairly safe in assuming that the Australian is far less intelligent than the Englishman" (Hooton 1946, 158). However, in an earlier treatment of the topic, he had said that a "race" is "characterized as a group by a certain combination of morphological and metrical features, primarily nonadaptive, which have been derived from their common descent" (Hooton 1926, 75). Twenty years later, he reversed himself on that view: "This insistence upon the use of 'non-adaptive' characters in human taxonomy now seems to me to be impractical and erroneous" (Hooton 1946, 452). Actually, his first view is closer to what led to the construction of dendrograms showing population similarities and differences, as illustrated in Chapter 1 (Fig. 1–7).

Halfway between the times he produced those conflicting statements, he articulated a view with which we can still agree: "Anthropologists have found as yet no relationship between any physical criterion of race and mental capacity whether in individuals or in groups" (Hooton 1936, 512). That was generated at the behest of Franz Boas of Columbia University and published by Hooton in *Science,* the official voice of the American Association for the Advancement of Science, on May 29, 1936 (Barkan 1988, 187). Subsequently, when a resolution denouncing the Nazi "racial" doctrine was presented to the annual meeting of the American Anthropological Association (AAA) in 1938, it was voted down because the membership thought it had been prepared by Boas and smacked of being self-serving. The president of the AAA then told them it had been written by Hooton. At the next session, it was read again and passed unanimously (Barkan 1992, 339). Obviously, Hooton was not replicating Sir Arthur Keith's approach toward "race."

Curiously enough, a very similar resolution condemning "the misuse of anthropological terms for political purposes" was presented by Ashley Montagu at the tenth annual meeting of the AAPA in Philadelphia, April 4, 1939, with Hooton serving as president pro-tem. It was moved and passed that Montagu's proposal be referred to the executive committee, where it vanished without further treatment (3). Hrdlička then took Montagu to task for the use of "intemperate language" (*Philadelphia Record* 1939, 6; Barkan 1992, 339). However, there were no hard feelings between the two. That evening at a dinner celebrating Hrdlička's 70th birthday, Montagu read an "illuminated resolution which was presented to Hrdlička" (4).

CARLETON COON ON "RACE"

Carleton S. Coon (1904–81) earned his Ph.D. under Hooton in 1928 and then became a colleague on the anthropology faculty at Harvard (Fig. 17–4). Subsequently, from 1948 until his retirement in 1963, he represented a kind of Hootonian biological anthropology at the University of Pennsylvania (Coon 1981; Giles 1997a, 294). Carl Coon was an outspoken and colorful character. While one description referred to him as "tall, lean, and lanky" (Trinkaus and Shipman 1992, 278), that would apply only if one could characterize a well-fed grizzly bear as "lanky." He was, in fact, rather bear-like in appearance.

When he was teaching at Harvard, the Macmillan Company contracted him to rewrite Ripley's *Races of Europe,* which he did (Coon 1939). This was the means by which

Figure 17-4   Carleton Stevens
Coon, 1904–81 (from Washburn
1952).

a vestige of Franco-American polygenism was reinforced in the middle of the 20th century. That book served as a springboard for what was to occupy his mind for the rest of
his career. Although one unsigned obituary notice called him a "distinguished social anthropologist" (*Newsweek* June 15, 1981, 107) and he did spread his attention across the
broad sweep of the several divisions of anthropology, still he was identified by most in
the business as more of a biological anthropologist than any other kind.

In fact, he was president of the AAPA in 1962 when it voted to condemn a blatantly
racist tract, *Race and Reason: A Yankee View,* written by a distant relative of his (Putnam
1961). The author, Carleton Putnam, was the former head of Delta Airlines and, alas, a
distant relative of mine also. Coon was the only member of the association to speak in
favor of that miserable manifestation of bigotry, and the membership voted 91 to 1 in
favor of the condemnation (Lasker 1999, 148). Coon then stormed out of the room, resigned his office, and never came back to the AAPA meetings. He also did not return to
the University of Pennsylvania (Lasker 1999, 148). *Race and Reason* was widely distributed in the South courtesy of the Pioneer Fund, about which I shall say more in the
next chapter (Tucker 2002, 106). The Louisiana State Board of Education made it required reading for all deans, professors, and other instructional personnel, as well as for
all students enrolled in anthropology, sociology, and psychology (H. M. [Mongolis]
1961, 1868). As shown later from the Coon correspondence housed at the Smithsonian,
he had exchanged a series of letters with Carleton Putnam prior to the publication of
Race and Reason (Tucker 2002, 115, 247). It appears that he had worked behind the

scenes to undermine the desegregation that followed the *Brown v. Board of Education* decision of 1954 (Tucker 1994b, 162–168).

Coon's magnum opus, *The Origin of Races,* came out the very next year, and it was dedicated to Franz Weidenreich (Coon 1963). Weidenreich (1873–1948) was justly famous for his descriptions of the *Homo erectus* fossils found in China from the late 1920s up to the outbreak of World War II in the Far East in 1937. Hooton himself had praised Weidenreich's descriptive competence while noting that his interpretive efforts "may be contested" (Hooton 1944, 317). The majority of the practitioners in the field have followed Hooton's thinking and ignored Weidenreich's interpretation of the evidence. A few who have dealt with that interpretation have seriously misrepresented it (as noted in Brace 1964b, 15; 1981, 423). Coon was one of the latter.

The reason he dedicated his book posthumously to Weidenreich was that Weidenreich had defended a view that human populations across the world reached their "modern" appearance in situ in each of the regions they inhabited. This was at the heart of Keith's approach, but there was a huge difference. In Coon's view, the status of *H. sapiens* had been reached independently and at different times in the various parts of the world because the inhabitants in each separate region had remained isolated from each other. In this, he represented continuity with the outlook of Keith (1936, 194; 1950, 631). Weidenreich's regional continuity scheme, however, showed what could be called "gene flow" between adjacent populations throughout the entire world of human occupation (Weidenreich 1947, 201). In this way, specific unity was maintained in the genus *Homo* since its initial appearance and an adaptively advantageous gene appearing in one population would, in the course of time, become the property of all (Weidenreich 1943, 253).

In Coon's view, each of the five "races" crossed the line into *H. sapiens* status at a different time. His "Caucasoids" and "Mongoloids" crossed it first and got a head start on exhibiting sophisticated and fully "modern" human characteristics (Coon 1962, 3–4). "Caucasoids" were the first to cross the line and presumably, therefore, are the most "advanced" (Coon 1962, 482): "If Africa was the cradle of mankind, it was only an indifferent kindergarten. Europe and Asia were our principal schools" (Coon 1962, 656). His two African "races," the "Congoids" of central Africa and "Capoids" from the south, like his "Australoids," crossed the *H. sapiens* line late, for whatever reason, and presumably are less sapient than northern people. Coon followed up with one more major work, *The Living Races of Man* (Coon and Hunt 1965), but this was just more of the same. At bottom, it was simply opinion unsupported by anything testable and clearly at odds with the archaeological evidence, which documents a picture of exchange between adjacent groups worldwide in the manner that Weidenreich had postulated (Clark 1977; Coles et al. 1999).

Starting in 1964, I deliberately applied Weidenreich's model to understanding the course of human evolution and how the differentiation that produced the variations in appearance of living human groups had come about (Brace 1964b, 1967, 1981, 1995, 2000). It seemed to me that starting with the expectation of "in situ continuity" and an examination of the circumstances that led to gradual change was likely to be "more useful" than assuming change occurred elsewhere for reasons unknown and then moved into areas that were already inhabited (Brace 1981, 423–424). That approach was picked up in partial form by Milford Wolpoff of the University of Michigan and, in a bit of verbal ineptitude, rechristened the "multiregional evolution" model (Wolpoff 1980; Wolpoff et al. 1984). Left out of that model were the mechanisms that produced the particular changes in form from the archaic to the "modern," which had been part of what I proposed, especially the reduction in robustness caused by mutations alone after particular aspects of selection had been relaxed. Weidenreich was an evolutionist, but he had been a somewhat uncertain Darwinian with hints of Lamarck and Haeckel in his outlook. His scheme of regional continuity, however, is perfectly compatible with the outlook of modern evolutionary biology, whose roots, of course, were firmly established by Darwin.

SCIENCE AND SOCIETY ON "RACE" AFTER WORLD WAR II

By the mid-point of the 20th century, it seemed to many people that the world could benefit from an informed statement on what "race" did and did not mean. Toward that end, the United Nations Educational, Scientific, and Cultural Organization (UNESCO) convened an international panel of anthropologists and sociologists at its headquarters in Paris late in 1949. The panel put together a statement on "race" in light of the latest scientific information available. There was some concern that other aspects of science had not been consulted (Snyder 1962, 98), so the chair sent copies to senior figures in biology, genetics, psychology, sociology, and economics, who responded with suggestions for strengthening and improving the text. Ashley Montagu, a member of the original panel, then rewrote the statement, incorporating the points suggested by the figures consulted. Over a span of 7 months, the statement went through five drafts. Clearly, Montagu, with the same impetus that he had shown at the AAPA meeting in 1939, was a main spark plug behind it; and some of its form shows his preferences—for example, the attempt to substitute the term *ethnic group* for *race* (Montagu 1951, 13). Finally, when all were happy to sign it, the statement was released to the press of all nations on July 18, 1950 (UNESCO on Race 1950; Beaglehole et al. 1951; Montagu 1951).

Much of what was covered was devoted to a consideration of the ethics of equal treatment, but there certainly was a concern for basic biology. A bit of that is worth quoting here:

> Statements that human hybrids frequently show undesirable traits, both physically and mentally, physical disharmonies and mental degeneracies, are not supported by the facts. There is, therefore, no *biological* justification for prohibiting intermarriage between persons of different ethnic groups. . . . intelligence tests do not enable us to differentiate safely between what is due to innate capacity and what is the result of environmental influences, training and education. . . . there is no proof that the groups of mankind differ in their innate mental characteristics, whether in respect to intelligence or temperament. . . . for all practical social purposes "race" is not so much a biological phenomenon as a social myth. (Montagu 1951, 14–17)

It would take another decade for the realization that "there are no races, there are only clines" (Livingstone 1962, 279) to seep into public consciousness or even into anthropological thinking (Littlefield et al. 1982). In the 1930s, well over half the published texts in anthropology accepted the biological reality of "race" and less than 20% rejected it. By the late 1970s, 50% of biological anthropologists but only 31% of cultural anthropologists accepted it. By the mid 1980s, over half of cultural anthropologists and 42% of biological anthropologists rejected the idea of a biological entity that could be called "race" (Lieberman et al. 1989). According to one analysis, there was a steady decrease in the number of texts supporting the existence of biological "races" over the last 60 years of the 20th century (Lieberman et al. 2003), although another look at the available evidence concluded that a more comprehensive treatment might not support that picture of change in belief (Cartmill and Brown 2003).

It is interesting to note, however, that, in 1996 the AAPA finally endorsed a 1964 revision of the UNESCO statement on "race." This had much in common with what Ashley Montagu had tried to get them to accept in 1939, only to have it disappear in the executive committee: "The human features which have universal biological value for the survival of the species are not known to occur more frequently in one population than in any other. Therefore it is meaningless from a biological point of view to attribute a general inferiority or superiority to this or that race" (AAPA Statement on Biological Aspects of Race 1996, 570).

18

THE LEGACY OF THE PIONEER FUND

THE PROMOTION OF "SCIENTIFIC" RACISM

The converse of Lippmann's outlook in the 1920s was given substance in the following decade with the establishment of the Pioneer Fund, supported financially by the "eccentric Massachusetts textile heir" and promoter of Nazi "race" policies Wickliffe Draper (1891–1972) (Kühl 1994, 5–6; Sedgwick 1995, 148; Tucker 2002, 29). The Draper fortune had not been made from the sales of textiles as such but from providing the machinery that made the production of textiles possible (Tucker 2002, 17). Draper had offered grant money to a number of prominent geneticists to conduct studies to prove black inferiority and promote repatriation to Africa (Tucker 1994b, 173). The organization for which he supplied the financial support was established in 1937 by the Nazi sympathizer Harry H. Laughlin and by Frederick Osborn, a nephew of Henry Fairfield Osborn (Lynn 2001, 555). Laughlin was chosen as its first president. His close personal friend Madison Grant also provided financial backing (G. E. Allen 1986, 246).

The stated aim of the Pioneer Fund was to promote the status of "white persons who settled in the original thirteen colonies prior to the adoption of the Constitution and/or from related stocks" and to support research on "race betterment with special reference to the people of the United States" (Kühl 1994, 6). When this was amended in 1985, the "white" was removed from the reference to those initial settlers, and the recent and euphemistically glossed over history of the fund does not mention the original wording or intent (Lynn 2001, 558). As one observer noted, "The fund's No. 1 priority is to establish the scientific validity of the hereditarian argument" (Mercer 1994, A29). Another added that "the pro-Nazi Pioneer Fund . . . has funded the work of every major advocate of racism, eugenics, and fascism since the late 1930s" (Rosenthal 1995, 44). In the words of yet another, "The list of . . . recipients of Pioneer Fund grants reads partly like a 'Who's Who' of scientific and political racism in the United States, Canada, Great Britain and Ireland" (Kühl 1994, 9). That roster is spelled out in sanitized fashion by the organization's carefully expurgated and recently published history of itself (Lynn 2001). The Pioneer Fund, in fact, has supported the continuity of the "scientific racism" represented by Francis Galton and his intellectual heirs, such as Arthur R. Jensen, J. Philippe Rushton, and Richard Lynn, who are alive and well and whose writings are being used in support of "racial" bigotry still in the 21st century. It has been the principal source of funding for the *Mankind Quarterly*, which has "churned out a steady stream of racism" ever since its founding in 1960 (Tucker 1994b, 176). That journal was founded by Robert Gayre, of the Scottish clans "of Gayre and Nigg," an eccentric white supremacist and Nazi sympathizer (Mehler 1989, 20–21; Lane 1994, 14; Linklater 1995). The former director of the Kaiser Wilhelm Institut für Anthropologie in Berlin and Nazi Otmar Verschuer was on the board of editors (Kühl 1994, 103). Verschuer had been the mentor of the infamous Auschwitz camp "doctor of death" Josef Mengele (Müller-Hill 1998, 76), who shipped the eyes and other organs of Jews who had not survived his "treatment" to Verschuer's institute during World War II (Müller-Hill,1998, 76). The current editor of *the Mankind Quarterly* is another white supremacist, anti-Semite, and neo-Nazi sympathizer, Roger Pearson, who has bragged that he helped to hide Mengele after the war's end (Anderson and Anderson 1986, 93; Mehler 1989, 20; Tucker 1994b, 257–258; 2002, 161–164). Pearson was inspired by the work and the stance of the Nazi anthropologist Hans F. K. Günther (1891–1968), the first professor of *Rassenkunde* (racial knowledge) in Germany and director of the Anstalt für Rassenkunde in Berlin in 1935 (Proctor 1988, 158; Tucker 2002, 159). Günther, for his part, had based his "understanding of race" on the writings of Madison Grant (Kühl 1994, 130).

One of the former presidents of the Pioneer Fund, Henry E. Garrett, a former president also of the American Psychological Association, was chair of the Psychology Department at Columbia University, retiring in 1956, the year Arthur Jensen got his Ph.D. in psychology from Columbia Teachers' College (Fig. 18–1). Garrett had been a witness for the segregationist side, first in a Virginia case in 1952, where segregation was upheld, and then in the landmark *Brown v. Board of Education* case of 1954. That was the case where the "separate but equal" philosophy of the *Plessy v. Ferguson* case of 1896 was overturned by a unanimous Supreme Court. The final and unanimous

Figure 18–1 Henry E. Garrett, 1894–1973 (from Lynn 2001, 60).

decision of the Court in *Brown v. Board of Education* was delivered by Chief Justice Earl Warren on May 31, 1955: "declaring the fundamental principle that racial discrimination in public education is unconstitutional" (Kluger 1977b, 744). Unfortunately, the educational inequality enforced in the past has shaped the American school system so that discrimination survives on a massive scale (Bay 2000, 24).

After Garrett retired from Columbia, he accepted a professorship at the University of Virginia. He had actually requested an appointment in the Department of Psychology but had been rejected because of his views on "race." The Department of Education, however, had no such qualms and was "pleased to have a person of such prestige" (Tucker 2002, 99). He was a native of the State of Virginia, and his bigotry fit into the continuing outlook of the region to the extent that he became a pamphleteer for the White Citizens Council, a racist organization founded barely 2 months after the *Brown v. Board of Education* decision (Edsall 1999, A03); this and other manifestations of his racism are unmentioned in the recent biographical treatment of him in the history of the Pioneer Fund (Lynn 2001, 600–676). Garrett represented a classic and unvarnished version of the racism of the American South, such as can be seen in written accounts from Thomas Jefferson's *Notes on the State of Virginia* in the 18th century to those of Josiah Clark Nott and Nathaniel Southgate Shaler. The full-scale manifestation of his bigotry can be seen in the comments he published in 1962 in the flagship journal of the American scientific community, *Science:* "No matter how low (in a socioeconomic sense) an American white may be, his ancestors built the civilizations of Europe; and no matter how high (again in a socioeconomic sense) a Negro may be, his ancestors were (and his kinsmen still are) savages in an African jungle. Free and general race mixture of Negro–white groups in this country would inevitably be not only dysgenic but socially disastrous" (Garrett 1962, 984). Presumably, "the civilizations of Europe" are an unalloyed plus and can be divorced from events such as Napoleon's rampage of conquest or the Nazi blitzkrieg and Holocaust. The stereotyping of the Africa from which America's slaves had been drawn as a "jungle" is just as unwarranted, and southern writers from Jefferson to Garrett regularly did this in complete ignorance of what the situation actually was. Nor were they the only ones. The equally bigoted Galtonian Hans J. Eysenck in London wrote the following: "White slavers wanted dull beasts of burden, ready to work themselves to death in the plantations, and under those conditions intelligence would have been counter-selective. Thus there is every reason to expect that the particular sub-sample of the Negro race which is constituted of American Negroes is not an unselected sample of Negroes, but has been selected throughout history according to criteria which would put the highly intelligent at a disadvantage. The inevitable outcome of such selection would of course be the creation of a gene pool lacking some of the genes making for higher intelligence" (Eysenck 1971, 42). This, however, was simply an off-the-cuff expression of wishful thinking—one might say "spitefulthinking"—rather than anything based on verifiable information.

The pragmatic practitioners of the slave trade tended to take what they could get, although there were factors that led them to value slaves from particular areas over those from other ones. Slaves from the western part of Africa were especially valued because of their skills in intensive hot-climate agriculture. Those raised in the knowledge of tropical cultivation were deliberately sought as slaves, and both the crops and their attendants were imported to the southeast coast of the United States. Beyond such matters, there is no excuse for judging living people by the accomplishments or thereof lack associated with their ancestors in another place and time.

After Auschwitz was liberated in January 1945, the outside world learned the extent of what had been going on in the name of eugenics or "racial hygiene" (Antelme [1947] 1992; Kevles 1985; Kühl 1994; Müller-Hill 1998). The business of sterilizing people by the thousand was hard enough to get used to, but slaughtering people by the million because of their "race" was such an enormity that many simply could not bring themselves to realize that it had actually been done. Then, there have been those who have stressed that the eyewitness reports on the Holocaust have largely been those of Jews and implied that they were simply making up the stories "to turn Germany into a 'cash cow' for Israel" (Reich 1993, 33). There are, however, some perfectly horrendous eyewitness reports from inmates who were non-Jews that leave no doubt concerning the reality and the magnitude of the Nazi-promoted genocide (Antelme [1947] 1992; Lengyel 1972). In sum, it seems transparently clear that "the primary motivation for most deniers is anti-Semitism, and for them the Holocaust is an infuriatingly inconvenient fact of history" (Reich 1993, 34).

The rest of this chapter deals with work that has been supported by the Pioneer Fund, mostly, although not entirely, done after the death of the fund's founder in 1972. Prior to that, however, Draper saw to it that millions of dollars were made available to citizens' councils in the American South via a series of alphabet soup-like committees, such as the CCFAF (Coordinating Committee for Fundamental American Freedoms), the FHU (Fund for Human Understanding), the IAAEE (International Association for the Advancement of Ethnology and Eugenics (where "ethnology" was considered the science of "race"), and some others less directly related to matters of civil rights and segregation that were the main issues of concern in the South in the 1950s and 1960s. Draper insisted on anonymity, so the funds for those various committees were transmitted in the form of cashier's checks and stock from the Morgan Guaranty Trust in New York, the bank that handled Draper's fortune (Tucker 2002, 122–123). In Mississippi, the money was funneled into the Mississippi Sovereignty Commission in an effort to maintain that state's right to perpetuate a segregated way of life. One of the ways in which that was promoted was the establishment of segregated private schools. Draper had supported the campaigns of Mississippi Senator Theodore G. Bilbo, "one of the most ardent racists ever to serve in the upper house" (Tucker 2002, 34), and his understudy and successor James Eastland (Tucker 2002, 67). Even though Draper's representatives were not successful in opposing *Brown v. Board of Education* in 1954 and the Civil Rights Act of 1964, one can see how such well-financed opposition slowed the pace of social justice in the South to such a reluctant crawl.

JENSENISM

As awareness grew of the enormities committed by German eugenicists during World War II, the ideals of eugenics acquired something of a malodorous taint. The association with racist practices made them more than faintly disreputable. Overt expressions of support for eugenics effectively disappeared, although the Pioneer Fund continued to support projects that fit within the framework of what had once been regarded as its

Figure 18-2   Arthur R. Jensen, b. 1924 (from Lynn 2001, 210).

specific aims. The activities of Henry E. Garrett obviously fit the pattern, but for the past third of a century the most visible recipient of Pioneer Fund support has been the University of California, Berkeley, professor (now professor emeritus) of educational psychology Arthur R. Jensen. Pioneer Fund grants have been awarded to him to the extent of more than a million dollars, which is an enormous amount of support for a scholar who is not pursuing the kind of work that requires maintaining a laboratory filled with expensive equipment (Miller 1995, 173; Tucker 2002, 155) (Fig. 18–2).

Since the Pioneer Fund gives money only to institutions and not particular individuals, Jensen obligingly created a nonprofit corporation, the Institute for the Study of Educational Differences, with himself as president and his wife as vice-president. That way he was able to accept huge sums without having to bother with the oversight of the Berkeley administration (Tucker 2002, 155). The technique was enthusiastically copied by University of Western Ontario racist J. Philippe Rushton, who is treated later in this chapter.

Jensen has repaid the investment with an outpouring of writing in the form of a formidable corpus of books and technical papers. That his productivity has no scientific value does not mean that it has not proved to be of great aid and comfort to the white supremacists and defenders of present levels of social inequality: "No one better typifies the return to scientific racist ideology in the period after World War II than eugenicist Arthur Jensen" (Graves 2001, 159). Jensen's single-minded efforts have achieved such widespread recognition that his name has been enshrined in the label applied to a doctrine (and see Miele 2002, Chapter 1): "Jensenism, n. The theory that an individual's IQ is largely due to heredity, including racial heritage" (*Random House Webster's Unabridged Dictionary*, 2nd ed. 2001, 1026).

Not only has his writing been copious, but it has been unswervingly consistent for a good third of a century since he first achieved notoriety in his issue-long report in the *Harvard Educational Review* (HER) (Jensen 1969b). His consistency has been in his unvarying loyalty to the racialist position. As I phrased it, recalling the similar assessment of Galton by Chase (1977, 103): "Arthur R. Jensen illustrates in the form of a single person an embodiment of the judgment applied by Talleyrand, that *politicien extraordinaire,* to characterize the Bourbons of the *ancien régime* in eighteenth-century France: He has learned nothing and forgotten nothing. . . . Jensen's outlook is a classic example of 'racialism' in Todorov's sense of the word (Todorov 1993:91). As a racialist, he takes it for granted a) that entities called 'races' exist, b) that there is a continuity between physical 'type' and behavioral capabilities, and c) that those capabilities can be ranked in hierarchical fashion among groups" (Brace 1999c).

Oddly enough, prior to that controversial article, Jensen had written that the lower tested achievements of blacks and Hispanics "cannot be interpreted as evidence of poor genetic potential." He recognized that because "powerful barriers to social mobility" existed, such "socioeconomic and cultural disadvantages" suggested the "reasonable hypothesis that their low-average IQ is due to environmental rather than to genetic factors" (Jensen 1967, 10).

Supported by a Guggenheim Fellowship, Jensen spent the 1966–67 academic year as a fellow of the Center for Advanced Study in the Behavioral Sciences located on the Stanford University campus (Tucker 1994b, 195; Lynn 2001, 210–230). There, in discussions with the Stanford physicist William Shockley (1910–89), he became a convert to the narrow hereditarian and eugenicist outlook that he has represented ever since. Shockley shared the Nobel Prize with John Bardeen and Walter Brattain in 1956 for the invention of the transistor in 1947. Supported by the Pioneer Fund, Shockley subsequently declared that poverty, crime, and illiteracy were perpetuated genetically and that the nation's "gene pool" is being "polluted by the black race" (Shockley 1972a, 303; 1972b, 415). While Jensen did not project the abrasive racism evident in Shockley's writings and speech, it is clear that he adopted the basic dimensions of Shockley's racist assumptions.

After 1969, however, Jensen never again referred to his 1967 study and has taken it as a given that "races" exist as valid biological entities and that they "differ, on average, in mental ability" (Jensen 1998, 2): "Nearly every anatomical, physiological, and biochemical system investigated shows racial differences. Why should the brain be any exception?" (Jensen 1969a, 80; 1969b, 213; 1976, 99; and quoted subsequently by one of Jensen's role models, Eysenck 1971, 15). That unsupported blanket statement, however, is simply untrue. A great many aspects of human biology are held in common throughout the human species on the average, although differing from person to person in any given population. If this were not the case, the practice of medicine as we know it would not be possible. The functioning of the liver and the spleen are the same in all human populations, blood pressure and salinity do not differ from one population to another, and the same is true for innumerable other aspects of human physiology that are essential for survival. As is realized in medical schools around the world, the basics of human anatomy, physiology, and histology are essentially the same. Traits that are associated with particular populations and which can be used to identify them, however, are simply the result of relatedness and have no adaptive value (Brace 1996a; Brace et al. 2001). One can even say that traits that are characteristic of particular human populations therefore have no significant adaptive meaning.

Mental capabilities, however, clearly do have survival value, and questions arise concerning whether one might expect differences in that realm. Jensen somewhat offhandedly assumed that such must have been the case. He declared that "races" are of "widely separated geographic origins and have quite different histories which have subjected them to different selective social and economic pressures [making] it highly likely that their gene pools differ for some genetically conditioned behavioral characteristics, including intelligence or abstract reasoning ability" (Jensen 1976, 99). However, he has not taken a single step in the direction of investigating or even speculating on why or how those different "origins" and "histories" might have selected for differences in "intelligence or abstract reasoning ability." Instead, "racial" inequality in mental capacity is simply assumed a priori. That is what makes his stance *racialist*.

In the fall-out from his 1969 paper, his views were treated at some length in *the New York Times Magazine* (Edson 1969), where his edited replies to some of the ensuing letters laid out his position. In one of those, his views on differences in "racial" intelligence were outlined. It was noted that he "approved" of the idea that intelligence is the ability to adapt to "civilization" and that "races" differ in this ability according to the civilizations in which they live: "The Stanford-Binet I.Q. test measures the ability to adapt to Western civilization. Orientals, he adds, show this ability better than American Negroes; the test does not measure the ability to adapt to cultures other than Western" (Jensen 1969a).

Implicit in this is the assumption that people of African origin have not had enough time to adapt to the selective pressures imposed by Western civilization and therefore would be expected to have lower intelligence quotient (IQ) scores. Consistent with that assumption is his declaration that "*at least*" one-quarter of the African American population is mentally retarded (Jensen 1992, 174)—shades of early Goddard and the outlook of intelligence assessors at the time of World War I! In his view, it is that inherent mental deficit, and not the legacy of slavery and a succeeding century of enforced inequality of opportunity, which accounts for the economic and social disparity between African Americans and the other groups to whom they are compared. With those as his expectations, he concluded that: "in the domain of cognitive abilities the g factor accounts for the largest mean difference between blacks and whites" and "the primary evolutionary differentiation and largest genetic distance between human populations is between the African populations and all others" (Jensen 1998, 443).

At this point, we need a bit of perspective from history and anthropology. There is more than a little reason to wonder whether indeed *any* living human population can be said to be adapted to the "civilization" with which it is associated. There is no culture in the world today that represents a way of life which continues unchanged from the survival strategy common to all humans at the end of the Pleistocene 12,000 years ago. Even those often-cited paradigms of "the primitive," the Australian aborigines, were pursuing a sophisticated post-Pleistocene Mesolithic way of life when first contacted by Europeans just over two centuries ago (Brace 1995, 130, 266). Throughout the nearly 2 million-year span of the Pleistocene, the problems of dealing with competing neighbors and of getting an adequate diet were essentially the same in the entire realm occupied by members of the genus *Homo*. Two million years of being shaped by the same selective forces should have produced cognitive capabilities that were identical on the average for all human populations (Brace 2000, see Chapter 12).

As for Jensen's vaunted Western civilization, it has only a scant two centuries to it in anything like its currently enhanced technological capacity. As Jensen has noted, mental capabilities are inherited "in much the same fashion as height" since both are "the result of a large number of genes each having a small additive effect" (Jensen 1967, 5), although stature can be specified in measurable units in a way that is not possible in assessments of mind. The probability that differences in way of life could have had any discernible selective effect on any such genetically complex entity in a couple of hundred or even several thousand years is effectively nil.

As an example of the rate of change of a human trait under polygenic control, consider skin color, which, although polygenic, is almost certainly less genetically complex than mental capability. Humans entered the Western Hemisphere from the northeast edge of the Asian continent somewhere around 15,000 years ago and spread throughout both North and South America, where they have remained ever since (Brace et al. 2001). Although skin color clearly is an adaptive trait and its differences between the tropics and the Temperate Zones in the Old World were produced by the long-term effects of selection, the fact that there is no significant gradient between the Arctic Circle and the Equator in the New World tells us that 15,000 years just is not enough time for selection to have had any impact. There is no way that anything as abstruse as IQ or as unmeasurable as Spearman and Jensen's *g* could be detected by selection and altered in discoverable ways in just a couple of centuries' time.

There is always the possibility that long-lasting residence at different latitudes in the Old World may have allowed enough time for cognitive differences to develop between tropical and Temperate Zone populations. As Jensen put it, "complex mental abilities were more crucial for survival of the populations that migrated to the northern Eurasian regions, and were therefore under greater selection pressure as fitness characters, than in the populations that remained in tropical or subtropical regions" (Jensen 1998, 436). Such views have been promoted by a number of figures over the last two centuries. William Diller Matthew (1915) and his mentor Henry Fairfield Osborn (1926) come to mind, as do Richard Lynn (1991) and J. Philippe Rushton (1995, 1997). Osborn spoke of life at the Equator, where "the quest for food is very easy and requires relatively little intelligence" and "intellectual and spiritual development is at a standstill. Here we have the environmental conditions which have kept many branches of the Negroid race in a state of arrested development" (Osborn 1926, 6).

As with the reification of the "original affluent society," such views reflect more the survival of a folklore faith in a primitive "Eden" than they do any kind of verifiable reality. It is an outlook that has been twitted as "*anthropologie naïve*" (Stoczkowski 1994). A golden age of ease and plenty was assumed, followed by an expulsion, and then survival by daily drudgery and the sweat of one's brow. If one looks at the rest of the animate world, it is clear that there is no support for such assumptions. Rodents, carnivores, and ungulates have occupied a geographic spread running from the arctic to the equator for tens of millions of years; yet, there is no evidence that northern mice, foxes, and deer are any smarter than their tropical counterparts. The same is true for a great many kinds of animal with representatives in both the colder and warmer parts of the world.

Underneath it all, one can suspect that there lurks a European ethnocentrism. Despite a century and more of attempts to gather "proof" of differences in "racial" intelligence from Josiah Clark Nott through Lewis M. Terman, Jensen realized at the beginning of his three decades of effort to document the intellectual inferiority of people of African origin that it had not yet been accomplished. After his controversial paper of 1969, he was interviewed for *Life Magazine:* "I simply say the idea of a genetic difference is not an unreasonable one because everything else that's ever been examined has shown differences and why should the brain be an exception? It's not an unreasonable proposition, but it has not been proved in any scientifically acceptable way. I think it *could* be" (quoted in Neary 1970, 62). Over a decade later, he acknowledged that there still was no genetic evidence for "racial" differences in IQ, but he supported the hypothesis that they were there nevertheless based on his "personal hunch" (Jensen 1981, 500). Clearly, the will to believe was alive and well, and it has lasted into the new millennium. That qualifies as prejudgment or, to give it a more precise label, "racial prejudice."

Throughout his long, highly visible, and amply funded career, Jensen has paid virtually no attention to the circumstances past or present that have influenced the development of human mental capacities. Instead, his energies have been single-mindedly devoted to refining the procedures by which those capacities are tested and measured. He has justified his approach metaphorically by declaring "One cannot treat a fever by throwing away the thermometer" (Jensen 1980, xi). His entire professional focus, then, has been involved with "the construction and refinement of an intellectual thermometer" (Brace 1999c).

What an odd metaphor to have chosen to justify his efforts. In the first place, a thermometer is never used as the means to "treat a fever." In the second place, readings that depart from a single species-wide level—for example, 37°C (98.6°F)—are considered an indication that something is wrong and not the result of inherited differences. Despite Jensen's declaration that "everything else that's ever been examined has shown differences," the one thing he chose to justify his focus on testing for differences—human body temperature—is something that is the same for all the human populations of the world. As every trained physician is well aware, this is also the case for a whole roster of basic human biological attributes. Could it be that the same is also true for the human intellect? The very suggestion that this might be so has elicited vehement denial: "genetic equality of human abilities is an altogether untenable belief in view of the evidence we already possess, as untenable as the geocentric theory in astronomy or special creation in biology" (Jensen 1972c, 427). However, if we actually consider "the evidence we already possess," we shall see that there is nothing "untenable" about it at all.

Jensen has said that "the assumption of equal or equivalent intelligence" across all human populations is "gratuitous" and "scientifically unwarranted" and merits being denounced as the "egalitarian fallacy" (Jensen 1980, 370), a stance that was only a slight rewording of that taken by his one-time mentor, the white supremacist Henry E. Garrett (1961, 484): "The egalitarian assumption obviously begs the question in such a way as to completely remove itself from the possibility of scientific investigation" (Jensen 1980,

370). Again, the absolute opposite is the case. Whether or not capabilities are the same, the appropriate way to test the question is to assume that they are and then proceed to see whether that hypothesis can be rejected. The initial assumption that there are no significant differences need not be based on an actual assessment of the evidence but is simply the classic scientific procedure of setting up a null hypothesis to be tested.

An appropriate test then demands that the conditions under which the test is performed be properly controlled. As the council for the Society for the Psychological Study of Social Issues (1969, 2) unanimously stated in response to Jensen's HER article, "We believe that a more accurate understanding of the contribution of heredity to intelligence will be possible only when social conditions for all races are equal and when this situation has existed for several generations." Jensen's response to this properly phrased scientific statement was to declare: "Since no operationally testable meaning is given to 'equal' social conditions, such a statement, if taken seriously, would completely preclude the possibility of researching this important question, not just for several generations but indefinitely" (Jensen 1971, 24).

What Jensen did then was proceed with his program of proving the innate intellectual inferiority of people of African origin without making the slightest effort to set up a scientifically credible test situation. My own response at that time was as follows:

> if in fact Jensen were really interested in an unbiased testing of the heritable component of intellectual differences between human groups, he should have been devoting his efforts to setting up a scientifically acceptable test situation. The very first step would involve engaging in an attempt to produce an operational definition of equal social conditions and the systematic effort to see that these be extended to all of those whom he might wish to test. . . . Then, and only then, could the question of inherited differences in ability be posed. In fact, whether or not the question is indeed 'important' could only be decided under such circumstances. . . . Viewed from a humanitarian perspective, it would substantially improve the lot of mankind if the energy currently being devoted to the dubious demonstration of innate human unworth were rechanneled to the task of removing the non-innate but very real social inequities that cripple the lives of the very people for whom Jensen professes such concern. (Brace 1971, 8)

In contrast, what Jensen has done is to set up what he calls his "default position" as the null hypothesis (Jensen 1998, 444). That position, or "hypothesis," starts with the assumption of inherent differences. By definition, there is nothing "null" about such a stance. Attempts to prove it do not conform to Popper's "falsifiability criterion" as the "demarcation between science and pseudoscience," although that by itself does not necessarily relegate Jensen's efforts to the realm of pseudoscience (Popper 1978, 52). In Jensen's defense, one could say that his approach is more along the lines of Bayesian statistics, where the effort is made to see whether a hypothesis is likely rather than "the superficially simple syllogisms of falsificationist logic" (Fisher 1987, 328). At the same time, one must constantly bear in mind that the default hypothesis is fully consistent with racialist assumptions.

Given that, however, the jump from the recognition of variation within groups to the assumption that this demonstrates the existence of comparable variation between groups as a whole has no logical justification. As Jensen put it, "The default hypothesis states that human *individual* differences and *population* differences in heritable behavioral capacities . . . are . . . controlled by differences in allele frequencies, and that differences in allele frequencies *between* populations exist for all heritable characteristics . . . in which we find individual differences *within* populations" (Jensen 1998, 444). This, however, is not based on Bayesian inference and, as has been pointed out by a number of scholars, is an unwarranted non sequitur: "The fundamental error of Jensen's argument is to confuse heritability of a character within a population with heritability of the difference between two populations. . . . The genetic basis of the difference between two populations bears no logical relation to the heritabilities within populations and cannot be inferred from it" (Lewontin 1976a, 89; and see similar critiques by Mercer 1988, 201; Dorfman 1995, 420; Tucker 1994b, 227).

This brings up a final matter in the consideration of Jensenism, and that is the duplicitous treatment of heritability. In spite of its name, the word *heritability* does not mean the extent to which something is inherited or under strict genetic control. It is actually a ratio of the environmental and the genetic contribution to a given trait in a population. Thus, it does not apply to individuals but to populations, and even if the genetic background of the trait is constant, the heritability figure will vary as circumstances change. One notation for heritability is as follows:

$$h^2 = \frac{\sigma^2_G}{\sigma^2_G + \sigma^2_E}$$

where h^2 is heritability, σ^2_G is genetic variance, σ^2_E is environmental variance, and the sum of the genetic plus the environmental variance is the phenotypic variance (Falconer 1961). Heritability then is genotypic variance divided by phenotypic variance. The eminent British geneticist Sir Ronald A. Fisher (1890–1962), warned of the "unfortunate" consequences of a ratio created by dividing the genetic variance in the numerator by such a "hotch-potch of a denominator" and noted that a given trait measured for a population could give very different estimates of heritability depending on the control and skill of the investigator (Fisher 1951).

From Jensen's discussion, it is apparent that he understands all the ifs, ands, and buts of heritability, noting that h^2 will be low for a genetically homogeneous population in a variable environment and high where the environmental variability is low (Jensen 1969b, 43). In fact, from his treatment of the matter, one could almost conclude that h^2 works better as an indicator of environmental favorability than as a measure of genetic contribution. Even one of his severest critics, the outspoken geneticist Richard Lewontin, grants that, although Jensen posits an estimate of the heritability of intelligence that is a bit on the high side, "he appears to have said just about everything that a judicious man can say." Yet, he goes on to observe that "the logical and empirical hiatus between the conclusions and the premises is especially striking . . . in view of Jensen's apparent understanding of the technical issues" (Lewontin 1976a, 88).

To repeat, a high heritability ratio does not have anything to do with whether a trait is strongly genetically determined. It means only that the environmental circumstances are favorable to its development for a given population at a given time. Calculation of heritability levels for a given population also does not allow one to say anything about the difference in the manifestation of that trait between that population and another population. Jensen, however, plunged right ahead and made those claims despite his apparent understanding of the nature of heritability: "the fact of the high heritability of IQ, therefore, makes it a very reasonable and likely hypothesis that genetic factors are involved in the Negro–white difference" (Jensen 1972b, 421). After his articulate and informed discussion of heritability, a statement such as this is completely unwarranted. That is why I have called his treatment "duplicitous." One physical scientist who looked at Jensen's treatment came to what should have been a definitive conclusion: "What does the alleged high heritability of IQ imply about genetic differences between ethnic groups? The answer to this question is unequivocal: nothing" (Layzer 1972, 270).

The high heritability figure he initially proposed was 0.8 (Jensen 1969b, 50–51), and he has regularly defended that figure, although other workers have presented data showing a spectrum of heritability values down to half that level (Scarr and Weinberg 1983, 264; Chipuer et al. 1990) and even 0 (Kamin 1981, 481). There are some other problems with the emphasis on heritability, particularly high heritability. For one thing, heritability levels appear to be inversely related to the survival value of the trait in question. Based on data ranging from pigs to fruit flies, this evolutionary generalization has been voiced: "On the whole, the characters with the lowest heritabilities are those most closely connected with reproductive fitness, while the characters with the highest heritabilities are those that might be judged on biological grounds to be the least important as determinants of natural fitness" (Falconer 1961, 167, 1985, 149–150). One might take this to indicate that the heritability figures stressed by Jensen show that the "intelligence" he is talking about is not an important element in human fitness, if indeed one can believe what he claims. Despite his apparent understanding of heritability, his repeated insistence on quoting the same high figure as though it were a fixed number does an injustice to the fact that "heritability is a variable, not a constant, and thus has no fixed or 'true' value" (Tucker 1994b, 222). One gets the feeling that his continued use of that high value is a deliberate ploy to bolster his position in the eyes of a public that really does not understand the meaning of heritability, even though he actually knows that it is not an intellectually defensible tactic. As one caustic critic put it, "Patriotism, we have been told, is the last refuge for scoundrels. Psychologists and biologists might consider the possibility that heritability is the first" (Kamin 1974, 3).

Finally, there is the realization that IQ is measured on a relative, and not an absolute, scale. There are no IQ units, such as centimeters of stature or grams of weight. Neither are there any units of g. This means that there is no legitimate way to calculate heritability for cognitive capabilities (Layzer 1972, 297). In fact, as with reifying aspects of morphology, the business of naming mental dimensions and presuming that particulate inheritance can be identified and heritability calculated for them has been called into question by modern developmental biology (Thorogood 1997; Lovejoy et al. 1999). Furthermore, the very groups for which heritability levels were calculated have no clear biological reality. Jensen in fact has recognized that "race" is a social construct and, for purposes of producing his figures, declared that "the social definition of race should be adequate and, in fact, should be the only appropriate definition" (Jensen 1995b, 42). The "racial" identity of his subjects, then, was what they declared it to be. This led me to the following query: "Can there be any validity in calculating the heritability of anything that is associated with a 'self-identified' construct that has no coherent biological existence?" (Brace 1999c, 8).

For all of these reasons and others I have not mentioned, the prolonged treatment of heritability that made up the bulk of Jensen's *HER* article in 1969 and his subsequent and continuing devotion to the topic has no scientific relevance. When Jensen's book *The g Factor: The Science of Mental Ability* was published in 1998, I was among the some two dozen asked to review it for the on-line journal *psycoloquy*. That review appeared on December 16, 1999, and contained many of the observations quoted in the past few pages. Jensen, who has been faithful in responding to his critics over the past three decades and more, wrote replies to the other reviews but chose to regard my effort as simply an *ad hominem* attack and did not deal with any of the points I raised, even though, as an anthropologist, I brought up a whole series of issues that were not mentioned by any other reviewer (Jensen 2000). My reaction is the same as that of the Harvard geneticist Richard Lewontin when Jensen accused him of maintaining a pervasive "ad hominem flavor" in a paper published over 30 years ago (Jensen 1976, 93). Here I can repeat Lewontin's rejoinder: "There is no *ad hominem* argument in my [text]" (Lewontin 1976b, 107).

THE BELL CURVE

In a fashion very similar to Jensen's perpetuation of the Galtonian tradition, there are three other major manifestations of that same kind of racism that appeared in the last decade of the 20th century and the beginning of the 21st. Easily the most notorious of these was the unlikely bestseller *The Bell Curve: Intelligence and Class Structure in American Life* by the late Harvard psychologist Richard J. Herrnstein and the right-wing "political analyst" Charles Murray in 1994 (see also De Parle 1994). I say "unlikely" because most works that are filled with graphs, statistical tables, and probability coefficients tend to bring a glazed look to the average reader's eyes.

The text, however, presents a graciously condescending "would-that-it-were-not-so" assessment of the supposed intellectual limitations conferred by an African ancestry, all the while denying that there is any racism implied. The stance obviously resonated with a large segment of the American public, and the eye-glazing quantity of statistics gave it an aura of the scientific even if the reading public—and the authors—did not really understand them. The book contains a massive compilation of largely irrelevant data from the National Longitudinal Survey of Youth and some very dubious statistical procedures applied in support of a set of "conclusions" which are said to be "beyond significant technical dispute" (Herrnstein and Murray 1994, 22). Those "conclusions" are actually stated as assumptions at the beginning and never discussed, justified, or tested against any real data. Those six assumptions are as follows:

1. Human cognitive ability is a single general entity—Spearman's *g*—in which there are individual and group differences.
2. IQ tests measure this accurately.
3. IQ tests measure how "intelligent" people are.
4. IQ scores are fixed for much of a life span.
5. IQ tests are *not* biased in regard to "race," ethnic group, or social or economic status.
6. Cognitive ability has a heritability of 40–80 percent.

The Distribution of IQ

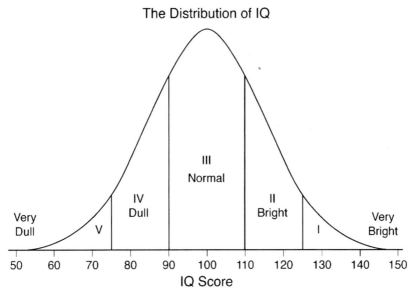

Figure 18-3   The "bell curve" redrawn from Herrnstein and Murray (1994, 121).

Actually, since point 1 is demonstrably not true, assumptions 2, 3, and 4 become irrelevant. Assumptions 5 and 6 are also demonstrably false (Brace 1996c, S156–S157).

The "bell curve" of the title is just the normal distribution which characterizes the spread of many measurable phenomena. For instance, they present as an example a graph showing that 50 percent of the population has an IQ between 90 and 110, with an average of 100 (Fig. 18–3). This is their "Normal" range. Another 20% of the population ranges down another 15 points and is referred to as "dull," while a comparable 20% ranges 15 points upward and is called "bright." The 5% ranging down from scores of 75 to 50 is referred to as "very dull," which "sounds better than the standard retarded" (Herrnstein and Murray 1994, 122), while the remaining 5% ranges upward from 125 and is called "very bright." What is depicted is a standard statistical picture of a normal distribution, but as it happens, IQ data are not distributed in normal fashion but, rather, skewed. Transforming the skewed data to "normalize" them renders them inappropriate for use by the methods the authors adopt. As one cautionary consideration put it: "Their use helps to obscure rather than elucidate the relative contributions of IQ and SES [socioeconomic status] in the various analyses. . . . Herrnstein and Murray's regression analyses are structured to sidestep any serious effort to explain how the effects of ability come about" (Devlin et al. 1995, 34).

In the Galtonian tradition and with the added ingrained American belief that skin pigment and brain power are negatively correlated, *The Bell Curve,* despite the authors' denial, is a ponderous exposition of racial prejudice. The lower average IQ scores of Americans with African, as opposed to European, ancestry is assumed to be genetically caused. The authors assume that IQ is a set figure fixed by heredity, but they report that IQ in Western Europe and the United States rose between 15 and 20 points in the four decades following the Great Depression of the 1930s. That change through time was greater than the average black–white difference. The change occurred between generations of a single continuing population in each place where it was tested. Genetic continuity was obvious, but the change was much too large to be accounted for by biological evolution.

No polygenic trait—and mental capability is certainly under the control of many genes—has ever been known to change by 20 percent in a couple of generations as the result of biological evolution. Stature, another polygenic phenomenon, underwent a profound change over the past century, but this was a "secular," not a genetic, change (Chamla 1964). Clearly, it had to indicate some environmental influence—adequate nutrition, for example—and something similar has to have been the case for the dramatic IQ change documented for Europe and the United States. The person who focused on the evidence for that change is a political scientist in New Zealand, James R. Flynn (Flynn 1984, 1987, 1998, 1999). Herrnstein and Murray (1994, 307) had no ready explanation to account for that dramatic change, and they refer to it in deprecatory fashion as "the Flynn effect," as though it had somehow been caused by the manipulations of Professor Flynn himself and could therefore be disregarded.

IQ scores are heavily influenced by experience and how this affects an individual's perception of the world. In the not too distant past, urban dwellers regularly looked down on the "backwardness" of rural "rubes," a condition they presumed to be a consequence of inherent stupidity. In a world where information was spread by word of mouth, urbanites, because of daily contact with many more people, were apt to know much more about what was happening in the human world than rural farmers. This began to change rapidly when radio became widespread starting in the 1930s and was only emphasized with the huge expansion of television a couple of decades later. Now, the "local yokels" are apt to know just as much about the goings-on in the world as the urban "sophisticates." That massive increase in IQ documented by Flynn may simply be a consequence of that effective information explosion. In any case, it is apparent that the quantum change in IQ over the last couple of generations cannot have been the result of a genetic change, and it lends credence to Flynn's suggestion that the black–white IQ difference also is unlikely to be genetically based.

The Bell Curve generated an enormous amount of interest and controversy. Other books published at the same time (Itzkoff 1994; Rushton 1995) also pushed the idea that programs such as Head Start and Affirmative Action were not justified by the findings of "science" and therefore should be terminated. The *New York Times,* as it does so often when reporting on matters of science, turned to a science journalist rather than a real scientist to review those three works. The result was a cautious, noncommittal waffle (M. W. Browne 1994). Other reviews were less restrained concerning *The Bell Curve'*s flaws. Even the *Scientific American,* which has become more journalism and less science over the past some years, ran a strong and highly critical review by the outspoken and supremely qualified Leon J. Kamin (1995a). Kamin also wrote a more extensive critique in a volume dedicated to the whole range of issues brought up by Herrnstein and Murray's book (Jacoby and Glauberman 1995; Kamin 1995b).

There were a great many more reactions, both pro and con, but a recounting of these would just take up more space without adding anything of value to the discussion. There is one review, however, that is well worth considering. Probably the most cogent treatment was provided by the late Stephen Jay Gould in the *New Yorker* in November 1994. Gould, a paleontologist and historian of science at Harvard, was a consummate essayist, and his stint of 300 consecutive monthly contributions to *Natural History* between 1974 and 2001 was a bravura performance even if some of us felt that the information tended to get less and less as the word count grew more and more. Gould, however, turned his whole mind and attention to the manifest flaws of Herrnstein and Murray's book in his essay "Curveball" (1994), and he entirely avoided the kind of slipshod errors that had characterized his assessment of Morton in 1981 (and repeated in 1996b).

Gould started by noting that the book's premises are "all asserted (but hardly discussed or defended)" and that "most of the premises are false" (Gould 1994, 139). He complained about the "pervasive disingenuousness. The authors omit facts" and "misuse statistical methods" (Gould 1994, 140). He grumbled that it "contains no new arguments and presents no compelling data to support its anachronistic social Darwinism" (Gould 1994, 139): "This book is in fact extraordinarily one-dimensional. It makes no attempt to survey the range of available data" (Gould 1994, 142). In his summary judgment, he declared: "It is a manifesto of conservative ideology; the book's inadequate and biased treatment of data displays its primary purpose—advocacy" (Gould 1994, 147). What the book advocates is "reduction or elimination of welfare, ending or sharply curtailing affirmative action in schools and workplaces, cutting back Head Start" (Gould 1994, 147–148). Nothing supports Gould's complaint about the "pervasive disingenuousness" better than the clear statement by the authors that "There is no such thing as an undeserving five-year-old" (Herrnstein and Murray 1994, 223) at the same time that they would take away public funds for the nutrition and education of 5-year-olds born to poverty. In their view, poverty is the result of innate stupidity. Undernourished and ill-educated 5-year-olds are in that position because of the presumed intellectual incompetence of their parents. Denying them public support in effect is regarded as deserved, which includes the prejudgment that they too have inherited the degree of mental incompetence attributed to their parents and therefore deserve the poverty and ignorance bestowed on them by circumstances over which they have no control.

My own reactions to the work were very similar to those of Gould, Kamin, and other critics, and it was this that led me to conclude the following: "As a whole, *The Bell Curve* is a massive manifestation of genteel bigotry" (Brace 1996c, S161).

J. PHILIPPE RUSHTON: APOSTLE OF APARTHEID

The a priori racial prejudice that pervades *The Bell Curve* is extended to an almost pornographic degree in the career and works of J. Philippe Rushton, professor of psychology at the University of Western Ontario in Canada (Fig. 18–4). Rushton earned his B.Sc. in psychology in 1970 at Birbeck College, University of London, followed soon by his Ph.D. at the London School of Economics in 1973 and subsequently his D.Sc. in 1992 (Rushton 1995, xvii). In his best known work, *Race, Evolution, and Behavior: A*

Figure 18-4 J. Philippe Rushton, b. 1943 (from Lynn 2001, 358).

Life-History Perspective (1995), he identifies himself as a product of the "London School" of Psychology, sometimes known as the "Galton School." That would certainly account for his racialism, but he evidently got a major head start in that direction earlier in life with 4 years in an all-white elementary school in South Africa before his father moved the family to London. As he put it: "I guess my upbringing led me to believe there really were genetically based class, ethnic, and racial differences" (A. Miller 1995, 170). His South African schooling occurred during the time *apartheid* was in effect. That Afrikaans word means "separateness," but it is not pronounced using the Germanic convention for *ei* in a word, a sound rendered in English as "aye." Instead, it is spoken as "apart-hate," which is eerily evocative of the "racial" prejudice that it symbolized. From that point on, Rushton's entire career has been devoted to providing proofs in favor of his childhood prejudice. As I have said before, this is not science but advocacy, specifically the advocacy of "racism."

To begin with, he accepts the sacrosanct trinity of Western racial designations— "Caucasoid," "Mongoloid," and "Negroid"—as appropriate and valid for the biological variation in *Homo sapiens* (Rushton 1995, 96; Brace 1996b, 177). His classification is not based on the analysis of data but, rather, on the assertion that this is what a team of "extraterrestrial scientists" would identify immediately if called upon to subdivide the human spectrum (Rushton 1991, 29; 1995, 1). When he actually alludes to biological data he refers to the racialist compilation *Races,* put together by John Baker (1974): "race is a biological concept. Races are recognized by a combination of geographic, ecological, and morphological factors and gene frequencies of biological components" (Rushton 1995, 96).

He does note that "races merge with each other through intermediate forms" (Rushton 1995, 96) and that "no claim is made however that races are discrete groups" (Rushton 1995, 42). He never mentions the biological data that document that "race" is not a valid biological entity, even though his attention has been directed toward the significance of crosscutting clines and a portion of the relevant literature (Weizmann et al. 1990, 1991). His "races," then, are social constructs based on his own initial prejudices— his own 19th-century political correctness (Lieberman 2001)—and not on anything that has a coherent biological existence.

He also accepts one of the standard assumptions of *anthropologie naïve,* that life in a cold climate is "more cognitively demanding" than life in the tropics and, consequently, the inhabitants of temperate environments are "more stringently selected for intelligence" (Rushton 1991, 39; 1995, 7). In addition, they were selected for "forward planning, sexual and personal restraint" and a reproductive strategy that concentrates on the care given to raising a small number of offspring as opposed to one that tries to assure the perpetuation of the species by generating offspring in vast profusion but playing no role in their nurturing. This contrast in reproductive strategies is referred to in the fields of ecology and evolutionary biology as the contrast between r as opposed to K selection (MacArthur and Wilson 1967; Stearns 1976, 1977, 1992): "Oysters, producing 500 million eggs a year exemplify the r-strategy, while great apes, producing only one infant every 5 or six years, exemplify the K-strategy" (Rushton 1985, 441).

In oversimplified terms, r strategy emphasizes rate of reproduction. Growth and sexual maturation occur early, many small offspring are produced, whether they survive or not is left to chance and not care, and the life span is short. The K strategy involves care. Growth and maturation occur slowly, sexual behavior comes late and sparingly, few but large offspring are produced, prolonged parental care is given to increase the chances of survival, and the life span is long. As one analyst noted, both r and K selection have been used as labels to indicate the combination of traits found together or "as an implied *explanation* of why those traits are found together. Which meaning is being used is rarely specified" (Stearns 1976, 4; 1992, 206). That lack of specification characterizes all of Rushton's writings.

The contrast between the r and K strategies does give some insight into the different means of species perpetuation in organisms as different as oysters and elephants, but there can be no legitimate reason for applying it within a species as Rushton (1995, xiii) does with unapologetic racism. He attributes a stronger sex drive, fertility, developmental precocity, lower intelligence, less "law-abidingness," and poorer family cohesion to tropical populations—his "Negroids," whom he treats as the oysters of the human realm (Rushton 1995, 157–160). Laws, of course, could not have been recorded until writing was invented, and the idea that human populations could have evolved differentially since that time is biologically absurd. To treat "law-abidingness" as though it had a genetic basis is as improbable as the Nazi assertion of "the hereditary criminal nature of Jewry" and is simply a manifestation of racial prejudice (Leers 1944, 8; Cohn 1967, 2007). In many instances, what he reports are simply assertions in the absence of data. "Facts" are cadged from a wide and disparate variety of sources with little concern for their documentation. Many of those sources are blatantly racist and unreliable. Some are misrepresented or selectively used without telling the reader that the authors in question have documented exactly the opposite of what Rushton uses them to support. The results of various different efforts are combined by "aggregation" in a manner that is statistically indefensible and masks within-group variation (Weizmann et al. 1991, 49; Cernovsky 1993, 284; Barash 1995; Lieberman 2001).

Although he consistently deals with data relating to his three "races" and regularly cites an alleged slight intellectual "superiority" of his "Mongoloids," the main point repeatedly emphasized is the lesser worth of his "Negroids." It is all related, as he would have us believe, to the different stresses generated by a tropical, as opposed to a cold, climate. It is his thesis that cold climates, both temperate and arctic, feature more cognitively demanding but also more predictable environments. The "subtropical savannahs" where humans first evolved were less cognitively challenging and "less predictable" (Rushton 1995, 231). Presumably, there is no point in being intelligent if the future is unpredictable. Intelligence and K strategy then supposedly were adaptive in cooler climates, whereas witless fecundity was advantageous in the tropics (Rushton 1995, 199). These are all just assertions in the absence of any support, and there is no reason to accept them.

There is nothing that demonstrates that the arctic is more predictable than the tropics, as anyone caught by an unexpected blizzard can testify; and try telling anyone who makes a living as a farmer in the Temperate Zone that the seasonal vicissitudes that have to be coped with are solidly predictable. In fact, a case has been made that reality is quite the reverse of Rushton's offhand assumption (Dobzhansky 1950, 220; Stearns 1976, 20–21). For all of Rushton's "life history perspective," the biologists who actually have dealt with life history in many different organisms have made the case that the situation is the opposite of what Rushton has claimed. The original proposer of the contrast between r and K selection noted that the more constant nature of tropical rain forest conditions was the reason the order Primates as a whole evolved a K strategy in the first place (MacArthur and Wilson 1967; Stearns 1992, 206).

As it happens, r/K theory fails in about 50% of between-species tests where the data are adequate for analysis, which makes offhand attempts to apply it within a species completely indefensible (Stearns 1992, 206). In addition to ignoring the efforts by biologists who have actually dealt with r and K selection, Rushton has been equally cavalier with the anthropological and archaeological assessment of life-ways in the tropics and Temperate Zones: "Peoples in tropical and subtropical latitudes were largely scavengers, while peoples in temperate environments relied more on hunting. . . . Hunting in the open grasslands of northern Eurasia was also more difficult than hunting in the woodlands of the tropics and subtropics where there is plenty of cover for hunters to hide in" (Rushton 1995, 228). These and other assertions are gratuitous and undocumented and have absolutely no justification. Scavenging evidently was being pursued by the African hominids of 2.5 million years ago, but it had clearly given way to hunting by 1.9 million years ago (Brace et al. 1973; Blumenschine and Cavallo 1992). It was the hunting technology developed in Africa that enabled members of the genus *Homo* to spread across the tropics of the Old World approximately 2 million years ago, and refinements of that same technology allowed northward movement to occur subsequently at both the eastern and western edges of that range of habitation in the Middle Pleistocene (Brain 1991; Walker 1984; Brace 1995).

Rushton has a couple of other fetishes that need to be mentioned. One is his pro-longed effort to show that "racial" differences in brain size are correlated with and presumably responsible for differences in IQ. He has indeed cited the statistical signif-icance of the differences between the brain sizes in his samples; but, as has been pointed out, when very large samples are used it is easy to find statistical significance in trivial differences, but that does not necessarily have anything to do with biological significance (Chisholm 1994, 44). None of his "racial" differences is as great as the male–female difference in any group, yet there is no evidence that females are lower in IQ than males. If one is going to argue, as Rushton does, that a less than 60 cubic centi-meters difference out of 1,300–1,400 cubic centimeters in brain size indicates a significant difference in average intellect, then one would have to defend the view that small men are dumber than large men and females are dumber on the average than males. The latter view is patently untrue, and there are no data that would support the former. While Rushton has drawn from the data collected by one of the most thorough treatments of brain size and its relations, he has chosen to use it in support of his need to believe that there are significant "racial" differences in brain size. That particular source, however, after testing brain size against all sorts of physical features such as bulk, stature, skin surface area, and such, came to the conclusion that brain size varies more in conjunction with climate than anything else (Beals et al. 1984).

His other major fetish is with supposed "racial" differences in sexual behavior. His assumption that "Negroids" are r-selected leads him to assume that they are more sexu-ally active than anyone else, produce more children, and take less care of them. In Africa, he opines, "biological parents do not expect to be the major providers for their children" (Rushton 1995, 156). Generalizing about an entire continent on the basis of one biased report made out of context is the antithesis of responsible scholarship. Even the most cursory sampling of the available literature based on primary investigations done in Africa paints a completely different picture. One could do no better than to start with the classic *African Systems of Kinship and Marriage* (Radcliffe-Brown and Forde 1950) and add more recent accounts from both hunting and gathering (Blurton Jones 1987) and polygynous agricultural (Strassmann 1997) groups.

Rushton's casual assertion that Africa lacked stable political systems with accepted legal codes is abundantly refuted in another classic, *African Political Systems* (Fortes and Evans-Prichard 1970). Reinforcing that is the observation that the Kongo state ranging from Angola up through the western part of the Congo had a political effectiveness that allowed a sophistication and even luxury that was not exceeded by anything in Europe until the slave trade and European armed conquest destroyed it (Bokie 2001).

Rushton's equally casual denial that religion and moral systems existed in pre-colonial Africa (1995, 100) is also abundantly contradicted by published records, such as *African Traditional Religions* (Parrinder 1954): "informed opinion has now swung round to the conviction that most, if not all, African people have had a Supreme Being as an integral part of their world view and practiced religion" (Parrinder 1969, 39). This is reinforced by a series of more recent works (Mbiti 1990; Nagesa 1997; Glazier 2001).

Denigration of African family values, political organization, and religion in the absence of even the most rudimentary effort to check the available records is a classic example of racially motivated and ethnocentric ignorance. The same is true for the assessment of African intellectual capabilities based on nonverbal scores on tests administered to children whose command of English was so marginal that in some instances instructions had to be given by gestures. Then, in spite of the fact that the testers indicated that this was indefensible (Owen 1992, 149; Lane 1994, 16; Kamin 1995a, 100), the scores of those nonverbal tests were converted into IQ numbers and used to characterize an entire continent. The tradition of Galtonian bigotry is alive and vigorous in this volume.

If Africans were denigrated for supposedly being deficient in brain power, on the one hand, then they were equally denigrated as being oversexed and lacking in the capacity to control their libidos, on the other hand. Rushton declares that "personal and sexual competitiveness" is indicated by "the size of breasts, buttocks, and male genitalia" (Rushton 1987; 1995, 231). In comparing the "salience of muscularity, buttocks, and breasts" between his "races," he ranks "Orientals least, blacks most" (Rushton 1995, 167).

In what could almost be characterized as an illustration of "penis envy," he pronounces upon the dimensions—length and thickness—and angles of erection and hardness of the tumescent male phallus for a spectrum of the world's populations. The source of all this "information" is *Untrodden Fields of Anthropology* by a "French Army Surgeon" writing under the pseudonym Dr. Jacobus *X* (1898). That production is more in the tradition of "anthropological pornography" than science (Davis and Whitten 1987, 70). The indefatigable "surgeon" never tells us how he got his information on the dimensions, angles, and hardness of such a profusion of erections. The reader, in fact, has no reason to believe that this long recitation of "information" has anything to do with science at all. For the Rushtons of the world it evidently has a prurient fascination, but a goodly proportion of the rest are justified in regarding it as nothing more than a prolonged exercise in "ethnopornography" (Weizmann et al. 1991, 49).

Rushton's enthusiasm for stressing the size of the African male member as an indicator of presumably overdeveloped sexual appetite is right in line with Western folk beliefs that go back centuries, but it is not supported by an actual assessment of the data (Masters and Johnson 1966, 191 ff.). Oddly enough, Rushton makes no mention of the evidence indicating sexual drive by the source of his "information" on genital characteristics, namely that same French Army Surgeon who concluded that sexual potency was demonstrated by the size of the testicles and not just the features of the phallus itself (*X* 1898, 2:429). That fount of "knowledge" observed that African testicles were not at the top of the worldwide range of size: Europeans were at least their equal, but Polynesian men were more generously endowed (*X* 1898, 2:428).

Rushton, however, remains true to the traditions of Western folklore and takes it as a given that sexual and intellectual capabilities are opposite poles of the same spectrum: "you know, it's a trade-off: more brain or more penis. You can't have everything" (Miller 1995, 170). That may be fine as folklore, but it is completely unacceptable as science. We are a long way from knowing the dimensions and genetic control of cognitive capabilities, although we can be assured that they are vastly more complex than the simple-minded *g* of Spearman, Jensen, Rushton, and the like. We can also be assured that they are completely unrelated to the dimensions and the genetic control of sexual capabilities and behavior.

Think for a moment of the ABO blood group system. This is controlled by a single genetic locus on chromosome 9, and there are three genes in the system (Race and

Sanger 1975). Every individual has one gene (allele) from one parent and another from the other parent. If one parent is AO at that locus and the other parent is BO, their child can have any possible combination known in the ABO system. An A from one parent and an O from the other makes an AO child, and since O is recessive, the child will be registered as having blood group A. In similar fashion, a B from one parent and an O from the other produces a child who will test as blood group B. An A from one and a B from the other produces an AB child since the A and B alleles are codominant. An O from each parent produces a child who tests as O. Now, if we let A stand for sexual ability, B stand for brains, and O stand for omission, we can see that a person could easily have one or the other or both or neither.

This example was set up using alleles at only a single locus on a chromosome. In the case of cognitive capabilities and sexual organ development, we know that the genetic control is far more complex, with multiple alleles at multiple loci, and that these are completely independent of each other. There is no theoretical reason a person could not have an abundance of brains or penis or neither or both. This is just basic high school biology. Even if the real biological control of both realms is orders of magnitude more complex, the principles are the same.

In his efforts to portray Africans as *r*-selected and therefore biologically geared to generate abnormal quantities of offspring, Rushton (1995, 165) has stressed their higher frequency of double ovulation and twin production, although the between-population differences are extremely small. Lost are the actual consequences of multiple births. In Africa, "twins are greatly feared among most people who subsist on hunting and gathering. . . . Even when twins survive the birth process, usually one or both are killed on the spot" (Kaplan 2001, 809). Rather than symbolizing a strategy of producing oyster-like quantities of newborns, twins actually result in a reduction of the number of surviving offspring.

Also stressed are the supposedly higher levels of the male sex hormone testosterone in people of African origin (Rushton 1995, 272–273). Once again, this is simply the result of a mind-set that is convinced that Africans are congenitally over-sexed. Testosterone is not set at different levels for different populations, and despite the folklore-based expectations of the Rushtons of the world, "there is no evidence that supranormal levels of testosterone produce exaggerated libido" (Ellison 2001, 263). Instead, it is the result of a great many influencing factors. Age is one such factor, and so is social stress. When representatives of over a half-dozen different careers were tested, the lowest average levels of testosterone were found among ministers. Professional football players were higher than average, which is hardly unexpected, but the highest average levels were found among stage actors (Dabbs et al. 1990). Winners in athletic contests and in nonathletic face-to-face competitions such as chess had higher levels than losers (Mazur et al. 1992). Of a whole series of Africans tested, the average level was significantly lower than that of males of a similar age in Boston, Massachusetts (Ellison et al. 1989, 22; Ellison 2001, 275). It is quite clear that the stress of the situation is what produces differences in testosterone levels, and it is not people with inherently different levels seeking careers that differ in stress. The same thing is almost certainly true for group differences in average IQ scores.

The authors of *The Bell Curve* as well as the science journalist who reviewed it along with Rushton's book for the *New York Times Book Review* referred to Rushton's work as "science" (Herrnstein and Murray 1994, 643; M. W. Browne 1994). This, however, drew a pointed rebuttal: "Nothing could be further from the truth. . . . The bulk of his controversial claims are published in journals that do not adhere to the standard scientific procedures of review and criticism by scientific colleagues" (S. Greene 1994, 75). One could say exactly the same thing in regard to the authors of *The Bell Curve.* My own conclusions were consistent with that critique: "*Race, Evolution, and Behavior* is an amalgamation of bad biology and inexcusable anthropology. It is not science but advocacy, and advocacy for the promotion of 'racialism'" (Brace 1996b, 176). Finally, "Quite evidently it is a manifestation of blatant bigotry" (Brace 1996c, S177). Even that was not quite as strongly worded as the occasionally scatological review which concluded the following: "Bad science and virulent racial prejudice drip like pus from nearly every page of this despicable book" (Barash 1995, 113). Not the least bit daunted, Rushton exulted: "I really do believe I have made a major breakthrough in understanding human evolution" (quoted in Platiel and Strauss 1989, A6). Then, to make sure that his message would be as widely circulated as possible, he prepared an abridged paperback edition of his book *Race, Evolution, and Behavior* (Rushton 1999). With the financial backing of the Pioneer Fund, he acquired the membership lists of the American Anthropological Association, the American Association of Physical Anthropologists, the American Psychological Association, the American Sociological Association, and the American Society for Criminology, ostensibly to send out fliers describing the book he had written 5 years previously. Instead, in what has been called a "bait-and-switch" operation, in November and December 1999, he sent a free copy of his poisonous racist screed to all who were on those lists (Rushton 2000, 104; Tucker 2002, 199). Those who were members of more than one of those professional societies received a copy for each one to which they belonged. This created such a reaction among the affronted members of those professions that Transaction Publishers in New Brunswick, New Jersey, declared that, despite the imprint on those volumes, they had not published them and demanded that Rushton destroy the remaining 60,000 copies, which Rushton did with some ill-tempered words. That was only a temporary setback for a richly funded racist, however; and an alternate printer was generated so that the bigotry could continue to be disseminated (Rushton 2000). The alternate publisher was Rushton's own Charles Darwin Research Institute in London, Ontario, Canada, which he had set up so that he could in effect directly receive Pioneer Fund support greatly in excess of what would have been possible had the money been given to the University of Western Ontario for its management. In financially supporting this gambit, the Pioneer Fund remained in accord with its long-term policy of publicizing previously held convictions rather than in backing anything that could be counted as actual research.

As a coda to this saga of racialist advocacy, the long-term president of the Pioneer Fund, Harry F. Weyher, died late in March 2002. Weyher had been the personal attorney of the founder of the Fund, the white supremacist and Nazi sympathizer Wickliffe P. Draper. When Draper died in 1972, Weyher continued as president until his own death. The board of directors then met to choose new directors and select a president. Richard Lynn and Rushton were added to the board, and the new president they chose was J. Philippe Rushton (Tucker 2002, 214). His "research" had been richly supported over the years by the Pioneer Fund (Kühl 1994, 8). Evidently, the traditional commitment to racial prejudice represented by the Pioneer Fund will continue with renewed

vigor: "Rushton's thinking, so redolent of Nazi-era political and scientific pronouncements . . . is nothing more than the most recent instance of genetic determinist ideology
promoted as science." It is: "poor science and represents a fatally flawed basis for pre-
scribing social policy" (Lerner 1992, 147).

RICHARD LYNN

Strictly speaking, Richard Lynn does not fit within the spectrum of American contributions to the idea of "race." Lynn was trained in psychology at Cambridge University,
with a B.A. in 1953 and a Ph.D. in 1956. Subsequently, he was on the staff of the
University of Exeter and the Economic and Social Research Institute in Dublin. In 1967
he became professor of psychology at the University of Ulster, Coleraine, Northern
Ireland, where currently he is emeritus. His writings, however, have been cited with
approval by racialists on both sides of the Atlantic Ocean (Herrnstein and Murray 1994;
Rushton 1995; Eysenck 1998), and his most recent production, *IQ and the Wealth of
Nations* (Lynn and Vanhanen 2002), has been lavishly praised by the new president of
the Pioneer Fund, J. Philippe Rushton (2002). That American fund itself has contributed
hundreds of thousands of dollars in support of his efforts, and he has now been selected
to serve on its board of directors.

It is relevant, then, to consider the nature of what he has produced with that support.
For years he has published papers in such journals as *Intelligence, The Mankind
Quarterly,* and *Personality and Individual Differences,* among others. These do not have
the standards of peer review comparable to those that are in place for such journals as
The American Anthropologist, The American Psychologist, Nature, Science, and a great
many other that have earned a reputation for scholarly respectability. Instead, the nature
of what they print is more a reflection of the views of their editors. Those editors seem
to be more interested in publishing support for their racialist assumptions than in the
pursuit of science for its own merit.

The nature of Lynn's interest—and his bias—is displayed in *IQ and the Wealth of
Nations* (Lynn and Vanhanen 2002). As the title would lead one to expect, there is an
informed bow to Adam Smith's 1776 treatise (Smith [1776] 1976) and a follow-up
treatment of what are called "psychological theories of economic development" (Lynn
and Vanhanen 2002, 6), such as *The Protestant Ethic and the Spirit of Capitalism* by
Max Weber ([1904] 1930). Lynn and Vanhanen (2002, 158) declare their enthusiasm for
"market economies" and the Enron kind of ideology that characterizes the economic
policy of the current American government. The unattractive consequences of their
ideology were presciently treated by Anthony Trollope in fictional form more than a
century ago in *The Way We Live Now* (Trollope 1875) and have recently been looked
at in the light of contemporary economic facts (Krugman 2002). Lynn, in fact, regards
individual rights and political freedom as "dysgenic" (Valone 2002, 534).

At the beginning of the book, the authors articulate their basic assumption: "We . . .
seek to show that there are large differences in intelligence between nations, that these
differences are systematically related to economic growth, and that this growth is causal"
(Lynn and Vanhanen 2002, xvi). The approach evidently is one of advocacy and not of science or scholarship. Although they occasionally make reference to an environmental

component in intelligence, they ignore this in practice and repeatedly emphasize the following: "We believe that national differences in intelligence have a substantial genetic basis" (Lynn and Vanhanen 2002, 193).

The volume presents a mass of data showing intelligence ratings collected from tests administered in 81 countries representing a goodly sampling of the peoples of the world. These ratings are presented as IQ figures, although IQ tests were not given to the people represented. Those subjects were not, in fact, given verbal tests at all. Instead, they were rated on their performance on "Standard Progressive Matrices" tests (Lynn and Vanhanen 2002, 197). The conversion from those scores to IQ figures is not considered justifiable or valid in the first place (Owen 1992, 149; Lane 1994, 16; Kamin 1995a, 100), and it is not at all clear that the children being tested in various less than affluent parts of the world had any real idea of what they were supposed to be doing. Generalizing about the genetic component of national IQ differences on such a flawed set of data is simply a reflection of a priori racist expectations.

The generalizations about Asian IQ levels regularly made by Rushton and Lynn were based on converting nonverbal Standard Progressive Matrices scores into IQ scores in unwarranted fashion for populations in Japan, China, and Singapore. Even the IQ tests done on Asian Americans showing higher scores than for European Americans were rigged by using the scores of a previous generation of European Americans compared to more recent Asian Americans. When compared against their contemporaries, Asian Americans came out just slightly lower than European Americans: "those studies which showed Oriental Americans scoring above white Americans for IQ had inflated Oriental IQ by scoring them against obsolete norms; they outscore the white of earlier generations but thanks to IQ gains over time, not the whites of their own generation" (Flynn 1989, 364).

It has repeatedly been shown that Asians score higher on tests of visuospatial ability than Westerners (Lynn 1987; Chan and Vernon 1988; Iwawaki and Vernon 1988). The Inuit and other Native Americans also score high on visuospatial tests, and more than one analyst has concluded that this indicates a "Mongoloid racial" phenomenon: "Any simple socioeconomic, cultural, or linguistic explanation is out of the question, given the diversity of living conditions, native languages, educational resources, and cultural practices experienced by Hong Kong Chinese, Japanese in Japan or the United States, Koreans in Korea or Belgium, and Inuit or American Indians. . . . Common genetic history of racial East Asians . . . cannot plausibly be dismissed as irrelevant" (Herrnstein and Murray 1994, 301). It has been pointed out, however, that learning a writing system based on ideographs (zi in Chinese and kanji in Japanese) provides a kind of practice and experience in visuospatial perception that has no counterpart elsewhere (Chan and Vernon 1988, 346; Brace 1996c, S160). The Inuit and other Native Americans tested were still pursuing a foraging way of life, which also emphasizes visuospatial perception in a way that is not generally true elsewhere. It is far more likely that continual practice in the use of visuospatial skills is the reason for those higher test scores, rather than anything produced by a special genetic background.

At the same time, those very populations showed a more limited vocabulary than was true for the European Americans with whom they were compared. The tests were administered in writing and in what for the Inuit and other Native Americans was a foreign language, which would account for the lower scores. Tests in Japan and China were in the native languages: "However, mastering a reading vocabulary in a language that is based on ideographs entails a process of rote memory to an extent that is not true in the Western world where, with the use of prefixes, suffixes, and roots, one can readily identify the meaning of words never before encountered. There is no such comparable possibility in Chinese and Japanese, and the number of words in the reading vocabulary of a literate East Asian is always less for a given educational level than is true in the West" (Brace 1996c, S160).

Finally, the attitudes and expectations of students and parents are very different in the groups being compared. When elementary school students were compared in cities of comparable size in the United States and China, American student performance was the lowest but both student self-rating and parental satisfaction were the highest. The American assumption is that ability is the key, whereas the Asian one is that the results are proportional to the effort applied (Stevenson 1992). There is a very good chance that tests are going to show the results of attitude, application, and parental expectations to a greater extent than innate ability.

Lynn has accepted the Galtonian assumption that wealth is an indicator of intellectual capability and that one can use this to compare not only individuals but whole societies and "races" as well. Quantities of information on gross national product (GNP) and gross domestic product (GDP) per capita are presented for various regions. Changes in these measures for various times are also presented in tabular form. By amalgamating the examples from the 81 countries for which mental test figures were collected with another 104 countries for which interpolated estimates were made and then analyzing correlations between the supposed national IQ and per capita income from 1820 to 1998, Lynn and Vanhanen (2002, 159) were able to show correlations of about 0.50 in 1820 and 0.70 in 1998.

Actually, there is a problem concerning the different time periods for which they calculate coefficients of correlation. They use estimated IQ figures of living people calculated with the economic figures of previous years, but there is every reason to believe that the IQ figures for these earlier intervals would have been unrelated to the figures of the living population. They are fully aware of Flynn's demonstration that IQ has changed dramatically since the 1930s, but they never even consider that it may well have changed even more drastically between 1820 and 1930. What they have erected, then, is a very flimsy house of cards.

However, there is another way of looking at the data they have compiled. They have assumed a causal relationship between IQ and income. There may very well be one, but if there is, it is almost certainly the complete reverse of what they have assumed. The long-term benefits from comfortable economic circumstances may well constitute one of the major contributions to an IQ that is higher than that of someone who has lived in socially and economically depressed circumstances—for instance, one whose ancestors were "made free" by the abolition of slavery in the United States in 1865.

As with Jensen and Rushton and going all the way back to Henry Fairfield Osborn and William Diller Matthew early in the 20th century, they have simply accepted the Garden of Eden mythology of *anthropologie naïve* and assumed that life in the tropics and subtropics was less challenging and that those who continued living there did not evolve the cognitive capabilities developed by those whose ancestors had long ago moved into the supposedly more challenging Temperate Zone: "We assume that differences in climatic and geographical conditions affected the evolution of human mental abilities in such a way that the average IQs are higher for the populations of temperate zones than for populations of the tropics" (Lynn and Vanhanen 2002, 165). Curiously, they assume that a nation with a large agricultural population will have a low IQ because farmers "do not require a high level of intelligence" (Lynn and Vanhanen 2002, 161). It would appear that neither Lynn nor Vanhanen has any real familiarity with the amount of knowledge and intelligence required to make a farm support a family; And one of their standards for Temperate Zone IQ level is China, where the figure is alleged to be above the worldwide average but where there are more farmers (i.e., peasants) than anywhere else in the world.

They take it for granted that the IQ differences they find for temperate and tropical people are simply the consequence of long-term residence in and adaptation to those different zones, although, as I have noted before, this was not the case for any other kind of animal which has variants that are long-term residents of those different latitudes. Their conclusion is as follows: "Intelligence differences between nations will be impossible to eradicate because they have a genetic basis and have evolved over the course of tens of thousands of years" (Lynn and Vanhanen 2002, 195). There is an enormous archaeological literature dealing with what the peoples of the world were doing at different times and in different places. None of this is mentioned. A familiarity with that corpus would lead one to conclusions that are exactly the opposite of what they have offhandedly assumed.

From surveys of that literature in a previous generation (Clark 1969) and more recently (Clark and Willermet 1997), it is apparent that the subsistence strategies of all human groups at any given time were essentially the same from one end of the inhabited world to the other from 2 million years ago until the first appearance of agriculture at the end of the Pleistocene some 10,000 years ago. Climate did differ from one area to another, but the constants of dealing with where the next meal was going to come from and how to handle human neighbors were everywhere the same. The same selective forces should have had the same consequences. The archaeological and anthropological record should lead to the expectation that human intellectual capabilities were the same everywhere that people survived (Brace 1999a, 2000).

Without any consideration of the actual nature of prehistoric life-ways, then, Jensen, Rushton, Lynn, and the like simply take it for granted that the average difference in IQ scores between Americans of European and African heritage is the result of a long evolutionary divergence. In their words, tests provided by cases of adoption simply confirm what they assert: "black infants reared by white middle class adoptive parents in the United States show no improvement in intelligence, contrary to the prediction of environmental theory and consistent with a genetic explanation of the lower average IQ of Blacks" (Lynn and Vanhanen 2002, 194).

That, however, is another statement made in the absence of any justification or citation, and it is simply false. There have been a number of adoption studies in the United States, and they all show what was evident in the first: that is, when children from underprivileged backgrounds are adopted by middle-class parents, those "children are consistently and unmistakably superior to their natural parents" (Skodak and Skeels 1949, 116). It is true that the children's scores "correlate" with the natural and not the adoptive parent, but that just says that they rise or fall in parallel and nothing at all about the magnitude of the scores. In that particular study, the average IQ of the natural parents was just shy of 86, while their children adopted into comfortable foster homes averaged a full 20 points higher, at 106 (Skodak and Skeels 1949, 110). That put the adoptees above the national average for children of European origin. Other adoption studies have shown the same thing (Scarr and Weinberg 1976, 1983; Horn 1983). These higher scores were not just temporary phenomena: "adoption studies actually demonstrate that *radical* interventions succeed in permanently raising the average IQ of adopted children over what it would have been if the children were reared by their natural parents" (Horn 1983, 274)—and this from a source whose work was supported by the Pioneer Fund (Lynn 2001, 324–334).

The continuing attempt of the Jensens, the Rushtons, and the Lynns of the world to claim that people of African origin are intellectually inferior on the basis of cooked figures, sheer assertion in the absence of evidence, or claims that are actually contrary to the known facts is nothing less than a demonstration of a surviving strain of the rampant racism of the recent past. With the publication of *IQ and the Wealth of Nations* and the appointment of its senior author to the board of directors of the Pioneer Fund, it is evident that white supremacy is alive and well and anxious to extend its noxious influence into the new millennium.

19

"OTHERISM"

AFTERTHOUGHTS

America has no monopoly on what produced the reification of the concept of "race," although the daily reinforcement of "racial" perceptions that is the legacy of the way in which the hemisphere was settled ensures that consciousness of "race" plays a more pervasive role in American thought than is true for most other societies in the world. All societies display a certain amount of ethnocentrism. That is, they tend to regard themselves as the "good guys" while looking on others with suspicion, ranging from dislike to fear and even hatred. Of all the various "*isms*," this mistrust of the "other"—one could call it "*otherism*"—is arguably the most problematic. Otherism, elsewhere called "otherness" (Taylor 1987, 34; Mason 1990, 1; Baldwin 2001, 170), in fact is the basis for racism.

There is no justification for discriminating against people just because they are different. One of the most insightful treatments of the denigration of the "other" was written in verse form by Rudyard Kipling. Although he is often remembered for the racism exemplified in his "White Man's Burden," I quoted the first stanza of his "We and They" in Chapter 15 since it exemplifies quite a different point of view. Here, it seems most appropriate to include the whole of that extraordinary poem:

> *We and They*
>
> Father, and Mother, and Me.
>   Sister and Auntie say
> All the people like us are We,
>   And every one else is They.
> And They live over the sea,
>   While We live over the way,
> But—would you believe it?—They look upon we
>   As only a sort of They!
>
> We eat pork and beef
>   With cow-horn-handled knives.
> They who gobble Their rice off a leaf,
>   Are horrified out of Their lives;
> While They who live up a tree,
>   And feast on grubs and clay,
> (Isn't it scandalous?) look upon we
>   As a simply disgusting They!

We shoot birds with a gun
  They stick lions with spears.
Their full-dress is un-,
  We dress up to our ears.
They like Their friends for tea.
  We like ours to stay;
And, after all that, They look upon We
  As an utterly ignorant They!

We eat kitcheny food,
  We have doors that latch.
They drink milk or blood,
  Under an open thatch.
We have Doctors to fee.
  They have Wizards to pay.
And (impudent heathen!) They look upon We
  As a quite impossible They!

All good people agree,
  And all good people say,
All nice people, like Us, are We,
  And everyone else is They:
But if you cross over the sea,
  Instead of over the way,
You may end by (think of it!) looking on We
  As only a sort of They!

(Kipling 1926, 277–278)

In many places, however, the "other" is not physically different from the people doing the evaluating. The socially despised Eta, or *Burakumin,* of Japan are biologically indistinguishable from the Japanese themselves (Price 1966). The "national minorities" in China, while often of longstanding provincial continuity and dialectical distinction, are simply local representations of the general Han Chinese population (Fairbank 1992). Even in India, where the famous caste system is arranged in a hierarchy, caste membership does not coincide with differences in appearance in spite of Western attempts to interpret it in such a fashion (Channa in press).

Inevitably, those countries that participated in the post-Renaissance colonization of what to Europe was the overseas world—and of course the predominant part of that was the Western Hemisphere—were the sources of the outlook that became crystallized by the daily social realities that sustain the American belief in the existence of "race" as a valid biological category. The United States of course, was a product of that widespread British Empire, on which the sun never set. Americans inherited British habits of thought along with the language in which these were expressed, so it was inevitable that the circumstances that reified the concept of "race" in the former colony would be absorbed as part of the common consciousness in Great Britain itself.

It was the artificial juxtaposition of people from widely separate places of origin that created the perception that categorical distinction was the normal way in which human physical differences occurred. The transoceanic travel that helped to create the Renaissance view of the world just reinforced the perception of human differences as being categorical. Those were the circumstances that destroyed the peasant perspective of the previous outlook, even though that latter, in retrospect, was far more sophisticated and defensible. In the Protestant portion of the colonized world, the compulsion of the individual to find out about the nature of his or her surroundings in order to gain an understanding of what God had provided for human benefit led to an attempt to evaluate everything in terms of its potential utility. That compulsion to evaluate, of course, extended to the artificially created human distinctions as well. This not only created categorical "racial" distinctions but also endowed them with differential worth.

As we saw in Chapter 1, biologically adaptive traits in which people differ are not distributed according to our perceptions of "racial" boundaries, and we can make no sense out of the meanings of their actual distributions if we use "race" as a starting point in our analysis. Some anatomical and physiological traits show graded distributions related to the distribution of the selective forces to which they represent adaptations. Skin color varies in conjunction with the intensity of ultraviolet radiation and long-term residence in areas where that intensity is notably different (Jablonski and Chaplin 2000). Reflecting a completely unrelated cline, human dental reduction is related to the time depth of particular food-preparation practices followed in different parts of the world (Brace et al. 1991). In comparable fashion, the distributions of hemoglobins C and S and the Duffy blood group alleles reflect the prevalence of different kinds of malaria (Livingstone 1980, 1983, 1984, 1985). The gradations or clines of those different inherited traits are unrelated to the skin color cline or the tooth-size cline. A great many adaptive traits are clinally distributed, but those clines have distributions that are completely independent, crossing population boundaries as though they did not exist and exerting no influence on each other (Brace and Hunt 1990). What governs those traits are the selective forces to which they represent responses, but those selective forces are completely unrelated to each other.

Obviously, people who are related to each other look more alike than they look like people to whom they are not related. What makes people look like each other is largely determined by traits that have no adaptive significance at all. What we are seeing has been called "family resemblance writ large" (Brace 1996a, 130). The concept of "race," then, is a product of colonization and, as such, is a social construct. From the perspective of evolutionary biology, there is no entity that corresponds to the social perception conveyed by the word "race." In that realm, as Frank Livingstone said 40 years ago, "There are no races, there are only clines" (1962, 279).

"Race" is not a valid biological category, even recently being called "biologically meaningless" (Schwartz 2001, 1392), yet it is a universal perception reinforced by the economic and military influence of the United States of America. Although America as a society was originally derived from European roots, it has taken on a life of its own, in part shaped by the out-of-context nature of its peopling. Because of its status as a major world power, this is influencing how the Old World now perceives things. As was mentioned in Chapter 4, it is a case of a New World tail wagging an Old World dog. Having unconsciously done so much to create the concept in the first place, perhaps the United States could help to redeem things by using its power to convince the rest of the world that there is no biological entity that corresponds to the word "race."

If "race" is strictly a social construct, then the treatment of "racial" matters should be governed only by what controls the social realm. This involves matters of ethics and politics, and the latter is completely beyond what is covered in this book. If what are perceived as "races" are not equally represented in different professions, schools, or income tax brackets, then we know that this is the result of past inequities. Yet, the idea of advocating some kind of quota for different "races" is seen as tantamount to assuring that "better-qualified candidates lose out to less-qualified ones" (Bolick 1996, 70). Where the goal is admission to high-status educational institutions, admission is in part dependent on SAT scores. As mentioned, these were once called the "Scholastic Aptitude Tests," but, in recognition of the fact that they test achievement at least as much as aptitude, they are now referred to as the "Scholastic Assessment Tests" (Schwartz 1999, 35). As it happens, the assumption that higher scores, above a threshold of 1100, indicate higher qualification turns out to be without foundation. Higher levels are not correlated with higher levels of graduation, prestige career appointments, or earnings (Bowen and Bok 1998, 65, 76, 133, 165).

It is somewhat analogous to the situation of applying for a driver's license. The person who gets a perfect score on the written test is no more likely to be a first-rate driver than the person who barely passes. Everyone who passes gets a license. In the case of the SAT, however, not everyone who gets above that key level can expect admission to Harvard, Michigan, or Princeton or to whatever law or medical school to which he or she applies. Schools can and do factor in other things to assure that they enroll a representative mix of the elements of the country. Some form of affirmative action for minorities who score well above the level that indicates that they possess the necessary capabilities would fit into the selection process without inflicting any injustices. How such decisions should be made is essentially a political question and beyond the scope of my treatment. Ethically, I can say that the situation should be fixed. How that should be done is for others to determine, but that determination should be made by those who are informed about the matters covered in this book.

At the moment, my own university has defended its use of a minor but significant form of affirmative action in the selection of its student body. The University of Michigan was sued in both an undergraduate admissions case and a law school admissions case. The suit was backed by the Center for Individual Rights, with the support of none other than the Pioneer Fund (Garber 2002, 33). The case was brought before the Supreme Court, and the outlook was, to say the least, uncertain. For one thing, there is no strong moral and legal presence representing minority interests in the manner of the former Justice Thurgood Marshall. His replacement, Clarence Thomas, has made it clear that he is firmly opposed to affirmative action, although he himself has admitted that were it not for just that he would never have been in a position to be nominated for a seat on that bench (Higginbotham 1998). Thomas's education in a Catholic seminary, at Holy Cross, and then at Yale Law School was made possible only by affirmative action, although Thomas has subsequently denied that this was the case (Mayer and Abramson 1994, 14, 50, 53, 58). In his view, affirmative action is "degrading in its implications that African-Americans needed assistance" (Mayer and Abramson 1994, 18).

In a great many instances, they *do* need assistance; but instead of this having degrading implications, it is quite the reverse. For over a third of a century I have been teaching undergraduates, among whom have been substantial numbers who have been products of the school system in nearby Detroit. Since Detroit is the most racially segregated city in America, most of those students are African Americans. Because of the poverty of the community in which their schools are located, they are miserably underfunded, and the education they provide is very far from first-rate. We get the best students those schools produce, and with SAT scores that show they are clearly college material, they are fully the equal in ability to any of our other students. However, they come in at a serious disadvantage, which it often takes them a year or two to realize. In most instances, they then buckle down and make a concerted effort to overcome the deficiencies in their previous preparation. After graduation, they go on to become citizens who will try to see to it that their own children will not suffer from the kind of educational inadequacies which they themselves unknowingly endured.

Without affirmative action, Thomas would never have graduated from a good university and law school, the extraordinarily productive Henry Lewis Gates, Jr., would never have become a department head at Harvard (see Gates 2003), and a substantial number of innately able but only partially prepared products of the Detroit public school system would never have had the advantages of an education at the University of Michigan.

In a decision handed down on June 23, 2003, the Supreme Court approved the admission policy of the University of Michigan Law School while rejecting the use of "racial" points toward admission to the Michigan undergraduate program. Although it was a narrow 5-to-4 decision, it did approve in principle of the benefits provided by a nonrigid form of affirmative action (Greenhouse 2003). Predictably, Thomas was firm in his opposition to giving anyone else the kind of opportunity that allowed him to achieve the position that he now occupies. The following question has been raised: "So why, despite his racial blessing, does he come across as an angry, bitter self-pitying victim?" (Dowd 2003, A27).

At bottom, devaluation of the "different" or "other" is a psychological matter. People are innately suspicious of those who look different, who have different beliefs, who value different kinds of behavior and consequently act differently, who speak with a different accent or use a different language, and who wear different kinds of clothes and eat different foods. When Herodotus wrote about the Persians, he noted that they gave most honor to those who lived nearest, and those who lived farthest away were assigned the least merit of all: "But at this rate, who among us is not Persian? Patriotism of this sort would merely be the transposition of individual egocentrism to the level of the group. . . . egocentrism is . . . 'the rule of Herodotus'" (Todorov 1993, 173). The perception of the "other," then, is completely self-centered: "There is no objective reality, no 'other' out there to be objectified. All others are part of the self. All so-called realities are subjective, and all of them are constructs" (Cartmill 1994, 2). While this is true of our perceptions of the human world—and I have made the case that this is exemplified in the concept of "race"—there is always the danger of taking it too far and denying that there is an objective reality in the physical world. Some of the extreme enthusiasts for what is called "postmodernism" have gone so far as to deny any absolute reality in the material world and claim that *everything* is just a "social construct."

In a sense, this is just a more extreme manifestation of the split between the "two cultures" discussed in Chapter 5. One physicist, Alan Sokal, played along with them in a hilarious but straightfaced spoof, suggesting among other things that the value of π, the nature of gravity, and the speed of light were not invariably fixed (Sokal 1996b). He was pulling their legs, of course, but the editors of a trendy cultural studies journal, *Social Text,* were completely taken in and published his parody in a special issue, "Science Wars," as though it were a serious contribution. Elsewhere, and almost simultaneously, Sokal gloated over the hoax, noting that he did indeed have a serious point to make in regard to the pompous verbosity in the fatuous misunderstanding and misuse of aspects of science exhibited by some highly regarded members of the literary world (Sokal 1996a, 2000; Sokal and Bricmont 1998). In response, one of the editors of *Social Text,* in very much the same vein of ignorant "vulgarity" that characterized F. R. Leavis's treatment of C. P. Snow a couple of generations earlier, called the physicist "ill-read and half-educated" (*Lingua Franca* 2000, 60, 76), a claim that might describe the editor in question but certainly not his target (Sokal and Bricmont 1998, 182 ff.). Even before that highly publicized episode, an equally effective twitting of the occasionally pretentious literary posturing was offered by a biologist: "Even the most dedicated postmodernist, when she descends from her ivory tower after a hard day denying reality, suspends her disbelief long enough to choose the stairs instead of the quicker way down afforded by her window" (Queller 1995, 488). Sokal himself offered the same opportunity to those who believe that "the laws of physics are mere social conventions," inviting them to transgress those conventions from the windows of his apartment, noting that he lives "on the twenty-first floor" (Sokal and Bricmont 1998, 268).

Where it is a matter of dealing with the human condition, however, it is completely within the realm of the subjective. There, not surprisingly, representatives of the literary world have been particularly effective. The endless roster of perceptions and misperceptions of human likenesses and differences constitutes the engine that drives much literary enterprise. To cite only a few English examples, William Shakespeare drew on this at the beginning of the 17th century for his Moor in *Othello,* his Shylock in *The Merchant of Venice,* and his Thane of Cawdor in *MacBeth.* In Victorian England, Charles Dickens in *Oliver Twist* and Anthony Trollope in *The Way We Live Now* dealt with perceived class and ethnic differences. In the 20th century, "racial," class, and ethnic perceptions are examined with insightful effectiveness in such works as Ralph Ellison's *Invisible Man,* Joyce Carol Oates's *Them,* and Salman Rushdie's *Satanic Verses,* just to mention single works by a tiny sample of extraordinarily prolific authors. The same is true for other parts of the world and not just European ones. Lady Murasaki's *The Tale of Genji,* set in 11th-century Japan, is an example, as is the 18th-century Chinese masterpiece *The Story of the Stone* (sometimes translated under the title *A Dream of Red Mansions*) by Cao Xueqin.

Travel writers from Herodotus on have recounted their perceptions of the habits and foibles of the "other." Almost without exception, the author and the author's natal group is assumed to be the exemplification of what is praiseworthy in the human spectrum. The extent to which others differ in appearance and behavior is generally taken as a measure of their assumed lesser worth. It is this that represents the essence of "otherism," and it is completely subjective. The pluses and minuses of human difference are simply asserted, with no effort made to test their relative merits.

It seems appropriate to end with an echo of some of the themes which underlie this book and how the conferral of a label can create a belief in an entity that has no objective reality.

The Name of a Race

When we ponder on the contours in the features of a face
Which resembles all the others that are from a given place,

What potential harm would follow if we use a single name,
To denote a group of people when we think they look the same?

But there are no implications that a common shape will bear,
Beyond the clear reminder of the kinship that they share;

For selection's not delimited by groups of kin alone,
Or confined within the boundaries of a continental zone.

Pigment in the skin will give protection from the sun,
But it doesn't give a clue to how another trait will run;

Both the desert and the arctic take the moisture from the air,
And people from both places have a nose with length to spare.

Features cannot tell us who is mad and who is sane,
Or nuance of the forehead say a thing about the brain.

Each trait that is adaptive will pursue a separate course,
Determined by the nature of its own selective force

Which crosses all the others in a fashion that defines
A pattern without meaning made of independent clines.

Since each selected feature has a different place of birth,
The mix within a region can have no collective worth.

When thoughtlessly we verbalize without the proper care,
Our words can make an entity that isn't really there;

How much pigment or how little will suffice to give the right
To warrant the conferral of the label "Black" or "White"?

And beware the added meaning in the tag we lightly give;
For it oftentimes determines who may have the right to live.

Acceptance of the concept and all that it can mean,
Gives credence to an image that could best be called obscene;

To use the very word is to be captured by its spell:
That which we call a "race," by any other name would smell . . .

(Echo 1996)

SOURCES CITED

Abrahams, Harold J. 1966. *Extinct Medical Schools of Nineteenth-Century Philadelphia.* University of Pennsylvania Press, Philadelphia. 580 pp.

Ackerknecht, Erwin H. 1953. *Rudolf Virchow: Doctor, Statesman, Anthropologist.* University of Wisconsin Press, Madison. 304 pp.

Ackerknecht, Erwin, and Henri V. Vallois. 1955. *François Joseph Gall et sa collection.* *Mémoires du Museum national d'histoire naturelle. Série A: Zoologie,* t. 10, fasc. 1. Museum national d'histoire naturelle, Paris. 92 pp.

Adair, Fred Lyman, 1970. Paracelsus. *Encylopaedia Britannica,* Vol. 17, p. 299.

Adelsteinsson, S. 1985. Human ABO blood groups and changes in Iceland. *Annals of Human Genetics* 49(3):275–281.

Agassiz, Louis, 1840. On glaciers and the evidence of their having once existed in Scotland, Ireland and England. *Proceedings of the Geological Society of England* 3:327–332.

———. 1845. Notice sur la géographie des animaux. Extrait de *La Revue Suisse.* H. Wolfrath, Neuchâtel. 31 pp.

———. 1850a. The geographical distribution of animals. *Christian Examiner and Religious Miscellany* 48:181–204.

———. 1850b. The diversity and origin of the human races. *Christian Examiner and Religious Miscellany* 49:110–145.

———. 1854. Sketch of the natural provinces of the animal world and their relation to the different types of man. In J. C. Nott and G. R. Gliddon (eds.), *Types of Mankind.* Lippincott & Grambo, Philadelphia. Pp. lviii–lxxvi.

———. 1857. *Essay on Classification.* Little, Brown, Boston. 381 pp.

Allen, Don Cameron, 1949. *The Legend of Noah: Renaissance Rationalism in Art, Science, and Letters.* University of Illinois Press, Urbana. 221 pp.

Allen, Garland E. 1986. The Eugenics Record Office at Cold Spring Harbor, 1910–1940: An essay in institutional history. *Osiris,* n.s., 2:225–264.

American Association of Physical Anthropologists. 1939. Proceedings of the Tenth Annual Meeting. *American Journal of Physical Anthropology* 25(1, Suppl.):1–7.

———. 1996. AAPA statement on biological aspects of race. *American Journal of Physical Anthropology* 101(4):569–570.

Anderson, Scott, and Jon Lee Anderson. 1986. *Inside the League: The Shocking Exposé of How Terrorists, Nazis, and Latin American Death Squads Have Infiltrated the World Anticommunist League.* Dodd, Mead, New York. 322 pp.

Antelme, Robert, [1947] 1992. *The Human Race.* Jeffrey Haight and Annie Mahler (trans.). Marlboro Press, Marlboro, VT. 298 pp.

Appel, John T. (ed.) 1971. *The New Immigration.* Pitman Publishing, New York. 215 pp.

Appel, Toby A. 1987. *The Cuvier-Geoffroy Debate: French Biology in the Decades Before Darwin.* Oxford University Press, New York. 305 pp.

Appiah, Kwame Anthony, 1990. Racisms. In David Theo Goldberg (ed.), *Anatomy of Racism.* University of Minnesota Press, Minneapolis. Pp. 3–17.

Appiah, Kwame Anthony, and Amy Gutmann. 1996. *Color Conscious: The Political Morality of Race.* Princeton University Press, Princeton. 191 pp.

Aquinas, Saint Thomas, 1994. *God and Creation. Selections from Summa Theologiae.* William P. Baumgarth and Richard J. Regan (trans.). Associated Universities Presses, Cranbury, NJ. 310 pp.

Armytage, W. H. G. 1953. Matthew Arnold and T. H. Huxley: Some new letters 1870–80. *Review of English Studies* 4(16):346–353.

Arnold, Matthew, 1869. *Culture and Anarchy: An Essay in Political and Social Criticism.* Smith, Elder and Co., London. 212 pp.

Audubon, John James, 1827–38. *The Birds of America.* Published by the author, London. 5 Vols.

Audubon, John James, and Rev. John Bachman. 1845–53. *The Viviparous Quadrupeds of North America.* G. R. Lockwood, New York. 3 Vols.

Bachman, Catherine L. 1888. *John Bachman. The Pastor of S. John's Lutheran Church, Charleston.* Walker, Evans and Cogswell, Charleston, SC. 436 pp.

Bachman, John, 1850. *The Doctrine of the Unity of the Human Race, Examined on the Principles of Science.* C. Canning, Charleston, SC. 312 pp.

———. 1854a. A notice of the "Types of Mankind," with an examination of the charges contained in the biography of Dr. Morton. *Charleston Medical Journal and Review* 9:627–659.

———. 1854b. An examination of a few of the statements of Prof. Agassiz in his "Sketch of the natural provinces of the animal world and their relations to the different types of men." *Charleston Medical Journal and Review* 9:790–806.

———1855a. An examination of the characteristics of genera and species as applicable to the doctrine of the unity of the human race. *Charleston Medical Journal and Review* 10(3):201–222.

———. 1855b. An examination of Prof. Agassiz's sketch of the natural provinces of the animal world, and their relation to the different types of man, with a tableau accompanying the sketch. *Charleston Medical Journal and Review* 10(4):482–534.

Bacon, Francis, 1605. *Advancement of Learning.* W. Washington, London. 335 pp.

Baker, John, 1974. *Race.* Oxford University Press, New York. 625 pp.

Baker, Lee D. 1998. *From Savage to Negro: Anthropology and the Construction of Race, 1896–1954.* University of California Press, Berkeley. 325 pp.

Baker, Timothy B., and Michael C. Fiore. 1992. Elvis is alive, the Mafia killed JFK, and smoking is good for you. Review of *Smoking, Personality, and Stress: Psychological Factors in the Prevention of Cancer and Coronary Heart Disease* by Hans J. Eysenck. *Contemporary Psychology* 37(10):1014–1016.

Baldwin, Neil, 2001. *Henry Ford and the Jews. The Mass Production of Hate.* Public Affairs, New York. 416 pp.

Baltzell, E. Digby, 1979. *Puritan Boston and Quaker Philadelphia: Two Protestant Ethics and the Spirit of Class Authority and Leadership.* Free Press, New York. 585 pp.

Banton, Michael, 1967. *Race Relations.* Tavistock Publishers, London. 434 pp.

———. 1998. *Racial Theories,* 2nd ed. Cambridge University Press, New York. 253 pp.

Banton, Michael, and Jonathan Harwood. 1975. *The Race Concept.* Praeger, New York. 160 pp.

Barash, David P. 1995. Review of *Race, Evolution, and Behavior* by J. P. Rushton. *Animal Behaviour* 49(4):1131–1133.

Barkan, Elazar, 1988. Mobilizing scientists against Nazi racism, 1933–1939. In George W. Stocking, Jr. (ed.), *Bones, Bodies, Behavior. Essays on Biological Anthropology.* University of Wisconsin Press, Madison. Pp. 181–205.

———. 1992. *The Retreat of Scientific Racism. Changing Concepts of Race in Britain and the United States Between the World Wars.* Cambridge University Press, Cambridge. 381 pp.

Barzun, Jacques, 1937. *Race: A Study of Modern Superstition.* Harcourt, Brace and Co., New York. 353 pp.

———. 1958. *Darwin, Marx, Wagner: Critique of a Heritage,* rev. 2nd ed. Doubleday Anchor Books, Garden City, NY. 373 pp.

———. 1965. *Race: A Study in Superstition,* rev. ed. Harper & Row, New York. 263 pp.

Basu, Amitabha, 1969. The Pahira: A population genetical study. *American Journal of Physical Anthropology* 31(3):399–416.

Battuta, Ibn, [1356] 1929. *Travels in Asia and Africa, 1325–1354.* Sir H. A. R. Gibb (trans.) R. M. McBride and Co., New York. 398 pp.

Battuta, Ibn, 1982. *Voyages.* C. Defremery and B. R. Sanguinetti (trans. 1858). Introduction et notes de Stephane Yerasimos. F. Maspero, Paris. 3 Vols.

Bay, Mia, 2002. A dream deferred, review of *The Broken Promise of the Brown Decision* by Peter Irons. *New York Times,* October 6, p. 24.

Beaglehole, Ernest, Joan Comas, L. A. Costa Pinta, Franklin Frazier, Morris Ginsberg, Humayan Kabir, Claude Levi-Straus, and Ashley Montagu. 1951. UNESCO statement by experts on problems of race. *American Anthropologist* 53(1):142–145.

Beals, Kenneth L., Courtland L. Smith, and Stephen M. Dodd. 1984. Brain size, cranial morphology, climate and time machines. *Current Anthropology* 25(3):301–330.

Bean, Robert Bennett, 1906. Some racial peculiarities of the Negro brain. *American Journal of Anatomy* 5(4):353–432.

Bedini, Silvio A. 1972. *The Life of Benjamin Banneker.* Charles Scribner's Sons, New York. 434 pp.

Beer, Gillian 1983. *Darwin's Plots. Evolution Narrative in Darwin, George Eliot and Nineteenth-Century Fiction.* Routledge & Kegan Paul, London. 295 pp.

Bell, David A. 2001. *The Cult of the Nation in France: Inventing Nationalism 1680–1800.* Harvard University Press, Cambridge, MA. 304 pp.

Bendyshe, Thomas (ed.) 1865. *The Anthropological Treatises of Johann Friedrich Blumenbach.* Longman, Green, Longman, Roberts and Green, London. 406 pp.

Benedict, Ruth, 1945. *Race: Science and Politics,* rev. ed. Viking Press, New York. 206 pp.

Bennett, Harry, and Paul Marcus. 1951. *We Never Called Him Henry.* Gold Medal Books, Fawcett Publications, Greenwich, CT. 180 pp.

Bentley, George R. 1955. *A History of the Freedmen's Bureau.* University of Pennsylvania Press, Philadelphia. 294 pp.

Berlin, Isaiah, 1980. *Against the Current: Essays in the History of Ideas.* Viking Press, New York. 394 pp.

Bernal, Martin. 1987. *Black Athena: The Afroasiatic Roots of Classical Civilization. The Fabrication of Ancient Greece 1785–1985,* Vol. I. Free Association Books, London. 576 pp.

Bernasconi, Robert, 2001. Who invented the concept of race? Kant's role in the Enlightenment construction of race. In Robert Bernasconi (ed.), *Race.* Blackwell Publishers, Malden, MA. Pp. 11–36.

Bernstein, Herman, 1921. *The History of a Lie, "The Protocols of the Wise Men of Zion."* J. S. Ogilvie Publishing Company, New York. 84 pp.

———. 1935. *The Truth About "The Protocols of Zion;" A Complete Exposure.* Covici Friede Publishers, New York. 397 pp.

Bessel, Richard, 1993. *Germany After the First World War.* Clarendon Press, Oxford. 325 pp.

Biasutti, Renato, 1959. *Le razze e i popoli della terra. Razze, popoli e culture,* 3rd ed., Vol. I. Unione Tipografico-Editrice, Torino. 721 pp.

Biddiss, Michael D. 1970. *Father of Racist Ideology: The Social and Political Thought of Count Gobineau.* Weidenfeld and Nicolson, London. 314 pp.

Bilger, Burkhard, 2002. Fortune hunters and gatherers. Review of *The Natural History of the Rich: A Field Guide* by Richard Conniff. *New York Times Book Review* October 27, p. 18.

Binet, Alfred, 1905. Analyse de C. E. Spearman, "The proof and measurement of association between two things" and "General intelligence objectively determined and measured." *L'Année Psychologique* 11:623–624.

———. 1910. *Les idées modernes sur les enfants.* Ernest Flammarion, Paris. 346 pp.

Binet, Alfred, and Théodore Simon. 1905. Méthodes nouvelles pour le diagnostic du niveau intellectuel des anormaux. *L'Année Psychologique* 11(1):191–244.

———. 1908. Le dévelopement de l'intelligence chez les enfants. *L'Année Psychologique* 14:1–94.

———. 1980. *The Development of Intelligence in Children (The Binet-Simon Scale)*, Elizabeth S. Kite (trans.). Facsimile of 1916 edition. Williams Printing, Nashville, TN. 336 pp.

Birnbaum, Jonathan, and Clarence Taylor (eds.) 2000. *Civil Rights Since 1787: A Reader on the Black Struggle.* New York University Press, New York. 936 pp.

Bishop, Katherine, 1988. Day of apology and sigh of relief. *New York Times,* August 11, p. 16.

Blanckaert, Claude, 1988a. J.-J. Virey, observateur de l'homme (1800–1825). In C. Bénichou and C. Blanckaert (eds.), *Julien-Joseph Virey, naturaliste et anthropologue.* J. Vrin, Paris. Pp. 97–182.

———. 1988b. On the origins of French ethnology: William Edwards and the doctrine of race. In G. W. Stocking (ed.), *Bones, Bodies, Behavior: Essays on Biological Anthropology. History of Anthropology,* Vol. 5. University of Wisconsin Press, Madison. Pp. 18–55.

Blumenbach, Johann Friedrich, 1790–1828. *Decades suae craniorum diversarum Gentium, illustratae.* I. C. Dietrich, Göttingen. 6 Vols.

———. 1825. *A Manual of the Elements of Natural History* Richard T. Gore (trans., from tenth German ed.). W. Simpkin and R. Marshall, London. 415 pp.

———. [1865] 1969. *On the Natural Varieties of Mankind. De Generis Humani Varietate Nativa* Thomas Bendyshe (trans., ed. from Latin, German and French originals). Bergman Publishers, New York. Pp. 145–276.

Blumenschine, Robert J., and John A. Cavallo. 1992. Scavenging and human evolution. *Scientific American* 267(4):90–96.

Blunt, Wilfrid, 2001. *Linnaeus: The Compleat Naturalist.* Princeton University Press, Princeton. 264 pp. (Originally *The Compleat Naturalist: A Life of Linnaeus.* Frances Lincoln Limited, London, 1971.)

Blurton Jones, Nicholas, 1987. Bushman birth spacing: A direct test of some simple predictions. *Ethology and Sociobiology* 8(3):183–205.

Boas, Franz, 1899. The cephalic index. *American Anthropologist* 1(3):448–461.

———. 1911. Changes in bodily form of descendants of immigrants. In *Reports of the Immigration Commission,* Vol. 38 (61st Congress, 2nd Session, Senate Document 208). Government Printing Office, Washington, DC.

———. 1912. Changes in the bodily form of descendants of immigrants. *American Anthropologist* 14(3):530–562.

———. 1918. Review of *The Passing of the Great Race: or the Racial Basis for European History* by Madison Grant. *American Journal of Physical Anthropology* 1(3):363.

———. 1919. Scientists as spies. *Nation* 109(Dec. 20):797. (Reprinted in G. W. Stocking, Jr. [ed.] 1974. *The Shaping of American Anthropology 1883–1911: A Franz Boas Reader.* Basic Books, New York. Pp. 336–337.)

———. 1920. Review of *The Rising Tide of Color: Against White World Supremacy* by Lothrop Stoddard. *Nation* 111:658.

Boesiger, Ernest, 1980. Evolutionary biology in France at the time of the evolutionary synthesis. In E. Mayr and W. B. Provine (eds.), *The Evolutionary Synthesis.* Harvard University Press, Cambridge, MA. Pp. 309–321.

Bokie, Simon, 2001. Kongo religion. In Stephen D. Glazier (ed.), *The Encyclopedia of African and African-American Religions.* Routledge, New York. Pp. 172–174.

Bolick, Clint, 1996. *The Affirmative Action Fraud: Can We Restore the American Civil Rights Vision?* Cato Institute, Washington, DC. 170 pp.

Boring, Edwin G. 1923. Intelligence as the tests test it. *New Republic* 35:35–37.

Bory de Saint Vincent, Jean Baptiste Geneviève Marcellin, baron. 1827. *L'Homme* (Homo) *Essai zoologique sur le genre humain,* 2nd ed. Rey et Gravier, Paris. 2 Vols.

Boule, Marcellin, 1911–13. L'homme fossile de La Chapelle-aux-Saints. *Annales de Paléontologie* 6:111–172, 7:21–192, 8:1–70.

Bowen, William G., and Derek Bok. 1998. *The Shape of the River: Long-Term Consequences of Considering Race in College and University Admission.* Princeton University Press, Princeton. 472 pp.

Bowler, Peter J. 1986. *Theories of Human Evolution. A Century of Debate 1844–1944.* Johns Hopkins University Press, Baltimore. 318 pp.

Boyd, James, 1970. Nixon's southern strategy. "It's all in the charts." *New York Times Magazine* May 17, p. 109.

Brabrook, E. W. 1881. Paul Broca, honorary member. *Journal of the Anthropological Institute of Great Britain and Ireland* 10:242–261.

Brace, Charles L. 1861. Ethnological fallacies. *Independent* 13:6.

———. 1863. *The Races of the Old World: A Manual of Ethnology.* Charles Scribner, New York. 540 pp.

Brace, C. Loring, 1963. Structural reduction in evolution. *American Naturalist* 97:729–741.

———. 1964a. A non-racial approach towards the understanding of human diversity. In M. F. A. Montagu (ed.), *Concept of Race.* Free Press of Glencoe, New York. Pp. 313–320.

———. 1964b. The fate of the "classic" Neanderthals: A consideration of hominid catastrophism. *Current Anthropology* 5(1):3–43.

———. 1967. *The Stages of Human Evolution: Human and Cultural Origins.* Prentice-Hall, Englewood Cliffs, NJ. 116 pp.

———. 1971. Introduction to Jensenism. In C. L. Brace, G. R. Gamble, and J. T. Bond (eds.), *Race and Intelligence. Anthropology Studies,* Vol. 8. American Anthropological Association, Washington, DC. Pp. 4–9.

———. 1974a. The "ethnology" of Josiah Clark Nott. *Bulletin of the New York Academy of Medicine* 40:409–438.

———. 1974b. Problems in early hominid interpretations. *Yearbook of Physical Anthropology* 17:202–207.

———. 1977. Occlusion to the anthropological eye. In J. A. McNamara, Jr. (ed.), *The Biology of Occlusal Development. Craniofacial Growth Series,* Monograph 7. Center for Human Growth and Development, University of Michigan, Ann Arbor. Pp. 179–209.

———. 1979. Krapina, "classic" Neanderthals, and the evolution of the European face. *Journal of Human Evolution* 8(5):527–550.

———. 1980a. Australian tooth size clines and the death of a stereotype. *Current Anthropology* 21(2):141–164.

———. 1980b. Review of *Bias in Mental Testing* by Arthur R. Jensen. *Behavioral and Brain Sciences* 3(3):333–334.

———. 1981. Tales of the phylogenetic woods: The evolution and significance of phylogenetic trees. *American Journal of Physical Anthropology* 56(4):411–429.

———. 1982. The roots of the race concept in American physical anthropology. In F. Spencer (ed.), *A History of American Physical Anthropology, 1930–1980.* Academic Press, New York. Pp. 11–29.

———. 1988. Punctuationism, cladistics and the legacy of medieval Neoplatonism. *Human Evolution* 3(3):121–138.

———. 1995. *The Stages of Human Evolution,* 5th ed. Prentice-Hall, Englewood Cliffs, NJ. 371 pp.

———. 1996a. A four-letter word called "race." In Larry T. Reynolds and Leonard Lieberman (eds.), *Race and Other Misadventures: Essays in Honor of Ashley Montagu in His Ninetieth Year.* General Hall Publishers, Dix Hills, NY. Pp. 106–141.

———. 1996b. Racialism and racist agendas: Review of *Race, Evolution and Behavior: A Life History Perspective,* by J. Philippe Rushton. *American Anthropologist* 98(1):176–177.

———. 1996c. Review of *The Bell Curve: Intelligence and Class Structure in American Life* by Richard J. Herrnstein and Charles Murray. *Current Anthropology* 37(Suppl.): S156–S161.

———. 1997a. Foreword. In *Man's Most Dangerous Myth, The Fallacy of Race,* 6th ed., by Ashley Montagu. AltaMira Press, Walnut Creek, CA. Pp. 13–23.

———. 1997b. The intellectual standing of Charles Darwin, and the legacy of the "Scottish Enlightenment" in biological thought. *Yearbook of Physical Anthropology* 40:91–111.

———. 1999a. An anthropological perspective on "race" and intelligence: The non-clinal nature of human cognitive capabilities. *Journal of Anthropological Research* 55(2):245–264.

———. 1999b. Beware the bigot brigade. *Anthropology Newsletter* 40(3):2.

———. 1999c. Racialism, racism and the bigot brigade: Review of *The g Factor* by Arthur R. Jensen. *psycoloquy.*99.10.026.intelligence-g-factor.11.brace (accessed Dec. 16).

———. 2000. *Evolution in an Anthropological View.* AltaMira Press, Walnut Creek, CA. 407 pp.

———. 2002. The concept of race in physical anthropology. In Peter N. Peregrine, Carol R. Ember, and Melvin Ember (eds.), *Physical Anthropology: Original Readings in Method and Practice.* Prentice-Hall, Upper Saddle River, NJ. Pp. 239–253.

Brace, C. Loring, Mary L. Brace, and William R. Leonard. 1989. Reflections on the face of Japan. *American Journal of Physical Anthropology* 78(1):93–113.

Brace, C. Loring, and Kevin D. Hunt. 1990. A non-racial craniofacial perspective on human variation: A(ustralia) to Z(uni). *American Journal of Physical Anthropology* 82(3): 341–360.

Brace, C. Loring, Paul E. Mahler, and Richard B. Rosen. 1973. Tooth measurements and the rejection of the taxon "*Homo habilis.*" *Yearbook of Physical Anthropology* 16:31–49.

Brace, C. Loring, and Ashley Montagu. 1965. *Man's Evolution: An Introduction to Physical Anthropology.* Macmillan, New York. 352 pp.

———. 1977. *Human Evolution: An Introduction to Biological Anthropology,* 2nd ed. Macmillan, New York. 493 pp.

Brace, C. Loring, A. Russell Nelson, Noriko Seguchi, Hiroaki Oe, Leslie Sering, Pan Qifeng, Li Yongyi, and Dastseveg Tumen. 2001. Old World sources of the first New World inhabitants. *Proceedings of the National Academy of Sciences USA* 98(17):10017–10022.

Brace, C. Loring, and Noriko Seguchi. In press. "Race": Social construct vs. biological reality. In Yasuko Takezawa (ed.), *Is Race a Universal Ideal? Nation-State and a Myth Invented.* Institute for Research in Humanities, Kyoto University, Kyoto, Japan. (Read at the Inter-Congress of the International Union of Anthropological and Ethnological Sciences, Tokyo, September 2002.)

Brace, C. Loring, Shelley L. Smith, and Kevin D. Hunt. 1991. What big teeth you had Grandma! Human tooth size, past and present. In Marc A. Kelley and Clark S. Larsen (eds.), *Advances in Dental Anthropology.* Wiley-Liss, New York. Pp. 33–57.

Brace, C. Loring, and David P. Tracer. 1992. Craniofacial continuity and change: A comparison of Late Pleistocene and Recent Europe and Asia. In T. Akazawa, K. Aoki, and T. Kimura (eds.), *The Evolution and Dispersion of Modern Humans in Asia.* Hokusen-Sha Publishing, Tokyo. Pp. 439–471.

Brace, C. Loring, David P. Tracer, Lucia Allen Yaroch, John Robb, Kari Brandt, and A. Russell Nelson. 1993. Clines and clusters versus "race": A test in ancient Egypt and the case of a death on the Nile. *Yearbook of Physical Anthropology* 36:1–31.

Brace, Emma (ed.) 1894. *The Life of Charles Loring Brace Chiefly Told in His Own Letters.* Charles Scribner's Sons, New York. 503 pp.

Brace, Gerald W. 1952. *The Spire.* W. W. Norton, New York. 380 pp.

Brain, Charles K. 1981. *The Hunters or the Hunted? An Introduction to Cave Taphonomy.* University of Chicago Press, Chicago. 365 pp.

Brandon, Robert N. 1999. The units of selection revisited: The modules of selection. *Biology and Philosophy* 14(2):167–180.

Breitman, Richard, 1991. *The Architect of Genocide. Himmler and the Final Solution.* Bodley Head, London. 335 pp.

Bridie, James, 1931. *The Anatomist.* Constable & Co., London. 73 pp.

Brigham, Carl C. 1923. *A Study of American Intelligence.* Princeton University Press, Princeton. 210 pp.

———. 1930. Intelligence tests of immigrant groups. *Psychological Review* 37(1):158–165.

Broc, Pierre-Paul, 1837. *Essai sur les races humaines considérées sous les rapports anatomique et philosophique,* Vol. 14. Établissement Encyclographique, Bruxelles. 41 pp.

Broca, Paul, 1858. Mémoire sur l'hybridité en général, sur la distinction des espèces animales et sur les métis obtenus par le croisement du lièvre et du lapin. *Journal de la Physiologie de l'Homme et des Animaux* 1(3):433–471, 1(4):684–729.

———. 1859a. Mémoire sur l'hybridité en général, sur la distinction des espèces animales et sur les métis obtenus par le croisement du lièvre et du lapin. *Journal de la Physiologie de l'Homme et des Animaux* 2(6):218–250, 2(7)345–396.

———. 1859b. Des phénomènes d'hybridité dans le genre humain. *Journal de la Physiologie de l'Homme et des Animaux* 2(8):601–625.

———. 1860a. Des phénomènes d'hybridité dans le genre humain. *Journal de la Physiologie de l'Homme et des Animaux* 3(10):392–439.

———. 1860b. *Recherches sur l'hybridité animal en général et sur l'hybridité humaine en particulier, considérées dans leurs rapports avec la question de la pluralité des espèces humains.* J. Claye, Paris. Pp. 433–664.

———. 1861a. Remarques sur la siège de la faculté de la parole articulée, suivies d'une observation d'aphémie (perte de parole). *Bulletin de la Société d'Anatomie* (Paris) 36:330–357.

———. 1861b. Sur le volume et la forme du cerveau suivant les individus et suivant les races. *Bulletins de la Société d'Anthropologie de Paris* 2:139–204, 301–321, 441–446.

———. 1862a. Sur le rapport de M. Dally concernant les Américains. *Bulletins de la Société d'Anthropologie de Paris* 3:423–427, 433–435.

———. 1862b. En réponse à M. Pruner-Bey sur les travaux anthropologiques de l'école américaine. *Bulletins de la Société d'Anthropologie de Paris* 3:456–457.

———. 1862c. La linguistique et l'anthropologie. Mémoire lu à la Société d'Anthropologie le 5 juin 1862. *Bulletins de la Société d'Anthropologie de Paris* 3:264–319.

———. 1864. *On the Phenomena of Hybridity in the Genus* Homo. C. Carter Blake (trans., ed.). Longman, Green, & Roberts, London. 76 pp.

———. 1865. Histoire des travaux de la Société d'Anthropologie (1859–1863). *Mémoires de la Société d'Anthropologie de Paris* 2nd tome, VII–LI.

———. 1870. Sur le transformisme. *Bulletins de la Société d'Anthropologie de Paris* 2nd series, t. 5:168–242.

———. 1873. Sur le mensuration de la capacité du crâne. *Mémoires de la Société d'Anthropologie de Paris* 2nd series, 1:92.

Browman, David L. 2002. The Peabody Museum, Frederic W. Putnam and the rise of U.S. anthropology. *American Anthropologist* 104(2):508–519.

Brown, Charles Michael, 1989. *Benjamin Silliman: A Life in the Young Republic.* Princeton University Press, Princeton. 363 pp.

Brown, F. Martin, 1955. Studies of nearctic *Coenonympha tullia* (Rhopalocera, Satyridae). *Bulletin of the American Museum of Natural History* 104(4):361–409.

Browne, Janet, 1995. *Charles Darwin: Voyaging. Volume 1 of a Biography.* A. A. Knopf, New York. 605 pp.

———. 2002. *Charles Darwin: The Power of Place. Volume 2 of a Biography.* A. A. Knopf, New York. 624 pp.

Browne, Malcolm W. 1994. What is intelligence and who has it? Review of *The Bell Curve: Intelligence and Class Structure in American Life* by Richard J. Herrnstein and Charles Murray; *The Decline of Intelligence in America* by Seymour W. Itzkoff; and *Race, Evolution, and Behavior: A Life History Perspective* by J. Philippe Rushton. *New York Times Book Review,* October 16, pp. 3, 41, 45.

Buchler, Justus (ed.) 1955. *Philosophical Writings of Peirce.* Dover Publications, New York. 386 pp.

Buffon, Georges-Louis Leclerc, comte de, 1799. *L'Histoire naturelle générale et particulière avec la déscription du cabinet du roi.* F. Dufart, Paris. 127 Vols.

Burrow, John W. 1963. Evolution and anthropology in the 1860's: The Anthropological Society of London, 1863–1871. *Victorian Studies* 7:137–154.

Burt, Cyril, 1925. *The Young Delinquent.* Appleton and Co., New York. 619 pp.

Bury, John Bagnall, 1964. *History of the Papacy in the 19th Century: Liberty and Authority in the Roman Catholic Church.* Schocken Books, New York. 217 pp.

Busey, Samuel C. 1856. *Immigration: Its Evils and Consequences.* De Witt & Davenport, New York. 162 pp.

Butterfield, Sir Herbert, 1931. *The Whig Interpretation of History.* G. Bell, London. 132 pp.

[Caldwell, Charles]. 1811. Review of *An Essay on the Causes of the Variety of Complexion and Figure in the Human Species &c. &c.*by Samuel Stanhope Smith. *American Review of History and Politics* 2:128–166.

———. 1814. Criticism—for the *Port Folio. An Essay on the Causes of the Variety of Complexion and Figure in the Human Species &c. &c.* by Samuel Stanhope Smith. D.D. LL.D. &c. &c. *Port Folio* IV(1):8–33, IV(2):148–163, V(4):362–382, IV(5):447–457.

———. 1824. *Elements of Phrenology.* T. T. Skillman, Lexington, KY. 100 pp.

———. 1838. *Phrenology Vindicated and Antiphrenology Unmasked.* Samuel Colman, New York. 156 pp.

———. 1852. *Thoughts on the Original Unity of the Human Race.* J. A. & U. P. James, Cincinnati. 165 pp.

———. 1855. *Autobiography of Charles Caldwell, M.D.* Harriot W. Warner (ed.). Lippincott, Grambo and Co., Philadelphia. 454 pp.

Calhoun, John C. 1848. Senate speech of January 4. *Congressional Globe* (30th Congress, 1st Session), n.s. 7, 18:97–100.

Camper, Pieter, 1791. *Dissertation physique de M. Pierre Camper sur les différences réelles que présentent les traits du visage chez les hommes de différents pays et de différents ages.* D. B. Q. d'Isjonval (trans.). B. Wild and J. Altheer, Autrecht. 114 pp.

Cann, Rebecca L., Mark Stoneking, and Allan C. Wilson. 1987. Mitochondrial DNA and human evolution. *Nature* 325:31–36.

Cardwell, Donald S. L. (ed.) 1968. *John Dalton and the Progress of Science.* Manchester University Press, Manchester. 352 pp.

Carlyle, Thomas, 1838. *Sartor Resartus. The Life and Opinions of Herr Teufeldröckh.* Chapman and Hall, London. 250 pp.

Carmichael, Emmett B. 1948. Josiah Clark Nott. *Bulletin of the History of Medicine* 22:249–262.

Carney, Judith A. 2001. *Black Rice: The African Origins of Rice Cultivation in the Americas.* Harvard University Press, Cambridge, MA. 240 pp.

Carson, Hampton L., Linda S. Chang, and Terrence W. Lyttle. 1982. Decay of female sexual behavior under parthenogenesis. *Science* 218:68–70.

Carter, Stephen L. 1991. *Reflections of an Affirmative Action Baby.* Basic Books, New York. 286 pp.

Cartmill, Matt, 1994. Reinventing anthropology: American Association of Physical Anthropologists annual luncheon address, April 1, 1994. *Yearbook of Physical Anthropology* 37:1–9.

Cartmill, Matt, and Kaye Brown. 2003. Surveying the race concept: A reply to Lieberman, Kirk, and Littlefield. *American Anthropologist* 105(1):114–115.

Cassirer, Ernst, 1945. *Rousseau, Kant, Goethe, Two Essays.* James Gutmann, Paul Oskar Kristeller, and John Herman Randall, Jr. (trans.). Princeton University Press, Princeton. 98 pp.

Casson, Stanley, 1939. *The Discovery of Man.* Harper & Brothers, New York. 339 pp.

Cavalli-Sforza, L. Luca, and Walter F. Bodmer. 1971. *The Genetics of Human Populations.* Freeman, San Francisco. 965 pp.

Cernovsky, Zack Z. 1993. J. P. Rushton's aggregational errors in racial psychology. *Journal of Black Psychology* 19(3):282–289.

Chamberlain, Houston Stewart, 1909. *Die Grundlagen der neunzehnten Jahrhunderts.* F. Brückmann, Munich. 2 Vols.

———. 1910. *The Foundations of the Nineteenth Century.* John Lees (trans.). John Lane, Bodley Head, London. 2 Vols.

Chamla, Marie-Claude, 1964. L'accroisement de la stature en France de 1800 à 1960; comparison avec les pays d'Europe occidentale. *Bulletins et Mémoires de la Société d'Anthropologie de Paris, Série 11,* 6:201–278.

Chan, J. W. C., and Philip E. Vernon. 1988. Individual differences among the peoples of China. In Sidney H. Irvine and John W. Berry (eds.), *Human Abilities in Cultural Context.* Cambridge University Press, Cambridge. Pp. 340–357.

Channa, Subhadra. In press. Colonialism, caste and the myth of race: A historical perspective on the interaction of Indian beliefs and Western science. In Yasuko Takezawa (ed.), *Is Race a Universal Idea? Colonialism, Nation-State, and a Myth Invented.* Institute for Research in Humanities, Kyoto University, Kyoto. Pp. 211–244.

Chapman, Paul Davis, 1988. *Schools as Sorters. Lewis M. Terman, Applied Psychology, and the Intelligence Testing Movement, 1890–1930.* New York University Press, New York. 228 pp.

Chase, Allan, 1977. *The Legacy of Malthus: The Social Costs of the New Scientific Racism.* A. A. Knopf, New York. 686 pp.

Chesebrough, David B. 1991. Slavery. In D. B. Chesebrough (ed.), *"God Ordained This War." Sermons on the Sectional Crisis, 1830–1865.* University of South Carolina Press, Columbia. Pp. 17–33.

Chipuer, H. M., M. J. Rovine, and R. Plomin. 1990. LISREL modeling: Genetic and environmental influence on IQ revisited. *Intelligence* 14:11–29.

Chisholm, James S. 1994. On life-history evolution. Reply to K. Hawkes and J. P. Rushton. *Current Anthropology* 35(1):42–46.

Clark, Geoffrey A., and Catherine M. Willermet (eds.) 1997. *Conceptual Issues in Modern Human Origins Research.* Aldine de Gruyter, New York. 508 pp.

Clark, Grahame, 1969. *World Prehistory: A New Outline,* 2nd ed. Cambridge University Press, New York. 331 pp.

————. 1977. *World Prehistory: A New Outline,* 3rd ed. Cambridge University Press, New York. 574 pp.

Clark, Ronald W. 1968. *The Huxleys.* William Heinemann, London. 398 pp.

Coffman, Edward M. 1968. *The War to End All Wars: The American Military Experience in World War I.* Oxford University Press, New York. 412 pp.

Cohn, Norman, 1967. *Warrant for Genocide; The Myth of the Jewish World-Conspiracy and the Protocols of the Elders of Zion.* Harper & Row, New York. 303 pp.

Colbert, Edwin H. 1994. Four giants of paleontology. *Natural History* 103(5):62–67.

Coles, John, Robert Bewley, and Paul Mellars (eds.) 1999. *World Prehistory: Studies in Memory of Grahame Clark.* Oxford University Press, Oxford. 246 pp.

Collini, Stefan, 1996. Outsiders and the "reformer's science." The heroic age of anthropology. Review of *After Tylor: British Social Anthropology 1888–1951,* by George W. Stocking. *Times Literary Supplement,* June 28, pp. 4–5.

Combe, George, 1834. *The Constitution of Man Considered in Relation to External Objects.* A facsimile reproduction, 1974, with an introduction by Eric T. Carlson. Scholars' Facsimiles & Reprints, Delmar, NY. 223 pp.

Conquest of a Continent, The, or the Expansion of Races in America. By Madison Grant, 1933. Scribner's, New York. 393 pp., anonymously reviewed in *Eugenical News* 18(6):113 (1933).

Conrat, Maisie, and Richard Conrat. 1972. *Executive Order 9066: Internment of 110,000 Japanese Americans.* California Historical Society, Special Publication 51, San Francisco. 120 pp.

Coon, Carleton S. 1939. *The Races of Europe.* Macmillan, New York. 739 pp.

————. 1962. *The Origin of Races.* A. A. Knopf, New York. 724 pp.

————. 1981. *Adventures and Discoveries: The Autobiography of Carleton S. Coon.* Prentice-Hall, Englewood Cliffs, NJ. 404 pp.

Coon, Carleton S., and Edward E. Hunt, Jr. 1965. *The Living Races of Man.* A. A. Knopf, New York. 344 pp.

Coon, Carleton S., Stanley M. Garn, and Joseph B. Birdsell. 1950. *Races: A Study of the Problems of Race Formation in Man.* Charles C. Thomas, Springfield, IL. 153 pp.

Cooper, Virginia M. 1946. *The Creole Kitchen Cookbook.* Naylor Co., San Antonio, TX. 248 pp.

Coughlin, Father Charles E., 1938a. Protocols of the Wise Men of Zion. *Social Justice* 2A(3):5.

————. 1938b. The fifth protocol. *Social Justice* 2A(9):5, 20.

Current, R. N. 1973. Review of *Stephen A. Douglas* by Robert W. Johannsen. *New York Times Book Review,* April 22, pp. 6–7.

Cuvier, Georges, 1817. *Le règne animal distribué d'après son organisation pour servir de base à l'histoire naturelle des animaux et d'introduction à l'anatomie comparée.* Deterville, Paris. 4 Vols.

————. 1821. Discours sur les révolutions de la surface du globe. In *Recherches sur les ossemens fossils.* G. Dufour et Editions d'Ocagne, Paris. 196 pp.

Dabbs, James M., Jr., Denise de La Rue, and Paula M. Williams. 1990. Testosterone and occupational choice: Actors, ministers, and other men. *Journal of Personality and Social Psychology* 59(6):1261–1265.

Dally, Eugène, 1862. En réponse à M. Pruner-Bey sur les travaux anthropologiques de l'école américaine. *Bulletins de la Société d'Anthropologie de Paris* 3:450–455.

Daniel-Rops, Henri, 1965. *The Church in an Age of Revolution, 1789–1870.* E. P. Dutton, New York. 509 pp.

Darwin, Charles R. 1839. Observations on the parallel roads of Glen Roy, and other parts of Lochaber in Scotland, with an attempt to prove that they are of marine origin. *Philosophical Transactions of the Royal Society of London* 129:39–81.

———. 1859. *On the Origin of Species by Means of Natural Selection, or the Preservation of the Favoured Races in the Struggle For Life.* John Murray, London. 502 pp.

Darwin, Francis (ed.) 1887. *The Life and Letters of Charles Darwin Including an Autobiographical Chapter,* Vol. I. Appleton & Co., New York. 562 pp.

———. 1961. *Charles Darwin's Autobiography with Notes and Letters Depicting the Growth of the* Origin of Species. Collier Books, New York. 245 pp.

Davenport, Charles B., and Morris Steggerda. 1929. *Race Crossing in Jamaica,* Publication 395. Carnegie Institution of Washington, Washington, DC. 516 pp.

Davenport, Guy, 1979. Review of *Investigations: Ezra Pound and Remy de Gourmont* by Richard Sieburth. *New York Times Book Review,* January 14, p. 9.

Davies, John D. 1971. *Phrenology, Fad and Science: A 19th Century American Crusade.* Archon Books, Hamden, CT. 203 pp.

Davis, D. L., and R. G. Whitten. 1987. The cross-cultural study of human sexuality. *Annual Review of Anthropology* 16:69–98.

Dawkins, Richard. 1976. *The Selfish Gene.* Oxford University Press, New York. 224 pp.

Dean, John W. 2001. *The Rehnquist Choice: The Untold Story of the Nixon Appointment that Redefined the Supreme Court.* Free Press, New York. 333 pp.

Deniker, Joseph, 1900. *Les races et les peuples de la terre: Éléments d'anthropologie et d'ethnographie.* Schleicher Frères, Paris. 692 pp.

Dennett, Daniel C. 1995. *Darwin's Dangerous Idea. Evolution and the Meaning of Life.* Simon & Schuster, New York. 586 pp.

De Parle, Jason, 1994. The most dangerous conservative: Daring research or "social science pornography"? Charles Murray. *New York Times Magazine,* October 9, pp. 48–53, 62, 70–71, 74, 78, 80.

Desmoulins, Antoine, 1826. *Histoire naturelle des races humaines du nort-est de l'Europe, de l'Asie boréale et orientale, et de l'Afrique australe, d'après des recherches speciales d'antiquités, de physiologie, d'anatomie et de zoologie, appliquée à la recherche des origines des anciens peuples à la science etymologique, à la critique de l'histoire.* Mequignon-Marvis, Paris. 392 pp.

Devlin, Bernie, Stephen E. Feinberg, Daniel P. Resnick, and Kathryn Roedel. 1995. Wringing *The Bell Curve:* A cautionary tale about the relationships among race, genes, and IQ. *Chance* 8(3):27–36.

Diamond, Jared, 1991. World of the living dead. *Natural History* 9:30–37.

———. 1997. *Guns, Germs, and Steel: The Fates of Human Societies.* W. W. Norton, New York. 480 pp.

Dickinson, Joshua Clifton, 1952. Geographic variation in the red-eyed towhee of the eastern United States. *Bulletin of the Museum of Comparative Zoology, Harvard University* 107(5):273–352.

Dobzhansky, T. H. 1950. Evolution in the tropics. *American Scientist* 38(2):209–221.

Donald, David H. 1960. *Charles Sumner and the Coming of the Civil War.* A. A. Knopf, New York. 392 pp.

Dorfman, Donald D. 1995. Soft science with a neoconservative agenda. *Contemporary Psychology* 40(5):418–421.

Dowd, Maureen, 2003. Could Thomas be right? *New York Times,* June 25, p. A27.

Duffy, John, 1953. *Epidemics in Colonial America.* Louisiana State University Press, Baton Rouge. 275 pp.

Dumond, Dwight Lowell, 1959. *Antislavery Origins of the Civil War in the United States.* University of Michigan Press, Ann Arbor. 130 pp.

Dupree, A. Hunter, 1959. *Asa Gray, 1810–1888.* Belknap Press of Harvard University Press, Cambridge, MA. 505 pp.

Durant, Will, and Ariel Durant. 1967. *Rousseau and Revolution: The Story of Civilization,* Part X. Simon & Schuster, New York. 1091 pp.

Dyer, Thomas G. 1980. *Theodore Roosevelt and the Idea of Race.* Louisiana State University Press, Baton Rouge. 182 pp.

Echo, Humbert O. 1996. The name of a race. *Connective Tissue* 12(5):6.

Eco, Umberto, 1989. *Foucault's Pendulum.* William Weaver (trans.). Harcourt, Brace, Jovanovich, San Diego. 641 pp.

Edsall, Thomas, 1999. With "resegregation," old divisions take new form. *Washington Post,* February 8, p. A03.

Edson, Lee, 1969. jensenism, n. The theory that I.Q. is largely determined by the genes. *New York Times Magazine,* August 31, pp. 10–11, 40–41, 43–47.

Edwards, Mike, 2001. The adventures of Marco Polo I. *National Geographic* 199(5):2–31. II, Marco Polo in China. 199(6):20–45. III, Journey home. 200(1):26–47.

Eickstedt, Egon Freiherr von, 1937–40. *Rassenkunde und Rassengeschichte der Menschheit. Erster Band: Die Forschung am Menschen.* Ferdinand Enke Verlag, Stuttgart. 624 pp.

Eisenhower, John S. D., with Joanne Thompson Eisenhower. 2001. *Yanks: The Epic Story of the American Army in World War I.* Free Press, New York. 353 pp.

Eldredge, Niles, and Ian Tattersall. 1982. *The Myths of Human Evolution.* Columbia University Press, New York. 197 pp.

Elkins, Stanley M. 1968. *Slavery: A Problem in American Institutional and Intellectual Life,* 2nd ed. University of Chicago Press, Chicago. 263 pp.

Ellis, Joseph J. 2000. *Founding Brothers: The Revolutionary Generation.* A. A. Knopf, New York. 288 pp.

Ellison, Peter, 2001. *On Fertile Ground: A Natural History of Human Reproduction.* Harvard University Press, Cambridge, MA. 368 pp.

Ellison, Peter T., S. F. Lipson, and M. D. Meredith. 1989. Salivary testosterone levels in males from the Ituri Forest of Zaïre. *American Journal of Human Biology* 1(1):21–24.

Elman, Robert, 1976. *The Living World of Audubon Mammals.* Grosset and Dunlap, New York. 272 pp.

Erickson, Paul A. 1977. Phrenology and physical anthropology: The George Combe connection. *Current Anthropology* 18(1):92–93.

———. 1981. The anthropology of Charles Caldwell, M.D. *Isis* 72:252–256.

———. 1986. The anthropology of Josiah Clark Nott. *Kroeber Anthropological Society Papers* 65–66:103–120.

Eysenck, Hans J. 1971. *The IQ Argument: Race, Intelligence and Education.* Library Press, New York. 155 pp.

———. 1980. *The Causes and Effects of Smoking.* Sage Publications, Beverly Hills, CA. 397 pp.

———. 1985. Personality, cancer and cardiovascular disease: A causal analysis. *Personality and Individual Differences* 6(5):535–556.

———. 1991. *Smoking, Personality, and Stress: Psychological Factors in the Prevention of Cancer and Coronary Heart Disease.* Springer Verlag, New York. 130 pp.

———. 1998. *Intelligence.* Transaction Publishers, New Brunswick, NJ. 227 pp.

Fairbank, John King, 1986. *The Great Chinese Revolution: 1800–1985.* Harper & Row, New York. 396 pp.

———. 1992. *China: A New History.* Belknap Press of Harvard University Press, Cambridge, MA. 519 pp.

Falconer, Douglas S. 1961. *Introduction to Quantitative Genetics.* Ronald Press, New York. 365 pp.

———. 1985. *Introduction to Quantitative Genetics,* 2nd ed. Longman, London. 340 pp.

Fancher, Raymond E. 1991. The Burt case: Another foray. Review of *Science, Ideology, and the Media: The Cyril Burt Scandal* by Ronald Fletcher. *Science* 253:1565–1566.

Faulds, Henry, 1880. On the skin furrows of the hand. *Nature* 22:605.

Field, Geoffrey G. 1981. *Evangelist of Race: The Germanic Vision of Houston Stewart Chamberlain.* Columbia University Press, New York. 565 pp.

Figes, Orlando, 1997. *A People's Tragedy: A History of the Russian Revolution.* Viking, New York. 923 pp.

Findley, George H. 1972. *Dr. Robert Broom, F. R. S. Palaeontologist and Physician, 1866–1951: A Biography, Appreciation and Bibliography.* A. A. Balkema, Cape Town, South Africa. 157 pp.

Finkelstein, Norman G. 1992. How we inspired Nazis [Letter to the editor]. *New York Times,* September 18, p. A34.

Fisher, Daniel C. 1987. Mastodont procurement by Paleoindians of the Great Lakes region: Hunting or scavenging. In Matthew H. Nitecki and Doris V. Nitecki (eds.), *The Evolution of Human Hunting.* Plenum Publishing, Chicago. Pp. 309–421.

Fisher, Ronald A. 1951. Limits to intensive production in animals. *British Agricultural Bulletin* 4:317–318.

Fitzpatrick, Thomas B., Michael M. Wick, and Kiyoshi Toda (eds.) 1986. *Brown Melanoderma: Biology and Disease of Epidermal Pigmentation.* University of Tokyo Press, Tokyo. 232 pp.

Fleming, Gerald, 1993. Engineers of death. *New York Times,* July 18, p. 19.

Fletcher, Robert, 1882. Paul Broca and the French school of anthropology. In *The Saturday Lectures, Anthropological and Biological Societies of Washington.* D. Lothrop & Co., Boston. Pp. 113–142.

Flynn, James R. 1984. The mean IQ of Americans: Massive gains 1932–1978. *Psychological Bulletin* 95(1):29–51.

———. 1987. Massive IQ gains in 14 nations: What IQ tests really measure. *Psychological Bulletin* 101(2):171–191.

———. 1989. Rushton, evolution, and race: An essay on intelligence and virtue. *Psychologist* 2(9):363–366.

———. 1998. IQ gains over time: Toward finding the causes. In Ulric Neisser (ed.), *The Rising Curve.* American Psychological Association, Washington, DC. Pp. 25–66.

———. 1999. Searching for justice: The discovery of IQ gains over time. *American Psychologist* 54(1):5–20.

Ford, Henry, and Samuel Crowther. 1922. *My Life and Work.* Doubleday, Page and Company, New York. 289 pp.

———. 1926. *Today and Tomorrow.* Doubleday, Garden City, NY. 281 pp.

Forrest, Derek W. 1974. *Francis Galton: The Life and Work of a Victorian Genius.* Elek, London. 340 pp.

Fortes, Meyer, and E. E. Evans-Prichard (eds.) 1970. *African Political Systems.* Oxford University Press, London. 302 pp.

Foster, Kenneth R., Mary F. Jenkins, and Anna Coxe Toogood. 1998. The Philadelphia yellow fever epidemic of 1793. *Scientific American* 279(2):88–93.

Frederickson, George M. 2002. *Racism: A Short History.* Princeton University Press, Princeton. 207 pp.

Freehling, William W. 1965. *Prelude to Civil War: The Nullification Controversy in South Carolina 1816–1836.* Harper & Row, New York. 395 pp.

Friedlander, Henry, 1996. *The Origins of Nazi Genocide. From Euthanasia to the Final Solution.* University of North Carolina Press, Chapel Hill. 421 pp.

Friedman, Robert J., Darrell S. Rigel, Alfred U. Kopf, Matthew Harris, and Daniel Baker (eds.) 1991. *Cancer of the Skin.* W. B. Saunders Company, Philadelphia. 620 pp.

Fuller, George N. 1939. *Michigan: A Centennial History of the State and Its People.* Lewis Publishing, Chicago. 5 Vols.

Gall, Franz Joseph, and Johann Gaspar Spurzheim. 1810. *Anatomie et physiologie du système nerveux en général, et du cerveau en particulier; avec des observations sur la possibilité de reconnoître plusiers dispositions intellectuelles et morales de l'homme et des animaux par la configuration de leurs têtes,* Vol. 1. F. Schoell, Paris. 352 pp.

———. 1812. *Anatomie et physiologie du système nerveux en général, et du cerveau en particulier; avec des observations sur la possibilité de reconnoître plusiers dispositions intellectuelles et morales de l'homme et des animaux par la configuration de leurs têtes,* Vol. 2. F. Schoell, Paris. 212 pp.

Galton, Francis, 1869. *Hereditary Genius: An Inquiry into Its Laws and Consequences.* Macmillan, London. 390 pp.

———. 1873. Hereditary improvement. *Fraser's Magazine,* n.s., 7:116–130.

———. 1875. *English Men of Science, Their Nature and Nurture.* D. Appleton & Co., New York. 206 pp.

———. 1883. *Inquiries into Human Faculty and Its Development.* Macmillan, London. 387 pp.

———. 1901. The possible improvement of the human breed under existing conditions of law and sentiment. 2nd Huxley Lecture of the Anthropological Institute, delivered Oct. 29, 1901. *Popular Science Monthly* 60:218–233.

——— 1908a. Eugenics, an address delivered in compliance with a request of Mr. Crackanthorpe, I.C., at 65 Portland-gate, on June 25, 1908. *Westminster Gazette* 31:1–2.

———. 1908b. *Memories of My Life.* Methuen, London. 339 pp.

———. 1914. *Hereditary Genius: An Inquiry into Its Laws and Consequences,* 2nd ed. Macmillan, London. 379 pp.

———. 1962. *Hereditary Genius: An Inquiry into Its Laws and Consequences.* World Publishing Company, Cleveland, OH. 446 pp.

Gannett, Robert T. 2003. *Tocqueville Unveiled: The Historian and His Sources for the Old Regime and the Revolution.* University of Chicago Press, Chicago. 246 pp.

Garber, Ken, 2002. Weird science. *Ann Arbor Observer* 26(6):29–33.

Gardner, Howard, 1983. *Frames of Mind: The Theory of Multiple Intelligences.* Basic Books, New York. 440 pp.

Garn, Stanley M., and Eugene Giles. 1995. Earnest Albert Hooton 1887–1954. *Biographical Memoirs of the National Academy of Sciences* 68:3–15.

Garrett, Henry E. 1961. The equalitarian dogma. *Perspectives in Biology and Medicine* 3(4):480–484.

———. 1962. Racial differences and witch hunting. *Science* 135:982–984.

Garton Ash, Timothy, 1993. *In Europe's Name: Germany and the Divided Continent.* J. Cape, London. 680 pp.

Gasman, Daniel, 1971. *The Scientific Origins of National Socialism: Social Darwinism in Ernst Haeckel and the German Monist League.* Macdonald, London. 208 pp.

Gates, Henry Louis, Jr. 1985. Editor's introduction. Writing "race" and the difference it makes. In H. L. Gates, Jr. (ed.), *"Race," Writing, and Difference.* University of Chicago Press, Chicago. Pp. 1–20.

———. 2003. Both sides now. The close reader. *New York Times Book Review,* May 4, p. 31.

Gaudry, Albert, 1878. *Les enchainements du monde animal dans les temps géologiques: Mammifères tertiares.* G. Masson, Paris. 293 pp.

Genesway, Deborah, and Mindy Roseman. 1987. *Beyond Words: Images from America's Concentration Camps.* Cornell University Press, Ithaca. 176 pp.

Ghiselin, Michael T. 1969. *The Triumph of the Darwinian Method.* University of California Press, Berkeley. 290 pp.

Gibbon, Charles, 1878. *The Life of George Combe, Author of "The Constitution of Man."* Macmillan, London. 2 Vols.

[Gibbon, John?] 1815. Review of *Anatomie et Physiologie,* by Franz Joseph Gall and Johann Gaspar Spurzheim, 1810, 1812. *Edinburgh Review* 25(49):227–268.

Gilbert, Bil, 1984. The obscure fame of Carl Linnaeus. *Audubon* 86(5):102–114.

Gilbert, Martin, 1989. *The Second World War: A Complete History.* Henry Holt & Company, New York. 846 pp.

Gilbert, Richard, 1998. Where love is: A case for same-sex marriage. www.rochesterunitarian.org/ 1997–98/980301.html (accessed Nov. 1, 2004).

Giles, Eugene, 1997a. Coon, Carleton S(tevens) (1904–1981). In Frank Spencer (ed.), *History of Physical Anthropology: An Encyclopedia,* Vol. 1. Garland Publishing, New York. Pp. 294–295.

———. 1997b. Hooton, E(arnest) A(lbert) (1887–1954). In Frank Spencer (ed.), *History of Physical Anthropology: An Encyclopedia,* Vol. 1. Garland Publishing, New York. Pp. 499–501.

Gillham, Nicholas Wright, 1956. Geographic variation and the subspecies concept in butterflies. *Systematic Zoology* 5(3):110–120.

———. 2001. *A Life of Sir Francis Galton.* Oxford University Press, New York. 397 pp.

Gillie, Oliver, 1979. Burt's missing ladies. *Science* 204:1035–1039.

Glazier, Stephen D. (ed.) 2001. *The Encylopedia of African and African-American Religions.* Routledge, New York. 452 pp.

Gliddon, George R. 1857. The monogenists and the polygenists being an exposition of the doctrines of schools professing to sustain dogmatically the unity or the diversity of human races; with an inquiry into the antiquity of mankind upon earth, viewed chronologically, historically, and palaeontolotically. In J. C. Nott and G. R. Gliddon (eds.), *Indigenous Races of the Earth.* J. B. Lippincott and Co., Philadelphia. Pp. 402–602.

Gobineau, Joseph-Arthur, comte de, 1853–5. *Essai sur l'inegalité des races humaines.* Didot Frères, Paris. 4 Vols.

Goddard, Henry H. 1913. The Binet tests in relation to immigration. *Journal of Psycho-Asthenics* 18(2):105–107.

———. 1914. *Feeble-Mindedness: Its Causes and Consequences.* Macmillan, New York. 599 pp.

———. 1917. Mental tests and the immigrant. *Journal of Delinquency* 2(5):243–277.

———. 1919. *Psychology of the Normal and Subnormal.* Dodd, Mead and Co., New York. 349 pp.

———. 1920a. *Human Efficiency and Levels of Intelligence.* Princeton University Press, Princeton, 128 pp.

———. 1920b. In the light of recent developments: What should be our policy in dealing with delinquents—juvenile and adult? *Journal of the American Institute of Criminal Law and Criminology* 11:426–432.

———. 1928. Feeble-mindedness: A question of definition. *Journal of Psycho-Asthenics* 33:2199–2227.

Goebel, Ted, Michael R. Waters, and Margarita Dikova. 2003. The archaeology of Ushki Lake, Kamchatka, and the Pleistocene peopling of the Americas. *Science* 301:501–505.

Goldhagen, Daniel Jonah, 1996. *Hitler's Willing Executioners: Ordinary Germans and the Holocaust.* A. A. Knopf, New York. 622 pp.

Goodman, Edward, 1990. *American Philosophy and the Romantic Tradition.* Cambridge University Press, Cambridge. 162 pp.

Gossett, Thomas F. 1963. *Race, the History of an Idea in America.* Southern Methodist University Press, Dallas, TX. 512 pp.

Gould, Stephen Jay, 1978. Morton's ranking of races by cranial capacity. *Science* 200:503–509.
———. 1980. Wallace's fatal flaw. *Natural History* 89(1):26–40.
———. 1981. *The Mismeasure of Man.* W. W. Norton, New York. 352 pp.
———. 1984. Carrie Buck's daughter. *Natural History* 93(7):14–18.
———. 1988. In a jumbled drawer. *Natural History* 97(8):12–19.
———. 1989. The chain of reason vs. the chain of thumbs. *Natural History* 7:12–21.
———. 1993. American polygeny and craniometry before Darwin: Blacks and Indians as separate, inferior species. In Sandra Harding (ed.), *The "Racial" Economy of Science: Toward a Democratic Future.* Indiana University Press, Bloomington. Pp. 84–115.
———. 1994. Curveball; review of *The Bell Curve* by Richard J. Herrnstein and Charles Murray. *New Yorker* 70(39):139–149.
———. 1996a. The dodo in the caucus race. *Natural History* 105(11):22–33.
———. 1996b. *The Mismeasure of Man,* rev. ed. W. W. Norton, New York. 444 pp.
———. 2002. *The Structure of Evolutionary Theory.* Belknap Press of Harvard University Press, Cambridge, MA. 1,433 pp.
Gould, Stephen Jay, and Richard C. Lewontin. 1979. The spandrels of San Marco and the Panglossian paradigm: A critique of the adaptationist programme. *Proceedings of the Royal Society of London B* 205:581–598.
Grant, Madison, 1916. *The Passing of the Great Race.* C. Scribner's Sons, New York. 245 pp.
———. 1918. *The Passing of the Great Race: or the Racial Basis of European History,* rev. ed., C. Scribner's Sons, New York. 296 pp.
———. 1920. Introduction to *The Rising Tide of Color: Against White World Supremacy* by Lothrop Stoddard. Charles Scribner's Sons, New York. Pp. xi–xxxii.
———. 1921. *The Passing of the Great Race, or the Racial Basis of European History,* 4th rev. ed., with preface by Henry Fairfield Osborn. C. Scribner's Sons, New York. 478 pp.
———. 1933. *The Conquest of a Continent, or the Expansion of Races in America.* Scribner's, New York. 393 pp.
Graves, Joseph L., Jr. 2001. *The Emperor's New Clothes: Biological Theories of Race at the Millennium.* Rutgers University Press, New Brunswick, NJ. 272 pp.
Greene, Edward L. 1909. Linnaeus as an evolutionist. *Proceedings of the Washington Academy of Sciences* 11:17–26.
Greene, John C. 1959. *The Death of Adam: Evolution and Its Impact on Western Thought.* Iowa State University Press, Ames. 388 pp.
Greene, Steven, 1994. Letter to the editor. *New York Times Book Review* November 13, p. 75.
Greenhouse, Linda, 2003. Justices back affirmative action by 5 to 4, but wider vote bans a racial point system. *New York Times,* June 24, pp. A1, A25.
Gregersen, Edgar A. 1977. *Language in Africa. An Introductory Survey.* Gordon and Breach, New York. 237 pp.
Gressman, Eugene, 1952. The unhappy history of civil rights legislation. *Michigan Law Review* 50(8):1323–1358.
Gribben, Alan, 1972. Mark Twain, phrenology and the "temperaments": A study of pseudoscientific influence. *American Quarterly* 24:45–68.
Gross, Samuel D. 1887. *Autobiography of Samuel D. Gross, M.D.,* Samuel W. Gross and A. Haller Gross (eds.), with *Sketches of Some Distinguished Contemporaries.* George Barrie, Philadelphia. 2 Vols.
Groves, Colin P. 1989. *A Theory of Human and Primate Evolution.* Clarendon Press, Oxford. 375 pp.
Guggisberg, Charles A. W. 1970. *Man and Wildlife.* Arco Publishing Company, New York. 224 pp.
Günther, Hans F. K. 1927. *The Racial Elements of European History.* G. C. Wheeler (trans.). E. P. Dutton & Co., New York. 279 pp.

Gyory, Andrew, 1998. *Closing the Gate: Race, Politics, and the Chinese Exclusion Act.* University of North Carolina Press, Chapel Hill. 354 pp.

Hagmeier, Edwin M. 1958. The inapplicability of the subspecies concept in the North American marten, *Martes americana. Systematic Zoology* 7(1):1–7.

Hall, E. Raymond, 1974. The graceful and rapacious weasel. *Natural History* 83(9):44–50.

Haller, John S., Jr. 1971. *Outcasts from Evolution: Scientific Attitudes of Racial Inferiority, 1859–1900.* University of Illinois Press, Urbana. 228 pp.

Hallowell, A. Irving, 1967. Anthropology in Philadelphia. In Jacob W. Gruber (ed.), *The Philadelphia Anthropological Society. Papers Presented on its Golden Anniversary.* Temple University Publications, Philadelphia. Pp. 1–31.

Hamilton, James, 2003. *Turner: A Life.* Random House, New York. 461 pp.

Hammer, Michael F., Tatiana Karafet, Alan J. Redd, Hamdi Jarjanazi, Silvana Santachiari, Himla Soodyall, and Stephen L. Zegura. 2001. Hierarchical patterns of global human Y-chromosome diversity. *Molecular Biology and Evolution* 18(7):1189–1203.

Hammer, Michael F., and Stephen L. Zegura. 1996. The role of the Y chromosome in human evolution. *Evolutionary Anthropology* 5(4):116–134.

Handlin, Oscar, 1959. *Boston's Immigrants: A Study in Acculturation.* Belknap Press of Harvard University Press, Cambridge, MA. 382 pp.

Hanke, Lewis, 1974. *All Mankind Is One: A Study of the Disputation Between Bartolomé de Las Casas and Juan Gines de Sepulveda in 1550 on the Intellectual and Religious Capacity of the American Indians.* Northern Illinois University Press, De Kalb. 205 pp.

Hannaford, Ivan, 1996. *Race: The History of an Idea in the West.* Johns Hopkins University Press, Baltimore. 448 pp.

Harlan, Jack R., Jan M. J. DeWet, and Ann Stamler. 1976. Plant domestication and indigenous African agriculture. In J. R. Harlan, J. M. J. DeWet, and A. Stamler (eds.), *Origins of African Plant Domestication.* Mouton, The Hague. Pp. 2–19.

Harris, Marvin, 1964. *Patterns of Race in the Americas.* Walker and Company, New York. 154 pp.

Hearnshaw, Leslie S. 1979. *Cyril Burt: Psychologist.* Cornell University Press, Ithaca. 370 pp.

Heffer, Simon, 1995. *Moral Desperado. A Life of Thomas Carlyle.* Weidenfeld & Nicolson, London. 420 pp.

Henneberg, Maciej, and C. Loring Brace. 2000. Human skin color as a measure of time in situ. *American Journal of Physical Anthropology* (Suppl. 30):177.

Herbert, Bob, 1999. "The real disgrace" in America. *New York Times,* January 10, p. WK21.

Herodotus. 1990. *The Histories of Herodotus.* A. D. Godley (trans). Harvard University Press, Cambridge, MA. 4 Vols.

Herrnstein, Richard J., and Charles Murray. 1994. *The Bell Curve: Intelligence and Class Structure in American Life.* Free Press, New York. 845 pp.

Herzl, Theodor, 1896. *Der Judenstaat: Versuch einer modernen Lösung der Judenfrage.* M. Breitenstein Verlags-Buchhandlung, Leipzig. 86 pp.

Higginbotham, A. Leon, Jr. 1978. *In the Matter of Color: Race and the American Legal Process: The Colonial Period.* Oxford University Press, New York. 512 pp.

———. 1998. Breaking Thurgood Marshall's promise. *New York Times Magazine,* January 18, pp. 28–29.

Higham, John, 1969. Social discrimination against Jews in America 1830–1930. In Abraham J. Karp (ed.), *The Jewish Experience in America,* Vol. V. KTAV Publishing House, New York. Pp. 349–381.

Higonnet, Patrice. 1988. *Sister Republics: The Origins of French and American Republicanism.* Harvard University Press, Cambridge, MA. 317 pp.

———. 1994. "A hard Republic to love," review of *The Locust Years: The Story of the Fourth French Republic, 1946–1958,* by Frank Giles. *New York Times Book Review,* June 19, p. 34.

Hing, Bill Ong, 1993. *Making and Remaking Asian America Through Immigration Policy, 1850–1990.* Stanford University Press, Stanford, CA. 340 pp.

Hitchcock, Edward, 1852. *The Religion of Geology and Its Connected Sciences.* Phillips, Sampson and Co., Boston. 511 pp.

Hitler, Adolf, 1943. *Mein Kampf.* Ralph Manheim (trans.). Houghton Mifflin, Boston. 694 pp.

Hole, Judith, and Ellen Levine. 1971. *Rebirth of Feminism.* Quadrangle Books, New York. 488 pp.

Holick, Michael F. (ed.) 2002. *Biological Effects of Light: Proceedings of a Symposium, Boston, Massachusetts, June 16–18, 2001.* Kluwer Academic Publishers, Boston. 500 pp.

Holloway, Ralph L., Jr. 1966. Structural reduction through the "probable mutation effect": A critique with questions regarding human evolution. *American Journal of Physical Anthropology* 25(1):7–11.

Honig, George R., and Junius G. Adams, III. 1986. *Human Hemoglobin Genetics.* Springer-Verlag, New York. 452 pp.

Hook, Andrew, 1975. *Scotland and America: A Study of Cultural Relations 1750–1835.* Blackie and Son, Glasgow. 260 pp.

Hooton, Earnest A. 1926. Method of racial analysis. *Science* 63:75–81.

———. 1931. *Up from the Ape.* Macmillan, New York. 626 pp.

———. 1936. Plain statement about race. *Science* 83:511–513.

———. 1944. Review of *The Skull of* Sinanthropus pekinensis: *A Comparative Study of a Primitive Hominid Skull* by Franz Weidenreich. *American Journal of Physical Anthropology* 2(3):317–319.

———. 1946. *Up from the Ape,* 2nd ed. Macmillan, New York. 788 pp.

———. 1947. Preface to *Evolution and Ethics* by Sir Arthur Keith. G. P. Putnam's Sons, New York. Pp. v–vi.

Hooykaas, Reijer, 1972. *Religion and the Rise of Modern Science.* Scottish Academic Press, Edinburgh. 162 pp.

Horine, Emmet Field, 1960. *Biographical Sketch and Guide to the Writings of Charles Caldwell, M.D. (1772–1853), with Sections on Phrenology and Hypnotism.* High Press, Brooks, KY. 155 pp.

Horn, Joseph M. 1983. The Texas adoption project: Adopted children and their intellectual resemblance to biological and adoptive parents. *Child Development* 54(2):268–275.

Horsman, Reginald, 1981. *Race and Manifest Destiny: The Origins of American Racial Anglo-Saxonism.* Harvard University Press, Cambridge, MA. 367 pp.

———. 1987. *Josiah Nott of Mobile: Southern Physician and Racial Theorist.* Louisiana State University Press, Baton Rouge. 348 pp.

Hosokawa, William K. 2002. *Nisei: The Quiet Americans,* rev. ed. University of Colorado Press, Boulder. 570 pp.

Howard, Oliver Otis, 1908. *Autobiography of Oliver Otis Howard, Major General United States Army.* Baker and Taylor Company, New York. 2 Vols.

Howard, Robert West, 1975. *The Dawnseekers: The First History of American Paleontology.* Harcourt, Brace, Jovanovich, New York. 314 pp.

Howe, Daniel Walker, 1970. *The Unitarian Conscience: Harvard Moral Philosophy, 1805–1861.* Harvard University Press, Cambridge, MA. 398 pp.

[Howells, William W.] 1954. Memoriam. Earnest Albert Hooton. *American Journal of Physical Anthropology* 12(3):445–453.

Hrdlicka, Aleš, 1907. Skeletal remains suggesting or attributed to early man in North America. *Smithsonian Institution Bulletin of American Ethnology* 83:1–113.

———. 1914. The most ancient skeletal remains of man. In *Annual Report of the Board of Regents of the Smithsonian Institution, for the Year Ending* 1913. Government Printing Office, Washington, DC. Pp. 491–552.

———. 1918. Recent discoveries attributed to early man in America. *Smithsonian Institution Bureau of American Ethnology Bulletin* 66:1–67.

———. 1919. *Physical Anthropology, Its Scope and Aims; Its History and Present Status in the United States.* Wistar Institute of Anatomy and Biology Press, Philadelphia. 153 pp.

———. 1927a. Leon Pierre Manouvrier. *American Journal of Physical Anthropology* 10(1):163–164.

———. 1927b. The Neanderthal phase of man. The Huxley Memorial Lecture. *Journal of the Royal Anthropological Institute* 57:249–269.

———. 1928a. The full-blood American Negro. *American Journal of Physical Anthropology* 12(1):15–30.

———. 1928b. Race deterioration and destruction with special reference to the American people. In *Proceedings of the Third Race Betterment Conference.* Race Betterment Foundation, Battle Creek, MI. Pp. 82–85.

———. 1929. American Association of Physical Anthropologists. *American Journal of Physical Anthropology* 12(3):519–521.

———. 1930. *The Skeletal Remains of Early Man. Smithsonian Miscellaneous Collections,* Vol. 83. Smithsonian Institution, Washington, DC. 379 pp.

———. 1935. Melanesians and Australians in the peopling of America. *Smithsonian Miscellaneous Collections* 94(11):1–58.

———. 1943. Contribution to the history of physical anthropology in the United States of America, with special reference to Philadelphia. *Proceedings of the American Philosophical Society* 87(1):61–64.

Hudnutt, William H., III. 1956. Samuel Stanhope Smith: Enlightened conservative. *Journal of the History of Ideas* 17(4):540–552.

Huelke, Donald F. 1961. The history of the Department of Anatomy at the University of Michigan: Part I. 1850–1894. *University of Michigan Medical Bulletin* 27:1–27.

Hull, David L. 1984. Evolutionary thinking observed. Review of *Dimensions of Darwinism,* Marjorie Greene (ed.). *Science* 223:923–924.

Huntington, Charles E. 1952. Hybridization in the purple grackle *Quiscalus quiscula. Systematic Zoology* 1(4):149–170.

Huntington, Samuel P. 1985. Will more countries become democratic? In Samuel P. Huntington and Joseph S. Nye, Jr. (eds.), *Global Dilemmas.* Harvard University Press, Cambridge, MA. Pp. 253–279.

Hutton, James, 1795. *Theory of the Earth, with Proofs and Illustrations.* William Creech, Edinburgh. 3 Vols.

Huxley, Aldous, 1963. *Literature and Science.* Harper & Row, New York. 118 pp.

Huxley, Julian, 1938. Clines: An auxiliary taxonomic principle. *Nature* 142:219–220.

———. 1951. Introduction. In *Human Fertility: The Modern Dilemma,* by Robert C. Cook. W. Sloane Associates, New York. Pp. vii–viii.

Huxley, Julian, and Alfred Cort Haddon. 1936. *We Europeans: A Survey of Racial Problems.* Harper, New York. 246 pp.

Huxley, Thomas Henry, 1894. Owen's position in the history of anatomical science. In Rev. Richard Owen (ed.), *The Life of Richard Owen,* Vol. II. John Murray, London. Pp. 273–332.

Imperato, Pascal James, 1984. The dubious gamble against smallpox. *Natural History* 89(7):8–18.

Inside Ann Arbor. 2002. The Jews did It. *Ann Arbor Observer* 27(2):11.

International Jew. 1920. *The World's Foremost Problem,* Vol. 1. Dearborn Publishing Company, Dearborn, MI. 235 pp.

———. 1921a. *Jewish Activities in the United States,* Vol. 2. Dearborn Publishing Company, Dearborn, MI. 255 pp.

———. 1921b. *Jewish Influences in American Life,* Vol. 3. Dearborn Publishing Company, Dearborn, MI. 256 pp.

———. 1922. *Aspects of Jewish Power in the United States,* Vol. 4. Dearborn Publishing Company, Dearborn, MI. 246 pp.

Irons, Peter (ed.) 1989. *Justice Delayed. The Record of Japanese American Internment Cases.* Wesleyan University Press, Middletown, CT. 436 pp.

Itzkoff, Seymour W. 1994. *The Decline of Intelligence in America.* Praeger, Westport, CT. 242 pp.

Iwawaki, Saburo, and Philip E. Vernon. 1988. Japanese abilities and achievements. In Sidney H. Irvine and John W. Berry (eds.), *Abilities in Cultural Context.* Cambridge University Press, New York. Pp. 358–384.

Jablonski, Nina, and George Chaplin. 2000. The evolution of human skin coloration. *Journal of Human Evolution* 39(1):57–106.

Jacoby, Russell, and Naomi Glauberman (eds.) 1995. *The Bell Curve Debate: History, Documents, Opinions.* Times Books, New York. 720 pp.

Jahoda, Gloria, 1975. *The Trail of Tears.* Holt, Rinehart & Winston, New York. 356 pp.

James, Thomas G. H. 1988. *Ancient Egypt. The Land and Its Legacy.* University of Texas Press, Austin. 223 pp.

Jefferson, Thomas [1787] 1800. *Jefferson's Notes on the State of Virginia with the Appendices— Complete.* W. Pechin, Baltimore. 194 pp.

Jenkins, William Sumner, 1935. *Pro-Slavery Thought in the Old South.* University of North Carolina Press, Chapel Hill. 381 pp.

Jensen, Arthur R. 1967. The culturally disadvantaged: Psychological and educational aspects. *Educational Research* 10(1):4–20.

———. 1969a. Edited reply to the letter by D. N. Robinson. *New York Times Magazine,* September 21, p. 14.

———. 1969b. How much can we boost IQ and scholastic achievement. *Harvard Educational Review* 38(1):1–123.

———. 1971. Can we and should we study race differences? In C. L. Brace, G. R. Gamble, and J. T. Bond (eds.), *Race and Intelligence. Anthropological Studies 8.* American Anthropological Association, Washington, DC. Pp. 10–31.

———. 1972a. Sir Cyril Burt [obituary]. *Psychometrika* 37(2):115–117.

———. 1972b. A reply to Gage: The causes of twin differences in I.Q. *Phi Delta Kappan* 53:420–421.

———. 1972c. The IQ controversy: A reply to Layzer. *Cognition* 1(4):427–452.

———. 1974. Kinship correlations reported by Sir Cyril Burt. *Behavior Genetics* 4(1):1–28.

———. 1976. Race and genetics of intelligence: A reply to Lewontin. In N. J. Block and Gerald Dworkin (eds.), *The IQ Controversy. Critical Readings.* Pantheon Books, New York. Pp. 93–106 (reprinted from the *Bulletin of the Atomic Scientists,* May 1970).

———. 1980. *Bias in Mental Testing.* Free Press, New York. 786 pp.

———. 1981. Obstacles, problems and pitfalls in differential psychology. In Sandra Scarr (ed.), *Race, Social Class, and Individual Differences in IQ.* Lawrence Erlbaum Associates, Hillsdale, NJ. Pp. 483–514.

———. 1992. Mental ability: Critical thresholds and social policy. *Journal of Social, Political, and Economic Studies* 17:171–182.

———. 1995a. IQ and science: The mysterious Burt affair. In N. J. Mackintosh (ed.), *Cyril Burt: Fraud or Framed?* Oxford University Press, New York. Pp. 1–12.

———. 1995b. Psychological research on race differences. *American Psychologist* 50(1): 41–42.

———. 1998. *The g Factor: The Science of Mental Ability.* Praeger, Westport, CT. 648 pp.

————. 2000. Name-calling is a disappointing substitute for real criticism. Reply to Brace on Jensen on Intelligence-g-Factor. *psycoloquy*.00.11.009.intelligence.g-factor.25.jensen (accessed Jan. 24).

Jensen, Arthur R., and Arlene R. Inouye. 1980. Level I and level II abilities in Asian, white and black children. *Intelligence* 4(1):41–49.

Jerrold, Walter, 1930. Introduction to *Candide or All For the Best*, by François Marie Arouet Voltaire. Treo & Jacobs, New York. Pp. xi–xviii.

Joint Committee on Reconstruction. *Report*. 1866. 39th Congress, 1st Session. Part III: Georgia, Alabama, Mississippi, Arkansas. Government Printing Office, Washington, DC. 187 pp.

Joly, Maurice, 1864. *Dialogue aux enfers entre Machiavel et Montesquieu, ou la politique de Machiavel au XIXe siècle. Par un contemporain*. A. Mertens et Fils, Bruxelles. 337 pp.

Jordan, Winthrop D. 1965. Introduction to *An Essay on the Causes of the Variety of Complexion and Figure in the Human Species* by Samuel Stanhope Smith. Belknap Press of Harvard University Press, Cambridge, MA. Pp. vii–lvii.

————. 1968. *White over Black: American Attitudes Toward the Negro, 1550–1812*. University of North Carolina Press, Chapel Hill. 651 pp.

Kames, Henry Home, lord. 1774. *Sketches of the History of Man*. James Williams, Dublin. 4 Vols.

Kamin, Leon J. 1974. *The Science and Politics of IQ*. Lawrence Erlbaum Associates, Potomac, MD. 183 pp.

————. 1981. Commentary. In Sandra Scarr (ed.), *Race, Social Class, and Individual Differences in IQ*. Lawrence Erlbaum Associates, Hillsdale, NJ. Pp. 467–482.

————. 1995a. Behind the curve; review of *The Bell Curve: Intelligence and Class Structure in American Life* by Richard J. Herrnstein and Charles Murray. *Scientific American* 272(2):99–103.

————. 1995b. The pioneers of IQ testing. In Russell Jacoby and Naomi Glauberman (eds.), *The Bell Curve Debate: History, Documents, Opinions*. Times Books, New York. Pp. 476–509.

Kant, Immanuel [1781] 1998. *Kritik der reinen Vernunft*. J. F. Hartnoch, Riga. 856 pp. *Critique of Pure Reason*. Paul Geyer and Allen W. Wood (trans., ed.). Cambridge University Press, New York. 785 pp.

Kaplan, Hillard S. 2001. Evolution and our reproductive physiology. Review of *On Fertile Ground: A Natural History of Human Reproduction*, by Peter Ellison. *Science* 293:809–810.

Keegan, John, 1999. *The First World War*. A. A. Knopf, New York. 475 pp.

Keita, S. O. Y. 1990. Studies of ancient crania from northern Africa. *American Journal of Physical Anthropology* 83(1):35–48.

Keith, Sir Arthur, 1911. *Ancient Types of Man*. Harper & Brothers, London. 151 pp.

————. 1913. Present problems relating to the origin of modern races. *Lancet* 2:1050–1053.

————. 1915a. *The Antiquity of Man*. Williams & Norgate, London. 519 pp.

————. 1915b. War as a factor in racial evolution. *St. Thomas's Hospital Gazette* 25:153.

————. 1916. On certain factors concerned in the evolution of human races [presidential address]. *Journal of the Royal Anthropological Institute of Great Britain and Ireland* 46:10–34.

————. 1919a. The differentiation of mankind into racial types. *Nature* 104:301–305.

————. 1919b. *Nationality and Race from an Anthropologist's Point of View. The Robert Boyle Lecture Given at Balliol College, Oxford, 1919*. Oxford University Press, London. 39 pp.

————. 1920. Galton's place among anthropologists. *Eugenics Review* 12(1):14–28.

————. 1924. Concerning certain structural changes which are taking place in our jaws and teeth. In J. C. Brash (ed.), *The Growth of the Jaws, Normal and Abnormal, in Health and Disease*. Dental Board of the United Kingdom, London. Pp. 133–147.

————. 1925. *The Antiquity of Man*, 2nd ed., Vols. 1, 2. Williams & Norgate, London. 753 pp.

————. 1928a. *Concerning Man's Origin.* G. P. Putnam's Sons, New York. 188 pp.

————. 1928b. The evolution of the human races. The Huxley Memorial Lecture of 1928. *Journal of the Royal Anthropological Institute of Great Britain and Ireland* 58:305–321.

————. 1931. *The Place of Prejudice in Modern Civilization (Prejudice and Politics). Rectorial Address to the Students of Aberdeen University.* Williams & Norgate, London. 54 pp.

————. 1935. The ordeal of Ernst Haeckel. *Rationalist Annual* pp. 3–12.

————. 1936. Origins of modern races of mankind. *Nature* 138:194.

————. 1943. Carlyle and Darwin as interpreters of the truth. *Rationalist Annual* pp. 17–24.

————. 1946. *Essays on Human Evolution.* Watts & Company, London. 224 pp.

————. 1950. *An Autobiography.* Watts & Company, London. 721 pp.

————. 1955. *Darwin Revalued.* Watts, London. 294 pp.

Kellog, Davida, 1988. "And then a miracle occurs"—weak links in the chain from punctuation to hierarchy. *Biology and Philosophy* 3(1):3–28.

Kessler, Harry Graf, 1971. *The Diaries of a Cosmopolitan: Count Harry Kessler, 1918–1937,* Charles Kessler (trans., ed.). Weidenfeld & Nicolson, London. 535 pp.

Kevles, Daniel J. 1985. *In the Name of Eugenics: Genetics and the Uses of Human Heredity.* A. A. Knopf, New York. 426 pp.

————. 2003. Here comes the master race. Review of *War Against the Weak: Eugenics and America's Campaign to Create a Master Race* by Edwin Black. *New York Times Book Review,* October 5, p. 8.

Kimbel, William H., and Lawrence B. Martin. 1993. Species and speciation: Conceptual issues and their relevance for primate evolutionary biology. In W. H. Kimbel and L. B. Martin (eds.), *Species, Species Concepts, and Primate Evolution.* Plenum Press, New York. Pp. 539–553.

Kimura, Motoo, 1968. Evolutionary rate at the molecular level. *Nature* 217:624–626.

————. 1969. The rate of molecular evolution considered from the standpoint of population genetics. *Proceedings of the National Academy of Sciences USA* 63(6):1181–1188.

King, Jack Lester, and Thomas H. Jukes. 1969. Non-Darwinian evolution. *Science* 164:788–798.

Kinnicutt, Francis H. 1923. *Testimony at the Hearings Before the Committee on Immigration, United States Senate, February 20.* Government Printing Office, Washington, DC. Pp. 80–81.

Kipling, Rudyard, 1907. *Collected Verse of Rudyard Kipling.* Doubleday, Page & Co., New York. 367 pp.

————. 1926. *Debits and Credits.* Doubleday Page & Co., Garden City, New York. 354 pp.

————. 1990. *Rudyard Kipling. The Complete Verse.* Kyle Cathie Limited, London. 704 pp.

Kitcher, Philip, 1985. *Vaulting Ambition: Sociobiology and the Quest for Human Nature.* Massachusetts Institute of Technology Press, Cambridge, MA. 447 pp.

Kluger, Richard, 1977a. Merely firm, fair and compassionate. Review of *The Memoirs of Earl Warren,* by Earl Warren. *New York Times Book Review,* June 5, pp. 15, 43–44.

————. 1977b. *Simple Justice. The History of Brown v. Board of Education and Black America's Struggle for Equality.* Vintage Books, New York. 823 pp.

Knox, Robert, 1862. *The Races of Men: A Philosophical Enquiry into the Influence of Race over the Destinies of Nations,* 2nd ed. R. Renshaw, London. 600 pp.

Koenig, Robert, 2001. Max Planck offers historic apology. *Science* 292:1881–1882.

Kreiling, Frederick C. 1968. Leibniz. *Scientific American* 218(5):95–100.

Kroeber, Alfred L. 1915. Frederick Ward Putnam. *American Anthropologist* 15(4):712–718.

Krugman, Paul, 2002. The class wars. Part I. The end of middle-class America. *New York Times Magazine,* October 20, pp. 62–67, 76–77, 141–142.

Kühl, Stefan, 1994. *The Nazi Connection: Eugenics, American Racism, and German National Socialism.* Oxford University Press, New York. 166 pp.

Lane, Charles, 1994. The tainted sources of the *Bell Curve*. *New York Review of Books* 41(20):14–19.

Larson, James L. 1971. *Reason and Experience: The Representation of Natural Order in the Work of Carl von Linné*. University of California Press, Berkeley. 172 pp.

Lasker, Gabriel W. 1989. Genetics in the journal *Human Biology*. *Human Biology* 61(5–6):615–627.

———. 1999. *Happenings and Hearsay: Experiences of a Biological Anthropologist*. Savoyard Books, Detroit, MI. 223 pp.

Laughlin, Harry H. 1914. *Report of the Committee to Study and to Report on the Best Practical Means of Cutting Off the Defective Germ-Plasm in the American Population*. Eugenics Record Office, Bulletin 10. Cold Spring Harbor, NY. 150 pp.

———. 1920. Biological aspects of immigration. Invited presentation to the Committee on Immigration and Naturalization, House of Representatives (67th Congress). April 16. Pp. 3–6; April 17, U.S. Government Printing Office, Washington, DC. Pp. 6–25.

———. 1922a. Analysis of America's modern melting pot: The determination of the rate of occurrence of the several definite types of social inadequacy in native population groups in the United States (67th Congress, 3rd Session). November 21. U. S. Government Printing Office, Washington, DC. Pp. 725–831.

———. 1922b. *Eugenical Sterilization in the United States*. Psychopathic Laboratory of the Municipal Court of Chicago. American Eugenics Society, New Haven, CT. 502 pp.

———. 1924. Europe as an emigrant-exporting continent and the United States as an immigrant-receiving nation. Statement before the Committee on Immigration and Naturalization, House of Representatives (68th Congress, 1st Session). March 8. U.S. Government Printing Office, Washington, DC. Pp. 1231–1240.

———. 1930. *The Legal Status of Eugenical Sterilization; History and Analysis of Litigation Under the Virginia Sterilization Statute*. Fred J. Ringley Co., Chicago. 83 pp.

———. 1939. *Immigration and Conquest*. Special Committee on Immigration and Naturalization of the Chamber of Commerce of the State of New York, John B. Trevor, Chair. Chamber of Commerce, New York. 267 pp.

Laughlin, William S. 1954. Obituary of Earnest A. Hooton. *American Antiquity* 20(2):158–159.

Lavater, Johann Caspar [1775] 1968–9. *Physiognomische Fragmente fur Beförderung der Menschenkenntnis und Menschenliebe* (Facsimile of the 1st ed.). Orell Füsli, Zürich. 4 Vols.

Lawrence, Sir William, 1819. *Lectures on Physiology, Zoology, and the Natural History of Man*. J. Callow, London. 579 pp.

Layzer, Daniel, 1972. Science or superstition: A physical scientist looks at the IQ controversy. *Cognition* 1:265–299.

Leavis, F. R. 1962. The two cultures?—The significance of C. P. Snow. The Richmond Lecture at Downing College, Cambridge. *Spectator* March 9, 6976:297–303.

Lee, Albert, 1980. *Henry Ford and the Jews*. Stein and Day, New York. 200 pp.

Leers, Johann von, 1944. *Die Verbrechernatur der Juden*. Paul Hochmuth, Berlin. 170 pp.

Lengyel, Olga, 1972. *Five Chimneys*. Mayflower, London. 221 pp.

Léonard, Jacques, 1988. Pour situer Virey. In C. Bénichou and C. Blanckaert (eds.), *Julien-Joseph Virey. Naturaliste et Anthropologue*. J. Vrin, Paris. Pp. 17–22.

Leonard, Jonathan N. 1932. *The Tragedy of Henry Ford*. G. P. Putnam's Sons, New York. 245 pp.

Lerner, Richard M. 1992. *Final Solutions: Biology, Prejudice, and Genocide*. Pennsylvania State University Press, University Park. 238 pp.

Levi, Primo, 1959. *Survival in Auschwitz: The Nazi Assault on Humanity*. Collier Books, New York. 157 pp.

———. 1986. *Survival in Auschwitz, and The Reawakening, Two Memoirs*, Stuart Wolf (trans.). Summit Books, New York. 397 pp.

Lewis, Bernard, 1990. *Race and Slavery in the Middle East: An Historical Enquiry.* Oxford University Press, New York. 184 pp.

Lewis, Herbert S. 2001. The passion of Franz Boas. *American Anthropologist* 101(2): 447–467.

Lewontin, Richard, 1976a. Race and intelligence. In N. J. Block and Gerald Dworkin (eds.), *The IQ Controversy: Critical Readings.* Pantheon Books, NY. Pp. 78–92. (Originally published in the *Bulletin of the Atomic Scientists* 26(3):2–8, March 1970.)

———. 1976b. Further remarks on race and intelligence. In N. J. Block and Gerald Dworkin (eds.), *The IQ Controversy: Critical Readings.* Pantheon Books, New York. Pp. 107–112. (Originally published in *Bulletin of the Atomic Scientists* 26(5):23–25, May 1970.)

Lieberman, Leonard, 2001. How "Caucasoids" got such big crania and how they shrank: From Morton to Rushton. *Current Anthropology* 42(1):69–95.

Lieberman, Leonard, Rodney C. Kirk, and Alice Littlefield. 2003. Exchange across difference: The status of the race concept. Perishing paradigm: Race—1931–99. *American Anthropologist* 105(1):110–113.

Lieberman, Leonard, Blaine W. Stevenson, and Larry T. Reynolds. 1989. Race and anthropology: A core concept without a consensus. *Anthropology and Education Quarterly* 20(2):67–73.

Limoges, Camille, 1980. A second glance at evolutionary biology in France. In E. Mayr and W. B. Provine (eds.), *The Evolutionary Synthesis.* Harvard University Press, Cambridge, MA. Pp. 322–328.

Lindroth, Sten, 1973. Linnaeus (or Von Linné), Carl. In Charles Coulston Gillispie (ed.), *Dictionary of Scientific Biography,* Vol. 8 Charles Scribner's Sons, New York. Pp. 374–381.

———. 1983. The two faces of Linnaeus. In Tore Frängsmyr (ed.), *Linnaeus: The Man and His Work.* University of California Press, Berkeley. Pp. 1–62.

Lindsay, J. A. 1917. Review of *The Passing of the Great Race* by Madison Grant. *Eugenical Review* 9(2):139–141.

Lingua Franca (eds.) 2000. *The Sokal Hoax: The Sham that Shook Academia.* University of Nebraska Press, Lincoln. 271 pp.

Linklater, Magnus, 1995. The barmy Laird of Nigg. In Russell Jacoby and Naomi Glauberman (eds.), *The Bell Curve Debate*: *History, Documents, Opinions.* Times Books, Random House, New York. Pp. 140–143.

Linnaeus, Carolus, 1956. *Caroli Linnaei, Systema naturae per regna tria naturae, secundum classes, ordines, species, cum characteribus, differentiis, synonymis, locis,* 10th rev. ed. of 1758. Laurentii Salvii, Stockholm. 2 Vols.

Lippmann, Walter, 1922a. Mental age of Americans. The first in a series of six articles on intelligence tests. *New Republic* 32:213–215.

———. 1922b. II. The mystery of the "A" man. *New Republic* 32:246–248.

———. 1922c. The reliability of intelligence tests. III. *New Republic* 32:275–277.

———. 1922d. The abuse of the tests. IV. *New Republic* 32:297–298.

———. 1922e. Tests of hereditary intelligence. V. *New Republic* 32:328–330.

———. 1922f. A future for the tests. VI. *New Republic* 33:99–11.

———. 1923. The great confusion. A reply to Mr. Terman. *New Republic* 33:145–146.

Litchfield, Henrietta (ed.) 1915. *Emma Darwin: A Century of Family Letters 1792–1896,* Vol. I. D. Appleton, New York. 289 pp.

Littlefield, Alice, Leonard Lieberman, and Larry T. Reynolds. 1982. Redefining race: The potential demise of a concept in physical anthropology. *Current Anthropology* 23(6):641–654.

Livingstone, David N. 1987a. *Darwin's Forgotten Defenders. The Encounter Between Evangelical Theology and Evolutionary Thought.* Scottish Academic Press, Edinburgh. 210 pp.

————. 1987b. *Nathaniel Southgate Shaler and the Culture of American Science.* University of Alabama Press, Tuscaloosa. 395 pp.

Livingstone, Frank B. 1958. Anthropological implications of sickle cell gene distribution in West Africa. *American Anthropologist* 60(3):533–562.

————. 1962. On the non-existence of human races. *Current Anthropology* 3(3):279.

————. 1967. *Abnormal Hemoglobins in Human Populations: A Summary and Interpretation.* Aldine, Chicago. 482 pp.

————. 1980. Natural selection and the origin and maintenance of standard genetic marker systems. *Yearbook of Physical Anthropology* 23:25–42.

————. 1983. The malaria hypothesis. In James E. Bowman (ed.), *Distribution and Evolution of Hemoglobin and the Globin Loci.* Elsevier, New York. Pp. 15–44.

————. 1984. The Duffy blood groups, *vivax* malaria, and malaria selection in human populations: A review. *Human Biology* 56(3):413–425.

————. 1985. *Frequencies of Hemoglobin Variants: Thalassemia, the Glucose-6-Phosphate Dehydrogenase Deficiency, G6PD Variants, and Ovalocytosis in Human Populations.* Oxford University Press, New York. 526 pp.

————. 1989. Who gave whom hemoglobin S: The use of restriction site haplotype variation for the interpretation of the evolution of the β^s-globin gene. *American Journal of Human Biology* 3(1):289–302.

Long, Edward, 1774. *The History of Jamaica, or General Survey of the Ancient and Modern State of that Island: With Reflections on its Situation, Settlements, Inhabitants, Climate, Products, Laws and Government.* Lowndes, London. 3 Vols.

Losee, John, 1980. *A Historical Introduction to the Philosophy of Science,* 2nd ed. Oxford University Press, New York. 248 pp.

Lovejoy, Arthur O. 1936. *The Great Chain of Being: A Study in the History of an Idea. The William James Lectures.* Harvard University Press, Cambridge, MA. 382 pp.

Lovejoy, C. Owen, Martin J. Cohn, and Tim D. White. 1999. Morphological analysis of the mammalian postcranium: A developmental perspective. *Proceedings of the National Academy of Sciences USA* 96(23):13247–13252.

Lurie, Edward, 1960. *Louis Agassiz: A Life in Science.* University of Chicago Press, Chicago. 449 pp.

Luther, Martin, 1543. *Von den Juden und jren Lugen.* Durch Hans Lufft, Wittenberg. 286 pp.

Lyell, Charles, 1863. *The Geological Evidences of the Antiquity of Man, with Remarks on Theories of the Origin of Species by Variation.* John Murray, London. 520 pp.

Lynn, Richard, 1987. The intelligence of the Mongoloids: A psychometric, evolutionary and neurological theory. *Personality and Individual Differences* 8(6):813–844.

————. 1991. Race differences in intelligence: A global perspective. *Mankind Quarterly* 31(3):254–296.

————. 2001. *The Science of Human Diversity. A History of the Pioneer Fund.* University Press of America, Lanham, MD. 581 pp.

Lynn, Richard, and Tatu Vanhanen. 2002. *IQ and the Wealth of Nations.* Praeger, Westport, CT. 298 pp.

MacArthur, Robert H., and Edward O. Wilson. 1967. *The Theory of Island Biogeography: Monographs in Population Biology.* Princeton University Press, Princeton. 203 pp.

McCullough, David, 1977. The American adventure of Louis Agassiz. *Audubon* 79(1):12–17.

————. 2001. *John Adams.* Simon & Schuster, New York. 751 pp.

MacDowell, E. Carlton, 1946. Charles Benedict Davenport, 1866–1944: A study in conflicting influences. *Bios* 17(1):3–50.

McFeely, William S. 1968. *Yankee Stepfather: O. O. Howard and the Freedman.* Yale University Press, New Haven, CT. 351 pp.

McKee, David R. 1944. Isaac de la Peyrère, a precursor of eighteenth-century critical deists. *Proceedings of the Modern Language Association of America* 59(4):456–485.

Mackintosh, Nicholas J. 1995. Does it matter? The scientific and political impact of Burt's work. In N. J. Mackintosh (ed.), *Cyril Burt: Fraud or Framed?* Oxford University Press, New York. Pp. 130–151.

Mackintosh-Smith, Tim, 2001. *Travels with a Tangerine: A Journey in the Footnotes of Ibn Battutah.* John Murray, London. 351 pp.

McPherson, James M. 1964. *The Struggle for Equality. Abolitionists and the Negro in the Civil War and Reconstruction.* Princeton University Press, Princeton. 474 pp.

———. 1982. *Ordeal by Fire: The Civil War and Reconstruction.* A. A. Knopf, New York. 694 pp.

———. 1991. *Abraham Lincoln and the Second American Revolution.* Oxford University Press, New York. 173 pp.

McShane, Damian, and J. W. Berry. 1988. Native North Americans: Indian and Inuit abilities. In Sidney H. Irvine and John W. Berry (eds.), *Human Abilities in Cultural Context.* Cambridge University Press, Cambridge. Pp. 385–426.

Mall, Franklin P. 1909. On several anatomical characters of the human brain, said to vary according to race and sex, with especial reference to the weight of the frontal lobe. *American Journal of Anatomy* 9(1):1–32.

[Margolis, Howard] 1961. Science and the news. Science and segregation: A dilemma for the anthropologists. *Science* 134:1868–1869.

Mark, Joan, 1980. *Four Anthropologists: An American Science in Its Early Years.* Science History Publications, New York. 209 pp.

Marszalek, John F. 1998. Review of *The Petticoat Affair: Manners, Mutiny and Sex in Andrew Jackson's White House* by Douglas A. Sylva. *New York Times Book Review,* March 15, p. 26.

Mason, Peter, 1990. *Deconstructing America: Representations of the Other.* Routledge, London. 216 pp.

Masters, William H., and Virginia E. Johnson. 1966. *Human Sexual Response.* Little, Brown and Company, Boston. 366 pp.

Mather, Cotton, 1721. *The Christian Philosopher: A Collection of the Best Discoveries in Nature, with Religious Improvements.* E. Matthews, London. 304 pp.

Matthew, William Diller, 1915. Climate and evolution. *Annals of the New York Academy of Sciences* 24:171–318.

Mayer, George H. 1967. *The Republican Party, 1854–1966.* Oxford University Press, New York. 604 pp.

Mayer, Jane, and Jill Abramson. 1994. *Strange Justice: The Selling of Clarence Thomas.* Houghton Mifflin Company, Boston. 406 pp.

Mayr, Ernst, 1959. Agassiz, Darwin and evolution. *Harvard Library Bulletin* 13:L171–L176.

———. 1982. *The Growth of Biological Thought: Diversity, Evolution and Inheritance.* Harvard University Press, Cambridge, MA. 974 pp.

———. 1991. *One Long Argument: Charles Darwin and the Genesis of Modern Evolutionary Thought.* Harvard University Press, Cambridge, MA. 195 pp.

———. 1996. The modern evolutionary theory. *Journal of Mammalogy* 77(1):1–7.

———. 2000. Darwin's influence on modern thought. *Scientific American* 283(1):78–83.

Mazur, Allen, Alan Booth, and James M. Dobbs, Jr. 1992. Testosterone and chess competition. *Social Psychology Quarterly* 55(1):70–77.

Mbiti, John, 1990. *African Religions & Philosophy,* 2nd ed. Heineman, Oxford. 288 pp.

Mead, Margaret, 1976. Towards a human science. *Science* 191:903–909.

Medawar, Peter B. 1975. Review of *Francis Galton: The Life of and Work of a Victorian Genius* by D. W. Forrest. *Times Literary Supplement,* January 24, p. 83.

Mehler, Barry, 1989. New eugenics. Foundation for fascism: The new eugenics movement in the United States. *Patterns in Prejudice* 23(30):17–25.

Meigs, Charles D., M.D. 1851. *A Memoir of Samuel George Morton, M.D., Late President of the Academy of Natural Sciences of Philadelphia.* T. K. and P. G. Collins, Philadelphia. 48 pp.

Mellars, Paul, and Chris Stringer. 1989. Introduction. In Paul Mellars and Chris Stringer (eds.), *The Human Revolution: Behavioural and Biological Perspectives on the Origins of Modern Humans.* Edinburgh University Press, Edinburgh. Pp. 1–14.

Mellow, James R. 1974. *Charmed Circle: Gertrude Stein & Company.* Praeger, New York. 528 pp.

Mengel, Robert M. 1967. Review of *The Original Water-Color Paintings by John James Audubon for The Birds of America. Scientific American* 216(5):155–159.

Mercer, Jane R. 1988. Ethnic differences in IQ scores: What do they mean. *Hispanic Journal of Behavioral Sciences* 10(3):199–218.

Mercer, Joyce, 1994. A fascination with genetics: Pioneer Fund is at center of debate over research on race and intelligence. *Chronicle of Higher Education* 41(15):A28–A29.

Merton, Robert K. 1938. Science, technology and society in seventeenth century England. *Osiris* 4:360–632.

———. 1970. *Science, Technology and Society in Seventeenth-Century England.* H. Fertig, New York. 279 pp.

Michael, John S. 1988. A new look at Morton's craniological research. *Current Anthropology* 29(2):349–354.

Miele, Frank, 2002. *Intelligence, Race and Genetics: Conversations with Arthur R. Jensen.* Westview Press, Boulder, CO. 243 pp.

Miller, Adam, 1995. Professors of hate. In Russell Jacoby and Naomi Glauberman (eds.), *The Bell Curve Debate: History, Documents, Opinion.* Times Books, New York. Pp. 162–178. (Originally published in *Rolling Stone,* October 20, 1994.)

Miller, John Chester, 1977. *The Wolf by the Ears: Thomas Jefferson and Slavery.* Free Press, New York. 319 pp.

Minton, Henry L. 1988. *Lewis M. Terman. Pioneer in Psychological Testing.* New York University Press, New York. 342 pp.

Monk, Samuel Holt, 1946. Samuel Stanhope Smith (1751–1819): Friend of rational liberty. In Willard Thorp (ed.), *The Lives of Eighteen from Princeton.* Princeton University Press, Princeton. Pp. 86–110.

Montagna, William, Giuseppe Prota, and John A. Kenney, Jr. 1993. *Black Skin: Structure and Function.* Academic Press, San Diego. 158 pp.

Montagu, Ashley, 1942. *Man's Most Dangerous Myth: The Fallacy of Race.* Columbia University Press, New York. 216 pp.

———. 1944. Hrdlicka, Aleš, 1869–1944. *American Anthropologist* 46(1):113–117.

———. 1951. *Statement on Race.* Henry Schuman, New York. 172 pp.

———. (ed.) 1964. *The Concept of Race.* Free Press of Glencoe, Collier-Macmillan, London. 270 pp.

———. 1997. *Man's Most Dangerous Myth: The Fallacy of Race,* 6th ed. AltaMira Press, Walnut Creek, CA. 699 pp.

Moore, John A. 1944. Geographic variation in *Rana pipiens* Schreber of eastern North America. *Bulletin of the American Museum of Natural History* 82(8):349–369.

———. 1949. Geographic variation of adaptive characters in *Rana pipiens* Schreber. *Evolution* 3(1):1–24.

———. 1986. Science as a way of knowing—genetics. *American Zoologist* 26(3):583–747.

Morton, Samuel George, 1834. *Synopsis of the Organic Remains of the Cretaceous Group of the United States.* Key & Biddle, Philadelphia. 88 pp.

———. 1839. *Crania Americana; or, a Comparative View of the Skulls of Various Aboriginal Nations of North and South America; to which Is Prefixed an Essay on the Varieties of the Human Species.* J. Dobson, Philadelphia. 296 pp.

———. 1844a. *Crania Ægyptiaca; or Observations on Egyptian Ethnography Derived from Anatomy, History and the Monuments.* John Pennington, Philadelphia. 67 pp.

———. 1844b. On a supposed new species of hippopotamus. *American Journal of Science and Arts* 47(11):406–407.

———. 1846. Observations on Egyptian ethnography, derived from anatomy, history, and the monuments. *Transactions of the American Philosophical Society* 9:93–159.

———. 1847. Hybridity in animals, considered in reference to the question of the unity of the human species. *American Journal of Science and Arts* 3:39–50, 203–212.

———. 1848. Account of a craniological collection; with remarks on the classification of some families of the human race. *Transactions of the American Ethnological Society* 2:215–222.

———. 1849a. *Additional Observations on a New Living Species of Hippopotamus, of Western Africa* (Hippopotamus liberiensis). Merrihew and Thompson, Philadelphia. 11 pp.

———. 1849b. *Catalogue of Skulls of Man and the Inferior Animals in the Collection of Samuel George Morton,* 3rd ed. Merrihew and Thompson, Philadelphia. 77 pp.

———. 1850a. Observations on the antiquity of some races of dogs. *Proceedings of the Academy of Natural Sciences of Philadelphia* 5:85–89.

———. 1850b. Observations on the size of the brain in various races and families of man. *American Journal of Science and Arts* 9:246–249.

———. 1850c. On the value of the word species in zoology. *Proceedings of the Academy of Natural Sciences of Philadelphia* 5:81–82.

———. 1851. Value of the word species in zoology. *American Journal of Science* 11:275–276.

Moynihan, Daniel Patrick, 1991. Two cheers for Solzhenitsyn. Review of *Rebuilding Russia* by Aleksandr Solzhenitsyn. *New York Times Book Review,* November 24, pp. 9, 11.

Muller, Hermann J. 1949. The Darwinian and modern conceptions of natural selection. *Proceedings of the American Philosophical Society* 93(6):459–470.

Müller-Hill, Benno, 1998. *Murderous Science: Elimination by Scientific Selection of Jews, Gypsies, and Others in Germany, 1933–1945.* George R. Fraser (trans.). Cold Spring Harbor Laboratory Press, Plainview, NY. 256 pp.

Nadel, Lynn, and Donna Rosenthal (eds.) 1991. *Down Syndrome: Living and Learning in the Community.* Wiley, New York. 297 pp.

Nagesa, Laurenti, 1997. *African Religion: The Moral Tradition of Abundant Life.* Orbis Books, Maryknoll, NY. 296 pp.

Nairn, Allan, and associates. 1980. *The Reign of ETS: The Corporation that Makes Up Minds. The Ralph Nader Report on the Educational Testing Service.* Ralph Nader, Washington, DC. 554 pp.

Neary, John, 1970. A scientist's variations on a disturbing racial theme. *Life* 68(22):58B–D, 61–62, 64–65.

Needham, Joseph, 1993. Poverties and triumphs of the Chinese scientific tradition. In Sandra Harding (ed.), *The "Racial" Economy of Science: Toward a Democratic Future.* Indiana University Press, Bloomington. Pp. 30–96.

Negus, Victor, 1958. *The Comparative Anatomy and Physiology of the Nose and Paranasal Sinuses.* Livingstone, Edinburgh. 402 pp.

———. 1965. *The Biology of Respiration.* Williams and Wilkins, Baltimore. 227 pp.

Nelson, Gareth, and Norman Platnick. 1984. Systematics and evolution. In Ho Mae-Wan and Peter T. Saunders (eds.), *Beyond Neo-Darwinism: An Introduction to the New Evolutionary Paradigm.* Academic Press, London. Pp. 143–158.

Neuberger, Max, 1916. Briefe Galls an Andreas und Nannette Streicher. *Archiv für Geschichte der Medizin* 10(1–2):3–70.

Neuffer, Claude Henry, 1960. John Bachman, a biography. In C. H. Neuffer (ed.), *The Christian Happoldt Journal. His European Tour with John Bachman. Contributions from the Charleston Museum 13.* Charleston Museum, Charleston, SC. Pp. 29–118.

Nevin, David, 1992. To the president, Peggy Eaton was chaste indeed. *Smithsonian* 23(2):84–97.

Nevins, Allan, and Frank Ernest Hill. 1957. *Ford: Expansion and Challenge 1915–1933.* Charles Scribner's Sons, New York. 714 pp.

———. 1963. *Ford: Decline and Rebirth 1933–1962.* Charles Scribner's Sons, New York. 508 pp.

Niceron, Jean Pierre, 1732. *Mémoires pour servir à l'histoire des hommes illustres dans le république des lettres,* Vol. 12. Braisson, Paris. 43 Vols.

Nicholson, Rob, 2002. A beautiful hand. *Natural History* 111(5):50–57.

Nilus, Sergei A. 1905. *The Great in the Small and Antichrist as a Near Political Possibility. Notes of an Orthodox Christian,* 2nd ed. Press of the Red Cross, Tsarskoye Selo. 110 pp.

———. [1920] 1948. *Protocols of the Meetings of the Learned Elders of Zion.* Victor E. Marsden (trans.). Christian Nationalist Crusade, Los Angeles. 80 pp.

———. [1920] 1963. *World Conquest through World Government: The Protocols of the Learned Elders of Zion.* Victor E. Marsden (trans.). Britons Publishing Company, London. 110 pp.

Nisbet, Robert A. 1980. *History of the Idea of Progress.* Basic Books, New York. 370 pp.

Noakes, Jeremy, and Geoffrey Pridham (eds.) 1988. *Nazism 1919–1945. Foreign Policy, War and Racial Extermination. A Documentary Reader,* Vol. 3. *Exeter Studies in History 13.* University of Exeter, Exeter. 1236 pp.

Noll, Mark A. 1989. *Princeton and the Republic, 1768–1822: The Search for a Christian Enlightenment in the Era of Samuel Stanhope Smith.* Princeton University Press, Princeton. 340 pp.

———. 1994. *The Scandal of the Evangelical Mind.* William B. Eerdmans Publishing Company, Grand Rapids, MI. 274 pp.

Noonan, John T., Jr., 2002. *Narrowing the Nation's Power. The Supreme Court Sides with the States.* University of California Press, Berkeley. 203 pp.

Nordenskiöld, Erik, 1928. *The History of Biology: A Survey.* Leonard Buckness Eyre (trans.). A. A. Knopf, New York. 629 pp.

Norwood, W. Frederick, 1966. Introduction to *Extinct Medical Schools of Nineteenth-Century Philadelphia* by Harold J. Abrahams. University of Pennsylvania Press, Philadelphia. Pp. 15–26.

Nott, Josiah Clark, 1843. The mulatto a hybrid; probable extermination of the two races if whites and blacks were allowed to inter-marry. *American Journal of Medical Science* 6(11):252–256.

———. 1844. *Two Lectures on the Natural History of the Caucasian and Negro Races.* Dade & Thompson, Mobile, AL. 53 pp.

———. 1847. Statistics of southern slave population with especial reference to life insurance. *Commercial Review of the South and West* 4:275–287.

———. 1849. *Two Lectures on the Connection Between the Biblical and Physical History of Man. Delivered by Invitation from the Chair of Political Economy of the Louisiana University in December 1848.* Bartlett & Welford, New York. 146 pp.

———. 1850. An examination of the physical history of the Jews, in its bearing on the question of the unity of the races. *Proceedings of the American Association for the Advancement of Science* 3:98–106.

———. 1854. Hybridity in animals, viewed in connection with the natural history of mankind. In J. C. Nott and G. R. Gliddon (eds.), *Types of Mankind.* Lippincott, Grambo & Co., Philadelphia. Pp. 372–410.

————. 1856. Appendix containing the latest scientific facts bearing upon the question of unity or plurality of species. In *The Moral and Intellectual Diversity of Races with Particular Reference to their Respective Influences in the Civil and Political History of Mankind* by Arthur comte de Gobineau. Henry Hotz (trans.). J. B. Lippincott, Philadelphia. Pp. 461–512.

————. 1858. A natural history of dogs. *New Orleans Medical and Surgical Journal* 15:484–500.

————. 1866a. Climates of the south in their relations to white labor. Characteristics of the negro races—their future at the south—white labor in its conflict with black—adaptation of the south to immigration and its splendid fields for future enterprise. *De Bow's Review, Devoted to the Restoration of the Southern States, and the Development of the Wealth and Resources of the Country. Journal of Literature, Education, Agriculture, Commerce, Internal Improvements, Manufactures, Mining and Statistics, the Question of the Freedmen. After the War Series* I:166–173.

————. 1866b. *Instincts of Races*. Reprinted from the *New Orleans Medical and Surgical Journal*. Graham, New Orleans. 28 pp.

————. 1866c. The Negro race. *Popular Magazine of Anthropology* (published with *Anthropological Review*) 1(3):102–118.

————. 1866d. The problem of the black races. What we have done—where we are drifting—and what of the freedmen and the Freedman's Bureau. *De Bow's Review, Devoted to the Restoration of the Southern States, and the Development of the Wealth and Resources of the Country. Journal of Literature, Education, Agriculture, Commerce, Internal Improvements, Manufactures, Mining and Statistics, the Question of the Freedmen. After the War Series* I:266–283.

————. 1866e. *Contributions to Bone and Nerve Surgery*. J. B. Lippincott, Philadelphia. 96 pp.

Nott, Josiah Clark, and George R. Gliddon. 1854. *Types of Mankind*. Lippincott, Grambo & Co., Philadelphia. 738 pp.

————. 1857. *Indigenous Races of the Earth*. J. B. Lippincott and Company, Philadelphia. 656 pp.

Novick, Sheldon M. 1989. *Honorable Justice: The Life of Oliver Wendell Holmes*. Little, Brown & Co., Boston. 522 pp.

Nutton, Vivian, 2002. Logic, learning and experimental medicine. *Science* 295:800–801.

Nyiszli, Miklos, 1960. *Auschwitz: A Doctor's Eyewitness Account*. Frederick Fell, New York. 222 pp.

O'Hanlon, Redmond, 1982. Review of *Darwin* by Wilma B. George, and *Darwin* by Howard Jonathan. *Times Literary Supplement*, June 18, pp. 653–654.

Ohno, Susumu, 1970. *Evolution by Gene Duplication*. Springer-Verlag, New York. 160 pp.

————. 1972. So much "junk" DNA in our genome. In Harold H. Smith (ed.), *Evolution of Genetic Systems. Brookhaven Symposium 23*. Gordon and Breach, New York. Pp. 366–370.

Olsen, Stanley J. 1985. *Origins of the Domestic Dog: The Fossil Record*. University of Arizona Press, Tucson. 118 pp.

Olson, Richard, 1975. *Scottish Philosophy and British Physics, 1750–1880. A Study in the Foundations of Victorian Scientific Style*. Princeton University Press, Princeton. 350 pp.

Osborn, Henry Fairfield, 1918. Preface to *The Passing of the Great Race: Or the Racial Basis of European History* by Madison Grant. Charles Scribner's Sons, New York. Pp. xi–xiii.

————. 1926. The evolution of human races. *Natural History* 26(1):3–13.

Osofsky, Gilbert, 1967. *The Burden of Race: A Documentary History of Negro–White Relations in America*. Harper & Row, New York. 654 pp.

Owen, Kenneth, 1992. The suitability of Raven's Standard Progressive Matrices for various groups in South Africa. *Personality and Individual Differences* 13(2):149–159.

Pagel, Walter, 1974. Paracelsus, Theophrastus Philippus Aureolus Bombastus von Hohenheim. In C. G. Gillispie (ed.), *Dictionary of Scientific Biography,* Vol. X. Charles Scribner's Sons, New York. Pp. 304–313.

Paine, Thomas, [1796] 1951. *The Age of Reason.* D. I. Eaton, London. 236 pp.

Paley, William, 1802. *Natural Theology, or evidences of the Existence and Attributes of the Deity Collected from the Appearances of Nature.* Wilks and Taylor, London. 586 pp.

Parrinder, Geoffrey, 1954. *African Traditional Religions.* Hutchinson's University Library, New York. 156 pp.

––––––. 1969. *Religion in Africa.* Penguin Books, Baltimore, MD. 253 pp.

Pasteur, Georges, 1971. Evolution in France. *Science* 171:751.

Pastore, Nicholas, 1949. *The Nature–Nurture Controversy.* Columbia University Press, New York. 213 pp.

––––––. 1978. The army intelligence tests and Walter Lippmann. *Journal of the History of the Behavioral Sciences* 14(4):316–327.

Patterson, Henry S. 1855. Memoir of the life and scientific labors of Samuel George Morton. In J. C. Nott and Geo. R. Gliddon (eds.), *Types of Mankind: or Ethnological Researches Based Upon Ancient Monuments, Paintings, Sculptures, and Crania of Races, and Upon their Natural Geographical, Philosophical, and Biblical History: Illustrated by Selections from the Inedited Papers of Samuel George Morton, M.D., and by Additional Contributions from Prof. L. Agassiz, LL.D.; W. Usher, M.D.; and Prof. H. S. Patterson, M.D.* Lippincott, Grambo and Co., Philadelphia. Pp. xvii–lvii.

Paul, Arnold M. 1972. Introduction. In Arnold M. Paul (ed.), *Black Americans and the Supreme Court Since Emancipation: Betrayal or Protection?* Holt, Rinehart & Winston, New York. Pp. 1–8.

Paul, Harry W. 1974. Religion and Darwinism: Varieties of Catholic reaction. In Thomas F. Glick (ed.), *The Comparative Reception of Darwinism.* University of Texas Press, Austin. Pp. 403–436.

Pauly, Philip J. 2001. *Biologists and the Promise of American Life: From Merriwether Lewis to Alfred Kinsey.* Princeton University Press, Princeton. 313 pp.

Pearson, Karl, 1914. *The Life, Letters and Labours of Francis Galton,* Vol. 1. *Birth 1822 to Marriage 1853.* Cambridge University Press, Cambridge. 246 pp.

––––––. 1924. *The Life, Letters and Labours of Francis Galton,* Vol. 2. *Researches of Middle Life.* Cambridge University Press, Cambridge. 425 pp.

––––––. 1930. *The Life, Letters and Labours of Francis Galton,* Vol. 3A. *Correlation, Personal Identification and Eugenics.* 432 pp. Vol. 3B. *Characterisation, Especially by Letters. Index.* Cambridge University Press, Cambridge. 232 pp.

Pearson, Roger, 1996. *Heredity and Humanity: Race, Eugenics, and Modern Science.* Scott-Townsend Publishers, Washington, DC. 162 pp.

Pennant, Thomas. 1781. *History of Quadrupeds.* B. White, London. 2 Vols.

Pettigrew, John D. 1986. Flying primates? Megabats have the advanced pathway from eye to midbrain. *Science* 231:1304–1306.

––––––. 1991. Wings or brain? Convergent evolution in the origin of bats. *Systematic Zoology* 10(2):199–216.

Philadelphia Record. 1939. Fascist doctrines stir rift among savants. April 5, p. 6.

Pickens, Donald K. 1968. *Eugenics and the Progressives.* Vanderbilt University Press, Nashville, TN. 260 pp.

Platiel, Judy, and Stephen Strauss. 1989. University chief defends professor's right to voice racist theory. *Globe and Mail,* February 4, p. A6.

Poliakov, Léon, 1974. *Aryan Myth: A History of Racist and Nationalist Ideas in Europe.* Basic Books, New York. 388 pp.

Polk, William M. 1913. Josiah C. Nott. *American Journal of Obstetrics* 67:957–958.

Polo, Marco, 1931. *The Travels of Marco Polo.* Aldo Ricci (trans., from the text of L. F. Benedetto), Sir E. Denison Ross (ed.). George Routledge & Sons, London. 439 pp.

———. 1968. *The Travels of Marco Polo, the Venetian.* William Marsden (trans.), Thomas Wright (ed.). AMS Press, New York. 508 pp.

———. 1998. *Milione: Redazione Latina del manoscritto Z a cura di Alvaro Barbieri.* Fondazione Pietro Bembo, Ugo Guando Editore, Padua. 704 pp.

Pool, James, and Suzanne Pool. 1979. *Who Financed Hitler: The Secret Funding of Hitler's Rise to Power 1919–1933.* Dial Press, New York. 535 pp.

Pope, Alexander, [1734] 1969. *An Essay on Man, Being the First Book of Ethic Epistles to Henry St. John, L. Bolingbroke* (facsimile). Scolar Press, Menston, UK. 75 pp.

Popper, Karl, 1978. *Unended Quest: An Intellectual Autobiography.* Fontana/Collins, Edinburgh. 256 pp.

Portères, Roland, 1976. African cereals: Eleusine, Fonio, black Fonio, teff, Brachiaria, Paspalum, Pennisetum, and African rice. In J. R. Harlan, J. M. J. de Wet, and A. B. L. Stemter (eds.), *Origins of African Plant Domestication.* Mouton, The Hague. Pp. 409–452.

Pouchet, Georges, 1864. *De la pluralité des races humaines; essai anthropologique,* 2nd ed. V. Masson et Fils, Paris. 234 pp.

Pressac, Jean-Claude, 1989. *Auschwitz: Technique and Operation of the Gas Chambers.* Beate Klarsfeld Foundation, New York. 563 pp.

Pretty, Graeme L. 1977. The cultural chronology of the Roonka Flat: A preliminary consideration. In R. V. S. Wright (ed.), *Stone Tools as Cultural Markers. Prehistory and Material Culture Series 12.* Australian Institute of Aboriginal Studies, Canberra. Pp. 288–331.

Price, John, 1966. A history of the outcaste: Untouchability in Japan. In George A. DeVos and Hiroshi Wagatsuma (eds.), *Japan's Invisible Race: Caste in Culture and Personality.* University of California Press, Berkeley. Pp. 6–30.

Prichard, James Cowles. 1813. *Researches into the Physical History of Mankind.* J. and A. Arch, London. 558 pp.

———. 1851. *Researches into the Physical History of Mankind,* 4th ed. Houlston and Stoneman, London. 5 Vols.

Proctor, Robert N. 1988. From *Anthropologie* to *Rassenkunde* in the German anthropological tradition. In George W. Stocking, Jr. (ed.), *Bones, Bodies, Behavior: Essays on Biological Anthropology.* University of Wisconsin Press, Madison. Pp. 138–179.

———. 1995. Atrocity begins at home. Review of *Death and Deliverance. "Euthanasia" in Germany c. 1900–1945* by Michael Burleigh. *New York Times Book Review,* February 5, p. 3.

Prudhomme, Paul, 1984. *Chef Paul Prudhomme's Louisiana Kitchen.* William Morrow and Co., New York. 351 pp.

Pruner-Bey, F. 1862. Sur le rapport de M. Dally concernant les Américains. *Bulletins de la Société d'Anthropologie de Paris* 3:417–421, 430–433.

———. 1863. Observations sur le crâne de Néanderthal. *Bulletins de la Société d'Anthropologie de Paris* 4:318–323.

———. 1864. The Neanderthal skull. *Anthropological Review* 2(4):223.

Pulzer, Peter G. J. 1964. *The Rise of Political Anti-Semitism in Germany and Austria.* Wiley, New York. 364 pp.

Putnam, Carleton, 1961. *Race and Reason. A Yankee View.* Public Affairs Press, Washington, DC. 125 pp.

Quammen, David, 1996. *The Song of the Dodo: Island Biogeography in an Age of Extinction.* Scribner, New York. 702 pp.

Queller, David C. 1995. The spaniels of St. Marx and the Panglossian paradox: A critique of a rhetorical programme. *Quarterly Review of Biology* 70(4):485–489.

Race, Robert R., and Ruth Sanger. 1975. *Blood Groups in Man,* 6th ed. Blackwell Scientific Publications, Oxford. 659 pp.

Radcliffe-Brown, A. R., and Daryll Forde (eds.) 1950. *African Systems of Kinship and Marriage.* Oxford University Press, London. 399 pp.

Rae, Isobel, 1964. *Knox the Anatomist.* Oliver & Boyd, Edinburgh. 164 pp.

Rainger, Ronald, 1978. Race, politics, and science: The Anthropological Society of London. *Victorian Studies* 22:51–70.

———. 1991. *An Agenda for Antiquity: Henry Fairfield Osborn and Vertebrate Paleontology at the American Museum of Natural History, 1890–1935.* University of Alabama Press, Tuscaloosa. 360 pp.

Ratzel, Friedrich, 1882. *Anthropo-Geographie oder Grundzüge der Anwendung der Erdkunde auf die Geschichte.* J. Engelhorn, Stuttgart. 506 pp.

———. 1897. *Politische Geographie oder die Geographie der Staaten des Verkehres und des Krieges.* R. Oldenbourg, Munich. 715 pp.

Raup, David M. 1986. *The Nemesis Affair: A Story of the Death of Dinosaurs and the Ways of Science.* W. W. Norton, New York. 220 pp.

Rauschning, Hermann, 1940. *Hitler Speaks: A Series of Political Conversations with Adolf Hitler on His Real Aims.* Thornton Butterworth, London. 287 pp.

Reich, Walter, 1993. Erasing the Holocaust. Review of *Denying the Holocaust* by Deborah E. Lipstadt, and *Assassins of Memory* by Pierre Vidal-Naguet. *New York Times Book Review,* July 11, pp. 1, 31, 33–34.

Reid, Thomas, 1764. *An Inquiry into the Human Mind on the Principles of Common Sense.* A. Kincaid and J. Bell, Edinburgh. 541 pp.

Richards, William C. 1948. *The Last Billionaire: Henry Ford.* Scribner, New York. 422 pp.

Rightmire, G. Philip, 1990. *The Evolution of* Homo erectus: *Comparative Anatomical Studies of an Extinct Human Species.* Cambridge University Press, Cambridge. 260 pp.

Ripley, William Z. 1897–8. The racial geography of Europe: A sociological study (the Lowell Institute Lectures of 1896). *Appleton's Popular Science Monthly* 50:454–468, 577–594, 757–780; 51:17–34, 192–209, 289–307, 433–453, 613–634, 721–739; 52:499–68, 145–170, 304, 469–486, 591–608.

———. 1899. *The Races of Europe: A Sociological Study.* D. Appleton & Co., New York. 624 pp.

Roberts, Richard G., Rhys Jones, Nigel A. Spooner, M. J. Head, Andrew S. Murray, and M. A. Smith. 1994. The human colonisation of Australia: Optical dates of 53,000 and 60,000 years bracket human arrival at Deaf Adder Gorge, Northern Territory. *Quaternary Science Reviews* 13(5–7):575–586.

Robins, Ashley H. 1991. *Biological Perspectives on Human Pigmentation.* Cambridge University Press, New York. 253 pp.

Roger, Jacques, 1970. Buffon, Georges-Louis Leclerc, comte de. In Charles Coulston Gillisipie (ed.), *Dictionary of Scientific Biography,* Vol. 2. Charles Scribner's Sons, New York. Pp. 576–582.

Rogin, Michael Paul, 1975. *Fathers and Children: Andrew Jackson and the Subjugation of the American Indian.* A. A. Knopf, New York. 373 pp.

Rose, Steven, 1992. The Burt business: Another view. *Times Literary Supplement,* September 18, p. 14.

Rosen, Jeffrey, 2001. "Renchburg's the one." Review of *The Rehnquist Choice. The Untold Story of the Nixon Appointment that Redefined the Supreme Court,* by John Dean. *New York Times Book Review,* November 4, p. 15.

Rosenthal, Steven J. 1995. The Pioneer Fund: Financier of fascist research. *American Behavioral Scientist* 39(1):44–61.

Rowley, Charles D. 1970. *The Destruction of Aboriginal Society.* Australian National University Press, Canberra. 430 pp.

Rudwick, Martin J. 1972. *The Meaning of Fossils: Episodes in the History of Palaeontology.* Macdonald, London. 287 pp.

Rupke, Nicolaas A. 1983. *The Great Chain of History: William Buckland and the English School of Geology (1814–1849).* Clarendon Press of Oxford University Press, New York. 322 pp.

Ruse, Michael, 2003. *Darwin and Design. Does Evolution Have a Purpose?* Harvard University Press, Cambridge, MA. 381 pp.

Rushton, J. Philippe, 1985. Differential K theory: The sociobiology of individual and group differences. *Personality and Individual Differences* 6(4):441–452.

———. 1987. Race differences in sexual behavior: Testing an evolutionary hypothesis. *Journal of Research in Personality* 21(4):529–551.

———. 1989. Evolutionary biology and heritable traits (with reference to Oriental–white–black differences). Presentation to the annual meeting of the American Association for the Advancement of Science, San Francisco, CA, January 19.

———. 1991. Do *r–K* strategies underlie human race differences? A reply to Weizmann et al. *Canadian Psychology* 32(1):29–42.

———. 1995. *Race, Evolution, and Behavior: A Life History Perspective.* Transaction Publishers, New Brunswick, NJ. 334 pp.

———. 1997. Race, intelligence, and the brain: The errors and omissions of the "revised" edition of S. J. Gould's *The Mismeasure of Man. Personality and Individual Differences* 23(1):169–180.

———. 1999. *Race, Evolution, and Behavior: A Life History Perspective,* special abridged edition. Transaction Publishers, New Brunswick, NJ. 108 pp.

———. 2000. *Race, Evolution, and Behavior: A Life History Perspective,* 2nd special abridged ed. Charles Darwin Research Institute, Port Huron, MI. 108 pp.

———. 2002. Review of *IQ and the Wealth of Nations* by Richard Lynn and Tata Vanhanen. http://www.vdare.com/misc/rushton_ig.htm (accessed March 5, 2002).

Sagan, Carl, 1979. *Broca's Brain: Reflections on the Romance of Science.* Random House, New York. 328 pp.

St. Aubyn, Giles, 1979. *Edward VII. Prince and King.* Collins, London. 555 pp.

Salmon, Philippe, 1896. L'École d'anthropologie de Paris (1875–1896). *Revue Mensuelle de l'École d'Anthropologie de Paris* 6:337–376.

Sampson, Scott D., David W. Krause, and Catherine A. Forster. 1997. Madagascar's buried treasure. *Natural History* 106(2):24–27.

Sarton, George, 1966. *Galen of Pergamon.* University of Kansas Press, Lawrence. 112 pp.

Saunders, J. B. de C. M., and Charles D. O'Malley. 1950. *The Illustrations from the Works of Andreas Vesalius of Brussels, with Annotations and Translations, a Discussion of the Plates and Their Background, Authorship and Influence, and a Biographical Sketch of Vesalius.* World Publishing Company, Cleveland, OH. 252 pp.

Scarr, Sandra, 1991. Sir Cyril Burt reconsidered: The science and politics of British psychology. *Contemporary Psychology* 36(3):200–201.

Scarr, Sandra, and Richard A. Weinberg. 1976. IQ test performance of black children adopted by white families. *American Psychologist* 31(10):726–739.

———. 1983. The Minnesota adoption studies: Genetic differences and malleability. *Child Development* 54(2):260–267.

Schelling, Friedrich Wilhelm Joseph von. 1800. *System des Transcendentalen Idealismus.* J. G. Gotta'schen Buchhandlung, Tübingen. 486 pp.

Schiller, Francis, 1979. *Paul Broca: Founder of French Anthropology, Explorer of the Brain.* University of California Press, Berkeley. 350 pp.

Schultz, Adolph H. 1945. Aleš Hrdlička, 1869–1943. *Biographical Memoirs of the National Academy of Sciences* 23:305–338.

Schwalbe, Gustav, 1906. *Studien zur Vorgeschichte des Menschen.* E. Schweizerbartsche Verlagsbuchhandlung, Stuttgart. 228 pp.

Schwartz, Robert S. 2001. Racial profiling in medical research [editorial]. *New England Journal of Medicine* 344(18):1392–1393.

Schwartz, Tony, 1999. The S.A.T. numbers game: The test under stress. *New York Times Magazine,* January 10, pp. 30–35, 51, 56, 63.

Sedgwick, John, 1995. Inside the Pioneer Fund. In Russell Jacoby and Naomi Glauberman (eds.), *The Bell Curve Debate: History, Documents, Opinion.* Times Books, New York. Pp. 144–161.

Segel, Binjamin, and Richard S. Levy (trans., ed.). 1995. *A Lie and a Libel: The History of the Protocols of the Elders of Zion.* University of Nebraska Press, Lincoln. 148 pp.

Shaler, Nathaniel Southgate, 1870. An ex-southerner in South Carolina. *Atlantic Monthly* 26:53–61.

———. 1886. Race prejudices. *Atlantic Monthly* 58:510.

———. 1891. *Nature and Man in America.* C. Scribner's Sons, New York. 290 pp.

———. 1893. European peasants as immigrants. *Atlantic Monthly* 71:646–651.

———. 1896. The Scotch element in the American people. *Atlantic Monthly* 77:508–516.

———. 1900. Our Negro types. *Current Literature* 29:44–45.

———. 1904. *The Neighbor: The Natural History of Human Contacts.* Houghton Mifflin, Boston. 342 pp.

———. 1909. *The Autobiography of Nathaniel Southgate Shaler.* Houghton Mifflin, Boston. 481 pp.

Shapiro, Alan E. 1991. The unfolding of philosophy. Review of *Numbers and Motion: The Scientific Career of René Descartes* by William R. Shea. *Science* 253:457.

Shapiro, Harry L. 1981. Earnest A. Hooton, 1887–1954 *in memoriam cum amore. American Journal of Physical Anthropology* 56(4):431–434.

Shockley, William, 1972a. Dysgenics, geneticity, raceology: A challenge to the intellectual responsibility of educators. *Phi Delta Kappan* 53:297–307.

———. 1972b. A debate challenge: Geneticity is 80% for white identical twins' I.Q.'s. *Phi Delta Kappan* 53:415–427.

Shryock, Richard Harrison, 1960. *Medicine and Society in America 1660–1860.* New York University Press, New York. 182 pp.

———. 1966. *Medicine in America: Historical Essays.* Johns Hopkins University Press, Baltimore. 346 pp.

Silverman, Kenneth, 1984. *The Life and Times of Cotton Mather.* Harper & Row, New York. 479 pp.

Singerman, Robert, 1981. The American career of the *Protocols of the Elders of Zion. American Jewish History* 71(1):48–78.

Skodak, Marie, and Harold M. Skeels. 1949. A final follow-up study of one hundred adopted children. *Journal of Genetic Psychology* 75(1):85–125.

Sloan, Douglas, 1971. *The Scottish Enlightenment and the American College Ideal.* Teachers College Press, Columbia University, New York. 298 pp.

Smedley, Audrey, 1993. *Race in North America: Origin and Evolution of a World View.* Westview Press, Boulder, CO. 340 pp.

Smith, Adam, [1776] 1976. *An Inquiry into the Nature and Causes of the Wealth of Nations,* E. B. Todd (ed.). Clarendon Press, Oxford. 2 Vols.

Smith, George H. 1968. *Who is Ronald Reagan?* Pyramid Books, New York. 173 pp.

Smith, Gerald L. K., n.d. *International Jew: The World's Foremost Problem.* Christian Nationalist Crusade, Los Angeles. 231 pp.

Smith, Samuel Stanhope, 1965. *An Essay on the Causes of the Variety of Complexion and Figure in the Human Species, to Which Are Added, Strictures On Lord Kaims's Discourse on the Original Diversity of Mankind* (reprint of 1810 ed.), Winthrop D. Jordan (ed.). Belknap Press of Harvard University Press, Cambridge, MA. 285 pp.

Snow, C. P. 1959. *The Two Cultures and the Scientific Revolution. The Rede Lecture, 1959.* Cambridge University Press, New York. 98 pp.

Snyder, Louis L. 1939. *Race: A History of Modern Ethnic Theories.* Longmans, Green & Co., London. 342 pp.

———. 1962. *The Idea of Racialism: Its Meaning and History.* Van Nostrand, Princeton. 123 pp.

Society for the Psychological Study of Social Issues. 1969. Council statement on race and intelligence. *Journal of Social Issues* 25:1–3.

Sokal, Alan D. 1996a. A physicist experiments with cultural studies. *Lingua Franca: The Review of Academic Life* 6(4):62–64.

———. 1996b. Transgressing the boundaries: Toward a transformative hermeneutics of quantum gravity. *Social Text* 14(1):217–252.

———. 2000. Revelation: A physicist experiments with cultural studies. In *Lingua Franca* (eds.), *The Sokal Hoax: The Sham that Shook the Academy.* University of Nebraska Press, Lincoln. Pp. 49–53.

Sokal, Alan, and Jean Bricmont. 1998. *Fashionable Nonsense: Postmodern Intellectuals' Abuse of Science.* Picador, New York. 300 pp.

Spearman, Charles, 1904. "General intelligence": Objectively determined and measured. *American Journal of Psychology* 15(2):201–292.

Spencer, Frank, 1979. Aleš Hrdlička, M.D., 1869–1943. A chronicle of the life and work of an American physical anthropologist. Ph.D. diss., University of Michigan, Ann Arbor. 2 Vols., 873 pp.

———. 1981. Review of *Paul Broca: Founder of French Anthropology, Explorer of the Brain,* by Francis Schiller. *American Anthropologist* 83(2):426–27.

———. 1983. Samuel George Morton's doctoral thesis on bodily pain: The probable source of Morton's polygenism. *Transactions and Studies of the College of Physicians of Philadelphia Series 5,* 5(4):321–338.

———. 1997a. Hrdlička, Aleš (1869–1943). In Frank Spencer (ed.), *History of American Physical Anthropology: An Encyclopedia.* Garland Press, New York. Pp. 503–505.

———. 1997b. Manouvrier, Léonce Pierre (1850–1927). In Frank Spencer (ed.), *History of American Physical Anthropology: An Encyclopedia.* Garland Press, New York. Pp. 642–643.

Spicer, Edward H., A. F. Hansen, Katherine Luomala, and Marvin Opler. 1969. *Impounded People: Japanese-Americans in the Relocation Centers.* University of Arizona Press, Tucson. 342 pp.

Spier, Leslie, 1959. Some central elements in the legacy. In *Memoir No. 89,* Walter Goldschmidt (ed.), *The Anthropology of Franz Boas. Essays on the Centennial of His Birth. American Anthropologist* 61(5, Part 2): 146–155.

Spurzheim, Johann Gaspar, M.D. 1832. *Phrenology or the Doctrine of the Mental Phenomena.* Marsh, Capen & Lyon, Boston. 2 Vols.

Squier, Ephriam G., and Edwin H. Davis. 1848. *Ancient Monuments of the Mississippi Valley: Comprising the Results of Extensive Original Surveys and Explorations. Smithsonian Contributions to Knowledge 1.* Smithsonian Institution, Washington, DC. 304 pp.

Stampp, Kenneth M. 1956. *The Peculiar Institution: Slavery in the Ante-Bellum South.* Random House, New York. 435 pp.

———. 1967. *The Era of Reconstruction 1865–1877.* A. A. Knopf, New York. 228 pp.

Stanton, William R. 1960. *The Leopard's Spots. Scientific Attitudes Towards Race in America, 1815–59.* University of Chicago Press, Chicago. 245 pp.

Stearns, Stephen C. 1976. Life history tactics: A review of the ideas. *Quarterly Review of Biology* 51(1):3–47.

———. 1977. The evolution of life-history traits: A critique of the theory and a review of the data. *Annual Review of Ecology and Systematics* 8:145–171.

———. 1992. *The Evolution of Life Histories.* Oxford University Press, New York. 249 pp.

Stebbins, Robert E. 1974. France. In T. F. Glick (ed.), *The Comparative Reception of Darwin.* University of Texas Press, Austin. Pp. 117–163.

Steel, Ronald, 1980. *Walter Lippmann and the American Century.* Little Brown, Boston. 669 pp.

Stein, Leon, 1950. *The Racial Thinking of Richard Wagner.* Philosophical Library, New York. 252 pp.

Steinberg, Mark D., and Vladimir M. Khrustalëv. 1995. *The Fall of the Romanovs: Political Dreams and Personal Struggles in a Time of Revolution.* Yale University Press, New Haven, CT. 444 pp.

Steinberg, Stephen, 1989. *The Ethnic Myth. Race, Ethnicity, and Class in America,* 2nd ed. Beacon Press, Boston. 317 pp.

Stevenson, Harold W. 1992. Learning from Asian schools. *Scientific American* 267(6):70–76.

Stocking, George W., Jr. 1968. *Race, Culture, and Evolution. Essays in the History of Anthropology.* Free Press, New York. 397 pp.

Stoczkowski, Wiktor, 1994. *Anthropologie naïve, anthropologie savante. De l'origine de l'homme, de l'imagination et des idées reçues.* CNRS Éditions, Paris. 242 pp.

Stoddard, Lothrop, 1920. *The Rising Tide of Color: Against White World Supremacy.* Charles Scribner's Sons, New York. 320 pp.

———. 1940. *Into the Darkness: Nazi Germany Today.* Duell, Sloan & Pierce, New York. 311 pp.

Strassmann, Beverly I. 1997. The biology of menstruation in *Homo sapiens:* Total lifetime menses, fecundity, and nonsynchrony in a natural-fertility population. *Current Anthropology* 38(1):123–129.

Straus, Lawrence Guy, 1989. On early hominid use of fire. *Current Anthropology* 30(4):488–491.

Stringer, Christopher B. 2000. Modern human origins: Where are we now? Distinguished Lecture, General Anthropology Division and Biological Anthropology, American Anthropological Association annual meeting, San Francisco, November 17.

Stringer, Christopher, and Robin McKie. 1997. *African Exodus: The Origins of Modern Humanity.* Henry Holt & Co., New York. 282 pp.

Strouse, Jean, 2001. Where they got their ideas. Review of *The Metaphysical Club* by Louis Menand. *New York Times Book Review,* June 10, p. 10.

Sue, Eugène, 1844. *Le juif errant.* Hauman, Bruxelles.

Sumner, Charles, 1856. *The Crime Against Kansas.* Greeley & McElrath, New York. 31 pp.

Sutherland, Arthur E. 1954. Segregation and the Supreme Court. *Atlantic* July:33–36.

Swanson, Gordon Ira, 1993. The hall of shame. *Phi Delta Kappan* 74(10):796–798.

Tattersall, Ian, 1998. *Becoming Human: Evolution and Human Uniqueness.* Harcourt Brace & Co., New York. 258 pp.

———. 1999. The abuse of adaptation. *Evolutionary Anthropology* 7(4):115–116.

———. 2001. *The Monkey in the Mirror: Essays in the Science of What Makes Us Human.* Harcourt and Brace, New York. 224 pp.

———. 2002. Paleoanthropology and evolutionary theory. In Peter N. Peregrine, Carol R. Ember, and Melvin Ember (eds.), *Physical Anthropology: Original Readings on Method and Practice.* Prentice-Hall, Upper Saddle River, NJ. Pp. 29–41.

Tattersall, Ian, and Jeffrey H. Schwartz. 2000. *Extinct Humans.* Westview Press, New York. 256 pp.

Taylor, Mark C. 1987. Descartes, Nietzsche and the search for the unsayable. *New York Times Book Review,* February 1, pp. 3, 34.

Temkin, Owsei, 1947. Gall and the phrenological movement. *Bulletin of the History of Medicine* 21(3):275–321.

———. 1952. The elusiveness of Paracelsus. *Bulletin of the History of Medicine* 26(3):201–217.

———. 1973. *Galenism: The Rise and Decline of a Medical Philosophy.* Cornell University Press, Ithaca, NY. 249 pp.

Ten Broek, Jacobus, Edward N. Barnhart, and Floyd W. Matson. 1968. *Prejudice, War and the Constitution: Causes and consequences of Evacuation of the Japanese Americans in the Second World War.* University of California Press, Berkeley. 408 pp.

Terman, Lewis M. 1916. *The Measurement of Intelligence: An Explanation of and a Complete Guide for the Use of the Stanford Revision and Extension of the Binet-Simon Intelligence Scale.* Houghton Mifflin, Boston. 362 pp.

———. 1917. The intelligence quotient of Francis Galton in childhood. *American Journal of Psychology* 28(2):209–215.

———. 1919. *The Intelligence of School Children, How Children Differ in Ability, the Use of Mental Tests in School Grading and the Proper Education of Exceptional Children.* Houghton Mifflin, Boston. 317 pp.

———. 1922. The great conspiracy or the impulse imperious of intelligence testers psychoanalyzed and exposed by Mr. Lippmann. *New Republic* 33:116–220.

———. 1926. *Genetic Studies of Genius,* Vol. 2. *The Early Mental Traits of Three Hundred Geniuses.* Stanford University Press, Stanford, CA. 842 pp.

———. 1940. Psychological approaches to the biography of genius. *Science* 92:293–301.

Thomas, John L. 1963. *The Liberator. William Lloyd Garrison, A Biography.* Little, Brown and Company, Boston. 502 pp.

Thorogood, Peter, 1997. The relationship between genotype and phenotype: Some basic concepts. In Peter Thorogood (ed.), *Embryos, Genes and Birth Defects.* John Wiley & Sons, Chichester, UK. Pp. 1–16.

Thurstone, Louis L. 1940. Current issues in factor analysis. *Psychological Bulletin* 37(4): 189–236.

Tiedemann, Friedrich, 1836. On the brain of the Negro, compared with that of the European and the orang-outan. *Philosophical Transactions of the Royal Society of London* 126:497–527.

Tishkoff, S. A., A. J. Pakstit, M. Stoneking, J. R. Kidd, G. Destro-Bisol, A. Sanjatila, R.-b. Lu, A. S. Deinard, G. Sirugo, T. Jenkins, K. K. Kidd, and A. G. Clark. 2000. Short tandem-repeat polymorphism/Alu haplotype variation at the PLAT locus: Implications for modern human origins. *American Journal of Human Genetics* 67(4):901–925.

Tocqueville, Alexis de, 1835–40. *Democracy in America.* Henry Reeve (trans.). Saunders & Otley, London. 2 Vols.

Todorov, Zvetan, 1986. "Race," writing and culture. In Henry Louis Gates, Jr. (ed.), *"Race," Writing, and Difference.* University of Chicago Press, Chicago. Pp. 370–380.

———. 1993. *On Human Diversity: Nationalism, Racism, and Exoticism in French Thought.* Catherine Porter (trans.). Harvard University Press, Cambridge, MA. 424 pp.

Topinard, Paul, 1879. De la notion de race en anthropologie. *Revue d'anthropologie,* série 2, 8:589–660.

———. 1888. Review of *Les ancêtres de nos animaux dans les temps géologiques* by Albert Gaudry. *Revue d'anthropologie,* série 3, 3:472–474.

Tozzer, Alfred M. 1936. Frederick Ward Putnam. *Biographical Memoirs of the National Academy of Sciences* 16(4):125–153.

Trefil, James, 1989. The survival of the luckiest. Review of *Wonderful Life. The Burgess Shale and the Nature of History* by Stephen Jay Gould. *Washington Post National Weekly Edition,* October 30–November 5, pp. 35–36.

Trinkaus, Erik, and Pat Shipman. 1992. *The Neandertals: Changing the Image of Mankind.* A. A. Knopf, New York. 454 pp.

Trollope, Anthony, 1875. *The Way We Live Now.* Chapman and Hall, London. 2 Vols.

Tucker, William H. 1994a. Fact and fiction in the discovery of Sir Cyril Burt's flaws. *Journal of the History of the Behavioral Sciences* 30(4):335–347.

———. 1994b. *The Science and Politics of Racial Research.* University of Illinois Press, Urbana. 371 pp.

———. 1997. Re-reconsidering Burt: Beyond a reasonable doubt. *Journal of the History of the Behavioral Sciences* 33(2):145–162.

———. 2002. *The Funding of Scientific Racism: Wickliffe Draper and the Pioneer Fund.* University of Illinois Press, Urbana. 286 pp.

UNESCO on Race. 1950. *Man* 50(220):138–139.

Vallois, Henri-Victor, 1940. Le laboratoire Broca. *Bulletins et Mémoires d'Anthropologie,* série 9, 11:1–18.

———. 1953. Race. In Alfred L. Kroeber (ed.), *Anthropology Today. An Enclyopedic Inventory.* University of Chicago Press, Chicago. Pp. 145–162.

Valone, David A. 2002. Review of *Eugenics: A Reassessment. Human Evolution, Behavior, and Intelligence,* by Richard Lynn (2001). *Isis* 93(3):534.

Van Rensselaer, Cortlandt, 1854. Review of *Types of Mankind* by J. C. Nott and G. R. Gliddon. *Presbyterian Magazine* 4(6):285–289.

Vilà, Carlos, Peter Savolainen, Jesús E. Maldonado, Isabel R. Amorim, John E. Rice, Rodney L. Honeycutt, Keith A. Crandall, Joakim Lundeberg, and Robert K. Wayne. 1997. Multiple and ancient origins of the domestic dog. *Science* 276:1687–1689.

Virey, Julien-Joseph, 1824. *Histoire naturelle du genre humain.* Crochard, Paris. 3 Vols.

Vogel, Friedrich, and M. R. Chakravarti. 1971. Blood groups and small pox in a rural population of West Bengal and Bihar (India). In Carl Jay Bajema (ed.), *Natural Selection in Human Populations: The Measurement of Ongoing Genetic Evolution in Contemporary Societies.* John Wiley & Sons, New York. Pp. 147–165.

Voltaire, François Marie Arouet, [1759] 1957. *Candide; ou l'optimisme.* André Morize (ed.). Librairie M. Didier, Paris. 237 pp.

———. 1773. *Essai sur les moeurs et l'esprit des nations; et sur les principaux faits de l'histoire depuis Charlemagne jusqu'à Louis XIII.* Garnier Frères, Paris. 8 Vols.

Wade, Nicholas, 1976. IQ and heredity: Suspicion of fraud beclouds classic experiment. *Science* 194:916–919.

Walker, Alan, 1984. Extinction in hominid evolution. In Matthew H. Nitecki (ed.), *Extinctions.* University of Chicago Press, Chicago. Pp. 119–152.

Wallace, Douglas C., Carol Stugard, Deborah Murdock, Theodore Schurr, and Michael D. Brown 1997. Ancient mtDNA sequences in the human nuclear genome: A potential source of errors identifying pathogenic mutations. *Proceedings of the National Academy of Sciences USA* 94(26):14900–14905.

Walsh, Anthony A. 1972. The American tour of Dr. Spurzheim. *Journal of the History of Medicine* 27(2):187–205.

Ward, Geoffrey C. 1991. Some fought for freedom, some for glory. Review of *On the Altar of Freedom. A Black Soldier's Civil War Letters from the Front,* by Corporal James Henry Godding, V. M. Adams (ed.), and *Fallen Leaves. The Civil War Letters of Major Henry Livermore Abbott,* R. G. Scott (ed.). *New York Times Book Review,* November 17, pp. 1, 36–37.

Ward, Robert De Courcy, 1904. The restriction of immigration. *North American Review* 179(2):226–237.

Warner, Marina, 1972. *The Dragon Empress: Life and Times of Tz'u-hsi 1835–1908, Empress Dowager of China.* Atheneum, New York. 247 pp.

Warren, Earl, 1977. *The Memoirs of Earl Warren.* Doubleday & Company, Garden City, NY. 394 pp.

Warren, J. Collins, M.D. 1921. The collection of the Boston Phrenological Society—a retrospective. *Annals of Medical History* 3(1):1–11.

Washburn, Sherwood L. 1952. Carleton Stevens Coon: Viking medalist for 1951. *American Journal of Physical Anthropology* 10(2):227–228.

Washburn, Wilcomb E. 1959. The moral and legal justifications for dispossessing the Indians. In James Morton Smith (ed.), *Seventeenth-Century America: Essays in Colonial History.* University of North Carolina Press, Chapel Hill. Pp. 15–32.

Watson, James D. 1998. Afterword: Five days in Berlin. In *Murderous Science: Elimination by Scientific Selection of Jews, Gypsies, and Others in Germany, 1933–1945* by Benno Müller-Hill. Cold Spring Harbor Laboratory Press, Plainview, NY. Pp. 187–200.

Wayne, John, 1971. Interview by Richard Warren Lewis. *Playboy* 80(5):75–82.

Wayne, Robert K. 1993. Molecular evolution of the dog family. *Trends in Genetics* 9(6):218–224.

Weatherby, Harold L. 1973. *Cardinal Newman in His Age: His Place in English Theology and Literature.* Vanderbilt University Press, Nashville, TN. 296 pp.

Weber, Max, [1904] 1930. *The Protestant Ethic and the Spirit of Capitalism.* Talcott Parsons (trans.). G. Allen and Unwin, London. 292 pp.

Webster, Charles, 1982. *From Paracelsus to Newton. Magic and the Making of Modern Science.* Cambridge University Press, New York. 107 pp.

Webster, Nesta, [1924] 1967. *Secret Societies and Subversive Movements,* 9th ed. E. P. Dutton, New York. 419 pp.

Weeks, Edward, 1966. *The Lowells and Their Institute.* Little, Brown, Boston. 202 pp.

Weidenreich, Franz, 1943. The skull of "*Sinanthropus pekinensis.*" A comparative study on a primitive hominid skull. *Palaeontologia Sinica,* n. s., 10:1–484.

———. 1947. Facts and speculations concerning the origin of *Homo sapiens. American Anthropologist* 49(2):187–203.

Weinberg, Albert K. 1958. *Manifest Destiny: A Study of Nationalist Expansion in American History.* Peter Smith, Gloucester, MA. 559 pp.

Weinreich, Max, 1946. *Hitler's Professors: The Part of Scholarship in Germany's Crimes Against the Jewish People.* Yiddish Scientific Institute, New York. 291 pp.

Weintraub, Stanley, 2001. *Edward the Caresser. The Playboy Prince Who Became Edward VII.* Free Press, New York. 429 pp.

Weizmann, Frederic, Neil I. Wiener, David L. Wiesenthal, and Michael Ziegler. 1990. Differential K theory and racial hierarchies. *Canadian Psychology* 31(1):1–13.

———. 1991. Discussion. Eggs, eggplants and eggheads: A rejoinder to Rushton. *Canadian Psychology* 32(1):43–50.

Wells, George A. 1967. Goethe and the intermaxillary bone. *British Journal of the History of Science* 3(4):348–361.

Wertenbaker, Thomas Jefferson, 1946. *Princeton 1746–1896.* Princeton University Press, Princeton. 424 pp.

Weston, R. F. 1972. *Racism in U.S. Imperialism: The Influence of Racial Assumptions on American Foreign Policy, 1893–1946.* University of South Carolina Press, Columbia. 291 pp.

Weyher, Harry F. 1999. The Pioneer Fund, the behavioral sciences, and the media's false stories. *Intelligence* 26(4):319–336.

Whewell, William, 1832. Review of *Principles of Geology, being an Attempt to explain the former Changes of the Earth's Surface, by reference to causes now in operation,* Vol. II, by Charles Lyell. *Quarterly Review* 47:103–132.

White, Charles, 1799. *An Account of the Regular Gradation in Man, and in Different Animals and Vegetables; and from the Former to the Latter.* C. Dilly, London. 146 pp.

White, John, 1983. Vita Paracelsus. Enigmatic doctor: ca. 1493–1541. *Harvard Magazine* 86(2):50.

Wiesel, Elie, 1972. *Night, Dawn, The Accident; Three Tales.* Hill and Wang, New York. 318 pp.

———. 1995. *All Rivers Run to the Sea: Memoirs.* A. A. Knopf, New York. 432 pp.

Wilkens, Horst, 1988. Evolution and genetics of epigean and cave *Astyanax fasciatus* (Characidae, Pisces). *Evolutionary Biology* 23:271–367.

Wilkinson, Elizabeth Mary, 1970. Goethe, Johann Wolfgang von. In *Encyclopaedia Britannica,* Vol. 10. William Benton Publisher, Chicago. Pp. 522–529.

Williams, Henry Smith, 1923. *The Story of Modern Science,* Vol. 7. *Bettering the Race.* Funk & Wagnalls, New York. 212 pp.

Wills, Garry, 1978. *Inventing America: Jefferson's Declaration of Independence.* Doubleday, Garden City, NY. 398 pp.

Wilshire, Bruce (ed.) 1968. *Romanticism and Evolution: The Nineteenth Century.* G. P. Putnam's Sons, Capricorn Books, New York. 320 pp.

Wilson, A. N. 1999. *God's Funeral,* 1st American ed. W. W. Norton, New York. 402 pp.

Wilson, Edward O., and William L. Brown, Jr. 1953. The subspecies concept and its taxonomic application. *Systematic Zoology* 2(3):97–111.

Wilson, John B. 1956. Phrenology and the transcendentalists. *American Literature* 28(2):220–225.

Wilton, George, 1938. *Fingerprints: History, Law and Romance.* William Hodge & Co., London. 317 pp.

Wimsatt, William C. 1980. Reductionist research strategies and their biases in the units of selection controversy. In T. Nickles (ed.), *Scientific Discovery,* Vol. 2. *Historical and Scientific Case Studies.* D. Reidel, Dordrecht, the Netherlands. Pp. 213–259.

Winrod, Gerald B. n.d. *The Truth About the Protocols.* Sons of Liberty, Hollywood, CA. 53 pp.

Wira, Joseph, 2002. On media exaggeration. *Credo* 7(20):11.

Wise, George, 1990. Reckless pioneer. *American Heritage of Invention and Technology* 6(1):26–31.

Wolf, Theta H. 1973. *Alfred Binet.* University of Chicago Press, Chicago. 376 pp.

Wolpoff, Milford H. 1980. *Paleoanthropology.* A. A. Knopf, New York. 379 pp.

Wolpoff, Milford, John Hawks, and Rachel Caspari. 2000. Multiregional, not multiple origins. *American Journal of Physical Anthropology* 112(1):129–136.

Wolpoff, Milford H., Wu Xin Zhi, and Alan G. Thorne. 1984. Modern *Homo sapiens* origins: A general theory of hominid evolution involving the fossil evidence from East Asia. In Fred H. Smith and Frank Spencer (eds.), *The Origin of Modern Humans: A World Survey of the Fossil Evidence.* Alan R. Liss, New York. Pp. 411–483.

Wood, George B. 1859. A memoir of the life and character of the late Joseph Parrish, M.D. In *Introductory Lectures and Addresses on Medical Subjects.* J. B. Lippincott, Philadelphia. Pp. 387–434.

Wood, Paul (ed.) 2000. *The Scottish Enlightenment: Essays in Reinterpretation.* University of Rochester Press, Rochester, NY. 399 pp.

Woodward, C. Vann, 1966. *The Strange Career of Jim Crow,* 2nd ed. Oxford University Press, New York. 205 pp.

———. 1969. American history (white man's version) needs an infusion of soul. *New York Times Magazine,* April 20, pp. 32–33, 108–114.

Wrangham, Richard W., James Holland Jones, Greg Laden, David Pilbeam, and NancyLou Conklin-Brittain. 1999. The raw and the stolen: Cooking and the ecology of human origins. *Current Anthropology* 40(5):567–594.

Wrobel, Arthur. 1975. Orthodoxy and respectability in nineteenth-century phrenology. *Journal of Popular Culture* 9(7):38–50.

———. (ed.) 1987. *Pseudo-Science and Society in Nineteenth-Century America.* University of Kentucky Press, Lexington. 245 pp.

Wynne-Edwards, V. C. 1962. *Animal Dispersion in Relation to Social Behaviour.* Hafner
    Publishing Company, New York. 653 pp.

———. 1986. *Evolution through Group Selection.* Blackwell Scientific, Palo Alto, CA. 386 pp.

X, Jacobus, a French Army Surgeon, 1898. *Untrodden Fields of Anthropology. Observations of
    the Esoteric Manners and Customs of Semi-Civilized Peoples; Being a Record of Thirty
    Years' Experience in Asia, Africa, America and Oceania.* Charles Carrington (ed.). Librairie
    de Medecine, Folklore et Anthropologie, Paris. Vol. 1, 343 pp.; Vol. 2, 502 pp.

Yerkes, Robert M. (ed.) 1921. *Psychological Examining in the United States Army.* Government
    Printing Office, Washington, DC. 890 pp.

Yoakum, Clarence S., and Robert M. Yerkes. 1920. *Army Mental Tests.* Henry Holt and Co.,
    New York. 303 pp.

Zia, Helen, 2000. *Asian American Dreams. The Emergence of an American People.* Farrar,
    Straus & Giroux, New York. 356 pp.

Zuckerman, Solly, baron, 1973. Sir Grafton Elliot Smith 1871–1937. In Professor Lord
    Zuckerman (ed.), *The Concept of Evolution. Symposia of the Zoological Society of London,
    Number 33.* Published for the Zoological Society of London by Academic Press, London.
    Pp. 3–21.

INDEX

Hereditary Genius: An Inquiry into Its Laws and
   Consequences (Galton), 179–80
Hereditary health law (Nazi Germany), 185
Herodotus, 19, 40, 82, 85, 272, 273
Herrnstein, Richard J., 252–55
Herzl, Theodor, 199
Heydrich, Reinhard, 187, 188
Hierarchical selection, 231
Hieroglyphics, 19, 84, 116, 125, 126, 128
Highland Clearances, 48
Himmler, Heinrich, 187, 188
Hippocrates, 19
Hispanics, 245
Histoire Naturelle (Buffon), 30, 31
Histoire Naturelle des Races Humains (Desmoulins), 41
Histoire Naturelle du Genre Humain (Virey), 41
Histories (Herodotus), 19
History of Jamaica, The (Long), 40
Hitler, Adolf, 1, 3, 119, 122, 173, 177, 178, 187, 189, 199,
   200, 203, 219, 223, 232; Ford's support of, 201–2;
   justification for Holocaust, 185–86; Laughlin's
   admiration for, 217
Holbrook, John Edward, 100
Holland, 32–33
Holmes, Oliver Wendell, Jr., 184
Holmes, Oliver Wendell, Sr., 74
Holocaust, 3, 59, 119, 177, 185–89, 219, 242, 243;
   ethos of, 197–203; Hitler's justification for, 185–86.
   See also Nazi Germany
Homo: Essai Zoologique sur le Genre Humain (Bory), 41
Homo erectus, 228, 237
Homo monstrosus, 27
Homo sapiens, 2, 21, 25, 26, 33, 46, 237, 256
Homo sapiens afer, 27
Homo sapiens americanus, 27
Homo sapiens asiaticus, 27
Homo sapiens europaeus, 27
Hooton, Earnest Albert, 225, 233–35
Hooton, Mary, 225
Hoover, Herbert, 177
Horner, William Edmonds, 112
Hottentots, 41
Hotz, Henry, 121
Howard, Margaret, 210
Howard, Oliver Otis, 137–38, 140, 142–43,
   144, 162, 175
Howard University, 137
Howells, William W., 226
Hrdlička, Aleš, 91, 92, 222–27, 228, 235
Human Evolution: An Introduction to Biological
   Anthropology (Brace and Montagu), x
Humboldt, Baron Alexander von, 44, 82, 106, 159
Hume, David, 48, 49, 53
Hunt, Catherine ("Kate"), 125, 126
Hunt, James, 138, 148–49, 154
Hunt, Leigh, 125
Hunt, Thornton, 126
Hutcheson, Francis, 47, 48
Hutton, James, 85
Huxley, Aldous, 63, 74
Huxley, Julian, 5, 8, 63
Huxley, Thomas Henry, 4, 41, 61–62, 63, 91, 234
Huxley Memorial Lectures, 182, 228, 231
Hybrid sterility: Broca on, 148–49, 151–52, 153; Morton
   on, 86–88, 108, 128; Nott on, 113, 114
Hyperselectionism, 12–13

Ibn Battutah, 19, 20
Ideographs, 264, 265

Immigration policy, 105, 122, 134, 177, 221, 225; Boas's
   influence on, 172–73; eugenics movement and, 173,
   178–79, 192–96; intelligence and, 204, 211,
   213–17; Shaler's influence on, 161, 163–64
Immigration Restriction Act, 195
Immigration Restriction League, 104, 163–64, 193, 194
Immigration Restriction Society, 214
India, 20, 165, 269
Indian Removal Act, 140
Indigenous Races of the Earth (Gliddon), 129–30
Inquiries into Human Faculty and Its Development
   (Galton), 178
Inquiry into the Human Mind on the Principles of
   Common Sense, An (Reid), 48, 49
Instincts of Races (Nott), 138
Institute for the Study of Educational Differences, 243
Intelligence, 182, 191–92, 204–10; Galton on, 182–83,
   205, 206, 207, 211; genetic predestination and,
   217–19; Herrnstein and Murray on, 252–55; Jensen
   on (see Jensen, Arthur R.); Lynn on, 263–67;
   Rushton on, 258, 259–61; statistical theology of,
   205–8
Intelligence (journal), 263
Intelligence quotient (IQ), 182, 208, 212
Intelligence testing, 102, 205, 211–21; fraud in, 208–10;
   Herrnstein and Murray on, 252; history of, 206–8;
   of immigrants, 204, 211, 213–17; Lynn on, 264–65;
   Rushton on, 259–60; in World War I military,
   211–12, 213–14, 216–17
Intermaxillary bone, contention over, 61
International Association for the Advancement of
   Ethnology and Eugenics (IAAEE), 243
International Jew, 200–201, 202, 203
Inuit people, 264
IQ and the Wealth of Nations (Lynn and Vanhanen),
   263–64
Irish, 134, 161, 208
Italians, 134, 213
Italy, 165

Jackson, Andrew, 92, 140
Jackson, Samuel, 112
Jacobus X, Dr. (pseudonym), 260
James, William, 99–100, 211, 220
Jameson, Robert, 85
Japan, 15, 20, 264–65, 269
Japanese Americans, internment of, 195–96
Jardin des Plantes, 30, 157
Jefferson, Thomas, 48, 76, 111, 122, 189, 191–92, 242
Jensen, Arthur R., 102–3, 154, 182, 191–92, 205, 208,
   240, 241, 243–52, 260, 265, 266, 267; conversion
   of, 245; default hypothesis of, 249–50; racialist
   stance of, 245, 246; treatment of heritability,
   250–52
Jensenism, 243–52
Jews, 39, 116, 183; Galton on, 180; Grant on, 174, 175;
   immigration policy on, 211, 213, 214; Nott on, 100;
   Stoddard on, 177. See also Anti-Semitism;
   Holocaust
Jim Crow laws, 192. See also Black Codes
John Birch Society, 203
Johns Hopkins University, 32, 166, 233
Johnson, Albert, 195, 214–15, 225
Johnson, Andrew, 137
Johnson-Lodge Act of 1924, 195, 213, 216
Joly, Maurice, 198
Jōmon, 15
Jones, Sir William, 120
Journal de la Physiologie, 148

CPSIA information can be obtained at www.ICGtesting.com
Printed in the USA
266969BV00003B/2/P